AJMER

AJMER

HISTORICAL AND DESCRIPTIVE

BY

DIWAN BAHADUR HAR BILAS SARDA

GYAN

Published by

GYAN

Gyan Publishing House
5, Ansari Road
Daryaganj, New Delhi-110002
Phone: 011-47034999, 9811692060
E-mail: books@gyanbooks.com

Distribution Network
gyanbooks.com
India, USA, Canada, UK, Australia, France

ISBN: 978-93-6920-157-0 (PB)

First Published, 1911

2nd Impression 2025

Printed at: Gyan Press, Delhi.

AJMER
Autor: DIWAN BAHADUR HAR BILAS SARDA

Air Commodore His Highness Raj Rajeshwar Saramad Raja-i-Hind
MAHARAJA DHIRAJ MAHARAJA SRI SIR UMAID SINGHJI BAHADUR,
G.C.S.I., G.C.I.E., K.C.V.O., L.L.D., A.D.C.,
MAHARAJA OF JODHPUR.

AJMER:

HISTORICAL AND DESCRIPTIVE

BY

DIWAN BAHADUR HAR BILAS SARDA, M.R.A.S., F.S.S.
SOMETIME MEMBER OF THE CENTRAL LEGISLATIVE ASSEMBLY, INDIA.

Author of

MAHARANA KUMBHA ; MAHARANA SANGA ; HINDU SUPERIORITY ;
HAMMIR OF RANTHAMBHOR ; SPEECHES AND WRITINGS, &C.

AJMER :
FINE ART PRINTING PRESS.
1941.

DEDICATED

BY KIND PERMISSION

TO

Air Commodore
His Highness Raj Rajeshwar Saramad Raja-i-Hind
Maharaja Dhiraj Maharaja Sri

SIR UMAID SINGHJI BAHADUR,

G. C. S. I., G. C. I. E., K. C. V. O., L. L. D., A. D. C.,

Maharaja of Jodhpur

PUBLISHER'S NOTE.

Ajmer: Historical and Descriptive, was first published in 1911 A.D. The present book, however, is practically a new one. Not only has every chapter of the book been rewritten, enlarged and brought upto date, but several new chapters have been added. Chapters XIII, XIV and XV of Part I, section V of chapter XVII, are new. Chapter XVIII, *Rulers of Ajmer*, giving complete lists, with dates, of the sovereigns of Ajmer, from its foundation to 1940, and of the Governors and the Chief Commissioners and the Commissioners of Ajmer from 1558, (beginning of Mughal Rule) to 1940 A.D. is new, as also the following Chapter, headed *Chronology of Ajmer* which records, in chronological order, all important events that have any bearing on the history of Ajmer.

Part III, *Administration*, (Chapters XX to XXVIII) containing a full account of the various branches of the Administration has been added for the first time. A Bibliography and several Appendices containing much useful information, have been added. Many new illustrations have been put in; and maps to illustrate battles and important places have been inserted. A new chapter, containing the history of the little known district of Merwara, including a full account of the acquisition in the nineteenth century, and retrocession in 1938 A.D., of the Mewar and Marwar portions of Merwara, has been given for the first time.

CONTENTS

CHAPTER X.—CHASHMA.

CHAPTER XI.—MAYO COLLEGE.

CHAPTER XII.—NASIYAN (OR RED TEMPLE).

CHAPTER XIII.—FOYSAGAR.

CHAPTER XIV.—RAJPUTANA MUSEUM.

CHAPTER XV.—AJAIPAL.

CHAPTER XVI.—MINOR SIGHTS.

PART II.—HISTORICAL.

CHAPTER XVII.—HISTORY.

I.—CHAUHAN PERIOD.

II.—PATHAN AND RAJPUT PERIOD.

III.—MUGHAL PERIOD.

IV.—RATHOR AND MAHRATTA PERIOD.

CHAPTER XXVIII.—B. B. & C. I. RAILWAY, METRE GAUGE.

PART IV.—PUSHKAR AND MERWARA.

CHAPTER XXIX.—PUSHKAR.

CHAPTER XXX.—MERWARA.

ILLUSTRATIONS

HAR BILAS SARDA.

INTRODUCTION.

Ajmer is one of the most beautiful cities in India. Picturesquely situated in a valley surrounded by high hills, and adorned with two fine lakes; abounding in romantic spots, hoary with age and historic associations, resting in the shadow of one of the most renowed fortresses in the East, nature has endowed Ajmer with the attractions of lake and hill scenery. British Political Officers who have come to Ajmer after serving in Kashmir, have said that Ajmer during the rains reminded them of Kashmir. Ajmer enjoys the distinction of having been the Capital of India during the twelfth century, when its Chauhan Kings were Emperors of India and ruled the whole of Upper India.

The splendid situation of Ajmer marking the highest elevation of the plains of Hindustan and the centre of a region inhabited by warlike races, famous for their unsurpassed courage and valour, has made Ajmer not only a place of supreme strategical and political importance, but the cynosure of all eyes. Traditions of chivalry unequalled in history; events occuring here, which decided the fate of the Indian empire more than once, and the first place it occupies in the religious sentiments of the people, both Hindus and Muslims, owing to Pushkar, the "King of Sacred places" of the Hindus, and the shrine of the "Chief of the Muslim Saints," Khwaja Muinuddin Chishti, have invested Ajmer with an importance, which added to its natural beauties, its superb situation, and its political distinction have placed it on a high pedestal amongst the cities of India.

Where'er we tread it is haunted holy ground
No earth of thine is lost in vulgar mould
But one realm of wonder spreads around
And all the muses' tales seem truly told.[1]

The far-famed fortress of Taragarh is as famous as the celebrated fort of Chitor. Its greater strategical importance however, made it a constant factor in the varied drama of political power in this great country, and also the aim of every one who sought supremacy in India, whether he was an Arab or an Afghan, a Mughal or a Marhatta or a Briton.

1. Byron: *Childe Harold*, Canto II.

The renowned Adhai-din-ka-Jhonpra, one of the greatest monuments of architecture in India, is a rare relic of the proud and palmy days, when, as the centre of political gravity, Ajmer became the premier city in India under Visaldeva Vigrahraj, whose glorious exploits are engraved on the Siwalik pillar in the Firozshah's Kotla at Delhi. The entrancing beauty, of the Anasagar Lake enchants the eye and charms the mind. When during the rains, the god of gladness, with a parting smile, sinks behind the Nagpahar, and its rays striking the crystal waters of the lake dissolve into the colours of the rainbow, the scene fills the mind with rapture, and Byron's famous lines come to mind:

> Slow sinks, more lovely ere his race be run,
> Along Morea's hills the setting Sun;
> Not, as in northern climes, obscurely bright,
> But one unclouded blaze of living light;
> O'er the hushed deep the yellow beam he throws,
> Gilds the green wave that trembles as it glows.[1]

With the fall of the Mughal Empire, the prosperity of this historic city suffered an eclipse. But with the advent of the British, and particularly since the coming of the Railway, Ajmer has, been making steady progress. This book tells the story of its foundation and its chequered career under the Afghans, the Mughals, the Mahrattas, the Rathors and the British, and its present condition, political, administrative, social and cultural.

Not only have the results of the latest researches, having any bearing on the history of Ajmer been incorporated in the book, but all desirable information about the place is given, the object being to make it as informing as possible to all classes of readers, to visitors to Ajmer, to students of its history, its administration and its institutions, as also to its residents, official as well as non-official.

I must acknowledge my obligations to the Hon'ble the Chief Commissioner, the Commissioner and the various officials of this province, as also to the Principal of the Mayo College, Ajmer and the Agent of the B. B. and C. I. Railway and other local Railway officials, and Mahamahopadhyaya Dr. G. S. Ojha who all kindly gave me the information I asked for. I am much obliged to Mr. P. Seshadri, Principal of the Government College, Ajmer for his valuable suggestions, and his help in seeing the book through the Press, as also for the foreword he has kindly contributed.

HAR BILAS SARDA

10th. May, 1941.

1. Byron: *Curse of Minerva.*

PART I.

DESCRIPTIVE.

CHAPTER I

AJMER-MERWARA

AJMER-MERWARA is a small province of British India lying in the centre of Rajputana—the land of chivalry and ancient tradition—and is surrounded by the Rajput States of Marwar on the west, Kishangarh and Marwar on the North, Jaipur and Kishangarh on the east, and Mewar on the south. It comprises a total area of 2,367·6 square miles, and has a population of 5,06,964.[1] It lies[2] between North Latitude 25° 24′ and 26° 42′ and East Longitude 73° 45′ and consists of the two sub-divisions, Ajmer and Merwara (areas 2,069 and 298 square miles respectively). Ajmer is 80 miles north to south, and 50 miles in breadth. Merwara is 48 miles long and 15 miles in breadth.

Hills.—The Aravalli Range runs through the province north to south, and divides the plains of the Rathors from the high tableland of the country of the Sesodias. The range commences at the ridge of Delhi—famous in the history of the Sepoy Mutiny of 1857 A.D.—lies low till it reaches the northern borders of Ajmer, and assumes its full height where stands the city of Ajmer. After a little break, a few miles south of Ajmer, it reappears in the form of a compact double-range, enclosing the Beawar Tahsil near Todgarh, where at Goramji it attains a height of 3,075 feet, the average level being 1,800 feet above the sea. Breaking thence into hills and valleys, it leaves behind the southernmost point of Merwara, and finally ends in the group of hills known throughout the country as Abu Raj, Mount Abu, the only hill-station in Rajputana, and the head-quarters of the Resident in Rajputana and Chief Commissioner of Ajmer-Merwara.

Rivers:—The hills between Ajmer and Nasirabad mark the watershed of India. The rain falling on the eastern side is drained off by the Chambal into the Bay of Bengal, and that on the western side is carried by the Luni river into the Ara-

1. The population and area have been reduced from 5,60,292 and 2710·689 miles respectively by the transfer of certain portions of Merwara to the Mewar and Marwar States.
2. Ajmer-Merwara Gazetteer, by C. C. Watson, 1904.

bian Sea. Being the centre of the watershed it could not have any rivers. The Saraswati comes from Marwar and after passing Pushkar joins the Sagarmati at Govindgarh. The Banas which rises in the Aravalli hills 40 miles north-east of Udaipur, passes near Deoli and falls into the Jumna, only touches the south-eastern frontier of Ajmer. The Khari[1] which originates in the hills near the village Brijal in Merwara, and falls into the Banas river in the Sawar estate, and the Dai which begins in the Rajgarh hills and joins the Banas near Deoli, also affect only a small south-eastern portion of the district. The Sagarmati, so called because it falls into the Sagar (Arabian Sea), takes its rise in the Ajaipal Hills, and after nearly circumscribing the town of Ajmer, flows by Bhaonta and Pisangan to Govindgarh, where the Saraswati from Pushkar meets it.[2] The united stream then enters Marwar, assumes the name of Luni, and after passing through and fertilizing a large portion of that State, discharges itself into the Gulf of Cutch. There are two other rivulets, the Balad river which originates in the Borwa hills and goes to Marwar, and the Nai which rises in the village Chang in Merwara and also goes to Marwar[3].

Lakes.—The natural lakes are only the two Pushkars in Ajmer, and those at Sargaon and Karantia in Merwara, the one at Sargaon alone being used for irrigation purposes. Of the artificial lakes, the majority were constructed by Colonel Dixon (Superintendent and Commissioner, 1842-57 A.D.), who has left his mark on the administration of the province.

Forts.—With the exception of the celebrated Garh Beetli or Taragarh at Ajmer there are no big forts in the district. Small forts exist at Rajgarh, Srinagar, Arjunpura and Sawar. In Merwara, there are forts at:—

1. Athoon, built by Duda Khan, about six hundred years ago.
2. Borwa, built by Maharana Bheem Singh about 1819 A.D.
3. Jhak, built by Thakur Devi Singh of Masuda in 1819 A.D.
4. Kot Kirana, built by Maharaja Man Singh of Jodhpur.
5. Bagdi, built by Maharaja Man Singh of Jodhpur in 1811 A.D.

6 and 7. Barar and Jaitgarh, built by the Thakur of Badnor (Mewar.)

Fauna (Wild animals).—There is little cover for large game. An occasional tiger is to be met with in the Pushkar

1. "Named from containing a quantity of *Khar* or carbonate of soda."—Some Account of the General and Medical Topography of Ajmer by Dr. R. H. Irvine M. D., 1841 A.D. 2. Thornton's Gazetteer, p. 18.

3. Besides these, there are some nallahs which flow during the rains. They are:—Balai Khera and Raitan Khera nallahs; Sangarwas nallah; Lulwa nallah; Shamgarh nallah; Biliawas nallah; Radhona nallah; Samel nallah; Mavela nallah; Ada nallah; Rai Kana nallah and others.

and Merwara forests. Leopards and hyaenas are to be met with in the hills. Wolves are rare. Wild hog, Black buck (antelope, cervicapra L.), Ravine deer, Chinkara (Gazella-bennetti, Sykes) and Nilgai or blue bull (Boselaphus trago-camelus-Pallas) are met with in Ajmer. There are only a few Sambhars (Rusa unicolor Kerr) and so their shooting is prohibited. Of small game, the following are found in Ajmer-Merwara :—

(*a*) Indian bustard. (*b*) Florican (during rains). (*c*) Small Sand grouse. (*d*) Large Sand grouse (rare). (*e*) Quail (fairly common). (*f*) Hares. (*g*) Grey partridges (common). (*h*) Pea-fowl (shooting prohibited). (*i*) Geese and ducks. (*j*) Snipe.

Flora.—Topographical features, drought and frost are the three important factors which militate against the growth of vegetation in Ajmer-Merwara. Owing to these adverse factors, its flora is of a xerophytic type. It consists of dry miscellaneous forest composed of a number of species common to Rajputana. This xerophytic type of vegetation is more vulnerable to bad treatment than other forests.

The above mixture of trees and bushes constitutes the prevailing type of vegetation for Ajmer-Merwara, particularly in all wastelands north of Billiawas forest. To the south of this forest other species come in sparsely. These include the following :—

1. Goliadho (Anogeussus latifolia).
2. Ghantolan (Randia dumetorum).
3. Passai (Dalbergia lanceolaria).
4. Umbia (Saccopetalum tomentosum).
5. Kankaran (Flacourtia spida).
6. Lemkana (Bridelia retusa).
7. Black Siris (Albizzia lebbek).
8. Kar (Sterculia urens).

The distribution of the species follows two or three more or less clearly marked zones of growth. The highest and steepest slopes carry almost pure salar (Boswellia thurifera). If the ridge is precipitous, it is devoid of all growth, as exemplified by the Nagpahar forests.

On the middle slopes and lower ridges and stretching down to the nallahs below is found the *Dhokra* (Anogeissus pendula) forest sometimes almost pure, but generally well mixed with its common associates. On the flat ground at the foot of hills are to be found Bor (Zizyphus numularia), Kumta (Acacia rupestris), and Arinja (Leucophloea) with Khejra (Prosopis spicigera) mixed with many shrubs and Falsas, Dhaman etc., (Grewias).

Large nallahs are stocked liberally with Dhak (Butea frondosa), Kadam (Mitragyna parvifolia), Jamun (Eugenia Jambolana); while the shrubs are chiefly Negan (Vitex negundo), and Jhaon (Tamarix gallica). Bamboo (Dendrocalamus strictus) is found on the higher slopes of the Nagpahar and Taragarh forests. There is a sprinkling of date-palm (phoenix Sylvestria) in some nallahs of the forests.

Forests.—In ancient times the hills about Ajmer were covered with scrub; and Merwara even in 1819, three years before it came under British rule, was described by Mr. Wilder, the first Superintendent of Ajmer, as an impenetrable jungle; but the province is now practically denuded of trees.[1]

The more important species composing the main type of the crop are as follow :—

Trees.

1. Kumta (Acacia rupestris).
2. Salar (Boswellia thuri-fera.)
3. Khejra (Prosopis spicigera.)
4. Arinja (Acacia leucophloea.)
5. Babool (Acacia arabica.)
6. Khair (Acacia catechu,)
7. Neem (Melia indica.)
8. Khoulasi (Dichrostachys cinera.)
9. Jharbor (*Zizyphus* nummularia.)
10. Dhokra (anogeissus pendula).
11. Barh (Ficus bengalensis.)
12. Semal (Bombax mala-baricum.)
13. Pipal (Ficus religiosa.)
14. Tambolia (Ehretia laevis.)

Shrubs and bushes.

1. Thor (Euhorbia nivuli.)
2. Firangan (Grewia pilosa.)
3. Gangan (Grewia ripulifolia.)
4. Halepan Salepan (Securinega obooata.)
5. Dhasna (Rhus mysorensis.)
6. Ber (*Zizyphus* jujuba.)
7. Arni (Clerodendron phlomoides.)

Mineralogy.—Lead, iron, copper, and silver are to be found in Ajmer; garnet and aquamarines in the Sawar Parganah; mica in Kharwa, Sanod, Goela and more so in Merwara, where also is to be found asbestos near Sendra, hæmatite near Saroth, and copper and lead in the south.

The lead mines of Ajmer yielded a revenue of Rs. 5,000 to the Mahrattas. Mr. Wilder, worked them, and annually produced 10,000 to 12,000 maunds of lead, which was sold at Rs. 11 per maund to the Ajmer Magazine. The mines were closed in 1846 A. D. Ajmer lead is purer and of a better quality than European piglead, but want of fuel and cheap transport militate against the mines being worked at a profit.

Iron is found in Ghugra ghati, Lohagal, Kabra hill in Pushkar. Col. Dixon obtained iron ore from Kishenpura and Lohagal. It is, however, nowhere remunerative.

1. "The demands of the town of Beawar, of the cantonment of Nasirabad, and for wood to burn lime for the tank embankments joined to the absence of all attempts at replacing what was destroyed, left but few trees in any accessible part of the district."—Mr. Watson's Ajmer-Merwara Gazetteer, page 58.

Thornton's Gazetteer says :—

> The mountain of Taragarh contains lodes of carbonate of lead, worked from time immemorial by the natives. The demand for the article is, however, so small, that little if any profit is derived from the working. There are also ores of manganese in the same mountain, and indications of copper, besides some lodes of ore of that metal *in situ*. Iron ore is abundant and yields a metal of good quality. The soil in many places is much impregnated with mineral salts, especially carbonate of soda.

Mica and garnet mines are at present being worked in Ajmer and Merwara, and the industry gives employment to several hundred people.

Stone is abundantly quarried in the district and is used in roofing houses, which in other parts of India is done by wood. Door-frames of stone are also made in Ajmer. Stone beams from 15 to 20 ft. long, and slabs 12 to 14 ft. long by 3 to 5 ft. wide are quarried in Srinagar, about 14 miles from Ajmer. Khodan also supplies stone slabs. Marbles of various colours are quarried in the vicinity of Ajmer.

Industry.—There are 33 Joint Stock Companies with an authorised capital of Rs. 1,18,76,940, and a paid capital of Rs. 37,31,642, and there are 49 factories in the province.

Trade and Commerce.—In the old days, not only was Ajmer the *entrepot* for the trade between Bombay and Upper India, but was the centre for the trade of Rajputana. In the early days of the East India Company, a factory was opened in Ajmer (1614 A.D.) by Mr. Edwards, subordinate to that of Surat. Ajmer was for many years the chief mart for the exchange of European goods and the produce and manufactures of Rajputana and Upper India. Pisangan, in Ajmer, was the principal mart for *Khajrod* tobacco, much appreciated in Rajputana, and which even now is exported largely to Marwar, Jaipur, Bikaner, Jaisalmer, and Upper India. Beawar, owing to its situation at the confluence of Marwar and Mewar territories, has supplanted Ajmer as the commercial centre of the Province.

People.—"The people are industrious, well-behaved, of fine physique, and possess powers of endurance." The total population of the province before the rendition of certain portions of Merwara to the Mewar and Marwar States was 5,60,292 (Census of 1931 A.D.) The rural population was

3,83,850 and urban 1,76,442. Of these, there were[1]:—

Hindus	4,54,006
Mussalmans	97,133
Christians (including British troops) ...	6,947
Sikhs	341
Parsees	301
Others (Buddhists, Jews, and tribal) ...	1,564

In other words, 81 p.c. were Hindus, and 17 p.c., Mussalmans.

Communications.—There is 106 miles of railway running through the district.

The total length of metalled roads is 248 miles and of unmetalled roads, 274 miles. These were made principally as famine works. There are dak bungalows for the use of Touring Officers.

There are at present (1-11-39), 53 Post Offices and Branch Post Offices, and eleven Telegraph Offices, in addition to those at the railway stations. A list of dak bungalows and Post and Telegraph Offices in Ajmer-Merwara is given in Appendix B.

1. Lupton's Settlement Report, p. 18.

CHAPTER II

CITY OF AJMER

THE city of Ajmer is situated at the foot of the hill on which is perched the renowned fortress of *Garh Beetli*, now called Taragarh (Star Citadel). The town covers the entire valley between the Taragarh and the Madar Hills, and lies between 26° 27′ North and 74° 37′ East.

The plateau, on which the city of Ajmer stands, marks the highest elevation of the plains of Hindustan, and from the hills which surround it, the country slopes to all points of the compass.

Remarkable for its picturesque situation and its strategical importance, the city of Ajmer lies hemmed in on all sides by hills, well guarded like a gem of peerless beauty and brilliancy, and is associated with hoary tradition and ages of chivalry and war that have gone for ever. Mr. Caine says:—

> "It is an ancient, beautiful city, full of interest, both historical and architectural, its gay busy bazars and its old houses with carved fronts, some of which are amongst the finest in India, giving added attraction to its superb situation. A well built stone wall with five gateways surround the city."[1]

> Mr. Victor Jacquemont, the French Naturalist who visited Ajmer in 1832, says: "Ajmer is the prettiest place I have seen in the plains of India."[2]

> "It is situated on a valley or rather basin, which, though rocky, is very picturesque and beautiful, and surrounded by hills. On the base and lower slope of one of the hills the town is built. It is surrounded by a wall of stone."[3]

Ajmer is at its best in the rains, when the surrounding hills are all draped in green; the lakes of Ana Sagar, Visla, and Foy Sagar are full; and the waterfalls of *Chashma*, *Antedh-ki-Mata*, and *Baij Nath* add to the beauty of the mountain scenery; the fine hill streams in the glens of *Chavanda*, *Agastaji*, *Gaukund*, *Panchkund* and *Kanbai*,

1. Picturesque India, page 77.
2. "Letters from India" by Victor Jacquemont, 1834 A.D.
3. Thornton's Gazetteer, p. 16.

and the trickling of water everywhere in the hills extend tempting and irresistible invitations to the citizens to visit them in merry picnic parties.

Ajmer is rich in beautiful and picturesque spots in the surrounding hills, where there are several small waterfalls, and *nallahs* run with water; wild flowers, shrubs, and grass abound, and the pleasure of hill-climbing and the enjoyment of beautiful scenery may be combined with worship. *Chavanda*, *Ajaipalji*, *Baij Nathji*, *Anted*, *Agastaji-ki-Gupha*, *Kanbai*, *Gaurikund-ki-Mata* and *Panch kund* are the principal sacred places of public resort. People go there picnicing all the year round, more frequently during the rains.

Though roses (for which Ajmer is famous) are at this time of the year in their decline, the much-prized and sweet-scented Ajmer *chameli* is in full bloom, and the whole atmosphere is charged with that sweet contentedness and enjoyment which beauty, combined with plenty, provides. Few sights afford more delight than the entrancing beauty of the scene from the Ana Sagar *bund* on a fair evening after rain, when, amid the play of endless colours, the sun veils itself behind the purple hills that surround the clear blue lake, and light slowly melts into darkness. This scene once enjoyed is never forgotten.

Owing to its situation and the natural strength of the fortress of Taragarh. which overlooks it, the town of Ajmer, like the famous Koh-i-Noor, has always been a prize in the hands of the victor. Being "the key to Rajputana," as Colonel Tod calls it, its importance as a *point d'appui*, in the midst of a country inhabited by a brave and warlike people, divided into clans and forming separate kingdoms and States, has always been readily recognised by those who have striven for the mastery of Upper India.

Ajmer is situated in the centre of the Rajputana-Malwa Railway line, being 305 miles north of Ahmedabad (677 miles from Bombay), 234 miles south west of Agra; 271 miles south of Delhi, *via* Jaipur and Bandikui and 235 miles *via* Phulera Rewari cord line; and 393 miles north of Khandwa—the four termini of the Railway system.

Climate.—The climate of Ajmer is one of the healthiest in India, particularly bracing in the winter; the seasons are all moderate, and the air is dry and hot in summer and cold and bracing in winter, particularly in December, January and February, when hoar frost not unfrequently covers the ground.

The level of the province varies from one thousand to two thousand feet above sea level. The average temperature is, therefore, much moderated and is generally lower than the latitude would indicate. The place is singularly free from cyclones, earthquakes and violent storms, and is a good place to live in in summer. A couplet says:—

सियालो खाटू भलो, उंदालो अजमेर ।
नागीनो नितका भलो, सावण बीकानेर ॥

"Khatoo (in Marwar) is pleasant in winter, and Ajmer in summer; Nagor is pleasant all the year round; Bikaner is good in the rains." This may be explained by a comparison of the mean temperature in summer of Ajmer with that of other cities in Upper India, as well as by the fact, strange as it is, that Ajmer never has more than a week of continuous heat. Four or five days of heat, and there is either a mild dust storm or a mild shower to cool the air. Writing in 1841 A.D., Dr. R. H. Irvine says[1]:—

> The close saturated atmosphere is not often experienced, though occasionally very close days and nights happen. The thermometer averages 84 degrees: whenever the mercury rises to 88 degrees or 90 degrees, rain speedily will fall.

Since then there has been a change. During the 58 years ending 1938 (1881-1938), the maximum temperatures recorded in the shade were 116·9 degrees in June 1894, and 114 in May 1912; the minimum being 27 on 15 and 16 January, 1935, (20 degrees below normal) and 29 on 20 January, and 30 on 1 February, 1905. A temperature chart giving the maximum and the minimum for the last 60 years is given in Appendix B.

The average maximum and minimum temperatures for the decades following 1901 A. D. are:—

Years	Maximum	Minimum
1901—1910	110·4	44·
1911—1920	109·9	37·6
1921—1930	108·7	34·6
1931—1937	109·7	32·4

The average mean temperature of four representative months at Ajmer for the last quarter of the nineteenth century was:—

January	...	...	...	59·4 degrees.
May	...	...	...	91·5 ,,
July	...	...	...	84·9 ,,
November	...	...	...	67·9 ,,

1. Medical Topography of Ajmer, p. 66. (1840 A.D.)

The average annual rainfall is 21·2 inches; the lowest recorded was 8·18 in 1891-92 A. D., and the highest, 41 inches in 1908 A. D.

Language.—The Hindus, with the exception of those who have come from outside Rajputana, speak either the Hindi or the Marwari dialect of it. The lower classes of Mussalmans speak Marwari and the upper classes, Hindustani. Learned pandits sometimes talk in Sanskrit, and the English educated Indians use the English language in official intercourse.

Arts and Manufactures.—Dyeing and lace-making are the principal manufactures of Ajmer. English muslins and *silks* are dyed in different colours and beautiful designs. and are used principally by ladies of higher classes for *aurahnas* and *kanchlees* (kind of bodice). These are not only used in Rajputana but exported to Malwa, the Berars, Khandesh, Gujrat, and to all places where Marwaries are to be found. Lace-making—*gota*, *kinari*, *lappa*, *gokhru*, etc.—is another industry of rising importance, and though the trade in both is in the hands of Mahajans, the manufacturers are almost all Muhammadans; and, in the case of lace-making, generally those of Delhi. Ajmer laces differ in colour, quality and shape from those manufactured at Delhi. They are preferred by the inhabitants of Rajputana to Delhi laces. Gold embroidery work—*salma sitara* and *kalabatoo*—on silks, velvets, and other cloths is also largely done in Ajmer.

An important industry of Ajmer is the making of various kinds of brass, copper and bell-metal utensils, such as dishes, *katordans*, *lotas* and cooking pots of different shapes and sizes.

Gold and silver ornaments for men and women are largely manufactured in Ajmer; and some of them are good specimens of the goldsmith's art. These ornaments[1] made in Ajmer are not only used by the higher classes in Ajmer-Merwara, but are largely exported to the different parts of Rajputana and other provinces where Marwaries have settled.

Another piece of art-work is the making of *jalees* in Nagor cement, called *kadhi*, with pieces of glass of different colours, in different designs and all kinds of geometrical figures—more generally rectangles, circles, and semi-circles. Some of these were exhibited in the Delhi Exhibition of 1902 A. D.

1. *Doras*, *Kanthees* and rings are the principal gold ornaments worn by men; *Timnias*, *Tussics*, *Mala*, *Har*, *Jhela*, *Jhutna*, *Bor*, *Bazu*, *Hathphul*, *Gokhru*, *Bangdi*, *Poonchi* *Goojri* and *Gujra* are the principal gold ornaments for women.

Salt used to be manufactured in large quantities in the Ramsar Parganah, but the manufacture was stopped by Government in 1870 A.D. The making of *lac* bangles used to be another industry in Ajmer, but it is also declining owing to the introduction of German and Austrian glass bangles. Ivory and wood bangles are made in Ajmer; also sandalwood combs and rosaries and small boxes, which are largely purchased and taken home by Mussalman pilgrims to the Dargah, along with *revdees* and *tillees* (sweets, of which the oilseed is the principal ingredient). Carpets (*qalins*) and durries of beautiful Kashmir, Persian, and Bokhara patterns are made in the Ajmer jail, and orders for them are received from distant stations.

Food.—The Hindus, with the exception of the Rajputs, some up-country Brahmins, Kayasthas, and some of the lower castes, are vegetarians. Wheat and barley, gram, maize and bajra are the staple food grains. People generally take two meals; breakfast at 10-11 a.m. and dinner at 6-8 p.m. The use of tea is spreading. All vegetarians and the Muhammadans, with the exception of some up-country Mussalmans, are total abstainers. The habit of drinking is increasingly spreading amongst low-caste Hindus. Unlike the natives of the United Provinces, who take fried dishes for dinner, Hindus of this province eat *rotis* at both meals. More ghee, sugar, and condiments, especially *chillies*, are consumed here than in the United Provinces, the Punjab or Gujrat. *Chowka*,[1] the distinctive feature of the United Provinces, is not strictly observed here, chiefly because Jain influence has always remained predominant in Rajputana.

Clubs.—There are 4 clubs (1) The Ajmer Club situated near the District Court House, of which higher European and a few Indian Officers are members, (2) The Indian Club in the Kaisar bagh, 'for the Indian intelligentsia; and the two Railway Institutes for railway employees, (3) The Railway Institute for Europeans and Anglo-Indians and (4) The Bisset Institute for the Indian employees of the Railway.

The Ajmer Club is situated in the north-east corner of the Kaiser Bagh, and has excellent facilities for all kinds of games. Here the Band of the Rajputana Auxiliary Force discourses music every Sunday evening. In front of the Club, stands the Saunders Memorial, a beautiful marble *chattri* with fountains in it.

1. The practice of taking food in the kitchen itself, sitting apart from and not touching one another is called *chowka*. When the food consists of fried dishes only, no chowka is observed.

Festivals and Fairs.—In addition to the Hindu national festivals of *Dashera* in October, *Holi* in March April and *Dewali* in November, observed throughout India, a number of other festivals are observed in Ajmer, amongst which the chief is that of *Gangaur*, which, with the two *Tij* festivals, are peculiar to Rajputana. These three are in reality ladies' festivals. The *Gangaur* festival, in honour of Gauri, wife of Siva, is celebrated by the Rajputs and the Mahajans. It celebrates the conjugal felicity of Hindu households, and all virgins and married women take part in it. It begins with the *Sil Saptami*—which comes seven days after the *Holi* (when the goddess of small-pox is worshipped by women)—and lasts for a fortnight, when in almost every muhalla (parish) inhabited by Mahajans, images of Gauri and Ishwara (female and male deities) fully adorned are exhibited. The places are decorated and ladies assemble and sing. Four times the images are taken out to the public gardens and brought back, accompanied by music.

Festivals are also held in honour of King Ajaipal, the founder of Ajmer when worship is offered to him at a place called after him, Ajaipal, seven miles away from Ajmer; and Goga Chauhan, who fell with his hundred and sixty sons and grandsons in attempting to bar the last inroad of Sultan Mahmud of Ghazni, in Rajputana.

A number of public fairs are held in Ajmer in connection with religious festivals, mostly in the rainy season, when Ajmer is at its best. The biggest fairs are:—

1. The Jaljhulni Ekadashi, the eleventh day of Bhadwa Sud (August September) when the idols in the temples of Ajmer are all taken out in a grand procession for a bath in the Anasagar lake.
2. The Sil Saptami Fair in honour of the goddess of small-pox held in the morning near the Daulat Bagh and in the evening at the Madar Gate.
3. The Savitri Fair held in Pushkar, is the most fashionable fair.
4. The Dashera or the Ravana Fair held in Asoj (September October) near the Carriage and Wagon Shops, and also outside the Usri Gate.
5. The biggest fair in the province is the Pushkar Kartik Fair in October November, when nearly a lakh of pilgrims bathe in the Pushkar Lake.

Tejaji-ka-Mela is another local festival of importance; though observed by all classes of Hindus, it is the principal festival of the peasantry. Beawar, Tabiji and Kekri are the chief places of worship of this deity. Tejaji is always represented as a warrior on horseback with a drawn sword and a snake biting his tongue; and the Jats and Gujars wear an amulet of silver or gold with this device round their necks to protect them from snakes. The festival is held with great *eclat* and ceremony in Kekri and Beawar, under the patronage of the district authorities.

The chief Muhammadan festivals, with the exception of the Mohurrum, the Shabrat, and the two Ids, are the Urs of Khwaja Sahib, and of Miran Sahib. Urs Khwaja Sahib attracts about 50,000 people from outside Ajmer.

The Kingdom of Ajmer, in its days of prosperity, was famous for four things, as the popular lines say:—

अजमेरा के मायने, चार चीज़ सरनाम ।
ख्वाजे साहब की दरगाह कहिये, पुष्कर का अस्नान ।
मकराणा में पत्थर निकले, साँभर लूण की खान ॥

TRANSLATION:—"Four things are famous in the territory of Ajmer—

1. Khwaja Sahib-ki-Dargah at Ajmer.
2. The sacred lake of Pushkar.
3. Marble mines of Makrana.
4. Sambhar salt mines."

RELIGION

The Hindus, who form about two thirds of the population of the city of Ajmer are divided into several sects, Vaishnavas, Shaivas, Jains, and others. The orthodox amongst them, follow their several creeds. In the seventies of the last century, Swami Dayanand Saraswati started a reformist movement in India, and told the Hindus that they were Aryas, as described everywhere in their religious books and not Hindus; that the foreigners originally called them Sindus, as they first came into contact with the Indians living near the river Sind (Indus). The term Sindus in time became Hindus by the law of phonetic change. The reformist movement is called, Arya Samaj (Society of Aryas).

The **Aryasamaj** is a body of Hindus whose aim is to restore Hinduism to its pristine purity. Accepting the Vedas alone as Revelation, the Arya Samaj rejects the authority of the Puranas and all other books held as Sastras by the orthodox Hindus. It rejects idol-worship, the caste system, the sanctity of places of pilgrimage, most of the rites, practices and customs which at present prevail among the Hindus, governing their lives and regulating their conduct in social and domestic life. It knows no untouchability, and gives women a status equal to men.

The special connection of the Aryasamaj with Ajmer is due to the fact that the founder of the movement, Mahrishi Dayanand Saraswati, breathed his last in Ajmer on the Diwali, the 30th September, 1883 A.D. Mahrishi Dayanand's remains were interred with great ceremony in a garden on the bank of the Ana Sagar presented to the Paropkarini Sabha by his disciple, the late Rajadhiraj Nahar Singh of Shahpura.

An Aryasamaj had been established at Ajmer in 1881. In 1886, it constructed a large building as its meeting place in Kaisar Gunj, with a lecture hall and a court yard. Additions have been made, from time to time, and the Arya Samaj Bhavan is now a double storeyed imposing building on the Seven Dials in Kaisar Gunj.

Swami Dayanand Saraswati had, in 1881, appointed by a will, a body of twenty three persons with His Highness the Maharana of Udaipur as president, to carry on his work after his death. This body called the Paropkarini Sabha held its first meeting in December, 1883 in the Udaipur House, Mayo College, Ajmer and decided to establish, in honour of Dayanand's memory, an Ashram (institute) consisting of a college, a library, a hospital, an orphanage and a lecture hall.

In 1888, by which time, a number of Arya Samajes had been established in the various towns of Rajputana and Malwa, a Pratinidhi Sabha composed of the representatives of these Samajes was formed with headquarters at Ajmer. It represents 167 Aryasamajes in these two provinces.

In 1889, the Paropkarini Sabha established a High School in the Aryasamaj building. It is affiliated to the Rajputana and Central India Board of Intermediate and High School Education. It contains about 1,250 boys including the Primary section (250) and the Middle School section (about 300). It employes 46 teachers. It has obtained recognition in Commerce and Drawing, besides Sanskrit and Science for High School Examination. It is now proposed to raise this school to an Intermediate College with sections for Agriculture and Technology. A site has already been acquired for the building on the Beawar Road.

The Paropkarini Sabha also established in 1889, as part of the Dayanand Ashram, an orphanage which is at present housed in two buildings, one for girls and the other for boys. It had 160 inmates in December, 1938 and is managed by a separate committee. Carpentry and tailoring are taught in it.

The Vedic Press, established by Mahrishi Dayanand Saraswati in Allahabad in 1875, to print his commentary on the Vedas was removed to Ajmer in 1890. A spacious building has been put up for it on the Seven Dials. It is one of the largest printing presses in Rajputana, and prints and publishes the works of Swami Dayanand Saraswati. On the west side of the Seven Dials, the Paropkarini Sabha has constructed the central building of the Dayanand Ashram, consisting of a splendid hall, sixty by twenty-eight by thirty-two feet, and side-rooms to accomodate the Vedic Library and the office of the Sabha. The Vedic Library or Pustakalaya contains a large collection of Sanskrit and English books on Vedic literature. It also contains books on history and general literature in Hindi, Gujrati, Marathi, English and Urdu. It is a free library. This Pustakalaya also sells the works of Swami Dayanand Saraswati, including his famous commentaries on the Vedas.

The Paropkarini Sabha[1] owns two gardens on the Anasagar lake, formerly known as the Shahpura Bagh and the Bakshiji-ka-Bagh. In the former, repose Swamiji's remains. Over the remains of the Mahrishi, there now stands a Yajna-Shala where *havan* with the chanting of Vedic Mantras is regularly performed every morning and evening throughout the year. In the other garden, a Saraswati Bhavan (Temple of Learning) has recently been built. It is an imposing double-storied building with a big lecture hall and commands a magnificent view of the Anasagar lake. It invariably catches the eye of those who go to Pushkar or the Foysagar.

In a building overlooking the lake and adjoining the Saraswati Bhavan is housed a Sadhu Ashram. The Paropkarini Sabha established a Sadhu Ashram about 1900 A.D. to train Sadhus to popularize Vedic teachings and establish Aryasamajes where they did not exist in the various provinces of India. The institution failed to take root at the time. The Arya Pratinidhi Sabha has now revived the scheme and established this Ashram.

The Aryasamaj has established a Widow's Home, in which widows from all over Rajputana and outside, find shelter till they re-marry or return home. A girls school in connection with the Arya Samaj was opened by Mrs. Gulab Devi, wife of Syt. Mathura Prasad, the then secretary of the Ajmer

1. In 1933, the Paropkarini Sabha held semi-centenary celebrations of the death of Swami Dayanand Saraswati at Ajmer, when over a lakh of people connected with the Aryasamajes of India, Africa and Burma, assembled to commemorate the occasion.

Aryasamaj in 1897 A.D. It is a most popular institution with 300 pupils, doing admirable work, and is personally supervised by Mrs. Gulab Devi, who has given away all her property for its maintenance.

Two weekly papers are published, one by the Arya Pratinidhi Sabha, Rajputana and Malwa, called the *Aryamartanda*, and the other, the *Vijaya*, by the Dayananda Orphanage Committee.

Jains.—The Jains are an important community in Ajmer. They are divided into three sects: (1) Swatambari, (2) Digambari, who worship idols in temples, and (3) Sthanak Vasies, or Dhoondias, who do not worship idols but who have their Thanaks (Sanskrit, Sthanak = place) where their preachers (male or female) reside. They move from place to place, but always on foot, never using the Railway or any other conveyance. The Jains, to which community, the principal *Seths* of Ajmer belong, have a free Dispensary and a High School.

Mussalmans.—The indigenous Mussalmans of Ajmer consist chiefly of the Khadims of the Dargah, and the Inderkotis and Deswalis, who are converted Hindus. The Deswalis are the latest converts, among whom Hindu ceremonies and rites are still observed. The Mussalmans, who have come from the Punjab, the United Provinces, and other parts of India are either artizans and workmen in factories, or are employed in Government or Railway service. The Khadims live on the offerings of the pilgrims and the income of two revenuefree villages granted by the Mughal emperors. The Inderkotis when not in the service of the Hindu seths, farm fruit gardens in Inderkot, Gughra, and other places. The Deswalis are either in the service of Government or are vendors of lime, stones and other building materials.

Parsees.—The Parsees have a Fire Temple of their own, on the Nasirabad Road opposite the Railway Institute, and a Tower of Silence outside the town, not very far from the Government distillery.

Sikhs.—The *Sikhs* are a body of Hindus who, while they respect all Hindu Sastras, look upon the Granth Sahib, a book containing the teachings and sayings of Sri Guru Nanak Deva, the founder of Sikhism, as their Sacred Book. The Sikhs in the city of Ajmer number 341 (1931 Census). The first printing press in Ajmer was started by a Sikh named Boota Singh in the eighties of the last century.

CHAPTER III.

GROWTH OF THE CITY OF AJMER

AJAIMERU Doorg, or the fortress of Ajmer, now called Taragarh, was built by King Ajaipal Chauhan, who was King of Sapadlaksh, with Sambhar as his Capital, early in the sixth century A.D. He also built the town of Ajmer. The village Ajaisar, to the south of Foysagar, commemorates his name.

The *Prithviraj Vijaya* says that Ajaideva II, the twenty third Chauhan King of Sakambhari, the first being Vasudeva, founded a town and named it after himself. On the strength of this statement, Dr. Buhler has, in his article on "Ajmer" in the Indian Antiquary, Vol. XXVI, pp. 162-63, concluded that the present city of Ajmer was founded by him.

The *Prithviraj Vijaya*, Sarga VIII, also says that Someshwar, the third son of Arnoraj or Anaji founded a town where his elder brother and predecessor Vigrahraj's palaces stood, and named it after himself. As these palaces stood in Ajmer, the town founded by Someshwar and named after Arnoraj, must have existed in or near Ajmer. No one, however, has heard of such a town, and there is no mention of it in any book. The fact evidently is, that several Chauhan kings repaired, renovated or improved the existing town, and the court poets, given to exaggeration, have stated that each of the kings founded this town. Ajaideva II made improvements and additions to the town of Ajmer, and probably transferred his Capital from Sakambhari (Sambhar) to Ajmer, and the poet gives him credit for foundng it.

A convincing proof that Ajmer existed long before Ajaideva II or Ajairaj was born, is furnished by the inscriptions in the *Thadas* and *Chhatrees* of the Digambar Jain religious leaders at Ajmer. An inscription in one of the Chhatrees built over the remains of Hemraj, disciple of Bhattarak Ratankirtiji at Ajmer, bears date S. 817. (A.D. 760). Three other inscriptions in these Chhatrees are dated the 845 A. D., 854 A. D., and 871 A. D. respectively. This was long before the time of Ajaideva II, who lived early in the twelfth century A. D. That these Jain Pandits and Bhattaraks died and were cremated in Ajmer proves that the town of Ajmer existed in the eighth century A. D. and must have been founded prior to that time.

The following poetic description of Ajmer as it existed in the twelfth century A.D. appears in the *Prithviraj Vijaya*, which was composed about 1190 A.D:—

"Ajaimeru (Ajmer) is full of temples of gods, and is thus, like Meru, the abode of gods. Anything situated on an elevation is visible to all; but Ajmer, though so situate, is quite invisible to the famine, which goes everywhere else. *Baoris*, wells, *talaos*, *pyavoos* (water stalls) are full of water here. People sitting in the *jharokas* enjoy the cool breeze of the Ganges of Paradise. The Vāruna (god of water) has come and taken shelter in the wells on the hill-fort of Ajmer. The smoke of fragrant things burnt by women to perfume their hair gather in thick clouds and hide the moon. The increasing prosperity of the city has laid low the pride of Amaravati (the mythical city of god Indra). Other cities where there are thieves, tyrannical rulers, and poor and famine-striken people, cannot come up to this city, which knows these things not. The camphor and musk which drop from the bodies of the citizens in the streets, make the clothes of the passers-by white-black (*pandurshyam*). The city Rama won after crossing the sea (the golden Lanka) and that founded by Krishna in the sea (Dwarka), are not fit to be slave girls of this city."

According to the *Prithviraj Vijaya*, Ajaideva's son, Anaji or Arnoraj (about 1130-1150 A.D.) built the Ana Sagar lake, to purify the land which had become impure owing to the spilling of Mussalman blood in a battle fought at that place. Anaji's son, Visaldeva (1151-1163 A.D.) constructed the Visalsar lake (Visla) with temples and palaces round it. He also built the College at Ajmer, later converted by Shahabuddin Ghori into a mosque, and now called the *Adhai-din-ka Jhonpra*. As Visaldeva conquered Delhi and the whole of Hindustan between the Vindhya and the Himalayas, Ajmer, having become the capital of the empire, naturally became a very flourishing city. Those were the palmy days of Ajmer; and it was during the reign of Visaldeva's grand nephew Prithviraj, that it attained the highest prosperity that it ever enjoyed prior to the advent of the English.

In 1192 A.D., Ajmer was taken by Sultan. Shahabuddin Ghori. The *Tajul Maasir*, the author of which was a contemporary of Shahabuddin Ghori, in its hyperbolic language, says of Ajmer of that time :—

"The gardens of Ajmer are robed in seven colours, and the face of the hills and the jungles is the envy of the famous Picture Gallery

THE VICTORIA JUBILEE CLOCK TOWER.

City of Ajmer.

of China. Flowers so adorn the gardens and the plains as if a garden had been sent to the earth from Heaven itself. The morning breeze sprinkles *attar* (otto) in the garden and the eastern breeze burns *ood* (a sweet-smelling wood) in it. The clothes of the jungle are perfumed by the *sunbal* and *banafsha* flowers, and the breasts of the morning are adorned with the clothes of roses and the poppy flowers. The dust of Ajmer has the perfume of musk of the deer of Tibet. The fountains of sweet water in Ajmer compete with the *kosar* (the spring water of Paradise). The water is so clear, that the smallest pebble is clearly visible in the bed of the fountain in the darkness of the night; in sweetness it is like *salsabil* (a spring in Paradise) and it is as wholesome as the water of life. The city and the suburbs are exceedingly beautiful, owing to general brightness and light, the beauty and purity of its flowers, the purity of its air and earth, and abundance of water and trees; it is a place of inestimable enjoyment and luxury."

During his short stay at Ajmer, the Sultan, "destroyed the pillars and foundations of the idol temples." Visaldeva's College was dismantled, and a portion of it converted into a mosque, to which Shamsuddin Altamash (1211-1236 A. D.) added the present screen of seven arches. The prosperity of the town declined so much in the middle of the fifteenth century A.D., that it is said that tigers used to roam where the tomb of Khwaja Muinuddin Chishti stands.

A mausoleum over the tomb of the Khwaja was built some time about 1464 A.D. Mallu Khan, Governor of Ajmer under the Mandoo Sultan, built about this time the two Malusar tanks and a garden to the south of Ajmer, at the foot of the eastern spur of the Taragarh hill.

In 1535 A.D., Rao Maldeva of Marwar took possession of Ajmer, strengthened the fortress and built the half-finished water lift to carry water from the Chashma into the fort of Taragarh. About 1558 A.D., Ajmer passed into the possession of Akbar; and in 1571 A.D., to improve the condition of the place, he ordered a strong wall to be built round it and a palace to be erected for his own residence.[1]

This palace, called the Daulat khana, is now known as the Magazine. The city wall, when Emperor Akbar built it, was only 4,045 yards in circumference. He also built the *Khas Bazar*, now called the Dargah Bazar. A gallery or passage ran right through the length of the street for the convenience of the ladies of the royal harem, when they went on foot from the Daulatkhana to the Dargah. On such occasions the shops were curtained off from the public gaze, the shop-keepers taking their stand on the street side of the partitions.

1. Elliot's History of India, Vol. V, p. 335. Also Tabqati Akbari.

Akbar added the Akbari Masjid to the Dargah in 1570. He built a Phul Mahal, of which only the gateway now stands at the back of the house of Seth Kalyan Mal Bhadagtia towards the Dhobi Muhalla. In 1569 A.D., Ismail Kuli Khan, Akbar's subedar at Ajmer, built the Buland Darwaza (high gateway) of the shrine of Miran Sayad Husain. The present mausoleum itself was built later in 1615 A.D, by Aitbar Khan. In 1569 A.D., Ghisu Khan built a mosque in Inderkot, now in ruins. In 1643 A.D , one Miya Bai built the mosque opposite the Motikatra. An inscription on an arch mentions Miya Bai and the date of construction as H. 1053; and Tilokdi, the daughter of Akbar's famous musician, Tansen, built another in the Dargah Bazar in 1652 A.D. It is a domed building. The inscription on the central arch gives the date, H. 1052, and the name and parentage of Tilokdi (Tilok Devi).

Ajmer, in Akbar's time, was bounded on the north by the Delhi Gate (still standing); on the east by the gate since rebuilt and called the Bansphad Darwaza (the western end of Naya Bazar); on the south by the Diggi Darwaza, demolished in 1883 A.D.; and on the west, by the Tripolia Gate (still standing). Thus, after a lapse of 376 years (1194-1570 A.D.), during which Ajmer had been neglected, it began to recover in Akbar's reign.

Jahangir, after he came to the throne in 1605 A.D., built the Daulat Bagh, and erected palaces in it, which have since disappeared. In 1615 A.D., he had the Visla lake which he called *Bisal Tal*, repaired and built a palace on its bank. He also built a residence for himself on the Pushkar lake which still stands, though in ruins, behind the Jodhpur Ghat. He added a small mosque to the Dargah, and presented a second *deg* (cauldron,) the first one having been presented by Akbar.

Sir Thomas Roe, who was in Ajmer from 22nd December 1615 to 1st December 1616 A.D., as the ambassador of King James I. of England to the court of Jahangir, gives a very poor description of Ajmer. In a letter dated the 17th January 1616 to Lord Carew, he says: "The king now resides in a base old city wherein is no house but of mud, not so great as a cottage on Hounslow Heath, only himself hath one of stone. His Lords live in tents."[1] He does not even mention the Dargah Khwaja Sahib or the Adhai-din-ka-Jhonpra or the Dargah Bazar, or even the city wall.

After Jahangir, came Shah Jahan, who built in 1637 A.D. the beautiful baradaries (pavilions) standing on the Ana Sagar

1. Journal (Hakluyt Society), Vol. II, page 113.

Lake and a Turkish bath, since demolished except the floor. He built the present mausoleum over the tomb of the Khwaja, and the Juma Masjid in the Dargah, both in white marble. He also repaired and extended the city wall. He laid out a garden to the west of Ana Sagar which, though in ruins is still called the Shah Jahani Bagh.

In Aurangzeb's time, the Visla Lake was destroyed during the war with Dara Shikoh; and the fortress of Ajmer, Taragarh, suffered great damage. Sayad Muhammad's mosque situated on the top of some shops in the Dargah Bazar was built by Sayad Muhammad in Aurangzeb's time in 1693 A D. (H. 1104), as stated in an inscription on the arches of the mosque. The chronogram is, بیت‌المقدس نیک زیا شد بنا

In 1704 A.D. Sayad Abdullah Khan built the Abdullahpura, consisting of a tomb for his wife, a garden and a mosque, with a high wall round them. His son, Husain Ali Khan, built a tomb to his father, Sayad Abdullah Khan, in 1710 A.D., during the reign of King Farrukhsayar. The place was used afterwards as a Government Jail, and later on, as a *sarai*.

The two tombs still stand on the Beawar road. The old gateway facing the north was dismantled when the present road was built. A new gateway. in lieu of the old one, was put up by the Railway facing the east. In 1769 A.D., Santooji, the Mahratta subedar of Ajmer, laid out a garden outside Madar Gate, called it Chishti-Chaman[1] and presented it to the Dargah. He built a bazar called Santupura near it.

In 1773 A.D. (H. 1187), the Idgah, (near the Government College,) was built by Mirza Chaman Beg, son of Adil Beg, Scindia's subedar of Malwa. The mosque in it is 130 yards long and 40 yards broad. The Idgah has five gates. In front of the mosque, there is open space 130 ft. long and 52 ft. wide. An inscription on a marble slab in the central arch of the mosque mentions Chaman Beg and the date in a chronogram شد آراستہ معبد اهل دین. His remains were interred in the Dargah near the water stall and a marble tomb built over it.

In 1791 A D, Sivaji Nana became governor of Ajmer, and built the Jhalra on the Taragarh hill called the "Nana Sahib ka Jhalra" (water reservoir). It was he who designed and started the construction of the present Naya Bazar. Shops began to spring up there in 1797 A.D. The street, however, was not completed when Colonel Tod in December 1819 A.D. passed through Ajmer.[2]

1. Now it has been transformed into a *sarai*.
2. Tod's Rajasthan, Vol. I, page 777.

In 1803 A.D., Bala Rao Inglia, the then Governor of Ajmer, demolished the Santupura built by his predecessor Santuji, as it provided access to the city *morchals* (entrenchments). When Santupura was demolished, the Mahratta governor of Ajmer, gave to the owners of the houses that were destroyed, the Sarai that Akbar had built for travellers, situated just inside the Madar Gate. There were 27 domed apartments in it with an imposing gateway which still stands. This place was named Ganpatpura after the image of god Ganpati placed above the doorway of the gate.

Bala Rao founded the village of Balapura, near the Madar Hill, strengthened the fortifications of Ajmer, repaired the city wall, and dug a ditch round it, some remnants of which near the Madar Gate still exist. Bapu Scindia, the last Mahratta governor of Ajmer, (1816-1818) built the Bapugarh and repaired the Bajranggarh temple.

In 1818 A.D., Ajmer was ceded to the English, and on 28th July, 1818, Sir David Ochterlony and Colonel Nixon, occupied the city, which was then at a very low ebb. With the advent of the English, bright days dawned on Ajmer. With peace, there has been continuous progress. Once the capital of an empire, Ajmer fell on evil days with the fall of that empire towards the end of the twelfth century. In the beginning of the nineteenth century, under the British Government, it began to regain its former position of prosperity, and we now find the city more populous than it had ever been before.

The population of the city, which in 1818 A.D., was about 24,000 souls all told, rose to 119,524 in 1931 A.D. The whole valley is filled with buildings, roads and gardens. The railway has now linked Ajmer with the United Provinces on the east, Punjab on the north, Bombay on the south, and Sindh on the west

Since 1818, the town has been greatly extended. The Naya Bazar was finished and the Agra Gate built about 1820. This bazar is now the finest street of Ajmer. The Moti Katra, so called after Moti Begum, the wife of Sir D. Ochterlony, was built about the same time. When founded, it was called Nasirgunj after General Sir David Ochterlony, on whom the title of Nasir-ud-daula had been conferred by the King of Delhi.[1] Mr. Cavendish (Oct. 1827 to Oct. 1831 A. D.) built the street outside Madar Gate, where the short-lived Santu-

1. Its gateway, which is the most conspicuous thing in the Dargah Bazar was built by the General. It was afterwards sold by Government to Seth Bagh Mal Bhadagtia.

pura once existed. It is named Cavendishpura, after the founder, and is now the busiest street of Ajmer. He also enlarged the city wall near the old Diggi Darwaza, and built the Usri Gate. This extension, begun in 1828, was finished on 18th October 1831. Mr. Edmonstone (1834-36 A.D.) extended the Dargah Bazar by building the Dhan Mandi (grain market). During the time of Mr. Macnaghten (July 1837-Feb. 1842 A.D.) and Colonel Dixon (1842-1857 A.D.) the Ana Sagar lake was adorned by a series of ghats and gardens. They are all on the south side of the lake, and abut the Pushkar road.

1. **Ramprasadji-ka-Ghat.**—This, with a garden attached to it, is the first ghat as we go from the city to the lake, and was built on a sanad being granted by the Superintendent of Ajmer on 12th July 1834 to Seth Askaran, father of Seth Ramprasad.

2. **Jagdish Ghat** with a temple attached to it. Seth Ram Narain Siriya, after obtaining a patta from the Teli shamlat, built the temple and a few steps near the edge of the water. The Marwari Agarwal Panchayat built the ghat later.

3. **Gulkhandiyon-ka-Ghat.**—It was originally built by Lakhmi Chand, son of Manak Chand and Mul Chand, son of Motilal in 1844 A.D., at Col. Dixon's request. It was later purchased by S. Ram Ballabh Gulkhandia from Manak Chand Milap Chand. A spinning and weaving factory worked by hand-machines is located in it in place of the old garden.

5. Next to it, is the open land, called the Dhobi Ghat. Dhobis wash clothes here and cattle drink water.

6, 7. The next two ghats, formerly known as **Bakhshiji ka-Ghat** and **Shahpura Ghat** are now owned by the Paropkarini Sabha of India. The Shahpura Ghat was built by the Raja of Shahpura in 1847-48, then an Istimrardar of Ajmer, at the request of Col. Dixon. In the garden attached to these ghats, now stand a Saraswati Mandir (Temple of Learning), a Yagya Shala and a Sadhu Ashram.

8. **Lodhan-ka-Ghat** lies next to these two ghats. It was built in 1848 A.D. by Seth Hamir Singh Lodha, at Col. Dixon's request. A garden is attached to it. An open space intervenes between it and the next ghat.

9. **Khazanchion-ka-Ghat** was built by Seth Radha Kishen of Muttra, Government Treasurer in Rajputana, after receiving a sanad dated the 6th November, 1839 A D. from Col. Dixon. A garden is attached to it. It is now owned by Seth Ratanlal.

10. **Navagraha Ghat** lies next to it. The ghat and garden attached to it were built by Seth Kishan Chand Kan Mal who were granted a sanad dated the 6th September, 1846. A fair used to be held here. This is the last ghat on the Anasagar lake.

At Colonel Dixon's suggestion, four reservoirs to supply water to the town were built, two outside the city wall—the Surajkund (in 1854) outside Madar Gate and the Chandkund between the Delhi and the Agra Gates—and two inside the town, the Nahar in the Nahar Muhalla and the Diggi at the foot of the Taragarh hill. Owing to the establishment of waterworks, Surajkund, Chandkund and the Nahar which received their supply of water from the Ana Sagar have been filled up. Colonel Dixon also deepened and repaired the Jhalra for the use of the town.

In the early thirties of the nineteenth century, a few rich families of Mahajans from Marwar and Jaipur came and settled in Ajmer owing to the security of life and property under the British Raj, and the facilities of business and concessions given by the early British administrators of Ajmer, who wanted to make Ajmer the centre of their influence in Rajputana. One of the first to come, was the family of Seth Ram Prasad Agarwala from Jhunjhunoo in Shekhawati. Seth Ram Prasad was a public-spirited citizen, and Ajmer benefited greatly from his benefactions. They were four brothers, sons of Seth Askaran. In the famine of 1834 A.D., he built the ghat on the Ana Sagar named after him, Ram Prasadji ka Ghat. Later, when Col. Dixon proposed to have water reservoirs constructed in Ajmer to provide water for all parts of the town, and suggested that public subscriptions should be raised for the purpose, Seth Ram Prasad offered to build, at his own expense, two of the four reservoirs. He built the Diggi at the foot of the Taragarh hill which still exists and supplies water to the southern part of the city, and the Nahar at a little distance behind the present Badshahi building in Naya Bazar, to supply water to the northern portion. He also dug the wellknown Shakkar Kui near the Dudiya well and the Daulat Bagh to supply water to the public, for which Government gave him a patta and a *parvana* dated 25th July, 1840. He also built the old Pushkar Ghati road and a kund at the top of the hill. The remains of the paved road and the kund are still visible. He built tibaras at the Hindu sacred places, Ajaipal and Baijnath in the environs of Ajmer. Seth Ram Prasad also built the Narsinghji temple in Nayabazar, Ajmer.

He rendered great assistance to Col. Dixon in populating the new town of Nayanagar, in recognition of which, Col. Dixon, by an order dated 31st August, 1840, granted him a remission of half court fees and one-fourth octroi.[1]

1. When Seth Ram Prasad went on pilgrimage to Gaya in Behar, the A. G. G., Rajputana and Commissioner of Ajmer gave him a note addressed to all British Officers on the way to help him. Captain Dixon also gave him a Circular letter dated 1 February 1837, mentioning that Seth Ram Prasad was going on a pilgrimage, taking a party of 900 pilgrims, 100 armed men, 75 bullock carts, 2 *Ruths*, 50 camels, 26 horses, 5 palkies and 3 chaprasis and asked all British Officers to help him.

Seth Ram Prasad persuaded his relative, Seth Pooran Mal of Ganeri, also to come to Ajmer. Seth Pooran Mal built three nohras and houses in the Nayabazar, one of which is the present Kharwa house and another by it, which now belongs to Karan Mal Bharagtya. He built the wellknown Rangji Temple at Pushkar, an account of which appears in the chapter on Pushkar.

A third well-to-do family, the Patwari family, came from Parbatsar. They were three brothers, Mohan Lal, Jawahar Lal and Chhotu Lal. Seth Mohan Lal built a big temple at Pushkar and endowed it with four shops situated in the Ghas Katla in Naya Bazar, Ajmer. Jawahar Lal built a big haveli in the Nahar Mohalla at the corner, where the Gajmalji ki Gali meets the Nahar Gali. Chhotu Lal built a haveli adjacent to that of Seth Karnidan, Seth Ram Prasad's brother.

Seth Ram Prasad's younger brother, Karnidan, built another haveli, adjacent to Ram Prasad's haveli. The fourth brother Dinanath built a haveli in front of the Nahar reservoir.

The following are the important *havelies* (big residential houses) in Ajmer. They were constructed during the Mahratta and the early British period in Ajmer.

1. The Patwa ki Haveli, built by Seth Magniram Zorawarmal Patwa of Jaisalmer in Karaka Chowk with its entrance in gali Nahar Muhalla at a cost of one lakh, seventyfive thousand rupees, between 1830 and 1840. This is the finest residential house in Ajmer and the carvings on the balconies overhanging the *Karaka Chowk* are the finest to be found anywhere.[1] It is said that the stone for the Jharokas and the masons who built them, came from Jaisalmer. The Patwa Seths have an equally beautiful house in Jaisalmer.

2. Narsinghdasji ki Haveli, also in Karaka Chowk built by Narsinghdas Agarwala, elder brother of Seth Ram Prasad between 1840 and 1850 A.D. It is now known as Deccani Vada.

3. Gajmalji ki Haveli built by Seth Gajmal Loonia, Oswal in Nahar Muhalla during the Mahratta times (1791—1818 A D.)

4. Ram Prasadji ki Haveli in Nahar Muhalla, built in 1840-1850.

5. Lodha House in Naya Bazar, built by Seth Hamir Singh father of Seth Sujan Mal Lodha about 1850 A.D,

6. Haji Muhammad Khan-ki-Haveli, built by Nawab Haji Muhammad Khan, Minister of Jodhpur, near Dhan Mandi about 1865 A.D. It was originally a small house of one Mubarak Mahal.

1. It is said that they were five brothers. The son of one of them was to be married to the daughter of Seth Gajmal Loonia of Ajmer. They sent a man from Jaisalmer asking Seth Gajmal to arrange accommodation for the marriage party and secure a house big enough to accommodate the five brothers in separate portions of it. As such a house was not available in Ajmer, the agent of the Jaisalmer Seths began to build such a house; and, though the preliminary ceremonies of the marriage had begun, the wedding itself had to be deferred for ten months till this house was ready.

7. Mamaiyon-ki-Haveli in Lakhan Kotri built during the Mahratta times (1791-1818).

Other wellknown havelies are Kanakmal Lodha's, Bahadurmal Agarwala's, Kesri Chand Mehta's, Sahaskaran Mehta's, Pratapmal Kanmal Mehta's, Jethmal Mehta's, and Mehta Kishan Chand's. They are all in Lakhankotri.

In 1843 A D. (H. 1259), Mir Saadat Ali, Mir Munshi of Rajputana Agency built the mosque opposite the present railway station. It has since been greatly enlarged. The inscription in four verses on an arch of the mosque beginning with میر سعادت‌علی کرد در اجمیر طارح مسجد و چاهی که هست از چشمهٔ آب بقا gives the date in the last half of the verse as H. 1269.

On 17th February 1868, Colonel Keating, Agent Governor General for Rajputana, laid the foundation stone of the present Government College building.

In Mr. Saunders' time (1871 to 1885), a new court-house and the Central Jail were built, and a hospital was opened in the Naya Bazar.

The Mayo College, with a number of Boarding Houses belonging to the various Rajputana States and residential houses for the Principal and the Head Master were built in 1875-82. Many new houses have since been put up in the Mayo College park, *vide*, Chapter on The Mayo College.

Telegraphic communication between Ajmer and Agra and Deesa was sanctioned in 1861-62 A.D. In June 1864, the wires, were brought down to Ajmer, and in September, carried on to Deesa.

The B. B. & C. I. Railway Company has filled up the entire area between the Visla lake and the Madar Hill with bungalows called *Fiftytwo Bungalows*, as also the area called the Hazari Bagh to the south of the Government College, Ajmer.

With the advent of the Railway and the transfer of the various offices connected with the Railway and, particularly, of the Locomotive and Carriage Shops to Ajmer from Agra and other places, and their subsequent extensions, the population of Ajmer began to increase by leaps and bounds. Plans were at once taken in hand to extend the town. The first extension planned by Mr. Saunders was towards the south, and Kaisarganj came into existence in 1884-5, with a large circle enclosing a park in the centre, and seven roads running out of the circle. The extension was beautifully planned, and within a very short time all available space was occupied by the shops and houses. This new extension, called Kaisarganj, is the most flourishing adjunct of Ajmer.

The Railway General office was built in 1884 and the railway workshops in 1879. The Adhai-din-ka-Jhonpra, the Magazine, and the Baradaries on the Ana Sagar Lake have been repaired and restored. In 1888 A.D., the Victoria Jubilee Clock Tower, opposite the Railway Station was built, to commemorate the Golden Jubilee of Her Majesty the Empress Victoria; and in 1898 A.D., the Victoria General Hospital was built in honour of Her Majesty's Diamond Jubilee.

In 1899-1901 A.D., the Trevor Town Hall was built to commemorate the connection of Colonel G. H. Trevor with Ajmer, first as Commissioner, and later, as Chief Commissioner of Ajmer-Merwara, from 1887 to 1895 A.D.

People began to settle down in the neighbourhood of the Railway shops; and Nagra, Jonesganj, Ramganj and Naraingañj sprang up in the early eighties of the last century. Jonesganj was established by the Railway about 1880, when the Railway Shops were erected in Ajmer. Land and other facilities were given by the Railway to its employees. The colony at Pal Bisla sprang up about 1890 A.D., and by it the settlement called, old Jadughar, between the Srinagar and Nasirabad roads. All these are now thickly populated areas.

As the population increased, the Ganj outside the Agra Gate, a very old extension, became congested, and Loongia and Bapugarh Muhallas sprang up near it. The area between the Imperial road to the Daulat Bagh, and the Jaipur and Katchery roads, which in old days had been covered by vegetable and fruit gardens, became a populous muhalla called Hathi Bhata. In the beginning of this century, a little later, Brahmpuri came into existence. These are now as congested areas as the walled city itself.

It was, however, chiefly towards the south, where the Railway shops are situated, that extensions took place in rapid succession; Bhagwan ganj, Asaganj (near the Tramway Station) Bheroonganj, Behariganj (near the cemetry on the Nasirabad road) and the Rabadya between the Mayo College and the Loco Shops, came into existence. Udaiganj and Bhajanganj on the Nasirabad road, and Ganeshganj to the south of Jonesganj sprang up, as also Paharganj, south of Asaganj. The Muhalla called Topdara between the Railway line and the Government High School also came into existence. Kalabagh and the adjacent gardens to the east of Daulat Bagh disappeared, and higher class people built houses there as also in the Civil Lines, which have all become well-populated areas,

THE GULAB BARI, behind the Mayo College, so called because roses grew here in hundreds of acres, contained a few huts prior to 1925. This colony was established about 1924. The residents are mostly people employed in public offices. The main road to it was constructed by the Municipality about the year 1934-35.

To the north of the Anasagar lake, between it and the *Anted ki Mata Temple*, has arisen Christianganj. There were a few isolated houses here prior to 1930. A survey with a view to townplanning was made in 1930-31, and it is now a well-populated suburb of Ajmer, inhabited by middle class people.

Ramnagar near Narsinghpura, and the Foysagar Road and Pushkar Road colonies, came into existence between 1925 and 1935. The Alwar Gate colony began to fill up about 1925, and is now a thickly populated area. Sringar Chanvri, Naya Bara, Bhopon ka Bara, Lohakan, Dongri Gehlotan, all old hamlets on the outskirts of the city of Ajmer and inhabited chiefly by Malees, to whom all the cultivated and uncultivated land around Ajmer except that to the west of Anasagar, originally belonged, and who have from ancient times formed the agricultural community of Ajmer, have all developed into small settlements.

Adarshnagar.—With a view to build a model town in Ajmer, the Adarshnagar Housing Society was formed by some enterprising persons living in the city in 1931. With the advice of Mr. Russel, the Architect to the Government of India, a plan was prepared and sanctioned by the Municipal Committee. A road 100 ft. wide and several 30 or 40 ft. wide and some smaller ones, have been provided, some of which have already been made by the Society. The lay out is practically a self contained one. They have provided for a school, a play-ground, a dispensary and shops to sell provisions. Though far from the city, this is a model colony of people of the upper middle class.

While these new colonies and the extensions were being constructed, many large and important buildings were constructed in Ajmer. The Roman Catholic Cathedral; the Dayanand Ashram; the Railway Institute and the Railway Hospital were built in Kaisarganj and on the Railway lands and Hazari Bagh, to the south of the city. The old Victoria Hospital, the new Court Houses, the General Post and Telegraph office, King Edward Memorial, the Government High School and the New Victoria Hospital in the Kaisarbagh and the Railway Bisset Institute were built towards the north and the east of the city.

CHAPTER IV

TARAGARH

THE celebrated fortress of Ajmer, famous in song as *Garh Beetli*, but commonly called Taragarh, is one of the most renowned fortresses in the East, and has played a prominent part in Indian history.

Name.—*Garh Beetli* is said to have been so called from the fact that the *garh* (fortress) was built on the Beetli hill. According to *Chahar Chaman Chitraman*,[1] however, the fort was called *Garh Bithali*, after Bithaldas Gor, the trusted general of Emperor Shah Jahan, who repaired the fort during his governorship of Ajmer from 1644 to 1656 A.D.

Situation.—The fort covers an area of 80 acres,[2] and is built on the crest of a towering hill "2,855 feet above sea level, and about 1,300 above the plain"[3] which, says Colonel Tod, "rises majestically from its base to the height of about 800 feet, its crest encircled by the ancient walls and towers raised by Ajaipal."[4]

This hill, which overhangs the city of Ajmer and commands it at every point, is the north-east end of one of the ranges of the Aravalli Mountains. The walls of the battlements, where they have not been built on the edge of an inaccessible precipice, are composed of huge blocks of stone cut and squared so as to make a plain stone wall 20 feet thick, and as many feet high, strengthened by round towers built at every declivity in the hill, except on the promontory which juts out of the main fortress to the south, and which is fortified by stronger bastions at very short distances. This

1. A history written in the 18th century A.D. 2. LaTouche's Gazetteer, p. 54.
3. Letters Written From a Mahratta Camp, p. 7. 4. Tod's Rajasthan, Vol. I, page 783.

Of the fortifications originally built by Hindus, only portions here and there remain. They are to be seen now a few feet at the base, where we find carefully-squared and dressed blocks of sandstone which often attain nearly one-fifth of the wall's entire height. The superstructure is all of later times, and generally consists of two independent walls, having been built each about 18" thick with mortar and boulders, some dressed, others undressed. The space left is then filled up by stones of all shapes and sizes tumbled in pell-mell from above, often without any mortar preparation whatever The rubble work is the hand-work of Hindu masons either of the time of the Mughal Emperors, or of the time of the Rathors and Mahrattas.

"The view of the fort is superb, especially in the early morning."—Caine's Picturesque India, page 81.

promontory is the point of the fortress most exposed to attack. The principal strength of the fortress lies in the ruggedness and acclivity of the hill upon which it is situated, and which, except on the south, is practically inaccessible.[1]

Bishop R. Heber says: "Above, on the mountain top is a very remarkable fortress called Taragarh, nearly two miles in circuit, but, from its irregular shape and surface not capable of containing more than 1,200 men. It is, however, a magnificent place of arms in many respects. The rock is in most parts quite inaccessible. It has an abundant supply of good water in all seasons from tanks and cisterns cut in the live rock. There are bomb proofs to a vast extent, and storehouses like wells, where corn, ghee, etc., used to be kept, and with very little improvement from European skill, it might easily be made a second Gibraltar."[2]

Col. Broughton says: "Its principal strength doubtless lies in the ruggedness and acclivity of the hill upon which it is situated."[3]

History.—The *Akhbar-ul-Akhyar* says that the first fort built on a hill in India was the fortress of Taragarh. Built in the seventh century of the Christian era, the *Ajaimeru Doorg*, as it was originally called, maintained its reputation for strength and strategic importance during all the political changes and upheavals this country has witnessed during the momentous period between the seventh and the nineteenth centuries.

The long sieges Taragarh has sustained bear witness to its immense strength. The first attack was made by Sultan Mahmud Ghaznavi in 1024 A.D., when he was wounded, and failing in his attempt to take it, he raised the siege and proceeded towards Naharwalla.[4]

Garh Beetli now enjoyed a repose of 170 years, and in the year 1192 A D., Emperor Prithviraj having been defeated on the fateful plains of Thaneshwar, Sultan Shahabuddin Ghori came to Ajmer and carried the citadel by assault.[5] The fort was retaken by Hariraj, the younger brother of Prithviraj, as soon as the Sultan turned his back on Ajmer. Qutbuddin re-took it[6] in 1195 A.D., and for the first time, a Mussalman

1. The circumference of the walls is two miles. The fort is approached by inclined planes of great length, at a considerable angle, roughly paved and parapeted; by which, when formerly in repair, guns and horses could be taken up. This ascent is well covered by the fort itself, and also by the out-works and the hill to the west.—Dr. R. H. Irvine's Medical Topography of Ajmer.
2. Heber's Journal, Vol II, page 48.
3. Letters From a Mahratta Camp, p. 253.
4. Tod'sRajasthan, Vol. II. p. 448.
5. Wheeler's History of India, Vol. IV, p. 41.
6. Raverty's Tabqati Nasiri, p. 519.

named Sayad Husain Mashedi was appointed its governor. Qutbuddin Aibak, after his defeat the same year by Bhimdeva, the King of Gujrat, fled to Ajmer and shut himself up in the *Garh Beetli*. The Mers and Rajputs invested the fort; the siege lasted six months, when reinforcements having arrived from Ghazni (Afghanistan), the siege was raised.

The Sesodias, under Rao Ranmal of Marwar, attacked and took possession of it some time between 1397 and 1409, A.D,[1] Ala-ud-din Khilji of Mandoo attacked it in 1455 A.D., and took it after the governor, Gajadhar Rai, was slain in his heroic defence of the fortress.[2] In 1505 A.D., Kanwar Prithviraj of Mewar took it by assault, slaying the Mussalman governor.[3] Bahadur Shah of Gujrat attacked it in 1533A.D. and took it from the Sesodias[4] Rao Viramdeva of Merta took it in 1535, but in a few months, Rao Maldeva of Jodhpur seized it.[5] Sher shah Sur took temporary possession of it in 1544.[6] In 1555 A.D. Haji Khan, an officer of the Sur dynasty, seized it;[7] but shortly after, Akbar's general, Sayad Kasim Khan Neshapuri, took possession of it without any resistance.[8]

During the rebellion of Aurangzeb, after the defeat of the Imperial armies near Dholpur, Dara Shikoh threw himself into this fort and fortified it against attack. Aurangzeb laid siege to it and conquered it after a stormy fight in 1659 A.D.[9] The fortress remained in the possession of the Mughals till 1720 A.D., in which year Maharaja Ajit Singh seized it.[10] In July 1722 A.D., the fortress was invested by the Imperial Army under Maharaja Jai Singh of Jaipur, Haider Kuli and Iradat Khan Bungash. It held out for four months, when Maharaja Jai Singh persuaded Ajit Singh "to surrender Ajmer."[11] Maharaja Abhai Singh of Marwar took possession of it after a siege in 1744 A.D., and incorporated it with Marwar.

During the reign of Maharaja Bijai Singh, the Mahratta general, Jai Appa, was assassinated at Nagor, and Ajmer was given in 1756 A.D. in *moondkati* (compensation for murder) to the Mahrattas. After the battle of Lalsot in 1787 A.D., when Scindia was defeated, the Rathors under Singhi Bhimraj seized Taragarh by a *coup de main*.[12] Scindia sent

1. Tod's Rajasthan, Vol. II, p. 16.
2. Brigg's Ferishta, Vol. II, p. 222.
3. Tod s Rajasthan, Vol. I, p. 674.
4. Bayley's Gujrat, p. 371.
5. Tod's Rajasthan, Vol. II, p, 24. Tarikhi Daudi. p. 238.
6. Elliot's History of India, Vol. III, p. 406.
7. Elliot's History of India, Vol. VI, p. 22.
8. Ibid, Vol. VI, p. 22.
9. Ibid, Vol. VII, p. 240.
10. Tod's Rajasthan, Vol. II, p. 89.
11. Ibid, p. 91.
12. Compton's European Military Adventurers of Hindustan, page 37.

another army to Rajputana under General De Boigne, who arrived at Ajmer on 15th August, 1790, and at once completed the investment; but owing to the impregnable nature of the fort, he was unable to take it. So leaving 2,000 cavalry and a sufficient force of infantry, he advanced to Merta.[1] The garrison held out till, peace having been made, the fort was surrendered in 1791 A.D.

In 1800 A.D., General Perron, who had succeeded De Boigne in the command of Scindia's regulars, sent Major Bourguien to capture Ajmer from Lakwa Dada, the Mahratta general, who had rebelled against Scindia. Major Bourguien arrived at Ajmer early in December, 1800, and endeavoured to storm Taragarh on the 8th, but was driven back by the garrison. He bombarded it, but to no purpose, and after five long months he gained possession of it by bribery on the 8th May 1801.[2] From that time till July, 1818, it remained in the possession of the Scindia, when it was ceded to the British Government. The Mahratta governor then evacuated it, and Colonel Nixon and Sir David Ochterlony took possession of it on 28th July 1818.[3]

From 1818 to 1832 A.D. Taragarh was occupied by a company of Native Infantry.[4] In 1832, Lord William Bentinck, Governor-General of India, visited the fort, and ordered it to be dismantled.[5] From 1860 A.D. till 1920 the place was used as a sanatorium for the European troops at Nasirabad, accommodation for whom was increased in 1873 A.D. so as to allow of the residence of 100 men.

Roads.—Before the British occupation, the only way to the fort was through Inderkot, which was steep, narrow and difficult. Colonel T. D. Broughton, who came to Ajmer in 1809, says: "The access to the fort is from the city, and is carried for more than half-a-mile over several smaller rocky hills, till it reaches the main wall of the fortress. Some of our people who obtained admission complained of the road being so very steep and rough that they were obliged to climb with difficulty for the greater part of the way."[6] Since the dismantling of the fort in 1832 A.D. and its conversion into a sanatorium, the access has been made easy, and two good metalled roads have been constructed, one on the south face of the hills for soldiers coming from Nasirabad, and the other through Inderkot. Writing in 1883 A.D., Mr. H. B. W. Garrick of the Archæological Survey of India, says: "The

1. Compton's European Military Adventurers of Hindustan, p. 55.
2. Ibid, p. 247.
3. Rajputana Gazetteer, Vol. II, p. 19.
4. La Touche's Gazetteer, p. 54.
5. Rajputana Gazetteer, Vol. II, p. 65.
6. Letters From A Mahratta Camp, p. 253.

ascent to the fort is gradual, and an excellent road for pedestrians is provided the whole way."[1]

In addition to the two metalled roads there are two footpaths, one from the city past the *Bada Pir* and the *Nana Sahib ka Jhalra* to the *Khidki Darwaza*; and the other through the *Khidki Burj* at the head of the promontory to Sambalpur.

Fortifications.—Passing through the Inderkot and the *kela baya* and *amba baya* (plaintain well and mango well) we ascend by an admirable winding path, and about midway we arrive at the Lakshmi Pol, the gate in the outermost line of fortifications which extend to the surrounding hills. This gate stands on the ridge between the Taragarh and the Chavanda hill, and gives access to the beautiful valley called the Chashma. It is this Pol about which the traditional couplet says:—

आना सागर पोल बिन्च, बड़ जितरो बिस्तार ।
लख गांडा को मार है, लीजो काल दुकाल ॥

TRANSLATION.—Between the Pol and the Ana Sagar Lake, a hundred thousand cartloads of treasure lie buried, which may be used in times of famine or stress.

Passing through the Lakshmi Pol we come to the second line of fortifications, the entrance to which is by a much-broken gate now known as the *phuta darwaza* (broken gate). Ascending by the winding road, near to the main gate of the fortress stands a small bastion and the remains of a wicket (*khidki*), which used to be called *gugandi ki khidki*, or the rubbish wicket. A little further on, is the main gate of the fortress now called the *bada darwaza* (principal gate). Originally this was the only gate to the fortress, a small postern or *khidki* having been afterwards opened in the centre of the fourth bastion, counting eastwards from the principal gate. This gate is so situated as to be easily made inaccessible.

The remaining portals are to the north-west, and serve to guard the passage from the plains across the lowest hills to the semi-circular road on the range above, which continues its southerly course to the fortifications thrown across the northern edge of a deep ravine on the west of Taragarh. These are named *Bhawani Pol*, *Hathi Pol* and *Arkot-ka darwaza* (the gate of the cross fortification).

1. Archaeological Survey Report for 1883-84, p. 36.

There are fourteen bastions in the wall of the fortress. Counting eastwards from the *Bara Darwaza*, the first three are the *Ghungat, Gugadi* and *Phuta* bastions. The fourth is the *Nakarchi ka burj*, in which is the small postern which gives the nearest access to the city. The fifth is the *Singar Chanvri Burj*, near the house built by Major Repton, Deputy Commissioner about 1865 A.D., now belonging to a firm of Hindu bankers. The sixth is the *Arparka Atta* or the bastion commanding both sides of the ravine. Near it, is the *Janu Naik ka Burj*, and next to it is the *Pipli-wala Burj*. The ninth is the *Ibrahim Shahid ka Burj*. The tenth is the *Dorai Burj*, called after the village *Dorai*, situated opposite to it three miles away. The eleventh is the *Bandra Burj*, (monkey bastion). The twelfth is the *Imli ka Burj;* so called from a tamarind tree which used to flourish near it. The thirteenth is the *Khidki ka Burj*, and the fourteenth is the *Fateh Burj*, near the principal gateway.

It is, however, on the promontory that fortified bastions with cannon-stands are to be seen. The bastion at the head of the promontory is the *Khidki ka Burj*. The next to the south of it is the *Hakani Bakani Sayad ka Burj*, which is the most important of the three bastions. It overlooks a line of rugged rocks, amongst which are two small water reservoirs. The bastion standing on the extremity of the promontory, the farthest of the outer works on the south, is called the *Husain Burj*, and overlooks the deep ravine by which runs the road leading to Nasirabad.

These ruined bastions alone remain to remind the visitor of the great deeds done and renown won by warriors long since forgotten. Not a piece of metal now remains to show that at one time they held their heads high, armed with deadly weapons of war, defying attack, and were the abode of heroes who had conquered death. Now,

> "There they stand as stands a lofty mind,
> Worn but unstooping to the baser crowd,
> All tenantless save to the crannying wind,
> Or holding dark communion with the cloud."

But, as Lord Byron says:

> "————there is a power
> And magic in the ruined battlement,
> For which the palace of the present hour,
> Must yield its pomp, and wait till ages are its dower.

Water Supply.—To store water, there are five reservoirs inside the fort and one outside it. The latter called the

Nana Sahib ka Jhalra, near the *Nakarchi ka Burj*, was built by Sivaji Nana, Governor of Ajmer, in 1791 A.D. There is another water reservoir within the fortress near this Burj called the *Gol Jhalra* (circular tank), also built by Nana Sahib. Another *jhalra* of about the same size as the *Gol Jhalra*, called the *Ibrahim Sharif ka Jhalra*, is situated near the bastion of that name. Near the *Bandra Burj*, is another large reservoir kept in good repair. In addition to these, there is the *Bada Jhalra*, the principal tank, perhaps of the same date as the fortress, situated in the centre of the citadel. Of the four *chhatrees*, that stood on the four corners of this tank, one alone remains. The marble remains of two of them lie in the enclosure round the shrine of Miran Sayad Husain. Unlike the Mussalmans of the city, who immerse their *tabuts* in water, the Mussalmans of Taragarh bury them in a corner of the *Jhalra* in front of the *Tibari*, in the enclosure called the *Karbala*. Near this *Jhalra*, were two reservoirs for ghee (clarified butter) and oil for the use of the besieged. Bishop Heber, who visited Ajmer in 1825 A.D., describes them as store-houses like wells, where corn, ghee, etc., used to be kept."[1] The reservoirs have since been filled up and now form a level open space between the barrrack lines.

Population—The permanent population of Taragarh consists of the Khadims of the Dargah of Miran Sayad Husain, about 80 families, 500 souls. There is a good government dak bungalow for travellers, as well as a rest-house belonging to the Rajputana-Malwa Railway for the use of its officers, and a bungalow for the use of the United Free Church missionaries. These and the house built by Major Repton and the military barracks are the only houses built during the English occupation of this fortress. The houses of the khadims are situated to the north and north-west of the Dargah.

Dargah Miran Sahib—The Dargah stands on the highest point of the fortress, and is an oblong building. Miran Sayad Husain Khangsawar,[2] Governor of the fortress, is said to have been slain on *Rajab* 17th, H. 598 (1202 A.D.) during an attack on the fort by the Rajputs,[3] and was interred along with the other Mussalmans killed at the time.

For four and a half centuries no Dargah of Miran Sayad Husain existed in the fort, and no sanctity was attached to his tomb.

1. Heber's Journal, Vol. II, page 48.
2. His father's name was Sayad Asghar Husain and mother's, Bibi Hajra.
3. This event is not related in any contemporary history.

The Tarikhi Daudi, describing Shershah Sur's visit to Ajmer after defeating King Maldeva of Marwar in 1544 A.D., says:

شیرشاه خود بزیارت حضرت خواجه معین‌الدین‌چشتی در اجمیر رفته بفقرا از خانقاه مبلغی گزراینده آنچه لازم طواف‌است بعمل آورده بالی قلعه بتفریح رفت— از کم آبی‌اندیشه خواست ما چشمه که‌اورا حافظ جمال گویند بالا برد و برای این‌کار دستکاران عجیب نامور گردانیدونامش شیرچشمه نهاد وغیره وغیره—

TRANSLATION—"Shershah himself went to Ajmer to have Ziarat of (offer worship to) Hazrat Khwaja Muinuddin Chishti, gave large alms to the *faqirs* of that Khanqah and performed the necessary ceremonies of going round it (طواف). He then went up to the fortress for بتفریح *recreation.* As there was scarcity of water in the fortress, he thought of bringing water from the Chashma called Hafiz Jammal to the fort. He appointed capable masons to do this and named the Chashma, Shir Chashma," etc , etc.

This clearly shows that no such thing as Dargah Miran Sahib existed on the Taragarh fort till 1544 A.D. and that the tomb of Miran Sahib dating from 1202 A.D. had no sacerdotal character but was looked upon merely as one of the tombs of soldiers and laymen.

It was when Akbar brought the Dargah Khwaja Sahib Ajmer into prominence, by coming to it as a pilgrim, that people began to hold Miran Sahib's tomb at Taragarh, Ajmer, also as sacred and put up a mausoleum.

Abul Fazal, the Prime Minister of Akbar, and author of the celebrated *Ayeeni Akbari* and *Akbarnama*, speaking of Akbar's visit to the shrine of Khwaja Muinuddin Chishti at Ajmer in 1870 A.D., says:—

و روز دیگر به تماشه‌قلعه اجمیر که برقلعه کوهی واقع است متوجه شدند ودران عالیمقام بزیارت سید حسین خنگ سوار که درزبان عوام از اولاد امام زین‌العابدین است پرداخته تبرک جستند—وتحقیق آنست که سید ازملازمان شهاب‌الدین غوری است هنگامی که فتح هندوستان کرده مراجعت نموده اورا بشقراری اجمیر گزاشت واو انجا نقد حیات سپرد بمرور ایام و هجوم عوام بولایت مشهور گشت و تربتش مطاف عالمیان شد—

TRANSLATION.—The next day he (the Emperor) set out on a pleasure trip to view the fortress of Ajmer, which is situated on the summit of a hill, and in that magnificent place paid his respects to Sayad Husain Khangsawar, who, according to the common report is a decendant of Imam Zainul Abdin, and sought *tabarruk* (gift from a sacred place) there. But the fact is, the Sayad was one of the servants (ملازمان) of Shahabuddin Ghori, and the time when he conquered Hindustan and returned, he (Sultan) left him (Sayad Husain Khangsawar) as the Revenue Collector (ملقدار) of Ajmer. He died there and after a lapse of time, and owing to people coming there in large numbers, became known as a saint (ولی) and his tomb became a place of popular worship (مطاف عالمیان).

The Dargah was built by the Jabbar Khan during the reign of Akbar. The access to the Dargah is from the east, through a portal called the *Dhol Darwaza* (drum gate). Facing this gate is the *Buland Darwaza* or the high gate, which is the principal entrance to the Dargah. This gate, which is 64 feet high and 17 feet wide, was built of red sandstone by Ismail Quli Khan,[1] subedar of Ajmer, in H. 976 (1569 A.D.) during the time of Akbar. This gate gives access to the outer court of the Dargah, wherein to the right of the gateway, is a *tibari* called the *nakkar khana*, a *sahan chirag*, courtyard lamp to light the courtyard, and dalans on the southern and northern sides of the courtyard to accomodate visitors. A small door facing the *Buland Darwaza* leads to the inner courtyard, in which is situated the mausoleum of Sayad Husain. At the door of the mausoleum is the tomb (always kept covered with green cloth) of the sayad's favourite horse named *Khang*, after whom the sayad is called *Khangsawar*.

1. The following lines are inscribed on a stone fixed in the northern wall of the gate:—

بمهد بادشاه آسماں قدر — پناه ملک و ملت ظل یزدان
جلال الدین محمد اکبر بادشاه — که دارد در نگین ملک سلیماں
بدیں درگه که همچو کعبه آمد — سوادش عین نور و نور اعیاں
بنا فرمود ایں ایواں عالي — کریم الذات اسمعیل قلي خاں
زکاخ دلکشا تاریخ اتمام — اگر خواهد کسے می بابد آساں—
کتبه الراجی درویش محمد الحاجی المشتهر برمزی

The mausoleum is a square building having *tibarees* towards the south and the west. The *tibari* to the south is partly of white marble, and was built by a Hindu governor of Ajmer, Balarao Inglia in H. 1222 (1807-8 A.D.); that to the west, by Gumanji Rao Scindia in H. 1227-29 (1812-14 A.D.), as the inscriptions in the tibarees show.[1]

1- The following verses are inscribed on a store fixed in the south *tibari*,

از بشارت سید الشهدا حسین خنگ سوار کرد دالاں راو بالا انگلیا پیش مزار
یک هزار دو صد و افزوں ازیں کن بست دو سال هجرت خانه بیت الهه باید شمار—

The following verse is inscribed on a stone in a wall of the west *tibari*.

معدن نور منبع اسرار هست درگاه شاه خنگ سوار
ساخت دالاں که هست رشک بهشت راو گمانجي سیندهیا بوقار

The tomb stands in the centre of this open square, and is surrounded by a marble screen (*katera*) about four feet high. Over the tomb is a cloth canopy. In the *katera*, two or three pieces of looking-glass are crudely fixed in mortar. At the head of the tomb on the *shahida* (a vertical piece of stone fixed on tombs of persons killed in warfare) is placed a round turban. The chronogram on the southern door of the *katera* gives the date of its construction as 1810 A.D. The first construction in lime masonry built over the tomb was in 1615 A.D., by Aitbar Khan, *alias* Mumtaz Khan, a Mughal officer of Akbar and Jahangir.[1]

In the open space in front of the northern entrance to the Dargah are two iron cauldrons (*degs*) to cook food for the poor. These are much smaller than those in the Dargah of Khwaja Muinuddin Chishti. One of them was presented by Emperor Jahangir and the other by Mulla Madari. Of the three villages bestowed on the Dargah for its maintenance, the average annual revenue of which is Rs. 4,367, two were given by Akbar and the third (*Dorai*) by Maharaja Scindia.

The only other thing in connection with Miran Sayad Husain in Taragarh is the *Ganj Shahidan* (Treasury of martyrs). It is a small enclosure outside the Dargah, and is full of small tombs, built over the Mussalmans, slain by the Rajputs in 1202 A.D., when the garrison to the last man was put to the sword.[2] The enclosure wall was built by Wazir Khan Kallan, an Amir of Jahangir in 1613 A.D.

Between the *Phuta* gate in the outer line of fortifications and the *Bada* or *Fateh Darwaza*, near a bend in the road, lies a large boulder called the *Adhar Silla* (unsupported slab). It is partly whitewashed, and the Khadims of the Dargah of Miran Sahib say that during an attack, the Hindus who were in the fort threw it by magic so as to fall on Miran Sahib; but that the latter saw it coming, and addressing it said: "If thou art come from God, fall on my head; if magic has sent thee, stay here." Marks of the Miran Sahib's two fingers and the stick with which he touched it, and of the place where it came in contact with his horse, are still shown to pilgrims.

1. Six verses are inscribed on the Southern door of the *katera* the last of which gives the date as H. 1225 (1810 A.D.).

از پے تاریخ او کردم سوال از عقل کل گفت جو تاریخ او از روضے سلطان دین

2. Watson's Gazetteer of Ajmer-Merwara. page 10.

Archæology.—There is little left in Taragarh to interest a student of archaeology. The sandstone basis of the circumvallation of the fortress, some of the outer fortifications on the adjoining hills and the names of the gates in such fortifications the *Bara Jhalra*, a pillared stone chamber called the *katchery* or court, are all of Hindu period. "This katchery" says Mr. Garrick,[1] the Assistant Archaeological Surveyor of India, "from its generally massive construction and the heavy—disproportionately heavy—capitals of its supporting columns, must belong to the Hindu period, and therefore is unique." The chamber is situated to the east of a range of barracks utilised as a church, and is exposed to full view from the western verandah of the dak bungalow. The stone slab-floor of this chamber, which was used as a reading room by soldiers, is considerably below the level of the church-room adjoining it. It is a flat-roofed compartment containing 30 stone pillars, each 11 feet high. A general belief exists on Taragarh that it was a *katchery* or court. It certainly looks as though the chamber was originally designed for a public building of some kind, either a law court, assembly-room, or hospital. The Dargah dates after the year 1557 A.D. and a great part of it has been built by the Hindus after the fall of the Mughal empire. Colonel Tod, writing on the 4th December, 1818, says: "The reader will see as much of this far-famed fortress as I did: the only temple visible was a modern-looking white-washed mosque lifting its dazzling minarets over the dingy antique towers of the Chauhan: he who seven times captured the Sultan and seven times released him."[2]

This far-famed fortress has sustained so many assaults, so many sieges, and has been occupied by so many masters that the character of the fortress is now completely changed; and even before its final dismantlement during the time of Lord William Bentinck, the place had lost much of the architectural interest usually attached to such places. The ancient walls and towers raised by Ajaipal are hardly of any account now. But—

"There was a day when they were young and proud
Banners on high, and battles passed below;
But they who fought are in a bloody shroud,
And those which waved are shredless dust ere now,
And the bleak battlements shall bear no future blow.

1. Archaeological Survey Report for 1883-84, page 42.
2. Tod's Rajasthan, Vol. I, page 782.

CHAPTER V

ANA SAGAR AND THE BARADARIES

THE most picturesque site in Ajmer is the famous Ana Sagar lake. It is an artificial lake formed by throwing up an embankment between two hillocks named *Bajrang Garh* and *Khobra Behrun*, after the respective Hindu temples built on them. The lake was constructed by King Arnoraja or Anaji (about 1135-1150 A.D.), the grandfather of Emperor Prithviraj. "The Ana Sagar," says Mr. Caine, "is one of the loveliest tanks in India."[1]

The lake when full has a circumference of eight miles.[2] Its capacity is 72'48 M. cft.; water spread 11377 M. sq. ft., depth now, 16 ft. Its catchment area[3] has been reduced since the construction in 1891 A.D. of another reservoir near the hills of Ajaipal, called Foy Sagar. It lies hemmed in on all sides by hills, with the lofty Nagpahar as its background. It is, says Dr. Fuhrer, "perhaps the greatest of the various natural beauties that combine to make Ajmer one of the most remarkable of the old native cities of India."[4]

On the southern side, Ana Sagar is fringed by ghats and gardens built mostly during the early days of British rule by wealthy Hindu residents of Ajmer. On the hill near its weir, stands the Residency, where the Honourable the Chief Commissioner of Ajmer-Merwara resides during his stay in Ajmer.

Ana Sagar supplied drinking water to the city of Ajmer[5] before the construction of Foy Sagar, by two underground masonry channels, one passing through the city to the Nahar reservoir and the other outside it to Surajkund, facing the Madar Gate and near the railway station. "Besides the beauty it adds to the vale of Ajmer," says Colonel Tod, "it has a source

1. Picturesque India, page 82. 2. Tod's Rajasthan, Vol. I, page 783.
3. Dr. R. H. Irvine, writing in 1841 A.D. says:—"The lake has gradually much diminished in depth." "The deepest portion is that near the bund varying at the greatest height from 15 to 20 feet."—Medical Topography of Ajmer, page 43.
4. Archæological Survey Report for 1902-03.
5. Bishop Heber says: "Ana Sagar supplies abundance of excellent water to the citizens of Ajmer, is full of fish, and should, if there were any boats, be an excellent place for sailing.',—*Journal*, Vol. II, page 49.

The Ana Sagar and the Baradaris.

A Baradari.

of interest in being the fountain of the Luni River, which pursues its silent course, until it unites with the eastern arm of the delta of the Indus. The point of outlet is at the northern angle of Daulat Bagh, laid out by Jahangir. The water is not unwholesome, and there are three outlets at this fountain-head for the escape of the water fitting its periodical altitude. The stream at its parent source is thence called the *Sagarmati*.[1] It takes a sweep northward by Bhaonta and Pisangan, and at Govindgarh is joind by the Saraswati from Pushkar, when the united waters (at whose *sangam* or confluence there is a small temple) is called the Luni."[2]

An interesting account of Ana Sagar during a storm of rain is given by Sir Thomas Roe in his Journal, under date the 20th August, 1616 A.D. He says: "The 20th day and the night fell a storm of rain called the elephant,[3] usual at going out of the rains, but this was extraordinary, for there ran such streams into the tank, whose head is of stone, in show exceeding strong, yet the water was so grown that it broke through one place, and there came an alarm and sudden fear that it would give way and drown all that part of the town where I dwelt, insomuch that Prince Khurram and all his women forsook their house; my next neighbour carried away his goods and his wife on his elephants and camels to fly to the hill-side. All men had their horses ready at their doors to save their lives, so that we were much frighted and sat up till midnight, for that we had no help but to flee ourselves and lose goods; for, it was reported that it would run higher than the top of my house by three feet and carry all away, being poor muddy buildings; fourteen years before, a terrible experience having showed the violence, the bottom of the tank being level with our dwelling and the water extreme great and deep, so that the top was much higher than my house, which stood at the bottom in the course of the water, every ordinary rain, making such a current at my door that it run not swifter in the arches of London Bridge, and is for some hours impassable by horse or man. But God otherwise disposed it in His mercy. The king caused a sluice to be cut in the night to ease the water another way, yet the very rain had washed down a great part of the walls of my house and so weakened it in divers places, that I feared the fall more

1. The stream takes its rise in the Ajaipal hills, and is known as the *Bandi Nadi* till it empties its waters into the Anasagar. 2. Tod's Rajasthan, Vol. I, p. 783.

3. Thevenot explains the name as derived from the shape of the clouds at the time of the storm. The early Portuguese appear to have given this name to the storm which they usually experienced every year upon the coast in the beginning of September.

than the flood, and was so moiled[1] with dirt and water that I could scarce lie dry or safe, for that I must be enforced to be at new charge in reparation. Thus were we every day afflicted; fires, smoke, floods, storms, heat, dust, flies and no temperate or quiet season."

The embankment built by Anaji is broad and massive and is faced with stone. It is 1,102 feet long. Dr. R. H. Irvine says:—"Fronting to the water it is 22½ feet in height. To the eastward it is much higher."[2] Nothing is known of the buildings which may have stood on it before the sixteenth century. "The beauty of the Lake Ana Sagar," says Captain Cole, "made it a favourite resort of the Mughal Emperors, and the valley became filled with their palaces and gardens."[3] Rousselet says: "One of the most beautiful is Daulat Bagh, or garden of splendour, built by Jahangir in the sixteenth century."

Emperor Jahangir, with the eye of an artist, at once saw the beauty of this spot and erected palaces, mentioned as "*Mahalat-i-Jahangiri* by contemporary historians of the Mughal period. These palaces are alluded to by Sir Thomas Roe in his account of the dinner given to him by a Mughal noble named Jamaluddin Hasan, as well as in the entry in his Journal under date the 19th June, 1616 A D., when he says that Jahangir removed his Court to Hauz Jammal,[5] and remained there from the 19th to the 23rd June.

Sir Thomas Roe says: "He (Jamaluddin Hasan) borrowed of the king his house and garden of pleasure, Hauz Jummal, a mile out of the town, to feast me in, and invited me over night. I promised to come. At midnight he went himself and carried his tents and all furniture, and fitted up a place by the tank-side very handsomely. In the morning I went. He met me with much civility and carried me into his room prepared for me, where he had some company and a hundred servants attending two of his sons, he having thirty. He showed me the king's closets and retiring rooms, which were painted *a la antique*, and in some panes were pictures of the French kings and other Christian princes."[6]

1 Moile, not too much underground.—Bacon's Essay on Plantations. Here it means "softened by moistening." 2. Medical Topography of India, p. 43.

3. Preservation of Ancient Monuments in Rajputana, by Captain Cole.

4. "India and its Native Princes."

5 The place was called Hauz Jammal evidently after the beautiful fountain reservoir, near the flight of steps leading from the second to the third terrace of the embankment. 6. Journal, Vol. I, page 238.

Of Jahangirs's palaces, the only remnant now standing is the masonry ruin by the side of the road leading from the embankment to the Kaisar Bagh, near where the surplus water of Ana Sagar emerges from under the road, and trickles down to the culvert at the northern entrance to Daulat Bagh. Shah Jahan, perhaps the greatest of the kings who adorned their countries with beautiful buildings with the eye of an artist, saw the superb beauty of the Ana Sagar Lake; put up a marble parapet on the embankment 1,240 feet long, and five Pavilions (*Baradaries*) of polished marble, incomparable in elegance and beauty, and a *hammam* or Turkish bath, in 1637 A.D.[1] During his visits to Ajmer, he resided here as appears from an account of the visit to Ajmer given by his favourite daughter, Jahan Ara Begum in her book *Munisul Arvah.* She says: By good fortune, I directed my course to the sacred town of Ajmer to attend on my venerable father, and remained on the way from the 18th Shaban to 7th Ramzan, H. 1053 (1643 A.D.), when I set my foot in the palace on the bank of the Ana Sagar Lake (داخل عمارت کنار تال آناساگر گشتم) These elegant marble Pavilions," says Captain Cole, the Curator of Ancient Monuments in India, "command an incomparable view of the town, and the mountain is reflected as in a crystal mirror. The garden is of great extent and full of venerable trees."[2]

Of the five Pavilions, the third from the south, the largest (46 feet long) and the best, built after the model of the Diwan-i-Khas in the Delhi Fort, was allowed to stand intact. The others were converted into offices and residences. The two Pavilions at the southern end (29 feet and 26 feet 6 inches long respectively) were fitted up as a house for the Superintendent of Ajmer, when Ajmer passed from the Scindia to the English in July, 1818 A D. It was in this house, that Col. Tod breakfasted with Mr. Wilder, the first Superintendent of Ajmer, on the 2nd December, 1819 A.D., and both discussed how best they could promote the prosperity of Ajmer and Bhilwara.[3] And it was in this house that Bishop Heber, when he came to Ajmer on the 7th February 1825 A.D., dined with Mr. Moore. He says in his Journal: "Mr. Moore lives in a small house fitted up out of a summer

1. According to the Muasir-ul-Umra, Vol. II, p. 816, Shah Jahan put up these buildings and those in Ahmedabad at an expense of ten lakhs of rupees.

2. Preservation of Ancient Monuments in Rajputana. "A beautifull park full of fine old trees."—Caine's Picturesque India, page 78.

3. Tod's Rajasthan, Vol. I, page 777.

house erected by Shah Jahan on the very bund of Ana Sagar, with its water beating against the basement."[1]

The fourth Pavilion (44 feet 6 in. long) was converted into a station reading-room and library, and subsequently used as the Municipal Office. The fifth Pavilion was converted into a bungalow, where the Deputy Commissioner of Ajmer, and later, the Civil Surgeon, generally resided.

The fourth Pavilion was the first to be restored to its original state. In 1892 A.D. the additions were demolished, the municipal office was removed to the south-eastern bastion of the Magazine, and the Pavilion restored at a cost of Rs. 1,234. The other Pavilions, the first, second and the fifth, however, were not touched till His Excellency Lord Curzon, during his visit to Ajmer in 1899 A.D., ordered the restoration of the embankment and the buildings on it, to the state in which the Mughals had left them. This has been done at a total cost of Rs. 40,062. The Commissioner's house was demolished and the first and second Pavilions were restored. But in the case of the fifth Pavilion, little of the original marble was found. The three arches fronting the lake alone remained, with corner wing-pieces, which latter were removed; and with the exception of the three arches (31'-6" long) the whole of the site has been turfed. The position of this Pavilion, standing as it did at the water weir, shows that a large Pavilion had been originally erected here, and that it was bodily removed from this place by the Mahratta rulers of Ajmer and used as a Hindu temple in the Magazine on the third story adjoining the south-western bastion. A comparison of this temple with the Pavilions on the Ana Sagar bund irresistibly points to the fact that this is the fifth Pavilion removed from the embankment to the Magazine and used as a Hindu temple, when the Mahratta governors took up their residence in the Magazine.

The Turkish bath, which for long was used as the Commissioner's office, was dismantled in 1902 and the ground floor alone preserved. It is to be hoped that care will always be taken of the old and "venerable trees" on the embankment, "beneath whose shades" Captain Cole supposes, though wrongly, that "the haughty Jahangir received the Ambassador of an English sovereign."

At the head of the stairs leading from the second to the third terrace, to the right, as we ascend them, there stood a palace surrounded by marble lattice work of the time of

1. Journal, Vol. II., page 49.

the Mughals, in which the Government Treasury was at one time located. The building was afterwards dismantled; and now a *chabutra* alone remains to mark the site of the palace.

The Daulat Bagh was laid out by Jahangir as a royal pleasure garden, and was in no sense a public garden. It was a walled enclosure constructed primarily for the use of the inmates of the *harem*. The walls were only demolished when the gardens were extended during the time of Mr. L. S. Saunders, Commissioner of Ajmer (1870-1884 A.D.). The square tank (50 feet by 50 feet) surrounded by a marble platform, in which fountains throw beautiful sprays of water from the centre and the corners, is of Jahangir's time, and is still in a good state of preservation.

Emperor Jahangir relates in his Memoirs that it was in Ajmer that the *otto* of roses was first manufactured in India during his reign, and that the invention was due to the observation and inventive faculty of his mother-in-law, the mother of the Empress Nur Jahan.[1]

The Daulat Bagh and Kaiser Bagh are now public gardens, maintained by the Municipality, where in their season, roses in rich profusion still continue to delight the eye and to perfume the atmosphere by their sweet fragrance. Several bathing ghats with gardens attached to them lie on the southern side of Anasagar. They were all built between 1835 and 1850 A.D., most of them at the suggestion of Colonel Dixon, Superintendent of Ajmer. They lie between the lake and the road to Pushkar.[2]

1. Tuzac-i-Jahangiri; also Elliot's History of India, Vol VI, page 338.
2. For a full account of the Ghats see the Chapter, "Growth of the City of Ajmer".

CHAPTER VI.

VISAL SAR

THIS beautiful lake now called Bisla, was in ancient times one of the most beautiful ornaments of Ajmer. Writing in 1840, Dr R. H. Irvine says; "when full of water, the Visala-talao is a beautiful object."[1] It is an artificial lake, oblong in shape, built by Emperor Visaldeva, who reigned about 1152-1163 A.D.

The celebrated *Prithviraj Rasa* says that the Emperor, returning from a hunting party one day, finding springs of water and hills amidst beautiful surroundings, called his ministers and ordered a lake like Pushkar to be built there.[2]

तव देखि नरिन्द अनुप ठाम, निर्भर गिरिन्द बनपूजीस राम ।
बुल्लाय लिए मन्त्री प्रधान, सर रच्यो इहां पहुकर समान ॥

And Visalsar was constructed accordingly. It received the overflow from Ana Sagar, built by Visaldeva's father, Annaji or Arnoraj (1135-1160 A D.), as well as the water flowing down the western and northern slopes of Taragarh and the adjacent hills this side of Lakshmi Pol, through Inderkot. It is about 2½ miles in circumference. The surrounding embankment was faced in stone, with steps leading to the bottom of the lake. Temples and houses stood all round, and there were two islands in the lake, on which stood palaces for the king.

Though the embankment remains all round in a more or less ruined state, as also the massive stairs on the eastern side, a short distance from the water weir, nothing is left of the temples and buildings to mark the ancient grandeur of the place.[3] Images were extant on the embankment during the time of the Mahrattas (1790-1818 A.D.), which sent forth jets, when the water rose to their lips.

The islands are hopelessly ruined, though marks of a reservoir and foundations of buildings on them remind the

1. Medical Topography of Ajmer, p. 49.
2. Prithviraj Rasa, Adiparva, Chhand 364.
3. "The vestiges of an island are yet seen in the lake, and upon its margin; but the materials have been carried away by the Goths."—Tod's Rajasthan, Vol. I, p. 783.

spectator that in old days the Visal Sar was a beautiful lake with island palaces fit to adorn the capital of an Emperor, distinguished as much for letters as for valour. This splendid place appears to have been destroyed partly because of the temples standing there, during the early Muhammadan invasions. Up to the time of Jahangir, the place had some pretension to beauty, as the Emperor in his memoirs (*Tuzak Jahangiri*) says that while at Ajmer in 1615 A.D., he ordered repairs to be executed to the lake.[2]

The English church now stands on the south-west embankment of the lake, where once stood the temples of the sun-god. In the north-east corner of the lake, on the embankment, is an enclosure containing *chhatrees* and *chabutras* built over the remains of the ancestors of the *Oswal* Seths of Ajmer, and now called the *Dada bari*.[3]

The Bisla Lake is unfortunately too far gone to ruin to admit of restoration; but it is earnestly hoped that this relic of ancient days, emblematic of the most glorious period of the history of Ajmer, when it was the capital of the Hindu Empire in India, may be protected from further assaults of the Railway, and preserved in a condition in which it existed when St. George's banner first began to float over the *Kangras* of Ajmer.

1. *Vide*, Chapter VII, p. 81.
2. Jahangir is said to have built a palace on the banks of this lake.
3. See Chapter on "Minor Sites."

CHAPTER VII.

ADHAI-DIN-KA-JHONPRA

FROM an antiquarian as well as an architectural point of view, the *Adhai-din-ka-Jhonpra* is one of the most important buildings in India. General Cunningham says: "There is no building in India which either for historical interest or archaeological importance is more worthy of preservation." Colonel Tod says that this, " relic of nobler days and noblest arts" is' 'one of the most perfect as well as the most ancient monuments of Hindu architecture"[1] still preserved.

In its conception and execution, this building was a fit monument of the reign of Emperor Visaldeva. As a work of art, it was an exquisite ornament of the Capital of his Empire. As a specimen of Hindu sculpture, this college building marks the high water-mark of excellence attained in the art. "For gorgeous prodigality of ornament, beautiful richness of tracery, delicate sharpness of finish, laborious accuracy of workmanship, endless variety of detail, all of which are due to the Hindu masons, this building," says General Cunningham, Director General of Archaeology, "may justly vie with the noblest buildings which the world has yet produced."[2]

"Nothing," says Mr. Fergusson,[3] "can exceed the taste with which the Kufic and Tugra inscriptions are interwoven with the more purely architectural decorations, or in the manner in which they give life and variety to the whole without ever interfering with the constructive lines of the design. As examples of surface decoration, the Jhonpra and the Mosque of Altamash at Delhi are probably unrivalled. Nothing in Cairo or in Persia is so exquisite in detail, and nothing in Spain or Syria can approach them for beauty of surface decoration."

1. Annals and Antiquities of Rajasthan, Vol. I, page 778.
2. Archaeological Survey of India, Vol, II, page 263.
3. History of Eastern and Indian Architecture, page 513.

THE ADHAI-DIN-KA JHONPRA.

INTERIOR VIEW OF THE ADHAI-DIN-KA-JHONPRA.

Dr. Fuhrer says: "The whole of the exterior is covered with a network of tracery so finely and delicately wrought that it can only be compared to fine lace."[1]

Name.—The name Adhai-din-ka-Jhonpra is not an old one. It nowhere occurs in any historical or other writing. The building was in Mughal days known only as a musjid, and for centuries, this was the only mosque in Ajmer. No mosque is anywhere known as a Jhonpra. The name, *Adhai-din-ka-Jhonpra* was given to it in the latter half of the eighteenth century when fakirs began to assemble here in the times of the Mahrattas to celebrate the *urs* anniversary of the death of their *Pir*, religious leader, Panjaba Shah (who had migrated to Ajmer from the Punjab) which lasted for two-and-a-half days, and *fakirs* residences are *Jhonpras* (huts).

History.—The Jain tradition is, that Seth Viramdeva Kala built a Jain temple in celebration of the Jain festival Panch Kalyan Mahotsava in S. 717 (A.D. 660) at a cost of seven lakhs of rupees. The foundation stone was laid by the Jain Bhàttarak, Sri Vishwanandji. The Jain Acharyas decided to give up their practice of not having a permanent place, but to tour about and preach Jainism. As there was no place in Ajmer for Jain priestly class to stay in Ajmer, this temple was built. Similar places for the abode of Bhattaraks were established at Delhi, Amber (Jaipur) and Nagor. Colonel Tod also supposed that the building was a Jain temple which was converted into a mosque by the early Mussalman invaders, while General Cunningham accepted the common belief that it was built in two-and-a-half days, as its name implies, of the spoils of Hindu temples[2] demolished by the bigotry of the conquerors. It was certainly not built in two-and-a-half days, of the materials of several temples. Even its conversion into a mosque took several years.

It was originally one building, as the design easily traceable plainly shows, and was used as a college-house. It was built in the form of a square, 259 feet each side, with cloisters on all the four sides enclosing a spacious court-yard, and four splendid star-shaped cloister towers on the four corners,

1. Archæological Survey Report (N.-W.P.) for 1893.

2. "In 1902, a large white marble *linga* was discovered in the course of excavation in the court-yard. This confirms the Brahmannical character of the early temple, often incorrectly described as Jain."—A.L.P. Tucker in the Archæological Survey Report for 1902-3, page 81.

Mr. Cousens, Superintendent, Archæological Survey, Western India, in his report, dated the 28th April, 1900, says: "The work is not of Jain origin. It is distinctly Brahmannical. Amongst the mutilated sculptures are those of Mahakali, Shiva, Parvati and Kuver."

surmounted by magnificent *chhatrees*. The stone used is fine-grained pure silicious sandstone coloured yellow by iron. The building stood on a high terrace, and was originally constructed against the scarped rock of the hill, having the *Saraswati Mandir* (temple of learning) on the western side, and entrances towards the south and east. The interior consisted of a quadrangle, 200 feet by 175 feet. The college was built about 1153 A.D. by Visaldeva, the first Chauhan Emperor of India.[1] A comparison of this building with an almost similar one at Dhar, also converted into a mosque, and which is still known as *Raja Bhoja's Pathshala* (school), would perhaps remove doubts regarding its origin. The towers, the exquisitely-designed fluting and ornamental bands of the columns, and the wonderful cloisters in the shape of a quadrangle, which originally extended to 770 feet, and of which only 164 feet are now left, were destroyed by the ignorant bigotry and fanaticism of the Afghans of Ghor, who attacked Ajmer under Shahabuddin Ghori in 1192 A.D.

They then began to convert it into a mosque; the alteration consisted principally of the addition of the magnificent screenwall, consisting of seven[2] arches fronting the western side, and the insertion in the back wall of the inevitable *mehrab* or arch inseparable from a mosque, and the erection of a pulpit or *mimbar* near it. The *imamgah* or *mehrab* in white marble was built in 1199 A.D., and the screen wall was added during the time of Sultan Shamsuddin Altamash, about 1213 A.D. The conversion was carried on under the management of different persons, the names of two of whom are recorded—Abubakar, the son of Ahmed (1200 A.D.), and Ahmed, son of Muhammad the Aariz. Thus, the work of reconstruction or conversion lasted from before 1199 to 1213 A.D., a period of more than fifteen years.

After the time of Shamsuddin Altamash, for about six centuries no one appears ever to have taken any notice of the *Jhonpra*. The slave dynasty disappeared; Lodies, Khiljees, Afghans, Sesodias, Rathors, came and went; Ajmer passed from the hands of one power to another, as it happened to be paramount in Upper India; the Mughals came, Akbar, Jahangir, Shah Jahan and Aurangzeb all reigned in splendour and disappeared; Rathors and Mahrattas then held temporary

1. Major Repton, Deputy Commissioner of Ajmer, in a printed report, says that a record in a Jain monastery in Ajmer states, that the buildng was completed on Magh Badi 9th, Samvat 1132 (1075 A.D).

2. The number of columns of the old pillared hall ill fit in with the size of the arches, and clearly shows what is old and what is new.

sway and passed away. The earliest history of the Slave Dynasty, the *Tajulmaasir*, makes no mention of the building further than that Sultan Shahabuddin Ghori during his stay at Ajmer, "destroyed the pillars and foundations of idol temples, and built in their stead, mosques and schools."[1] Nor does the *Tabqat-i-Nasiri* of Minhaj-ul-Siraj make any mention of it. The *Akbarnama*, *Tuzak-i-Jahangiri*, the *Badshahanama*, the *Alamgirnama* are all silent about it. Strangely enough, Sir Thomas Roe, who lived in Ajmer during Jahangir's time for about a year (23rd December, 1615, to 1st December, 1616 A.D.), does not appear even to have known of its existence. Bernier says nothing about it, and even Colonel Broughton, who came to Ajmer in the train of Daulat Rao Scindia in 1810 A.D., and who describes the Dargah, makes no mention of it in his "Letters from a Mahratta Camp." In 1818 A.D., Ajmer passed into the hands of the British, and in the following year, Colonel James Tod visited it. At his hands the *Jhonpra*, for the first time, received its due appreciation. Bishop Heber followed Tod in 1825 A.D., and though he has described the Fort of Taragarh, the Dargah and the Ana Sagar, he has not a word to say about the *Jhonpra*. General Cunningham, Director-General of Archæological Survey, inspected it in 1864 A.D., and gave a detailed description of it in the Archæological Survey Report for that year.

Daulat Rao Scindia was the first ruler to take measures to protect this magnificent edifice, by restoring the central dome and prohibiting the removal of stones from it. A slab was fixed to the left of the entrance gate of the *Jhonpra* forbidding Hindus and Muhammadans, in the name of their respective religions, to remove stones[2] from this ancient building. This slab inscription is dated, Savan Sudi 14th, S. 1866 (1809 A.D.). People, however, continued their depredations up to the time of Lord Mayo. Neglect and ill-treatment were now followed by solicitude and care; and repairs, though "not always very happy," were executed to the *Jhonpra* in 1875-1878 A.D., at a cost of Rs. 23,128. Restoration on more thoughtful lines was carried out in 1900-1903, at a cost of Rs. 7,538, under the supervision of Mr. A. L. P. Tucker, Commissioner of Ajmer-Merwara.

Description.—The mosque proper, which forms a part of the western side of the quadrangle, and which originally

1. Elliot's History of India, Vol. II, page 215.
2. We find stones, dressed and carved, from this building in almost every house in Inderkot.

was the Temple of Learning, is 185 feet long by 57½ feet broad, inclusive of the screen wall, which is 185 feet long, 11½ feet thick, and rises to a height of 56 feet.

This screen wall, which Tod calls "a superb screen of Saracenic architecture," but which General Cunningham assigns to "a higher and nobler style of art than the Saracenic architects ever reached," consists of seven arches.[1] The three central arches are surrounded by three lines of writing, which are divided from each other by two bands of rich arabesque ornament. The two inner lines of writing are Arabic and the outer line is square Tughra or Kufic. The whole of the ornament[2] is boldly and deeply cut in a hard yellow limestone, and although somewhat discoloured by the weather, it still retains all its original sharpness of outline. "The central arch," says Colonel Tod, "is of that wavy kind characteristic of what is termed the Saracenic, whether the term be applied to the Alhambra of Spain or the mosques of Delhi, and I am disposed on close examination, to pronounce it Hindu." It is 22 feet 3 inches wide. The remaining arches are all 13′-5¼″ wide.

These arches were not only constructed by Hindu masons but are of Hindu origin. Some European archæologists and students of architecture have wrongly supposed that the arch was unknown to Hindu architecture. The untenability of this view must be clear to those who are acquainted with the remarkable achievements of the Hindus in geometry, conic sections, mechanics and sculpture. All lingering doubt, however, has been removed by the discovery near Mirpur (Sindh) in 1909 A.D., of the Buddhist *Vihar* of the sixth century A.D, containing true arches, with keystones and domes, during an excavation by Mr. Cousens, late Superintendent of the Archæological Survey, Western Circle.

Colonel Tod thinks that the early Mussalman invaders learnt the art of constructing arches from the Hindus.[3] Speaking of the ruins of Anhalwarra Patan, he says:

"About one hundred and fifty yards from the Jain Towers of Time stands the skeleton arch of a noble gateway. Were we to take this magnificent relic as a specimen of what the city of Anhal had been, we might at once solve a great problem in architecture; for it is one of the finest outlines of what is termed the Saracenic arch that I ever saw; and could we prove it to be Hindu in origin, we might discover in it the prototype

1. Archæological Survey Report, Vol. II, page 263.
2. "The decoration of the whole facade of this wonderful screen is of unique beauty."—Caine's Picturesque India, page 79.
3. Tod's Travels in Western India, pages 224-26.

of those in the Alhambra, and the varieties of the pointed style, denominated Gothic, spread over Europe. If, originally, it formed part of the circumvallation raised by Vansraj in 746 A.D., it would be nearly the period of the Alhambra, '*the edifice*,' *par excellence*, raised by Haroun in the kingdom of Granada . . . I have elsewhere stated that so early as the eighth century, the arms of Islam were both on the Indus and the Ebro; but where did the Arab learn to turn this arch? Not from the Visigoth in Spain, nor from the architraved edifices of the ancient Greeks or Persians; not from Tadmor in the desert, nor from Persepolis; neither from Hauran nor from Haleb. Did they then invent and spread it over Europe; or did they acquire the knowledge of it from the Silpi or architect of the Hindus, who had their Vitruvius before Romulus was born? Of one thing we are confident, that this arch was erected by a Hindu mason, and that its ornaments are purely Hindu, and if the Arabians had anything to do with it, their merit was confined to the design. Can we reasonably concede even so much to probability? . . . The character of this architecture is of a much earlier date, being nearly that of the Ghorian dynasties preceding Alla, which afterwards gradually softened down until it attained the florid embellishments and effeminate though striking distinctions of the Mughal. The varied conceptions of the pointed style in Europe are much less easy to discriminate than those of the Indo-Saracenic, a term we may be permitted to use. in order to distinguish it from the simple Saracenic, as found in the Western conquests of the Arabians, who, as they and their successors invariably destroyed every edifice of religion, or converted it to the worship of Islam, have left us no means of determining what was purely Hindu. Were any artist, or any curious enquirer, to go to ancient Delhi, and live for a few months amongst the inexhaustible ruins of its various dynasties, he would be enabled to distinguish these with more accuracy from the architecture of the tombs, than from the pages of the historian, each having its character more clearly defined than the styles which we divide into Gothic, Byzantine or Tedesque, Saracenic, and Saxon. We may, I think, claim for the Hindus the invention of the Ogee or contracted arch, of which the pointed horse-shoe arch, as the Saracenic is not inaptly termed, is a modification, as this is the commonest form of their *torun*, the nuptial or triumphal arch. It is at least far more probable that the wealthy and scientific Hindu—whose claims to discoveries in the highest walks of astronomy, algebra, and all the subtleties of metaphysical lore, are placed upon an indisputable foundation—should be the inventor, than the roving Bedouin of the desert.

On entering the mosque by the central arch, we see a vast pillared hall 248 feet long by 40 feet wide, covered by a flat recessed roof, which is divided into nine octagonal compartments, corresponding with the seven arches of the screen wall and the two corners of the cloisters. In this hall there are five rows of columns, of which one row is placed against the back wall. Altogether there are 70 pillars now standing. These pillars have a greater height than those at the Kutub, and are more elegant in their sculpture and general appearance than the converted mosques in Malwa and Ahmedabad.[1]

1. Captain H. H. Cole's Preservation of National Monuments in Raiputana (1881).

"After confessing and admiring the taste of the vandal architect," says Colonel Tod, "we passed under the arch to examine the more noble production of the Hindu. Its plan is simple and consonant with all the more ancient temples of the Jains. It is an extensive saloon, the ceiling supported by a quadruple range of columns, those of the centre being surmounted by a range of vaulted coverings; while the lateral portion, which is flat, is divided into compartments. But the columns are most worthy of attention. They are unique in design, and with the exception of cave temples, probably among the oldest now existing in India. On examining them, ideas entirely novel, even in Hindu art, are developed. Like all these portions of Hindu architecture, their ornaments are very complex, and the observer will not fail to be struck with their dissimilarity; it was evidently a rule in the art to make the ornaments of every part unlike the other, and which I have seen carried to great extent. There may be forty columns, but no two are alike. The ornaments of the base are peculiar both as to form and execution; the lozenges, with the rich tracery surmounting them, might be transferred, not inappropriately, to the Gothic Cathedrals of Europe. The projections from various parts of the shaft (which on a small scale may be compared to the corresponding projections of the columns in the *Duomo* at Milan), with the small niches still containing the statues, though occasionally mutilated, of the Pontiffs of the Jains, give them a character which strengthens the comparison, and which would be yet more apparent, if we could afford to engrave the details. The elegant *Camacumpa*, the emblem of 'the Hindu Ceres, with its pendant palmyra branches, is here lost, as are many emblematical ornaments, curious in design and elegant in their execution. Here and there occurs a richly-carved corbeille, which still further sustains the analogy between the two systems of architecture; and the capitals are at once strong and delicate. The central vault, which is the largest, is constructed after the same fashion as that described at Nadole; but the concentric annulets, which in that are plain, in this are one blaze of ornaments, which with the whole of the ceiling is too elaborate and complicated for description."[1]

The *Jhonpra* is the earliest specimen of a converted mosque having mazzina (towers for calling the Mussalmans to prayer), placed in the shape of two small *minars* on the top of the central arch in the screen wall. In the Kutub Mosque at Delhi, the Muazin's tower is a separate building (the

1. Annals and Antiquities of Rajasthan, Vol. I., page 780.

famous lofty Kutub Minar), as those in the two mosques at Ghazni, which had only one minar each. In the Delhi mosque, the screen wall being only eight feet thick, no *minar* could be placed on it; but in the *Jhonpra*, with its massive screen wall 11½ feet thick, the architect found it possible to erect two minars 10½ feet in diameter. These minars are in a ruined state now—"crumpled away to mere stumps," as Mr. Caine[1] says; but what remains shows that they were sloping hollow towers with 24 faces or flutes alternately right-angular and semi-circular, just like those of the celebrated Kutub Minar at Delhi; and like their prototype, they were divided into separate stages or storeys by horizontal belts of writing, of which two belts of the northern minar still remain partly legible. Of the Southern minar only one storey is left, while the northern has two; and a part of the horizontal belt of writing, separating the second from the third storey, containing the name of Sultan Altamash with his titles, is lying in the open courtyard.

Inscriptions.—The *Adhai-din-ka-Jhonpra* is rich in inscriptions. While all of them are of importance, a few of them found buried in the court-yard in 1875-6 A.D. are of exceptional interest to the historian as well as to the student of Sanskrit literature. These, and the two small inscriptions, which refer to the construction of the original building are of great historical importance, and are in Sanskrit. The two small inscriptions being fixed in an out-of-the-way place long escaped observation, and probably saved them from destruction at the hands of vandals. They are placed on the lintels of the small stair-cases by the back wall of the cloistered hall, leading from the roof of the hall to the top of the Imamgah Mehrab of white marble. The one in the northern staircase is fading fast, while the other one is in good condition, and is श्रीविग्रहराजदेवेन कारितमायतनमिदं, which means: "This building was constructed by the illustrious King Vigraharaj." The other one simply says, "made by the illustrious King Vigraharaj."

The other Sanskrit inscriptions recovered during excavations in 1875-6 A.D. consist of six tablets of polished basalt, inscribed in Devanagri of the twelfth century A.D., and are in fragments. Four of these tables contain fragments of two old plays in Sanskrit and Prakrit, hitherto unknown. On slabs one and two, are engraved parts of a play called the *Lalita Vigraharaja Nataka.* "The lovely play of

1. Picturesque India, page 79.

Vigraharaj," composed by the learned poet Somadeva, in honour of Emperor Vigraharaj of Ajmer. Dr. Keilhorn, who has edited these inscriptions in the Indian Antiquary, Vol. XX, page 201, says: "The two tablets (I and II) contain large portions of the *Lalita-Vigraharaja Nataka*, composed evidently in honour of the King Vigraharajadeva of Sakambhari, by the Mahakavi, the learned Somadeva. It opens with a conversation between Sasiprabha and the king (Vigraharaja), from which we may conclude that the king was in love with Desaldevi, a daughter of Prince Vasantapala[1] (who resided in Indrapur). The two lovers, one of whom apparently has seen the other in a dream, being separated, Sasiprabha, a confidant of the lady, is sent to ascertain the king's feelings; and having attained her purpose, she is about to depart to gladden her friend with her tidings, when the king confesses that he cannot bear to part with Sasiprabha, and proposes to send Kalyanavati to the Princess instead. Accordingly, Kalyanavati is despatched with a love-message, in which the king informs the lady that his march against the King of the Turushkas, a battle with whom appears to be impending, will soon give him an opportunity of joining her. Suitable preparations having been made for making Sasiprabha's stay with the king comfortable, the latter goes to attend to his mid-day ceremonies. Thus ends the third act.

At the opening of the fourth act, two Turushka prisoners appear on the scene, which represents the camp of the king Vigraharaja at Sakambhari, or a place close to it, in search of the royal residence. In their perplexity they luckily meet with a countryman, a spy, sent to the camp by the Turushka King. This man tells them how he has managed to enter the enemy's camp in the guise of a beggar, together with a crowd of people who went to see the god Somesvara. He also informs them that the army of the Chahumana (Vigraharaja) consists of a thousand elephants, a hundred thousand horses, and a million of men; in fact, that by the side of it, the ocean would appear dry. And having pointed out the king's residence, he departs. The two prisoners take their places near the royal quarters; they meet with the king, who is thinking of his beloved, address him (in verses which unfortunately are damaged in the text), and are sent away richly rewarded.

Vigraharaja now expresses his surprise that his own spy, whom he has sent to the camp of the Hammira,[2] has not

1 "I know of no prince Vasantapala who lived in the twelfth century A.D., but the name looks as if it might belong to one of the Tomara princes of Delhi."—Dr. Keilhorn, Indian Antiquary, Vol. XX, page 201. 2. Sanskritised form of Amir.

returned yet. But just then the spy comes back and informs his master of what he has been able to learn regarding the enemy's forces and his movements. According to his account, the Hammira's army consists of countless elephants, chariots, horses and men, and his camp is well provided. On the previous day it was three *yojanas* distant from Vavverna, the place where Vigraharaja then is, but it is now located at a distance of only one *yojana*. There is also a rumour that the Hammira, having prepared his forces for battle, is about to send a messenger to the king.

The spy having been dismissed, Vigraharaja sends for his maternal uncle, the Raja Simhabala, and having explained the state of affairs, consults with him and his chief minister, Sridhara, as to what should be done. The cautious minister advises not to risk a battle with the powerful adversary. But the king intimating that it is his duty to protect his friends, is too proud to enter upon peaceful negotiations, and is encouraged by Simhabala to act according to his own views. While they are still consulting, the arrival of the Hammira's messenger is announced. The stranger is admitted into the royal presence, expresses his wonder at the splendour and the signs of power which surround the king, is struck with Vigraharaja's own appearance, and cannot conceal from himself that the task entrusted to him will be a difficult one to perform.

Here the inscription ends. "It may be assumed," says Dr. Keilhorn, that Vigraharaja and the Hammira on the present occasion did not fight, and that the king eventually was united with his lady love From the Delhi Siwalik Pillar inscription we know that in reality Visaldeva-Vigraharaja successfully made war against the Muhammadan invaders," and finally drove them out of Hindustan.

Slabs three and four contain portions of a play by Vigraharaja himself in honour of Siva, called *Harakeli Nataka*, or the play of Hara (Siva). The play is partly in imitation of Bharavi's *Kiratarjuniya*. There is praise of the Emperor by Siva for the play. The date of the play as given in theinscription corresponds to Sunday, the 22nd November, 1153 A.D.

These inscriptions were engraved by Bhaskar, son of Mahipati and grandson of Govinda (a favourite of King Bhoj), belonging to a family of Hun chiefs who had been admitted into Hinduism.

The fifth slab has engraved on it the beginning of a poem, the name of which is not given. It contains the *Stuti*, invocation to and praises of various *devatas* (gods), and finally comes to Surya, from whom, says the poem, the Chauhans are descended. The remaining portions appear to have been engraved on other stones, which undoubtedly still lie buried in the debris of the *Jhonpra.* This inscription is in pure Sanskrit.

The sixth slab, or rather the few pieces of this slab that have been found, show that it was a *Prasasti* concerning the Chauhan Kings of Ajmer. The available pieces have been put together. The inscription mentions that "Ajmer was made for his residence by King Ajaideva," that he conquered Narvarma (King of Malwa) on the border of Avanti (Ujjain), and that after giving his throne to his son, he became a *Vanaprastha* and took up his abode in the forest of the sacred Pushkar. It is further stated that his son adorned the land of Ajmer with the blood of Turushkas, as a woman whose husband returns alive and victorious from war adorns herself in clothes of red *kusunbh* colour. It is also stated that the warriors of this king captured the elephants of the King of Malwa. The name Kumar Pal is also found engraved on one of the pieces, but for want of the next connected piece nothing further can be made out of this name.

These inscriptions are of the greatest importance to the historian, and it is hoped that Government will see their way, to taking in hand regular excavations in the *Jhonpra,* with a view to recover, if possible, the remaining portions of these important inscriptions. These inscriptions serve a threefold purpose. Firstly, they show that Vigraharaj (Visaldeva) fought against the invaders of India from the north-west, and thus supports the Delhi Siwalik inscription of the same monarch, and tends to show that the event took place about 1153 A.D. or soon after it. Secondly, they show that Visaldeva was not only a great king, but was a great scholar and poet, and was a patron of learning. "Actual and undoubted proof is here afforded," says Dr. Keilhorn, "to us of the fact that powerful Hindu rulers of the past were eager to compete with Kalidasa and Bhavabhuti for poetical fame."[1]

Dr. Keilhorn adds: "And it shows the strange vicissitudes of fortune that the stones on which a royal author, who could boast of having repeatedly exterminated the barbarians (Turushkas, Mussalmans) and conquered all the land between the Vindhya and the Himalaya, made known to his people the products of his muse, should have been used as

1. Indian Antiquary, Vol. XX, p. 201.

common building material" by the descendants of those barbarians."

Thirdly, the inscriptions help us in fixing the date of the building, which would be some time before 1153 A.D.; and, if we remember the design of and similar inscriptions in the famous Pathshala of Bhoj, which was evidently the prototype of the *Adhai-din-ka-Jhonpra*, also in showing that the building was originally a college building.

Another inscription in Nagri characters, but in the Hindi language, is to be found on the marble pillar of the northern balcony at the entrance gate, which records the visit of one Dharma, Master mason of Boondi, in Sambat 1462 (1405 A.D.), during the reign in Ajmer of Rana Mokal. The inscription simply says: "Sambat 1462 Varshe Jeth badi 8 Sutradhar Dharma Boondiko" (Samvat year 1462, Jeth Badi 8th, Master mason Dharma of Boondi).[1] Near this inscription are recorded in rude Nagri, measurements of the *Jhonpra*, as—Hath 172, hath 167. "These numbers" says General Cunningham, "curiously corroborate my measurements, for as 172: 167 272·6: 264·517 feet, or less than one-quarter of an inch different from my breadth of the enclosure. The two dimensions together give an average length of 19·0088 inches for the old *hath* or cubit of Ajmer. I am inclined to ascribe these measurements to a mason named Dharma.

All the remaining inscriptions are in Arabic, and in a way record the history of the building after it came into the hands of Shahabuddin Ghori and his successors. The earliest Arabic inscription is on the Imamgah, or the arch built of white marble in the back wall of the *Jhonpra*, beside which stands the *mimber*, or an elevated stand for the speaker. This inscription begins with a verse from the Koran, and ends with the date of its construction. It is as follows:—

"But he only shall visit the temples of God who believes in God and the last day, and is constant at prayer, and pays the legal alms, and fears God alone. These perhaps may become of the number of those who are rightly directed. Do ye reckon the giving of drink to the pilgrims and the visiting the holy temples to be actions as meritorious as those performed by him who believeth in God and the last day, and fighteth for the religion of of God? They shall not be held equal with God; for God directeth not the unrighteous people. Erected on the 21st Jamadi-ui-Akhir H. 595" (1199 A.D.).

A tradition (*hadis*) is also inscribed round the arch which says:

"The prophet has said that haste should be made for prayers before they are missed and for *toba* (repentance) before death comes."

1. Archaeological Survey Report, Vol. II, page 259.

A little removed from the above inscription in the back wall of the *Jhonpra*, and immediately under the roof of the second dome from the centre towards the north, there is another inscription in two lines in Kufic characters, which translated means: "(This was built) under the management (Darogai) of Abubakar, the son of Ahmad, entitled Jamal-ul-Fazilat, in the month of Zilhijah 596." (September 1200 A.D., Katik and Mangsar S. 1257). This inscription has been built up upside down during the repairs.

Of the three belts of writing that surround the central arch and the two beside it of the screen, the two inner ones are Arabic and the outer one square Tughra or Kufik. The Kufik lines, however, go in straight lines on the two sides of the arches, but do not go round the arch proper. The outer of the two Arabic lines round the central arch contains the same verse from the Koran as is inscribed on the marble Imamgah above described. The innermost line is of great historical importance, and shows that the screen was built during the reign of Sultan Shamsuddin Altamash (1210-1236 A.D.). It says:

"This building was ordered to be built by the King of the World, the just, the magnificent; the King, the great, superior Lord of the heads of the people, chief of the King of Arabia and Persia; he is the shadow of God in this world, the sun of the faith and the world. The defender (one who attends to the complaints of Islam and Muhammadans; the crown of the nobles and the kings, the extirpator of the unbelievers and the irreligious; ever ready to clear off the darkness of unbelief and the idolators, the supporter of Islam, the mighty Government and the crown of the bright religion, master of land and water, the King of the Eastern Continent; Heaven helps him; victorious over his enemies; his title Abdul Muzaffar Altamash Sultan, the right hand of the Caliph of God, the ally of the chief of Muhammadans, he is sublime in everything, and every moment a new proof of his greatness is forthcoming. This was written on the 20th of Rabi-ul-Akhir———,"

The stone bearing the year has been lost, presumably during the repairs of 1875-76 A.D.

Round the two side arches, are inscribed the following verses from the Koran in two lines. On the northern arch:

"Verily we have granted thee a manifest victory, that God may forgive thee thy preceding and thy subsequent sin, and may complete his favor on thee and direct thee in the right way; and that God may assist thee with a glorious assistance. It is he who sendeth down secure tranquillity into the hearts of the true believers, that they increase in faith beyond their former faith: (the hosts of heaven and earth are God's; and God is knowing and wise): that he may lead the true believers of both sexes into gardens beneath which rivers flow, to dwell therein for ever, and may remove their evil deeds from them: (this will be great felicity with God): and that he may punish the hypocritical men and women and the idolators and idolatresses who conceive an ill opinion of God. They shall experience a term of evil fortune; and God shall be angry with them and curse them, and has prepared hell for them; an ill journey shall it be thither." "Praise be unto him who transported his servant by night from the sacred temple of Mecca to the farther temple of Jerusalem, the circuit of which we have blessed, that we might show him some of our signs; for God is he who heareth and seeth, and we gave unto Moses the book of the law, and appointed the same to be a direction unto the children of Israel, commanding them, saying, 'take not any other patron besides me.' O posterity of those whom we carried in the ark with Noah; verily he was a grateful servant and was expressly declared unto the children of Israel in the book of the law, saying, ye will surely commit evil in the earth twice, and ye will be elated with great insolence."

Round the southern arch are inscribed the following verses:

"Blessed be he who has placed the twelve signs in the heavens and has placed therein a lamp by day and the moon which shines by night. It is he who has ordained the night and the day to succeed each other for the observation of him who will consider or desires to show his gratitude. The servants of the merciful are those who walk meekly on the earth; and when the ignorant speak unto them, answer, Peace: and who pass the night adoring their Lord and standing up to pray unto him; and who say, 'O Lord avert from us the torment of hell, for the torment thereof is perpetual:' verily, the same is a miserable abode, and a wretched station."

"If we had sent down the Koran on a mountain, thou wouldst certainly have seen the same humble itself, and cleave asunder for fear of God. The similitudes do we propose unto men that they may consider. He is God besides whom there is no God; who knoweth that which is future and that which is present; he is the most merciful; he is God; besides him there is no God; the King, the most Holy, the Giver of Peace, the Faithful, the Guardian, the Powerful, the Strong, the most High. Far be God exalted above the idols which they associate with him! He is God, the Creator, the Maker, the First. He has most excellent names, Whatever is in heaven and in earth praiseth him: and he is the Mighty, the All-wise."

Behind the second arch from the south, on the flat stone lintel, as we enter the pillared hall, is a small inscription to the following effect:

"During the time when the management was in the hands of Ahmad, son of Muhammad the Aariz" (the officer of the court whose duty it is to present people to the king).

The two ruined minarets on the central arch are divided into separate stories by horizontal belts of writing. In the lower belt round the north minar, we read;

"The father of victory, Sultan Altamash, ally of the chief of Muhammmadans, may God ever keep the country and government in his hands; the Chief of all Chiefs; he is exalted above all in the East and the West."

In the upper belt is a verse from the Koran which says:

"We are your friends in this life, and in that which is to come: therein shall ye have that which your souls shall desire, and therein shall ye obtain whatever ye shall ask for; as a gift from the gracious and merciful God. Who speaketh better than he who inviteth unto God and worketh righteousness, and saith, I am a Muslim? God and evil shall not be held equal."

Over the entrance gate-way to the east, as we ascend the steps of the *Jhonpra* and before we enter it, are inscribed two traditional sayings of Muhammad, one regarding Friday and the other in praise of the virtuous act of erecting a mosque. The first says:

"The prophet said: Friday prayers are equal to an exalted kind of pilgrimage; so long as he who regularly says his prayers is in the world, the beneficent effect of the prayers is with him; and if he is in the company of those in Heaven, it is with him there."

The other says:

"The prophet said: for him who erects a place for the worship of God with means righteously acquired, the Almighty God builds a place in Heaven."

On several stones in the arches, are engraved stray words in Arabic as *Alkhaqani*, *Alkhalafa* in a number of places, and some in Sanskrit, as *Sri Sinhaldeva* and other Hindu names. The word *Alkhalafa* probably marks the place where the Khalifa or the leader of a group of those who stood to say their prayers, took his stand at the time of prayer.

CHAPTER VIII

DARGAH KHWAJA SAHIB

THE Dargah of Khwaja Muinuddin Chishti, popularly known as Khwaja Sahib, is a place of worship of the Mussalmans. The Khwaja is sometimes called the Sultan-ul-Hind (chief of the saints of India) and the Dargah is one of the chief holy places of the Muhammadans in India.

Khwaja Muinuddin Chishti.—Khwaja Muinuddin Chishti was a native of Afghanistan, and was born on a Monday in H. 537[1] (1143 A.D.) in the village Sijiz in Sistan (Sans. *Shak-sthan*, country of the Shaks), near Ghor. His father was a Husaini Sayad, and was named Sayad Ghiasuddin Ahmad, and his mother, Bibi Mahanur.[2] The boyhood of Khwaja Muinuddin was passed in Khurasan, to which his father had migrated. Khwaja Ghiasuddin Ahmad died in H. 551 (1156 A.D.) at Nishapur, leaving his son a garden and a water flour-mill as his sole inheritance. Khwaja Muinuddin came under the influence of Ibrahim Qandozi, sold the garden, distributed the proceeds amongst the poor, became a fakir and went away towards Bokhara and Samarkand. He became a pupil of Hisamuddin Bokhari, and committed the Koran to memory. Thence he proceeded *via* Nishapur to a village in its neighbourhood, called Haroon. There, he became on 10th of Shawal (Thursday) H. 560 (1165 A.D.), a disciple of Khwaja Usman Chishti Harooni, whose mausoleum is at Mecca. As Khwaja Usman was a follower of the Chishtia sect[3] of fakirs, Khwaja Muinuddin has also come to be known as Chishti. Chisht is a village near Herat, now called Shaqlan; and as four[4] of the eminent teachers of this sect of fakirs were natives of Chisht, their disciples have come to be styled Chishti. Khwaja Muinuddin thus became the Khalifa of Khwaja Usman, disciple of Haji Sharif Zindani, who was a follower of the school of Khwaja Ishaq Shami, the founder of

1. Some say the Khwaja was born in H. 527 (1133 A.D.).
2. Others say her name was Bibi Khasul Malka.
3. The four sects of fakirs are (1) Qadirya, (2) Nakshbandia, (3) Chishtia, and (4) Shorwardia.
4. (1) Khwaja Abu Ahmad (2) Khwaja Nasaruddin Abu Ahmad, (3) Khwaja Yusuf. (4) Khwaja Qutbuddin Modud.

the Chishtia sect. After an attendance of 20½ years on Khwaja Usman Harooni, Khwaja Muinuddin went to Mecca, Medina and Sanjar, and thence to Baghdad, where he met Sheikh Ziauddin and Shahabuddin Saharwardy, and became a disciple and Khalifa of Khwaja Ahaduddin Kirwani. In Jeel, near Baghdad, Khwaja Muinuddin stayed a short time with Sheikh Abdul Kadir Gilani, called Piranpir. Passing Hamadan and Tabrez—where he met Abu Said Tabrezi—he came to Ispahan, where Khwaja Qutbuddin Bakhtyar Kaki became a disciple of Khwaja Muinuddin. After staying two years in Khurqan, where he preached in the town and suburbs, he went to Astrabad, and there met Sheikh Nasiruddin Astrabadi, and lived with him for a time. Thence, he migrated to Hirat and Sabzwar, the *Hakim* of which place, Yadgar Muhammad, became the Khwaja's disciple, and accompanied him to Hissar Shadman. The Khwaja thence proceeded to Balkh. There, Hakim Ziauddin became his disciple. The Khwaja went to Ghazni. From there he came to India with the army of Shahabuddin Ghori, and at the age of 52, took up his abode in Ajmer.

It has been wrongly stated that Khwaja Muinuddin came to Ajmer several years before the conquest of Ajmer by Shahabuddin Ghori, and while Prithvi Raj was still King of Ajmer. As a matter of fact he came with Shahabuddin's army to India. The *Tajul Maasir*, the earliest history of Shahabuddin Ghori by Hasan Nizami, who was a contemporary writer, while writing about Ajmer, makes no mention of the Khwaja. The *Tabkati Nasiri*, admittedly the most authentic history of the period, the work of Minahaji-Siraj, who was also a contemporary writer, speaking of Shahabuddin's invasion of India when Prithviraj was killed, says:—

> "The author heard from a trustworthy person, a distinguished man of the highland district of Tulak, whom they used to style by the title of Muinuddin Ushi,[1] who said: 'I was in that army along with the Sultan-i-Ghazi, and the number of cavalry composing the army of Islam that year was one hundred and twenty thousand arrayed in defensive armour.'"

The author of *Muntakhabul Tawarikh*, Maulana Abdul Qadir Badayuni[2] a contemporary of Emperor Akbar, also says: "Khwaja Muinuddin Chishti came with Sultan Shahabuddin

1. "The person here referred to is no other than the celebrated Muinuddin Chishti, whose tomb is at Ajmer."—Major Raverty, Tabqati Nasiri, page 465.

2. Muntakhabul Tawarikh, page 15. The text is.

حضرت خواجه معین‌الدین چشتی قدس‌الله سره العزیز که سرچشم اولیا بداکبار و مشایخ
عظام دیار هند است و مزار متبرک وے در اجمیر واقعه است‌درین نوبت باسلطان همراه
بود و این فتح بموجب راندن نفس مبارک رحمانی آب قطب زبانی نزمی نموده—

Dargah of Khwaja Muinuddin Chishti, from the Bazar (1914 A. D.)

THE BALAND DARWAZA AND A DEG.

when he invaded India again in 588 H. (1192 A.D.)." The author of another history of the Mughal period, *Charchman Chatraman*, also says that Khwaja Muinuddin came with Shahabuddin Ghori, when he defeated Prithviraj The famous historian, *Ferishta*, says that when Khwaja Sahib first arrived at Ajmer, "the Sardar of Sardars, Sayad Husain Mashhedi, who was khown as Khangsawar and followed the Shia religion, and who had been appointed *darogha* of that town, received the Sheikh (Khwaja Muinuddin) with great respect and honour."[1] The *Khulasat-ul-Tawarikh*, written in 1695 A.D., says: "When Sultan Shahabuddin Ghori conquered Hindustan, he (Khwaja Muinuddin Chisti) came to Delhi and afterwards went to Ajmer for the purpose of retirement"—Jadunath Sarkar's, *The India of Aurangzeb*, p. 58. This settles the matter.

The Khwaja Sahib is said to have died on the 6th of Rajab, H. 633[2] (March, 1233 A.D.) at the age of 97. Seven years before his death, he married the daughter of Sayad Wajiuddin Muhammad Mashhedi. The Khwaja's two wives were named Amatullah and Asmat Bano. Khwaja Muinuddin had three sons, Khwaja Fakhruddin, Khwaja Abu Said, and Khwaja Hisamuddin, and a daughter named Bibi Hafiz Jammal, whose piety has procured her a *Chilla* in the Chashma, Ajmer, and whose tomb is to the right of the southern entrance to the Khwaja Sahib's mausoleum. His eldest son, Fakhruddin, died twenty years after him, in Sarwar (now in Kishangarh State), 32 miles from Ajmer, and was buried there. Fakhruddin's son, Hisamuddin Sokhta, died in Sambhar. The tomb of the Khwaja's second son, Abu Said, is in the Dargah, on the platform near the Carnataki Dalan.

Khwaja Muinuddin lived a life of piety. He is said to have passed days together in devotion and meditation. His diet was simple and spare, and his dress consisted of a simple tunic, which when torn in any place was patched by himself.

1. Tarikhe Farishta, Vol II, page 377. The original text says:—

سیدالسادات سید حسن مشهدی المشهور خنگ سوار که شیعه مذهب بود وبصلاح
وتقوی آراسته در سلک اولیاء الله اِنتظام داشت وسلطان قطب الدین ایبک آورا داروغه آن
بلده ساخته بود قدوم شیخ را باعزاز و اِکرام تلقی فرمود—

2. As a matter of fact, he was found dead on the 6th Rajab in his cell, and as the cell had not been opened for six days it could not be said with certainty on which of the six days, he had died. Hence the Urs, or anniversary of his death, takes place from the first to the sixth Rajab, every year.

Sheikh Fariduddin Ganjshakar says that he sometimes ate only one *chapatee* weighing five misqals on the eighth day, and Sheikh Nizamuddin Aulia says that the Khwaja Sahib used, during his initiation, to cover himself with a *dutai* (two sheets of cloth stitched together) patched in many places. He never preached aggression, was a man of peace and good-will towards all God's creatures. His chief disciples were Sheikh Hamid-uddin Soofi of Nagor (Marwar), entitled Sultan-ul-Tarkeen, who died on 29th Rabi-ul-sani H. 673 (1275 A.D.), and Khwaja Qutbuddin Bakhtyar Kaki, who settled in Delhi[1] and died there.

On the death of the Khwaja, his remains were interred in the cell in which he lived, but no masonry tomb was built over them. In fact, he appears to have been forgotten in Ajmer.[2] For nearly 250 years nothing more is heard of him, till the time of Sultan Ghiasuddin son of Sultan Mahmud Khilji of Mandoo. At the instance of Khwaja Husain of Nagor in H. 868 (1464 A.D.) he built a *pucca* tomb and a small dome over it. In 1570 A.D., Akbar built the magnificent Akbari Masjid in the Dargah, and often came on pilgrimage to the shrine during the first twentyfive years of his reign, and gave alms to the *khadims*. The Dargah being thus firmly established, additions were made to it by his successors. His grandson, Shah Jahan. built the present splendid dome and added the Juma Masjid in white marble, and added a gateway for the *Nakkar Khana*, and generally beautified the place It did not receive much attention from Aurangzeb, and is said to have been badly treated during the succeeding Rathor Raj in Ajmer. The Nizam of Hyderabad built the imposing gateway in 1915 A. D., which is now the principal entrance. The Dargah as a whole is an ornament to the town.

Description.—The Dargah is situated at the foot of the north-eastern spur of the Taragarh hill and separated from it by the Jhalra tank. It is an irregular rectangle, with its principal entrance to the north. It has also five small entrances, two towards the east, opening into the Khadim Muhalla, and three towards the west—one into the burial ground of the Diwan's family, another from the Akbari Masjid into the street leading to the Tripolia Gate, and the third through the Mahfilkhana to the Khanqah. Before

1. Qutbuddin Bakhtyar Kaki came to Ajmer during the Khwaja's last illness. The Khwaja died 20 days after Qutbuddin's departure.

2 It is said that the descendants of Sheikh Hamiduddin Nagori sometimes came to Ajmer to pay their respects to the Khwaja's tomb.

the Nizam's gateway was built, the main entrance was a small gateway built during the time of Shah Jahan, as the inscription above the gate shows. Its wooden doors have recently been replaced by nickel plated ones presented by a resident of Bombay. The raised steps now covered by the Nizam's Gate were erected in Akbar's time to prevent water from Inderkot flowing into the Dargah during the rains. This gateway is called, the Nakkar-khana, because on the gate are kept two pairs of *nakkaras* (big drums). The larger of the two is wrongly stated to have been presented along with the *sahan chirag*, the brass lamp to the south of the *Buland Darwaza*, by Akbar from the spoils of Chitor. As a matter of fact, neither of these *nakkaras* nor the *sahan chirag* ever belonged to Chitor. The *nakkaras* were no doubt presented by Akbar and were trophies of war, but they had belonged to the army of Daud Khan, Sultan of Bengal, and were presented long after the capture of Chitor. The matter is thus explicitly stated by a contemporary Muhammadan historian, Maulana Nizamuddin, in his well-known history, Tabqat-i-Akbari[1]—

وقائیع سال هیزدهم الهي—اکبر از دهلی روانه شد باجمیر—در اوایل رمضان المبارک هواے اجمیر از غبار نعال مراکب مشک بیز وعنبر آمیز گردید ازگرد راه بمزار مورد الانوار خواجه معین الحق والدین قدس سره فرمود لوازم زیارت وشرایط طواف بجاآوردند واز غنایم بنگاله یک جفت دمامه را واوراک روز اول نزد حضرت خواجه قدس سره جدا فرموده بودند آورده داخل نقارخانه حضرت قدس سره فرمودند و بهر روز بدستور قدیم بمزار فایض الانوار تشریف برده ازصدقات اوند و خیرات فقرا واهل احتیاج را از نوال بے نیاز میگردا نیدند—

TRANSLATION:—Early in Ramzan (1574 A.D.) the atmosphere of Ajmer became fragrant from the storm raised by the musk like hoofs of (royal) horses. (The king) went straight to the shrine of Khwaja Muinuddin and duly observed the necessary religious ceremonies there; and from the spoils of Bengal, two big drums, which from the first day had been kept apart to be presented to the Khwaja, were brought and presented to the Nakarkhana of the Khwaja Sahib. According to old custom, (the emperor) went every day to the shrine and made the beggars and the needy, rich by charitable presents and alms.

To the right as we enter the main door, is the Akbari Masjid, which is a square 140 by 140 feet, built by Emperor Akbar in H. 978 (1571 A.D.). The central arch of this masjid facing the east, is 56 feet high, and reminds one of the magnificent gate-way of the mosque at Fatehpur Sikri. Its northern cloisters are at present used as a day school for the Dargah primary school, and the southern and eastern ones are clo...

1. Tabqati-i-Akbari, p. 322. See also Elliot's History of India, Vol. V.,

into cells and used as store-rooms. Repairs were executed to this mosque in 1320 H. (1901 A.D.), at the expense of Nawab Gafur Ali of Danapur.

The visitor next passes under the *Buland Darwaza* or high gateway, so called because it is disproportionately high. It is 75 feet from the ground to the top of the two *chhatrees* over the gate. Towards the north, this gate is supported on either side by three-storied *chhatrees* of carved stone, the spoils of some Hindu building. The materials and the style of these *chhatrees* plainly betray their Hindu origin. Their excellent surface carving is unfortunately hidden from view by coats of colour and whitewash, which should be removed. It is also stated that these *chhatrees* and the gate—which is of red sandstone (raised higher and arched by Mussalmans), with the eastern cell continuation of it—formed part of an old Jain temple, which was demolished.

Nothing is known for certain regarding the date of the building of the gate. It is, however, stated that it was built in the time of Sultan Ghyasuddin Khilji (1469-1500) of Mandoo. To the south of the gate, on either side, is a big cauldron in which a mess of rice is prepared and looted. The *Buland Darwaza* and the cauldrons are thus described by Colonel Broughton[1]:—

"The entrance to the outer court passes under an arched gateway, remarkable only for its preposterous height; and one of the exhibitions with which you are indulged during a visit to the tomb is to be mounted on the top of this archway by a flight of steps so steep and narrow as to be really frightful to one not accustomed to them; and when seated there, to scatter handfuls of cowries and copper coin among the crowd of *peer-zadas* and beggars of all description, who flock below and scramble and fight for the money, to the great amusement of the exalted spectators. On either side of this archway, within the court, is an enormous copper boiler fitted into solid masonry, the larger of which is capable of holding seventy maunds or five thousand four hundred pounds of rice, and the smaller twenty-eight maunds. When princes or other great men visit Ajmer, it is usual for them to order these vessels to be filled, which is accordingly done with rice, sugar, butter, sweetmeats etc. It requires the whole night to boil this mess, which is distributed in the morning among the hungry peer-zadas. The mode in which the distribution is conducted affords the chief amusement to the pious donor, who is generally seated half-way up the gateway, to witness the extraordinary spectacle. Some of the oldest of the *peer-zadas* are entitled to certain portions of the composition, and when this quantity is taken out and distributed, large shovelfuls are thrown among the rest of these holy persons, who scramble for them with such avidity that they soon begin fighting, while some, who have taken the precaution to wrap old clothes around their bodies and limbs, plunge boldly into the boilers, where a battle-royal takes place for every handful; but should an unfortunate stranger

1. Letters From a Mahratta Camp.

presume to intrude upon their prescriptive rights, and try his luck for a share of the *tabarruk* (for it is all consecrated), they join instantly to drive away the intruder and make him pay dearly for his temerity. The *tabarruk* is afterwards sold by the *peer-zadas.* Scindia, whose devotion to Muhammadan saints and religious customs. I have more than once had occasion to mention, has given this favourite entertainment three times since our arrival."

Tom Coryat says: "When at Ajmer he (Jahangir) went afoot to the tomb of the prophet, Hod Moinuddin, there buried, and kindled fire with his own hands and his Nur Mahal under that immense and Heidelbergian œquipollent brass pot, and made *khichri* for five thousand poor, taking out the first platter with his own hands and serving one; Nur Mahal, the second, and so his ladies all the rest."[1]

One of these two cauldrons was presented by Akbar in 974 H. (1567 A.D.), when he made a grant of 18 villages for the maintenance of the *langar* or daily distribution of cooked food to the poor. The other cauldron was presented by Emperor Jahangir in 1022 H. (1613 A.D.). He states in his *Tuzaki Jahangiri.*[2] "I had a big cauldron made in Agra and presented to the Dargah. Five thousand men were fed out of it." The original cauldrons in time became unserviceable, and Mulla Madari, a minister of Scindia, paid for two new cauldrons, which were made at Ajmer under the supervision of Seth Akhey Chand Mehta.[3] These cauldrons too in time became unserviceable, and Sir Asman Jah, Nawab Bashir-udaula, had a new one built in H. 1307 (1889 A.D.) to replace the larger of the two. Nawab Alam Ali Khan had the smaller one renewed in H. 1314 (1896 A.D.).

The courtyard between the *Buland Darwaza* and the inner courtyard covers underneath it, cellars of old Hindu temples of which many rooms remain intact. In fact, the whole of the Dargah appears to have been built, as was usual in the times of the early Mussalman rulers, on the ruins of old Hindu temples, partly by converting and partly by adding to the structures already existing.

To the west of the court is situated the Mahfilkhana, which was only recently built by Bashirudaula Sir Asman Jah in H. 1306-9 (1888-1891 A.D.). Previous to this, the place was an open court, and a big *shamiana* called *dalbadal* used to be fixed here during the *Urs* Fair for the Mahfil. It is lighted up every year during the *Urs* at Sir Asman Jah's expense. The building is a hall, 46 feet square, with a gallery 14 feet wide, running round it. In front of the Mahfilkhana,

1. Purchas, Vol. I., p. 601. 2. Tuzaki Jahangiri, vol. I, p. 256.
3. The circumference of the edge of the larger of the two cauldrons is three and half yards.

is a small reservoir of water for the Mussalmans to wash their hands and feet before saying their prayers. This was repaired and roofed with Rs. 1500 presented by Her Majesty Queen Mary in 1911 A.D.

From the courtyard two small gateways lead into the inner court, wherein are situated the Khwaja Sahib's mausoleum, and the *Juma Masjid*. Inside the gate, which faces the *Buland Darwaza*, to the right, is the mosque, variously stated as having been built by Sultan Muhammad Khilji of Mandoo and Jahangir. Jahangir is said to have built a mosque in 1610 A.D., and this may be the building he put up. It is called the *Sandal Khana*, from the fact that sandal prepared here is daily placed, morning and evening, on the Khwaja's tomb. It was repaired and painted at the expense of Nawab Ishaq Khan of Jahangirabad in H. 1314 (1897 A.D.)

To the north of this mosque grow *Chameli* plants; the remains of the two wives of the Khwaja Sahib are said to repose here. Behind the Sandal Khana is the doorway that leads by an underground passage to the cellar, where the remains of the Khwaja were interred, and over which an ordinary *kachcha* tomb in brick was at first raised. Tradition says that inside the cellar is the image of Mahadeva in a temple, on which *sandal* used to be placed every day by a Brahman, whose family is still maintained by the Dargah as *gharhyali* (bell-striker).

Adjacent to the *Sandal Khana* and to the south of it, is the mausoleum of Khwaja Muinuddin Chishti, with its principal entrance to the east, and another towards the south. Though Sultan Ghiasuddin of Mandoo is credited with furnishing the means of building the mausoleum, the building itself was not completed till H. 939 (1537 A.D). This is the *sanctum sanctorum* of the Dargah, and into it only Muhammadans and Hindus are admitted, but no Christians.

The illustration on the opposite page gives the ground plan of this mausoleum,[1] the principal entrance to which is towards the east through the *Begumi Dalan*. This dalan was built in H. 1053 (1643 A.D.) by the accomplished Princess Jahan Ara Begum, the favourite daughter of Shah Jahan and his constant companion in his captivity. During the rebellion of Aurangzeb and his younger brothers against their father, Shah Jahan, her loyalty and faithfulness were marked features of the imperial harem life, as against the conduct of her younger sister, Roshan Ara. Jahan Ara was a

1. The present crown-like kalas on the apex of the dome was presented in 1896 A.D. by Haidar Ali Khan, younger brother of the late Nawab of Rampur.

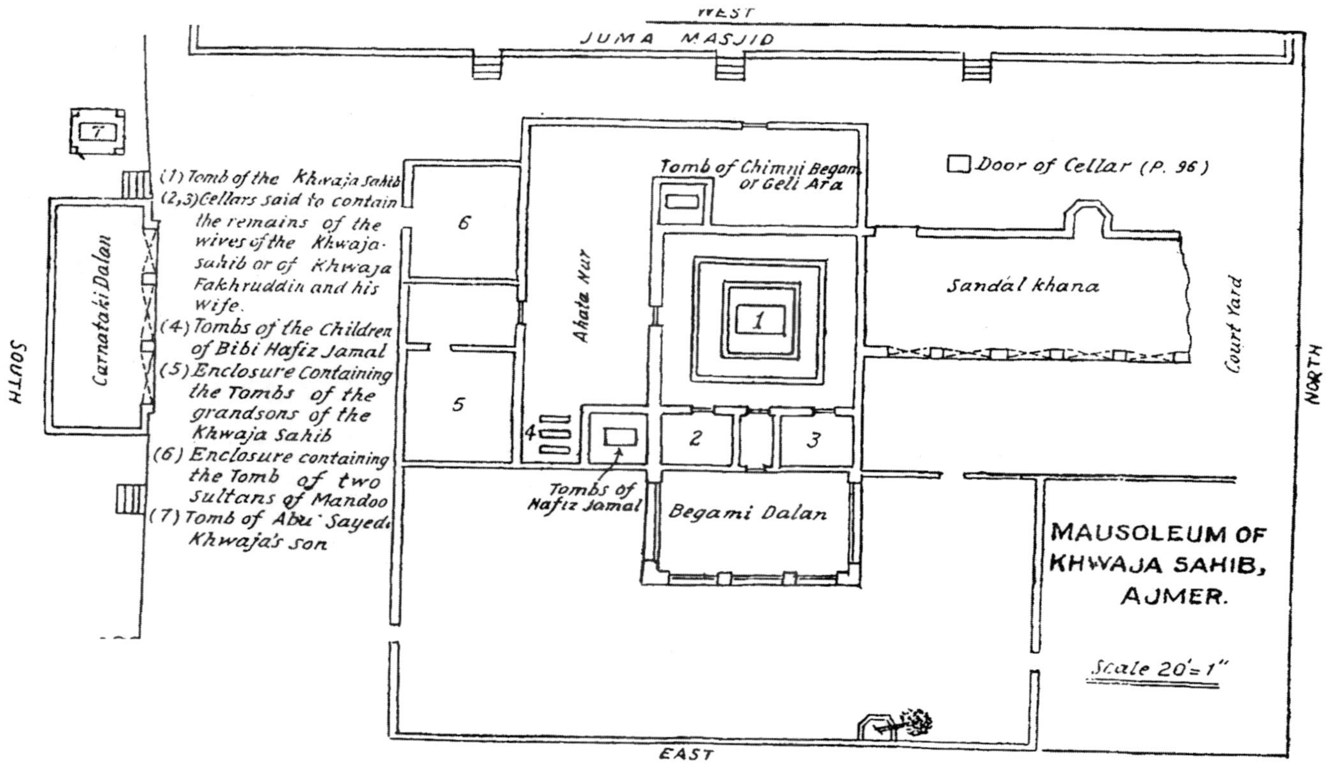

WEST
JUMA MASJID
Door of Cellar (P. 96)
Tomb of Chimni Begam or Geli Ara
Sandal khana
Court Yard
NORTH
Ahata Nur
1
2
3
4
5
6
7
Tombs of Hafiz Jamal
Begami Dalan
Carnataki Dalan
SOUTH
EAST
(1) Tomb of the Khwaja Sahib
(2,3) Cellars said to contain the remains of the wives of the Khwaja-sahib or of Khwaja Fakhruddin and his wife.
(4) Tombs of the Children of Bibi Hafiz Jamal
(5) Enclosure Containing the Tombs of the grandsons of the Khwaja Sahib
(6) Enclosure containing the Tomb of two sultans of Mandoo
(7) Tomb of Abu Sayed Khwaja's son
MAUSOLEUM OF KHWAJA SAHIB, AJMER.
Scale 20'=1"

disciple of the Chishtia sect, and her book, *Munis-ul-Arvah*, is replete with expressions of devotion and love for the Khwaja. Jahan Ara presented to the Dargah, her own attendants connected with the *Farrash Khana*, *Tosha Khana*, &c.

The *Begumi dalan* is of white marble, and the walls and pillars were painted in gold and colours in 1888 A.D. with money given by the late Nawab Mushtak Ali Khan of Rampur, and the roof by a Mussalman merchant of Bombay. The floor of this *dalan* is of white marble, interspersed with the rare *bichhya* and *habur* stones of Jaisalmer. This *dalan* is the portico to the square domed building containing the Khwaja's tomb. In the central arch over the doorway leading to the tomb is fixed a horseshoe-like ornament, and visitors are gravely informed that it is a neck ornament of the Empress Nur Jahan!

The inner doorway (eastern) has doors plated in nickel[1] In the centre of the domed building, is the tomb of Khwaja Muinuddin Chishti, with the head towards the north. As already stated, the actual remains of the Khwaja lie in an underground cellar, covered with a few bricks, several feet below this tomb. The tomb is in white marble inlaid with pieces of coloured stone, and it is said that near the place corresponding to the heart is fixed a rubylike stone of the size of an eight-anna silver piece. This tomb is daily bestrewed with sandal, and is always kept covered with a piece of *kinkhab* (brocade), and over it are placed *chameli* flowers. Above the tomb is an old wooden *chaparkhat* inlaid with pieces of mother-of-pearl, said to have been presented by Jahangir. Between the four poles which support this *chaparkhat* is a silver-plated railing with an opening towards the south. A second similar railing runs round the first railing at a distance of about two feet, also with an opening corresponding to that of the first. At the openings, always sit Khadims of the Dargah in turn, to receive offerings tendered by pilgrims and to bestow *tabarrukh* on them.[2] Between the

1. Both the eastern and southern doors of the mausoleum are nickel plated, and were given by one Saadatullah Khan of Jaora in 1901 A.D., while those fixed in the west gate of the Abata Nur were presented by one Haji Muhammad Ali Khan of Rampur.

2. "Here it is usual for visitors to present some of the rupees with which they should come well supplied to answer the numerous demands made upon their purses. When the offering is made, the Khadim or priest, who attends to show the place, just lifts the pall high enough to discover the lower step of the tomb, and lets it fall again immediately: the tomb itself, which is of white marble inlaid with cornelian, jasper, and various other coloured stones, being totally uncovered only on seven days in the year. A clamorous host of sturdy fellows are always thronging about, each of whom asks for some benefaction for himself in a tone and manner more resembling the demands of a footpad than the supplication of a beggar."—Col Broughton's Letters From a Mahratta Camp, p. 255.

two railings, Hindu and Muhammadan men are admitted, but women are excluded. Under the dome is always hung a velvet shamiana. On the northern wall of the mausoleum is inscribed the following, giving the date of its decoration as H. 939 (1532-33 A.D.):—

ازپے تاریخ نقش گنبد خواجہ معین—گفت ہاتف گو معظم کعبہ عرش برین

In the eastern wall of this domed building, are two cellars, one on either side of the doorway, containing two tombs. These are the tombs of Khwaja Fakhruddin and his wife, who are said to have come with the saint from Afghanistan. The Khadims say that they are the descendants of Khwaja Fakhruddin, a fellow disciple of the Khwaja Sahib. The northern one is now used as a store-room for the tomb-covers, sandal-utensils, etc., required for daily use; and the southern for silver utensils etc., used during the *Urs*.

It is difficult to determine who built the first mausoleum. Babur, and Humayun had nothing to do with the Dargah. It is said that Sultan Ghiasuddin Khilji of Mandoo (1469-1500 A.D.) had invited Khwaja Makhdum Husain, a descendant of Shaikh Hamiduddin of Nagor, the chief disciple of Khwaja Muinuddin to visit him, and that he gave him a large donation, which was used in building (*a*) a brick mausoleum on the Khwaja's tomb at Ajmer, and (*b*) the *Buland Darwaza* of the Dargah of Shaikh Hamiduddin at Nagor (Marwar).

There have always been two *kateras*, round the tomb. In place of a wooden inner *katera*, Jahangir had a gold-plated one made in H. 1025 (1616 A.D.), at a cost of Rs. 1,10,000. This, with the original outer one and other valuable things appear to have been taken away by the Rathors of Jodhpur at the time, when all the mosques in Marwar, except that of Hamiduddin in Nagor, were razed to the ground[1] and the Koran wherever found thrown into wells, in retaliation for similar conduct of Aurangzeb towards the Hindu sacred places. The present outer *katera* was built under the orders of His Highness Maharaja Sawai Jai Singh, the founder of the city of Jaipur, about 1730 A.D., under the supervision of Muhammad Hayat and Haji Manzur Ali Khan, *mutwalis* of the Dargah. It contains 42,961 tolas of silver. The shamianas now in use and some of the tomb coverings were presented by H. H. the Gaekwar of Baroda.

1. See Sairul Mutakharin, Vol II, page 396; also, Elliot's History of India, Vol VII, pages 404 and 446.

To the west and south of the domed building there is an enclosure called the *Ahat-i-Nur* (enclosure of light), in which there are two tombs, and where people retire to repeat the Koran. The two tombs are those of Bibi Hafiz Jammal, the daughter of Khwaja Muinuddin, and of the princess Hurul Nisa[1] or Chimni Begam, daughter of Shah Jahan and grand-daughter of Jahangir, who died of smallpox in her childhood on 29 Jamadul Awal, H. 1025 at Ajmer. Jahangir, in his memoirs, records his grief at her death. The tomb of Hafiz Jammal is of white marble, in a small room about six feet square, near the southern entrance to the domed building; near the door of this room, lie the remains of her three children, who had died in infancy. The tomb of Geti Ara, adjacent to the western wall of the mausoleum, is built in white marble beautifully polished, with a masonry domed roof over it, and closed by marble *jalis* on all sides for fear of the removal of a large topaz fixed on the tomb of the princess On the two sides of the southern gate of this enclosure of light, are walled spaces about 10 feet square, in which purdah women stand or sit to pay their devotions to the saint. In the eastern of these two enclosures, there are two tombs, said to be of the two sons of Khwaja Hisamuddin, grandson of Khwaja Muinuddin. The western enclosure is said to contain the tombs of two Sultans of Mandoo.

The courtyard to the east of the *Begumi Dalan*, separated from the enclosure containing the Khwaja's mausoleum by a marble *katera*, is studded with tombs, two of which deserve notice. The most prominent tomb in the courtyard, built of white marble $10\frac{1}{2}' \times 8\frac{1}{2}'$ with a *jali-katera* (trellis work) about two feet high running round it, is that of Nizam, the famous *bhishti*, or water-carrier, who saved the life of Humayun when he was nearly drowned in the Ganges, near Kanauj, after his defeat by Sher Shah in 1590 A.D. This Nizam is renowned as having reigned by the order of Humayun for half a day on the Mughal throne, when to commemorate the event, he issued leather coins in place of silver ones, which were current during his few hours' reign.

This pretty tomb was at one time studded with precious stones and had a beautiful silk canopy over it, supported by silver-plated stands. Emperor Aurangzeb, on his first visit to the Dargah, mistook this tomb to be that of the Khwaja himself; and when he was told, that the tomb, to which he was making his obeisance, was the tomb of

1. According to some the name of the princess was Geti Ara.

Nizam, the famous water-carrier, he ordered the canopy and ornamentation to be removed. Near this tomb, is the *Kalandari* mosque, known as the *Auliya Masjid.* It consists of a marble floor 20′×6½′, in which the usual three arches are marked in black stone, with a small marble balustrade about three feet high to the west. It is said that the Khwaja on his arrival at Ajmer first alighted at this place. Some say that this was the place, where royal camels used to be tethered in the time of Emperor Prithviraj.

Further east, near the *Khidki Darwaza*, lie the remains of Sheikh Mir, the commander of Dara Shikoh's forces (and father-in-law of Aurangzeb) and of Shah Nawaz Khan, Alamgir's general, who were both killed in the famous battle of Ajmer, in Hijri 1069 (1659 A.D.), between Dara Shikoh and Aurangzeb. The remains of Mallu Khan, Governor of Ajmer during the reign of Sultan Ghiasuddin of Mandoo, were also laid in this court, but his tomb was demolished and the remains dug out and thrown away after the defeat of his son, Mallu Iqbal Khan, who had proclaimed his independence on the death of the Sultan.

To the south of the mausoleum, there is an open space where musicians, male and female, sit and sing; and every Thursday afternoon finds some dancing girl from some part of India doing *mujra*[1] to the Khwaja Sahib. Beyond this, to the south, is situated a *dalan* built in white marble, in H. 1207 (1793 A.D.), by the Nawab of Carnatic, and hence called the *Carnataki Dalan.* Ten verses inscribed under the *chhajja* over the three arches give the name of the Nawab as *Walajah*, and the date as H. 1207 (1793 A.D.).

To the east of the dalan on the platform there is a *sabil* or water-depot. This raised platform or *chhabutra*, which runs east to west separates the Dargah from the Jhalra. In the south-eastern corner of this long platform and due east of Jhalra, stands the mausoleum built by Muhammad Tāfi Buksh, on whom the title of Shah Quli Khan had been conferred by Emperor Akbar. During Akbar's reign, while he was Subedar of Ajmer, he had this place built to allow of his remains being interred there after his death. This wish of his, however, was never gratified, as he died in H. 1008 (1605 A.D.) at Agra, and was buried there. This building is of white marble except the domed roof, which is of lime masonry. The floor is inlaid with Jaisalmer *bichhya*

1. When the singer squats on the floor while singing, it is called *mujra*.

and *habur* stone. To the north of the *Makbara* on the platform are several tombs with inscriptions on them, but none is of any importance. One of these is the tomb of Mirza Aadil, an officer of the Mahrattas who served in Malwa and who died in 1769 A.D. Another is of Asadul Mulk, Mirza Abdul Rahim Khan, who died in 1800 A.D.

The western end of this platform was originally a ghat, built by Shah Jahan, to descend into the Jhalra. In 1901 A.D., this ghat was converted into a square *hauz* (tank), which is daily filled with water from the Jhalra for the faithful to wash their hands and feet before entering the Juma Masjid to say their prayers. To the south of this *hauz*, and between it and the burial ground called the *charyar*, was open space till recently, when some cells were put up there by Sarwar Jung, a noble of Hyderabad.

The *charyar* (four companions) is an enclosure containing a number of small tombs (some of which are of marble), and is so called from the fact that the remains of the four companions of Khwaja Muinuddin who are said to have come with him from Afghanistan to Ajmer were laid in this enclosure. It also contains tombs of the ancestors of the Mutavali and the Khadims of the Dargah. The oldest tomb here bears an inscription on a pillar of a domed *chhatri* over it, which gives the date of the tomb as 16th Rajab, H. 1022 (1613 A.D.)

The finest building in the Dargah, however, is the Juma Masjid, situated to the west of the mausoleum. This was built by Shah Jahan, in the tenth year of his reign (1638 A.D.), as stated by his daughter, Jahan Ara Begum, in the *Munis-ul-Arvah*, at an expenditure of two lakhs and forty thousand rupees. It is of white marble, and though inferior in design and dignity to the famous Moti Masjid in the Agra Fort—also built by Shah Jahan—it is nevertheless an excellent structure, and is a suitable ornament to the Dargah. The Masjid proper is 148'×25'-3½". What, however, imparts beauty to the mosque and adds to its dignity, is the enclosure 156 feet by 53¼ feet in front of it, paved in polished marble and surrounded on three sides by an elegant balustrade having five openings for ingress and egress.[1] The screen wall of the mosque has eleven pointed arches of uniform height. Inside the Imamgah, there are five niches in which the *kalma* is inscribed in letters of gold. An inscription in black runs along the whole length of the building under the eaves. Besides containing 99 different names

1. Abdul Rahman, the author of Mirat-ul-Israr, says that the mosque took fourteen years to build.

of God. it contains 33 verses, which give the date of its erection as H. 1047 (1638 A.D.), and says that Shah Jahan, on his return from the campaign (1617 A.D.) against the Maharana of Mewar, while his father, Jahangir, was still on the throne, feeling the want of a mosque in the Dargah, had vowed that he would build one, should he succeed in getting the throne, a vow that was carried out as soon as he became emperor.

"This building," says Mr. Caine, "will charm the traveller who has not yet reached Delhi and Agra."[1]

Between the Dargah and the northern spur of the Taragarh hill, is an artificial reservoir of water formed by putting two dams across the old nullah which drained the rain water of Inderkot. and diverting the course of the nullah from behind to the front of the Dargah, during the time of Akbar. As the two approaches which are both outside the limits of the Dargah show, it is not a part of the Dargah. "This great tank," says Mr. Caine, "all in warm shadow, surrounded by white marble tombs intermixed with the deep green foliage, topped with the lofty hills that surround Ajmer, ablaze with sunlight. forms a picture not easily forgotten."[2] Colonel Dixon (1843-57 A.D.) repaired this Jhalra, and demolished the small reservoir of water that stood near the Tripolia Gate. He built in its place, quarters for the police constables, stationed at the gate. Only some drains falling into the Jhalra now mark the course by which the nullah water used to go to the Jhalra.

Behind the Mahfilkhana and the Juma Masjid, is situated the burial ground wherein lie, the remains of the former Diwans of the Dargah and members of their families. Two structures in this enclosure, deserving passing notice, are the mausoleums of Khwaja Hasan and of Sheikh Allauddin, commonly called, the *sola khamba* (sixteen pillars). The plan of the former is similar to that of the mausoleum of Khwaja Muinuddin, and consists of a square chamber roofed by a more prominent dome than that of Allauddin's tomb behind it, with a sixteen-sided drum. An ante-chamber is attached to the west side of the square chamber, and in the centre of the antechamber to the east, is a gateway, large in proportion to the rest of the facade. The gateway has a pointed arch carved on the soffit with bold buds, and around it forming a kind of architrave are rows of little niches. It was built in H. 1047 (1638 A.D.), as shown by the lines[3] inscribed on the entrance door. The building is not kept in good repair. Its inside is congested with small tombs.

1. Picturesque India, p. 80. 2. Picturesque India, p. 80.

3. بنائے مقبرہ باصفاے خواجہ حسین بلفظ مغز شدہ سال خاتمیت این.

THE JHALRA TANK AT AJMER.

View of the Dargah of Khwaja Muinuddin Chishti, from Bada Pir Hill.

The tomb of Allauddin, or *sola khamba*, is so called because its three domes rest on sixteen pillars in addition to the eight, that stand against the eastern and western walls. It is an imposing building of white marble of the middle Mughal period. It is rectangular in plan, the sides being respectively about 40 × 20 feet. It is open on three sides, on the north and south, are three bays divided by groups of four columns united by a solid base, with arches turned between them, while on the east side are three arched openings separated by piers. On the west side, there is a solid wall containing three *mehrabs*, an arrangement which is frequently met with in the tombs of Muhammadan saints from the period of Firoz Shah downwards. A noticeable feature in this building is the zig-zag pattern of black marble inlay adorning the *guldastas*, which run up from the ground at each corner of the building. The shafts of the columns are all octagonal, thirteen inches in diameter, and the arches between them are heavily cusped. The transverse arches connecting the groups of columns are similarly treated, and from them springs a dome carried on pendentives, the soffits of which are ornamented with prismatic groining characteristic of Mughal architecture. On the piers at the ends of the north and south facades, and again above the groups of four columns, inlaid patterns in black marble occur. This inlay work was evidently never completed, as is shown by the abrupt termination of the chases or grooves cut to receive it. In certain cases too, one can see where the workman had marked out the line of the groove by a scratch without proceeding to cut it out. This is an interesting indication that in ancient work, the masons did not finish each stone on the bench, but that they left a certain amount of carving and decorative work to be done after their structures were erected.

Allauddin is said to have been a descendant of Khwaja Muinuddin Chishti, and was a religious dignitary during the reign of Shah Jahan. He died in H. 1011 (1633 A.D.) at the age of 75. An inscription containing the above date appears on the eastern wall of the *mukbara*. At its north-east corner, Allauddin's tomb is connected by a wall to a stone gateway surmounted by a *chhatree* balanced on the wall in a curious fashion. The *chhatree* has four columns, one at each angle; and these rest upon a slab, which forms the floor of the *chhatree*, and which in turn is supported on two stone lintels, which cross the wall at right angles. The lintels, therefore, which carry all the weight of the *chhatree*, are only supported on the wall at their centres, and the whole *chhatree* is balanced upon them. As the wall is only a span or *balisht* broad, the *chhatree* is called "*ek balisht ki chhatree* (one-span *chhatree*). It is a constructional freak which, happily for the public safety, is not commonly employed. The floor of the *chhatree* is already cracked, and is not likely to remain standing for many more years. Earth has accumulated very considerably at this point, since the head of the gateway is only about three feet above the present ground level. Probably there are some steps leading down to it, all buried in the soil.

Dargah Endowment

The Dargah was first endowed by Akbar, and the first Sanad on record is dated the year 1567 A.D., granting 18 villages and one per cent on the sale of salt at Sambhar "wakf langar-i-mazar." Of these villages, however, only two, Nawab and Kanea, are now in the possession of the Dargah. In A.D. 1637, Shah Jahan cancelled this old firman, and gave a new Jagir of the annual value of 25, 780; of this, 10,057 was cash payment, and the remainder 15,723, was the estimated rental of 17 villages, of which 14 are in Ajmer-Merwara. Emperor Farrukhsayar added two villages to the grant.

In the year 1769, Shah Alam issued a firman granting Hokran and Kishanpura to the Dewan Sayad Imam-ud-din. In 1802, Daulat Rao Scindia granted Dantra to Meer Azim-ul-lah Mutvalli, "ba-iwaz rozina Mutvalli" (to the Mutavalli instead of daily allowance). The annual value of Hokran and Kishanpura, on an average of ten years collections, is Rs. 3,534 that of Dantra Rs. 3544/-. An account of the endowment appears in the chapter, "Land Revenue" under head *Jagirs*.

Akbar left Agra on 20 January, 1570 and arrived at Ajmer on the 16th day, walking on foot. The Akbarnama says:—

> He distributed gifts among the attendants of the shrine. As on the occasion of the division of the gifts, which came to a large amount, those who claimed to be descendants of the Khwaja, and who had the superintendence of the shrine—their chief was Sheikh Husain—took possession of the whole of the money, and there were disputes and quarrels between him (Sheikh Husain) and the attendants of the shrine, and there was the allegation that the Sheikhs who had charge of the shrine had told falsehoods with regard to their descent, and as this dispute had gone on a long time, His Majesty appointed trustworthy persons to inquire into the matter and to report thereon. After much investigation, it was found that *the claim of sonship was not genuine*. Accordingly, the charge of the shrine was made over to Sheikh Muhammad Bukhari, who was distinguished among the Sayads of Hindustan for knowledge and fidelity. His Majesty also arranged for the management of the shrine, and for the treatment of pilgrims."[1]

1. Akbarnama, translated by H. Beveridge, vol. II, p. 511.

The management of the endowment was entrusted to the Mutvalli. The Mutvalli has thus two-fold functions to perform in the Dargah, to conduct the religious ceremonies and practices, and to manage the Jagir. His office is a hereditary one.

In 1863, when the Religious Endowments Act XX, was passed, a Committee of five people was appointed to manage the endowment. A new Act "to make better provisions for the management of Dargah and its endowments", Act No. 23 of 1936, has recently been passed superseding the old act. This contemplates a Dargah Committee of 25 members as below :—

One representative of Mutvalli.

One representative of Dewan.

Two representatives of the Khadims of the Dargah.

One representative of the Nizam of Hyderabad.

Five members to be elected by theMuslims of Ajmer.

Four Sajjada Nashins of the Chisti shrinesa.

One member to be elected by the Muslim Members of each of the N. W. F., Bombay, United Provinces, Behar, Bengal, Punjab, Sindh, and Madras Legislatures; and three by the Central Legislature of India. It also provides that the Mutvalli will always be the manager of the Dargah estate.

His Exalted Highness the Nizam has been giving since Fasli year 1302 (A. D. 1893), a part of the Vakf income of the Hyderabad State towards the expenses of this Dargah. This income is about 12000/- a year. This is divided into three shares: one share comes to the Mutvalli and is used for *Langar* (free porridge given to fakirs) once a day and to provide scents, sandal etc, for the tomb; one share goes to the Dewan and the third to the Khadims of the Dargah. The Nizam's Government gives 300/- a month, Hyderabad Currency, to the Mutvalli in lieu of a jagir. In addition to the above, the Nizam gives a grant of 1200/- a year to the Dargah Moinia Usmania School, and about 600/- a month for the new *Naqqar Khana* etc. He also pays the expenses (about 1500/-) of the food prepared in the smaller of the two Degs once during the Urs Fair.

CHAPTER IX

THE MAGAZINE

OR

AKBAR'S PALACE

THE Magazine is one of the most prominent objects in the landscape from all parts of the valley of Ajmer, and is of historical importance. Its stones, were they able to speak, could tell a tale of political intrigue and the court life of one of the most interesting periods in Indian history, that in romantic interest would vie with the best productions of its kind anywhere.

The Magazine is a massive rectangular structure with four imposing bastions at the corners, an audience chamber in the centre, and a magnificent gateway towards the west, facing the town. Mr. J. D. La Touche, in his Settlement Report, 1875, p. 16. says:—"This is a massive square fortified palace built by Akbar, on the north side of the city which from 1818 to 1863, was used as the Rajputana Arsenal, but has now been turned into a Tahsil and Treasury."

Mr. (later Sir Charles) Watson's Ajmer-Merwara Gazetteer, 1904, page 18, says:—"It is a massive square building with lofty octagonal bastions at each corner. It was used as the residence of the Mughal Emperors during their visits to Ajmer, and was the head-quarters of the administration, both in their time and in that of the Mahrattas The main entrance faces the city and is lofty and imposing."[1]

It is said that there was a small garden surrounding the inner Audience Chamber. A well existed between the south-east corner of the Chamber and the bastion near it, into which were thrown unserviceable cannon and other things in 1857 A.D., when the place was fortified in consequence of the army at Nasirabad having joined the Sepoy Mutiny.

To the west of the Magazine, there was an open space for elephant fights and similar other amusements for the emperors, who witnessed them from the window in the gate, as also for the execution of criminals. Sir Thomas Roe

1. Thornton's Gazetteer, (published about 1850 A.D.) says:—"Beyond the city wall is the ruined palace of Shah Jahan. Another of Akbar has been converted into an arsenal."

The Main Gate of the Magazine (or Akbar's Palace) at Ajmer.

THE MAGAZINE IN 1818 A. D. (AKBAR'S PALACE.)

says in his Journal: "At this window, the king sits in judgment, never refusing the poorest man's complaint. He hears with patience both parties, and sometimes sees, with too much delight in blood, the execution done by his elephants."

The Audience Chamber or the building in the centre of the Magazine now used as the Rajputana Museum, is of *khattu* sandstone from the quarries in the town of that name in Marwar, except the Agra redstone brackets which project from the walls, and which have been recently restored. It was a Hindu[1] building in early times, rectangular in shape, 73′-9″ × 59′-6″, the four *facades* being alike in all details. The principal features of the building are the lofty square pillars of the verandah, which occur in the centre of each *facade*, and the heavy cutstone *chhajja* with its massive ornamental brackets. The building consists of a central hall, with four *tibaras* on its four sides, two staircases and four small square corner rooms. The roof is 19 feet above floor level, but the corner rooms have an intermediate roof, nine feet above floor level. These four rooms are double-storied.

This building with the bastions and the rooms built against the high walls between the bastions, provided a complete set of apartments usually found in a palace of the Mughal Emperors, who often visited Ajmer. Of the four bastions, (greatest length of each is 74′) those to the north-east and south-east are similar, each providing the same accommodation as the other, while the other two—those towards the city—are open in the centre, and must have been used by the Emperor himself. It is difficult, in the absence of any records, to determine what portions were allotted to the harem, and where the *ghusal khana*[2] was situated, which figures so prominently in the life of the Great Mughal, and to which Sir Thomas Roe was so often invited, and which he must have long remembered as the place, to which he was summoned one night (2nd September 1616) with the picture of his lady-love, and there deprived of it.[3]

1. Archæological Survey Report, Vol. XXIII, P. 46.

2. The *ghusal khana* was a chamber for private audience and was so called as it was adjacent to the Emperors' bath.

3. "Sir Thomas Roe had shown the picture to the king's painter as a work of art. The painter spoke to the king about it in the gushal khana, where he had company, it being his birthday (2nd September 1616). Jahangir instantly summoned Roe with it. It was past 10 P. M. and Roe had gone to sleep. He was awakened and given the king's message. He took two pictures with him. Jahangir instantly selected the one Roe prized most. Jahangir asked for it and Roe gave it, answering, "I was not so in love with anything that I would refuse to content His Majesty: I was extreme glad to do him service, and if I could give him a better demonstration of my affection, which was in my heart to do him service, I was ready to present it to him. At which he bowed to me and replied, it was sufficient; I had given it." On enquiry, Roe said the lady was dead, and Jahangir said he would have copies made and return the original if Roe could recognise it from the copies."—Sir T. Roe's Journal, Vol. II, page 252.

Was the open porch, as we enter the main gate, roofed at the time, and the large open space on the first floor thus provided, was enclosed and roofed for the use of the harem, which included the celebrated Nur Jahan? This appears probable from the fact that the walls of the open porch were painted in colours, marks of which still remain, which could not have been the case, if they had been left exposed to the sun and rain. And the fact that those who had to interview the Emperor while he sat in the window had to climb up the scaffolding erected under it, also shows that the rooms on the space behind the window were closed to all except the Emperor. That the room was utilised for the *harem* is shown by the following extract from Roe's Journal:—

"The king comes every morning to a window looking into a plain before his gate, and shows himself to the common people. One day I went to attend him. Coming to the palace, I found him at the Jharoka window, and went up on the scaffold under him." On two tressles stood eunuchs with long poles headed with feathers fanning him. He gave many favours and received many presents. What he bestowed, he let down by a silk string rolled on a turning instrument; what was given him, a venerable fat deformed old matron, wrinkled and hung with grimbelles like an image, pulled up at a hole. With such another clue at one side in a window were his two principal wives, whose curiosity made them break little holes in a grate of reed that hung before it to gaze on me. I saw first their fingers, and after laying their faces close, now one eye, now another, sometime I could discern the full proportion. They were indifferently white, had black hair smoothed up, but if I had no other light, their diamonds and pearls had sufficed to show them. When I looked up they retired, and were so merry that I supposed they laughed at me."

Finding no suitable residence for himself, in the sixteenth year of his reign, Akbar ordered one to be built. The *Tabqati-Akbari*, a contemporary history, says:—

"Akbar left Agra on 8th Rabiul Akhir A. H. 978 (1571-72 A.D.),and after staying twelve days at Fatehpur Sikri, came to Ajmer. Here he ordered that a strong and durable wall be built round Ajmer and a magnificent palace constructed for his own residence. The Amirs, Khans and attendants at the court vied with one another in erecting buildings. His Majesty distributed villages and lands attached to the Ajmer administration amongst his Amirs to enable them to pay the expenditure on new buildings."[1]

1. Mr. La Touche, in his Settlement Report, and Mr. Watson, following Mr. La Touche, in his Gazetteer, call Akbar's Daulat Khana a fort, partly because the structure with its bastions looks like a fort, and partly because the British after coming to Ajmer in 1818, used the place as an arsenal till 1863 A.D. From 1570 to 1818 A.D., no garrison was ever kept in it, nor arms. The Mughals used it only as a Royal residence. Akbar, Jahangir and Shah Jahan (the last till the marble, baradaries on the Anasagar were built), and Aurangzeb always lived in it during their stay in Ajmer. Of the later Mughals, only Bahadur Shah came to Ajmer once and it is not recorded where he resided. The Mahrattas, and the Rathors used it as the Subedar's residence and for administrative offices and courts.

The city wall and the palace or Daulat Khana took three years to build.

Akbar never stayed long in Ajmer, though he visited it oftener than any of his successors. Jahangir stayed here for three years, the longest period that any ruler of India except the Chauhans has ever stopped in Ajmer. The austere Aurangzeb, whose two important visits to Ajmer were in connection with important wars, and who perhaps was never so uncomfortable in his life as on these two occasions, chose this fortified building for his residence during the rebellion of prince Akbar.

The Mahratta governor took up his residence in this building and altered the central place to suit his requirements. It was most probably then that a *baradari*, 22'-9" × 21'-9", probably the northernmost marble pavilion, was removed from the Ana Sagar embankment and put up on the roof of the room to the north of the western bastion and used as a temple, by which designation it is still known. The English followed the Mahrattas in 1818 A. D.; and while the District Officers took up their residence in the marble *baradaries* on the Ana Sagar Lake, they converted this place into an arsenal, and as such it remained up to 1863 A. D. Hence the name Magazine, by which it is now universally known.

In 1857 A. D., however, when the great mutiny broke out, and the forces at Nasirabad rebelled, the Europeans in Ajmer took refuge in the Magazine and fortified it. The original entrance in the outer wall between the bastions in front of the Naya Bazar was closed up, cannon were mounted on those bastions, and a temporary opening made for egress and ingress in the wall further south, which still stands near the Veterinary Hospital. As daily worship could not be carried on during the mutiny in the Hindu marble temple near the top of the South Western bastion, the idol was removed to the temple of Laxminarainji, near the Agra gate, where it is still kept and worshipped.

In 1863 A.D., the arsenal was removed and the Tahsildar of Ajmer installed in the Audience Chamber of the mighty Akbar. In 1903 A. D., the Tahsildar and his office were shifted to a bastion, and the central chamber restored as far as possible to its original state, consistent with its use as a Museum of Antiquities, at a cost of Rs. 66,860. The main gateway, 84 feet long and 43 ft. wide, too, has been repaired at a cost of Rs. 5,853. To the north of the Magazine, there is a Hindu temple of Shiva, largely visited by people. An annual fair is held here.

CHAPTER X

THE CHASHMA

ONE of the most beautiful sights of Ajmer, illustrative alike of the beauty of its natural scenery and its historical associations is the *Chashma*. It is a valley to the west of the historic fortress of Taragarh; and, possessing as it does all the lovely features of beautiful mountain scenery, it was from the earliest times a place where the more prosperous of the residents of Ajmer built themselves pleasure houses, and to which all went for pleasure.

The Chashma proper is the place bounded on the north by the Chanvanda Hill, on the east by the Taragarh Hill, on the west by the hills of Ajaipal, and on the south by the hill on the south-eastern slope of which stand the tombs of Tagha and Targhan. The valley to the east narrows down to a pass between two high hills and is called, *Chashma ki gal*, at the entrance to which, stand the ruins of Jahangir's palace. This serpentine valley winds round the rugged Taragarh Hill towards the south-west and ends[1] amidst hillocks, the scene of the famous battle of Ajmer, fought in 1659 A.D., which sealed for ever the fate of the accomplished but unfortunate Dara Shikoh, the rightful heir of Shah Jahan, and placed on the throne, Aurangzeb, the last real Mughal Emperor of India.

The name by which this place was originally known is one of the secrets of history, which time or circumstances may yet unfold. Hafiz Jamal, the daughter of Khwaja Muinuddin Chishti, lived for some time as a religious recluse here. Jahangir came to Ajmer in 1613 A.D.; and he built a hunting palace here and christened the place, *Nur-Chashma*, (spring of light), after his own name, Nur-uddin (light of faith.)

The earliest relic of any historic or archaeological importance standing in the Chashma (besides the insignificant cellar on the western side of the southern spur of the Taragarh Hill, pointed out as the place where Jamal Bibi, the pious

1. During Colonel Dixon's time a *bund* was constructed here to form the "Chashma ka talao."

daughter of Khwaja Muinuddin, passed days of devotion and prayer) is the massive unfinished water lift, built by Rao Maldeva of Marwar, who took Ajmer in 1535 A.D. The lift was to consist of a chain of towers, one overlooking the other, and water was to be raised from the Chashma to the fort of Taragarh.[1] The work, however, was never finished; only three links of the chain were made. But they still stand as solid as on the day they were built, though nearly four hundred years have passed, and they have never been repaired. The construction of the lift also shows that the Chashma was then a perennial spring of water.

It was, however, Jahangir who appreciated the beauty of the place; and as he lived in Ajmer for nearly three years (1613 to 1616 A.D.)[2] he built a residence here, laid out a garden, constructed tanks and generally improved the place. The Emperor himself thus describes the place in his celebrated *Tuzaki Jahangiri:*—

"Near the town of Ajmer there is a beautiful valley or pass. In it there is a spring of sweet water, and this water is excellent and better than the water of any other place in Ajmer.. This valley and spring are named after Hafiz Jamal. When I went there, I ordered that a house suitable to this place be built. In one year, that building was so nicely built that people do not speak of a similar building anywhere else. The masons built a large water reservoir (حوض) there, and took the water into this tank by a fountain. The water in the fountain rises twelve yards, and the tank is 40 by 40 yards, and there is a nice *dalan* on the edge of the tank. Similarly, above it, where there are the lake and the spring, and suitable chambers and sleeping apartments, pleasing and delightful. Some of them are illuminated and adorned with pictures by masters and experts in the art of painting. I desired that a name should be given to it, having some connection with my name, hence I named it *Chashma-i-Nur*. The only drawback in this Chashma is that it is not within the town, nor situated on a highway. Generally on Thursdays and Fridays I live here. In accordance with my wish, the poet composed verses to give the date of its construction by the numerical value of the letters in the words. Saadai Gilani Zargabashi has cleverly brought out the date (H. 1024=1615 A.D.) in the following excellent line:—

MAHAL SHAH NUR-UD-DIN JAHANGIR

(Palace of the King Nur ud din Jahangir). I ordered that this be inscribed on a stone and the stone to be fixed over the arch of the lower building."[3]

1. Speaking of Maldeva, Colonel Tod says: "He also erected that bastion in Garh Beetli (Citadel of Ajmer) called the Kot Burj, and showed his skill in hydraulics by the construction of a wheel to bring water into the fort."—Annals and Antiquities of Rajasthan, Vol. II, page 25.
2. 18 November 1613 to 10 November 1616 A.D. *Vide*, Roger's Tuzaki Jahangiri, Vol. I, P. 340.
3. Roger's Translation, Vol. I., P. 269.

The line "Mahal Shah Nur-ud-din Jahangir" is the last of the fourteen lines composed by the above-named poet, and they still stand inscribed on the summit of the arch (vault) of the *dalan*. They are engraved on three pieces of marble stone:—

بلندا اقبال شاه هفت کشور — که وصف او نمي گنجد به تقدیر
فروغ خاندان شاه اکبر — شهنشاه زمان شاه جهانگیر
درین سر چشمه چون آصدز فیضش — روان شد آب و خاکش گشت اکسیر
شهنشه کرد نامش چشمه نور — شده آب خضر زو چاشني گیر
دهم سال از جلوس شاه غازی — بحکم بادشاه نیک تدبیر
بطرف چشمه نور این عمارت — جهان آرای شد زروي تقدیر
خود تاریخ اتمامش رقم زد — محل شاه نورالدین جهانگیر—

TRANSLATION.—"High is his fortune; He is king of the seven regions. His virtues cannot be contained in the records of Fate. Light of the family of King Akbar: Emperor of his time, King Jahangir. As he came to this spring, from his favour, water began to flow, and its very dust became *Aksir* (Elixir of Life). The Emperor named it *Chashma-i-Nur*: The water of life derived its virtue from it. In the tenth year from the accession of the brave king, under the orders of the wise king, this building towards the *Chashma-i-Nur* became the ornament of the world, as it was predestined to be. *Khirad* (the surname of the poet) recorded the date of its completion as "The Palace of the King Nur-ud-din Jahangir." [1]

Sir Thomas Roe, who was in Ajmer in 1616 A D., thus describes the place in his Journal:—

"The 1st of March (1616 A.D.) I rode to see a house of pleasure of the king's, given him by Asaf Khan,[2] two miles from Ajmer, but between mighty rocks so defended from the sun that it scarce any way sees it; the foundation cut out of them and some rooms, the rest of free stone; a handsome little garden with five fountains; two great tanks, one thirty steps over the other. The way to it is inaccessible but for one or two in front, and that very steep and stony: a place of much melancholy delight and security, only being accompanied with wild peacocks, turtles, fowl and monkeys that inhabit the rocks hanging every way over it."[3]

The monkeys are still to be seen, especially near the *Chilla* of Bibi Hafiz Jamal, but the gardens and the fountains have disappeared; and of the tanks, only one remains, and that is in ruins—an octagonal tank in front of the *dalan* cut out of a rock spoken of above. A staircase leads to the roof of this *dalan*, and two rooms (also *dalans*) stand separated by a broad passage for water which falls into the tank below. These *dalans* are of red stone. That towards the east has three openings in front and one towards the staircase. There was marble plastering inside the *dalan*, which was decorated in colours, marks of which still remain near the eastern door.

1. With the aid of field glasses, one is able to read on the last piece, the name of the engraver of the inscription, as "Abdulla."
2. Jahangir's brother-in-law, and brother of the celebrated Empress Nur Jahan.
3. Sir Thomas Roe's Journal, Vol II.

The western part of this structure is in a dilapidated condition, and though the support to the lintel of the western opening has long disappeared,

> "Self poised, the top stone seems to rock
> But ages past have seen it mock
> The winter's storm or earthquake's shock."

The southern *dalan* is in a better state of preservation, and reminds the visitor of the old days, when the famous Nur-Jahan and Jahangir, sitting in these *dalans* enjoying the beautiful scenery around them, and breathing the air heavily laden with the sweet smell of mountain flowers watched the water fall over the roof of the *dalan* below into the octagonal tank.

Further down the valley, on the hill to the west, there are the tombs of Tagha and Targhan, commonly called Taga and Toga, who are said to have been slain by the Rajputs during the reign of Qutub-ud-in Aibak, or at some subsequent period. There is nothing of importance about these and the other tombs there, except that at one time the place appears to have been inhabited. Excavations have discovered big earthen pots in the neighbourhood of this place, all found buried with the mouth downwards.

The Chashma valley widens a little towards the end, and at its mouth, there are two or three small hillocks commanding the entrance to the valley. It was here that the historic battle between Dara Shikoh and Aurangzeb was fought. The hillock on which Dara Shikoh planted his artillery still commands the entrance to the valley, and the ruins of the battlements and entrenchments defended by his generals, Shah Nawaz Khan, Feroz Mewati and Mustafa Khan, as well as the remains of the fortifications thrown across the hills, and which are fully described in Part II, "History", may still be seen.

These picturesque hills, which have witnessed political convulsions that more than once altered the course of history, seen dynasties of kings come and go like spring and autumn leaves; which have seen proud rulers of men like Visaldeva, Prithviraj, Akbar and Aurangzeb, appear and disappear before the irresistible blasts of doom, leaving little trace of their triumphs, still stand quiet, mocking the puny efforts of man to impose his will on the forces which a Higher Power employs to rear and destroy empires, races and civilizations, in furtherance of His own inscrutable design.

CHAPTER XI

THE MAYO COLLEGE

THE Mayo College, sometimes called the "Eton of India", is situated in an extensive park on the south east outskirts of Ajmer, at a distance of about two miles from the Post Office, on an elevation of 1570 feet above sea level. Founded under the auspices of Lord Mayo, the Viceroy of India (1869-72), exclusively "for the education of the sons of Chiefs, Princes and leading Thakurs", it opened in 1875 with one pupil, who lived outside the College and proceeded to his studies daily on an elephant. Since then, it has developed into the premier Princes College of India with over 150 pupils, who come not only from Rajputana but from all parts of India; and in the course of its history, the College has drawn recruits even from outside India, from the Persian Gulf.

Surrounded on all sides by Indian States, Ajmer is naturally suited for an institution like the Mayo College. Hardly twelve years had passed since the assumption by the Sovereign of England of the Crown of India, when Colonel C. K. M. Walter, the then Agent to the Governor General for Rajputana, put forward the idea of founding an institution to educate the sons of the aristocracy of India. The proposal was taken up by the Government of India, and on 22nd October, 1870, Lord Mayo held a Durbar at Ajmer, at which he laid the proposed scheme before the Princes and Thakurs of Rajputana; and it was agreed that the Government of India would contribute to the endowment of the College, a sum equal to that contributed by the States. On the States contributing six lakhs, the Government of India agreed to donate a like sum, part of which was to be devoted to buildings and the rest to endowment. The Government of India undertook to construct the Main Building, Houses for the Principal and the Head Master, a Boarding House for the sons of the Istimrardars of Ajmer, and the necessary roads, while the States of Rajputana were asked to build Boarding Houses for pupils from their States. Ten of the States agreed, both to build and to maintain such Houses.

The Mayo College at Ajmer.

In 1871 A.D., land measuring 167 acres was acquired and building work started in 1873. It was possible to open the College on 21 October, 1875. The College building designed by Major Mant, was taken in hand in July 1877, and was finished in February, 1885. For the first ten years of its existence, the College had to hold its classes in a house, since pulled down, which had formerly been the residence of the Agent to the Governor General for Rajputana; and the first Principal, Captain (later) Colonel Sir Oliver St. John, lived at first in a house adjoining the former Residency. Since those early days, considerable additions have been made both to the College buildings and to the estate. In 1910, during the principalship of Mr. C. W. Waddington, an Annexe to the Main Building, designed by Sir Swinton Jacob and nearly as large as the original building, was constructed. The College Building is a noble structure of unpolished white marble found near the city of Ajmer, with bands of black introduced at intervals in the Hindu Saracenic style. It contains a large Hall, 68'×40'×37½' beautifully coloured in oils and richly decorated by Mr. Freyberger. In the ceiling, two stained glass sky lights are introduced. The design on one, copied from the banner of His Highness the Maharana of Udaipur, represents the Sun. The other design represents the Moon. They are emblematic of the Solar and Lunar Races, to which most of the Rajput clans belong; the walls are hung with the portraits and Shields of Arms of the Ruling Princes of Rajputana. Rising above the building is a delicately proportioned Clock Tower, 127 feet high.

In front of the main entrance to the Building, on a pedestal six feet high, stands an imposing statue, in carrara marble, of Lord Mayo in the robes of the Grand Master of the Order of the Star of India, the work of Mr. Noble, and its nobly-worded inscription still conveys its message to India.

Round the Main Building are grouped in the form of a horse-shoe, most of the Boarding Houses, namely, the Kotah, Ajmer, Jodhpur, Bikaner, Tonk, Bharatpur, Alwar and Udaipur Houses, while in the centre of the horse-shoe is the principal Cricket ground with a hand-some pavilion, the gift of His Highness the present Maharaja of Bikaner, an Old Boy of the college. Other buildings in the horse-shoe, are the four houses of the English staff, a Boarding House for the Senior or Post-Diploma students, called the Colvin House, after Sir Elliot Colvin, Agent to the Governor-General for Rajputana (1905-1917) A.D., and a staff and old Boy's club, the latter a recent addition.

Outside the horse shoe, are the Jaipur Boarding House and three houses, the Kashmir, New Jodhpur and New Bharatpur Houses constructed for boys who live with their own private guardians and called after either the original or present occupants, and a recently constructed Hindu Temple which has replaced an older building outside the grounds. In the western corner of the grounds are a Sanatorium presented by His Highness the Maharao of Kotah, an Old Boy of the College and a set of recently constructed houses for members of the Indian staff. This latest addition made together with the Temple during the tenure of the present Principal, Mr. V. A. S. Stow has enabled the College to achieve fully its aim of being a self-contained residential institution. The accommodation for boys has also been recently enlarged by the construction, by the Jodhpur and Jaipur Durbars, of additional wings to their State Boarding Houses.

In former days, the control of the College was largely in the hands of the Political Department of the Government of India; but by a new constitution introduced in 1931, the control is now mainly in the hands of the Ruling Princes and Old Boys. His Excellency the Viceroy, who was formerly President of the General Council, is now Patron, and the Hon'ble the Resident in Rajputana who used to be Vice-President, is Visitor. The College under the new constitution is governed by a General Council consisting of all Ruling Princes of Rajputana, a number of Ruling Princes elected from outside Rajputana, four representatives of the Old Boys' Association, and four members nominated by Government consisting of a Political Officer, a representative of Ajmer-Merwara, the Educational Commissioner with the Government of India, and a Financial Adviser. The President of the Council is a Ruling Prince of Rajputana, elected by the council, and the present holder of the office is His Highness the Maharaja of Jaipur who succeeded His Highness the Maharaja of Jodhpur, while the Vice-President is His Highness the Maharaja of Jodhpur. There is also a Working Committee consisting of five Ruling Princes elected by the General Council, two representatives of the Old Boy's Association, and a Political Officer nominated by Government. The Committee elects its own Chairman, who is at present His Highness the Maharaj Rana of Dholpur. The Principal is Secretary of both bodies.

The staff of the College consists of an English Principal and an English Vice-Principal and three English Assistant Masters, twenty Indian Assistant Masters, nine Motamids, i. e.

Boarding House Superintendents, a Resident Doctor, a Public Works Overseer, a Games Superintendent and an Assistant Games Superintendent and an Assistant Games Superintendent, Riding and P. T. Drill Instructors, and Office establishment. The post of the Principal has been held in succession by the following officers:—

1. Col. Sir O. B. C. St. John, K.C.S.I., R.E. 1875-1878
2. Lt. Col. W. Loch, C.I.E., A.D.C. 1878-1903
3. Mr. C. W. Waddington, M.A., C.I.E., M.V.O., I.E.S. ... 1903-1917
4. Mr. F. A. Leslie-Jones, M.A., C.B.E., I.E.S. ... 1917-1929
5. Mr. S. F. Madden, B.A., C.I.E., O.B.E., I.E.S. ... 1929-1931
6. Mr. V. A. S. Stow, M.A., C.I.E., I.E.S. ... 1931-present day.

The College is divided into two sections, School and College. The latter has recently developed from classes started for training in administration after completing the School course into a Degree College. In addition to providing training in administration for those, for whom such a training is considered desirable, and preparing candidates for entry into the Public Services including admission to the Indian Military Academy, for which a Special Army Class has recently been started, it prepares candidates for the Intermediate Examination of the Board of Intermediate Education for Rajputana, Central India and Gwalior, and the B. A. Degree of the Agra University, to which it has recently been affiliated. The College is the only one of the five Chiefs' colleges in India, which gives instruction upto the Degree standard.

The curriculum in the School Section leads up to an examination, different from that of other schools, but equivalent to Matriculation, namely the Chiefs Colleges Diploma Examination conducted by the Government of India. The syllabus includes English, modern Indian languages (whatever the boy's language may be and this often demands the teaching of as many as five different languages in the College,) History both Indian and British, Geography, Arithmetic and either Advanced Mathematics or Law and Administration, and a choice of one more subject from Science, a Classical Language, and Drawing.

The College Section of the Mayo College is organized on the lines of a residential university College, while the School Section is organised on English Public School lines adapted to Indian conditions. In former days, it was considered by parents necessary for the dignity and often the safety of a boy in the School, that he should have his own messing arrangements and be surrounded by a retinue of servants; and, in fact, one distinguished present Ruling Prince of Rajputana when he first joined the College was accompanied by over 200 followers for whom, a special village had to be built adjoining the College grounds. In recent years, however, it has been found possible to reduce the number of private servants in the majority of cases to one (though even that may sound an anomaly to English ears) and to introduce a common messing system in all the nine School Houses, which are organized in three groups of each under the supervision of a member of the English staff as House Master. The Monitorial system is in force, there being at present five Monitors, while there is a House Captain in each House to assist the House Master and Motamid, and Deputies perform similar functions in the College Section. General training outside class-work receives special attention; and Debates, Lectures Special Activities such as Motor Instruction, Rifle shooting. Carpentry, First Aid, Swimming and Holiday tours are regular features. Religious instruction is given both in and outside the class-room, and attendance daily at the temple is compulsory for all Hindu boys, while similar arrangements are in force for Muhammadan boys.

Physical training has from its early days been a prominent feature of the Mayo College. Games are organized on a compulsory basis for the School section and on a voluntary one for the College section. On working days, there is a Morning Parade of half an hour, at which the members of the College squadron receive a varied training in Riding, while non-riders do physical drill. In the afternoon, Cricket, Polo, Association Football, Hockey, Squash Tennis, and Basket Ball are played according to the season of the year. With recent additions, the college is now admirably equipped as to its grounds. Most of them are situated to the west of the Main Building, and include a large Riding instruction area, part of which serves as a private landing ground for æroplanes, a grass Polo ground, the water installation for which was recently presented by His Highness the Maharaja of Jodhpur, an Old Boy, five cricket grounds, three of which are turfed, four Hockey grounds, five Squash Courts, two of which are electrically lit, and eight Tennis Courts besides courts in certain Boarding Houses. In addition there are a Miniature Rifle Range and a well-equipped open air Swimming Bath at both of which regular instruction is given.

The Mayo College is unique among schools in India, and in fact in most parts of the world, in including Polo among its regular games and has proved a nursery for a number of fine players. Among them may be mentioned the late Maharaja of Alwar, His Highness the Maharaja of Kashmir, and His Highness the Maharaja of Jaipur.

At Cricket, the College has produced a number of good players, if not many of wide repute; the Maharaj Kumar of Vizianagram who captained the All-India team in England in 1936, is an Old Boy of the College, and His Highness the Maharawal of Dungarpur has captained successive Rajputana sides against visiting teams from overseas.

The motto of the College is, *Let there be Light*, and the College can fairly claim that it has spread its light over a wide area. Of the twenty Ruling Princes in Rajputana at present, no less than twelve are Old Boys of the College, namely.—

H. H. the Maharawal of Banswara,
H. H. the Maharaja of Bikaner,
The Maharana of Danta,
H. H. the Maharaj Rana of Dholpur,
H. H. the Maharawal of Dungarpur,
H. H. the Maharaja of Jaipur,
H. H. the Maharawal of Jaisalmer,
H. H. the Maharaj Rana of Jhalawar,
H. H. the Maharaja of Jodhpur,
H. H. the Maharaja of Kishengarh,
H. H. the Maharao of Kotah,
H. H. the Maharawat of Partabgarh;

and of the Ruling Princes outside Rajputana, who were educated at the College, may be mentioned:—

H. H. the Maharaja of Kashmir,
H. H. the Maharaja of Panna,
H. H. the Raja of Sailana,
H. H. the Nawab of Baoni,
H. H. the Maharaja of Orcha,
H. H. the Maharaja of Charkhari,
H. H. the Raja of Narsingarh,
H. H. the Raja of Bilaspur,
H. H. the Maharaja of Tehri-Garhwal,
H. H. the Maharaja of Idar.
H. H. the Maharaja of Manipur,
H. H. the Maharaja of Sikkim,
H. H. the Nawab of Junagadh,
H. H. the Yuvraja of Mysore,
H. H. the Sultan of Muscat.

While Old boys of the College other than the Ruling Princes and Thakurs who have their own estates to manage, may be found holding responsible positions in States not only through out Rajputana but outside.

CHAPTER XII

THE NASIYAN
OR
THE RED TEMPLE

THE Nasiyan is a modern Jain building, consisting of a Jain temple and an imposing double-storied Hall. The temple or Sidhkut Chatalaya, to call it by its orthodox name, is a Digamber Jain temple. Its foundation was laid on 10th October, 1864 and it was completed in 1865 A.D.

Just behind this temple is the *Svarna Nagari Hall*, containing gilt wooden representations of scenes from Jain mythology. These representations were manufactured at Jaipur and installed in the Svarna Nagari Hall in 1896.

The hall, which measures 80 ft. by 40 ft., is richly painted in beautiful colours, and the walls and the roofs are covered with glass mosaic work. It contains representations illustrative of the birth and life of Rishabdeva or Adinath (Eternal Lord), the first propagator of the Jain religion. Adinath, the first Jain incarnation of God, was born in Ajodhia, and was the son of King Nabha, by his queen, Moradevi. At Adinath's birth, god Indra and his consort Indrani (followed by other gods in airships), came on an elephant and took away the infant to Mount Sumeru (which is in the centre of the earth), in procession, and gave him a bath there, by pouring over him an immense quantity of the contents of the *Khshir Samudra*—the fifth of the oceans which surround the earth—and then returned him to the queen's palace, leaving several child gods with the prince as his playmates. Adinath grew up to manhood and succeeded his father on the throne of Ajodhia. As he became engrossed in worldly affairs and did not attend to his mission, Indra appeared before him with the *Apsara* Tilotma. She danced before him and suddenly disappeared, throwing off her mortal coil. This reminded Rishabdeva of the transitoriness of the world and he determined to renounce it. Installing in his place his eldest son, he left the palace, followed by four thousand other Rajas. The god Indra, followed by other gods, took Rishabdeva in procession to the *Tribeni*, the confluence of the Ganges, the Jamna and the Saraswati at Allahabad, where under the shade of the *Akshyabat* (sacred banyan tree), Rishabdeva gave up the world, even the clothes which covered his body, and gave himself up to contemplation. Six months passed, without food or drink: his followers could no longer suffer these privations, and headed by his grandson, Mareech, they returned to the town and founded the various sects of *sadhus* such as *Khakis*, *Sanyasees*, *Kanphatas*, &c. Rishabdeva after one thousand years of devotion, attained salvation (*kewal gyana*). The above broad features of his career are represented here. The contents of this hall consist of two parts, the circular one, nearest the landing from the staircase, is the Jain representation of the creation, circular in shape, with a high mountain called Sumeru in the centre. Round this mount is the *Jambudweep*, which is surrounded by an ocean, round which is another *dweep* (island) having two Sumeru mounts. This, again, is surrounded by an ocean, and that again by a continent having two Sumeru mounts, and so on. The present representation shows thirteen such oceans and continents, which latter oceans and continents thus follow one another; but there are no more than five Sumeru mounts containing the 458 chaitalayas (temples) that are eternal. Man who resides in the *Jambudweep* can go as far as the middle of the third encircling continent: gods alone can go further. The trees in the thirteenth continent are all of stone, but bear eatable fruits. The oceans are of water, milk, honey, ghee and similar articles. The central *Sumeru* is twenty crores of miles high and the next four are 168,000,000 miles each.

The southern half of the hall contains a representation of the city of Ajodhia, with palaces in the centre and mansions for the nobles and citizens. To the south of Ajodhia is a representation of the city of (Prayag) Allahabad, the *Tribeni*, and the sacred banyan tree, and Rishabdeva in contemplation, having renounced the world.

Gods are represented as sailing in the skies in *vimans* or airships; and on the northern wall of the hall is painted the *aphsara* Tilotma, in the act of dancing before Rishabdeva.

A Manstambha (pillar), 85 ft high, plastered in white cement and marble chips was erected in the Nasiyan, in front of the Sidhkut Chatalaya in 1937 A.D.

CHAPTER XIII

FOYSAGAR

ANOTHER beautiful sight in Ajmer, partaking of lake scenery like the Anasagar, is the Foysagar. This lake was constructed in 1891-92 by the Municipal Committee of Ajmer as a famine work at a cost of Rs. 2,68,900/- primarily to supply drinking water to the people of Ajmer. It was constructed by damming up the river known as *Bandi Nadi* in Ajmer, near its source, by the village of Ajaisar about five miles from Ajmer, lying between two high hills, the Nagpahar and the Taragarh hills. It takes its name from Mr. Foy, the Executive Engineer who was in charge of the construction.

The lake is 24 feet deep and has a cubic capacity of 150 million feet and water spread of 14 million square feet. The height of the embankment is 39 feet. Its catchment area is about nine miles. In normal times, it supplies from six to seven lakhs gallons of water daily, and in seasons of drought 3,50,000 gallons only. As the lake is at a level higher than the general city level, water comes in by pipe by gravitation. When full, it contains sufficient water for the city for 18 months. There is a small garden to the north of the embankment. The whole scenery, owing to the close proximity of the hills on three sides, is very picturesque.

A small pavilion stands at the eastern end of the embankment for visitors to enjoy the sight. A boat is kept there. Buildings are springing up on both sides of the road to Foysagar, mostly pleasure gardens and country houses, as is also the case with the road to Pushkar which lies to the north of it, and on which a number of dharmshalas and garden houses have been built.

The village Ajaisar, founded by king Ajaipal the founder of Ajmer, lies to the south of Foysagar about a mile away. The way to another beautiful site of Ajmer, Ajaipal, lies by the Foysagar Lake.

The Begami Dalan in the Dargah, Khwaja Muinuddin Chishti at Ajmer.

THE RAJPUTANA MUSEUM, AJMER.

CHAPTER XIV

THE RAJPUTANA MUSEUM

THE Rajputana Museum at Ajmer was started as a Central Museum for the benefit of the whole of Rajputana, the British territory of Ajmer-Merwara as well as the surrounding Indian States. All those, who were interested in archaeology or history, keenly felt the want of a Museum to house the rare antiquities and works of art of Rajputana, which lay neglected in various places and were likely to be lost to future generations. In the year 1903, the Director-General of Archaeology in India put forward a proposal to start a Museum at Ajmer, financed by the Government of India. This idea appealed to Lord Curzon, the then Governor-General of India, who paid a visit to Ajmer in November 1902 and evinced great interest in the antiquities and ancient buildings of this historic city. The central building of the Magazine (Akbar's palace) at Ajmer built in 1572 or 1573 A.D. was selected for the Museum. Lord Curzon ordered all ancient and historic buildings in Ajmer to be restored to their original shape, and the Magazine and the Marble Baradaries on the Anasagar were restored in 1907. This unique building was handed over by the Government for locating the proposed Museum for Rajputana. Mahamahopadhyaya Pandit Gaurishanker H. Ojha, D. Litt. (Benares) the Curator and Librarian of the Victoria Hall Museum and Library at Udaipur, Mewar, was appointed Curator of the Museum in March, 1908. He began at once to collect exhibits, and when a fine collection was made, the opening ceremony of the Museum was performed in October, 1908, by the Honourable Mr. (later Sir) E G. Colvin, the then Agent to the Governor-General for Rajputana.

The Museum had in the beginning, two sections, one containing Antiquities, ancient coins etc., and (II) Objects illustrative of the arts and industries of Rajputana. Subsequently, however, the arts section was abolished on account of financial stringency and want of sufficient accomodation for the proper display of the collected exhibits. The scope of the Museum was thus restricted to archaeological objects only. The assiduous efforts of the curator who was well known in Rajputana and whose knowledge of the history and antiquities of this province was very extensive, soon resulted in making the Rajputana Museum one of the best Museums of antiquities in India. It attracted distinguished scholars and visitors from all parts of India on account of its exhibits. The central building was found too small to accommodate all the collected objects and a number of the southern, northern and western side rooms of the Magazine had to be utilized for keeping the exhibits.

Images.—The central building contains about one hundred rare images ranging in date from the Gupta period to the sixteenth century A. D. Of the Brahmannical images, special mention may be made of a number of unique panels representing the marriage of Siva and Parvati (Kalyanasundarmurti), an image of Yama, a number of images of Surya, interesting images of Siva and Vishnu in different varieties, images of Brahma, Lakulisha, Revanta, Lakshmi, Chamunda, Mahishasura, Mardini, Ganga, a curious figure of some form of Kali with fiftyfour hands. The last named image is a unique one on account of its ten heads, of which only one is human and the others, animal. The fiftyfour hands carry different weapons and attributes and a garland of human heads dangles down to the knees. Her short dress is composed of several hands adorned with bell-like objects. This image appears to represent some *tantric* conception of 'Shakti'. We have evidence of the 'Shakti' element of Hinduism penetrating as far west as Rajputana from Bengal, and this interesting image discovered in Rajputana itself proves a historical fact. The images of Surya (sun-god), the god of war, corresponding to the god Apollo of the Greeks are notable in that they have long boots of modern pattern going up to the knees. The images corroborate the story in the *Puranas* that the image of Surya was first made in India by the Magas who came from Persia.

An image of Siva has got five faces, four of which represent four different gods facing four directions, namely, the image of Surya faces the east and has got boots of Indian pattern; those of Brahma, Vishnu and Rudra facing the north, west and south respectively. The fifth face of Siva, representing the universe, is symbolised by a globular shape on the top. The image of Indra (rain-god) has a thunderbolt in one hand, and a goad in the other by the side of his elephant. These images afford good material for a study of Hindu Iconography.

In the room containing Jain images, there are rare images of a number of Tirthankaras, the goddess Saraswati, Gomukh-

Yaksha and other beautiful panels pertaining to Jainism, of which Rajputana is a stronghold even now.

In the north-west corner room of the central building, are exhibited a number of casts of seals and sealings of the prehistoric period discovered in the excavations at Mohenja-daro, district Larkana, Sind. On most of these seals, there is a line of pictographic writing which was prevalent in the Indus Valley about the third millennium B.C. Of the seals, one with a figure seated on a stool in a typical 'Yoga' attitude deserves special notice. This deity is surrounded by animals such as tiger, rhinoceros, buffalo and elephant, and represents god Siva in his aspect of Pashupati or Lord of beasts. The worship of Siva, it appears, dates back to prehistoric period, and the Siva cult is one of the oldest living cults in the world. Of the other seals exhibited in the Museum, we may specially note seals with a Brahmani bull having a garland around its neck, tree-goddess standing inside a *Pipal*, a hero grappling two tigers and an unicorn standing in front of a manger.

In the picture room, are exhibited copies of portraits of famous Rajput sovereigns of Mewar, Marwar and other states, whose achievements have redounded to the glory of Rajputana in the past. Besides these, there are portraits of Akbar, Farrukhsayar, Birbal, a Muhammadan princess, and others.

Inscriptions—The inscriptions are exhibited in two southern side rooms, which were probably used originally as residences for the retinues of the Mughal Emperors. About fifty inscriptions ranging in date from the 5th century B. C. are exhibited in these rooms. The earliest inscription in the Rajputana Museum—the Barli Inscription—is from Bhilot Mata's temple near Barli, about 36 miles south-east of Ajmer. This pre-Asokan inscription is in Brahmi script, and is of the 5th century B. C. It is one of the oldest inscriptions in Rajputana. It makes mention of a place called Majhimika which has been identified by scholars with modern Nagari, about eight miles north of Chitor. Another interesting inscription found at Samoli, is the inscription of Siladitya (published in Ep. Indica, vol. XX, p. 97). It is helpful in tracing the present Mewar dynasty to the seventh century A.D. This inscription of Vikrama Samvat 703 (646 A.D.), establishes the fact that the Gohila kings founded their kingdom in Mewar about 200 years before the foundation of the Persian Empire, thus disproving the theory mentioned by Col. Tod and others that the Guhilots of Mewar are descended from the kings of

Persia. A third inscription mentions the name of a new ruler Mahendrapala II in the genealogy of the Pratihars of Kanauj.

Another very important find exhibited here is a collection of seven stone tablets discovered in the Adhai-din-ka-Jhonpra, Ajmer, which are fully described in the chapter on that famous building in this book. They are dated the 12th century A.D., and throw light on the history of the Chauhans. Other inscriptions in this Museum are useful to the history of the Pratihars, the Paramaras and others.

Coins—In the coin cabinet of the Rajputana Museum, there are more than two thousand gold, silver, copper, lead, and nickel coins. The earliest coinage of India—the Punch marked of the prehistoric times—is represented by more than fifty rare pieces assignable to the second or third century B. C. After them, come the Bactrian, the Hun, Kushan, and the coins of Mahakshtrapas Rudrasena, Damsena, Yasodaman and others. There are also coins of the Guptas, Kalchuris, of the Chauhan Emperors Vigrahraja and Prithviraj of Ajmer. The Rajputana Museum also possesses a fairly large collection of coins of the Pathan Kings of Delhi, Malwa, Gujrat, and the Mughal Emperors of India.

Arms and Library—There is also a collection of old arms and armours in the coin-room, adjoining the Museum office. The library attached to the Museum office contains many valuable books.

The Museum is maintained by a Government grant supplemented by contributions from the Municipalities of Ajmer, Beawar and Kekri, and the District Board of Ajmer-Merwara. The Museum has a working committee with the Commissioner of Ajmer-Merwara as President, and the following gentlemen as members:—

(1) The Executive Engineer, Ajmer.
(2) Mahamahopadhya, Dr. P. Gauri Shanker Ojha, D. Litt.
(3) Diwan Bahadur Har Bilas Sarda.
(4) Rai Sahib Munshi Gopi Nath Mathur.
(5) Rai Sahib Pt. P. B. Joshi, M.A., Ajmer.
(6) The Assistant Superintendent, Archæological Survey, Central India and Rajputana.
(7) Mr. U. C. Bhattacharya, Curator of the Museum, Secretary.

The total income of the Museum during the year 1937-1938 was Rs. 5462 and the expenditure, Rs. 5345.

CHAPTER XV

AJAIPAL

AJAIPAL or Ajaipalji, as it is commonly called, is a most picturesque spot in the environs of Ajmer, situated about four miles to the south of Foysagar, and is held in great sanctity by the Hindus. It is named after King Ajaipal, the founder of Ajmer, who, after a long reign in the sixth century A. D., became in his old age, a *sannyasi*, retired to this place and passed the evening of his life in religious devotion.

The western end of the Serpent Mountain gradually lowers itself near Ajaipal to greet the sloping spurs of the chain of hillocks, which enclose the Chashma on the west and the south. The place is cool, quiet, full of tranquillity, with rills of water trickling down the slopes of the enclosing hills which are draped in green during and after the rains. There are two tanks, the upper one discharges its water over a miniature waterfall into the lower one, from which flows a small stream under the refreshing shade of big trees. This beautiful glen attracts hundreds of men and women from Ajmer during the rains, and is a popular place for picnics all the year round.

Passing the Foysagar and the village of Ajaisar, as one descends into the valley, a stone *ghani* (oil-press) meets his eye in which, according to tradition, King Ajaipal used to throw non-Hindus who attacked or disturbed Hindus in the performance of their religious rites. The next object that comes into view is the *Chakra Kund*, full of sweet water, which flows into another tank, lying a few feet below it. Near the upper tank is the temple, dedicated to Ajaipal Baba. The King's image with a *sota* (big stick) standing by it, is worshipped here, and the offering made is *khopra* (copra). On Bhadrapad Sudi 6th (6th day of the second half of the month of Bhadrapad), a big fair is held here, and people from Ajmer, Pushkar, Ajaisar, Bhaonta and villages nearby, pour into the valley to pay homage and offer worship to the Founder of Ajmer. *Jogees*, that day, go round the houses of the Hindus in Ajmer and other places, asking for *Ajaipal Baba Ka Rot* (loaf of bread of Ajaipal Baba).

Near this temple and overlooking the Chakra kund, is an old temple of Siva,[1] built in the seventh century, and since repaired, the stone used and the carving being similar to the buildings of that period. A little below the Siva temple, is the temple of *Ruthee Rani* (offended queen). The architecture of these temples resembles that of the Chauhan buildings at Delhi and Ajmer. Another small-temple of Siva stands here. A few feet away, on a higher level, several *tibaras* have been built for the use of pilgrims and picnic goers. Descending a few steps, we come to a small piece of level ground, where the inviting shade of big trees and a meandering stream of water provide comfort and rest. The way from Pushkar to Bhaonta passes through the valley.

A difficult, and at times steep, passage about three miles long through the hills, connects *Chashma* with Ajaipal. Entering the western *pol* (gate) of the Chashma valley, one goes through a thick and dense jungle and emerges into the valley of Ajaipal. This hill forest is called *badi nal.*

To preserve the sanctity of the place and guard against non-Hindus polluting this religious place, a stone inscription recognising it as a sacred place of the Hindus has been fixed by Government over the gate of the Siva temple. It prohibits non-Hindus from polluting it by taking there flesh or meat, or otherwise acting in any way against the behests of the Hindu religion.

1. According to the Prithviraj Vijaya, King Anaji built a temple of Siva here.

CHAPTER XVI

MINOR SIGHTS

I—The Chhatrees.

NEAR the mouth of the *Antedh Mata ki gal* glen, on a small hillock, to the north of Anasagar lake, stands a group of Chhatrees and Chabutras (*thadas*), belonging to the Digambar Jains of Ajmer. Their *gurus*, Acharyas, Bhattaraks, and Pandits were cremated here, and *thadas* (chabutras) and Chhatrees with foot-marks were erected on their remains. On every chattree except one, and on all the *thadas* except one or two, there are *padukas* or foot-marks with small inscriptions. These inscriptions are of great historic value, in as much as they show that in the eighth century of the Christian era, the town of Ajmer existed, and Jainism flourished here.

The oldest inscription is dated the S. 817 (A.D. 760) in a Chhatree commemorating the death, at Ajmer, of P. Hemraj, disciple of Bhattarak Ratna Kirtiji. Next in time, come the three inscriptions of the ninth century A.D:—

V.S. 905 (A.D. 845) commemorating the death of Bradh Chandji, (chabutra),
V.S. 911 (A.D. 854) " " " Shiveramji (chabutra),
V.S. 928 (A.D. 871) " " " P. Tulsiramji,
disciple of Hemrajji on Jeth Sud 5th, Sunday (chabutra)

After these come two other inscriptions, dated V. S. 973 (A.D. 916) in Bhattarak Vijaya Kirtiji's Chhatree, and that dated the Jeth Vadi 9th, S. 1027 (A D. 970) of Mandalacharya. Sri Ratna Kirtiji's death (Chabutra).

These are followed by an inscription of the twelfth century, dated the Vaishakh Sudi 13th, V.S. 1228 (A.D. 1171) in the Chhatree on Acharya Sri Rajkirtiji. Then there is a break, and the next inscription is of the sixteenth century, of Phalgun Vadi 5th, S. 1572 (A.D. 1515) in the Chhatree on Bhattarak Ratnakirtiji. Then follow two inscriptions of Magh Sudi 5th, S. 1766 (1709 A.D.) and Ashadh Sudi 5th, S. 1782 (1725 A.D.) on the Chabutras built over the remains of

Bhattarak Ratnakirtiji and Acharya Vishalkirtiji respectively. Next follow ten inscriptions as below:—

That dated Phalgun 11th s. 1801 (A.D. 1744) on Bhattarak Vijaya Kirtiji.
„ „ s. 1810 (A. D. 1753) on Bhattarak Annant Kirtiji.
„ „ Magh Sudi 1st, s. 1810 (1753) on Bhattarak Vidyanandji.
„ „ Mangsar Sudi 13, s. 1813(A.D. 1756) Acharya Ratna Bhushanji.
„ „ Shrawan Vadi 1st, s. 1814 (A.D 1757) Acharya Devendra Kirtiji.
„ „ s. 1828 (A.D. 1771) Acharya Raj Kirtiji.
„ „ Kartik Sudi 2nd, s. 1821 (A.D. 1764) Acharya Tilak Bhushanji.
„ „ Magh Sudi s. 1810 (A.D. 1753) Bhattarak Bhuvan Bhushanji (Chhatree)
„ „ Phalgun Vadi 4th, s. 1829 (A.D. 1772) on Vijai Kirtiji (Chhatree).
„ „ Asoj Vadi 14th, s. 1837 (A.D. 1780) on Tilokendra Kirtiji (Chhatree).

Then follow three inscriptions of the nineteenth century, one Maha Sudi 5th, V.S. 1892 (A.D. 1835) on Bhattarak Ratna-Bhushanji (Chhatree). The second dated V.S. 1901 (A.D. 1844) on P. Pannalalji, and the third dated 1928 (A.D. 1871) on Bhattarak Padmanandji, disciple of Navnidhi.

An Utsava or religious gathering of the followers of the sect takes place here on Ashwin Vadi 4th, every year.

II—The Dadabari.

The Dadabari is a memorial to the Svetambar Jain divine, Jindatta Suri, who was born in s. 1179 (1122 A.D.) and died at Ajmer on Ashadh sudi 11, s. 1211 (1154 A.D.). Mohan Lal Duli Chand Desai in his Gujrati *Short History of Jain Literature*, p. 233, says that Jinvallabh Suri's disciple, Jindatta Suri converted a large number of Rajputs to Jainism. He was known as Dadaji. Agar Chand Nahata of Bikaner in his *Yuga Pradhan Jinchandra Suri*, says: "In the Khartargachha sect of the Jains was born Abhaideva Suri whose disciple was Jinvallabha Suri, who died on Kartik Vadi 12, s. 1167 (1112 A.D.). Jinvallabha Suri's disciple was Dada Jindatta Suri, who died and was cremated at Ajmer on Ashadh Sudi 11th, s. 1211 (1154 A.D.). After Dada Jindatta Suri, the place came to be known as Dadabari or the Garden of Dada.

The Dadabari is an enclosure, standing on the eastern embankment of the Visla lake at Ajmer, and contains a temple of Paraswanath. On the image is inscribed, "s. 1535, Asar Sudi 6th." (1478 A.D.). Mr. Puran Chand Nahar, in his collection of Jain Inscriptions, quotes this inscription and says that on Asar Sudi 6th, s. 1535, Oswal Sahasajan and his wife Paru, and their son and the son's wife Lalande, installed in the temple, the idol of Shantinath of Tapogachha sect through Lakhshmi Sagar Suri.

Inside the inner compound of the temple, there are some chhattrees and Deolis (Chabutras) built over the remains of Dada Anopchand, dated s. 1871 (1814 A.D.) and Seth Dhanrup Mal, dated s. 1909 (A.D. 1852). Outside this inner compound, there are *chhattrees* and deolis built over the remains of some Oswals; the earliest is dated the s. 1872 (1815 A.D.) on a chabutra of Sagar Chand's footmarks, and the latest, of 1916 (A.D. 1859) on Seth Vaghmal's chabutra.

III—Jharna.

This is a beautiful spot in Inderkot ensconced in a depression in the Taragarh hill. A temple of Jharneshwar Mahadeva and a spring of sweet water, refreshing and cool, attract hundreds of Hindus every day. During the seasons of scarcity of water in Ajmer, Jharna is a great help.

IV—Anted Ki Mata.

To the north of the Anasagar lake, about a mile and a half from the Residency, in a small valley between two hills, stands the temple of Anted Ki Mata. It is a picturesque place and during the rainy season, almost every day people go picnicing there. At the mouth of the valley, the people of Ganpatpura (inside Madar Gate) and the shop-keepers of Cavendishpura, Ajmer, have built Tibaras and a gate and dug a well for the convenience of people who frequent the place. A fair is held here every year on the Rakshabandhan day (August), when groups of people recite *Kavitas* (Hindi poems) all the way returning from the temple to the Daulat Bagh.

V—Chavanda Mata.

On the western slope of the hill, which separates the Foysagar from the Chashma, in a declension, there is a pretty spot, well wooded and restful, with water running down the hills during the rains. A temple dedicated to the goddess Chavanda stands there, with a couple of tibaras and a reservoir, full of water. It is a favourite resort of people who go for an outing. Visitors to Chashma often come to this place, and then descend to Foysagar. Every year on Sravan Sudi 8th, a fair is held here, when *the goddess* is worshipped by the people of Ajmer.

VI—Koteshwar.

On the western bank of the Bandi (Sagarmati) river, as it emerges from the Foysagar and goes to the Anasagar, there is a configuration of large flat rocks, bare of all vegetation, about fifty feet above ground, commanding an excellent view of the valley between the Serpent Mountain and the Taragarh hills. A temple of Koteshwar Mahadeva stands there, and an annual fair is held on Sravan Sudi 13th (thirteenth day of the second half of the month of Sravan). A feature of this fair is that people recite poems in Hindi all the way from the temple to the city.

VII—Bapugarh.

On the hill called Bapugarh, to the left side of the Pushkar Road at the Anasagar Ghati (pass), is situated a temple of Balaji. The hill appears to have derived its name from Bapu Scindia, the last Mahratta Subedar of Ajmer (1816-18 A. D.). A big Hindu fair takes place here on Sravan Sudi 3rd, every year. Near the temple, there are *samadhis* of Hindu Sadhus resembling tombs, similar to the Samadhis in the *Nagphanees* to the left as we go to Foysagar. A room near the western edge of the hill was long used for *Chilka* (heliograph) till 1880 A.D. and later.

VIII—Bajrang Garh.

This is another sacred place of the Hindus, on the hill which stands at the head of the Anasagar Lake near the water weir. It commands a magnificent view of the whole valley of Ajmer. The Hanumanji temple on the hill is an old one. The Mahratta governor of Ajmer improved the place. Hundreds of people go there every morning and evening to worship the god, and enjoy the superb scenery. It commands a fine view of the Anasagar Lake and the Daulat Bagh. A big fair is held here every year on Bhadrapad Vadi 3rd. (August or September).

IX—Khobra Bheroon.

This is a Hindu temple of Bheroonji, and is situated in a very picturesque place on a promontory near the southern end of Anasagar embankment, and commands an excellent view of the lake and the Daulat Bagh. It is one of the oldest places in Ajmer. Jahan Ara Begum, in her account of Khwaja Muinuddin, mentions that the Khwaja on his arrival at Ajmer took up his residence near this temple. She and the Mussalman writers generally call the Bheroonji, "Shadideva" (marriage god), as it is customary with Hindu bridegrooms to visit this temple with their brides after the conclusion of the marriage ceremony. The significance of the name is interesting. *Khobra* is a Marwari term meaning mischievous, and Bheroonji is a god. Tradition has it that unless a newly-married couple promptly proceed to pay their respects to him, this naughty god will play some prank to disturb their domestic felicity.

X—Hathi Bhata.

This is a Hindu temple, and is situated on the Imperial road opposite the old Victoria General Hospital, now the Municipal office. Since the advent of the Railway, rooms have been built all around it, where Hindu pilgrims to Pushkar, and others stay and take rest. It is called the *Hathi Bhata* (elephant stone) because the image is shaped like an elephant in a sitting posture. It appears to have been a rock jutting out of the earth. Emperor Jahangir had it shaped like an elephant. The couplet—

تاریخ فیل سنگ شد از حکمت اله
این کوه پارہ فیل جہانگیر بادشاہ

engraved on the right side of the "Elephant Stone" gives the date of its construction as 1613 A.D. (H. 1022).

XI—Bada Pir.

Baḍa Pir is situated on the northern spur of the Taragarh Hill, just above the Dargah and is a prominent sight of Ajmer. The place is of recent origin. A hundred and fifty years ago, it was a bare rock. A Mussalman fakir, named Soonda, who lived in the ruins of a *morchal* (entrenchment) of the fort of Taragarh, is said to have gone from Ajmer to Baghdad; and on his return, brought with him a brick from a building in the Dargah of Piran Pir there. At his death (about 1770), he asked that the brick might be buried with his remains. This was done. Dr. R. H. Irvine, writing a hundred years ago, and less than seventy years after the fakir's death, says that the Fakir brought two bricks (from Baghdad) with him as relics; placing these under a tree, he lived there with great sanctity, and at length dying during Mahratta rule, both Hindus and Muhammadans combined to erect the Dargah."—*Medical Topography of Ajmer*, p. 62.

An old manuscript "Account of Ajmer" in the Rajputana Musuem, Ajmer, says:—

"As 60 years have not yet passed since the above occurrences, the enquirer has ascertained the real state of the case; but after a few years, it is probable that people will fix on this spot, as having been the hermitage of Ghaus-ul-Azam, ignorant of the fact that Hindustan was never visited by that saint."

Bishop Heber says[1] :—

"And in Malwa it is not uncommon for pilgrims, who have been at the Ajmer Dargah, to set up a brick or a stone taken from the sanctuary, near their dwelling and to become saints themselves, and have pilgrimages made to them in consequence of such a possession."

One Shaikh Madoo put up a small building here, and as the site commands a good view of the city of Ajmer, people began to frequent it, and the place became known as the Chilla of Piran Pir.

The *Ajmer Regulations*, Vol. H to L, page 563, says:—

"From the evidence recorded by Mr. Cavendish, Superintendent of Ajmer in 1829 A. D., it appears, that when Nawab Amir Khan of Tonk came to Ajmer, he requested Bala Rao, the then Governor of Ajmer (1803-1808) to give an endowment of Re one a day to this shrine. Accordingly, Bala Rao gave a sanad, which was subsequently confirmed by Daulat Rao Scindia in 1810, enjoining Shaikh Asghar Ali who had a farm from Government, to make over the revenue of Makhopoora for *illuminations* and the other requirements of the shrine, the balance, if any, to be spent on the building. In this way, Shaikh Asghar Ali became Manager, and on his death and of that of his brother Fuzal Ali, the son-in-law of the latter, Mir Irshad Ali obtained the management. On the 5th May, 1821, Mr. Wilder, by order of Government resumed the grant and included the village in the Khalsa, giving a fixed revenue of Re. 1 a day to the shrine; but in 1822, the village was again made over to Irshad Ali, who was ordered to file papers of yearly receipts and expenditure. The average annual receipts from the village are now Rs. 1,553, from which the manager takes Rs. 200, as his perquisities as Manager, in accordance with an arrangement of Mr. Wilder."

Jamshed Khan, an officer of Nawab Amir Khan, the first Nawab of Tonk, built the *dalans* facing the north. Later Asghar Ali, Mutwali of the place, built the present domed structure and the mosque and paved the courtyard. His successor, Hakim Irshad Ali, built a reservoir for water near the entrance gate and a *dalan*, and generally improved the place in 1859 A. D.

XII—The Badshahi Building.

The Badshahi Building was originally a Hindu building. to which verandahs were afterwards added. As it stands, it is a structure of the early Mughal period, without any pretention to architectural beauty, and is so similar to the Audience Hall in the Magazine in its style and the materials used, that both appear to be of the same period. The two are

1. Narrative of a Journey Undertaken in the Northern Provinces of India, Vol. II, p. 49.

"very similar in size and almost precisely similar in detail."[1] The pillars, brackets and *chhajas* of the Badshahi Building agree in almost every particular with those of the Audience Hall in the Magazine. The building was not intended to contain a tomb, and it never contained one. A heap of debris in a corner of a room is now sometimes wrongly pointed to as a tomb. Nowhere do we find a tomb existing in an insignificant corner of a room in a building expressly built as a mausoleum. Moreover, as Mr. Nickolls says: "The existence of two elaborately-carved balconies—one on the north, the other on the south side of one of the chambers—seems to indicate that the building was intended for habitation". And when we remember, as is recorded in the *Tabkat-i-Akbari*, that in 1870 A.D., Emperor Akbar built the Daulat Khana, *i.e.*, the Magazine, and "his Amirs, Khans and other attendants at the Court vied with one another in erecting buildings, and that His Majesty distributed villages and lands attached to the Ajmer administration amongst his Amirs to enable them to pay the expenditure on new buildings," we can safely infer that this building, recently christened "The Badshahi Building" for want of a more appropriate name, was built or converted by one of Akbar's Amirs for his residence.

The building is situated in the Naya Bazar, not far from the Magazine. It is set back some twelve feet from the street, and is above the street level. The verandah and the main room are roofed with Pokhriawas greystone slabs, supported by a series of Khatoo and Agra cut-stone square pillars, with Agra cut-stone brackets supporting a heavy *chhaja* round the building, which is surmounted by an ornamental cut-stone parapet. The entrance is through the east verandah, and thence into a square chamber, roofed by a dome supported on pendentives and arches turned across the angles of the square. Immediately behind this chamber on the west side of it, is the room in which the balconies occur, supported on four moulded brackets corbelled out from the north and south walls. This chamber, too, has a domical roof, while the two smaller rooms on either side of it have vaulted ceilings. In all the four chambers, there are traces of painted patterns on the plastered walls, which are of lime-masonry, and plastered three to four inches inside and outside, with numerous shelves and niches, decorated with coloured edging and dado, similar to those under the main

1. "The similarity between the two buildings is so remarkable that there is ample justification for restoring the one and only doubtful feature in the Tahsil to match the corresponding part of the Badshahi Building." — Annual Progress Report of the Archaeological Survey, Northern Circle for 1905 A.D.

gateway of the Magazine. There are three staircases in the thickness of the west walls of the three rooms to the west of the central chamber, two of which lead to the upper floors of the smaller side chambers, the floor level of which is the same as that of the galleries in the chamber between them, while the third staircase leads up to the roof of the building. The roof is of concrete (flat), but the portion over the two larger chambers is higher than that over the verandahs, and there is no sign of the domed ceilings on the roof above, the raised roof over them being also flat—another sign that the building never contained a tomb. The building seems to have undergone further additions during the time of the Mahrattas, and was lately used as a municipal godown. The front portion of the building was used as an Indian Reading Room and Library for several years. It was restored in 1906-9 A.D., at a cost of Rs. 22,790.

XIII—Edward Memorial.

The Edward Memorial was built in 1912-13, to commemorate the memory of His late Majesty King Emperor Edward VII. The representatives of the various States in Rajputana including two ruling princes met on 29, August, 1910 at Ajmer, to consider a proposal to erect a provincial memorial to commemorate the reign of King Edward, and unanimously decided to construct a Dharamshala for the benefit of the visitors to Ajmer. The plans for the building were prepared by the Jodhpur Durbar, and the foundation stone was laid on 16, November, 1912 by H.E. Lord Hardinge, Viceroy and Governor General of India. The Memorial subscriptions to the amount of Rs. 1,32,078 were collected, the Udaipur and Jodhpur Darbars each paying Rs. 20,000/-. The buildings were put up at a cost of Rs. 91,592. Some additions have since been made.

The Memorial is a double-storied building with an imposing facade and a big gate in the centre, as its main entrance facing the east and a garden in front. It encloses a very spacious court-yard. There are in it, quarters and rooms for visitors of all ranks. Apart from a large suite of rooms intended for very rich people with a daily rent of 7/4, there are eight first class, fifteen second class, and eight third class rooms. The first three classes of visitors pay a fee of Re. 1/4, -/8/- and -/4/- a day for lodging. The fourth class of visitors for whom two rooms, two halls and four *dalans* are reserved, get free lodging. Food, in Indian style, can be had on payment, as also Electric fans and Radios.

A superintendent is in-charge of the Memorial and lives on the premises. It is under the control of a general committee, consisting of representatives of the various States in Rajputana, with the Commissioner of Ajmer as Chairman. The management is in the hands of a managing committee of seven members, with the Assistant Commissioner of Ajmer as ex-officio president.

The report of the Managing-Committee for 1938-39 shows that in the years 1929-30 to 1937-38, more than a lakh and a quarter visitors found shelter in it every year. In 1938-39, the total number of travellers who used the Memorial was 73,693, of whom 4349 belonged to the 1st class, and 56678 to the fourth class. The daily average of the four classes being 11·9, 19·18, 15·42 and 155·09. The fee collected in the year was Rs. 5463-10-8. The total income and expenditure of the Memorial in 1938-39 were Rs. 9976-7-7 and Rs. 8567-7-7 respectively. The Memorial fund now amounts to Rs. 67052 of which, Rs. 54425 are in Government Securities.

XIV—Tombs of Abdulla Khan and His Wife.

The tomb of Abdulla Khan is an ordinary building, of the later Mughal type, and is situated on the Beawar Road. It is a square, the sides measuring about 35 feet. At the four corners are piers with half columns upon two of their sides. The columns are octagonal, and with the exception of the interior of the dome over the centre, which is plastered, the whole structure is of unpolished white marble. The building stands on a platform surrounded by a plinth about three feet above the ground level. Between the columns are heavily-cusped arches, and the ceiling between the outer and the inner squares is flat, being formed of long slabs of marble. The tomb is in the centre of an inner square, at the four corners of which, are smaller piers and half columns, with cusped arches between them.

The tomb is said to be of Abdulla Khan, commonly called Miya Khan,[1] a resident of Barha in the United Provinces, and father of Husain Ali Khan, the Minister of King Farrukh-sayar (1712-1719 A.D.).

In 1704 A.D., Abdulla Khan built a mosque, which still stands behind the tomb, laid out a garden (as is shown by the inscription on the *Mehrab*), built a water channel from the Ana Sagar to this garden, and his wife's tomb, and

1. Elliot's History of India, Vol. VII, page 506.

enclosed all by a wall, having a gateway which still stands blocked up to the north of Allarakha & Son's shop. After his death, his tomb was built by his son, Husain Ali Khan in 1710 A.D., under the superintendence of Hidayatullah Khwajasara. Opposite to it, and separated from it by the road and a recently-built white stone gateway, is the tomb of Abdulla Khan's wife, in polished white marble, which, though small in size, yet in elegance, purity of design and workmanship, equals the best buildings existing anywhere. Mr. Garrick, the Assistant Archæological Surveyor of India, says: "I found an exquisitely-sculptured tomb of white marble; the perforated screens surrounding the sarcophagus of this tomb are equal in workmanship to anything I have seen, and the marble is of the finest quality"[1].

In plan, this mausoleum is a quadrangle of 15′-1″ sides or 60′-4″ in circuit, standing upon a marble platform 4′-6½″ high and measuring 128′ in circuit. The quadrangle consists of a small court containing the tomb, enclosed by marble *jali* screens with a parapet and *guldastas* (pinnacles), but without any roof. It is 9′-5″ high above the platform, and 13′-11¼″ above the ground. The platform had a balustrade, as is evidenced by the *mutakka* holes which still remain, although the balustrade has now disappeared.

XV—Chilla Madar Shah.

This is situated on the Madar Hill, to the east of the city of Ajmer. It was originally a Jain monastery of Jaman *yati*, the *chhatree* raised over whose remains still stands. It is said that one Sayad Badiuddin, *alias* Shah Madar, passed some time in devotion at this place, and that he afterwards migrated to Makanpur, near Kanauj. There is a tree near the *chhatree* which is called "the gram tree," because its leaves resemble the leaves of the gram plant. The place is unpretentious, but its position on the summit of the hill, which is about seven hundred feet high, makes it a prominent object in the landscape. The date of the original Hindu monastery or of the present *Chilla* is unknown; but it appears that the present small domed building was put up some time during the Mughal rule in Ajmer. The hill is mentioned in *Fatooh Alamgiri* as *Madar Dunger.*

XVI—Salar Ghazi.

A small domed building on a *chabutra* containing a tomb, on the summit of the hill to the right of the road to Pushkar,

1. Archæological Survey Report for 1883-84, page 47.

as it ascends the Ana Sagar Ghati, has come to be known as the hermitage of Salar Ghazi. As a matter of fact, Salar Ghazi never came to Ajmer; and nobody knows who lies buried in the tomb. Salar Ghazi, the son of Salar Sahu, died at Bharaich (Oudh). This place appears in time to have come to be known as Chilla Salar Ghazi, in the same way as the cell of Soonda fakir, has come to be called Piran Pir or Bada Pir. The place has been greatly improved during the last ten years by new additions.

The manuscript "Account of Ajmer" (written about 1830 A.D.) whilst mentioning the Madar Shah and Chilla Piran Pir, makes no mention of this place.

XVII—Chilla Khwaja Sahib.

On the way to the Hindu temple of *Khobra Bheroon*, near the Ana Sagar Ghati, is a building called the Chilla Khwaja Sahib. It is said that the Khwaja on his arrival at Ajmer took up his abode at this place and resided here till he moved to the place where he lies buried. For four hundred years, a cell and a flat stone slab marked this place as associated with the Khwaja. In 1628 A.D., Daulat Khan, a relative of Mahabat Khan, Subedar of Ajmer, built a small enclosure and paved the floor[1]. During the last ten years, the hermitage has been greatly extended by the addition of new buildings.

XVIII—Chilla Qutab Shah.

This is situated near the Ana Sagar embankment, opposite the western entrance to the conservatory of the Daulat Bagh and is said to be the place where Khwaja Qutbuddin Bakhtiar Kaki, the disciple of Khwaja Muinuddin Chishti used, during his visits to his preceptor at Ajmer, to pass his time in devotion. Khwaja Qutbuddin lived in Delhi and died there in H. 634 (1237 A.D.)[2] In 1776 A.D., Maulvi Shamsuddin, a disciple of Maulvi Fakharuddin of Delhi, built a mosque with a domed roof here. In the courtyard, at a lower level than the mosque, is an enclosure containing the tomb of Muhammad Shah Khan, an officer of Amir Khan, Nawab of Tonk. Muhammad Khan, the deputy of Muhammad Shah Khan, built a mosque here in 1824 A.D.

1. An inscription of six verses on the door says that it was put up during the time of Shah Jahan by Daulat Khan in H. 1037 (A.D. 1628).
2. Tarikhe Ferishta, Vol, II, page 382.

XIX—Villa of Sayad Ahmad.

At the foot of the hill, to the north-east of Ana Sagar, stand the remains of the garden of Sayad Ahmad, who was governor of Ajmer in 1669 A. D. The *baori* in it, however, is called the baori of Asad Khan, who was Sudedar of Ajmer in H. 1092 (1681 A. D.), and on whom the titles of Umdatul Mulk and Madarulmuham were conferred when he became minister at Delhi.

At a little distance to the south of these remains, on an elevation, stands a ruined mosque, built by one Sheikh Yaha during the reign of Aurangzeb, for the upkeep of which, Asad Khan made a grant of forty bighas of land in the neighbourhood. During recent years, additions have been made to it.

XX—Ganpatpura.

Ganpatpura is an old place of the early Mughal times, situated inside Madar Gate. It was a square with twentyseven domed apartments on its four sides, enclosing a large open space and an imposing gate. On both sides of the gate, there were vaulted *dalans* (sitting rooms with the fronts open). Behind the gate and connected with it, there was a domed porch with two vaulted dalans, one on either side. Akbar had built it as a *Sarai* for travellers.

Rao Balarao Inglia. the Mahratta Subedar (governor) of Ajmer from 1803 to 1808 A.D., gave the place in 1806 A.D. to the Mahajans of Jatiawas—a muhalla outside the Madar Gate just then demolished,.with a Sanad dated the Kartik Sudi 2nd, S. 1863 (12 November, 1806 A.D.) authorizing them to build houses for themselves in it. The gate, the domed porch and the vaulted dalans still exist, but the twenty seven domed apartments have disappeared, and in their place, big residential houses adorn the place.

Part II.

HISTORICAL

CHAPTER XVII

HISTORY

I—CHAUHAN PERIOD

THE early history of Ajmer is, shrouded in mystery. It is, however, admitted on all hands that the city was founded by the Chauhan King Ajaipal, or Ajairaj.[1] He is known as Ajaipal Chakwa (the universal potentate), who flourished late in the sixth or early in the seventh century, A.D. The supreme strategical importance[2] of the position of Ajmer—according to Colonel Tod, "the key of Rajputana," and the impregnable nature of the hill on which the fortress is situated, (Heber says, it could with very little European skill be made a second Gibraltar), could not but have been early recognised by the kings of Sambhar, whose dominions extended far beyond Ajmer towards the west. History tells us that from the twelfth to the nineteenth century, Ajmer was not only the cynosure of all eyes, but adorned the brow of the victor in the race for political supremacy in India. The possession of Ajmer by a Power is the index to its political predominance in Upper India, so much so that the history of Ajmer is, in one sense, the epitome of the history of India, just as, in another sense, India is an epitome of the world.[3]

King Ajaipal was the son of Samant Deva, and the grandson of Vasudeva, who came to Sambhar from Ahichetrapur or Nagor in Marwar. According to the *Vansavali* given at the end of *Prabandhkosh*, he flourished in S. 608 (551 A.D.). Vasudeva was descended from Chahuman, the founder of the clan, whose date is unknown.

1. According to the Prabandhkosh genealogy, this Ajairaja was the founder of Ajmer.

2. Heber's Journal, Vol. II., p 49: This very enviable strategical importance of Ajmer has exposed it to constant attack, and, as it was several times destroyed and several times rebuilt, the names of the rebuilders have been preserved as the founders of Ajmer, just as Badami in the Deccan, the capital of the Solankees, came to be known as having been founded by Kirtivarma (567-591 A.D.), though as a matter of fact the city had been the capital of his predecessor, Fulake-hi I Thus, while tradition assigns the foundation of Ajmer to Ajaipal Chakwa, the Prithviraj Rasa describes its rebuilding to Anaji, and the Prithviraj Vijaya says that the city was founded by Ajaideva, father of Anaji.

3. Chambers' Encyclopaedia, p. 337.

Chahuman belonged to the Solar dynasty of Rajputs. The *Hammir Mahakavya* says that he ruled over the heads of kings as his ancestor, the Sun, ruled over the heads of mountains. The *Prithviraj Vijaya*, and the stone inscription of the time of Visaldeva IV. (1153-1163 A.D.), in the Rajputana Museum, Ajmer, describe the Chauhans as descendants of the Solar race of kings.[1]

The Hansi inscription of 1167 A.D., as well as the inscription of 1320 A.D., in the Achleshwar temple on Mount Abu, however, describe the Chauhans as belonging to the Lunar dynasty. The *Gotracharya* of the Chauhans "*Sam Veda Soma Vansa Vatsagotra...........*"shows them as belonging to the Lunar race. Whether they belong to the Solar or the Lunar race, they assuredly do not belong to the Agnikula, as the Prithviraj Rasa wrongly describes them to do.

King Ajaipal was called *Chakri* from the fact of his conquering the *Chakra* (disposition of troops in battle in the form of a hollow circle) of the enemy. He was perfect in archery, and was a great warrior. In his old age, he retired from the world and lived as a religious recluse in the Ajaipal Valley, about four miles south of Foysagar. He seems to have lived in the sixth or seventh century A.D. Ajaipal is worshipped in Ajmer under the name *Ajaipal Baba*, and the sixth day of Bhadrapad *sudi*, every year, is sacred to his name. On that day a fair takes place, and the inhabitants of the city pour out into the beautiful valley where he ended his days, in order to do homage to the memory of the founder of this celebrated city, who is believed still to preside over the destinies of Ajmer and protect its citizens from ills, especially the attacks of venomous reptiles and animals.

Ajaipal was succeeded by his son, Vigraharaj I, after whom came his sons, Chandraraj and Gopendra, the latter also called Govindraj who was the first king of Ajmer to fight against the Mussalmans, and is recorded to have defeated[2] a Mussalman army and captured Sultan Beg Varis. Govind was succeded by Durlabh Rai, popularly called Doola Rai.

1. See Chapter on Adhai din ka Jhonpra, Sub head, Inscriptions.

2. According to tradition, it was during his time that Ajmer was first attacked by the Muhammadans. "Doola Rai was slain, and his only child Lot, then an infant seven years of age, was killed by an arrow while playing on the battlements. The importance of this event deeply impressed the Chauhans, who have deified the youthful heir of Ajmer. The day on which he was killed is sanctified, and his effigy then receives divine honours."—Tod's Rajasthan, Vol. II, p 445. Lot is said to have been killed on Monday, the 12th day of Jeshta (May-June). "This invasion was probably the one undertaken during the time of Junaid, son of Abdul Rahman al Marri, Commander of the Sindhian frontier, under Khalifa Hasham (H. 105 125), (724-743 A.D.). From facts which need not be discussed here, it appears that this invasion took place sometime between 724 and 726 A.D. Doola Rai also fought with the Gor Rajputs. Miss Duff' in her Chronology of India, p. 62, gives 724 A.D., as the year of this expedition.

Genealogy of the Chauhan Kings of Ajmer

- (1) Vasudeva.
  - (2) Samantaraja.
    - (3) Ajayaraja (Ajayapala).
      - (4) Vigraharaja.
        - (5) Chandraraja I.
          - (7) Durlabharaja I.
            - (8) Govindaraja or Guvaka I.
              - (9) Chandraraja II.
                - (10) Guvaka II.
                  - (11) Chandanaraja.
                    - (12) Vakpatiraja I.
                      - (13) Sinharaja.
                        - (14) Vigraharaja II (A. D. 973).
                        - (15) Durlabharaja II.
                          - (16) Govindraja II.
                            - (17) Vakpatiraja II.
                              - (18) Viryarama (about A. D. 1040).
                              - (19) Chamundaraja.
                                - (20) Durlabharaja III (about A. D. 1075).
                                - (21) Vigraharaja III.
                                  - (22) Prithviraja I. (A. D. 1105).
                                    - (23) Ajayaraja also called Salhana.
                                      - (24) Arnoraja (Anaji) (A D. 1140.)
                                        - (25) Jugdeva
                                          - (28) Prithvibhata (A. D. 1167-69).
                                        - (26) Vigraharaja IV. (about A. D. 1153-1164)
                                          - (27) Aparagangeya (A. D. 1167)
                                        - (29) Somesvara (A. D. 1170-71).
                                          - (30) Prithviraja the Great (died A. D. 1192).
                                          - (31) Hariraja (A. D. 1193-95). (the last Chauhan King of Ajmer.)
        - (6) Gopendraraja.

1. The genealogy given at the end of the Prabandhakosh MS., which is stated to be four or five centuries old, gives v. s. 608 (A. D. 551) as the date when Vasudeva flourished. *Vide*, *Gaudavahi* (Bombay Sanskrit Series, No. XXXIV), Introduction, p. CXXXV, note.

Durlabhraja was succeeded by his son, Guvaka I, who was a famous warrior, and who, owing to his valour, received about 756 A.D., the title of *Vir* (hero) in the assembly of Raja Nagavalok. After him, came Chandraraj II, and then Guvaka II, on whose death, Chandanraj came to the throne. He invaded Tanwaravati (a district near Delhi), and slew its king, Rudrena or Rudrapal of Delhi.[1] Chandanraj was succeeded by Vakpatiraj, also called Bappraj. His reign was a prosperous one, and he greatly extended his dominions, the southern boundary stretching to the Vindhya mountains. He was a great warrior, and won 188 battles.[2] King Tantrapal attacked him, but sustained a severe defeat. Vakpatiraj had three sons, Sinharaj, Lakshmanraj and Vatsaraj; Sinharaj succeeded him and Lakshmanraj, called Lakhansi, got Nadole and eventually established a separate principality there.

Sinharaj was a great king. The Tomars, with the assistance of Raja Lavana attacked his dominions but were defeated and put to flight. He is said to "have kept as many princes in his prison as he did in his house." He was as famous for his hospitality as for his military exploits. Speaking of him, the *Hammir Mahakavya says*: "When the drum announcing his starting on an expedition sounded, the King of Carnatak flattered him, the King of Lat (doab between the Mahi and Narbada rivers) would open his door to him. The Chola King (Madras Presidency) trembled; the King of Gujrat lost his head, and the King of Western Bengal (Anga[3]) lost heart." He repeatedly fought with the Mussalmans. In one encounter, he slew a Mussalman general named Hatim[4], and captured his elephants. On another occasion, he utterly routed a Muhammadan army under Sultan Hajiuddin, which had penetrated as far as Jethana, about 25 miles from Ajmer. He bore the title of *Sultan Grahi* or King Seizer. He "overcame Nasiruddin, from whom he captured twelve hundred horse." Nasiruddin was the title of Subuktagin, who repeatedly invaded India during the fifteen years' reign of his predecessor Alptagin, who died in 963 A.D. The Harsha[5] Stone Inscription says, that he "annihilated in war, rulers of men in all directions." Sinharaj was alive in 956 A.D., when, according to the Harsha Stone Inscription, the Harsha temple was completed.

1. Harsha Stone Inscription published in Epigraphia Indica, Vol. II, p. 177.
2. Prithviraj Vijaya, sarga V.
3. Bengal in old days was divided into two divisions; (*a*) Western Bengal called Anga, (*b*) Eastern Bengal called Banga.
4. Hammir Mahakavya, sarga I, verse 102.
5. Epigraphia Indica, Vol. II, p. 127.

Sinharaj was succeeded by his son, Vigraharaj II, (A.D. 973) who greatly enlarged his kingdom. The kingdom of Ajmer has from the earliest times been known as Sapadlaksh (a lakh and a quarter), evidently from the fact that the territory contained a hundred and twenty-five thousand towns and villages. It included the whole of eastern and southern Rajputana, a great part of Marwar, and extended to beyond Bhatner on the north. Sapadlaksh became Siwalik in Hindi, by which name, the part of Rajputana containing Nagor, Ajmer and Sambhar was long known.[1]

Vigraharaj invaded Gujrat between 973 and 996 A. D. King Mulraj abandoned his capital and fled to Cutch, but made his submission later, when Vigraharaj returned to his capital.[2] He conquered the country to the south as far as the river Narbada, and built a temple to the goddess Asapurna (Fulfilment of Hope) at Broach. The *Prabandha Chintamani* of Merutunga also mentions this event (Tawney's translation, pp. 23-24.) The *Hammira Mahakavya* (written in the fourteenth century) says that he killed Mulraj, king of Gujrat. This was the beginning of the conflict which ended in the overthrow of both by a third power, the Afghans. After Vigraharaj, came Durlabh II, who was succeeded by Govindraj II.

According to the *Prabandhkosh* (*Gaudavaho*, Introduction, p. CXXXVII) Govindraj II defeated Sultan Mahmud. Govindraj II was succeeded by his son, Vakpatiraj II, who, as the Chitor inscription of s. 1331, (published in the *Indian Antiquary*, Vol. XXII, p. 80) says, killed King Ambaprasad of Ahad (old capital of Mewar). After him, came Virya Ram, who was a contemporary of the famous King Bhoj of Malwa (1010-1055 A.D.). Virya Ram invaded Malwa, but was defeated and killed by Bhoj.[3] It was probably during Virya Ram's reign that Mahmud Ghaznavi attacked Ajmer, but was wounded and retired to Anhalwara in 1024 A. D.[4]

Virya Ram was succeeded by Chamundraj,[5] who captured Hejamuddin, Lord of the Shaks[6] (Mussalmans). Durlabhraj III

1. For Sapadlaksh, see "Speeches and Writings of Har Bilas Sarda," p. 224.
2. See Forbes' *Ras Mala*, page 38. Also *Bombay Gazetteer*, Vol. I, page 159.
3. Prithviraj Vijaya, sarga V.
4. Duff's Chronology of India, p. 113. When Sultan Mahmud of Ghazni had attacked Anangpal in 1008 A.D., "the Rajas of Ujjain, Kalingar, Gwalior, Kanauj, Delhi and Ajmer entered into a confederacy and united their forces and advanced to meet the invader—"The Hindu women sold their jewels, melted down their golden ornaments and sent their contributions to furnish resources."—Elphinstone's Histoy of India, pp. 320-21.(Ed. 1911).
5. Bijolian Inscription, v. 14, (Journal, Bengal A.S., Vol. LV, pt. 1, p. 40.
6. Later Hindu writers apply the term Shak, indiscriminately to Shaks, Huns and Mussalmans.

or Dusal succeeded him about 1075 A.D. and defeated a Mussalman general named Shahabuddin.[1] He invaded Gujrat and slew its king, Karna, sometime between 1061-1093 A.D. Durlabh was killed by Rawal Veri Singh of Mewar in a battle at Kowario.

Visaldeva III succeeded Durlabhraj, and distinguished himself in arms. It must have been this Visaldeva, who, according to Ferishta, headed a confederacy of Hindu kings and drove the governors of Modud from Hansi, Thaneshwar and Nagarkot. As the king of Gujrat did not join this confederacy, King Visaldeva III prepared to invade Gujrat when the Chaluca prince of Anhalwara Patan, King Karna, advanced to meet him. A battle was fought near Sojat in Marwar, when Karna having been defeated, fell back on Jalor, which also he was forced to relinquish. Visaldeva pursued the enemy to Girnar, the heart of the peninsula. Visaldeva, finding that the enemy did not face him, returned to his capital, when he received an embassy from King Karna, who had re-formed his army in the meantime, saying that he was Visaldeva's equal, and adding, "that the only tribute should be the sword whose fragments Visaldeva might collect, if he, Karna, were again defeated. With the chivalry, characteristic of a Chauhan, Visaldeva sent back the prisoners and the spoils he had taken, and advanced to give Karna another chance to win. Visaldeva formed his army in a circular array, and, in the first onslaught, killed 2000 Chalucas. The next day, a treaty was made and king Karna gave his daughter in marriage to Visaldeva. Visaldeva founded a town on the spot to commemorate his victory. Visalnagar still exists.[2] Visaldeva was succeeded by Prithviraj I, who attacked and killed five hundred Chaluka Rajputs who had come to plunder Pushkar.[3] He built an alms-house on the road to Somnath.

Ajaideva succeeded Prithviraj I. He lived about 1140 A.D. He conquered and killed three kings named Chachik, Sindhul and Yashoraj.[4] "He captured the Commander in Chief of Malwa, named Sulhana, brought him to Ajmer and consigned him to a strong fortress." He defeated the Mussalmans with great slaughter. He conquered the country up to Ujjain.[5]

1. Hammir Mahakavya, sarga II. V. 28.
2. Tod's Trave's in Western India, p. 172. Also Hammir Mahakavya.
3. Prithviraj Vijaya, Sarga V.
4. Prithviraj Vijaya, Sarga V. verse 15.
5. Stone inscription in the Rajputana Museum, Ajmer.

The Prithviraj Vijaya says that Ajaideva "filled the world with coins," and that his queen, Somaldevi was fond of designing new coins.

Ajaideva was succeeded by his son Arnoraj, or Anaji. Anaji annihilated a Muslim army that came *via* the desert at Ajmer.[1] "In order to purify the place of battle, Anaji performed a *havan* there and constructed the lake Ana Sagar, and filled it with the river Chandra which rises in the forest of Pushkar." Anaji built the temple of Siva in the Ajaipal Valley.[2] Arnoraj or Anaji's reign was an eventful one. He not only defeated the Muslim invaders, who came across the desert, but fought three wars with Anhalwara Patan, one with the celebrated Sidhraj Jaisingh, and the other two with the still more powerful king Kumarpal, successor of Jaisingh. Sidhraj Jaisingh invaded Ajmer, but the action fought was evidently an indecisive one. According to the *Kirti Kaumadi* (Bombay Sanskrit Series) canto II, p. 11, verses 2-29, Jaisingh was defeated and gave his daughter, Kanchandevi, in marriage to Arnoraj. This marriage was the cause of the first war with Jaisingh's successor, Kumarpal. Jaisingh left no son and the astrologers told him that Kumarpal, son of Tribhuwanpal of Dahithali, belonging to a younger branch of the royal family, would succeed him. Jaisingh became angry and attacked and destroyed Dahithali. Kumarpal, the sole survivor, fled in disguise and after many adventures came to Patan after Jaisingh's death, and was crowned king in 1143 A.D. As he was looked upon as an usurper. Arnoraj who was Jaisingh's son-in-law, espoused the cause of Bahad, the adopted son of Jaisingh and invaded Patan sometime between s. 1200 and 1202 (A.D. 1145). The result of the war was unfavourable to Kumarpal, who made peace with Arnoraj, to whom he gave his sister Devaldevi to wife. Kumarpal made this peace, as King Ballala of Malwa was advancing against Anhalwara Patan, having won over two generals of Kumarpal.

The second war in s. 1207 (1150 A.D.) was caused by Devaldevi instigating her brother, Kumarpal to attack Arnoraj, as the latter, while playing *chaupar* with her, had insulted her, and kicked her on her calling him *Ganwar* (rustic). Kumarpal invaded Ajmer and defeated Arnoraj, *vide* the Chitor Mokalji temple inscription[3] of Kumarpal of s. 1207 (A.D. 1149-50) which says that after defeating Arnoraj, Kumarpal visited Chitor and put up the inscription.

1. Prithviraj Vijaya, Sarga VI.
2. Ibid.
3. Epigraphia Indica, Vol II, p. 422. Also Tod's Travels in Western India, p. 504.

The wellknown historical work, *Ras Mala*, says that the Ajmer army was led by Govind Raj, and that while there was confusion in Kumarpal's army during the battle, an iron shaft felling Arnoraj, gave the victory to Kumarpal.[1]

The *Prithviraj Rasa* says that later, Bhola Bhim (A.D. 1179-1242), the Solanki ruler of Anhalwara, invaded Ajmer to avenge the death of Pratapsingh Solanki, whom Kanrai, younger brother of Someshwar (father of Emperor Prithviraj) had killed in open Darbar at Ajmer owing to a misunderstanding, and that Someshwar was killed in the fight.[2] The *Ras Mala* mentions the incident of Pratap Singh's death at the hands of Kanrai, but says that Bhim postponed the invasion owing to a Mussalman invasion of Anhalwara. According to the *Prithviraj Rasa*, Prithviraj invaded Gujrat to avenge his father's death and defeated and killed Bhim. The *Prithviraj Vijaya* does not mention Bhim's invasion of Ajmer, nor Prithviraj's victory over Bhim.

Arnoraj was a generous, discriminating and just king. He had three sons, Jugdeva and Visaldeva Vigraharaj by queen Sudhava of Marwar, and Someshwar by Kanchandevi, daughter of Sidhraj Jai Singh of Anhalwara Patan. Someshwar was brought up in the court of Sidhraj Jaisingh and Kumarpal. Arnoraj was murdered by his son Jugdeva sometime between 1150 and 1151 A.D. Jugdeva, however, was expelled by Visaldeva-Vigraharaj, who ascended the throne about 1152 A.D.

His reign is a landmark not only in the history of Ajmer, but also in the history of India. He conquered Nadole, Jalor and Pali, invaded and conquered Delhi[3], between 1155 and 1163 A. D., subjugated the country up to the Himalayas, clearing it of the last vestiges of Mussalman rule. The famous Sivalik Pillar Inscription dated the s. 1220 (A. D. 1164) states that he had conquered the country between the Himalayas and the Vindhia mountains and cleared the country of Aryavarta of Mussalmans and again made it *Arya bhumi*, the abode of the Aryas. He then commands his successors to drive the Mussalmans beyond the Attock.[4]

The *Prabandhkosh* calls him "the vanquisher of the Turushkas."—*Vide Gaudavaho*, Introduction, p. CXXXVII. Mr. Edward Thomas says:—"Delhi became a mere kingship

1. Ras Mala, Vol. II, p. 179, Oxford University Press.
2. Tod's Travels in Western India, (1839) p. 199.
3. Bijolian Inscription, verse 22.
4. Indian Antiquary, Vol. XIX, p. 215, Also Asiatic Researches, Vol. VIII, P. 130.

subject to Ajmer."[1] He was the first Chauhan Emperor of India, as his nephew, the renowned Prithviraj, son of his younger brother Someshwara—was the last. He had a large army consisting of a thousand elephants, a hundred thousand cavalry and a still larger force of infantry.

He was as great a scholar and a poet as he was a warrior, and his drama, *Harkeli Natak* is a composition "not unworthy of the great poet Bhavabhuti." Dr. Keilhorn says: "Actual and undoubted proof is here afforded to us of the fact that powerful Hindu rulers of the past were eager to compete with Kalidasa and Bhavabhuti for poetical fame."—The *Indian Antiquary*, Vol. XX, p. 201. He built the great college at Ajmer now called the Adhai Din Ka Jhonpra. "As in Dhar, so in Ajmer, the Adhai Din Ka Jhonpra mosque is an old Sanskrit School, recent excavations having brought to light slabs with entire dramas carved on them."—*Bombay Gazetteer*, Vol. II; p. 180 (1896 A.D.) 'Vigraharaja built in Ajmer as many temples as the forts he had conquered."

He constructed the lake Visalsar, now called Visla, at Ajmer. Visaldeva died about the year 1163 A. D., and was succeeded by his minor son, Amargangeya, who, however, was deposed by the parricide Jugdeva's son, Prithviraj II. (Prithvibhatta), who ascended the throne. An unpublished inscription, dated the Jaishta Vadi 13, V. S. 1225 (A. D. 1168), on a pillar in the temple of Ruthi Rani at Dhod, in the Jahazpur district of Mewar, says that Prithviraj (Prithvibhata) "obtained a victory over the king of Sakambhari by the strength of his arms". This shows that he defeated Amargangeya, the son and successor of Vigraharaja IV (Visaladeva) and took back the kingdom, which his father (Jugdeva) had lost to Vigraharaj. This inscription says that Suhavadevi was the queen of Prithvibhata. Prithviraj II is wellknown for his charities. He defeated King Vastupal, conquered the Mussalmans, and erected a palace in the fort of Hansi, which stood there till the guns of Mons. Perron destroyed it in 1801 A.D. along with the schemes of George Thomas to found a kingdom there.

On the death of Prithviraj in 1169 A.D., Someshwara succeeded him. He was a man of great prowess, and appears to have conquered all his enemies. According to the *Prithviraj Vijaya*, he was present in Kumarpal's campaign against the Raja of Konkan, whom Someshwara himself killed in battle. This event took place before he came to the throne. Someshwar (Prithviraj Vijaya, Sarga VIII) built a very big temple

1. Chronicles of the Pathan Kings of Delhi, p. 65.

of Vaidyanath which towered above the palaces of Visaldeva. In it, he placed an effigy of his father on horseback, with his own effigy in front, facing his father's. He placed the images of Brahma, Vishnu, and Siva in one place in a temple. He built five temples, and Ajmer vied with Meru, which boasted of its five *Kalpbrikshes.* He built so many temples in Gaugnak (Gangwana, 9 miles north east of Ajmer) and other places that the population of the city of gods dwindled away.

According to the Bijolian inscription, his surname was Pratap Lankeshwara. He married a Kalchuri Rajput princess named Karpurdevi, daughter of King Achalraj of Cheddi *desh* (country round Jubbalpur) who ruled at Tripuri, and had two sons by her, Prithviraj and Hari Raj. Someshwara died in 1179 A.D. Prithviraj being young, his mother Karpurdevi ruled the empire as regent for some time, with the assistance of the minister, Kadamb Vas. The description of Ajmer given in sarga IX of the Prithviraj Vijaya, during the regency of Queen Karpurdevi says:—

> "The city was so densely populated and there were so many gardens, tanks, and wells, that not more than one-tenth of the earth was visible to the sun, and water in the wells was only two cubits from the ground surface. Karpurdevi also founded a town."

The *Prithviraj Vijaya* (Sarga IX) says that Prithviraj was carefully educated under the direction of the minister Kadamb Vas. He was extremely handsome in body. The book mentions that Bhuvanaik Malla, the younger brother of Karpurdevi's father, who was a hero and a great gift-giver came to Ajmer and served Prithviraj and watched over his welfare. One of the earliest exploits of Prithviraj was to attack Nagarjuna, who had taken possession of Gudpur. Nagarjuna fled and Prithviraj, slew the warriors and conquered the fort.

Prithviraj reigned for thirteen years, from 1179 to 1192 A.D., and was the last Hindu Emperor of India.[1] He was the flower of Rajput Chivalry. His whole life was one unbroken chain of chivalrous deeds and glorious exploits, which have won for him eternal fame and a name that will last as long as chivalry itself. Colonel Tod says: "Although the Chauhans had always ranked high in the list of chivalry, yet the seal of the order was stamped on all who have the name of Chauhan since the days of Prithviraj, the model of every Rajput."[2]

1. Annals and Antiquities of Rajasthan, Vol. I, p. 445.
2. Annals and Antiquities of Rajasthan, Vol. I., p. 696.

EMPEROR PRITHVIRAJ.

Maharana Pratap.

A Jain book, *Khartargachha Gurvavali* (mss.) by Jinpalodaya says that there were several learned men in the court of Emperor Prithviraj, and that discussions on literary and religious subjects used to be held there. The book contains an account of a Sastrartha held at Ajmer between the Jain Acharya Jinpati Suri of Khartargachha,[1] and Padamprabha of Ukeshgachha, temple dweller, on Kartik Shukla 10th, S 1239.[2] The book also states that Prithviraj invaded Bhaddanak (Bhadrapura) and won a victory.

Emperor Prithviraj defeated the King of Gujrat and invaded Mahoba and vanquished the king, Parmaldeva. whose generals, Ala and Udil, fought with great valour. He carried away the princess Sanjogta, the daughter of King Jai Chandra of Kanauj, from amidst the united heroism and chivalry of Hindustan, as Sanjogta in a Swayamber had chosen Prithviraj as her husband. The bards made him the general theme of their songs, his personal appearance and actions were lauded at every court in India, and he became the *beau ideal* of every princess of the time. The Rathors of Kanauj and the Solankees of Gujrat conspired together, and invited Sultan Shahabuddin Ghori to invade the dominions of Prithviraj. "Six invasions by Shahabuddin occurred," says Colonel Tod, "ere he succeeded. He had been often defeated and twice taken prisoner by the Hindu sovereign of Delhi who, with a lofty and blind arrogance of the Rajput character, set him at liberty."[3]

1. About s. 1070 (1013 A.D.), Durlabharaj king of Anhalwara Patan gave the title of Khartargachha to Jineshwer Suri after winning a Sastrartha.

2. The account says that in S. 1239 (1182 A.D.) Jinpati Suri went to Phalodi (Marwar) and after staying there for a few months, proceeded to Ajmer. A Jain scholar Padam Prabha of Ukeshgachha lived in Phalodi, and after Jinpati Suri's departure, gave out that he had defeated the latter in a Sastrartha. Seth Ramdeva of Ajmer went to Emperor Prithviraj and prayed that a Sastrartha (learned disputation) be held in the Emperor's Court at Ajmer between Padamprabha and Jinpati Suri. The Emperor, who was at Narain (Naraina now a railway station on the B B. & C.I.R.) sent men to Phalodi to bring Padamprabha to Ajmer and himself started for a digvijaya (a victory in all directions) On his return to Narain, Seth Ramdeva reminded him of the Sastrartha. The Emperor fixed Kartik Shukla 10th. for the Sastrartha. Jinpati Suri, accompanied by Jainmatopadhyaya, P. Sthirchand, & Manchand went to Narain, and PadamPrabha also came there. When both the parties came to Court, Prithviraj told Mandleshwar (a subordinate ruler) Kaimasp, that he (Prithviraj) would take a little rest and that the Sastrartha should begin in court in the presence of the scholars Vidyapati, Janardhan Gor and Vageshwara. The subject of discussion was whether the *Arti* should be done from left to right or the reverse. Jinpati Suri contending that it should be from left to right. The Emperor on his return, was told by Kaimasp that "Suriji had won.' Further discussion on grammar took place and some Samasyas were given, Jinpati Suri was declared to have won. Later, Jinpati Suri was taken to Ajmer. The Emperor followed him after two days. The Emperor proceeded on an elephant to *Panshedha Shala* of Suriji and presented to him a *Vijayapatra* (Certificate of victory.). Suriji then went away to Vikrampur. Seth Ramdeva spent rupees sixteen thousand on the Sastrartha.

Jinpati Suri was a disciple of Jinchandra Suri *alias* Manidhari, who was the disciple of Jindatta Suri alias Dada Sahib who had died at Ajmer on 11th Ashadh, S. 1211 (1154 A.D.). The place of cremation is known after him as Dadabari.

3. Transactions of the Royal Asiatic Society of Great Britain and Ireland, Vol. I., pages 147-8.

Shahabuddin, after his last defeat by Prithviraj at Tirauri in 1191 A.D., was assiduous in raising another army, and in 1192 A.D., he advanced with an army of one hundred and twenty thousand horse.[1] Reinforced by the forces of the Rajas of Jammu and Kanauj[2] he took up his position at Thaneshwar. Prithviraj, says Abul Fazal, hurriedly "collected together only a small number of troops, and with these he marched out to attack the Sultan. But the heroes of Hindustan had all perished in the manner described above: besides, Jaichand, who had been his ally, was now in league with his enemy."[3] Another of his vassals, the Haoli Rao Hamir turned traitor and joined the Sultan. Prithviraj[4] was defeated and taken prisoner, and was killed. Shahabuddin advanced and took Ajmer, but leaving Prithviraj's son, Govindraj on the throne, he returned to Ghor.

Prithviraj's younger brother, Hari Raj—called Hemraj by Ferishta, and Hiraj by Hasan Nizami, the author of *Tajul Maasir*—drove his nephew from the throne, as he had acknowledged the supremacy of the Mussalmans, and himself became King. He sent his general, Chatar Raj, to invade Delhi, which had been seized by Qutbuddin Aibak. Qutbuddin met and defeated Chatar Raj, who retreated in good order to Ajmer and joined Hari Raj. Qutbuddin followed Chatar Raj to Ajmer. Hari Raj advanced and met him, but was defeated; Qutbuddin took possession of Ajmer and appointed a Mussalman[5] as governor of the place in 1195 A.D.

The mint at Ajmer which turned out coins of the Chauhans continued to produce currency after the Chauhan empire came to an end. The existence of a coin in the joint names of Prithviraj and Muhammad Bin Sam "mentioned by Mr. Edward Thomas[6], probably belongs to the time when Shahabuddin (Muhammad Bin Sam) left Ajmer in the possession of Prithviraj's son and returned to Ghor. The script used in the coins is Hindi. See the reverse of the coins containing.[7] **श्री हमीरमहमद साम** and **श्री महमदवने साम ।**

Sultan Shamsuddin Altmash's own coin[8] struck at Ajmer has the legend, **श्री हमीर** and on the reverse, **श्री समसीरलदेष**, and in another coin as **श्री हमीर** and **सुरिताण श्री सम्सदिण ।**

1. Tabqati Nasiri, by Major Raverty, page 465. 3. Akbar Nama.
2. Raverty's Tabqati Nasiri, page 467. 4. Tod's Rajasthan, Vol. I, page 560.
5. It is said by Mussalmans that on the death of Qutbuddin in 1209 A.D., the Rajputs attacked Garh Beetli and put the Mussalman garrison to the sword, and that Sayad Husain Khangsawar obtained martyrdom on that occasion. This event, however, is not recorded in any authentic history
6. Chronicles of the Pathan Kings of Delhi, p. 17.
7. Ibid, p. 20. 8. Ibid, pp. 70-71.

II—PATHAN & RAJPUT PERIOD

Qutbuddin now set out from Ajmer to conquer Anhilwara, but the Mers combined with the Rajputs, and inflicted a severe defeat on him. He fled wounded, pursued by them to Ajmer, and shut himself up in the Ajmer fortress. The Rajputs laid siege to the fortress: re-inforcements, however, arrived after many months from Ghazni, when the siege was raised, and the Rajputs retired.

Little is known of the history of Ajmer during the thirteenth and the fourteenth centuries. It remained sometimes in the possession of the Sultans of Delhi and sometimes in that of the Maharanas of Mewar. Maharana Kshetra Singh of Chitor captured it between 1364 and 1382 A.D.[1] Saleem Khan, governor of Multan, after helping the Bhatis of Poogal against Rao Chonda, King of Marwar, in 1423 A.D., took possession of Ajmer for the Sultan of Delhi. Chonda's son Ranmal, who was in Mewar, sent Pancholi Khimsi from Chitor, with 500 cavalry and 400 infantry against Saleem Khan. Khimsi, by a stratagem, killed Saleem Khan and took Ajmer. Ajmer thus came under Maharana Mokal. Col. Tod says: Maharana Mokal (1420 to 1433) "took Ajmer[2] and Sambhar from the Sultan of Delhi". Maharana Mokal gave the village of Bandanwara near Ajmer, for the upkeep of the Eklingji temple in Mewar.

Ajmer remained under the Maharana till 1455 A.D., when war broke out between the Maharana of Mewar and Mahmud Khilji, Sultan of Mandoo. The Sultan, sending the bulk of his army towards Mandsaur to keep the Maharana engaged, himself attacked Ajmer. Gajadhar Singh,[3] the governor of Ajmer, defended Taragarh for four days; and then, despising the enemy's forces, came out of the fort and attacked the Sultans' army. In the action, he was killed. As his men retired into the fortress, the Sultan's men mixed themselves amongst the Rajputs and entered the fort, and took possession of it. The Sultan appointed Khwaja Naimatullah with the title of Saifkhan, governor of Ajmer.

1. *Maharana Kumbha*, p. 26-27. 2. Tod's Rajasthan, Vol II, p. 16.
3. Ferishta's *History of India*, Vol. II, p. 222.

Maharana Kumbha recaptured Ajmer after a few months, when he went to Nagor to place Shamskhan on the throne there. Ajmer, however, appears to have been taken again by the Sultan of Mandoo after Maharana Kumbha's death.

Bir Singh, ruler of Merta and brother of Rao Santal of Marwar, attacked Sambhar. On this, Mallu Khan, governor of Ajmer, with Siryakhan and Mir Ghadula, officers of the Sultan of Mandoo, invaded Merta in 1491 A.D. Bir Singh fled to Jodhpur. Mullukhan captured the *Tijnias*[1] of Pipar. Pipar being a part of Marwar, Rao Santal of Marwar with his brother Duda, Bar Singh and Varjang Bhinot came with an army to release them. A battle was fought at *Kosana* between Rao Santal and Mallukhan and Mir Ghadula. Duda attacked Siryakhan, and Santal killed Mir Ghadula. Mallukhan and Mir Ghadula were defeated, and the *Tijnias* were released. The custom of young girls carrying a *Ghadula*[2] on Chaitra vadi 8th, has come into vogue since then.

In 1505 A.D., Prince Prithviraj, the eldest son of Maharana Raimal of Chitor, attacked Ajmer, slew the governor Mallukhan, and carried the citadel of *Garh Beetli* (Taragarh) by assault, thus restoring it to Mewar.[3]

Daulat Khan, ruler of Nagor having been defeated by Maldeva, took shelter in Ajmer. In 1533 A.D., Bahadur Shah of Gujrat, during his expedition against Chitor, sent Shamsherul Mulk with a large force to reduce the fortress of Ajmer,[4] and appears to have succeeded in doing so. But this acquisition was short-lived; for, in less than two year's time, Rao Viramdeva of Merta, drove out the Gujrat governor and took possession of Ajmer in 1535 A.D. Ajmer, however, was too great a prize to be left in the possession of a minor chieftain. Rao Maldeva, King of Mandor (Marwar), asked for it. Viramdeva declined to give it Maldeva attacked Merta and drove out Viramdeva, who took up residence at Ajmer. Viramdeva then attacked Riyan in Marwar. Maldeva sent reinforcements, and Viramdeva was defeated. Maldeva sent Kupa and Jaita, his army Chiefs, to take Ajmer. Viramdeva fought with great bravery, but was driven out of Ajmer in 1535. Maldeva gave Ajmer as *jagir* to Kupawat Mahesh Gharsinghot.

1. Married women go outside the town to worship Siva's wife, Gauri, on Chaitra vadi 3rd. As this worship takes place on Tij, or the 3rd of Chaitra, these women are called, Tijnias.

2 To commemorate this defeat, young girls carry an earthern pot called Ghadula, with innumerable holes in it and a lamp inside it, to personify Mir Ghadula, who had received innumerable wounds and died of them. The girls throw the Ghadula into a tank.

3. Tod's Rajasthan, Vol. I, pp., 633-4. 4. Bayley's Gujrat, p. 371.

Merta, Lachman Bhadawat, Prithviraj Kupawat and othe Sardars to assist Haji Khan, himself remaining in Jaitaran The Maharana advanced with an army and came to Harmara Raja Kalyanmal of Bikaner and Jaimal of Merta were witl him. Against the advice of his military chiefs, the Maharan attacked Haji Khan at once. A battle was fought on Falgur *krishna* 9th, S. 1613 = 24 January, 1557 at Harmara[1] in th vicinity of Ajmer. Rao Durga was wounded, and as an arrov struck the Maharana, his army took to flight. Rao Tej Singl ·Dungersinghot, Balisa Suja, Dodiya Bhim, Chondawat Chhita and other Mewar sardars were killed. Haji Khan retaine Ajmer. Maldeva attacked Merta and took it on Falgan vad 12th. He destroyed the old town and founded a new one nea Kindal.

After sometime, Akbar's army under Kasim Khar Nishapuri came to take Ajmer. Haji Khan, deeming discre· tion the better part of valour, evacuated Ajmer and went awa to Marwar, where Maldeva gave him shelter in the villag Latoda in the Jaitaran pargannah.

III—MUGHAL PERIOD

Akbar's general Kasim Khan Nishapuri obtained peacefu possession of Ajmer.[2] There is difference of opinion witl regard to the date of this event. Mr. Elphinstone, in his *History of India*,[3] says:—"In the third year (March, 1858 tc March, 1859 A.D.) he (Akbar) acquired Ajmer without a battle." The *Akbarnama*[4] says: "Ajmer was taken in the first year of Akbar's reign (March, 1856 to March, 1857.)" Dr. Vincent Smith in his *Akbar, the Great Mughal*, says (p. 449) that Ajmer fell into Akbar's hands in 1556-57 A.D. Dr. Beni Prasad, in his '*History of Jahangir*', p. 244, says:—"Ajmer had been annexed to the Mughal Empire in 1561 A. D." As the battle of Harmara was fought early in 1557 and Akbar sent an expedition from Ajmer against Jaitaran on Chaitra vadi 9th, s. 1616 (1559) under Hashim and Qasim, and Raja Bharmal of Jaipur, Jugmal and Prithviraj Kachhwaha, and

1. Muhnot Nainsi's *khyat*, Vol. I., p. 56. Elliot's History of India, Vol. VI.p. 22.
2. The *Maasirul Umra* says (Vol. II, p. 375) that Sayad Mahmud Khan Barha was appointed by Akbar to attack Haji Khan and take Ajmer and Nagor.
3. Page 489.
4. Elliot's History of India, Vol. VI, p. 22.

Jaimal and Isar, sons of Viramdeva of Merta; and again on Ashadh vadi 5th, s. 1616, sent Pir Muhammad, who looted fifteen villages of Merta; it is clear that Ajmer fell into Akbar's hands between 1557 and 1559 A. D. The probable time is, March, 1558 to March, 1559.

On Falgun vadi 15th, s. 1616 (1560 A.D.), Jaimal son of Viramdeva took Akbar's army under Mir Jahan and laid siege to Malkot (Merta). Maldeva's forces came out of the fort on Chaitra sudi 2nd, 1617 (1761 A D.) and fought gallantly, but were defeated. Jaimal regained Merta.

Emperor Akbar made Ajmer the head-quarters for his operations in Rajputana and Gujrat. He made it a *subha*, making Jaipur, Jodhpur, Bikaner, Jaisalmer and Sirohi subordinate to it. According to the *Ain-i-Akbari*, the length of the Ajmer *subah* was 336 miles, and breadth 300 miles; and it was bounded by Agra, Delhi, Multan and Gujrat. It contained 7 Sarcars and 197 Parganahs, with a total revenue of 28,61,37,968 *dams*,[1] or Rs. 72,10,038-14-9, out of the total revenue of the empire of Rs. 28,38,19,161.[2] The subah was to furnish 86,500 cavalry and 347,000 infantry,[3] of which Ajmer Sarcar containing 28 Mahals, was to contribute 16,000 cavalry and 80,000 infantry. The revenue of the Ajmer Sarcar was 6,21,83,890 *dams*, or Rs. 31,09,169-8.[4]

During the sixth year of Akbar's reign, in 1561 A.D., Akbar came to Ajmer and sent an expedition, under Mirza Sharafuddin Husain, Jagirdar of Ajmer, against Merta, which was held by the celebrated Jai Mal. In 1563 A.D., Mirza Sharafuddin, who had become Amirul Umra, revolted, and leaving Delhi, came to Ajmer and fortified the place. Akbar sent Husain Kuli Beg Khan to remonstrate with him and take him back to court, but to punish him if he did not submit. When Sharafuddin heard of it, he left Tarkhan Diwana in Ajmer and went away towards Jalor (Marwar). The imperial forces invested Ajmer, and after two or three days, Tarkhan Diwana capitulated.[5]

In the twelfth year of his reign, Akbar came to Ajmer on 7th Ramzan, H. 974 (Sunday, 6th March, 1568 A.D.),[6] and after staying two days, returned to Delhi. In the fourteenth year of his reign (11th March, 1570—11th March, 1571) he came to Ajmer on foot, walking twelve to fourteen miles every day, as a

1. Blockman's *Ain-i-Akbari*, Vol. II, p. 272.
2. *Chronicles of the Pathan Kings of Delhi*, pp. 433-34.
3. Blockman's *Ain-i-Akbari*, Vol. II, p. 272
4. Ibid.
5. Elliot's *History of India*, Vol. V, page 283.
6. Count Noer's *Akbar*, Vol. II, p. 170.

Viramdeva, thus ousted from his dominions, went to the Sultan of Mandoo for help against Maldeva. Meeting with no success, he went to Sher Shah Sur, who had defeated Humayan and become King of Delhi. He persuaded him to invade Marwar.

Sher Shah started from Agra with an army of 80000 horse in January, 1544 A.D. News of this, was sent by Kupa, who held the fief of Didwana, to Jodhpur. The Sardars rejoiced at the prospect of a war, and gave the messenger, rich rewards. Umande, Queen of Maldeva well known in history as the *Ruthi Rani* (the offended queen), who was at the time in Garh Beetli at Ajmer, wrote to her husband Maldeva, to leave the defence of the fortress to her, and himself go to defend Jodhpur. Maldeva wrote back, asking her to go and defend the Jodhpur fort, and leave Ajmer to him to defend. The Ruthi Rani then went towards Jodhpur. Maldeva came to Ajmer with 50,000 men, but fell back on Girri to take up a better position.

Sher Shah used to dig trenches and throw up redoubts around his camp. When, however, he reached the sandy tracts of Marwar, he could not throw up redoubts; at the suggestion of his son, he ordered the ground to be fortified by surrounding it with piles of sand bags. This form of protection is now extensively employed in Europe in war-time.

Sher Shah remained in the neighbourhood of Ajmer facing Maldeva for a month, (*Tabqati Akbari*, pp. 231-32) and (Qanungo's *Shershah*, p. 323). He, however, soon repented of his rashness in invading Marwar. "The admirable dispositions of the Rajputs made him dread an action, and from a position when he found it impossible to retreat."[1] Despairing of success, Sher Shah thought of retiring to Delhi, but Viramdeva dissuaded him from taking that course.

Sher Shah then asked Maldeva not to fight a battle, which would entail great slaughter, but that he and Maldeva should select champions, and let them decide the issue. Maldeva accepted the challenge and selected Bida Bharmalot and informed Sher Shah. Sher Shah consulted Viramdeva, who told the Sultan that there was no one in his army to fight Bida, except himself (Viramdeva). Viramdeva was Sher Shah's chief advisor, and Sher Shah declined to take the risk of losing Viram. He was then in despair. On this, Viramdeva, who knew Rao Maldeva's character, said that he would

1. Tod's Rajasthan, vol. II, p. 23, Calcutta edition, 1879 A.D.

have recourse to a stratagem and the Rao would flee. By forged letters, he would make Maldeva suspect his army chiefs and retire to Jodhpur. The stratagem[1] succeeded. Maldeva retired to Jodhpur; but Kupa, Jaita and others refused to fall back and fought a battle on Paush sudi 11th, s. 1660 (1544 A.D.). Their irresistible charge evoked great admiration in Sher Shah, who, when all was over, exclaimed, that he had almost lost the kingdom of Hindustan for a handful of *Bajri*.

Sher Shah sent troops to take Jodhpur, but himself returned from Merta to Ajmer in March, 1544. *Tarikhi Daudi*[2] is the only history which mentions Sher Shah's visit to Ajmer. It says (p. 238) that Sher Shah came to Ajmer and paid a visit to the Dargah Khwaja Sahib and went up to Taragarh to enjoy the scenery.

On the decline of the Sur dynasty, Haji Khan, took possession of Ajmer. Haji Khan, a slave of Sultan Sher Shah Sur, on being defeated by Akbar's general Nasirul Mulk Pir Muhammad Khan Sarvani at Alwar, came to Ajmer and took possession of it in 1556 A. D. As he plundered some villages of Marwar, Rao Maldeva sent an army under Prithviraj Jaitawat to attack Ajmer. Haji Khan appealed to Maharana Udai Singh of Chitor for help, acknowledging his suzerainty. The Maharana came with five thousand cavalry. The Marwar forces were defeated, and Prithviraj fell back on Bagdi (a village in Marwar near Sojat). Rao Surjan Hara of Bundi and Rao Jaimal Mertia and Rao Durga Sisodia were present in the Maharana's army. Rao Maldeva, in retaliation, attacked Merta, as Rao Jaimal of Merta had assisted Haji Khan. But he was defeated. Later, Maharana Udai Singh sent Tej Singh son of Dungar Singh and Balisa Suja, in spite of the protests of his sardars, to Haji Khan at Ajmer and demanded as price of his aid against Rao Maldeva, forty maunds of gold and a beautiful dancing girl named Rang Rai, who was in Haji Khan's keeping. Haji-Khan declined to surrender her saying, that she was his wife, and that he had no gold.

As he incurred the Maharana's displeasure by this refusal, Haji Khan now appealed to Rao Maldeva for help against the Maharana. Rao Maldeva sent fifteen hundred horsemen with Devidas Jaitawat, Rawal Meghraj, Jugmal son of Viramdeva of

1. The *Tarikhi Daudi* describes on page 97, the stratagem.

2. I could not get *Tarikhi Daudi* in India, and had to write to Dr. Codrington of the Royal Asiatic Society of Great Britain & Ireland, London, for it. At his request Mr. Edwards of the British Museum, London, very kindly had two pages of the book containing an account of this visit, photographed and sent to me. I am beholden to him for this. I must acknowledge my obligations both to Mr. Edwards and Dr. Codrington. *Tarikhi Daudi* was written by Abdullah during the reign of Jahangir.

EMPEROR AKBAR.

EMPEROR JAHANGIR.

EMPEROR SHAH JAHAN.

pilgrim to the shrine of Khwaja Muinuddin Chisti, in consequence of the birth of Mirza Salim (Jahangir) in fulfilment of a vow, Akbar had taken that he would come on foot to pay homage to the Khwaja, if a son was born to him. He left Agra on 20th January, 1570 and arrived at Ajmer on 5th February, 1570.[1] From 1570 to 1582 A.D., Akbar visited Ajmer every year; but after 1582, he never came to visit the Dargah, though he lived till 1605 A.D.

On 1st April, 1576 A.D. Akbar sent from Ajmer, Kunwar Man Singh against the celebrated Maharana Pratap of Mewar, who never submitted to Akbar. It was during this compaign that, as the following couplet says, K. Man Singh of Amber nearly lost his life at the hands of the Rana:

बाही राण प्रतापसी बखतर में बरछी। जाणे झींगर जाल में मुंह काडे मच्छी ॥

TRANSLATION:—Rana Pratap pierced the armour (of Man Singh) with his spear; it looked as if a fish had thrust its head through the net.

Jahangir, who succeeded Akbar, came to Ajmer in 1613 A.D., and made it the base of his operations against Maharana Amar Singh the son of Rana Pratap of Mewar. He resided here for three years (December 1613-1616 A.D.)[2] It was while the Emperor was in Ajmer that he conferred the title of Shah Jahan on his son, Prince Khurram, and the title of Nur Jahan on his favourite empress, Nur Mahal. Dara Shikoh, the eldest son of Shah Jahan, was born in Ajmer during Jahangir's residence here in December, 1615 A.D.; and it was at Ajmer in 1659 A.D., that he lost the throne.

When Jahangir came to Ajmer in 1613, Maharaja Sur Singh and K. Guj Singh of Jodhpur also came to Ajmer. One day, Raja Kishen Singh of Kishengarh complained to Jahangir, that Rathor Gopal Das, his brother, had been killed by Bhati Govind Das. Jahangir said, "you kill Govind Das." Kishen Singh said "Govind Das was Maharaja Sur Singh's Sardar." The king said, "Go and kill him there." Then on Jeth sudi 8th., s. 1671 (A.D. 1613) Kishen Singh with his followers went to Govind Das's tent in Maharaja Sur Singh's camp and killed Govind Das Bhati. Sur Singh was asleep. The noise awoke him. When he heard of Govind Das's murder, K. Guj Singh was sent in pursuit. They overtook the enemy

1. *Akbarnama*, Vol. II, p. 511.

1. That Jahangir was a pleasure-loving man rather than religious, is clear from the fact that though he lived in the city of Ajmer for three years, he seldom went to the shrine of Khwaja Muinuddin Chishti. He says in his autobiography (Vol I, p. 341.) "While at Ajmer, I visited *nine times* the mausoleum of the revered Khwaja, and *fifteen times* went to look at the Pushkar Lake; to the Chashma i-Nur, I went 38 times; I went out to hunt tigers, fifty times. I killed 15 tigers, 1 cheetah, 1 black ear (lynx), 53 Nilgao, 33 gazzalle, 90 antelopes, 80 boars and 340 water fowl."

on the way to Kishengarh and slew Raja Kishen Singh.[1] Maharaja Sur Singh was sent from Ajmer to Mewar to assist Prince Khurrum. In 1615, the Maharaja again went to Ajmer and presented two elephants and 100 Mohars and Rs. 43000/- to Jahangir.

Sir Thomas Roe came to Ajmer on 23rd December 1615 A. D. as ambassador from King James I of England to the court of the Great Mughal, and stayed at Ajmer for nearly a year to negotiate a treaty granting freedom of trade to the English East India Company. His first interview with Jahangir took place on 19th January, 1616. It is well known that though he was received with his usual courtesy by the emperor, his mission proved a failure.[2] Jahangir does not even mention Sir Thomas Roe or his mission in his Memoirs.

There was an English factory under Master Edwards at Ajmer (subordinate to that at Surat) when Roe arrived here. Tom Coryat, the "odcombian leg stretcher," had arrived in Ajmer in June, 1615 A. D.; and while[3] here, he wrote and published his pamphlet entitled, "Thomas Coryat, Traveller for the English wits: Greeting, from the Court of the Great Mughal at Asmer," London, 1616 A. D." In July, 1615, another traveller, Mr. Withingdon came to Ajmer.[4] On 19th August, 1616 A. D., Rev. John Hall, the minister in attendance on Sir Thomas Roe, died—probably the second European who died in Ajmer, the first being John Middenhall, English traveller who died in June, 1514.[5]

In 1616 A. D., Jahangir, while at Ajmer, gave K. Gajsingh, Jalor, which was in the possession of the Behari Mussalmans. Gajsingh attacked them. The Pathans fled to Palanpur, and founded the present dynasty of Nawabs there.

Shah Jahan succeeded Jahangir, on the latter's death, on 28th October, 1627 A. D. Shah Jahan was in Ajmer[6], having come out of his sanctuary at Udaipur, when the news of Jahangir's death reached him. He at once raised his standards and declared his succession. In 1632, Shah Jahan appointed Raja Bithaldas Gor, *faujdar* of Ajmer, and in 1634, *Subedar*

1. *Muasirul Umra*, Vol. I., p. 402.

2. For a full account of the doings of Sir Thomas Roe at Ajmer, see "The Embassy of Sir Thomas Roe."

3. Tom Coryat remained in Ajmer for fourteen months.—Foster's *Early Travels in India*, p. 236 4. Ibid, p. 194.

5. Foster's *Early Travels in India*, p. 52. Also. Crofton's *Inscriptions on Tombs and Monuments in Rajputana and Central India*. He was buried in Agra as he was a Roman Catholic. Thomas Kerridge, afterwards president at Surat; reached Ajmer on the day of Middenhall's death.

6. *Muasirul Umra*, Vol II, p. 213.

(governer) of Ajmer. In 1654 A.D., Shah Jahan sent an army under Asadullahkhan to destroy the repaired bastions of Chitor and himself came to Ajmer. The *Muasirul Umra* says that he sent Alami Saadullahkhan from Ajmer to do so.[1] Shah Jahan used to stay at Ajmer in the palaces on the Ana Sagar embankment, where he constructed five marble pavilions and apartments for the harem.[2] During Shah Jahan's time, the revenue of the Ajmer subah, according to the *Shah Jahan Nama*, was one and half crores of rupees.

THE BATTLE OF AJMER.

A historic battle was fought between Aurangzeb and Dara Shikoh at the mouth of the *Chashma* valley and the feet of the eastern spurs of the hills crowned by the celebrated Gurh Beetli (Taragarh) fortress of Ajmer on 11, 12 and 13 March, 1659 A.D.

In 1657 A.D., Emperor Shah Jahan became seriously ill at Agra, and rumours spread all over the country that Shah Jahan was dead or dying. Prince Dara Shikoh, the heir-apparent did his best to allay alarm, which appeared everywhere on rumours that the succession would be disputed. Dara Shikoh's three younger brothers, Shuja, Aurangzeb and Murad Baksh who were in Bengal, Deccan and Gujrat respectively, marched towards the capital, Agra, each claiming the throne. After the battles of Fatehabad and Samugarh, Dara Shikoh was driven out of Agra, and Aurangzeb imprisoned his own father Emperor Shah Jahan, who remained interned in a building in the Agra Fort till his death in 1664 A.D.

Dara, a fugitive in Gujrat, hearing that Maharaja Jaswant Singh of Jodhpur had deserted Aurangzeb and returned to Jodhpur, appealed to him for help. He advised Dara to proceed to Ajmer, so that Rajputs from all sides may go to his side. Dara started for Ajmer. He sent Thakur Dubin Singh from Merta to Jaswant Singh, who was ten miles from Jodhpur. Jaswant Singh said that his army was not assembled and he was waiting for his men. Tartib Khan, Nazim of Ajmer, was powerless to oppose Dara. He evacuated Ajmer before Dara's arrival, when he heard of it and went and joined the Emperor.

1. *Muasirul Umra*, Vol. II, p. 447.

2. According to the *Muasirul Umra*, Vol II., p. 816. Shah Jahan spent ten lakhs on the buildings in Ajmer and Ahmedabed; fifty lakhs on the Taj Mahal, Agra; fifty two lakhs, on other buildings in Agra; fifty lakhs on the Delhi fort (Lal Killa); ten lakhs on the Jama Masjid at Delhi; fifty lakhs on buildings at Lahore; twelve lakhs on buildings in Kabul; eight lakhs on buildings in Kashmir; and eight lakhs on buildings in Kandahar.

Hearing that Maharaja Jaswant Singh had promised support to Dara Shikoh, Aurangzeb asked Jai Singh of Jaipur to detach Jaswant Singh from Dara. Jai Singh, who was Dara's enemy owing to an affront[1] publicly administered by Dara, and was determined to compass his ruin, sent messengers to Jaswant Singh and cajoled him to desert Dara. The French traveller, Bernier, was in India at this time. He says that Jai Singh wrote to Jaswant Singh to say: "I, who am also a Raja, conjure you to spare the blood of Rajputs. If you leave Dara to his own resources, Aurangzeb will bury all the past in oblivion; will not reclaim the money you obtained at Khajua (near Allahabad), but will at once nominate you to the government of Gujrat. You can easily appreciate the advantage of ruling a province so contiguous to your own territories: there, you will remain in perfect quiet and security."[2]

The Jodhpur *khyat* says: "Jai Singh wrote to Jaswant Singh and informed him of Aurangzeb's request, and asked him to send a man to receive assurance from the Emperor himself. Jaswant Singh sent Angoliya (servant of the bath) Asa Madhawat. Jai Singh took him to Aurangzeb, who gave Asa, a firman with his *Panjah*,[3] giving Jaswant Singh his Munsab and territory, and asked him to return to Jodhpur and not help Dara. On Chaitra vadi 11th, the Firman came to Maharaja Jaswant Singh, and the Maharaja returned from Raodiawas to Jodhpur".

Dara again sent Dubin to Jaswant. He reached Jaswant Singh when he was twenty cos (forty miles) from Jodhpur. There he found that Jaswant was not going to join Dara and was retreating to Jodhpur. He returned to Ajmer. Dara again sent Prince Sipahar Shikoh with hundred men to bring Jaswant Singh, but in vain. Sipahar Shikoh returned to Ajmer disappointed. At last Dara had to depend upon his own forces against the army of Aurangzeb, reinforced by the forces of Jaipur and Jammu. Dara moved his force in the defiles, blocked up the roads with barriers of stone and earth, constructed *morchas* (entrenchments), distributed the bastions to his men and fortified them all with "weapons of war." Dara appointed one of his chiefs to each *morcha*. On his right hand, the first *morcha*, which was adjacent to Garh Beetli was placed under the charge of Sayad Ibrahim, (who had received the title of Mustafakhan) and Askar Khan and Jan Beg and his son who was at the time, the Commander of the Artillery. The

1. When Jai Singh appeared one day elaborately dressed in the Durbar at Delhi, Dara smiled and said Jai Singh looked like a musician. Jai Singh was offended.
2. Bernier's *Travels*, p. 86.
3. A Firman with the Emperor's *panjah* (impression of hand) is authoritative.

morcha next to it, was placed under Firoz Mewati who was one of his ablest and most reliable chiefs. Beside it, on the elevation commanding the view of the pass, a few bigger pieces of ordinance were placed, and Dara fixed his residence near that place. On his left side, a second *morcha* was constructed and Shah Nawaz Khan, his sons' attendants and relations, and Muhammad Sharif, who had been given the title of Qileej Khan and who had been appointed Pay Master General, as well as Barkandaz Khan and others were appointed to guard and protect it. Beyond this *morcha*, Sipahar Shikoh was placed in charge of another which was contiguous to the hill.

Four miles to the south of Ajmer, the hills of the Taragarh range are cleft by a narrow gorge, known as the Chashma, through which a track leads from the city, by the valley of Inderkot, west of Taragarh, to the plain of *village* Deorai. Dara occupied a position astride the entrance to this gorge, his left flank resting on the crags of Garh Beetli (Taragarh), his right on the almost equally lofty and inaccessible hill named the Kokla, and his front, (save where this was broken by the ravine of the Chashma), defended by a wall of massive masonry, a portion, probably, of the outer line of fortifications of the ancient fortress-city of Inderkot. This rampart, though its crest was dismantled and partly ruinous, was built of huge blocks of solid rock, which still at this day defy the attacks of time; and placed as it is on a commanding and well-defined ridge, it formed a most formidable obstacle to a direct assault. Dara quickly repaired it, mounted guns on the bastions, and constructed trenches and redoubts to cover the lines of approach. In this position, his communication with Ajmer, whence his army drew its supplies, was secure; he covered the weakest point of the defences of the city, that by which they have so often been penetrated, the back-door of the Inderkot valley; and he threatened the flank of his opponent, should Aurangzeb move directly on Ajmer. The natural strength of the position was very great; but its disadvantages lay in the narrow and difficult line of retreat, and in the fact that the line was cut in two by the gorge of the Chashma, which rendered it difficult to move troops from one part to another, or to reinforce a threatened flank. To compensate for this, the line was strongly posted, and the attacking force would have to advance on a narrow front, along valleys which were raked from end to end by Dara's guns. In this all but impregnable position, he could await with some degree of confidence, in spite of his inferiority in numbers, the attack of his redoubtable enemy.

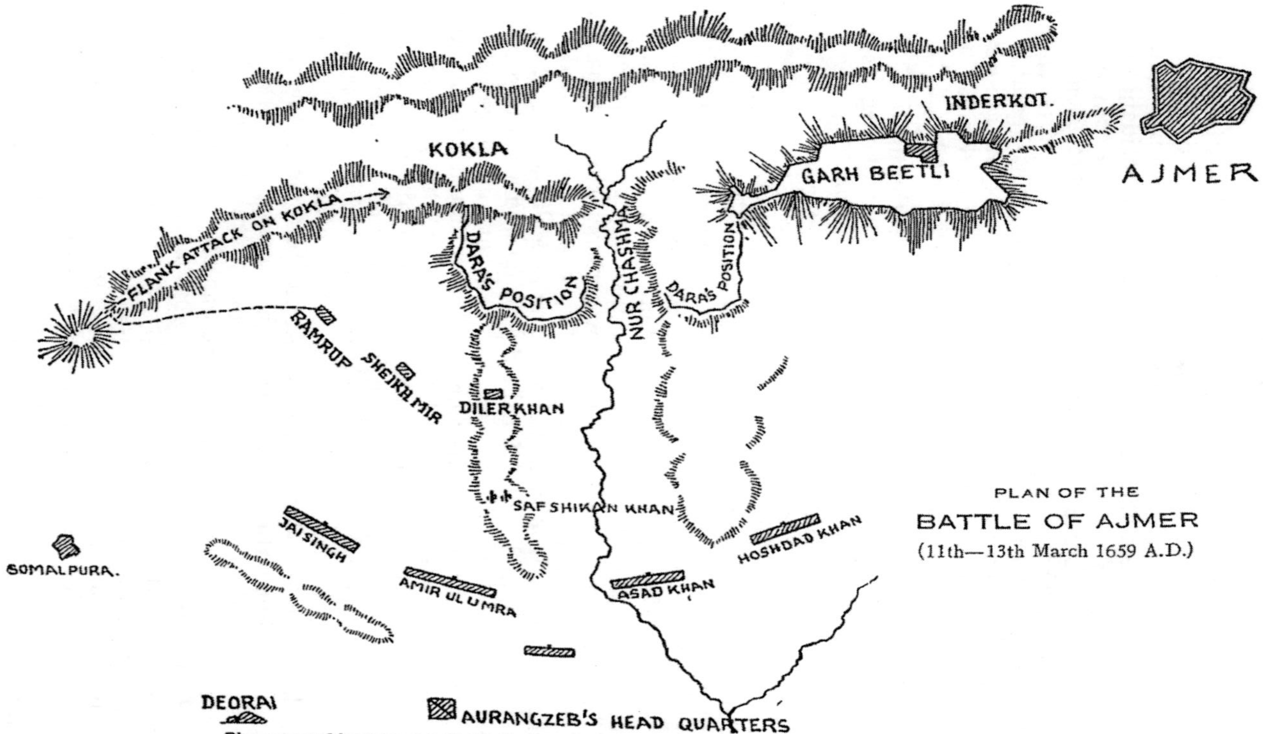

Plan prepared by Colonel J. C. M. Hoskyn, J. A. Commanding Officer, 44th Merwara Infantry, Ajmer.

Aurangzeb advanced *via* Ramsar and pitched his tents at Deorai, *four* miles from Ajmer. The artillery under Saf Shakin Khan was sent forward to take up a position in front of Dara's entrenchments. Raja Jai Singh, in command of the vanguard, took up a position to the right of Aurangzeb. Aurangzeb, on his part, cared little for advantages or disadvantages of position. Elated by his recent victories, and with an immense superiority in men, material and morale, he was confident of victory, and was only anxious to bring his adversary to bay. He hastened westward by forced marches, reached Ramsar, twenty two miles from Ajmer, on the 25th of the month (Jamadi-ul-Akhir), and the next night encamped at Deorai, two miles from Dara's position. Purdil Khan, with a piquet of 150 men, was at once sent forward to get in touch with the enemy. He advanced to a low hill, half way between the two armies, and occupied it. The enemy, discovering him at dawn, tried to dislodge him; but Aurangzeb sent up reinforcements. Dara's men were driven back; and the Imperial artillery, under the well-named Saf Shikan Khan, were speedily established on the hill, whence they opened fire at long range on the enemy's defences. A strong escort under Sheikh Mir and Diler Khan was posted to guard the artillery from a surprise attack.

Aurangzeb's army now deployed into position for a general attack. The Amir-ul-Umra and Rajah Jai Singh were posted on the left flank, facing the Kokla hill. Asad Khan and Hoshdad Khan, on the right were ordered to attack the defences north of the valley, beneath the cliffs of Garh Beetli. Owing to the narrowness of the frontal approaches to Dara's position, it was impossible to deploy the whole of the Imperial army; the remainder of it was therefore kept in reserve with Aurangzeb's head-quarters near Deorai. While these preliminary movements, which occupied nearly the whole day, were being carried out, Saf Shikan Khan carried his guns forward another three hundred yards or so, within effective range of the enemy's entrenchments.

Towards evening, the battle commenced in earnest with a heavy artillery fire on both sides, which lasted through the night and for the greater part of the next day. "The powder-smoke hung in the air like a thunder-cloud, through which the flashes of the guns shone like lightning, while the earth became sulphureous with flame and fire." The artillery duel was interrupted by the sallies of the besieged, who attacked the guns with great bravery, but were driven back to cover by storms of grape and round-shot, and whirlwinds of sword and lance. Still the general attack of Aurangzeb's army hung fire. The sight of those grim ramparts, far above them on the hillside, bristling with steel and belching fire and smoke, exercised a remarkably sedative effect on the ardour of the Imperial troops. Prudence is often the specious pretext for hesitation, and Aurangzeb's leaders excused their unwillingness to advance, on the ground that it would be wiser to wait until the artillery had done its work and effected a breach. But the ancient walls, solid as the rock on which they stood, defied bombardment; and Dara's artillery kept up a lively fire of reprisal, which did much damage to the exposed troops of the Imperial army, while his own men remained unharmed under cover. At the close of the second day's fighting, no progress at all had been made by the assailants, and the idea began to gain ground that the position was impregnable. "In the looking-glass of the hearts of Aurangzeb's generals, there was no reflection of an assault; and success did not seem attainable early or easily."

Aurangzeb now began to realise the seriousness of the situation. His careless confidence had encountered the check with which, in war, that frame of mind is so often visited. His troops were wavering. Many of the chiefs who led them were bound to him merely by loose ties of temporary policy; they followed him because they believed that his was the winning side; but secretly they admired the character, and sympathised with the misfortunes of his elder brother; and even an indecisive battle might have led to serious defections in the Imperial army. On the morning of the third day of the combat, Aurangzeb determined to make a supreme effort. He assembled his generals, rebuked them for their want of energy, and urged them to deliver a combined assault without further delay. Early the same morning, a fresh development had occurred, of which Aurangzeb was quick to avail himself, and which finally decided the issue of this doubtful struggle. Raja Ramrup, a chief from the mountains of Jammu, reported to the Emperor that some of his men, who were expert hill-men, had discovered a path by which they could ascend the Kokla hill from the south-west, in rear of Dara's position, and thus turn the enemy's right flank. A party of these men, with a company of musketeers, picked men from the Imperial body-guard, were promptly detached on this enterprise; while Raja Ramrup himself, with another party of his men, moved out to the foot of the Kokla hill, in order to withdraw the attention of the defenders on this flank from the summit of the hill. In this stratagem, he was rather more successful than he bargained for; for, seeing this small body of troops apparently isolated, a thousand horsemen suddenly swept out from behind the defenders' lines and charged down the slopes upon them. The men of Jammu were no match, in the open, for mail-clad men-at-arms. They gave way in confusion, and Raja Ramrup would have been cut to pieces with his party; but at this moment, the whole of the Imperial army, their leaders smarting under Aurangzeb's fiery reproaches, commenced a general forward movement; and the sally was quickly recalled. Diler Khan and Sheikh Mir led the attack, the former advancing from the artillery position along the spur, which forms the southern boundary of the Chashma valley, while Sheikh Mir advanced up the valley on the left of the guns. The two wings of the main army, under Raja Jai Singh and the Amir-ul-Umra on the left, and Asad Khan and Hoshdad Khan on the right, also moved forward as if to make a general attack along the whole line. The parties led by Diler Khan and Sheikh Mir converged on the south-eastern salient, the weakest point of Dara's line, where Shah Nawaz Khan, the father-in-law of Aurangzeb, held command. Here for a hundred yards or so, the ground in front of the rampart is level, forming a neck where the long spur springs from the main hill. Across this level ground, the Imperialists, gallantly led, again and again hurled themselves on the rampart, while the guns from the ridge behind them poured a hail of cannon balls over their heads into the enemy's position. The desperate attack began to make an impression. Shah Nawaz Khan was killed by a cannon-ball.[1] His son, Sayadad Khan, was wounded. The storm of shot, sweeping over the hillside, prevented Dara from moving reinforcements to the threatened point. On the attacking side, Sheikh Mir, who was sitting on an elephant and encouraging his men, was shot; but a retainer, who was in the howdah with him, supported the dead body of his chief in a life-like posture until the struggle was over. The slaughter among the assailants, was great; but the valour and resolution of Diler Khan and his Afghans were not to be denied. Battered, crushed, and decimated, they clung like limpets to the wall; and at last succeeded in effecting a lodgment within that terrible rampart.

Dara with his son, Sipahar Shikoh, was standing on an eminence in the centre of his line, whence he could command a view of the whole battle-field. Seeing the

1. He was buried in the courtyard of the Dargah Khwaja Sahib at Ajmer.

success of Diler Khan on his right flank, and the approach of Jai Singh who was moving up in support, he concluded hastily that the battle was going against him. The situation was indeed critical, but not desperate. The centre and left of his line were not even seriously threatened, and he still had 7,000 men in reserve. A swift counter-attack might have driven the exhausted troops of Diler Khan from their position, before Jai Singh, whose advance was unaccountably slow, could arrive to help him. But, while Dara stood there, "taking counsel of his fears", a wild shouting and firing from the summit of the Kokla hill announced that the enemy had seized that point of vantage, from which they threatened his right rear and his line of retreat. This new disaster decided the issue in Dara's mind. Unlike Aurangzeb, he had not the resolution to make a supreme effort to avert defeat. No doubt the strain of three days' fighting had told on his nerves. Perhaps, also, since the defection of Jaswant, he had expected to lose, and resigned himself easily to the inevitable decree of *kismet*. In the gathering dusk he stole away, leaving his unbeaten army to its fate. Not even venturing to return to Ajmer, where his *harem* and treasure loaded on elephants and ready for the worst, were awaiting news of the battle, he fled westward over the hills towards Merta. The harem followed him.

Meanwhile, the night fell upon a scene of the utmost confusion. Aurangzeb's generals did not at first realise the extent of their success. Diler Khan had indeed pierced the enemy's line, but his position was precarious. Sheikh Mir's troopers had discovered the death of their leader, and had forthwith lost all discipline and dispersed in search of plunder. Jai Singh's advance was still marked by extreme deliberation. On the right, Asad Khan and Hoshdad Khan had not ventured to press home their attack, and the defending troops on that flank had been idle spectators of the struggle on the left. But with the flight of Dara, all was lost. As the fatal news passed from man to man, the stubborn ranks which had held their ground for three days melted into a spate of undisciplined humanity, which quickly blocked the narrow gorge, their only road of escape. For, with the arrival of Jai Singh, at last it was apparent that resistance was at an end; and a general slaughter began, which lasted far into the night.

Thus ended the battle which, but for Jaswant Singh's defection and desertion, would have finally defeated Aurangzeb; and Marwar, Jaswant Singh's country, would have been spared the horrors of the Thirty Years' War. Who knows but that, if Dara had succeeded Shah Jahan on the throne, the Hindus would not have been alienated, and the Mughal empire lasted much longer. It is vain and futile to consider what course history would have taken, had Aurangzeb's religious bigotry not reacted on the Sikhs, the Mahrattas and the Rajputs in the way it did. Jaswant Singh's backsliding and Aurangzeb's intolerant bigotry changed the course of history; and, while the former's indefensible conduct eventually brought ruin to his country; the latter's intolerant bigotry shattered to pieces the empire which the Great Akbar had wisely built with the help of the Rajputs.

Dara retired towards Ahmedabad with his son, his harem, and Firoz Mewati. His generals continued to fight and some hours passed before Dara's flight became known. It was during this flight from Ajmer that the French traveller Bernier met Dara.[1] The French jeweller, Tavernier, who was in India at the time, says:—

> "As he (Dara) approached Ahmedabad, Monsieur Bernier, a French physician, who was on his way to Agra to visit the Court of the Great Mughal ....was of great assistance to one of the wives of this prince, who was attacked with erysipelas in one leg. Dara Shah having heard that an accomplished European physician was at hand, sent immediately for him, and Monsieur Bernier went to his tent, where he saw this lady, examined into her ailment, for which he gave a remedy and quick relief." [1]
>
> Bernier himself thus mentions the incident: "I had now been three days with Dara, whom I met on the road by the strangest chance imaginable; and being destitute of any medical attendant, he compelled me to accompany him in the capacity of physician............During the time that I remained in this prince's retinue, we marched, nearly without intermission, day and night; so insupportable was the heat and so suffocating the dust, that of the three large oxen of Gujrat which drew my carriage, one had died, another was in a dying state, and the third was unable to proceed from fatigue. Dara felt anxious to retain me in service, especially as one of his wives had a bad wound in her leg; yet neither his threats nor entreaties could procure for me a single horse, ox or camel, so destitute of power and influence had he become. I remained behind, therefore, because of the absolute impossibility of continuing the journey." [2]

All his brothers, having been disposed of there was nobody left to bar Aurangzeb's way to the throne of India, except his father Emperor Shah Jahan himself, who had been in occupation of it for thirtytwo years, but who was now powerless and friendless. Aurangzeb, therefore, imprisoned Shah Jahan and kept him in close confinement in an apartment in the fort of Agra, where he was subjected to great privations. Shah Jahan lingered in prison for seven years, when death relieved

1. Tavernier's Travels, Vol. I, p. 349.
2. Bernier's Travels, pp. 90-91.

him of his sufferings. On one occasion, as the place he lived in was locked up every evening and opened only the next morning, there was no water in his room, and Shah Jahan passed the night in great thirst. Next morning, he sent the following couplet to Aurangzeb:

آفرین باد هندواں هر باب   مردہ را دهند دایم آب
اے پسر تو عجب مسلمانی   زندہ را باب ترسانی

TRANSLATION:—The Hindus be praised in every way that they give water all their lives even to the dead: Thou, O son, art a strange Mussalman; thou deprived the living (father) of water.[1]

The inhuman treatment accorded to Shan Jahan by his son Aurangzeb, brings home to people the vicissitudes of life from which even the highest are not exempt. Whether Aurangzeb in his treatment of his father acted as a good Mussalman or a bad one, though his father reproaches him with being the latter, Shah Jahan with his past had little reason to complain of the hard fate which met him in the last years of his life. If lust of power impelled Aurangzeb to kill his brothers and dethrone and imprison his father, Shah Jahan himself was deeply dyed with similar guilt. The couplet current in Rajputana recounts how he waded through blood to the throne :

सवल सगाई नहीं गिरणे, नहीं सबलासुं सीर । खुरम अठारह मारिया, कै काका कै वीर ॥

TRANSLATION :—The powerful respect no relationship: nor do they share power with others who are also powerful. (Prince) Khurrum (Shah Jahan) murdered eighteen (people), either uncles or brothers and cousins.

"How do you", wrote, Aurangzeb, the embodiment of filial duty, in one of his letters to his captive father, "still regard the memony of Khusrau and Parvez, whom you did to death before your accession, and who had threatened no injury to you."—Sir J. N. Sarkar's *History of Aurangzeb*, Vol. III, p. 155. Whether it was poetic justice that was meted out to Shah Jahan or not, the mind contemplates with awe, the lot of those born in the purple in the Mughal times. What a wonderful advance, however, has the world witnessed since. Not three hundred years have passed since Aurangzeb's usurpation of the throne, in circumstances repugnant to the mind, and what an amazing change in social and political conditions has occurred in countries, where people have won their freedom and cast off the chains of despotism. In the seventeenth century, a designing, intriguing, artful prince filled with lust for power, kills his brothers and imprisons his father

1. Shah Jahan here alludes to the yearly *Tarpan* of the Hindus.

to usurp a throne, and the people, the chief party concerned in the matter of government, stand stupified and helpless. The twentieth century, when still young, presents the amazing spectacle of a lawful sovereign, popular and loved, compelled to resign his kingship, surrender his throne, and retire into private life in deference to the views and prejudices of his people, because he insisted on marrying a divorced woman, which outraged the sentiments of the ruling class in Britain.

The Mughal, or correctly speaking, the Turkish Empire in India began with the accession of Akbar to the throne in 1556, and may be said to have come to an end with the death of Bahadur Shah in 1712 A D. Though the tradition of the Empire lingered on for another fifty years, the reality ended with the last *few gasps* with the reign of Bahadur Shah (1707 to 1712).

During this period of about one hundred and fifty five years (from 1556 to 1712 A.D.) when the Mughal Emperors Akbar, Jehangir, Shah Jahan, and Aurangzeb and Bahadur Shah reigned in India, Ajmer enjoyed comparative peace. It was not attacked by any enemy. Its experience of war in those days was limited to the great and decisive battle fought between Dara Shikoh and Aurangzeb in 1678, the Rathor attack on Ajmer in 1679, and the fact that it was the base of military operations when Akbar, Jehangir, Shah Jahan and Aurangzeb, one after another, invaded Mewar to humble the Maharana, the *bulwark* of Rajput chivalry, as he flatly refused to bow his head to them. With the accession of Aurangzeb, the Imperial policy underwent new orientation and became imbued with religious bigotry against Hinduism. The Rajputs, with whose assistance, the Mughal Empire had been built up by Akbar, became disaffected. The death in December, 1678, at Jamrud near Peshawar, of Maharaja Jaswant Singh of Marwar, the most powerful of the Rajput Kings of the time, who had always been a thorn in Aurangzeb's side, furnished Aurangzeb with an opportunity to wreak his vengeance on Marwar. As Jaswant had left no son, the Emperor sent Khidmatguzar Khan from Delhi to be governor of the fort of Jodhpur, and himself left Delhi for Ajmer on Chaitra vadi 5, s. 1735 (February 19, 1679 A.D.) to make preparations to take possession of Jaswant's kingdom of Marwar. While he was on his way to Ajmer, he sent on 7th February, Khwaja Bahadur and Hasan Ali Khan in advance to take possession of Marwar. He called Prince Azam from Multan, Shaista Khan, Subedar of Agra, Muhammad Khan from Ujjain, Nawab Bahadur Khan, Rao Inder Singh from the Deccan, and the Subedar of Gujrat to assist him in this work. Word was sent to Jodhpur that Imperial officers were coming to take possession of Jodhpur. Reply came to the effect that, as Jaswant's Maharani was expecting, the result may be awaited. A deputation also came from Jodhpur but Aurangzeb had left Ajmer for Delhi.

While the Emperor was still in Ajmer, the Marwar Vakil at the Imperial Court informed him that the two Ranis of Jaswant Singh had given birth to two sons at Lahore. Aurangzeb laughed and said, "Man desires one thing: God does another."

Aurangzeb left Ajmer on the 7th March, 1679, leaving Bahadur Khan in charge, and encamped at Kishengarh. Bahadur Khan, Subedar of Ajmer, who understood the Rajputs well, recommended to the Emperor that Jodhpur be given to Ajit Singh. The Emperor turned down his request, and ordered him to stay in Ajmer. Bahadur Khan sent his son from Ajmer to Delhi with the Rathor deputation that had come from Jodhpur, to plead for the Rathors.

The deputation with Bahadur's son, reached Delhi in April, 1679. On 10 June, 1679, the Emperor gave Jodhpur to Rao Inder Singh. The Emperor ordered the Jodhpur people, who were in the Jodhpur House at Delhi, to vacate it. A few of the Rathors shifted to the Kishangarh House in Delhi, and the rest left for Jodhpur.

The two queens of Jaswant Singh had given birth to two sons at Lahore, and the boys were named Ajit Singh and Dalthamban. Ajit Singh was born of the Yadav Rani, Jaskanwar, daughter of Raja Chhatra Singh of Harauti. When the Ranis came to Delhi from Lahore, Aurangzeb, placed guards round the Jodhpur House to see that the two infant sons of Jaswant Singh were not taken away. Being convinced of the evil designs of Aurangzeb, the two boys were smuggled out of the House, by Gokaldas Khichi disguised as a snake charmer, and sent to Marwar with the Bagheli Thakurani of Rathor Mohkam Singh, son of Jagat Singh under the charge of Mukand Das Khichi. The *Ajitodaya* says that this brave lady gave her baby daughter to Ajitsingh's nurse and took Ajit Singh and went to Jodhpur. Dalthamban died on the way, and Ajitsingh was sent to the village of Kalindiri in Sirohi territory to the house of Jaideva Pushkarna (Jagguji), as his wife was a *Pativrata*. Khichi Mukand Das disguised as a *sannyasi* took up his residence in the neighbourhood to keep a watch on the young Maharaja. Ajit was brought up by Jaideva.

In Delhi, Aurangzeb sent the City kotwal, Faulad Khan Siddhi, to demand the surrender of Ajit and his brother. The Kotwal, with twenty thousand men and artillery, surrounded the Rathor Camp. The Rathors came out, placed the two Ranis on horseback and fell on the Imperial forces. When hard pressed, Jodha Chandra Bhan killed the Ranis to prevent their falling into the hands of the enemy. The battle was fierce and bloody, and is said to have been fought outside the Delhi Gate. Five hundred of the Imperial army were killed and seven hundred wounded. The Rathors under the leadership of Durga Das, Rup Singh and Ranchod Das with three hundred men, cut their way through the Mughal forces and departed for Marwar. Aurangzeb ordered every house in Delhi to be searched for Ajit and Dalthamban.

News of this event reached Jodhpur in July, 1679, and the Rathors prepared to attack the Jodhpur fort, in which there were Rahim Khan, Tahir Beg Fozdar and Dindar Khan Qazi, and two hundred Muslims. Rahim fled to Nagor. Tahir Beg and Dindar Khan surrendered to the Rajputs, who chivalrously sent them under an escort to Ajmer. Saadullah Khan, the Hakim of Merta, who happened to be there, was arrested and killed. The treasure in the fort was taken away by the Rajputs, who under Raj Singh now attacked Ajmer. Padshah Quli Khan, entitled Tahwar Khan, who had been appointed Fojdar of Ajmer in place of Iftikhar Khan,[1] was at Pushkar, where a battle was fought on the 19-21 August, 1679. It lasted for three days. The artillery duel was followed by archery practice and the Rajputs advanced nearer. From guns and arrows, recourse was had to small arms.[2] Tahwar Khan fled, and his army was destroyed. During the action, Raj Singh was killed by a stray shot, and the Rathors retired to Jodhpur.

Thus began the Thirty Years' War between the Rathors and Aurangzeb, which came to an end only with the death of the latter and the recovery of Jodhpur by the Rathors. Knowing well Aurangzeb and his religious bigotry, the Rathors made preparations for a long war. Jaswant Singh's other Ranis were sent to their fathers' houses, Bhatyaniji to Jaisalmer and Jadonji to Mewar. Maharana Raj Singh of Mewar prepared to join the war on the side of the Rathors. Durga Das, who had been wounded in the battle at Delhi, was under-going a cure in the village of Salwa. He went with Mukand Das Khichi to Sirohi to see the young Ajit growing up.

1. *Muasire Alamgiri*, p. 173.
2. *Muasirul Umra*, Vol. I, p. 447.

The Rathors reinforced by the Maharana's forces attacked Jalor. In November, 1679, Aurangzeb himself came to Ajmer, which he made his headquarters. From here, he sent an army against the Maharana. Fighting against this force, Gora Singh son of the famous warrior, Ballu Champawat, fell at Debari. the pass that leads to Udaipur, A Chhatree marks the place, where he fell fighting. After a month's stay in the palace on the Anasagar lake at Ajmer, Aurangzeb left for Udaipur, personally to direct the operations. Prince Akbar, who had come with his army from Meerut, joined the emperor at Deorai (four miles from Ajmer), and was sent to protect the environs of Chitor. On his return from Udaipur the emperor took up his residence in the Daulat Khana (Magazine) at Ajmer.

Prince Akbar witnessed, how, during this war, the Rajputs chivalrously released Aurangzeb, when he was hemmed in on all sides and surrender was the inevitable sequel, by themselves generously retiring and allowing Aurangzeb to escape. He (Akbar) himself had been treated chivalrously by the Rajputs. During the operations, Akbar with his harem fell into their hands. They did not touch him but escorted him to a place of safety, and then retired. Struck with admiration by the chivalrous conduct of the Rajputs in the war and comparing it with the cruelty and ruthlessness, with which his father, Aurangzeb, was carrying on the compaign against the Rajputs, Prince Akbar felt disgusted in fighting against such chivalrous foes, who had given no cause of offence whatever. He decided to make friends with the Rathors.

On the 26th Zi-l-hijj, news reached the king that Prince Akbar had gone over to the Rajputs and was advancing upon Ajmer. This greatly alarmed Aurangzeb. Baharmand Khan was appointed in command of the defence operations at Ajmer, and was instructed to erect fortifications round the small army the king had with him, and to guard the passes. Asad Khan Batlaya was appointed to guard the Pushkar Pass and Lake, and Abu Nasar Khan was appointed his deputy to keep watch towards the west of Ajmer.[1] The streets of Ajmer near the Magazine were fortified with cannon, and Hafiz Muhammad Amin, Nazim of Ahmedabad, and other officers were warned to remain under arms, ready to protect their several charges. Umdatul-Mulk was appointed to inspect the fortifications, and the vakils of the prince, Shujaat Khan and Badshah Kuli Khan, who were his advisers, were ordered to be imprisoned in

1. Muasir ul Umra, Vol. I, p. 292.

Emperor Aurangzeb.

THAKUR DURGA DAS, THE RATHOR LEADER.

Garh Beetli, (Ajmer fort) which was placed under the command of Himmat Khan.

The Rathors and Akbar started from Desuri to attack Aurangzeb at Ajmer and encamped at Budhwara, a village twenty two miles south of Ajmer, on the 17th January, 1681 A.D. Aurangzeb had only a small force with him. Tyber Khan was with Akbar. Aurangzeb ordered Inayat Khan, Tybar's father in law, to kill Tybar's family, owing to his betrayal. Inayat Khan wrote at once to Tybar who immediately left Prince Akbar and started for Ajmer. In his extremity, Aurangzeb, "had recourse to the same artifice which had raised him to empire, in order to ward off this danger. Akbar was but one day's march distant; his elder sons, Mauzum and Azim, yet far off.[1] Not a moment was to be lost: he penned a letter to his son, which by a spy was dropped in the tent of the Rajput leader Durga-Das. In this letter, he applauded a pretended scheme by which, Akbar was to fall upon them (Rajputs) when they engaged the emperor. The same scheme had saved Sher Shah in this country from king Maldeva of Marwar, and more recently, had been put in practice, with like success, in the war with Sivaji. It succeeded. The Rajputs detached themselves from the prince, who had apparently betrayed them. Tyber Khan, in despair, lost his life in an attempt to assassinate the emperor."[2]

The emperor who was at Dumada (eight miles from Ajmer, on the road to Saradhna) awaiting the result of his stratagem, now returned to Ajmer. Of the confederates of Akbar, some were imprisoned in the Gwalior and Kangra forts, Khwaja Mazhar and Mahram in Garh Beetli, Ajmer; and Qazi Khubullah, Mohammad Qayum and Mir Gulam Muhammad, after receiving corporal punishment, were also sent to the Ajmer fortress.

Akbar was asleep in his tent when the Rathors suddenly left him, without apprising him of the letter. When he awoke in the morning, he found the Rathors gone. He too hastily followed them taking his jewels, one of his wives and twenty five mistresses. The Mers of Merwara barred his way. The women and men with the prince, fought the marauders with bows and arrows but to no purpose. Eventually Akbar pur-

1. "The armies of Mauzam and Azam were advancing hastily to his aid; but Akbar was two days nearer and within one of Ajmer. This day was the 11th of January, 1681, Aurangzeb bribed the astrologer to prescribe it, and contrived a letter to be intercepted by the Commander of the Rajputs."—Orme's *Historical Fragments of the Mughal Empire*, Section I, p. 128.

2. Tod's Rajsthan, Vol. I, p. 300 (Cal. edition.)

chased his safe passage by giving the box of jewelry to the Mers. He overtook Durga Das at the village of Rabdya. Durga Das then came to know the truth of the matter. He sent his men to the Mers who restored the box of jewelry.

Aurangzeb sent Prince Alam from Ajmer to bring back Akbar. When Alam's camp was pitched at Jalor, the Rathors attacked and captured it. The emperor imprisoned Kileez Khan, and finding that Inder Singh was unequal to the task of retaining Jodhpur, took it away from him. He also took away Jalor from Ram Singh of Rutlam. Inder singh retired discomfited to Nagor on 17 April, 1681.

Prince Akbar, knowing the implacable character of his father, sought safety in flight, and asked the Rathors to help him to go to Persia. Durga Das, the great Rathor leader, escorted Prince Akbar to the Deccan. Akbar left his family with the Rathors, who sent it to Barmer and asked the Bhomias there to protect it. Akbar reached Sambhaji on 28 April, 1681 A.D. Sambhaji's man Chatkuji received Akbar on 27 April, 1681 A.D. (Jeth vadi 5th, s. 1737) at Suhalra. Durga Das stirred the Mahrattas up against the Emperor, and infused new energy in them. Durga Das remained with the Mahrattas for seven years. He rejoined Ajit Singh on Bhadrapad sudi 10, s. 1744 (6 September, 1687 A.D.).

Aurangzeb now decided to make peace with the Maharana and sent Bhim Singh with overtures to Udaipur. The Maharana accepted them. All parts of Mewar seized during the war were restored. The *Muasir-ul-Umra*, vol. I, p. 789 says that in 1680, the learned men of Burhanpur gave-up Friday prayers owing to Sambhaji having taken possession of Bahadurpura and Burhanpur, and sent an affidavit to the King that the honour of the Mussalmans had been taken away by Sambhaji. Aurangzeb left for the Deccan on the 8th September, 1681 (5th Ramzan, H. 1092) leaving Azimuddin son of Prince Shah Alam, and Vazir Asad Khan at Ajmer, instructing them to make peace also with the Rathors. Aurangzeb reached Burhanpur on 12 Ziqad, H. 1092 (1681 A.D.) He lived for twenty six years longer, but never returned to Upper India, dying at Ahmadnagar on 21 February, 1707 A.D.

On the 23rd March 1687, Ajit Singh, while yet only eight years old, emerged from his seclusion, the village of Palri, and the nobles of Marwar flocked to his standard. An attack was made on Sojat. Inayat Khan came from Jodhpur and handed over Sivana to Ajit Singh, and agreed in 1689 A.D.

to give *chouth* (one fourth of the revenue) to him throughout Marwar. Durga Das later returned from the Deccan *via* Rutlam and looted Malpura and Kekri. Aurangzeb disapproved of giving *chouth* to Ajit Singh and instructed Inayat Khan, governor of Ajmer, to capture Ajit Singh. Inayat Khan, however, died soon after, and the Viceroy of Gujrat succeeded him at Ajmer. Ajit Singh after making his *debut* and assuring the people of Marwar that their king was alive, retired to the *Chhapan-ka-pahar* in Mewar.

In 1690 (S. 1747), Shafi Khan tried to entrap Ajit Singh and asked him to come to Ajmer. Ajit came with 20,000 horse. Shafi Khan was non-plussed. The Rajputs prepared to give Ajmer to the flames. Shafi Khan gave jewels, horses and money as tribute to Ajit Singh and saved Ajmer.

On June 1692, the Subedar of Ajmer attacked Durga Das at the Bhartya village near Parbatsar, but had to retire discomfited. In January 1693, Aurangzeb still in the Deccan, tired of the war in Marwar and unable peacefully to hold possession of it, sent orders to Shafi Khan, Subedar of Ajmer, to make peace with Ajit Singh and settle his *munsab* and rank in *Hazari*. At the request of Nawab Shafi Khan, Ajit Singh came to Shamgarh near Beawar and sent Mukanddas Khichi to Ajmer. Shafi Khan offered Ajmer to Ajit, which the latter refused. Negotiations broke down and Ajit Singh moved to Seriari (Merwara). Ajit Singh now took the field. He attacked and took possession of the city, on 9 March, 1707 and the fort, of Jodhpur on the 20th.

In Aurangzeb's time, according to Father Catrau's list, the revenue of the province of Ajmer was Rs. 2,19,00,002. Bernier says, Ajmer stood only below Agra and Lahore in matters of revenue. The *Mirat-i-Alam* says that Ajmer had 235 mahals, with a revenue of 63,68,94,882 dams, or Rs. 1,59,22,372.

After Aurangzeb's death in 1707 A.D., five kings ascended the throne of Delhi within twelve years. Bahadur Shah, who succeeded Aurangzeb, came towards Ajmer and invited Ajit Singh to meet him. Ajit Singh met the new emperor in the village Kalu, and from there both came to Ajmer on 20 March, 1708 A.D., Ajit Singh encamping at the village of Nareli. A treaty of peace was made. Ajit Singh was recognised as King of Marwar and assigned the *munsab* of four thousand. Maharaja Jai Singh of Jaipur, who had been deprived of his State, which had been given in January 1708 to his younger brother, Bijai Singh, and on whom the title of Mirza Raja was later conferred on 30 April 1708, had also come with the emperor to Ajmer. All the three left on 2 April, for Ujjain reaching Mandsaur on 14 April, 1708. The emperor moved on towards the Deccan; but Ajit Singh and Durga Das and Jai Singh determined to return to their respective States. They left Bahadur Shah's camp at Mandsaur on 30 April, and arrived at Deolia Pratapgarh, and thence went to the Maharana at Udaipur to ask for help to restore Jaipur to Jai Singh. The Maharana gave two thousand men and four guns, and gave his daughter in marriage to Jai Singh. They all proceeded to Jodhpur, reaching there on 3 July, 1708.

Taking twenty thousand Rathors with him, Ajit Singh left Jodhpur to place Jai Singh on his throne at Amber and arrived on the 6th August 1708, at Pushkar near Ajmer. As the two Maharajas had deserted the Emperor, the latter was angry with them. Shujaat Khan, Governor of Ajmer, assured the two Maharajas that he would get them reconciled to the Emperor and obtain for them suitable *munsabs*. But he secretly sent to the Emperor for reinforcements. For a month no reply came from the Emperor, and the two Maharajas moved to Jaipur. In the meantime, imperial forces came from Agra, Delhi, Muttra and Karnal. The Mughal garrison in Amber, Jai Singh's capital, also came out to fight the Rajputs. The two armies met at Sambhar. Though the Mughal army had the advantage of possessing artillery, it was defeated and lost two thousand men and four elephants. Ajit Singh proceeded with Jai Singh to Amber (Jaipur), and put him on the throne there. . . .

Durga Das formulated a plan and proposed that Amber (Jaipur) Jodhpur and Udaipur should combine and destroy the Badshai, *i. e.*, Mughal Empire. He, therefore, went to Udaipur to enlist the Maharana's support. Ajit Singh returned to Jodhpur to make preparations for war. Raja Raj Singh of Rupangarh (now part of Kishengarh), fearing Ajit Singh's predominence, went to Deolia-Pratapgarh to inform the Emperor of the intentions of Ajit Singh. The Emperor, fearful of such a combination, decided to conciliate Ajit Singh, and sent him *firmans* for himself and Jai Singh with Raj Singh, who thus armed, went to Ajit Singh at Jodhpur.

Shujaat Khan, Governor of Ajmer, informed Ajit Singh that he (Shujaat Khan) had been dismissed from service, and that if Ajit Singh wished to take Ajmer, he should proceed to do so at once. Ajit Singh collected an army of twentyfive thousand men and plundered the villages attached to Ajmer. Accompanied by Bithaldas Bhandari, he proceeded towards Ajmer. As Mewati Firoz Khan's son, who was Thanedar of Mandal and Nahar Khan and Husain Khan had come to Ajmer and had fortified the approaches to the city of Ajmer, Ajit halted for a while at the village of Dantra near Pisangan, about twenty miles from Ajmer, and sent to Jodhpur for artillery. He moved on to Ajmer on the 19th February, 1709 and the fighting commenced. Ajit Singh plundered the northern part of the city of Ajmer called Ganj, outside the Agra Gate. Husain Khan was killed. Ajit Singh took the city and laid siege to Taragarh, the fortress of Ajmer. Shujaat Khan now asked Raj Singh to intervene. Peace was then made and Shujaat Khan gave elephants and horses and a fine of fortyfive thousand rupees to Ajit Singh who left for Deolia Pratapgarh to wed the daughter of the Maharawat there.

Bhandari Khimsi, one of Ajit Singh's officers took Deogaon (Ajmer district) and received fifteen thousand rupees as *nazrana* from T. Nahar Singh, whose son agreed to serve Ajit Singh. On his return after the marriage, Ajit Singh marched to Kishengarh and planted his banner there, and then advanced to take Rupangarh on Bhadrapad sudi 9th, s. 1765 (13 August 1709). Raja Raj Singh showed fight; but an amicable settlement was made, by which Raj Singh gave two guns to Ajit Singh and renounced his allegiance to the Emperor. Raj Singh's heir-apparent agreed to serve Ajit Singh. As the Chiefs of Pisangan and Junia had taken sides against Ajit Singh, the latter attacked both these places, drove out the rulers and took possession of the estates.

Hearing of these turmoils, the Emperor returned to Rajputana and encamped at Dandwa, 60 miles from Ajmer. Emissaries were sent to Ajit Singh. On 26 May, 1710, Ajit Singh's reply was presented to the Emperor, who gave khillats to Ajit Singh's messengers. The Emperor sent the Imperial Prime Minister's son, Mahabat Khan, to Ajit Singh requesting him to come to Ajmer. On the 20th June 1710, the Prime Minister himself went to Ajit Singh and gave him assurances. Then Ajit Singh and Jai Singh came and were presented with robes of honour.[1] They both went to Pushkar and from there to Jodhpur and Jaipur respectively. (*Later Mughals*, Vol. I., p. 73). The emperor having made peace with Ajit Singh, went to Delhi.

1. All the hills and plains of Ajmer were full of Rajputs, to attack Bahadur Shah if he acted treacherously.—*Later Mughals*, Vol. I, p. 73.

Bahadur Shah died on 27 February, 1712, and on 29 March 1712, Jahandar Shah succeeded him. He was defeated on 11 February, 1713 by Farrukhsayar, who thus became Emperor.

As Ajit Singh refused to give up Ajmer, Farrukhsayar sent Sayad Husain Ali with an army against Ajit Singh. Peace, however, was negotiated at Merta, by which Ajit Singh was appointed governor of Sindh, and his eldest son, Abhai Singh was to be sent to Delhi. As Ajit Singh declined to go to Sindh, the province of Gujrat, and Kekri, Marot, Parbatsar and other districts in Rajputana were given to him instead. The *Tarikhi Muzaffri* says that Ashratuddaula Iradatmand, by concession and conciliation persuaded Ajit Singh to give up the fortress of Ajmer and send Abhai Singh to Delhi (*Maasirul Umra*, Vol. III., p. 758). Ajit Singh went to Ahmedabad and Abhai Singh returned to Jodhpur. The Emperor gave Abhai Singh, Nagor, which Aurangzeb had given to Rao Inder Singh.

As Nawab Abdullah Khan became too powerful at Court, the Emperor appealed to Ajit Singh for protection against that turbulent noble, and sent Chela Nahar Khan with a *firman* to Jodhpur inviting Ajit Singh to Delhi. When Ajit Singh reached near Delhi, the Emperor sent Shamsuddaula to escort him. Farrukhsayar later sent Tarbiat Khan to receive him. Next day, when Ajit Singh encamped at Moti Bagh, the Emperor sent Aitbar Khan, Nawab Khan Dauran, Maharao Bhim Singh of Kotah and other Munsabdars to welcome Ajit Singh. When Ajit Singh went to see the Emperor, he was loaded with honours. He was received with the *banhapasar*[1] greetings (when the parties embrace each other).

As Ajit Singh was dissatisfied and angry owing to an incident, the Emperor "sent Zafar Khan on 23 December, 1718 to apologise to him. "The Emperor himself went to Ajit Singh's camp to reconcile him," and gave presents. Reconciliation thus took place.[2]

On 7 January, 1719 A.D., the title of *Raj Rajeshwar* was conferred upon Ajit Singh. He was presented with the highest *Saropao* and a crore of *dams*. The Emperor sent Khan Dauran and Sarbuland Khan to the Maharaja's camp. Ajit Singh was appointed Viceroy of Ahmedabad.[3] As Ajit Singh was anxious to return home, he left Delhi and reached Jodhpur *via* Amber.

1. Equals greet each other by *banhapasar*.
2. *Later Mughals*, Vol. I, p. 363.
3. *Later Mughals*, Vol. I, p. 364.

Ajit Singh remained Viceroy of Ahmedabad, and it was formally announced on 5 November 1719 (23rd Zil Hijja) that he was appointed Subedar of Ajmer too.[1]

One day when Ajit Singh was returning to his camp from the Durbar at Delhi, Nawab Abdullah Khan invited the Maharaja to sit with him on his own elephant, and escorted him home. Suspecting treachery, Ajit Singh being alone, Thakur Amar Singh of Nimaj took up his seat in *khawasi* (behind the Maharaja). The Nawab had conversations with the Maharaja, and both entered into a pact.

When the Emperor came to know of it, he determined to take the life of the Maharaja in the *durbar* by a stratagem. News of this having reached the Empress (Ajit's daughter), she had it carried to Ajit Singh. Thus warned, Maharaja Ajit Singh took his seat in another place and returned safely to his camp. Two more attempts having failed, the Emperor determined to go out on the pretence of hunting, and then suddenly to attack Ajit Singh in his camp. Nawab Abdullah Khan getting wind of it, came with twenty thousand men to protect Ajit Singh. Finding a large army round Ajitsingh, Farrukhsayar turned back and entered the fort. Abdullah Khan, aware of the Emperor's attitude, sent for his brother Husain Ali Khan who was in the Deccan. Husain Ali Khan returned with forced marches. Maharaja Jai Singh of Jaipur, foreseeing trouble, skulked away to Amber (Jaipur).

One day, while Ajit Singh went out riding, some one pointed out to him, the place where his mother and his brother Dalthamban's mother and the Marwar nobles had been killed, fighting to save him when he, as a baby, was taken away to Marwar. Ajit Singh then and there took a vow to be avenged.

Foiled in all his attempts to get rid of the Sayad brothers, Emperor Farrukhsayar tried to conciliate them and asked them what their wishes were. They said that they should be appointed *kiladars* of the Delhi fort and governor of the artillery. The Emperor put the Sayads in charge of the artilerry and the fort. Thus strengthened, Ajit Singh and the Sayad brothers resolved to remove the Emperor.

On Falgun sudi 10, s. 1776 (8 March, 1720) Nawab Abdullah Khan, Maharaj Ajit Singh, Maharao Bhim Singh of Kotah, and Raja Raj Singh of Rupangarh took up positions in the *Diwan-Am*. The Emperor fled into the *zenana* quarters; and sent a garland of flowers to Maharaj Ajit Singh with a

1. *Later Mughals*, Vol. II, p. 4.

note in it saying that he was indebted to Ajit Singh for his Badshahi (empire) and his life; and swore by the Quran that he would ever remain grateful to him if he helped him at that juncture. The Maharao of Kotah, the Raja of Rupangarh, and Bhandari Khimsi, after consultation among themselves, interceded for the Emperor and advised Ajit Singh to save the Emperor saying, that they would lose nothing and would be able to excrcise influence over the empire in future, as they were strong enoughto resist the Sayads and others. But Ajit Singh, resolved to avenge the deaths of his mother and his nobles, and full of anger at the attempts made by the Emperor to murder him, said that if Sayad Abdullah Khan had not come to his help, the Emperor would have attacked and killed him in his camp. He declined to help the Emperor.

The Sayads' men dragged the Emperor out of the zenana and imprisoned him.[1] Ajit Singh remained in possession of the Delhi fort for four days, when he remained night and day in the *Diwan-Am*, where he performed his worship. Morning and evening the *conch* was loudly sounded, and *Jhalar* was rung morning and evening in the Diwan-Am and cries of *Jai*, victory to Hindu gods were raised. A poet has said,

अजो दिली को बादशाह राजो तो रघनाथ ।

(Ajit was the Badshah at Delhi, and Rughnath, Ajit's minister, was Raja of Jodhpur).

The Sayads killed Farrukhsayar by strangulation on 28th April, 1719[2] (9 Jamadi II, H. 1131). Ajit Singh and the Sayads placed Rafiuddarjat, and later Rafiuddaula, on the throne. Both, however, died within a few months. In *Aswin* Samvat 1776, (September or October 1719), Ajit Singh sent his minister Bhandari Khim Singh and the Sayads' diwan, Raja Ratan Chand from Agra to Delhi to select a successor to the throne.

They collected the Shahzadas, young princes, in Salemkot in Delhi, and selected Muhammad Shah, who was twentytwo years old. His mother, knowing how the last two or three Emperors had died after occupying the throne only for a few months, declined to send her son saying she did not want him to become emperor. Bhandari Khim Singh gave all assurance to the would-be queen-mother and took Muhammad

1. Ajit Singh got his daughter, Inder Kunwar, who had been married to Farrukhsayar on 27 September 1715, out of the zenana, performed *Shuddhi*, reconverted her to Hinduism and sent her away to Jodhpur with all her personal possessions. "She performed a ceremony of purification in the Hindu fashion and gave up her Muhammadan attire"—Irvine's *Later Mughals*, vol. 1, p. 429.

2. *Later Mughals*, vol. I, p. 393. The *Sayarul Mutakharin* gives H. 1132, as the year.

Shah to Agra. When Muhammad Shah was brought to the Durbar to sit on the throne, Maharaja Ajit Singh took him by one arm and Sayad Abdullah Khan by the other, and they thus placed him on the throne.

Nawab Abdullah Khan now resolved to punish Maharaja Jai Singh and marched against Amber taking Ajit Singh with him. Jai Singh's vakil came to Ajit and pleaded with him to spare Jai Singh. Ajit Singh, generous as he was, interceded with Abdullah Khan. Abdullah Khan asked Ajit to send for his son, so that Amber may be given to him and the Kachwahas be completely uprooted from Amber, and the Rathors made masters of both Jodhpur and Amber. But Ajit declined to accept this and pleaded hard for Jai Singh. Sayad Abdullah was very sorry and said they would all regret it later. Ajit Singh insisting on leaving Jai Singh free. The Sayad returned to Agra and let the Maharaja proceed to Gujrat, of which he had been appointed Viceroy. Jai Singh went with Ajit Singh to Jodhpur.

IV—RATHOR AND MAHRATTA PERIOD

Ajit Singh sent Anoop Singh son of Rughnath, to take charge of Ahmedabad. Ajit Singh gave his daughter, Suraj Kunwar, in marriage to Jai Singh in Jaisht, s. 1777 (June 1720) and the ceremony was performed with great eclat. Ajit Singh prohibited slaughter of cows in the provinces of Ajmer and Gujrat.[1]

In the meantime, intrigue developed in Delhi, Sayad Husain Ali was assassinated and Abdullah Khan was imprisoned; and Nizamulmulk, the head of the enemies of the Sayads became Chief Minister. Jai Singh, coming to know of this, secretly left for Delhi without even informing Ajit Singh. On this, Ajit Singh left Jodhpur with his army of 30,000 horse, captured Ajmer and took up residence in the Anasagar palace and sent his son, K. Abhai Singh, and Rughnath Bhandari with a large army to attack Delhi. Abhai Singh, after a rapid march of one hundred and forty miles, attacked Narnaul and defeated the Imperial forces.[2] Narnaul

1. *Later Mughals*, Vol. II, p. 108.
2. *Sayar-ul Mutakharin*, Vol. I, p. 233.

Alwar, Tijara and Shahjahanpur were plundered. The Rathors advanced to Sarai Aliverdikhan, less than sixteen miles from Delhi (Later Mughals, II., p. 110). Col. Tod thus describes the event:—"He drew his sword, and swore he would possess himself of Ajmer. In twelve days after, Ajit reached Merta. In the face of day, he drove the Muslim from Ajmer and made it his own. He slew the king's governor and seized on Taragarh. Once more the bell of prayers was heard in the temple, while the *bang* of the Masjid was silent. Where the Koran was read, the Purana was now heard, and the *mandir* took the place of the mosque. The Kazi made way for the Brahmin, and the pit of burnt sacrifice (homa) was dug, where the sacred kine were slain. He took possession of the salt lakes of Sambhar and Didwana, and the records were always moist with inserting fresh conquests.

"Ajit ascended his own throne; the umbrella of supremacy, he waved over his head. He struck coins in his own name, established his own *guz* (measure) and seer (weight) his own courts of justice, and a new scale of rank for his chiefs, with *nalkees* and mace-bearers, *nobuts* and standards, and every emblem of sovereign rule. Ajmal in Ajmer, was equal to *Aspati* in Delhi. The intelligence spread over the land; it reached even Mecca and Iran, that Ajit had exalted his own faith, while the rites of Islam were prohibited throughout the land of Maroo."

"In s. 1778, (1722 A.D.) the emperor determined to regain Ajmer. He gave the command to Muzaffur who, in the rains, advanced towards Marwar. Ajit entrusted the conduct of this war to his son, the 'Shield of Maroo,' the 'fearless' (Abhai), with the eight great vassals, and thirty thousand horse. At Amber, the Rathors and the Imperialists came in sight; but Muzaffur disgraced himself, and retired within that city without risking an encounter. Abhai Singh, exasperated at this display of pusillanimous bravado, determined to punish the king. He attacked Shahjahanpur, sacked Narnaul, levied contributions on Patun (Tuarvati) and Rewari. He gave the villages to the flames, and spread conflagration and consternation even to Aliverdi's Serai. Delhi and Agra trembled with affright; the *Asoors* fled without their shoes at the deeds of Abhai, whom they styled Dhonkul, the *exterminator*."[1]

Shamsudaulla, Haider Kuli Khan and Qamruddin Khan were appointed by the Emperor to oppose the Rathors but one after another, they felt unequal to the task and kept back.

1. Tod's Annals and Antiquities of Rajasthan, Vol. II., p. 77.

In his alarm, Emperor Muhammad Shah[1] asked Ajit's agent, Khim Singh to persuade Ajit Singh to desist from spreading confusion in the country but to come to Delhi and receive honours. Ajit Singh proposed that the *Jaziya* be abolished and Sayad Abdullah Khan be released, before he would come to Delhi. The Emperor abolished the Jaziya and promised to release Abdullah Khan as soon as Ajit Singh reached Delhi. The Emperor sent Nahar Khan to invite Ajit Singh who was at Sambhar. Ajit refused to move till Abdullah Khan was released and informed the Emperor through Nahar Khan.

Maharaja Jai Singh, fearing Ajit's advent to Delhi, conspired with Khan Dauran and Tamardi Khan, and persuaded Nahar Khan, promising to make him *Haft Hazari* to tell Muhammad Shah that Ajit will not come to Delhi while Abdullah Khan was alive. The Emperor then had Abdullah Khan murdered in the prison, and sent Nahar Khan again to Ajit Singh. Ajit Singh, hearing of it, was furious when Khim Singh told him the whole story. Ajit Singh sent his men to kill Nahar Khan. They looted the camp and killed Nahar Khan and his brother Rohilla Khan.[2] Muhammad Shah then sent Hasan Kuli Khan and Jai Singh against Ajit Singh in 1723 A.D. Amar Singh, Thakur of Nimaj, governor of the Ajmer fortress and Bhandari Vijai Singh son of Khim Singh Bhandari were in charge of Ajmer. Ajit advanced to Manoharpur and prepared to fight. Jai Singh sent his men to Ajit Singh asking him not to fight an open battle. Ajit Singh returned to Merta.

The Imperial forces under Haider Kuli Khan, who was appointed governor of Ajmer, laid siege to the Ajmer fortress. One day, Nawab Haider Kuli Khan, Sarbaland Khan and Maharaj Jai Singh mounted on an elephant, were going to Dargah Khwaja Sahib, when a *gola* (shell) from a gun in the Taragarh Fort struck the howdah of the elephant, killing the *mahawat* and wounding others. This scared them and Jai Singh opened negotiations with Ajit Singh and persuaded him to make peace. Ajmer was ceded to the Mughals and K. Abhai Singh went to the Imperial Court.

Soon after this, when Abhai Singh reached Delhi, he created a scene in the Durbar. "Knowing that his father Ajit Singh, held the first place on the king's right hand, he (Abhai Singh) considered himself, as his representative, entitled to the same honour; and little heeding the unbending etiquette of the proudest court in the world, he unceremoniously

1. According to the *Sayarul Mutakharin*, Khan Dauran represented to the Emperor that it was impolitic to quarrel with Ajit Singh.
2. *Ajitodaya*, sarga 30, slokas 31-33.

hustled past all the dignitaries of the state, and had even ascended a step of the throne, when, checked by one of the nobles,[1] Abhai's hand was on his dagger, and, but for the presence of mind of the monarch, "who threw his own chaplet round his neck" to restrain him, the *Dewan* would have been deluged with blood."[2]

As Abhai Singh was an unexperienced youth, Jai Singh worked on his mind and told him that the Emperor was angry with Ajit Singh and would, as soon as an opportunity appeared, take away Marwar; but that, if Ajit were out of the way, Abhai Singh would become king of Marwar and the Emperor would be pleased. The *Tarikhi Muzaffari* says that Wazirul Mulk Aitmaduddaula Qamaruddin persuaded Abhai Singh on promise of giving all Marwar to him to kill Ajit Singh (*Muasir Ul-Umra*, vol. III, p. 758). Abhai Singh swallowed the bait and wrote to his younger brother, Bakht Singh to do away with Ajit, promising Nagor to him. On Ashadh sudi 13, s. 1781 (23 June, 1724) Bakht Singh entered at night the palace where Ajit Singh was sleeping and murdered him. The following popular verse refers to the evil deed of Bakht Singh:

वाहरे वखता वावरा क्यां मारयो अजमाल । हिन्दवाणी को सेहरो तुरकाणी को साल ॥

TRANSLATION:—Oh mad Bakhta, why did you kill Ajit Singh. He was the crown of the Hindus and a dagger for the Turks.

Another outspoken verse uttered by a *charan* when Bakht Singh was fondling his favourite horse, also confirms the perpetration of this deed:

वापा मत कह वखतसिंह कांपत है कैकाण । अब के बापा फिर कहयेा झट छोड़ेगो प्राण ॥

TRANSLATION:—Bakht Singh, don't say *bappa* (father) the horse is trembling. Say *bappa* once again, and the horse will give up his ghost.

Abhai Singh was in Delhi when Ajit Singh died. He was proclaimed King of Marwar there on Friday, Sravan vadi 8th, s. 1781 (2nd July, 1724). The Emperor was pleased with Abhai Singh for ridding the empire of Ajit Singh and gave him, on ascending the *Gadi*, Nagor, Kekri, and other pargannas to be added to his domain.

Maharaja Ajit Singh was one of the most powerful Kings that Rajputana produced during the Mughal times. His father, Maharaja Jaswant Singh was the most powerful of the Rajput potentates of his time, and was always an object of fear and suspicion to Emperor Aurangzeb. Ajit Singh was born and brought up in adversity, and his early youth was passed,

1. Mir Tuzak. 2. Tod's Rajasthan, Vol. II, page 78.

not in the luxuries of a royal household, but in a frugal and simple village life, if not in privation and poverty. His father, Jaswant Singh was not only a powerful king but was a man of learning and high culture. Aurangzeb the Mughal emperor hated and feared Jaswant Singh, and tried to destroy the independent kingdom of Marwar after his death. But Marwar defied the Emperor, who used all the resources of the most powerful empire of the time to crush the Rathors. The war was long and protracted, but after thirty years of fighting, Marwar emerged triumphant and the Mughal empire sank so rapidly that in twenty years, it lost its power and virility and succumbed to the attacks of the Hindus—the Mahrattas in the south, the Sikhs in the north and the Rajputs in the centre.

The momentous period of forty years in India, from 1680 to 1720 A D., enfolds a drama before our eyes, so full of events, so rich in incidents, so full of political lessons, so illustrative of the vicissitudes of fortune, as to lead the mind to the contemplation of those higher truths of humanity which history teaches. Little did Aurangzeb think that the magnificent empire he had inherited from Shah Jahan, would crumble to pieces as soon as he closed his eyes; that his generals and ministers, who shared his power and authority would, before they leave the scene, see the Imperial Rule defied and despised by those, who only a little while ago, respected and feared it. Sitting in splendour on the famous Peacock Throne, the monarch of all he surveyed, master and ruler of the most powerful and prosperous empire of his time, could Aurangzeb, even imagine that his sons and grandsons within thirty years of his death, would depend for their subsistence on the allowances made by those whom, he had tried to exterminate.

A great political lesson that the history of those times teaches, is that the greatest of the empires, as the Mughal Empire was in the seventeenth century, would fall and disappear in no time, if, like Aurangzeb, the head of the State, pursues a policy based on religious intolerance and utter disregard of the cherished beliefs of the people. Another lesson which the events of the time teaches is, that a people thoroughly united and devoted to their motherland like the people of Marwar after Jaswant Singh's death, though subjected to untold suffering, desolation and death would, if they remained true to themselves, eventually emerge triumphant, though the enemy be the most powerful tyrant of the time.

When Aurangzeb took the fort of Jodhpur and installed a Muslim governor there, and the *qazi* led the prayers facing the west in the stronghold of Jaswant, the rightful owner, the infant Ajit, had to take refuge in the Chhapan Mountains. It was not long, however, before time brought its own compensations and revenges. It was this very Ajit Singh, who lived to put his foot down on the dying body of the Mughal empire writhing in its death agony; made and unmade the Mughal emperors, seated and unseated them, and achieved the distinction and the glory of blowing the conch and ringing the *Jhalar* at the worship of Hindu gods in the holy of holies of the Mughals, the Diwan-Am in the Imperial fort of Delhi. And before another twenty years passed, the celebrated peacock throne of Shah Jahan and the magnificent collection of diamonds, rubies and other precious stones including the diamond *Regent*, and the world famous *Kohi-Nur* which now adorns the English crown, and the untold wealth which the great Mughal emperors Akbar, Jahangir, and Shah Jahan had collected from all over the then richest country in the world, were taken away by the Persian king, Nadir Shah in 1739 A.D.

Ajit Singh achieved a position in the seat of the Imperial Mughal Empire, which no Hindu sovereign of Mewar, Marwar or Jaipur or any other place did. Had he possessed the political ability and the intellectual power of Maharana Kumbha or Sanga; or, the foresight, the high character and the strength of will of Maharana Pratap, he would have installed a Hindu dynasty on the throne of Delhi and ended the Mughal rule in 1720 A.D.

Thus closed the career of one of the most distinguished princes who ever pressed the 'cushion' of Maroo; a career as full of incident as any life of equal duration. "Born amidst the snows of Kabul, deprived at his birth of both parents, one from grief, the other by suicidal custom; saved from the Herodian cruelty of the king by the heroism of his chiefs, nursed amidst the rocks of Abu or the intricacies of the Aravallis until the day of danger passed, he issued forth, still an infant, at the head of his brave clans, to redeem the inheritance so iniquitously wrested from him. In the history of mankind, there is nothing to be found presenting a more brilliant picture of fidelity, than that afforded by the Rathor clans in their devotion to their prince, from his birth until he worked out his own and his country's deliverance. It is one of those events which throw a gleam of splendour upon the dark picture of feudalism, more prolific perhaps in crime than

MAHARAJA AJIT SINGH OF JODHPUR.
(Inset Thakur Durga Das.)

MAHARAJA ABHAI SINGH OF MARWAR

MAHARAJA BAKHAT SINGH OF MARWAR.

in virtue. That of the Rajputs, indeed, in which consanguinity is superadded to the other reciprocalties which bind a feudal body, wears the more engaging aspect of a vast family. How affecting is the simple language of these brave men, while daily shedding their blood for a prince whom, until he had attained his seventh year, they had never beheld. '*Without the sight of our lord, bread and water have no flavour.*' The prodigality with which every clan *lavished* its blood, through a space of six and twenty years, may in part be learned from the chronicle; and in yet more forcible language from the cenotaphs scattered over the country, erected to the *manes* of those who fell in this religious warfare. Were other testimony required, it is to be found in the annals of their neighbours and their conquerors; while the traditional couplets of bards, familiar to evey Rajput, embalm the memory of the exploits of their forefathers.

"Ajit Singh was a prince of great vigour of mind as well as of frame. Valour was his inheritance; he displayed this hereditary quality at the early age of eleven, when he visited his enemy in his capital displaying a courtesy which can only be comprehended by a Rajput. Amongst the numerous desultory actions, of which many occurred every year, there were several in which the whole strength of the Rathors was led by their prince. The battle of Sambhar in S. 1765, (A.D. 1708) fought against the Sayads, which ended in an union of interests, was one of these; and, for the rest of Ajit's life kept him in close contact with the court, where he might have taken the lead, had his talent for intrigue been commensurate with his boldness. From this period until death, Ajit's agency was recognised amongst the occupants of Timoor's throne, from Farrukhsayar to Muhammad Shah."[1]

Ajit Singh's eldest son and successor, Abhai Singh was born at Jalor on Mangsar vadi 14, s. 1749 (26 November 1692) and died at Ajmer on Ashadh 15th, s. 1805 (29th June, 1748). As he had come under the influene of Maharaja Jai Singh of Jaipur while at Delhi, one of his first acts on his accession to the throne was to marry Jai Singh's daughter at Muttra on Bhadrapad sudi 8th, 1781 (16 August, 1724) inspite of the protests of his Sardars, many of whom then left him and returned to Marwar. Soon after returning to Jodhpur, Abhai Singh made his brother Bakht Singh, independent sovereign of Nagor, and tried to pacify the people whom his conduct had given great offence.

1. Tod's Rajasthan, Vol. II, p. 81.

He returned to Delhi in Ashadh, 1782 (June, 1725 A.D.). In his absence, the emperor had given his position in the Durbar to Roshanudaullah Turrabeg Khan. When the first public durbar was held, Abhai Singh elbowing out Roshanudaullah took his stand above him. On Roshanudaullah protesting, Abhai Singh, laying his hand on the dagger prepared to attack him. On this, Nawab Khan Dauran placed Abhai Singh above himself and the durbar was closed. When the next durbar was announced, Abhai Singh went prepared to fight and sent word to the Emperor that the latter should stay in the palace and he and Roshanudaullah would have a fight and whoever survived should occupy the disputed place. The Emperor was alarmed and pacified the Maharaja with the result that so long as the Maharaja lived in Delhi, no public durbar was held.

In s. 1785 (1728), T. Devi Singh Khangrot of Parsoli, one of the Jaipur nobles, incurred Maharaja Jai Singh's displeasure and fled to Merwara and took shelter with the Mers. As the Mers refused to surrender T. Devi Singh, Jai Singh invaded Merwara with a large army. Rajadhiraj Bakht Singh came to his aid from Nagor, and the Maharana of Udaipur also sent his troops. Jhak and Shamgarh were destroyed, and Jai Singh established a *thana* (military outpost) at Chang. Failing to make further progress, Jai Singh, after doing worship at Nathdwara went to Pisangan near Ajmer, to wed the daughter of the Raja there. From Pisangan he returned to Jaipur *via* Pushkar. Bakht Singh returned to Nagor.

In 1729 A.D., Sarbaland Khan, Viceroy of Ahmedabad, rebelled against the Emperor. As no one in the Imperial Court at Delhi felt equal to the task of subduing him, Maharaja Abhai Singh offered to do so. The Emperor gave him in June, 1730 costly presents, eighteen lakhs cash, fifty pieces of artillery and troops under Nawab Azimullah Khan. Abhai Singh returned to Jodhpur *via* Jaipur, which city was under construction at the time. He took possession of Ajmer. Taking Bakht Singh and twenty five thousand cavalry and other Sardars and their levies, Abhai Singh invaded Ahmedabad. A contingent from Ajmer, under Amar Singh, went with the army. Passing by Palanpur and Sidhpur, he encamped at Sarkhej. A battle was fought there on Asoj sudi 10, s. 1787 (10 October, 1730) when Sarbuland Khan was defeated, and his standards, artillery and the elephant named Fateh Jung, were captured by Abhai Singh.

In Jesht s. 1791 (May, 1735), Maharaja Abhai Singh came to Pushkar, and after staying there for a month, came to Ajmer and took up residence in the Anasagar palaces. Jai Singh came and took Abhai Singh to Jaipur. Next year, 1735, the rulers of Jaipur and Kotah and Nagor attended the coronation of Maharana Jagat Singh at Udaipur, and from there came to Hurda in Mewar, where Abhai Singh also joined them. Consultation took place there as to the means to be adopted to check the inroads of the Mahrattas into Rajputana. As Abhai Singh had pitched red tents for himself at Hurda, Roshanu-daullah, Abhai Singh's enemy, complained to the Emperor that Abhai Singh was assuming Imperial airs, and had incited the heir-apparent and brought together the Rajput rulers of Rajputana. The Emperor spoke to the prime minister, Khan Dauran, who spoke to Bhandari Amar Singh, Abhai Singh's vakil at the Imperial Court. Amar Singh, with great adroitness, replied that the whole thing was designed to assist the Emperor; that the Rajas had assembled to concert measures to check the advance of the Mahrattas from the Deccan and that the royal red tent was put up so that all Rajas might meet under royal auspices to take suitable action against the common enemy. The Emperor was pleased with this reply and sent a *Khas Rukka* (letter in his own hand) and a pearl necklace to Maharaja Abhai Singh as a token of his pleasure.

From Hurda, Abhai Singh came to Deolia, which had belonged to the Bhinai estate (Ajmer) but which Umed Singh, Raja of Shahpura, had wrested and given to his brother, Ishwar Singh. Abhai Singh took it from Ishwar Singh and gave it to Jodha Rughnath Singh. The Maharaja (Abhai Singh) resided there for three months and looted Shahpura villages. At last, the Chief of Shahpura came to Abhai Singh and made his submission. In s. 1793 (1736 A.D.), Abhai Singh again came to Ajmer and resided there for a year in the Anasagar palaces. From there, he went to Merta in September, 1737 A.D. Before leaving for Merta, he sent Pancholi Ram Kishen against Bhinai. Ram Kishen took Bhinai. Abhai Singh also took Rajgarh from Amar Singh Gor, and Ghatiali and Piplad and Chonthal from the Thakur of Sawar.

Jai Singh having in the meantime secured the viceroyalty of Ajmer from the Emperor, Abhai Singh and Bakht Singh resolved in 1740 A.D., to invade Jaipur and take Ajmer from Jai Singh. In May, 1740 A.D., the Rajas of Bhinai and Pisangan (Ajmer district) were summoned to join Bakht Singh with their levies at Merta. Bakht Singh advanced to Ajmer, drove out the governor and took possession of the city.

Battle of Gangwana.

News of this reached Jai Singh at Agra, and he started with an army of fifty thousand men. Advancing rapidly, he came up to the village of Oontra, fourteen miles north of Ajmer. Bakht Singh, who had only five thousand horsemen with him, sent to Maharaja Abhai Singh for reinforcements. As, however, no reinforcements arrived, Bakht Singh determined to attack Jai Singh with his small army, and came upon him at Gangwana, about nine miles north-east of Ajmer. The vanguard of Jai Singh's army was commanded by Raja Umed Singh of Shahpura. On 28 May, 1741 A.D., a great battle was fought at Gangwana, between the Rathors under Bakht Singh and the Cutchwahas under Jai Singh. Colonel Tod thus describes the battle: "Soon as the hostile lines approached, Bakht Singh gave the word, and, in one dense mass his gallant legion charged with lance and sword the deepened lines of Amber, carrying destruction at every pass. He passed through and through his host: but when he pulled up in the rear, only sixty of his band remained round his person. At this moment, the chief of Gujsinghpura, head of all his vassals, hinted there was a jungle in the rear. "And what is there in front," said the intrepid Rathor, "that we should not try the road we came?" And, as he espied the *Pacharanga*, or five coloured flag, which denoted the head-quarters of Amber, the word was given. The cautions Khoombani advised his prince (Jai Singh) to avoid the charge: with some difficulty, he was made to leave the field, and, as a salve to his honour, by a flank movement towards Khandailah north, so that it might not be said that he turned his back on his foe. As he retreated, he exclaimed, "Seventeen battles have I witnessed, but till this day, never one decided by the sword." Thus, after a life of success, the wisest, the most learned and the ablest prince of Rajwara incurred the disgrace of leaving the field in the face of a handful of men, strengthening the adage that "one Rathor equalled ten Cutchwahas."

Describing this battle, Sir Jadunath Sarkar says: "A levee 'en masse' of Jaipur vassals and allies, including Hadas, Jadavas of Karauli, Sisodias of Shahpura, Khichi Chauhans and Jats as well as three Muslim generals, who had been sent by the Emperor from Agra to assist Jai Singh in keeping the Mahrattas out of the North, marched by way of Ajmer towards Marwar. With this vast but disjointed host of a hundred thousand men, Jai Singh reached Gangwana, eleven miles north-east of the Pushkar lake, and encamped, with his guns planted in front. The Marwar army was hopelessly outnumbered. But Bakht Singh, at the head of only one thousand Rathor horsemen, desperate like himself, charged the enemy, swept through the line of guns, and fell upon Jai Singh's troops, "like tigers among a flock of sheep." Nothing could stand their onset. Many thousands of the Jaipur troops were slain and many more wounded, mostly without fighting. The Kachhwaha army fled away, and within four hours the field, covering some square miles, was entirely cleared as by magic of all save the dead and the wounded.

"Jai Singh fell back two miles and stood for some time almost alone and in perplexity. The three imperial generals, who had not been attacked, coolly kept their places in the field (near Pahari), though their followers had caught the panic and fled away, leaving only a hundred men out of nearly ten thousand to support them. By this time, Bakht Singh's gallant band had been reduced from a thousand to seventy men only and he himself was wounded. Jai Singh, thus miraculously saved from a field where his army had reaped nothing but shame, took the road to his capital."[1]

A similar heroic charge was made by the "Rathor horsemen upon the still more modern and powerful artillery of General De Boigne near Merta on 11 September, 1790 with the same butchery."[2]

Bakht Singh, with the remnants of his army joined his brother Abhai Singh at Pushkar. From Pushkar, both brothers marched against Jai Singh, who had moved to Ladpura, a village eight miles east of Ajmer. Jai Singh, feeling unequal to meeting the Rathors a second time in the field, sent Rugnath Bhandari to Abhai Singh and peace was concluded, Jai Singh ceding seven pargannas including Kekri, Parbatsar, Ramsar and Ajmer to the Rathors. Possibly actual possession of the fortress of Ajmer was not given; for, we find that on the death of Jai Singh, on the 3rd October, 1743 A.D., Maharaja Abhai Singh sent from Merta, Bhandari Surat Ram with Thakur Suraj Mal of Alniawas and Bahadur Singh son of the Raja of Rupangarh to take Ajmer. They took Ajmer, slaying the Fozdar, Khangrot Binai Singh, the *hakim*, having fled. Raja Suraj Mal Gor was also driven out of Rajgarh at the same time.

Maharaja Ishwari Singh, the successor of Sawai Jai Singh, with a view to regain the lost possession, advanced with an

1. Sarkar's *Fall of the Mughal Empire*, Vol I., p. 281-82. Harcharan Das author of *Chahar Gulzar*, who was an eyewitness of the battle, gives "a horrid picture of the battlefield as it looked when he walked among the dead the next day."

2. Sarkar's *Fall of the Mughal Empire*, Vol. I, p. 281.

army. Abhai Singh hearing of it, came to Ajmer with Bakht Singh, and was there joined by Bhat Govind Ram with five thousand cavalry from Kotah. Abhai Singh now had with him at Ajmer an army of thirty thousand horses. Ishwari Singh came up to Dhani, a village sixteen miles from Ajmer, and a battle was imminent when, through the efforts of Rai Mal of Jaipur and Purohit Jaggu of Jodhpur, peace was concluded in 1744 A.D. Bakht Singh disapproved of the peace and left for Nagor. Abhai Singh gave Rajgarh with twelve villages to his brother Raja Kishor Singh.

In 1745 A.D , Abhai Singh came to Ajmer and took up residence in the garden of Khwaja Danish, outside the town. In 1747 A.D., Malhar Rao Holkar who had invaded Jaipur, made peace with Ishwari Singh, the ruler of Jaipur, and came to Ajmer to see Maharaja Abhai Singh. He then returned to Bundi. On *falgun sudi* 6th, S. 1805 (11 February, 1749), Abhai Singh's queen, Rani Vichitra Kumari Kachhwaiji died at Ajmer. After four months, Abhai Singh also died there on Ashadh sudi 15, s. 1805 (1749 A.D.) and was cremated at Pushkar. His son Ram Singh succeeded him at Jodhpur.

On Abhai Singh's death, the Emperor gave the *Subah* of Ajmer to Salabat Khan. Bakht Singh, Rajadhiraj of Nagor, who had for some time been cultivating good relations with the Imperial Court, obtained Salabat's aid to attack and wrest Jodhpur from his nephew Ram Singh. Bakht Singh advanced to Merta, where Salabat Khan from Ajmer joined him. Ram Singh with reinforcements from Maharaja Ishwari Singh of Jaipur met him there. An artillery skirmish took place at the village Chursiawas on *kartik vadi* 14, s. 1806 (19 October, 1749 A.D.), in which Raja Shambhu Singh of Pisangan was killed. Salabat Khan was won over by Ram Singh, who paid him a lakh of rupees, and rupees fifty thousand to his Diwan, the revenue minister at Ajmer. Peace was made and the parties returned to their respective homes.

In 1751 A.D., Bakht Singh drove Ram Singh from Jodhpur and himself became ruler of Marwar. He gave Ramsar and Srinagar (now parts of the Ajmer district) to Bahadur Singh of Rupangarh, and took forty four villages of Rajgarh and gave them to the Thakur of Ras. Ram Singh, exiled from Jodhpur, took possession of Marot and seized Sambhar, and called in Holkar Malhar Rao's aid. Appa Scindia offered aid to Ram Singh and sent ten thousand troops under Sahaba Patel. Ram Singh, Sahaba and the Mertia Rajput supporters of Ram Singh, attacked Ajmer and captured Amar Singh Gor, who had prepared to fight, and buried him alive. Bakht Singh came to Alniawas and had recourse to the same stratagem as had worked successfully in the hands of Shershah Sur and Aurangzeb. He wrote letters to the Sardars of Ram Singh asking them to arrest Ram Singh on hearing the sound of drums. The Mahrattas seeing the letters, suspected treachery and marched away taking Ram Singh with them. The Sardars followed and asked for the reason of this departure, when the Mahrattas showed them Bakht Singh's letter. The Sardars told him that it was a stratagem. Bakht Singh took Ajmer[1] in 1752. He, however, died of poison the following year at village Sonali on 21 December, 1752[2] and was cremated there, thus fulfilling the curse pronounced by Ajit Singh's queen, when Bakht Singh murdered Ajit, that the two parricides, Abhai Singh and Bakht Singh, may leave their bones outside Marwar.

Bakht Singh's son, Bijai Singh ascended the *gadi* of Marwar at Marot. Ajmer remained incorporated with Marwar till 1756 A.D. In 1752 A.D. Maharaja Ajit Singh's third son, Raja Kishor Singh with the assistance of the Raja of Banera (Mewar) took possession of Bhinai (Ajmer district). Hearing of this, Maharaja Bijai Singh sent Thakur Kesri Singh of Ras with an army against Kishor Singh. A battle took place at the village Niaran near Bagsuri, where Kishor Singh was killed.

During the Civil War between Ram Singh, son of Abhai Singh, and Bijai Singh, son of Bakht Singh the former called in the aid of the Mahrattas to assist him. Jai Appa Scindia, who was at Ujjain, readily seized this opportunity of getting a footing in Rajputana, and advanced with his army towards Nagor. The combined armies of the Scindia and Jaipur, with the followers of Ram Singh came to Ajmer and took possession of it. Of the Istimrardars of Ajmer, Kharwa and Masuda sided with Ram Singh; while Bhinai, Deolia and Tantoti espoused the cause of Bijai Singh. Two officers were appointed to administer Ajmer—Ram Karan Pancholi on behalf of Ram Singh, and Govind Rao on behalf of the Scindia. From Ajmer, the armies advanced and encamped at Pushkar and sent a summons to Bijai Singh to surrender Marwar. "Battle, battle!" was shouted in reply, wnen the summons was read in the Durbar. The cavalry of Marwar, reinforced by the forces of Bikaner and Kishengarh, met the enemy near Merta. The Mahrattas at the first shock of battle wavered and were going to fall back, when treason began to show its head. Bikaner

1. Sarkar's *Fall of the Mughal Empire*, Vol. III, p. 317.

2. Sir Jadunath Sarkar's *Fall of the Mughal Empire*, Vol. III, p. 319, gives the date as 23, September 1752 and the place as Sindboliya.

and Kishengarh left the field. Scindia had actually prepared to quit the field, when the false news that Maharaja Bijai Singh had been killed, started by Sardar Singh, the expropriated Chief of Rupangarh now with the Mahrattas, spread like wildfire among the Rathors, who left the field panic-stricken. Bijai Singh thus left alone, fled to Nagor. After a short time, however, Jai Appa who was besieging that place was assassinated by Chauhan Khokar Kesar Singh in front of his tent. The siege was raised. After negotiations, peace was concluded, and Ajmer was ceded in 1756 A.D. as *Moondkati*, (price of the murder of Jai Appa), whose remains were brought to Pushkar, where a beautiful chhatri and temple, stand on his remains at the Gwalior Ghat.

From 1756 to 1758 A.D., the city of Ajmer remained under the joint possession of the Mahrattas and Maharaja Ram Singh. Marwar was partitioned between Ram Singh and Bijai Singh, Ram Singh getting Merta, Parbatsar, Marot, Sojat, Jalor, Bhinai, Kekri, Deolia with sixteen villages, and Masuda with twenty seven villages. In addition to Ajmer, Scindia got six lakhs[1] cash, thirty elephants and a tent valued at one lakh, and jewels valued at two lakhs. Of the share of Ram Singh, Scindia took a small portion. Kharwa, Masuda and Bhinai remained in Ram Singh's possession. The rest of the district was administered by Jankuji and Dattaji, brothers of Jai Appa.

The fact of partition of the district area of Ajmer shows that these parganas were at the time a part of Marwar. Bijai Singh's attempt to recover these parganas from Ram Singh failed. In 1756, Khan Jadu was sent by Scindia to Ajmer with four thousand men. Ram Singh took three thousand of his own men with him, and both invaded Marwar, but were defeated and had to retreat to Ajmer. Bijai Singh advanced and encamped at Pisangan.

In 1758 A.D., Ram Singh retired to Jaipur and the Mahratta subedar Govind Rao, drove out Ram Karan, Ram Singh's representative, and took exclusive possession of Ajmer. Maharaja Bijai Singh as Ram Singh's heir, laid claim to Ram Singh's share of the district. Govind Rao accepted the claim and handed over Masuda, Kharwa and Bhinai to Maharaja Bijai Singh, who established his *Thana* at Tantoti. In 1759 A.D., the Mahratta subedar having treated the Istimrardars of Ajmer harshly, the latter imprisoned him in a fort belonging to Gulab Singh, son of Kalyan Singh of Khawas. Mahratta reinforcements, however, arrived after three months and the subedar was released.

1. Rieu's *History of Marwar*, p. 375, says twenty lakhs.

The Mahrattas under Sadashiva Rao Bhau, having been defeated at Panipat in 1761 A.D. by Ahmed Shah Ibdali, king of Kabul, their power and prestige sustained a severe blow; and Maharaja Bijai Singh deeming it a good opportunity to recover Ajmer, sent Baloo Joshi in 1761 A.D. with a strong force to take possession of it. Govind Rao the Mahratta governor, shut himself up in the fort, Garh Beetli, and fortified the place. Baloo laid seige to it and sat before it for two months, when a Mahratta force arrived from the Deccan, and Baloo raising the siege, retired to Jodhpur. The same year, Maharaja Bijai Singh sent Baloo Joshi to the Khari river. He recovered *Peshkashi* as follows:—

From Pisangan	Rs.	20,000/-	From Masuda	Rs.	20,000/-
„ Govindgarh	„	7,000/-	„ Deolia & Tantoti	„	17,000/-
„ Kharwa	„	20,000/-	„ Bhinai	„	22,000/-

Peshkashi was also recovered from Barli and Junia, Kekri, Sawar and Para. Rajgarh was attacked and plundered, and the Marwar forces moved on to Ajmer. Here the Thakurs of Ras, Nimaj, Nibol and Lambia joined Baloo Joshi. Rs. 7,00,000 were sent to Merta. The Mahrattas, who were in possession of Ajmer, fought for three days and then retired to the hill-fort Garh Beetli. The city of Ajmer passed into Maharaja Bijai Singh's possession and the troops encamped on the Visla lake. Messengers were sent to Madhaji Scindia to send reinforcements at once, otherwise, Garh Beetli would surrender to the Rathors. Madhaji asked the garrison to hold out for ten days, when he would reach Ajmer. Sher Singh, Thakur of Tantoti, was in charge of the *morcha* at the city gate and Bishen Das was in charge of Amba Bao in Inderkot. Artillery was also stationed. Jamadar Sahib Khan was in charge of Chand Pol and the Hakim of Marot and other Sardars were in Nurchashma. On Jeth 10, s. 1818 (12 June, 1761), the garrison made a surprise attack at night from the fort and attacked the Amba Bao *morcha* (in Inderkot) and killed some men. Chandawat Ratan Singh and Jagram advanced from the town to Katan Bao (Inderkot) and made a counter attack and drove the garrison into the fortress. Then Baloo Joshi came with a contingent and stayed all day at Amba Bao in Inderkot. As news arrived that Scindia was coming by forced marches and had arrived near Ajmer, the Marwar artillery was sent away to Merta. When Madhaji Scindia arrived at Sambhar, Baloo Joshi raised the siege and retired to Bhaonta, ten miles from Ajmer. Dhabhai Jaggu, the Commander in Chief of Marwar, who was at Merta, sent Gulab Rai Asop to negotiate peace. Scindia came to Budhwara and went towards Baloo Joshi's camp. Firing began. In the meantime, the Udawat, the Surtanot and the Keshadasot Sardars went over to the Scindia and told him that they would arrest Baloo Joshi at midnight. Baloo got information of it, and with Thakur Fateh Singh went towards Samel, and reached Balunda a little after nightfall, and next morning joined Jaggu at Merta. From 1761 to 1787, the city of Ajmer remained in the possession of the Scindia. In 1767, Maharaja Bijai Singh came to Pushkar and met Maharaja Jawahir Singh of Bharatpur, and agreed to help him against Maharaja Madho Singh of Jaipur.

In 1787, the Mahrattas attacked Jaipur, and Maharaja Pratap Singh asked the Maharaja of Jodhpur for help. A Rathor army under commander Singhi Bhimraj was sent. The combined forces of Jaipur and Jodhpur defeated Scindia at Tunga.[1] Scindia fled to Agra, pursued by the Rajputs.

1. Describing the battle of Tunga, Sir Jadunath Sarkar says: "Then a tumultuous shout was heard on the enemy's right, and through the smoke screen burst four thousand Rathor horsemen at the gallop. The *desperadoes*, after taking a *last lingering pull at their pipes of opium*, drew their swords and charged the Mahratta left with wild cries of "Han ! Han ! Kill them ! Kill them.—*Fall of the Mughal Empire*, Vol. III, p. 377. Sir Jadunath Sarkar's condemnation of these valiant men as desperadoes is unfair and unjust. These Rajput warriors were not *desperadoes*, but brave men of unsurpassed courage. There was nothing criminal or lawless about their conduct or acts. The four thousand Rathor horsemen who made a magnificent cavalry charge at Tunga were chivalrous and honourable fighters. Then the words "after taking a last lingering pull at their pipes of opium", are equally wrong and inapplicable. The Rathors or other Rajputs never smoke opium, and are strangers to "pipes of opium". The Rajputs eat opium, or sip it dissolved in water.

Mr. Compton, a European historian, describes the Rathor charge at the battle of Tunga thus: "The Rathors of Jodhpur were the very flower of Rajput bravery, and celebrated throughout Hindustan for their splendid courage and their handsome mien. They were a warrior clan, whose past achievements had marked them out as the *first and the finest of all the fighting races of the East*, and won for them the proud distinction of being without fear. As they came within sight of De Boigne's two battalions, drawn up ready to receive them, they converged upon the little band, rending the air with fierce and exulting shouts of anticipated victory. Their flags flaunted in the breeze, the sunshine glistened on their plumed helmets and chain armour, and their swords and spears flashed aloft as they thundered over the sun-baked plain. *Never yet in the history of battle, had footmen dared to oppose the might of Marwar mounted for the fray*, and when the chief of Rian (in Marwar) saw the compact formation, steady as the stone around, awaiting his onslaught, he determined to punish this insolence of courage. "It was a terrible baptism of battle for De Boigne's young battalions. Armies had melted and dispersed before these on-charging warriors, who seemed as if they had but to ride to annihilate the little square, that

Singhi Bhimraj, the Commander of the Rathor force at Tunga, while returning to Jodhpur after the victory, took the city of Ajmer from Mirza Anwar Beg, Scindia's governor, who shut himself up in Garh Beetli, which was besieged.

Rajput reinforcements arrived from Nagor with four guns, and a thousand men under Mehta Rai Chand; from Jalor, two thousand men left for Ajmer. The siege lasted for two months.[1] When provisions failed, the Mahratta governor of the fort sent to Scindia for relief. Scindia sent seven thousand men under Bastaji, whom he asked to act according to the advice of the Raja of Kishengarh. The Mahrattas were able to send provisions to the fortress, but were unable to take the city. Two thousand men from Jalor and two hundred horsemen under Bhandari Shiv Chand came to Pushkar, and Thakur Bishen Singh of Chanod, Ram Datta Ojha and several young nobles with their contingents arrived to assist the Marwar forces in possession of the city of Ajmer. From Jodhpur came Singhi Akhai Raj.

Ambaji Inglia, the Mahratta commander, marched against them, and pitched his camp at Kayar (eight miles from Ajmer). Twenty rifles of Chandawats defended themselves till night-fall, when Ambaji returned to Kishengarh. The Marwar forces under Akhai Raj advanced to Gangwana. The Raja of Kishengarh persuaded Ambaji to attack the Marwar forces. The Marwar forces divided themselves into two parts, one under Akhai Raj and the other under Ram Datta Ojha and Sawai Singh, the Jalor contingents in the centre guarding the camp. The Mahrattas divided their army into three portions, and attacked the centre to plunder the camp, and thus cause confusion. A severe fight took place. The Mahrattas lost ground and fled. Ambaji's attack on Ojha's

held its place and awaited the shock with splendid courage."—*European Military Adventurers of Hindustan*, by H. Compton, p. 35.

Of the bravery shown by the Rathors at Merta in 1790 A.D., Mr. Compton says:—"It is impossible for me to describe the feats of bravery performed by the *Zard Kapde Wallahs* or the Forlorn Hope, of the enemy (Rathors). I have seen, after the line was broken, fifteen or twenty men return to charge a thousand Infantry, and advance to within ten or fifteen paces before all were shot".—*European Military Adventurers of Hindustan*, by H. Compton, p. 61. Saffron coloured clothes are put on by Rajputs when they go to battle, resolved to win or die.

Dr. Beni Prasad in his *History of Jahangir*, p. 221, says: "As one glides through Rajputana tradition, the mind staggers at the *heights of valour, devotion and altruism, to which human soul can soar.*"

1. According to Sarkar's *Fall of the Mughal Empire*, three months and twenty eight days.

army also failed. The armoured troops of Jalor, after a front attack, defeated the Mahrattas and pursued them for two miles. Coming to a river, the Marwar troops halted. The Mahrattas lost one hundred and fifty killed and one hundred and twenty wounded. Ambaji left the wounded in Sarwar, and with his army, went home (Malwa). The Marwar forces got Srinagar evacuated and taking Ramsar, came to Ajmer. Mirza Anwar Beg who was defending Garh Beetli, now evacuated the fort, and gave Rupees twenty thousand, and forty-five horses in order to be allowed to depart in safety.

The Rajputs after taking possession of Ajmer, approached the Emperor at Delhi and asked him to take the lead and drive away the Mahrattas beyond the river Narbada. The Emperor replied that *he was helpless*, that *the Scindia paid him five thousand rupees a day for his maintenance; and that if Jaipur and Jodhpur would pay him the same amount, he would be guided by them.* The Emperor came to Alwar during these negotiations. As there was no money to pay to the Emperor, Daulat Ram Haldiya persuaded the Emperor to return to Delhi. In the meantime, cholera broke out in the Marwar forces and large numbers died. While returning to Jodhpur, the Sardars went from Pushkar to their respective homes, and Bhimraj to the capital.

To avenge the defeat at Tunga in 1787, Scindia began to make preparations, and after three years, again marched against Jaipur in 1790 A.D. Madhaji Scindia having defeated the Rajputs at Patan (Shekhawati) on 20th June, 1790 A.D., the Mahratta army under Lakwa Dada and General De Boigne advanced against Jodhpur. "De Boigne decided first to attempt the capture of Ajmer, which, lying as it did, half-way between Jaipur and Jodhpur, was the key of the country. On the 15th of August, he reached it and at once completed the investment; but, owing to the impregnable nature of the fort, he was unable to take it by a *coup de main.* He therefore left two thousand cavalry and a sufficient force of infantry to cover it, and marched with the rest of the army towards Jodhpur.[1]

Singhi Dhanraj and Thakur Surajmal of Kharwa, the Raja of Bhinai, Bakht Singh of Deolia, Thakur Gulab Singh of Tantoti and Bhopal Singh of Masuda were in charge of the town of Ajmer. Scindia invoked the god Hanuman and spent three lakhs of rupees in *Jap* (incantations). Holkar's army

1. Compton's *European Military Adventurers of Hindustan*, page 55.

reinforced Scindia's at Ajmer. Scindia told De Boigne that the Rathors had spoiled his game of dominating the Imperial Rule in Delhi, and he wished to be revenged on the Rathors, and was willing to undergo any expense to humble them. General De Boigne placed his guns on the hills of Anasagar, and bombarded the town. The city walls gave way. Ten thousand Mahratta horse charged the infantry in the town. The Mussalmans inside the city, treacherously opened the gates and the Mahrattas rushed in and looted the place. This took place on 22 August, 1790[1] A.D. Dhanraj with one hundred and one Sardars ascended the fort and fortified it. Two assaults were made, but no impression was made on the fort.

An officer in De Boigne's brigade, in a letter dated Ajmer Camp, the 1st September 1790, and published in the *Calcutta Chronicle*, says:

> "Although we have invested this fort for fifteen days very closely, yet we can make no impression upon it; our guns from the very great elevation they are placed at, and the distance make no visible impression, and the narrow paths which lead to the fort are so defended by nature, that a few large stones thrown down must carry everything before them; the noise they make in rolling I can compare to nothing but thunder. Indeed, I am afraid we must turn the blockade into a siege, as they have six months' water and a year's provisions in the fort."[2]

The fortress held out for more than six months, and defied the efforts of the besiegers to take it. Credit for this heroic defence of the fortress was due to Singhi Dhanraj and Thakur Suraj Mal of Kharwa, who received the thanks of the Maharaja of Jodhpur for bravery and skill. In the meantime, the Jodhpur forces were defeated at Merta, and peace having been concluded, Ajmer was ceded to the Scindia, who gave it in jagir to Lakwa Dada, the Mahratta Commander-in-Chief. In a letter dated Falgun vadi 1st, S. 1847 (19th February, 1791 A.D.), Maharaja Bijai Singh wrote to Thakur Suraj Mal of Kharwa to hand over the fort of Ajmer to the "Deccanis."

Singhi Dhanraj, the governor of Ajmer, however, scorned thus tamely to surrender Ajmer, and not willing to disobey the orders of his prince, 'swallowed diamond powder.' "Tell the Maharaja," said this faithful servant, "thus only could I testify my obedience; and over my dead body alone could a Southron (Mahratta) enter Ajmer."[3]

The fort which had successfully stood the long siege was thus surrendered to the Mahrattas. The city of Ajmer and the fortress of Garh Beetli never again passed into Rathor hands,

1. *Hindustan Under the Free Lances*, by H. G. Keene, p. 49, (1907 A.D.).
2. Compton's *European Military Adventurers of Hindustan*, p. 55.
3. Tod's *Rajasthan*, Vol, II, p. 136.

though most of the district area of Ajmer remained for some time, part of Marwar.

From the facts given above, it is clear that except for the first few years of the eighteenth century, when the Mughal governor remained in precarious possession of it, the town of Ajmer, remained in the possession, either of the Rathors of Jodhpur or the Scindia of Gwalior throughout that century. The district area of Ajmer containing the Istimrari estates which form three-fifths of the district, remained part of Marwar throughout that century. It was in the beginning of the nineteenth century that most of the rural area forming the district of Ajmer came into Mahratta possession, and after a dozen years, passed into that of the British.

Except Sawar, all the Istimrardars of Ajmer are off-shoots of the royal family of Marwar, and they always acknowledged the Maharaja of Jodhpur as their liege lord. The people even of the town of Ajmer when the British came in 1818, were all from Marwar. Their language, dress, their social usages and customs, their entire culture and traditions are those of Marwar. Ethnologically, socially, culturally and politically, Ajmer has been a part of Marwar. The district of Merwara, geographically a part or continuation of the Mewar hilly territory, forms the barrier between Mewar and Marwar. In olden days it acknowledged the supremacy of Mewar, but for administrative purposes, it always enjoyed full autonomy.

General Perron remained in Ajmer to settle the district, which work he carried out with considerable ability.[2] In 1792 A.D., he left Ajmer for the Doab to join the army of the Scindia.

Sivaji Nana, known as Nana Sahib, who had been appointed subedar of Ajmer in 1791 A.D. was held in great respect by the Mahrattas. He ruled Ajmer with a strong hand and restored order. He turned his attention to the turbulent Mers and established some *thanas* in Merwara. He garrisoned Shamgarh and imposed fines on the Istimrardars who had joined Jodhpur in the late war. He levied three lakhs of rupees from Shahpura, forty-eight thousand from Sawar, and three years' revenue from the others, and demolished their forts. He deprived Bhinai of Ratakot and incorporated it in the Khalsa. In 1797 A.D., his son Bishwapat Rao Bhau imprisoned Udai Bhan, Raja of Bhinai, in Ajmer, owing to non-payment of revenue. The Rajputs of Bhinai, thereupon,

1. Tod's *Rajasthan*, Vol. II, p. 136.
2. Compton's *European Military Adventurers of Hindustan*, page 223.

imprisoned Ram Bhau, Tahsildar of the place, threw off their allegiance and took to plundering the district. The subedar thereupon released Udai Bhan of Bhinai, reduced the revenue payable by the Talukdars and made a permanent settlement with them. The Rajputs of Bhinai also released Ram Bhau.

In 1800 A.D., owing to a domestic intrigue, Lakwa Dada, the Commander-in-Chief of the Mahratta army of Hindustan, whose *Jaidad* (Jagir) Ajmer was, was superseded by Ambaji Inglia. Lakwa Dada went into rebellion, and General Perron was ordered to reduce him to submission. As Perron had been invited to join the marriage on 26th November of Maharaja Pratap Singh of Jaipur, he determined first to go there and then to return to Ajmer to attack Lakwa. On 14th November 1800, he heard at Balahera that Lakwa had gone away to Malwa. He, therefore, sent Major Bourguien to capture Ajmer, and himself proceeded to Jaipur.[1] Having arrived before the fort (of Ajmer) in December 1800, Major Louis Bourguien endeavoured to storm it on the 8th of the month, but was driven back by the garrison. He then, in expressive oriental phraseology, "sat down" before it and after fruitlessly attempting its reduction by siege, bombarded it with a more powerful metal than iron, and after five months, gained possession of the place by bribery on the 8th of May, 1801.[2]

Mons. Perron now became subedar of Ajmer, and appointed one, Mr. Low, to administer the district. In 1801 A.D., Maharaja Bhim Singh of Jodhpur married at Pushkar the sister of Maharaja Pratap Singh of Jaipur, and the latter married there Ajab Kanwar, grand daughter of Maharaja Bijai Singh. Thakur Bhairun Singh of Masuda, Raja Udai Bhan of Bhinai, Nathu Singh of Pisangan and Sawai Singh of Kharwa were in attendance on the Maharaja of Jodhpur, being his Sardars.

In 1802, Maharaja Bheem Singh of Jodhpur sent Bhandari Dhiraj Mal to take Ajmer but met with failure. In 1803, at the coronation of Maharaja Man Singh, Thakur Ajit Singh of Deolia, Raja Udai Singh of Bhinai, Devi Singh of Kharwa and Bherun Singh of Masuda being Sardars of Marwar, were in attendance at Jodhpur.

In 1803 A.D., war was declared between Scindia and the English Government, and Maharaja Man Singh of Marwar,

1. Compton's *European Military Adventurers of Hindustan*, page 244.
2. Ibid, 246. "Captain Symes was sent to supersede Bourguien who had been fruitlessly endeavouring to capture Ajmer."—*European Military Adventurers of Hindustan*, page 416.

regarding this as a good opportunity to regain Ajmer, established *thanas* (military outposts) in the district and kept possession of it for three years. The Mahrattas, however, got it back, in 1806 A.D. and remained in possession till, by virtue of the treaty of 25th June, 1818, Ajmer was ceded to the British Government. General Sir David Ochterlony, Resident at Delhi, and Col. Nixon, with eight regiments of infantry, one of cavalry and a proportionate amount of artillery,[1] came to Ajmer on 29th June 1818, encamped at the foot of the Madar Hill and sent the order (hukmnama) of the Scindia to the subedar to give up possession of Ajmer. The subedar, Bapu Scindia, did not comply with the demand at once, and began to prepare for hostilities. Sir David Ochterlony also prepared his force for an action, when Bapu Scindia gave in and evacuated the fort, and left with his family for Gwalior. General Ochterlony at once took possession of Ajmer on 28th July, 1818 A.D., and established a Cantonment between the villages of Bir and Nandla, fourteen miles from Ajmer, on 20th November 1818 A.D., and named it Nasirabad after his title Nasir-ud-daula, conferred on him by the king of Delhi in 1804 A.D.

V.—THE BRITISH PERIOD.

From 1195 A.D., when Afghan rule was established in Ajmer, to 1818 when the British took it, for a period of 623 years, Ajmer, owing to its strategical position of supreme importance, was the arena of constant warfare. Out of this period of 623 years, Ajmer enjoyed a sort of peace for 162 years from 1558 to 1720 A.D., when it was under Mughal rule. During the remaining period of 461 years, Ajmer was ruled sometimes by the Pathan Sultans of Delhi, sometimes by the Rathor Rajputs of Marwar or the Sisodias of Mewar (Udaipur), sometimes by the Scindia of Gwalior and, for very brief periods, by the Sultans of Mandoo and Gujrat.

The Pathan Sultans of Delhi were in no sense of the term, Emperors of India. They ruled in Delhi from 1193 to 1526 and again from 1542 to 1555, and belonged to several dynasties and exercised power according as the rulers were strong or weak. A powerful ruler like Allauddin Khilji extended his rule

1. Dixon's *Sketch of Merwara*, p. 18. According to Col. Dixon, one of the objects of this march of General Ochterlony was to effect the dispersion of Amir Khan, Nawab of Tonk's forces.

over several provinces and dominated a large part of Northern India; while weak rulers, like Allahuddin Masudshah and Nasiruddin Mahmudshah of the slave dynasty, held precarious rule even in the city of Delhi, when, as Edward Thomas' *Chronicles of the Pathan Kings of Delhi*, p. 131, says, *the gates of Delhi were shut at 6 p.m., for fear of the Mewatees raiding it.*

The Mughal (Turkish) empire of India had an active life of one hundred and sixty four years from 1556[1] to 1720, and then a dormant life of thirty five years from 1720 to 1755. After that year, the supreme power in Delhi passed into the hands of the Mahrattas. In 1757 A.D., Malhar Rao Holkar conquered Delhi, and the Mughal Emperor practically surrendered at discretion on the 3rd of September of that year. Sir Jadunath Sarkar[2] says:

"The completeness of the Mahratta supremacy over Delhi is seen from the entry in the official history of the reign. 'The Emperor, as requested, sent robes of honour to Malhar Rao (Holkar) to make new appointments at his own discretion. The persons thus inducted to office, after putting their *Killats* on, made their bows to Raghunath Rao in his tent."

Describing the Mahratta attack on Delhi and the battle of Purana Qila in 1772, under the heading, "§16 Complete Submission of the Emperor to the Mahrattas", Sir J. N. Sarkar[1] says:—

"The Emperor had no stomach for fighting left, his troops hopelessly outnumbered, and his city was completely enveloped by the Mahratta army with the Ruhela troopers of Zabita Khan and the Jat soldiers and Samru's battalions and guns which had arrived to the aid of the Mahrattas......... So the Emperor made a complete surrender and signed a promise to grant all his enemy's demands."

In his *Life of Madhava Rao Scindia*, p. 182 (Rulers of India Series), Mr. H. G. Keene says:—

"Shah Alam still wore the crown of Akbar in the palace of Shah Jahan; but he was a blind septuagenarian with no voice in the disposal of events beyond the palace walls. Elsewhere the affairs of peace and of war obeyed the orders of Scindia, from the Sutlej to the Narbada."

The Mahratta supremacy ended, when the British in 1803 A.D. acquired a dominant position in the Mughal Court. This continued till the year 1857, when the British removed the Mughal puppet and established their own rule in India.

Having been an arena of constant warfare for a long time, prosperity, which depends upon peace, always remained a stranger to Ajmer. The city which was the capital of the

1. Akbar was the real founder of the Mughal empire. He ascended the throne of Delhi in 1556, but took Ajmer in 1558 A.D.
2. J. N. Sarkar's *Fall of the Mughal Empire*, Vol. II, pp. 152-153.
1. J. N. Sarkar's *Fall of the Mughal Empire*, Vol. III, p. 74.

Hindu Empire of Northern India in the twelfth century, dwindled to a town of 24,000 souls in 1818 A.D. A new era of peace dawned on it with its occupation by the British Government, and peaceful progress became possible. The establishment of peace not only in Rajputana, but throughout India made social, industrial and educational progress possible.

An account of Ajmer-Merwara from 1818 A.D. to 1940 A.D., falls under two heads: (1) Historical survey of Ajmer, and (2) The British Administration of Ajmer-Merwara.

Historical Survey.

The historical survey of Ajmer is an account of the chief events that occurred in Ajmer-Merwara, and the administrative and other measures taken for the improvement and prosperity of this small province, and the consequent development of the city of Ajmer.

The first Trigonometrical[1] survey both of Ajmer and Merwara containing 591 villages and 19 pargannas, area, 2661½ square miles, (Ajmer 2059, and Merwara 602.599 sq. miles) was made by Lt. D. C. Varierence from 23rd. October, 1847 to April 1848 A.D. A Topographical[2] survey of the province of Ajmer-Merwara was commenced in 1868 and finished in 1875 A.D., and showed the areas of Ajmer and Merwara, to be 2069.816, and 640.864 sq. miles respectively.

Of the British province of Ajmer-Merwara, the Ajmer division has now an area of 2070 square miles and a population of 4,23,918 souls. It is 80 miles long and 50 miles broad.[3] It contains one city, Ajmer (population, 1,19,524), three towns, Nasirabad (population 21,397), Kekri (population 7179) and Pushkar (population 3781), and 518 villages, of which 140 lie in the Khalsa area, 51 in Jagir and 327 in the Istimarari area. Merwara with a population of 82,947, has one town, Beawar, (population 28,342), and 214 villages, all Khalsa.[4]

The story of the progressive development of Ajmer is summed up in the one fact, that the shrunken town of 24,000 souls in 1818, all cooped up in a short space enclosed by a city wall, at the foot of the famous Garh Beetli (Taragarh hill) became in 1931, a flourishing city of 1,19,524 souls, five

1. La Touche's *Settlement Report*, p. 136.
2. Ibid.
3. The farthest village from Ajmer is Dewair, 97 miles; and the longest distance between any two villages is 121 miles, between Harmara and Dewair.
4. Portions of Merwara were retroceded to the Mewar and Marwar States in 1933 A.D. reducing the area and population of British Merwara.

times its size in 1818 A D. The city of Ajmer now completely fills up the northern part of the beautiful valley formed by the eastern and western chains of converging hills, enclosing a space about twelve miles long, by two to four miles wide. And but for the great handicap of scarcity of water, from which it has always suffered, Ajmer would have rivalled Delhi, or Lucknow, both of which stand on the banks of rivers—Delhi on the Jumna and Lucknow on the Gomti.

With the establishment of security of life and property, people turn their attention to the improving of agriculture, the spreading of education, the starting of Industry, the opening of communications, and the developing of trade and commerce.

Edmund Burke, the most distinguished of the English political philosophers lays down the dictum that population and wealth are the two standards, by which to test the good or bad Government of a country. The population of the province of Ajmer-Merwara as well as the city of Ajmer has been steadily increasing since the British came to Ajmer in 1818 A.D. There have been about eleven or twelve censuses in Ajmer-Merwara. The result of the 1837 census, one of the early ones, is given in Dr. R. D. Irvine's *General and Medical Topography of Ajmer*, p. 41, as below :—

District.	PARGANNAS.		Towns and villages having more than 4,000 inhabitants.		No. of villages of not more than 4,000 inhabitants in each Pargannah
	Names.	Population.	Name.	Population.	
Ajmer.	1. Ajmer Town.	23,432			3
	2. Pushkur.	9,228	1. Ajmer.	23,432	19
	3. Gangwana.	10,866	2. Kekri	4,025	32
	4. Harmara.	2,130	3. Pushkur.	4,334	3
	5. Ramsar.	21,569	4. Pisangun.	4,174	65
	6. Pisangun.	15,740	5. Shahpura.	5,000	33
	7. Masuda.	20,599	6. Sawar.	4,100	93
	8. Rajgarh.	12,340			42
	9. Bhinai.	27,340			93
	10. Kekri Phooleya[1] Sawar.	67,080			159
	Total.	210,324	6	45,065	548

SUPERINTENDENT'S OFFICE, *Ajmer, 8th April, 1838.* (Signed) J. D. MACNAUGHTEN, *Superintendent of Ajmer.*

1. Now in the Shahpura State.

Population of Ajmer-Merwara as given in the Census Reports.

Census year.		Ajmer District.	Merwara District.[1]	Ajmer-Merwara.
December.	1837	2,10,324[2]	...	...
	1848	2,24,891[3]	...	...
	1865	...	...	4,26,178
	1872	...	...	3,16,590[4]
	1876	3,09,914	86,417	3,96,331
17th Feb.	1881	3,59,288	1,01,434	4,60,722
	1891	4,22,359	1,19,999	5,42,358
1st March.	1901	3,67,453	1,09,459	4,76,912
	1911	3,80,384	1,21,011	5,01,395
	1921	3,78,960	1,16,311	4,95,271
16th Feb.	1931	4,23,918	1,36,374	5,60,292

During the fifty years between 1881 and 1931, the population of the Ajmer district increased by 64630 or 20.7% and that of Merwara, by 34940 or 34%. For Ajmer and Merwara taken together, the increase is 21.6%.

In 1881 the mean density of population was 157 9[5]
In 1931 „ „ „ „ „ „ 207 per mile.

Ajmer-Merwara.

Census year.	Hindus	Muslims.	Christians.	Others.	Total.
1872	2,52,996	62,456	558 Europeans.	...	3,16,590
1876	3,48,248	47,310	715	58	3,96,331
1881	4,00,519	57,809	2,225	169	4,60,722
1891	4,65,140	74,265	2,683	270	5,42,358
1901	4,01,005	72,031	3,712	164	4,76,912
1911	4,10,660	81,035	5,432	3,979 289 4,268	5,01,395
1921	3,82,983	1,01,776	5,531	4,736 245 4,981	4,95,271
1931	4,54,006	97,133	6,947	2,206	5,60,292

1. Inclusive of the portion since transferred to Jodhpur and Udaipur 2. Dr. Irvine's *Medical Topography of Ajmer*, p 41. 3. Thornton's *Gazetteer*, p. 18. 4. Mr. La Touche in his *Settlement Report* says that in 1872, Hindus were 80%, Muslims, 20%, and that there were 558 Europeans. 5. Density of population of Ajmer, 169.96; of Merwara, 146.

That the increase in the population of Ajmer-Merwara is due principally to immigration from the surrounding States, is clear from the fact that, according to the 1931 Census Report, Appendix Table VI., p. 13, out of 5,60,292 persons, 1,06,444 were born outside Ajmer-Merwara. In other words, 19 out of 100 were immigrants. Out of 1000 immigrants, 718 were from the Indian States of Rajputana; 148 from the United Provinces, and 11 from Delhi. In the city of Ajmer, out of every 1000 immigrants, 870 were from Rajputana, 35 from United Provinces, 29 from the Punjab and 3 from Delhi. We find that in the city of Ajmer, out of its population of 1,19,524, only 67579 were born in Ajmer, and as many as 51,945 were born outside. Another interesting fact mentioned in the Census Report is that 60,903 persons, born in Ajmer-Merwara were enumerated in other provinces.

In 1881, out of the total population of Merwara, (1,01,434)

the population of British	Merwara	was	57,309
,,	Mewar	,,	38,514
,,	Marwar	,,	5,611

In 1931, out of the total population of Merwara, (1,36,374)

the population of British	Merwara	was	83,065 :	increase	25,756
,,	Mewar	,,	44,463 :	,,	5,949
,,	Marwar	,,	8,846 :	,,	3,235

In the whole of Merwara, the increase was 34,940, or 34%.

In British Merwara	the increase was	44%
Mewar ,,	,,	15%
Marwar ,,	,,	57%

By the return of Mewar Merwara and Marwar Merwara to the States of Udaipur and Jodhpur, Ajmer-Merwara has lost 53,309 of its population.

Of the total population of Ajmer-Merwara 5,60,292, according to the 1931 Census Report:

Hindus	are	4,54,006	or	81'032%
Muslims	are	97,133	or	17'333
Christians	are	6,947	or	1'244
Sikhs	are	341	or	0'060
Parsis	are	301	or	00'537
Buddhists	are	4	or	
Jews	are	49	or	0'008
Tribal and others	are	1,471	or	0'2%

The following table shows the population of Hindus, Muslims and Christians, per ten thousand of population, in Ajmer-Merwara:

Year	1881	1891	1901	1911	1921	1931
Hindus	8,689	8,562	8,413	8,173	8,128	8,103
Muslims	1,255	1,369	1,516	1,616	2,055[1]	1,734
Christians	48	50	78	108	112	124

1. This high proportion is due to inclusion of 15,000 Muslim pilgrims.

Ajmer District.

The increase in the population of the city of Ajmer and the three important towns in the district of Ajmer is as below:-

		1881	1891	1901	1911	1921	1931
Ajmer in 1872 A.D.	26,569[1]	48,735	68,843	73,830	86,222	99,364[2]	1,19,524
Beawar in 1847 A.D.	9,000	15,829	20,978	21,928	22,800	22,362	28,342
Nasirabad	...	21,320	21,710	22.494	20,241	19,651	21,397
Kekri	...	6,119	7,100	7,053	5,926	5,698	7,179

Increase between 1881 and 1931, (fifty years) :

Ajmer city is 70789 or 145%[3]
Beawar is 12513 or 72.6%
Nasirabad Cantt. is only 77. (stationary.)
Kekri 1060 or 17%

In the city of Ajmer the increase of population by religion is as under:

City of Ajmer 1891-1931 (40 years).

Census of	Total.	Hindus.	Muslims.	Christians.	Others.
1872	26,569[4]	...	...	...	...
1881	48,735	29,270	18,702	720	43
1891	68,843	40,755	26,433	1,497	158
1901	73,839	46,298	25,569	1,871	101
1911	86,222	52,678	30,654	5,677	...
1921	99,364	55,079	38,470	3,193	1,770
1931	1,19,524	74,526	40,548	4,161	289

Increase during the last 50 years Hindus 254.6 p. c.
" " " Muslims 216.8 p. c.
" " " Christians 578 p. c.

1. Mr. Macnaughten, Superintendent of Ajmer held a census of the town of Ajmer on 26 February, 1837. The population then was 23,432 only. But 1832 and 1834 were famine years.

2. Exclusive of about 15.000 Urs pilgrims in Ajmer.

3. The suburban population of Ajmer is increasing very fast. In 1901 it was 21,765. In 1921, it was 28,249; in 1931 it increased to 48,459 and including the Mayo College, 55,238.

4. La Touche's *Gazetteer*, p. 50, It gives the population of Ajmer in 1876 as 30,583.

The population of the Ajmer city in 1931 was composed of:

Hindus	74,526	or	62 p. c.
Muslims	40,548	or	33 p. c.
Europeans and Anglo Indians	1,860	or	1.5 p. c.
Indian Christians	2,301	or	1.9 p. c.
Sikhs	270		
Parsis	240		
Others	about 49		

Another interesting fact that emerges is, that in the city of Ajmer, the number of Hindus has risen during ten years, 1921 to 1931, by 35% while the Mussalmans have increased only by 5.4%.

After taking possession of Ajmer, Sir D. Ochterlony sent for Mr. Wilder, an Assistant Resident at Delhi, and appointed him first Superintendent of Ajmer. About his administration Mr. La Touche says:—

"In the middle of the famine year 1824 A. D. he was promoted to the charge of the Saugor and Narbada territories. His six years' administration was not productive of any great results. He made no radical inquiry into any of the institutions of the province. He called all the Istimrardars of Ajmer and the Thakurs of Athoon, Shamgarh and Jhak and assured them of protection. He continued many old abuses both in the Customs and the Revenue Departments, simply because they brought in money. It cannot be said that he took much pains to ascertain the value of the land he assessed or the condition of the people, and the era of material improvement had not yet dawned. He united in his person the offices of Superintendent of Ajmer, and of Political Agent for Jodhpur, Jaisalmer, and Kishangarh, and kept up a semi-regal state with elephants, horsemen, and chobdars. On the other hand, his administration was rather starved. The whole cost of the Revenue and Police establishment of the district was Rs. 1,374 a month, or less than half of Mr. Wilder's salary, which was Rupees 3,000. There was not a copy of any Regulation in the Office in 1823, and a copy of the *Calcutta Gazette* was refused."[1] After a time an European Assistant was appointed. The great solicitude of Mr. Wilder was to develop the trade of Ajmer, and he invited merchants from all quarters to come and settle in the city."

Merwara had for centuries been independent territory, part of it owing nominal allegiance to the Maharana of Udaipur. It was subjugated in 1821-22,[2] by the British and Udaipur forces, and Col. Hall was appointed Superintendent of Merwara. He ruled wisely. In 1836, Major Dixon was appointed to succeed him. He laid the foundation of the town of Nayanagar, (Beawar) four miles from the old village of Beawar.

1. La Touche's *Settlement Report*, p. 71.
2. For an account of this campaign, see Chapter "Merwara."

Currency.

The company's coins were not current in Ajmer. Coins of six mints were current. (1) Ajmer mint, established in Akbar's time, turned out yearly about a lakh and a half of rupees called *Sri Shahi* (2) *Kishengarh rupees*, minted in Kishengarh, (3) *Kuchaman* rupees minted by the Thakur of Kuchaman in Marwar (4) *Shahpura* (5) ***Chitori*** (Mewar currency) and (6) *Jhadshai* or Jaipur currency. Mr. Wilder recognised only Furrukhabad rupees.

Mr. Wilder was succeeded by Mr. Henry Middleton in December, 1824. On 24 October, 1827 the latter made over charge to Mr. Cavendish. Mr. Middleton found that Mr. Wilder's settlement was very high. He advocated the system of taking revenue dues in kind. "Many cultivators who had come to the district in the first year of the British rule had been driven away again by bad harvests and high assessments."[1] Mr. Cavendish was a reformer, and left the impress of his energy on the administration. He made an extension of the city to the east, just outside the Madar Gate, called after himself, Cavendishpura. He left Ajmer on 28, November, 1831 giving over charge to his assistant, Mr. Moore. He was succeeded by Major Speirs, who was transferred to Neemuch, and in his turn was succeeded by Mr. Edmunstone, who describes the people of Ajmer as "reckless, improvident and poverty striken."[2] In January, 1831 A.D., the Mewar Political Agency was abolished and the temporary charge of relations with the Maharana was vested in the Superintendent and Political Agent, Ajmer.

In 1832, Ajmer was placed under the Governor of the N. W. P. (now United Provinces of Agra and Oudh). In this year, the Governor General of India, Lord William Bentinck, visited Ajmer, and ordered the dismantling of the Taragarh fort, which had played such conspicuous part in the history of Rajputana.

Lord William Bentinck was the first Governor General of India to visit Ajmer. He invited all the Princes of Rajputana to meet him at Ajmer. It took him nearly three months to come and go back to Agra. Elephants, camels, horses, *Palkies* were used, and the luggage was carried in bullock carts. Ten to twelve miles were covered each day.

1. La Touche's *Settlement Report*, p. 71.
2. La Touche's *Settlement Report*, p. 74.

great solicitude for the welfare of the people. "He often dressed like an Indian gentleman, used an Indian saddle for his horse. He adopted the *Janeu* (sacred thread) and had Brahmin cooks and often sat down to take his meals with a *dhoti* on." He was very charitable and gave large gifts. Raja Chaman Singh of Rajgarh was a great friend of Mr. Macnaughten, who used to go to Rajgarh and join Indian amusements. The people of Ajmer loved him. He used to call Bhawanji Chita of Nausar (near Ajmer) as Bhawanji *kaka* (uncle). He generally conversed in the Marwari language, which he spoke fluently. He often went to Pushkar to bathe in the lake. He collected a lakh of rupees by public subscription and excavated the present Pushkar pass in 1840 A.D. The date of this excavation is given in the chronogram "Himmate Hakime Dauran Kamare Koh Shakist."

Major Dixon was appointed Superintendent of Ajmer in 1842, in addition to Merwara. About him, Mr. La Touche says: "From the date of his assuming charge, a new era—one of prosperity—commences in the history of the administration of the country. Old tanks were repaired and new ones constructed at an expense of 4,52,707/-. Both Major Dixon and Col. Sutherland wanted to reduce the rate of revenue to one third, but Government refused to sanction this. It was, however, reduced from one half to two fifths." When Major Dixon commenced the construction of his tank embankments in 1842, he acted as a steward to a great estate. He founded hamlets where he thought fit; he gave leases at privileged rates to those who were willing to dig wells, and distributed the lands under the new tanks to strangers whom he located in hamlets in the waste."[1]

In 1847 A.D., Mr. Thompson,[2] Lt. Governor of the N. W. P., visited Merwara. In this year, the Mewar share

1. J.D. La Touche's *Gazetter of Ajmer-Merwara*, page 20 Colonel Dixon had an Indian wife and had a son by her, who, when six years old, was sent to London for education and is said to have lived and died there, leaving three or four sons. Colonel Dixon's widow was living at Beawar in 1875 A.D. and receiving a pension from the property left by her husband.—*Vide* Maharaja Kishen's Urdu *Tarikhe Ajmer*, p. 126. (1875 A.D.) Colonel Dixon's *Chhatri* in the principal bazaar of Beawar is still venerated by the Mers of Merwara, who sing his praises as *Dixon Baba*.

Colonel Dixon, a native of Scotland, was appointed an officer of the Bengal Artillery in 1812 A.D., and had taken part in the subjugation of Merwara. He was appointed Dy. Commissioner of Ordinance and placed in charge of the Ajmer Magazine. He remained there till 1836, when he was appointed Superintendent of Merwara. In 1842, he became Superintendent of both the Ajmer and Merwara districts. In 1853, he was appointed Commissioner of Ajmer-Merwara, with an Assistant in each district. He administered the districts till 1857, when he died after 45 years of service at Beawar on 25th June, 1857, after having heard of the outbreak of the Mutiny. He was buried in the cemetry there. He always lived in Beawar during the summer and the rains.

2. La Touche's *Settlement Report*, p. 77.

of Merwara revenue began to be appropriated towards the maintenance of the Mewar Bhil Corps.

In 1847 A.D., the paragannah of Phooleya, a part of Ajmer, held by the Chief of Shahpura, as Istimrardar of Ajmer, was severed from Ajmer, and the connection of Shahpura with Ajmer ceased. The statement of the population of Ajmer contained in Dr. R. Irvine's *Medical Topography of Ajmer* and given above, shows that Phooleya was a part of Ajmer and held by the Chief of Shahpura as one of the Istimrardars of Ajmer. The state of Shahpura consisted of two pargannahs (1) Kachola in Mewar and (2) Phooleya in Ajmer. Kachola which had been given by the Mewar Darbar was recently resumed by H. H. the Maharana of Udaipur. Now, only Phooleya, which till 1847 was an Istimarari estate of Ajmer, forms the Shahpura State. Mr. J. D. La Touche says:

"The pargannah of Phooleya was originally part of the Khalsa of Ajmer and was given as *jagir* by Shah Jahan to the Raja of Shahpura, a scion of the royal house of Mewar. For many years, the Superintendent of Ajmer exercised an interference in the affairs of the pargannah; but in 1847, it was permanently assessed at Rs. 10,000/- and the Raja of Shahpura is no longer reckoned among the Istimrardars of Ajmer."—*Settlement Report of Ajmer*, p. 65, (1875.)

In 1848 A.D., a census of Ajmer-Merwara was taken. Mr. Thornton, in his *Gazetteer* (1850), p. 18, says:—

"The entire population, as returned by a recent census (1848), amounts to 224,891, something more than 110 to the square mile. Of the above number, 118,533 are returned as Hindu agricultural, 79070 as Hindu non-agricultural; 7,172 Muhammadans and others not being Hindus, agricultural; and 20,116 non-agricultural. The Superintendant reports that the *population* was taken by native officers and that it may be considered as an approximation to the truth."

Col. Dixon laid the foundation of the prosperity of Ajmer and Merwara. He built hundreds of *talaos*, put up embankments and dug wells to protect the districts from famines. He was the first and the last British Officer, who indentified himself with the people of Ajmer-Merwara, mixed with them freely, joined their social functions, and took part in the everyday life of the people. Under him, the town of Ajmer made great progress. All the *ghats* on the Anasagar lake were built under his inspiration. He constructed four big reservoirs of water in the town of Ajmer; namely, (1) the Surajkund opposite the Madar gate, (2) Chandkund outside the city wall between the Delhi and the Agra gates, (3) the Nahar near the Ghaskatla, and (4) the Diggi at the foot of the Taragarh hill, and connected the first three of them with pucca masonry channels with Anasagar. These have now been filled up and disappeared. The Diggi alone remains.

The Sepoy Mutiny.

In 1857 A.D. the famous Sepoy Mutiny took place, which spread throughout Upper India. It broke out at Meerut on 10 May, 1857. The sepoys of the Bengal Army came to believe that the British Government intended to tamper with their religion, by compelling them to use cartridges in which beef had been used. Great disaffection spread among the sepoys and eventually they rebelled. News of the out-break reached Abu on 19th May and Colonel George St. Patrick Lawrence, who had come to Abu, as Officiating Agent to the Governor General in Rajputana in April 1857, sent an urgent message to the Deesa Cantonment for a light field force to be sent to Nasirabad at once, in order to over-awe the sepoys there. On 23rd May, he issued a proclamation to the princes of Rajputana to keep order in their States and concentrate their forces on their borders to assist the British.[1] On the same date, the artillery and the cavalry portion of the light field force marched from Deesa for Nasirabad. Col. Lawrence sent his assistant, Captain Forbes, to accompany it. The first detachment of this European Force reached Nasirabad on the 12th of June. The forces at Nasirabad consisted of a battery (Indians), the same that had fought with General Sale at Jallalabad, and earned undying fame at that glorious siege; the 1st Bombay Lancers, and the 30th Native Infantry which force was increased on the 1st May by the advent of the 15th Regiment, Native Infantry.

The 15th Native Infantry had come to Nasirabad from Meerut where the sepoy forces had all become disaffected. Except the 83rd Foot at Deesa, which was European, the rest of the army in Rajputana, was wholly Indian. The troops at Neemuch consisted of the 72 Regiment Native Infantry, the 7th Regiment of Gwalior contingent and a wing of the 1st Bengal Lancers and fourth troop First Brigade, Horse Arbillery.[2] At Erinpura, one hundred miles from Ajmer, there was a force of irregular troops called the Jodhpur Legion. The two local corps under British Officers, one recruited from the Bhils at near Udaipur, and the other, Merwara Battalion raised by Kherwara Colonel Dixon at Beawar, thirty two miles south of Ajmer, remained loyal. At Kherwara, there was a troop of the 1st Bengal Infantry which mutinied but was disarmed by the, Bhil corps and disbanded.

At Ajmer, the Magazine was in the hands of two companies of the 15th Regiment, Bengal Infantry which had lately

1. *A chapter of the Indian Mutiny*, by Col. Trevor, A.G.G, Rajputana, p. 3.
2. Pritchard's *Mutinies in Rajputana*, p. 107.

come from Meerut to Nasirabad. Fortunately, there were few bungalows and European residents outside it, only an Assistant Commissioner, the Civil Surgeon and his wife, the Principal, Government College, and one of his assistants, and perhaps half a dozen conductors or non-commissioned officers attached to the Magazine. Colonel Dixon, the Commissioner of Ajmer, who was at Beawar, knew that there was disaffection in the Nasirabad garrison, and determined to save the Ajmer Magazine from falling into the hands of the mutineers. The Magazine was a fortified building, the walls of which were so old and rotten that it was generally believed a gun being fired from any one of the bastions would have brought them down. It stood close to the large and thickly populated city of Ajmer, and commanded by the heights outside the town and contained an arsenal large enough to supply the troops in the whole of Rajputana, capable of furnishing a siege train of great strength, guns, ammunition, besides an immense quantity of treasure, for the protection of which nothing more than a company of sepoys was allowed. When the excitement began, in consequence of the news from Meerut, the Grenadier Company of the 15th Native Infantry was sent for, ostensibly to reinforce the light company in the fort, in reality to act as a check upon it.

With Brigadier Macau's concurrence, Colonel Dixon sent his officiating second-in-command, Leiutenant W. Carnell, with two companies of the Merwara Battalion, which was considered reliable. to take charge of the Magazine by a forced march leaving Beawar at night. Lt. Carnell appeared before the Ajmer Magazine the next morning. The English Officer-in-Command refused to vacate the Magazine, but Lt. Carnell insisted on occupying the arsenal and took possession of the Magazine, turning out the 15th Indian Infantry. This relief was destined to be of the highest consequence. He brought into it the European residents of the place, mounted old cannon on every bastion, dug a well in the middle of the quandrangle, lay a stock of provisions and prepared for contingencies. The 15th Indian Infantry, on return to Nasirabad were hissed by their comrades there for giving way to the low caste *Mers*. Col. Lawrence sent hundred men of the 83rd (Europeans) on his arrival on 12th June at Nasirabad out of the first detachment of that regiment from Deesa.

The cantonment of Nasirabad was drawn out in a contiguous line. On the right, were the lines of the 1st Bombay Lancers; to their left, those of the 15th regiment, Native

Infantry.[1] To the left of them again was a large space of ground devoted to the artillery, containing lines for Indian sepoys as well as barracks for European gunners; and to the left of this again,. were the lines of the 30th regiment Native Infantry.

On the 28th May 1857, at 4 P. M., the two regiments of infantry and the company of Bengal artillery at Nasirabad went into mutiny. They took possession of the artillery. The 1st Bombay Cavalry advanced when ordered within a few yards of the guns but would not go further. They, however, allowed the officers to go on. Captain Spottiswoode[2] fell, Col. Newbury was cut to pieces, and Lt. Lock and Capt. Hardy were badly wounded. The remaining English Officers except Captain Fenwick of the 30th, took the road towards Ajmer. The sepoys urged Captain Fenwick to go away. When he shewed unwillingness and they did not want to hurt him, they used force and took him under an escort of four sepoys and an officer to the end of the cantonment and left him there. The officers with a body of lancers who remained loyal, left the road to Ajmer when so directed by the Brigadier Macau, and went towards Beawar. A party of the 30th Native Infantry under an Indian Officer, one hundred and twenty strong, followed the officers to Beawar. Col. Penney, Commandant of the Lancers died on the way to Beawar.[3]

Immediately after it was known that the European Officers had all abandoned the place, the work of destruction commenced in real earnest. There was immense confusion and disorder, as may be supposed. Having got rid of their legitimate commanders, the men had no mind to subject themselves to any new authority till they had had a fling first, and tasted the sweets of liberty. So they set to work, burning and plundering. The church was the first to go, and right merrily it blazed away as soon as fire was set to the dry thatch. The neighbouring bungalows went next, and Lt. Pritchards', being in close proximity to the Lines, was among the earliest destroyed. The treasure-chest was brought down, and put under a guard; very shortly after, it was broken open, and pay, as it was called, distributed among all the sepoys and registered camp-followers who chose to go and take it; and there were not many, we may be sure, who neglected so good an offer. But the whole night was spent by the bulk

1. Letter No. 107—A—784 dated 27th July, 1858, from the Agent, Governor General, Rajputana, to the Government of India.
2. Pritchard's *Mutinies in Rajputana* p. 49.
3. Letter of 29 May 1857, from the Commandant of Rajputana Field Force, to the Agent to the Governor General, Mt. Abu. Also, letter No: 107 - A—784 D/ 27 July 1858 from the Agent, Governor General, Rajputana, to the Government of India.

of the men in plunder. "After plundering the officers' houses, they next approached to loot the shops and planted a cannon at the head of the Sudder Bazar, threatening to open fire, if the inhabitants did not submit quietly to having their houses sacked and property taken away. It was a reign of terror. "But amid all this riot and disorder," says Lt., Pritchard, "I never heard that any blood was wantonly shed; indeed, in this respect, the Nasirabad mutiny forms an exception to the rest; two officers had been killed at the guns, and two wounded, and several of the sepoys had fallen, either killed or badly wounded by some of the cavalry officers who got among them, but there was no massacre, no butchery in cold blood like that which disgraced so many scenes of the rebellion."[1]

After electing their own officers and collecting the plunder, the mutineers took the way to Delhi.[2] Why they did not attack the Magazine at Ajmer, but passed by to Delhi is a mystery. Lt. I. C. Pritchard says: "The Magazine was a fort, but what means had we of maintaining a siege, for the plunder of so rich a city as Ajmer, and the possession of so valuable an arsenal as that in the fort with an almost inexhaustible supply of arms, ammunition, military stores, and all the materials of war, were likely to tempt them in that direction. It is said that they were so loaded with loot and were so anxious to join the mutineers at Delhi, that they did not care to undertake an attack on the Magazine which would be defended by the contingent of the Merwara Battalion."[3]

"The mutineers," says Lt. I. C. Pritchard in his *Mutinies in Rajputana*,[4] "were closely pursued by two officers, Lt. Walters, the Assistant Commisssioner of Ajmer, and Lt. Heathcote, Deputy Assistant Quarter-Master-General of the Rajputana Field Force, as the Nasirabad garrison was called. These officers were accompanied by one thousand men, called Raj troops, which signifies armed retainers of the neighbouring independent chiefs; some belonging to the Jodhpur and some to the Jaipur States. The men would not fight, and they were too much afraid of the sepoys and the guns to attack them, if they had wished, but they made no secret of the fact that their sympathies were with the rebels; they believed that we had tried to tamper with the religion of our men, and evidently thought they were right to act as they

1. Pritchard's *Mutinies in Rajputana*, p. 66.
2. They reached Delhi cn 18th June carrying six guns with them—Kaye's *Sepoy War*, vol. II, p. 550. These Nasirabad troops "were the very flower of the rebel army" Ibid, p. 551.
3. Lt. Pritchard's *Mutinies in Rajputana*, p. 58.
4. Ibid, pp. 89, 90.

did. Still, they went along with these two British officers cheerily enough, and, keeping just behind the rebel column, followed it nearly up to Delhi. It is a strange thing that though they were on the look-out for stragglers, they found none. The rebels made good long marches, the roads were in many places very heavy, the men were encumbered with immense quantities of plunder, and must have been badly off for carriage, yet the pursuers could pick up no stragglers. They parted with a quantity of the plundered property in the villages as they went along, from which a portion was subsequently recovered; but that they should have managed to carry along their sick and women and children and baggage in their hasty march, ill-equipped as they were, is not one of the least curious parts of their strange history."

The officers escorted by the 1st Bengal Lancers reached Beawar on Friday, the 29th May. As soon as the mutineers left Nasirabad for Delhi and the tidings of this reached Beawar, some of the fugitives returned to Nasirabad from Beawar about thirty-six hours after the sepoys left for Delhi. They found the houses blackened ruins, the compounds and roads strewn with papers, letters, notes and fragments of books. The ditches round most of the compounds were also full of papers. A house here and there had been set on fire. The inhabitants of the bazaar were reassured. Half the houses had been locked, the owners having gone away.

In a few days after the return of the fugitives to Nasirabad, the reinforcement promised to the inhabitants of the bazaar arrived; a detachment of the Jodhpur Legion, a wing of the 12th Bombay Native Infantry, a detachment of the 2nd Bombay Cavalry, three guns, Bombay Horse Artillery (European), and about two hundred men of H. M.'s 83rd. The officers who had been left at Beawar accompanied this part of the detachment, as also did the Brigadier and his staff.

On 12 June, a trooper of 1st Bombay Lancers mounted his horse, rode in front of the lines and called upon his comrades to mutiny. As the Bombay Lancers pursued him, he fled to the lines of 12th Bombay Native Infantry, where he was sheltered. Brigadier Henry Macau ordered the 12th to come out, only 40 obeyed. The Brigadier called out the guns and proceeded to the lines of the 12th with a compass of 83rd. The rebel trooper was shot by an Artillery Officer and the leaders of the disaffected court martialed. Five were hanged, three sentenced to life imprisonment, and twenty-five deserted. Arms were restored to others.

The light field force from Deesa, consisting of four hundred of Her Majesty's 83rd Foot, the 18th Bombay Native Infantry, and one troop of Horse Artillery, reached Nasirabad on June 12.[1] Colonel Lawrence, A. G. G., accompanied by his assistants, Capt. Hardcastle and Lt. Impey, had hurried down from Abu on the 1st of that month, as soon as he heard of the outbreak at Nasirabad, arriving at Beawar on the 5th. There he found a warrant from the Lt. Governor of Agra, nominating him Brigadier General, to command the troops in the province, which command he held till Major General Roberts was appointed to the command of Rajputana Division, in March 1858. Col. Dixon dying on 25 June, he assumed charge, by the desire of the same authority, of the Commissionership of Ajmer-Merwara.

On 10th July, Col. Lawrence sent one hundred men of Her Majesty's 83rd Regiment, two hundred men of 12th Bombay Native Infantry, one squadron of 2nd Bombay Cavalry from Nasirabad and two guns from Ajmer Magazine to Neemuch as urgently required there.[2] By this time, the Magazine had been put into as good a state of defence as was possible, breaches having been repaired and provisions for six months laid in. Making Ajmer his headquarters, and residing close to the city, with only a guard of the Mers round his house, Col. Lawrence paid frequent visits to Nasirabad and Beawar, instilling confidence by the calm way in which he carried out the usual duties of the Commissioner in open court during June and July.

On the 9th August 1857, an outbreak took place in the Ajmer Jail, and about fifty prisoners of the criminal class broke loose; the city remained perfectly quiet, and the civil Mounted Police (a portion of the same body which at Neemuch had joined the mutineers)[3] promptly pursued and mercilessly cut down the run-aways.[4]

On August 10, an incipient mutiny at Nasirabad among the Hindustani portion of the 12th Bombay Native Infantry, one of the corps sent from Deesa was suppressed by disarming most of the regiment and making an example of the ringleaders, five of whom were hanged on 25th August.

Maharaja Takht Singh of Jodhpur, at the request of the Political Agent, Captain Monck Mason, sent two thousand men

1. *A Chapter of the Indian Mutiny* by Col. Travor, A. G. G. Rajputana, p. 8.
2. Letter D/ 27 July, 1858 from the A. G. G. Rajputana to the Goverment of India.
3. Ibid.
4. Col. Trevor's *Chapter of the Indian Mutiny*, p. 8.

and six guns to help Lieutenant Carnell at Ajmer. This force encamped near the Anasagar and was not admitted in the Magazine. Thakur Kesri Singh of Kuchaman, Marwar, with his retainers came to help the British and remained for several weeks in the Magazine.

The crowning mercy of the year 1857 to Rajputana was the preservation of the arsenal, the treasury and the city of Ajmer, due to Lieutenant Carnell's forced march from Beawar to Ajmer, "backed by the loyalty of the *Mers* and the measures taken by Lt. Carnell to resist the attack from the Sepoys and over-awe the large and populous city." The report of Brigadier General Lawrence to the Government of India in 1858, says: "The importance of Ajmer cannot be over-estimated. It is to Rajputana what Delhi was to India, and an insurrection there would have been a focus for all the disaffected of the country." Lieutenant Pritchard says: "It was generally believed that if Ajmer had fallen, the Rajputana states would have gone too; for the possession of the arsenal and all the military stores aad treasure in the fort, besides the prestige which would accompany the acquisition of one of the most famous cities in India would have given the insurgents cause in that part of the country such an accession of influence and actual strength that it would have won over to its side one or more of the independent chiefs—the rest would have followed suit, and British interest and power would have ceased from that time to exist."[1]

It is no part of this narrative to give an account of the mutiny as it spread in other places in Rajputana; how the mutiny broke out on June 3, at Neemuch, where a troop of Horse Artillery, the left wing of the 1st Bengal Cavalry, the 72nd Regiment, Bengal Native Infantry, and 7th Regiment of the Gwalior Contingent, were stationed; how the European officers and their families, after vain attempts to resist and rally a portion of the troops were obliged to flee, and all got away safely except the wife of a sergeant and two children, who were murdered; how they shot some Sepoys of the 7th Regiment Gwalior Contingent, who had rejoined the column after seeing their officers to a place of safety; how on 9th June, a body of cavalry of the Mahidpur contingent, sent to Neemuch to assist the Kotah Raj troops, mutinied, murdered two of its officers, Lt. Hunt and Brodie, and joined the Neemuch mutineers beyond Deoli; how on 21st August, a band out of a contingent of the Erinpura Jodhpur Legion stationed at

1. *Mutinies in Rajputana*, p. 39.

Anadra,[1] stole up to Mt. Abu, and opened fire on the European soldiers in the Hospital there, and on Col. Hall's bungalow wounding his son Mr. A. Hall, but retired when the soldiers returned the fire; how they returned and joined the whole Legion in open mutiny at Erinpura, looted cantonments, imprisoned Lt. Conolly and marched to Ajmer, but finding that their way was barred at Pali by the Jodhpur State forces, entered into the service of the Thakur of Ahwa; how this legion attacked on 8th September the Marwar State troops who fled losing their commander, guns, camp and ammunition; how Colonel Lawrence failed to dislodge the mutineers and how the Agent, Captain M. Mason was killed; how the Kotah garrison rebelled, attacked the Residency, killed the doctor, Mr. Sadler, set fire to the palace, cut off the Political Agent Major Burton's head and that of his two sons and imprisoned the Maharao of Kotah, till relieved by the troops from the Karauli State; how General Roberts invested Kotah with 5500 men on March 25, 1858, and delivered an assault on 30th, but found the place evacuated, the rebels having all escaped unscathed; how the celebrated Tantia Topi appeared with an army of twelve thousand men and besieged Tonk, but retreated later and was defeated by General Roberts at Burwas and fled to Jhalrapatan, where he obtained a large amount of jewels and treasures, twenty-seven guns with elephants and horses which enabled him to take the field again; how Tantia Topi reappeared in Mewar and again with eight thousand cavalry crossed the Chambal and threatened Tonk and Jaipur, but was defeated at Dausa on 14 January 1859 by General Showers from Agra; and lastly, how a column of infantry under Colonel Holmes surprised the rebel camp at Sikar and dispersed them.

From 1857, Ajmer-Merwara became a Deputy Commissionership under the Agent Governor General, Rajputana, who became Commissioner of Ajmer, and remained subordinate to the government of the N. W. P. till 1871 A.D. The first Deputy Commissioner was Captain B. P. Lloyd, who had been Col. Dixon's Assistant from 1849 to 1853. He went on leave, and during his absence, Captain Brooke officiated for him.

In 1858, the whole of the rainfall took place between 16 July and 1 August. "All the tanks were filled and many of them burst. Anasagar overflowed, and the houses on the

1. The Jodhpur Legion at Erinpura consisted of artillery, two ninepounders; cavalry, three troops; and eight companies of infantry and three companies of Bhils. *vide*, Pritchard's *Mutinies in Rajputana*, pp. 208-9. A detachment had been distributed in villages".

bund were all under water."[1] The Kharif failed. Major Lloyd returned from leave on 12 July, 1859.

In June 1864, Ajmer was connected by telegraph with Agra. In September, the telegraph was extended to Deesa. Major Davidson succeeded Major Lloyd. Captain Repton succeeded Major Davidson in April, 1868 A.D.

The years 1868 to 1870 saw a famine in Ajmer-Merwara, which, for its tragic consequences, is unequalled in the history of the province.[2] Col. J. C. Brooke, Agent, Governor General, Rajputana, says that 25% of the population or one in every four human beings died.

Lord Mayo's Durbar at Ajmer.

In October, 1870 A.D. Lord Mayo, Viceroy of India, came to Ajmer *via* Bharatpur, Jaipur and Sambhar, and held a Durbar at Ajmer, to which all the Rulers of the Indian States of Rajputana, were invited. This was the first "Governor General's Durbar" at Ajmer, and the second occasion, when the Governor General invited the rulers of the Indian States in Rajputana to meet him, the first being the occasion when Lord William Bentinck[3] had done so on 17, January, 1832. The following princes came to Ajmer to attend the Durbar:

H. H. Maharana of Udaipur	H. H. Maharaja of Karauli
H. H. Maharaja of Jodhpur	H. H. Nawab of Tonk
H. H. Maharao of Kotah	H. H. Maharaja of Kishengarh
H. H. Maharao of Bundi	H. H. Maharaj Rana of Jhalawar

His Excellency the Viceroy arrived in the afternoon on the 20th of October, 1870 and his camp was pitched at the Mirshali gardens. He was taken in procession in the city of Ajmer, which he entered by the Agra Gate and passing through the Naya Bazar, Cavendishpura, Madar Gate, Ghaseti Bazar, Durgah Bazar came out by the Delhi Gate. The procession dispersed at the Residency, where the Mayo College now stands.

The Indian rulers of Rajputana paid visits to His Excellency on 21 October; and a Durbar was held on the 22nd, when an untoward incident occurred. Maharaja Takht Singh of Jodhpur felt offended at a lower seat being given to him

1. La Touche's *Settlement Report*, p. 82.
2. Col. Brooke's *Account of the Famine in Rajputana including Ajmer-Merwara*, p. 22. A full account of this famine is given under the chapter. "Famines in Ajmer-Merwara."
3. While Lord William Bentinck took several weeks to come to Jaipur from Bharatpur, Lord Mayo travelled 112 miles and came there in one day.

than he was entitled to, and left Ajmer without informing the Governor General or attending the Durbar. Maharaja Takht Singh's salute was reduced by two guns. The Maharaja represented matters to the Secretary of State for India, who accepted the Jodhpur claim, and matters were amicably settled and the salute restored.

His Excellency advised the princes present to protect and respect the rights of their subjects, as the British Government was doing the rights of Indian States themselves. He then proposed the founding of a college at Ajmer for the education of the princes and the thakurs of Rajputana, which was accepted by all. He left for Nasirabad on 25 October, 1870.

In 1871 A.D., a great administrative change occurred. Ajmer-Merwara was taken away from the N. W. P. Government and placed under the Foreign and Political Department of the Government of India to facilitate the work of that department in the Indian States of Rajputana. The Agent to the Governor-General, Rajputana, was made ex-officio Chief Commissioner of Ajmer-Merwara, and Mr. L. S. Saunders, a deputy commissioner in the Punjab was appointed the first Commissioner of Ajmer-Merwara. He had come to Ajmer from the Punjab in 1869 A.D. Both Ajmer and Merwara were given, an assistant commissioner each. They, like the Commissioner, were officers of the Political Department. This arrangement was slightly modified in 1914 A.D, when the assistant commissioner of Merwara was replaced by an extra assistant commissioner.

In 1873-74, earth-works for the Rajputana State Railway were commenced, and the Railway from Agra came to Ajmer on 1st August, 1875 A.D. and taken to Nasirabad on 14, February, 1876 A.D. The main line was continued to Ahmedabad. A branch line from Ajmer to Khandwa was opened on 1st December, 1881 A.D., and the Railway assumed the name of Rajputana Malwa Railway.

In honour of the Imperial Durbar held at Delhi in 1877, when Queen Victoria assumed the title of Empress of India, T. Pratap Singh of Pisangan was given the title of Raja and the Thakurs of Masuda, Kharwa, Bandanwara, and Junia were made Rao Sahibs.

With the advent of the Railway, the population of Ajmer began rapidly to increase. A new extension of the town of Ajmer was planned, and Kaisarganj came into existence in 1884-85. Other population centres began to spring up.

In 1886, the Ajmer-Merwara Municipalities' Regulation was enacted introducing the principle of election for the first time in Ajmer. On the 17th February 1890, H. R. H. Prince Albert Victor, Duke of Clarence, during his tour in India, came to Ajmer from Jaipur at 8-30 a.m., and left for Chitor the same evening at 11-36 p m. The Istimrardars of Kharwa, Bhinai, Masuda, Pisangan, Junia and Bandanwara were presented to him.

Two severe famines took place in Ajmer-Merwara, one in 1890-92, and another in 1899-1900. During the 1890-92 famine, the Municipal Committee, Ajmer constructed the Foysagar lake as a famine work, for water-supply for Ajmer.

In October 1890, the Czarewitch (later Czar of Russia) and Lord Lansdowne, Viceroy of India, visited Ajmer.

Under the Ancient Monuments Preservation Act of 1904, the following were declared as preserved monuments:
(1) Marble Baradaries on the Anasagar Bund. (2) Badshahi Building in the Naya Bazar. (3) Adhai-din-ka-Jhonpra. (4) Abdullah Khan's tomb on the Beawar Road near the Railway goods-shed. (5) Sola Khumba in the Dargah Khwaja Sahib and (6) Kos-Minars.[1]

H. H. Amir Habibullahkhan of Afghanistan paid a visit to Ajmer. He arrived by special train at 10 a.m. on 3rd January 1907, and left in the evening after ten hours' stay. He paid a visit to the Dargah Khwaja Sahib. He went straight from the Railway station to the Dargah and walked right-up to the tomb of the Khwaja Sahib with boots on. He was the first man to break the convention that people either should go into the Dargah without shoes on or with cotton covers over them. He and his fortyfour sardars were accommodated in the Baradaries on the Anasagar embankment, which were fitted out for his reception. He lunched at Ajmer, and had his dinner in the Railway train.

Her Majesty the Queen Empress Mary paid a visit to Ajmer. She came to Ajmer on 21st December, 1911 at 3-30 p.m. and was accommodated in the Residency. She paid a visit to the Mayo College in the after-noon the same day. The next day, at 10 a.m., she went to Pushkar; and after returning from there, she went to the city and paid a visit to

1. These are masonry pillars about twenty feet high, built by Emperor Akbar, every kos. or two miles, when he came from Agra to Ajmer in 1570 A.D. Eight of these minars still exist on or near the road from Ajmer to Kishengarh.

the Dargah and the Adhai-din-ka-Jhonpra at 4 p.m. She left at 10 a.m. on the 23rd, for Deoli. The Duchess of Devonshire, the Earl and Countess of Shaftesbury and the Hon'ble Venetia Baring were members of the party.

No change in the administration of Ajmer-Merwara took place when the Minto Morley Reforms were introduced in 1911 A.D., which largely affected the administration of the major provinces of India. The breaking out of the Great War in August, 1914 A.D. stirred life in Ajmer-Merwara along with the rest of India. In the Great War, AjmerMerwara rendered great assistance to Britain. Merwara supplied soldiers for the war, till almost every one capable of bearing arms in Merwara, enlisted and went to the front in Mesopotamia or some part of Africa. Large sums of money were subscribed in Ajmer and Beawar towards the War Loan. A sum of Rs. 2,12,810-12-4[1] was contributed towards the war and various relief funds. A sum of Rs. 20,45,349/- was subscribed towards the War Loan. A Committee was appointed to carry on publicity work and war propaganda in this small province, with Mr. Leslie Jones, Principal, Mayo College, Ajmer as President and the author of this book as Secretary.

The influenza epidemic, from which the whole of India suffered in 1918 took a toll of 19835 persons from Ajmer. A Government of India Act was enacted in 1919, but Ajmer-Merwara was again ignored.

H. R. H. the Prince of Wales[2] came to Ajmer on 28, November, 1921 at 8-30 a.m. and departed the same day at 11 p.m. Lord Cromer and Admiral Halesey were with him. He visited the Mayo College.

In 1920, the Government of India appointed a committee with Mr. Ashworth of the United Provinces Civil Service as President, to report on the administrative and judicial arrangement in Ajmer-Merwara so as to give the people a voice in the administration. This committee, after taking official and non-official evidence, reported that "the only way to make the

(1)

(a) Imperial Indian Relief Fund, Rajputana Branch,	Rs.	96,565	11	8
(b) St. John Ambulance Fund	,,	22,442	10	1
(c) Rajputana Aeroplane Fund	,,	46,187	2	6
(d) Indian Soldiers Fund	,,	22,279	4	1
(e) Motor Ambulances	,,	20,540	0	0
Others	,,	4,796	0	0
	Rs.	2,12,810	12	4

(2) Col. Worgan, Military Secretary to H. R. H. the Prince of Wales came to Ajmer on 15 August, 1921 A.D-

administration efficient in Ajmer-Merwara, and to let the province have the benefit of the reforms", recently introduced in other provinces, was to amalgamate it with the United Provinces. Nothing so far has come out of it. In 1924 A.D., Ajmer-Merwara was allowed to return a member, to represent it in the central Legislative Assembly. The author of this book was the first member so elected. In 1926, a Judicial Commissioner was appointed for Ajmer-Merwara, and the Chief Commissioner of Ajmer-Merwara was divested of his judicial functions.

In 1935, a new Government of India Act was passed. Part III of this Act was brought into force on 1 April, 1937. This has effected another change in the administration of the province. Ajmer-Merwara has been placed under the administrative control of the Home Department of the Government of India, as the Political Department, having been placed under the Viceroy as Crown Representative, has ceased to have any thing to do with British India. It has also been arranged that the Commissioner and Assistant Commissioner of Ajmer shall in future be two U. P. Civilians, whose services shall be borrowed from the United Provinces for three years at a time, to work under the Agent to the Governor-General for Rajputana, now designated "the Resident in Rajputana and Chief Commissioner, Ajmer-Merwara." Another little change, the Act of 1935 has introduced is that when the Federal Legislature is formed, Ajmer-Merwara and Panth Piploda will jointly return one member to the Federal Assembly and one to the Federal Council of State. A change necessarily entailed by the Home Department taking charge of the Ajmer-Merwara is that in future all legislation for the province will be passed by the Federal Legislature instead of the Governor-General in Council, which at present enacts laws for Ajmer-Merwara without reference to any legislative body. The Scheduled Districts Act has ceased to have any effect from 1 April, 1937. Another change, though a nominal one, is that the Police force in Ajmer-Merwara, railway lands in Rajputana and the Abu leased areas, which prior to the 1st April, 1937 was under the control of the Agent to the Governor General in Rajputana and Chief Commissioner, Ajmer-Merwara, has, with effect from the aforesaid date, been brought under the administrative control of the Chief Commissioner, Ajmer-Merwara.

A very important and material alteration in the area and population of Ajmer-Merwara was made in 1938 A.D. Those portions of Merwara which had originally belonged to the Mewar and Marwar States and which had been handed over temporarily between 1823 and 1830 A. D. to the British Government to restore order in Merwara, were retroceded to the two States. Thus an area of about 343 miles with a population of 53,328 has been retroceded to the Mewar and the Marwar States, reducing the area of Ajmer-Merwara from 2710 to 2367·9 sq. miles, and the population from 5,60,292 to 5,06,964.

CHANGES IN ADMINISTRATION

District.	Period.	Local Officer.	Local Government		Highest authority.
Ajmer.	1818-1832	Superintendent	Resident at Delhi. Later A G.G. Malwa and Rajputana, and later A. G. G. Rajputana as Commissioner.		Government of India.
,,	1832-1846	,,	A.G.G., Rajputana as Commissioner	N.W.P. Govt.	,,
Merwara.	1822-1846	,,	Resident at Delhi. Later A.G.G. Rajputana as Commissioner of Ajmer.		,,
Ajmer-Merwara.	1846-1853	Superintendent	A G.G. Rajputana as Commissioner.	N.W.P. Govt.	,,
	1853-1857	Commissioner		N.W.P. Govt.	,,
	1857-1871	Deputy Commissioner	A.G G. Rajputana as Commissioner.	,,	,,
	1871-1937	Commissioner	A G.G. Rajputana as Chief Commissioner.		Government of India Foreign and Political Department; & later, Political Department, Government of India.
	1937	,,	Resident in Rajputana as Chief Commissioner.		Government of India, Home Department.

A comparison of the financial aspects of the administration in 1849-50, with that of 1937-38 (which is the last normal year, the years 1938-39 and 1939-40 being famine years) will enable one to appreciate the great development, the administration of Ajmer-Merwara has undergone.

1849-50. A.D.

The income of Ajmer-Merwara in 1849-50, as given in Col. Dixon's

Settlement Report, p. 177, was:

1.	Land Revenue, Khalsa and Istimrar villages	2,86,913	10	7
2.	Customs	96,919	13	2
3.	Abkari	4,920	10	9
4.	Stamp	16,173	6	6
5.	Miscellaneous	6,106	0	4
		4,11,033	9	4
6.	Realised repairs of talaos and roads ...	6,306	0	0
		4,17,339	9	4

1937-38 A.D.

1.	Income tax	2,59,865	4	3
2.	Land Revenue	2,83,438	9	3
3.	Irrigation	1,01,790	4	11
4.	Stamps	2,84,565	8	6
5.	Excise	7,39,914	10	6
6.	Education	60,770	5	4
7.	Forest	85,979	0	0
8.	Others	1,01,173	11	8½
		19,17,497	6	5½

Statement of revenue and expenditure of Ajmer-Merwara for the year 1873-74.[1]—J. D. La Touche's *Gazetteer of Ajmer-Merwara*, page 47.

Heads of Receipts.	Amount.	Heads of Expenditure.	Amount.
IMPERIAL		Revenue	74,705 3 7
		Judicial	57,993 11 5
Land revenue... ...	3,68,831 3 3	Forest	16,352 0 6
		Settlement charges ...	75,344 12 7
Excise on spirits and drugs	30,769 9 9	Abkari	1,164 1 10
		Stamps	4,252 10 4
Assessed taxes... ...	710 9 2	Assessed taxes	24 0 0
Stamps	1,35,419 7 6	Commissioner, with establishment and contingencies.	62,821 10 1
		Meteorology	625 0 0
Law and Justice ...	25,776 9 11	Police	74,602 7 1
		Medical	15,045 5 10
Total Imperial...	5,71,507 7 7	Education	41,070 1 2
		Jail	16,671 13 10
LOCAL		Registration	2,067 4 3
		Cemetery and Church ...	425 0 0
District funds	82,429 14 1	Refunds	6,144 12 10
		Miscellaneous	17,075 7 7
Municipal	44,536 2 2		
		Total Imperial ...	4,66,425 6 11
		Districts funds	98,765 0 3
		Municipal	60,880 9 3
		Total Local ...	1,59,645 9 6
		Grand Total ...	6,26,071 0 5
		Surplus over Expenditure ...	74,402 7 0
Total ...	6,98,473 7 10	Total ...	6,98,473 7 10

1. "Deducting settlement charges, which are temporary, and refunds, the surplus of revenue over expenditure for this year is Rs. 1,58,892-0-10."

A remarkable feature is the increase. in Excise from Rs. 4,920-10-9 in 1849-50, to Rs. 7,39,914-10-6 in 1937-38.

	1849-50.			1937-38.		
Excise	4,920	10	9	7,39,914	4	9
Stamps	16,174	6	0	2,84,565	8	6
Land Revenue	2,86,913	10	7	3,85,228	14	2

The income and expenditure of Ajmer-Merwara[1] in 1937-38 were Rs. 19,17,497-6-5½ and Rs. 18,91,041-6-7 respectively as below.

Income.

	Rs. 18,31,518	6	5½
(with forest)	Rs. 85,979	0	0
Total	Rs. 19,17,497	6	5½

Expenditure.

	Rs. 35,12,173	10	10	
deduct	„ 14,51,853	0	0	paid out as interest on Government Securities.
	Rs. 20,60,320	10	10	
deduct	Rs. 2,41,454	4	3	pensions paid to army officers etc.
	Rs. 18,18,866	6	7	
Add Forest expenditure	„ 72,175	0	0	
Total	„ 18,91,041	6	7	

If the income and expenditure of the Municipal and other local funds be added, the total income and expenditure of Ajmer-Merwara will stand as under:

	Income.			Expenditure.		
Imperial ...	19,17,497	6	5½	18,91,041	6	7
Municipal 1838-39 ...	5,57,666	3	11	6,14,467	15	8
District Fund ...	1,13,721	0	0	1,17,110	0	0
Total ...	25,88,883	10	4½	25,22,619	6	3

1. The income and expenditure of the famine year 1939-40 A.D. were about fourteen and half lakhs and sixteen and half lakhs respectively, exclusive of famine expenditure.

CHAPTER XVIII

RULERS OF AJMER.

I—DYNASTIES OF RULERS.

Chauhan Rajputs	... ... about	600 to 1194 A.D.
Pathans Sultans of Delhi	... ...	1195 to 1400 ,,
Maharana of Mewar	... ...	1400 to 1455 ,,
Sultan of Mandoo	... ...	1456 to 1504 ,,
Maharana of Mewar	... ...	1505 to 1533 ,,
Sultan of Gujrat	... ...	1533 to 1535 ,,
Rathors of Marwar	... ...	1535 to 1544 ,,
Sur Sultans of Delhi	... ...	1544 to 1556 ,,
Mughal Emperors	... ...	1556 to 1719 ,,
Rathors of Marwar or Emperor of Delhi		1720 to 1755 ,,
Scindia of Gwalior and Maharaja Ram Singh		1756 to 1758 ,,
Scindia[1] (or Rathors for brief periods)		1758 to 1787 ,,
Rathors of Jodhpur	... ...	1787 to 1790 ,,
Scindia of Gwalior	... ...	1791 to 1818 ,,
East India Company of London	...	1818 to 1857 ,,
Kings of England	... ...	1857 to 1940 ,,

II—SOVEREIGNS.

CHAUHAN KINGS ABOUT 600 TO 1195 A.D.

1	Ajaipal or Ajairaja	16	Viryarama	(1040 A.D.)
2	Vigrahraja I	17	Chamundraja	
3	Chandraraja I	18	Durlabhraja III	(1075 A.D.)
4	Gopendraraja	19	Vigrahraja III	
5	Durlabhraja I	20	Prithviraja I	(1105 A.D.)
6	Govindraja or Guvaka I (820)	21	Ajaideva or Ajairaja	(1130 A.D.)
7	Chandraraja II	22	Arnoraja or Anaji	(1140 A.D)
8	Guvaka II	23	Jugdeva	
9	Chandanraja	24	Vigrahraja IV	(1153-64 A.D.)
10	Vakpatiraja I	25	Appargangeya	(1167 A.D.)
11	Sinharaja (950 A.D.)	26	Prithvibhatta	(1167-69 A.D.)
12	Vigrahraja II (973 A.D.)	27	Someshwar	(1170-79 A.D.)
13	Durlabhraja II	28	Prithviraja the Great	(died 1192 A.D.)
14	Govindraja II			
15	Vakpatiraja II	29	Hariraja	(1193-95 A.D.)

1. During this period, only the city of Ajmer was under the Scindia; the rural areas were under the Rathors of Jodhpur.

PATHAN KINGS,[1] MAHARANAS OF MEWAR, SULTANS OF MANDOO AND GUJRAT, AND RATHORS OF MARWAR 1195 TO 1556 A.D.

A.H. SULTANS OF DELHI (1195 to 1400 A.D.)

No.	A.H.	Name	Period
1.	589	Muizzuddin Muhammad bin Sam (1st Dynasty)	... 7th Jan., 1195 to 18th Aug., 1205
2.	602	Kutbuddin Aibak	... 18th Aug., 1205 to 25th June, 1210
3.	607	Aram Shah	... 25th June, 1210 (few months)
4.	607	Shamsuddin Altamash	... 1210 to 16th Sept. 1235
5.	633	Ruknuddin Firoz Shah I,	... 16th Sept. 1235 to 14th Aug., 1236
6.	634	Sultana Raziah Begum	... 14th Aug, 1236 to 3rd Aug., 1239
7.	637	Muizzuddin Bahram Shah	... 3rd Aug., 1239 to 12th July 1241
8.	639	Alauddinmasud Shah	... 12th July, 1241 to 19th May, 1246
9.	644	Nasiruddin Mahmud ...	... 19th May, 1246 to 13th Oct., 1265
10.	664	Ghiasuddin Balban ...	... 13th Oct., 1265 to 16th Feb., 1287
11.	686	Muizzuddin Kaikubad ...	... 16th Feb., 1287 to 14th Jan., 1290

Second Dynasty—KHILJIS.

No.	A.H.	Name	Period
12.	689	Jalaluddin Firuz Shah II	... 14th Jan., 1290 to 10th Nov., 1295
13.	695	Ruknuddin Ibrahim	... 10th Nov. (few months) 1295
14.	695	Alauddin Muhammad Shah	... 1295 to 7th April 1315
15.	715	Shahabuddin Umar ...	... 7th April, 1315 to 26th March 1316
16.	716	Kutbuddin Mubarak Shah I	... 26th March 1316 to 12th Feb. 1320
17.	720	Nasiruddin Khusru (few months)	12th Feb., 1320

Third Dynasty—TUGHLAQS.

No.	A.H.	Name	Period
18.	720	Ghayasuddin Tughlaq Shah	... 1320 to 18th Dec., 1324
19.	725	Muhammad Bin Tughlaq	... 18th Dec., 1324 to 28th Feb., 1351
20.	752	Firoz Shah III Bin Salar Rajab.	28th Feb., 1351 to 11th Jan., 1388

The following were the later Sultans of Delhi, but their rule was too precarious even in Delhi to admit of its extension to Ajmer. We come on firm ground after Kumbha's conquest of Ajmer.

No.	A.H.	Name	Period
21.	790	Tughlaq Shah II ...	... 11th Jan., 1388 to 31th Dec., 1388
22.	791	Abubakra Shah	... 31st Dec., 1388 to 20th Dec., 1389
23.	792	Muhammad Shah Bin Firoz Shah.	20th Dec., 1389 to 17th Nov., 1392
24.	795	Sikandar Shah	... 17th Nov., (45 days only) 1932
25.	795	Mahmud Shah II	... 1392 to 27th Oct., 1394
26.	797	Nusrat Shah, (Interregnum) Mahmud restored	... 27th Oct., 1394 to 13th April, 1410
		Maharana Kumbha of Chitor	 1400-1455
		Mahmud Khilji of Mandoo	 1456
		Maharana Rai Mal of Chitor	 1505
		Bahadur Shah of Gujrat ...	 1533
		Rao Viramdeva of Merta ...	 1535
		Rao Maldeva of Jodhpur ...	 1535-1544
		Sher Shah Sur, Sultan of Delhi	 1544
		Haji Khan, slave of Sher Shah Sur	 1556-58

1. Though no historical evidence is available that every one of the Sultans Ruknuddin Firoz Shah I to Firoz Shah III (number 5 to 20 above) actually ruled in Ajmer, yet it is presumed that they or their officers held away in Ajmer.

MUGHAL EMPERORS (1558 to 1719 A.D.)

Akbar	1558 to 1605
Jahangir	1605 to 1628
Shan Jahan	1628 to 1658
Aurangzeb	1658 to 1707
Bahadur Shah	1707 to 1712
Jahandar Shah	1712 to 1713
Farrukhsayar	1713 to 1719
Rafiuddarjat	1719 to 1719 (7th June)
Rafiuddaula (Shah Jahan II)	1719 to 1719

RATHORS OF JODHPUR, OR EMPERORS OF DELHI (1719 to 1755 A.D.)

Maharaja Ajit Singh of Jodhpur ...	1719 to 1722
Emperor Muhammad Shah	1722 to 1734
Maharaja Abhai Singh of Jodhpur ...	1735 to 1740
Emperor Muhammad Shah of Delhi ...	1740 to 1743
Maharaja Abhai Singh	1743 to 1749
Emperor Ahmad Shah	1749 to 1751
Maharaja Bakht Singh	1751 to 1752
Maharaja Bijai Singh	1752 to 1755

RATHORS OF JODHPUR, OR SCINDIA OF GWALIOR (1755-1818 A.D.)

Scindia of Gwalior and Maharaja Ram Singh	1756 to 1758
Scindia of Gwalior (and Rathors for brief periods)	1758 to 1787[1]
Maharaja Bijai Singh of Jodhpur ...	1787 to 1791
Madhava Rao Scindia	1791 to 1794[2]
Daulat Rao Scindia	1794 to 1818

BRITISH (1818 TO 1940).

The East India Company of London ...	1818 to 1857
Queen Victoria of Great Britain ...	1857 to 1901
Edward VII	1901 to 1910
George V	1910 to 1936
Edward VIII (only few months) ...	1936
George VI	1936

1. During this period except the town of Ajmer, the district of Ajmer was under the Rathors of Jodhpur.

2. When Ajmer was under Madhavarao Scindia, part of the district was under Jodhpur.

GOVERNORS AND VICEROYS

(1558 to 1940 A.D.).

Sovereign.	Subedar or Governor.	Date Hijra.	Date A.D.
	Mughal Governors.		
Akbar.	Muhammad Kasim Nishapuri ...	965	1558
,,	Mirza Sharfuddin Husain ...	967	1559-60
,,	Kazi Mad	970	1562-3
,,	Julal Boo Kasie	981	1573-4
,,	Raja Madho Singh... ...	987	1579
,,	Raja Man Singh	989	1581
,,	Madho Singh	1000	1591-2
,,	Mir Kalan	1008	1599-1600
,,	Shahbaz Khan	1012	1603-4
Jahangir.	Mirza Masud	1017	1608-9
,,	Sayad Ali	1018	1609-10
,,	Safdar Khan	1020	1611-2
,,	Karimdad Khan	1027	1618
,,	Sardul Singh	1034	1624-5
,,	Mirza Munnoo	1036	1626-7
,,	Hasub Khan	1038	1628-9
,,	Sardul Singh	1039	1629-30
,,	Raja Bhim Singh Sisodia ...	1046	1636-7
,,	Sayad Bagha	1047	1637-8
,,	Muhammad Murad... ...	1048	1638-9
,,	Bhagwan Singh	1050	1640-41
,,	K. Arjun Singh	1053	1643-4
Shah Jahan.	Mirza Doo	1054	1644-5
,,	Raja Bithal Das	1054	,,
,,	Rup Singh and Ram Singh ...	1066	1655-6
Aurangzeb.	Hafiz Nazir Shah	1068	1657-8
,,	K. Ram Singh	1069	1658-9
,,	Tarbiat Khan	1070	1659-60
,,	Murawat Khan	1073	1662-63
,,	Usman	1073	,,
,,	Hafiz Nazir	1075	1664-5
,,	Rashid Ahmad	1076	1665-6
,,	Maharaja Udaibhan ...	1076	,,
,,	Maharaja Raj Singh ...		
,,	Mir Sayad Umaid		
,,	Abid Khan	1078	1667-8
,,	Mir Sayad Umaid	1079	1668-9
,,	Nawab Surat Khan ...	1080	1669-70
,,	Jafir Khan	1080	,,
,,	Nawab Izat Khan	1081	1670-71
,,	Maharaja Raj Singh ...	1081	,,
,,	Rup Singh	1082	1671-2
,,	Nawab Durab Khan ...	1088	1677-8

Sovereign.	Subedar or Governor.	Date Hijra.	Date A.D.
Aurangzeb.	Tyber Khan	1090	1679
"	Maharaja Raj Singh ...	1091	1680
"	Asad Khan	1092	1681
"	Maharaja Madho Singh ...	1093	1682
"	Raja Pirthi Singh	1097	1685-6
"	Sipahdar Khan	1100	1688-9
"	Khudabad Sher	1100	"
"	Muhammad Khan	1102	1690-91
"	Alayar Khan	1104	1692-3
"	Shafi Khan	1105	1693-4
"	Muhammad Sharif... ...	1105	"
"	Muhammad Khan	1106	1694-5
"	Narsingh Das	1106	"
"	Saleh Muhammad	1109	1697-8
"	K. Amud Ali	1110	1698-9
"	Kesri Singh	1110	"
"	Amir Ali Khan	1112	1700-1701
"	K. Ram Chand	1113	1701-2
"	K. Kesri Singh	1114	1702-3
"	Muhammad Sayad son of Sheikh Qutab	1115	1703-4
"	K. Atmaram	1116	1704-5
Bahadur Shah.	Nawab Ghayasali Khan ...	1119	1707-8
Jahandar Shah.	Shah Ullah Khan	1122	1710
"	Ram Singh	1122	..
Farukhsayar.	Najabat Khan	1123	1711
"	Baz Khan	1123	..
"	Khan Jahan	1128	1716
"	Azizuddaula Khan Alam ...	1130	1717-8
"	Samandar Khan	1130	..
Muhammad Shah	Maharaja Sawai Singh ...	1131	1718-9
"	Maharaja Man Singh ...	1133	1720-21
"	Zafar Kuli Khan	1137	1724-5
"	Sheikh Rahmat Ullah ...	1141	1728-9
"	Wali Muhammad Khan ...	1142	1729-30
	(not known)	1143	1731-42
"	Mir Muhammad Islam ...	1156	1743
	Rajput and Mahratta Governors.		
Maharaja Abhai Singh.	Mir Muhammad Islam ...	"	"
Maharaja Bakht Singh.	"	"	"
	(not known)		
Maharaja Bijai Singh.	Balu Jyotshi	1176-1176	1762-63
Madhava Rao Scindia.	Bapurao Pandit	1177-1180	1763-1767

Sovereign.	Subedar or Governor.	Date Hijra.	Date A.D.
"	Shambhuji	1180-1182	1767-1769
"	Anwar Beg	1183-1183	1769-1770
"	Shambhuji	1184-1187	1770-1773
"	Jivaram	1188-1192	1774-1778
"	Anwar Beg	1197-1201	1783-1787
Maharaja Bijai Singh.	Dhanraj Singhi	1201-1205	1787-1791
		V. Sambat	
Madhavrao Scindia.	Sivaji Nana[1]	1849	1791-1797
Daulat Rao Scindia.	Jaswant Rao Bhao (Sivaji Nana's son)	1854	1797-1799
"	Mr. Simpson (3 months) Mr. Low (9 months) on behalf of General Perron... ...	1857	1800-1801
"	Goginbeg Khan, on behalf of General Perron... ...	1858-9	1801-1802
"	Balarao Inglia	1860-65	1803-1808
"	Hira Khan (3 months) Gumanji *alias* Tantia Scindia	1865	1809
"	Gumanji alias Tantia Scindia ...	1866-73	1809-1816
"	Bapu Scindia	1874	1816-1818
	British Governors General.		
East India Coy.	Marquis of Hastings		1818-1823
"	Lord Amherst		1823-1835
"	Sir Charles Metcalfe		1835-1836
"	Lord Auckland		1836-1842
"	Lord Ellenborough		1842-1844
"	Lord Hardinge		1844-1848
"	Lord Dalhousie		1848-1856
Queen Victoria.	Earl of Canning		1856 1862
"	Earl of Elgin		1862-1863
"	Lord Northbrook		1872-1876
"	Earl of Lytton		1876-1880
"	Marquis of Ripon		1880 1884
"	Marquis of Dufferin		1884-1888
"	Lord Lansdowne		1888-1894
"	Earl of Elgin		1894-1899
King Edward VII.	Lord Curzon		1900-1905
"	Lord Minto		1905-1910
King George V.	Lord Hardinge		1910-1916
"	Lord Chelmsford		1916-1921
"	Marquis of Reading		1921-1926
"	Lord Irvin		1926-1931
"	Lord Willingdon		1931-1936
King Edward VIII	Lord Linlithgow		1936
King George VI.			

1. From 1791 to 1806, most of the district of Ajmer was under Jodhpur.

IV-AGENTS TO THE GOVERNOR GENERAL

IN RAJPUTANA AND COMMISSIONERS OF AJMER MERWARA (1832 to 1853 and 1857 to 1871), AND CHIEF COMMISSIONERS OF AJMER-MERWARA (1871 to 1940 A.D.)

S. No.	Name.	Date of assumption of office.	Remarks.
1	Lieutenant-Colonel A Locket.	1832	Proceeded on leave 29th November 1833, making over charge to his First Assistant, Major A. Spiers.
2	Major Nathaniel Alves.	18th April, 1834 ...	Proceeded on leave 1st February, 1839, making over charge to Captain John Ludlow, Assistant to the Agent to the Governor-General and officiating Political Agent, Haraoti.
3	Lieutenant Colonel John Sutherland.	12th February, 1839.	Officiating. Confirmed 15th February, 1841. Major C. Thoresby officiated as Agent to the Governor-General during Lieutenant Colonel Sutherland's absence on leave from 26th February 1844 to 2nd March 1846. Lieutenant Colonel Sutherland died at Bharatpur on 24th June 1848. Lieutenant C. L. Showers, Assistant to the Agent to the Governor-General was in charge of the office until the arrival of Lieutenant Colonel Sutherland's successor.
4	Colonel John Low, C.B.	20th November, 1848.	Afterwards General Sir John Low, G.C.S.I., K.C.B., subsequently Resident at Hyderabad and Member of the Council of the Governor-General. Major D. A. Malcom officiated as Agent to the Governor General during Colonel Low's absence on short leave in Simla from the 8th September 1851 to the 1st December 1851. Lieutenant-Colonel G. St. P. Lawrence officiated as Agent to the Governor-General on Colonel Low's transfer to Hyderabad on the 25th December 1852 until th arrival of his successor.
5	Lieutenant Colonel Sir Henry Montgomery Lawrence, K.C.B.	5th March, 1853 ...	Transferred to Lucknow, as Chiet Commissioner, Oudh, March 1857.

S. No.	Name.	Date of assumption of office.	Remarks.
6	Colonel George St. Pierre Lawrence.	17th March, 1857 ...	Afterwards Lieutenant General Sir George Lawrence, K.C.S.I., C.B. Major W. F. Eden Officiated as Agent to the Governor-General during Colonel Lawrence's furlough in England from the 10th April 1859 to the 24th November 1860.
7	Lieutenant-Colonel E.K. Elliot.	15th April, 1864 ...	Previously Chief Commissioner of the Central Provinces. Confirmed as Agent to the Governor General in Rajputana with effect from the 1st November 1864. Died at Nasirabad on the 27th March 1865. Lieutenant A. R. Bruce, Assistant to the Agent to the Governor-General was in charge of the office until the arrival of his successor.
8	Lieutenant-Colonel William Frederick Eden	3rd April, 1865 ...	Died at Ahmedabad on the 14th November 1867 on his way to England on furlough.
9	Lieutenant-Colonel R H. Keating, V.C., C.S.I.	4th November, 1867.	Afterwards officiating Chief Commissioner of the Central Provinces and Chief Commissioner of Assam.
10	Colonel J C. Brooke ...	15th June 1870 ...	
11	Colonel Lewis Pelly, C.S.I.	21st June 1873 ...	Cofirmed as Agent to the Governor-General on the 6th February 1874. Afterwards Lieutenant-General Sir Lewis Pelly, K.C.B., K.C.S.I., M.P. Colonel W. H. Beynon officiated as Agent to the Governor-General during Colonel Pelly's absence on leave from the 6th April 1874 to the 7th July 1874.
12	Mr. Alfred C. Lyall, I.C.S.	12th November, 1874.	Afterwards the Right Hon'ble Sir Alfred Lyall, K.C.B., Foreign Secretary to the Government of India and member of the India Council 1888-1903. Major C. K. M. Walter officiated as Agent to the Governor-General from the 18th August 1876 to the 8th March 1877 during Mr. Lyall's absence from Rajputana.
13	Major Edward R. C. Bradford, C S.I.	23rd March, 1878 ...	Confirmed 12th December 1878. Afterwards Colonel Sir Edward Bradford, Bart, G.C.B, G.C V.O., K.C.S.I., Commissioner of the London Metropolitan Police, Lieutenant-Colonel C.K.M. Walter officiated as Agent to the Governor-General from the 17th March 1881 to the 29th November 1882 during Colonel Bradford's absence from Rajputana.

S. No.	Name.	Date of assumption of office.	Remarks.
14	Colonel C. K M. Walter.	27th March, 1887 ...	Confirmed on the 1st April 1887.
15	Colonel G. H. Trevor, C S.I.	20th March, 1890 ...	The following officers officiated as Agent to the Governor-General during Colonel Trevor's tenure:— (1) Colonel P. W. Powlett from the 27th August 1891 to the 27th November 1891, in addition to his own duties as Resident Western Rajputana States during Colonel Trevor's absence on privilege leave. (2) Lieutenant-Colonel W. H. Curzon Wyllie C.I.E., (afterwards Sir W. H. Curzon Wyllie, K.C.I.E., M.V.O., Political aide-de-Camp to the Secretary of State for India) in charge of current duties of Agent to the Governor-General from 5th November 1893 to 22nd November 1893. (3) Colonel W. F. Prideaux (afterwards C S.I.) from 22nd November 1893 to 9th January 1894 during Colonel Trevor's absence on privilege leave. (4) Lieutenant-Colonel H. B. Abbott from the 20th March 1895, on departure of Colonel Trevor till the arrival of his successor on the 28th October 1895.
16	Mr. R. J. Crosthwaite, I.C.S.	28th October, 1895...	Afterwards Sir Robert Crosthwaite, K.C.S.I., Agent to the Governor-General, Central India.
17	Mr. A.H.T. Martindale, I.C.S.	1st March, 1898 ...	Afterwards Sir Arthur Martindale, K.C.S.I. The following officers officiated as Agent to the Governor-General during the absence of Mr. Martindale on leave;— (1) Lieutenant-Colonel C. E. Yate, C. S. I., C. M. G., (afterwards Colonel Sir Charles Yate Bart, C.S.I., C.M.G., M. P. and Agent to the Governor-General in Baluchistan) from the 27th August 1898 to the 21st October 1898. (2) Lieutenant-Colonel W. H. Curzon-Wyllie, C.I.E., from the 1st May 1900 to the 31st March 1901. (3) Lieutenant-Colonel A.P. Thornton from the 1st April 1901 to the 2nd February 1902.

S. No.	Name.	Date of assumption of office.	Remarks.
18	Mr. Elliot Graham Colvin, I.C.S.	1st April, 1905 ...	Confirmed on 1st October 1906. Afterwards Sir Elliot Colvin K.C.S.I. The following officers officiated as Agent to the Governor-General during the absence of Mr. Colvin on leave:— (1) Lieutenant-Colonel Charles Herbert (afterwards C.S.I.) from the 12th July 1906 to the 7th January 1907. (2) Lieutenant-Colonel A. F. Pinhey, C. I. E., (Afterwards Sir Alexander Pinhey K.C.S.I., C.I.E., Resident at Hyderabad) from the 6th November 1908 to the 18th October 1909. (3) Lieutenant-Colonel W. C. R. Stratton C.I.E., from the 4th May 1912 to the 3rd November 1912. (4) Lieutenant-Colonel J. L. Kaye from the 30th September 1915 to the 15th October 1915.
19	Lieutenant-Colonel John Manners-Smith, V.C., C.V.O., C.I.E.	12th November, 1917.	Confirmed on 4th January 1918. The following officers officiated as Agent to the Governor-General after Lieutenant-Colonel Manners-Smith's departure and before the arrival of his successor: (1) Mr. A. T. Holme, I.C.S., from the 21st April 1919 to the 27th November 1919. (2) Lieutenant-Colonel P. T. A. Spence from the 28th November 1919 to the 21st December 1919. (held charge of current duties only).
20	Mr. Robert Erskine Holland C.I.E., I.C.S.	22nd December, 1919.	Afterwards Sir Robert Holland, K.C.I.E., C.S.I., C.V.O., Member of the Council of the Secretary of State for India. The following officers officiated as Agent to the Governor-General during Mr. Holland's absence on leave:— (1) Lieutenant-Colonel R. A. E. Benn from the 14th May 1920 to to the 23rd June 1920 (in charge of current duties only).

S. No	Name.	Date of assumption of office.	Remarks.
			(2) Mr. A. T. Holme, C.I.E., I.C.S., from the 24th June 1920 to the 18th November 1920. (3) Mr. C. C. Watson, C.I.E., I.C.S., (afterwards Sir Charles Watson K.C.I.E., C.S.I., Agent to the Governor-General, States of Western India. Later, Political Secretary to the Government of India) from the 6th March 1923 to the 27th October 1923. (4) Lieutenant-Colonel A. D. Macpherson from the 11th March on the departure of Sir Robert Holland until the arrival of his successor on the 7th August 1925.
21	Lieutenant-Colonel Stewart Blakely Agnew Patterson, C.I.E.	7th August, 1925 ...	Afterwards Sir Stewart Patterson, K.C.V.O., C.S.I., C.I.E., Political Aide-de-Camp to the Secretary of State for India.
22	Mr. Leonard William Reynolds, C.I.E., M.C., I.C.S.	14th March, 1927 ...	Afterwards Sir Leonard Reynolds, K.C.I.E., C.S.I., M.C. The following officers officiated as Agent to the Governor-General during Mr. Reynolds' absence on leave:— (1) Mr. A. N. L. Cater, I.C.S., (afterwards Sir Norman Cater, K.C.I.E., Agent to the Governor-General in Baluchistan) from the 16th April 1929 to the 3rd November 1929. (2) Lieutenant-Colonel R. J. Macnabb from the 3rd October 1930 to the 18th October 1930. (3) Lieutenant-Colonel D. M. Field from the 19th October 1930 to the 8th February 1931 and (during Mr. Reynold's severe illness) from the 20th August 1931 to the 8th September 1931. Afterwards Resident, Mysore.1
23	Lieutenant-Colonel George Drummond Ogilvie, C.S.I., C.I.E.	28th October, 1932...	Afterwards Sir George Ogilvie, K.C.I.E., C.S.I. Mr. A. C. Lothian, C.I.E., I.C.S., officiated as Agent to the Governor-General during Sir George Ogilvie's absence on leave in England from the 6th April 1934 to the 6th October 1934.
24	Mr. A. C. Lothian ...	28th October, 1937...	Mr. C.L. Corfield, C.I.E., M.C., I.C.S. officiated for Mr. A.C. Lothian as Resident in Rajputana from 12th May 1939 to 29th September 1939.

1. After retirement, Chief Minister at Jodhpur.

V—LOCAL OFFICERS

(1818 to 1940 A.D.)

SUPERINTENDENTS OF AJMER.

	From	To	Duration. Y.	M.	D.
Colonel Nixon ...	... 9th July 1818	17th July 1818 ...			9
Mr. Wilder ...	... 18th July 1818	15th Dec. 1824[1]...	6	4	28
Mr. Moore (incharge)	... 16th Dec. 1824	21st Apr. 1825 ...		4	6
Mr. Middleton ...	... 22nd Apr. 1825	23rd Oct. 1827 ...	2	6	2
Mr. Cavendish ...	... 24th Oct. 1827	28th Nov. 1831 ...	4	1	5
Mr. Moore ...	... 29th Nov. 1831	1st July 1832 ...		7	3
Major Alexander Speirs[2]...	2nd July 1832	16th Apr. 1834 ...	1	9	15
Mr. Edmonstone	... 17th Apr. 1834	30th June 1836 ...	2	2	14
Mr. Trevelyn ...	... 1st July 1836	25th July 1837 ...	1	0	25
Mr. Macnaughten...	... 26th July 1837	17th Feb. 1842 ...	4	6	23
Colonel Dixon ...	... 17th Feb. 1842	1853 ...	11		

SUPERINTENDENTS OF MERWARA.

Colonel Hall ... ... 1823—1835
Colonel J. Dixon... ... ... 1835—1853

COMMISSIONERS OF AJMER-MERWARA.

Colonel Dixon (Sir Henry Lawrence acted for a while, on Col. Dixon's death) ... ... 1853—1857

DEPUTY COMMISSIONERS.

(From 1857 to 1870, Deputy Commissioners were in charge, and the Agents to the Governor-General Rajputana, were Commissioners.)

	From	To
Major Lloyd[3]		1857
Captain J. C. Brooke	1857	Feb. 1859
Major Davidson (officiating)	Feb. 1859	11th July 1859
Major Lloyd	12th July 1859	14th Aug. 1862
Major Davidson	15th Aug. 1862	1868
Major Repton	Apr. 1868	1871

1. He was also Political Agent for Jodhpur, Jaisalmer and Kishengarh. See Watson's *Rajputana Gazetteer*, p. 94.

2. Mr. La Touche says (p. 73) that Major Speirs made over charge, to Mr. Edmonstone in Decr., 1833.

3. He was Col. Dixon's assistant from 1849 to 1853. He went on furlough when appointed Deputy Commissioner.

COMMISSIONERS OF AJMER-MERWARA.

	From	to
Mr. Leslie S. Saunders, I.C.S. ...	... 1871	3rd Mar. 1885
Colonel W. Tweedie, C.S.I., I.A. ...	4th Mar. 1885	25th June 1885
Mr. T. C. Plowden, I.C.S.	26th June 1885	13th Nov. 1885
Colonel G. H. Trevor, C S.I., I.A. ...	14th Nov. 1885	19th Mar. 1890
Colonel K. J. L. Mackenzie, I.A., officiated in August, September and October of 1888 when Colonel Trevor was on privilege leave.		
Captain A. F. DeLassoe, C.M.G.,C.I.E.,I.A.	20th Mar. 1890	15th Apr. 1890
Colonel John Biddulph, I.A.	15th Apr. 1890	3rd July 1891
Captain A. F. DeLassoe, C.M.G.,C.I.E.,I.A.	4th July 1891	16th July 1891
Major W. H. C. Wyllie, C.I.E., I.A. ...	17th July 1891	1st Dec. 1891
Mr. John Biddulph, I.A., ...	2nd Dec. 1891	13th Apr. 1892
Mr. A. H. T. Martindale, I.C.S. ...	14th Apr. 1892	19th Mar, 1895
Lt. Colonel A. P. Thornton, I.A. ...	20th Mar. 1895	27th Oct. 1895
Mr. A. H. T. Martindale, I.C S. ...	28th Oct. 1895	1st Mar. 1896
Mr. H. V. Cobb, I.C.S.	2nd Mar. 1896	8th Aug. 1896
Lt. Colonal A. P. Thornton, I.A. ...	9th Aug. 1896	15th Dec. 1896
Mr. A. H. T. Martindale, I.C.S. ...	16th Dec. 1896	6th April 1897
Lt. Colonel Thornton, I.A.	7th Apr. 1897	5th Oct. 1897
Captain C. H. Pritchard, I.A.	6th Oct. 1897	12th Nov. 1897
Lt. Colonel A. P. Thornton, I.A. ...	13th Nov. 1897	9th June 1899
Mr. J. Lang, I.C.S.	10th June 1899	21st June 1899
Lt. Colonel C. W. Ravenshaw, I.A, ...	22nd June 1899	28th Aug. 1899
Mr. A. L. P. Tucker, I.C.S.	29th Aug. 1899	4th June 1903
Lt. Colonel P. T. Melvill, I.A.... ...	5th June 1903	18th Nov. 1906
Major H. B. Peacock, I A.	19th Nov. 1906	12th Dec. 1906
Lt. Colonel C. H. Pritchard, I.A. ...	13th Dec. 1906	19th Mar. 1909
Major R. E. A. Hamilton, I.A.... ...	20th Mar. 1909	4th April 1909
Lt. Colonel W. C. R. Stratton, I.A. ...	5th Apr. 1909	30th April 1912
Captain W. G. Hutchinson, I.A. ...	1st May 1912	9th June 1912
Mr. A. T. Holme, I.C.S....	10th June 1912	24th June 1914
Mr. H. D. Graves Law, M.A., I.C.S. ...	25th June 1914	8th July 1914
Mr. A. T. Holme, I.C.S.	9th July 1914	28th Oct 1915
Mr. C. C. Watson, C.I.E., I.C.S.... ...	29th Oct. 1915	20th Dec. 1916
Mr. H. C. Greenfield, I.C.S.	21st Dec. 1916	2nd Jan. 1917
Mr. L. W. Reynolds, C.I.E., M.C., I.C.S.	3rd Jan. 1917	31st Oct. 1918
Lt. Colonel S. B. A. Patterson, I.A. ...	1st Nov. 1918	2nd Feb. 1920
Mr. E. C. Gibson, I.C.S....	3rd Feb. 1920	5th Mar. 1920

	From	To
Major D. M. Field, I.A....	6th Mar. 1920	25th May 1920
Major R. A. Lyall, I.A....	26th May 1920	5th Dec. 1920
Lt. Colonel S. B. A. Patterson, I.A. ...	6th Dec. 1920	31st Jan. 1922
Mr. P. B. Warburton, I.C.S.	1st Feb. 1922	19th Mar. 1922
Mr. C. C. Watson, C.I.E., I.C.S. ...	20th Mar. 1922	4th Mar. 1923
Mr. J. A.O. Fitzpatrick, C.I.E., C.B.E., I.C.S.	5th Mar. 1923	31st Oct. 1923
Mr. C. C. Watson, C.I.E., I.C.S.... ...	1st Nov. 1923	20th Jan. 1924
Mr. E. C Gibson, I.C.S.	21st Jan. 1924	4th Mar. 1925
Lt. Colonel R. J. W. Heale, O.B.E., I.A.	5th Mar. 1925	1st May 1926
Captain W. F. Q. Shuldham, I.A. ...	2nd May 1926	11th June 1926
Lt. Colonel R. J. W. Heale, O.B.E., I.A.	12th June 1926	20th April 1927
Mr. E. C. Gibson, I.C.S....	21st Apr. 1927	23rd Oct. 1927
Lt. Colonel R. J. W. Heale. O.B.E., I A.	24th Oct. 1927	3rd Mar. 1928
Captain I. W. Galbraith, M.C., I.A. ...	4th Mar. 1928	12th Mar. 1928
Lt. Colonel C. H. Gabriel, I A.	13th Mar. 1928	10th May 1928
Captain I. W. Galbraith, M.C., I.A. ...	11th May 1928	13th May 1928
Mr. E. C. Gibson, I.C.S.	14th May 1928	30th April 1930
Captain I. W. Galbraith, M.C., I.A. ...	1st May 1930	2nd Nov. 1930
Mr. E. C. Gibson, I.C.S.	3rd Nov. 1930	24th Mar. 1933
Captain L. A. G. Pinhey, I.A.	25th Mar. 1933	31st Mar. 1933
Major G. L. Betham, C.I.E., M.C. ...	1st April 1933	2nd Sept. 1934
Captain I. W. Galbraith, M.C., I.A. ...	3rd Sept. 1934	30th Sept. 1934
Major D. G. H. De La Fargue ...	1st Oct. 1934	7th Nov. 1934
Mr. G. H. Gidney, C.I E., I.C.S. ...	8th Nov. 1934	21st April 1936
Mr. L. C. L. Griffin, I.C.S.	22nd April 1936	31st Mar. 1937
Mr. B. J. K. Hallowes, I.C.S.	1st April 1937	...

CHAPTER XIX

CHRONOLOGY OF AJMER

Fifth Century B. C. The Barli Inscription in Brahmi script discovered in the Bhilot Mata Temple in the Barli Istimrari estate, Ajmer, thirty six miles south east of the city of Ajmer.

Second Century B. C. Four inscriptions in the Sanchi Stupa (Bhopal) mentions Pushkar and its inhabitants as having built cells in the Stupa:

Sanchi Stupa Inscription no. 294 (Ep. Indica, vol. II, p. 387).

"The gift of Isidatta (Risidatta), the wife of Leva from Pokhara (Pushkar)".

Ibid no. 297.

"The gift of Sangharakhita from Pokhara" (Ep. Indica, vol. II, p. 388).

Sanchi Stupa Inscription, Tope II, No. 30.

"The gift of the venerable Budharakhita, inhabitant of Pokhara" (Ep. Indica, vol. II, p. 398).

Ibid, Tope II, No. 42.

"The gift of Aya (Arya), inhabitant of Pokhar" (Ep. Indica, Vol. II, p. 398).

A. D.	
125	Pandu Lena Cave inscriptions in the hills of Trirashmi near Nasik mentions that Vishvadatt, son of Dinik of the Shak dynasty gave a village and cows after a bath in the sacred lake of Pushkar, near Ajmer.
551	V.S. 608. King Vasudeva, the first Chauhan king of Sambhar, and grandfather of Ajaipal, founder of the city of Ajmer, flourished.
About 590	Ajaimeru or Ajmer was founded by the Chauhan king Ajaipal or Ajaideva
724-726	King Durlabh Rai, great grandson of Ajaipal, was slain during an invasion of Ajmer.
760	P. Hemraj, disciple of Bhattarak Ratnkirtiji (Jain) died at Ajmer. Inscription in his *chhattree* at Ajmer.
805	Goovak I received the title of *Vir* (hero) in the assembly of Nagbhatta, king of Marwar and Kanauj, who died in 833 A.D.
845 854 871	Inscriptions in the *chhattrees* on Jain Bhattaraks at Ajmer.
950	King Singhraj, thirteenth from King Vasudeva, defeated the Tomars. He killed the Muslim general, Hatim and, on another occasion, defeated Sultan Haji-ud-din.

A. D.	
956	The Harshnath temple in Shekhawati containing the famous Harsh Stone Inscription, of A. D. 956 (Ephi. Ind. vol. II, p. 116), which gives the geneology of the Chauhan kings of Ajmer, was completed.
973	King Vigrahraja II invaded Gujrat, whose king Mulraj fled to Cutch.
	Inscription of V. S. 973 and S. 1027 (916 A.D. and 970 A D.) in the chhatrees of Vijaikirtiji and Ratnkirtiji.
1020	King Viryaram of Ajmer invaded Malwa. He was later defeated by King Bhoj of Dhar (Malwa).
1024	Sultan Mahmud of Ghazni attacked Ajmer and laid siege to its fortress Garh Beetli, but was wounded. Raising the siege, he went away to Anhilwara.
1075	Durlabh Rai III defeated Shahabuddin. He assisted Udayaditya, king of Malwa, to take Gujrat and kill its king, Raja Karan.
1105	King Prithviraj I of Ajmer mentioned in *Jin Mata temple* inscription of V. S. 1162 in Shekawati. (P. R. of R. S. I. W. Circle for 1909-10, p. 52.)
1108-1123	King Ajaideva II of Ajmer captured Salhana, Commander-in-Chief of Malwa. He defeated the Mussalmans with great slaughter.
1124	Sidhraj Jai Singh of Anhilwara attacked King Arnoraja. After the war, he gave his daughter in marriage to Arnoraja. Later, Kumar Pal, Sidhraj Jai Singh's successor, invaded Ajmer and defeated Arnoraja.
1135	King Arnoraja or Anaji defeated the Muslim invaders, and on the scene of battle, constructed the Anasagar lake at Ajmer.
1140	Inscription in Rajputana Museum, Ajmer of about 1140 A. D. of Ajaideva II, king of Ajmer.
	Inscription in the temple of Mokalji at Chitor (Ep. Indica, vol. II, p. 422) of S. 1207 (1149-50 A. D.) of Kumarpal about his invasion of Ajmer.
1150	Arnoraja was murdered by his son Jugdeva.
1152	Visaldeva Vigrahraja IV drove away the parricide Jugdeva from the throne and became king of Ajmer His reign is a landmark in the history of Ajmer. He conquered Nadole, Jalore and Pali. He conquered Delhi between 1155 to 1163. Emperor Visaldeva Vigrahraja IV's famous *Siwalik pillar inscription* dated 9th April, 1164 A D., says that he had cleared the country of all Mussalmans, and commanded his successors to drive them beyond the river Attock. He was the first Chauhan Emperor of India. He was a great scholar. Visaldeva built the Saraswati Mandir (College) at Ajmer, now known after conversion into a mosque, as Adhai-din-ka-Jhonpra. He also constructed the lake Visalsar in Ajmer. The stone inscription of Visaldeva IV of Ajmer in the Rajputana Museum, Ajmer, describes the Chauhans as belonging to the solar race.
	Two Sanskrit inscriptions in Adhai din ka-Jhonpra on the lintels of the two staircases leading from the roof to the top of the Imamgah stating that the building was constructed by King Vigrahraja.
	Six inscriptions of twelfth Century A. D. of Vigrahraj. Harkeli Nataka of 22 November, 1153 A. D.

A. D.	
1154	Jain Acharya, Jindatta Suri died at Ajmer, and Dadabari was built on his remains.
1157	Sannyasis attacked the Gujars, who were in possession of Pushkar and expelled them on the Diwali day, and appointed their own representatives in the principal temples.
1163	Vigrahraja's minor son, Amar Gangeya, became king of Ajmer but was deposed by Prithvibhatt, son of Jugdeva, uncle of Amar Gangeya.
1164	The Siwalik Pillar Inscription of 9th April 1164 A.D. of Emperor Vigrahraja (*Indian Antiquary*, vol. XIX, p. 215) in Delhi.
1167	The *Hansi inscription* of 1167 A. D. describes the Chauhans as belonging to the lunar race. (Vide *Indian Antiquary* for 1912, p. 19).
	Inscription of Jaishta Vadi 13, S. 1225 (1168 A. D.) on a pillar in the temple of Ruthi Rani at Dhod, Mewar, says that king Prithvibhatta, defeated the king of Sakambari (Amargangeya) and himself became the king (of Ajmer.)
1169	King Prithvibhatt died. King Someshwar, third son of Arnoraja succeeded Prithvibhatta.
	The Mynal inscription (J. B. A. S. vol. LV, pt. I, p. 64.)
1170	Bijolian inscription of Falgan v. 3 (5th Feb 1170 A.D) see J.B A.S. vol LV, pt. I, p. 40, gives an account of Chauhans of Ajmer.
	Anvalda inscription of Bhadrapad vadi 4, V. S. 1134 of King Someshwar's time.
1171	Inscription of V. S. 1228 (1171 A. D.) in Chhatree of Rajkirtiji, Jain Acharya.
1179	Someshwar died and his son, Prithviraj, ascended the throne. He defeated the king of Gujrat, conquered Mahoba which was defended by the famous generals Alla and Udal.
	Sati pillar inscription of Asadh V. S. 1236 in Lohari (Mewar) of Emperor Prithviraja's time.
1190	*Prithviraj Vijaya*, the famous epic poem, composed at Ajmer by Jayanak.
1191	Emperor Prithviraj defeated Shahbuddin Ghori of Ghor (who had invaded India) at Tarain near Thaneshwar.
1192	Shahbuddin Ghori again invaded India with 1,20,000 horse and defeated Prithviraj at Thaneshwar. Prithviraj was killed in the battle. Sultan Shahbuddin came to Ajmer, the seat of the Chauhan Empire, and sacked it. He placed Prithviraj's son Govindraj on the throne and returned to Ghor. Prithviraj's younger brother Hari Raj drove away Govind Raj from the throne for accepting Muslim supremacy, and himself became king of Ajmer.
1193	King Hariraj sent his general, Chatur Raj, to invade Delhi, which was in the possession of Qutubuddin Aibak, slave of Shahbuddin Ghori.
1194	Qutubuddin Aibak defeated Chaturraj and attacked Ajmer.
	Vaisakh Vadi 4th, V.S. 1251. The Tantoti Inscription on an image now in the Rajputana Museum, Ajmer about a grant of land by Queen Pratapdevi of King Hariraj, brother of Emperor Prithviraja.

A. D.	
1195	Qutubuddin Aibak retook Ajmer and the fort of Taragarh, and appointed a Mussalman governor of Ajmer. Khwaja Muinuddin Chisti came to Ajmer.
1196	Qutubuddin started from Ajmer to attack Anhilwara but the Mers and the Rajputs defeated him on the way. Qutubuddin shut himself in the Ajmer fortress, Taragarh.
	Inscription of H. 595 (1199 A. D.) on the Imamgah in the Adhai-din-ka-Jhonpra, Ajmer.
	Inscription of Zilhijj 596 (September 1200) in the Adhai-din-ka-Jhonpra about its conversion into a mosque.
1202	17 Rajab H. 598. The Rajputs made a night attack on the fortress of Ajmer and put the Mussalman garrison to the sword along with their commander Sayad Miran Husain Khangsawar.
	Inscription on the central arch in the Facade of Adhai-Din-ka-Jhonpra about its building in Shamsuddin Altimash's reign (1210-36).
1213	*Facade* (screen wall) of seven arches was finished in the Adhai-din-ka-Jhonpra, Ajmer.
1233	6th Rajab H. 633. In March, Khwaja Muinuddin Chisti died at Ajmer, leaving three sons, one daughter and two wives.
1280	The Chitor inscription of S. 1331 (1280 A. D.) (*Indian Antiquary*, vol. XXII, p. 80) recording that king Vakpatiraj II of Ajmer killed king Amba Prashad of Ahad (Mewar).
1320	Mt. Abu Achleshwar Temple inscription describes the Chauhans as belonging to the lunar race of Rajputs.
1364	Maharana Kshetra Singh of Chitor took Ajmer.
1400	Rao Ranmalla, administrator of Mewar during Maharana Mokal's minority, sent Khimsi with a Sisodia army, who attacked and took Ajmer.
1455	Muhammad Khilji, Sultan of Mandoo captured Ajmer from its Sisodia governor, Gajadhar Rai.
1464	First pucca tomb built on the remains of Khwaja Muinuddin Chisti at Ajmer.
	Inscription consisting of date S. 1535, Asadh Sudi 6, (1478 A. D.) on the image of Paraswanath in the Dadabari, Ajmer.
	Inscription of H. 939 (1532-33) on the northern wall of the Mausoleum of Khwaja Sahib giving date of its decoration.
1505	K. Prithviraj, son of Rana Rai Mal of Chitor attacked Ajmer, slew the governor Mallu Khan, and took possession of it.
1509	Guru Nanakdeva, Founder of Sikhism, visited Pushkar on Kartik sud 15th.
1523	Ramsar lake was constructed by Ramdeva of Dhar (S. 1580).
1533	In March, Bahadur Shah of Gujrat sent Shamsher-ul-mulk to reduce the fortress of Ajmer.
1534	Rao Viramdeva of Merta took Ajmer.

A. D.	
1535	Rao Maldeva of Marwar took possession of Ajmer.
1544	H. 951. Sher Shah Sur took Ajmer after defeating Rao Maldeva.
1556	Haji Khan, a slave of Sultan Salem Shah Sur, captured Ajmer.
1558	Akbar's general, Qasim Khan Nishapuri came to Ajmer and took it, Haji Khan having evacuated it.
1558	Masuda Istimarari Estate was founded in Ajmer District.
1561	Akbar came to Ajmer and sent Mirza Sharfuddin against Merta.
1563	Sharfuddin, Jagirdar of Ajmer revolted and came from Delhi to Ajmer. Later, when Akbar's army arrived, he left for Jalor, leaving Tarkhan Dewana in the fort of Ajmer. Tarkhan handed over the fort to Akbar's general.
1564	Akbar appointed Husain Kuli Beg as Jagirdar of Ajmer and Nagor in place of Sharfuddin, who had fled from Ajmer.
1567	(H. 974), Akbar made a grant of 17 villages to Dargah Khwaja Sahib, Ajmer.
1569	Akbar came to Ajmer after reducing Ranthambhor and appointed Shaikh Muhammad Bokhari as Mutavalli of Dargah Khwaja Sahib and rejected the claim of Shaikh Husain to be a descendant of Khwaja Sahib. The Buland Darwaja in Dargah Miran Sahib at Taragarh was built by the Subedar of Ajmer, Ismail Kuli Khan.
	Inscription of Akbar's time on Buland Darwaza in Dargah Miran Sahib, H. 976 (1569 A. D.)
1570	Akbar left Agra on 20th January to go on foot for Ajmer. On the sixteenth day, he came to Ajmer. He built the Akbari mosque in the Dargah.
	Akbar went from Ajmer to Nagor, where Rao Chandrasen of Jodhpur was invited to meet the Emperor.
1571	Emperor Akbar built the Ajmer citywall. He built a palace for his residence at Ajmer, now known as the Magazine.
1572	9th March. Prince Danyal was born to Akbar at Ajmer.
	Akbar came to Ajmer and made preparations to invade Gujrat. He sent Khan Kallan in advance.
1576	On 1 April, Akbar sent from Ajmer an army under K. Man Singh of Amber against Maharana Pratap.
1594	Sheruya Khan, son of Sherafghan Khan was made Khan and appointed *Pasban* of Ajmer.
1595	On accession to the throne of Jodhpur, Maharaja Sur Singh received the following pargannas of Ajmer:—Pisangan, worth Rs. 20,000/-, Samel, worth Rs. 4,000/ ; Naroo, worth Rs. 800/-; Bhadsurio, worth Rs. 800/-; Merwara, worth Rs. 87,631/- (12 villages); Terwara, worth Rs. 54,525/- (14 villages); Jharwasa and Adhwasa, worth a lakh.
1598	Shahbaz Khan, deputy of Mirza Salem (Jahangir) in administration came to Ajmer to go against Mewar. He died at Ajmer in 1599.
1602	Amanat Khan was appointed Bakhshi and chronicler of Ajmer.

A. D.

1605 Gokaldas received Sawar (Ajmer) as *Jagir* from Emperor Jahangir.

1610 Mahabat Khan started from Ajmer against Udaipur, but Maharana Amar Singh defeated him. (M. U. I. 402).

1613 Jahangir came to Ajmer and sent his son, Shahjahan against Mewar. Wheat sold at a rupee a seer at that time, owing to famine.

Inscription consisting of a couplet of H. (A. D. 1613) on the Hathibhata at Ajmer.

Inscription of 16 Rajah H. 1022 (1613 A.D.) giving date of a tomb in *charyar*, Dargah Khwaja, Ajmer.

1614 John Mildenhall, merchant, who had come from England, died at Ajmer, probably the first Englishman, who died here.

A factory under the Surat factory was opened by Mr Edwards at Ajmer.

Maharaja Sur Singh of Jodhpur was sent from Ajmer by Jahangir against Udaipur. He blockaded the mountain passes of Mewar.

1615 Jahangir repaired the Visla Lake at Ajmer.

The mausoleum of Miran Sahib at Taragarh built by Jabbar Khan.

June. Thomas Coryat, English traveller, arrived at Ajmer.

22nd December. Sir Thomas Roe, ambassador King James I of England came to Ajmer.

Jahangir built two pavilions at Pushkar. Inscription on the Southern pavilion giving the date of the building and saying that it was put up under Jahangir's order.

Inscription of H. 1024 (1615 A.D.) on the summit of the arch at the Dalan in Chashma, giving date of its building by order of Emperor Jahangir.

1616 Prince Shuja was born to Shahjahan at Ajmer on 24. June.

19th August, Rev. J. Hall died at Ajmer.

Muhammad Razabeg, Persian ambassador, came to the court of Jahangir at Ajmer on 19th October.

Sir Thomas Roe left Ajmer on return journey to London on 1st December, and encamped at Ramsar.

The Mers plundered the camp of Emperor Jahangir.

Jahangir, while at Ajmer, gave Jalor to Maharajkumar Gaj Singh of Jodhpur. Gaj Singh had taken it from the Biharee Pathans who had been in possession. The Pathans fled to Palanpur and founded there the present dynasty of Nawabs. Jahangir granted patta of Pushkar as Jagir to Brahmans.

1627 On the death of Jahangir in 1627, Shahjahan came to Ajmer from Udaipur and proclaimed himself King and left for Delhi. He gave Raja Bithaldas Gaur of Srinagar (Ajmer) all forts and cities from Ajmer to Ranthambhor.

1628 Shahjahan appointed Mahabat Khan, Subedar of Ajmer and gave him the title of *Khan Khanan* and made him *Haft Hazari*.

1629 Motkid Khan was appointed Fojdar of Ajmer. (M. U. III, 473).

A. D.	
1630	Ikhlas Khan Husain Beg was appointed Fojdar of Ajmer.
1632	Maharaja Gaj Singh of Jodhpur sent Muhnot Nainsi on a punitive expedition against Merwara. He burnt fifteen villages.
	Bithaldas Gaur was appointed Fozdar of Ajmer, and his son Aniruddha, his deputy, on retirement of Muzaffar Kirmani.
1634	Mahabat Khan died at Ajmer, and gave all his property to his Rajput followers.[1] Vithal Das Gaur was appointed Governor of Ajmer.
1636	Jama Masjid was built in the Dargah at Ajmer by Shah Jahan.
1637	Marble Baradaries on the Anasagar Lake were built by Emperor Shah Jahan.
	Inscription consisting of 33 verses under the eaves of the Juma Masjid, Ajmer giving date of the building H. 1147 (1638 A.D.)
1638	Inscription on the entrance to Allauddin's tomb in Dargah Khwaja at Ajmer of H. 1047 (1638 A.D.)
1640	Meerak Muinuddin Ahmad was appointed Bakshi of Ajmer and news writer of the Ajmer Subah.
1643	Princess Jahan Ara, daughter of Shah Jahan, built the Begumi Dalan in the Dargah Khwaja Sahib, Ajmer.
1645	S. 1702. Maharaja Jaswant Singh sent his minister Muhnot Nainsi to punish Rawat Narain. Nainsi destroyed Kot Kirana, Kukda and other villages in Merwara.
1649	Mirza Abu Said, son of Nur Jahan's brother, was made Fojdar of Ajmer; but as he was ill, after a few days stay, he left for Agra.
1654	Shah Jahan came to Ajmer and sent Allami Sadullah Khan to demolish the bastions of Chitor, which had been repaired by Maharana Raj Singh.
1657	Tarbiyat Khan Barlas was made *charhazari*, 4,000 horsemen, with 3,000 horse and was appointed Governor of Ajmer.
1658	Jeth sudi 13th, S. 1714. On 5th June, Maharaja Jaswant Singh came to Ajmer, and stopped here for 40 days. During his stay, he appointed Muhnot Nainsi as minister of Marwar in place of Mian Farasat.
1659	11, 12, 13 March. A battle was fought between Dara Shikoh and Aurangzeb at Ajmer
	After Dara's defeat, Tarbiyat Khan was, as before, appointed Hakim of Ajmer on the transfer of Lashkar Khan.
1667	Bandanwara Istimrari estate (Ajmer), was founded by Surajmal.
	Khwaja Kuli Khan was appointed Subedar of Ajmer.
1670	Mehroon and Junia, Istimrari estates, were founded by KishenSingh.

1. M. U. III. p 406-7 He said: "The Rajput know how to die. At his death, he addressed them thus: "With your help, I have been able to make a name. 'See that all my things go to you, and that the king's officers do not confiscate my property: take my coffin to Delhi and bury it there."—Jodhpur *Khyat*, and *Muasirul Umra*.

A. D.

1672 Darab Khan was appointed Governor of Ajmer.

1676 S. Hamid Khan son of Murtiza Khan was appointed Subedar of Ajmer, on S. Ahmad Khan's transfer.

1677 Iftkhar Khan Sultan Hussain was appointed Hakim of Ajmer, and later, companion of Prince Akbar. (M. U. I. 254.)

1678 Aurangzeb, appointed Padshah Kuli Khan, entitled Tahwar Khan, as Fojdar of Ajmer in place of Iftkhar Khan.

Aurangzeb, on his arrival at Ajmer, appointed Hasan Ali Khan Bahadur with Khan Jahan Bahadur to take possession of Jodhpur.

Aurangzeb sent an army of ten thousand cavalry under Bahadur against Jodhpur. From Jodhpur, Rathor Roop Singh, Ram Kumavat Bhati and Narsingh Das Rathor advanced, and a battle was fought at Gura.

The Marwar Sardars deputation left Ajmer and reached Delhi the same month.

1679 Ranchhod son of Govind Das, Istimrardar of Kharwa, was killed at Delhi when the Sardars of Marwar fought their way out of the siege which Aurangzeb had laid round the Jodhpur camp to take possession of Ajit Singh.

29 Shaaban H. 1090. Aurangzeb came to Ajmer and stopped in the palace at Anasagar. On 2nd February (Chet vadi S. 1735) Aurangzeb called his generals from various places to take possession of Marwar.

The Thirty Years' War began between Aurangzeb and Marwar.

Aurangzeb left Ajmer for Udaipur, sending a large army towards Udaipur under Hasan Ali Khan.

In July, the Rathors attacked the Jodhpur fort which was in the possession of Rahim Khan. Rahim Khan fled to Nagor. Rathors advanced to attack Ajmer

21 August. a battle was fought at Pushkar between Tahwar Khan, Governor of Ajmer and the Rathors. Tahwar Khan fled and his army was destroyed.

1679 Aurangzeb sent Tahwar Khan from Ajmer to attack Mandal (Mewar) and himself followed him.

On 17 January, Prince Akbar and Durgadas Rathor encamped at Budhwara near Ajmer. At night, owing to Aurangzeb's stratagem, Durgadas quietly left the camp, deserting Prince Akbar.

1680 Inayat Khan was appointed Fojdar of Ajmer. (M. U. I. 816.)

1681 8 Sep., (5 Ramzan H. 1092,) Aurangzeb left Ajmer for the Deccan to fight with Sambhaji who had given shelter to Prince Akbar. He left Jumlat-ul-mulk Asad Khan with Prince Azimuddin in Ajmer to guard it against the Rajputs.

Aitqad Khan went from Ajmer to attack the Rathors at Merta.

1685 Nahar Singh founded the Istimrari estate of Deogaon Baghera.

1689 Aurangzeb's governor of Jodhpur agreed to give *chauth* (one fourth of revenue as tribute) throughout Marwar to Maharaja Ajit Singh.

A. D

1690 S. 1747. Ajit Singh came with 20,000 horse to Ajmer and prepared to give the town to the flames; but the subedar, Shafi Khan, submitted and gave jewels and horses as tribute, and thus saved Ajmer.

1692 Subedar of Ajmer attacked T. Durgadas at the village Bhartiya near Parbatsar (Ajmer) but was defeated.

1693 Ajit Singh came to Shamshergarh near Beawar and was offered Ajmer by Nawab Shafi Khan on behalf of Aurangzeb. Ajit Singh refused it.

1704 Zabardast Khan, eldest son of Ibrahim Khan, was appointed Governor of Ajmer with the rank of 4,000 with 3,000 horse. Sayad Abdullah Khan, father of the future premier of Farrukhsayar, built Abdullahpura and his wife's tomb at Ajmer.

1705 Haji Khan of Athoon raided Hurda in Mewar. T. Jaswant Singh of Badnor killed Haji Khan and destroyed the fort of Chang.

1707 February 21. Aurangzeb died at Ahmednagar.

March. Ajit Singh took the city and fort of Jodhpur. Qutubul-Mulk Husain Ali Khan was appointed Subedar of Ajmer.

1708 March 24. Emperor Bahadur Shah arrived at Ajmer from Merta. Ajit Singh also came and was recognised as the king of Marwar.

2nd April. Maharaja Ajit Singh, Jai Singh and Bahadur Shah left for Mandsaur. Later, Ajit Singh and Jai Singh left the Emperor's camp at Mandsaur and went to Udaipur to ask for help to place Jai Singh on the throne of Jaipur.

August 6. Ajit Singh arrived at Pushkar on his way to Jaipur to place Jai Singh on the throne there.

1709 Feb. 19. Ajit Singh with twenty thousand men attacked Ajmer and took the city. The Governor of Ajmer, Shujaat Khan, gave a fine of 45,000/-, and Ajit Singh left for Pratapgarh.

1710 June 20. Ajit Singh came to Ajmer and was presented with robes of honour by the Emperor.

Abdullah Khan's tomb was built by his son Husain Ali Khan in Abdullahpura, Ajmer, near the Railway goodshed.

1713 Athoon (Merwara) was attacked by T. Jawahar Singh of Badnor.

1719 Maharaja Ajit Singh captured Ajmer.

1720 March 8. Maharaja Ajit Singh took up his residence in the Diwan-i-am at Delhi and worshipped Hindu gods there with bells ringing. Ajit Singh was ruler in the fort for three days. The Emperor Farrukhsayar fled into the Zenana.

1721 Emperor Muhammad Shah determined to regain Ajmer from Ajit Singh and sent an army under Muzzaffar Khan. Maharaja Jai Singh of Jaipur joined the Imperialists.

1722 Haidar Quli Khan was appointed Governor of Ajmer.

1723 Haidar Quli Khan died and Najmuddin Ali Khan appointed Governor of Ajmer. Maharaja Sangram Singh II of Mewar invaded Merwara.

A. D.

1725 Maharaja Jai Singh of Jaipur invaded Merwara, as the Mers refused to surrender T. Debi Singh of Parsoli, who had taken refuge with them.

1730 Maharaja Abhai Singh came to Ajmer and took possession of the fortress, Taragarh.

Maharana of Udaipur sent T. Jai Singh of Badnor against Athoon. T. Sultan Singh of Masuda, who had gone to assist T. Jai Singh was killed.

1731 Maharaja Abhai Singh appointed his own officers at Ajmer.

1735 May. Maharaja Abhai Singh came to Pushkar, and after staying a month there, he came to Ajmer and resided in the Anasagar palace.

1736 Maharaja Abhai Singh again came to Ajmer and resided there for an year and went to Merta in September 1737.

1737 Maharaja Abhai Singh of Jodhpur took Bhinai (Ajmer district).

1740 Maharaja Abhai Singh of Jodhpur and Rajadhiraj Bakht Singh of Nagor resolved to invade Jaipur, and took Ajmer from Maharaja Jai Singh.

1741 May 28. Rajadhiraj Bakht Singh attacked Sawai Jai Singh of Jaipur and defeated him at Gangwana, nine miles from Ajmer.

1743 Maharaja Abhai Singh sent from Merta, Bhandari Suraj Singh and T. Suraj Mal of Alniawas, who captured Ajmer.

1744 Maharaja Abhai Singh and Bakht Singh came to Ajmer and peace was made between Jaipur and Jodhpur.

1745 Maharaja Abhai Singh came to Ajmer and put up in Khwaja Danish's house.

1747 Malhar Rao Holkar came to Ajmer to see Maharaja Abhai Singh.

1748 Saadat Khan was appointed Governor of Ajmer. Saadat Khan marched into Marwar but was defeated, and had to return to Ajmer.

1749 Feb. 11. Abhai Singh's queen Vichetra Kumari, daughter of the Maharaja of Jaipur, died at Ajmer. In June, Maharaja Abhai Singh died at Ajmer, and was cremated at Pushkar.

On 19th October, an indecisive battle was fought at Chursiawas, nine miles from Ajmer, between Maharaja Ram Singh and Bakht Singh, the latter being assisted by Salabat Khan, Subedar of Ajmer.

1751 Ramsar and Srinagar (Ajmer district) were given to the Raja of Rupnagar (now in Kishengarh State).

1752 Bakht Singh took Ajmer. He died on 21st December at Sonali.

Ajit Singh's third son Kishor Singh captured Bhinai.

1755-1756 Ajmer was ceded by the Rathors to Scindia after the assassination of Jai Appa Scindia at Nagor.

1756 Scindia sent Khan Jadu with 4,000 men to Ajmer. Khan Jadu and Maharaja Ram Singh from Ajmer invaded Marwar, but were defeated, and retreated to Ajmer.

A. D.

1758 Maharaja Ram Singh left Ajmer and retired to Jaipur.

Ram Karan, Ram Singh's representative at Ajmer was driven out of Ajmer by his colleague, the Mahratta Subedar, Govind Ram, who henceforth became sole governor of Ajmer.

1759 The Mahratta governor of Ajmer was imprisoned in a fort belonging to the Thakur of Khawas by the Istimrardars of Ajmer.

1761 Baloo Joshi on behalf of Maharaja Bijai Singh of Jodhpur attacked Ajmer, took the city and laid siege to Taragarh.

1767 Maharaja Bijai Singh received Maharaja Jawahar Singh of Bharatpur at Pushkar, and agreed to help him against Jaipur.

1769 Santuji, the Mahratta governor of Ajmer, built the garden Chisti Chaman at Ajmer (near the Rly. Station) and gave it to Dargah Khwaja Sahib. It is now a *Sarai*.

1770-1773 Village Makhupura was given by Shimbhooji Mahratta for maintenance to Dargah Bada Pir at Ajmer.

1773 The Idgah near the Government College, Ajmer was built by Mirza Chaman Beg, Maharaja Scindia's subedar of Malwa.

1778 Maharaja Bijai Singh of Jodhpur sent an army against Chang (Merwara).

1779 Kot Kirana (Merwara) was attacked by the Jodhpur army under T. Arjun Singh of Raipur. The Jodhpur army was defeated.

1787 Singhi Dhanraj took the city of Ajmer from the Mahratta governor Anvar Beg and laid siege to the fort, and took it in December. A battle was fought between the Rathors and the Mahrattas at Gangwana near Ajmer. The Mahrattas were defeated and retired.

1790 August 15. General De Boigne took the city of Ajmer and laid siege to Taragarh fort. The fortress held out for more than six months, when peace was made between Maharaja Bijai Singh and the Mahrattas, and Ajmer was ceded to Scindia.

The Thakur of Kotario attacked Bhalain in Merwara, but was defeated.

1791 Sivaji Nana was appointed Subedar of Ajmer by the Scindia. He built the Nana Sahib-ka-Jhalra at Taragarh.

1792 General Perron, Subedar of Ajmer left for the Doab to join the Mahratta army.

1793 T. Jai Singh of Badnor conquered Athoon, destroyed the forts of Sarot and Ajitgarh, and excavated a lake at Ajitgarh.

Inscription consisting of ten verses of H. 1207 (1793 A.D.) on the Carnataki Dalan, Dargah, Ajmer, by Nawab Walajah.

1797 Vishwapat Rao Bhau, son of Sivaji Nana imprisoned Udai Bhan, Raja of Bhinai. The Istimrardars imprisoned Ram Bhau, the Tahsildar of Ajmer.

The construction of Naya Bazar, the principal street of Ajmer, was begun by Sivaji Nana, governor of Ajmer.

A. D.

1800 Lakwa Dada, Jagirdar of Ajmer, revolted against the Scindia and was superseded by Ambaji Inglia. General Perron, Scindia's Commander in Chief in Hindustan, sent Major Bourguien on 14 November to capture Ajmer.

Major Bourguien arrived at Ajmer and stormed Taragarh in Decr., but was driven off. He than laid siege to it.

1801 May 8. Major Bourguien gained possession of the Ajmer fort by bribery, and Mons. Perron was appointed governor of Ajmer by the Scindia.

Maharaja Bhim Singh of Jodhpur married at Pushkar the sister of the Maharaja of Jaipur.

1802 Maharaja Bhim Singh of Jodhpur sent Bhandari Dhiraj Mal to take Ajmer, who failed to do so.

1803 War was declared between the Scindia and the English. Maharaja Man Singh of Marwar took possession of certain areas of Ajmer, kept them for three years, and established *Thanas* (military outposts) in the district of Ajmer. The Mahratta governor, Bala Rao Inglia, demolished Santupura at Ajmer and founded the village of Balapura near the Mayo College. He repaired the citywall of Ajmer and dug a ditch round it.

1806 The Mahrattas retook that part of the territory of Ajmer of which the Maharaja of Jodhpur had taken possession.

Ganpatpura muhalla of Ajmer was built inplace of Akbar's *Sarai* by *mahajans* on a Sanad being given to them.

1807 Bala Rao, the Mahratta governor in Ajmer invaded Merwara with sixty thousand men but was defeated.

Inscription dated H. 1222 (1807-8 A.D.) in the south *tibari* of the mausoleum of Miransahib at Taragarh built by Balarao Inglia.

1809 The present *Brahmaji ka temple* at Pushkar was rebuilt.

Daulat Rao Scindia came to Ajmer and put up an inscription in the Adhai-din-ka-Jhonpra which was in the possession of the Mahratta government, forbidding removal of stones from it.

1810 Muhammad Shah Khan and Raja Bahadur, dependants of Nawab Amir Khan of Tonk, invaded Jhak, but were unsuccessful.

Incription on the southern door of the Katera of the tomb of Miran Sahib of H. 1225.

Inscription in the west Tibari of H. 1227-29 (1812-14 A.D.) built by Gumanji Rao Scindia in Dargah Miransahib.

1816-1818 Maharana Bhim Singh of Udaipur sent an army against Barar (Merwara), but failed to take it.

Bapu Scindia, governor of Ajmer, built the Bapugarh temple and repaired the Bajranggarh temple at Ajmer.

1818 Ajmer was ceded by the Scindia to the British.

July 9. Sir David Ochterlony took possession of Ajmer and occupied Taragarh on 28 July.

A. D.

1818 November, 20th, A Cantonment was established at Nasirabad by Brigadier Knox. The Magazine at Ajmer was fortified and made an arsenal.

Col. James Tod came to Ajmer and put up with the Superintendent, Mr. Wilder. He left on 5 December.

1819 The citywall of Ajmer was extended and the Naya Bazaar was finished.

In March, the army from Nasirabad, invaded Merwara. Maharana's army also came and established *thanas* in various places.

1820 The Agra Gate of Ajmer was built.

First Revenue Settlement of Ajmer was made by Mr. Wilder.

The Mers sieged Lulua and Jhak, and destroyed the thanas established by the British. Merwara was again invaded by the Udaipur forces. British forces under Lt. Col. Maxwell from Nasirabad also invaded Merwara. They took Shamgarh, Jhak and Borwa. The British attack on Athoon was repulsed. But later, Borwa was taken.

1822 Second Revenue Settlement was made by Mr. Wilder.

June 28. The Merwara Battalion was raised with Captain Hall as Commandant.

1823 Merwara was finally subjugated by the British and Udaipur forces. In May, Maharana Udaipur handed over the Mewar portion of Merwara to the British for administration.
Col. Hall was appointed Superintendent of Merwara.

1824 March. Jodhpur Durbar handed over the pargannahs of Chang and Kot Kirana to the British for administration.

1825 Bishop Heber visited Ajmer in February.

The temple of Bihariji was built at Pushkar.

1827 October 24. The third Settlement was made by Mr. Middleton. Mr. Cavendish was appointed Superintendent of Ajmer.

1828 Mr. Cavendish extended the Ajmer citywall in the south and built the Usri Gate. This work was finished in 1831 A.D.

1829 Mr. Cavendish made an enquiry into the Rentfree tenures of Ajmer.

1829-1831 Mr. Cavendish built the bazar, Cavendishpura, outside Madar Gate at Ajmer, where Santupura had formerly stood.

1832 Ajmer-Merwara was placed under the N. W. P. Govt. (now U. P.)

January 18. Lord William Bentinck, Governor General of India came to Ajmer, to which place the Chiefs of Rajputana were invited. Maharana Jawan Singh of Udaipur, Maharaja Sawai Singh of Jaipur, Maharao Ram Singh of Bundi, Maharao Ram Singh of Kotah, Maharana Kalyan Singh of Kishengarh and Nawab Amir Khan of Tonk came to Ajmer to meet the Governor General.

Lord William Bentinck ordered the dismantling of the Fort of Taragarh at Ajmer. Lord Clare, Governor of Bombay came to Ajmer. Col. Skinner with the *Skinners Horse* also came to Ajmer in January.

A. D.	
1832	Victor Jacquemont, the famous French naturalist, visited Ajmer and Merwara.
1832-1840	The *Patwan-ki-haveli* in *Karakka Chowk* at Ajmer, famous for its carved balconies, was built.
1833	Mr. Edmonstone became Superintendent of Ajmer. During his time, 1833-36, the Dargah Bazar was extended by the addition of Dhan Mandi. An English School was opened at Ajmer.
	The present Diggi (water reservior) at Ajmer was built.
1834	Ram Prasadji-ka-Ghat on the Anasagar lake was built, during the famine in Ajmer.
1835	General Hall, Superintendent of Merwara, resigned owing to ill health, and Capt. Dixon was appointed by Sir Charles Metcalfe as Superintendent of Merwara.
	Mr. Edmonstone's Ten Years' Settlement was made.
	Col. Dixon founded the town of Nayanagar (Beawar).
1836	Merwara was also placed under the N. W. P. Government.
	The English school, which had been closed in 1834 A.D., was again opened at Ajmer.
	The principal Bazaar in Beawar was built and opened.
1837	February 26. Census of the district of Ajmer was taken by Mr. Macnaughten, Superintendent of Ajmer.
1839	The *Khazanchion-ka-Ghat* on the Anasagar was built by S. Radha Kishen of Muttra, Government Treasurer.
	Col. Sutherland, Commissioner of Ajmer, took a British force to Jodhpur and held that town for some months.
1840	A cart road to Pushkar by cutting a rock in the Pushkar Ghati was built by Mr. Macnaughten with public subscriptions.
1842	February. Mr. Macnaughten left and Major Dixon was appointed Superintendent of Ajmer also. Thus Ajmer and Merwara were united and placed under Major C. Dixon, Supdt. of Ajmer-Merwara.
1842	Various Ghats were built on the Anasagar lake, Ajmer.
1844	Rangji temple at Pushkar was built.
	Lakhmi Chand and Mul Chand built the Ghat on Anasagar at Ajmer now known as Gulkhandyon-ka-Ghat.
1846	Mr. Thomason, Governor of the N. W. P. visited Ajmer.
	Seth Kishan Chand Kanmal built the Navagrah Ghat on the Anasagar Lake.
1847	October, 23. The first Trigonometrical survey of Ajmer-Merwara was made by Lt. D. C. Varierence.
	The East India Company opened a High School at Ajmer.
	The pargannah of Phooleya which had been an Istimrari Estate, was separated from Ajmer.
1847-1848	The Shahpura Ghat, now the Paropkarini Sabha Ghat, and the Lodhon-ka-Ghat were built on the Anasagar Lake.

A. D.	
1848	A Census of the town of Ajmer was taken.
1850	Col. Dixon's Twenty One Years Settlement was made, but brought into effect later.
1851	The Sadar Charitable Dispensary, the first public dispensary was opened at Ajmer near Balaji's temple, Agra Gate, Ajmer.
1853	Vaccination was first introduced by Dr. Lord.
	Col. Dixon, Superintendent of Ajmer-Merwara was made Commissioner of Ajmer-Merwara.
1854	Suraj Kund, a reservior of water, (now filled up) was constructed with the Ajmer Seths' subscriptions at Ajmer.
1857	May 28. The troops at Nasirabad Cantonment joined the Mutiny. Captain Spottiswoode and Col. Newbury were killed. The mutineers plundered the bungalows, burnt the records, and left for Delhi.
	Col. Dixon, Commissioner of Ajmer-Merwara, died at Nayanagar (Beawar) on 25 June. The Tahsils of Saroth and Rajgarh were abolished.
	August 9, an outbreak took place in the Ajmer Jail. The Magazine at Ajmer was fortified.
	Ajmer-Merwara became a Deputy Commissionership, and the Agent to the Governor-General, Rajputana, became Commissioner of Ajmer.
1860	The United Presbyterian Church of Scotland opened mission work at Nayanagar (Beawar).
1862	January. A regular Police Force of 548 men was established in Ajmer.
	The U. P. Church of Scotland began work at Ajmer.
1863	The Magazine at Ajmer ceased to be an arsenal. The Tahsil Court was opened in it.
1864	General Cunningham, Director General of Archaeology visited Adhai-Din-ka-Jhonpra. He describes it in the Archaeological Survey Report.
	June. Telegraph was brought from Agra to Ajmer.
1865	Haji Muhammad Khan's *haveli* in the Dhan Mandi was built.
1868	February 17. General Keating, A. G. G., Rajputana laid the foundation of the present Government College building.
1868-1870	The great famine, *pachisiya Kal*, took place in Ajmer-Merwara; when 25% of the population died.
	Major Repton became Deputy Commissioner of Ajmer.
1869	A Municipal Committee was established in Ajmer.
	Sir D. Brandis, Inspector General of Forests, visited Ajmer and made a report on the forests of Ajmer.
1870	20 October. Lord Mayo, Governor General of India, came to Ajmer.
	On 22 October, Lord Mayo, held a Durbar at Ajmer to which the princes of Rajputana had been invited. Maharana of Udaipur,

A. D.	
	Maharao of Bundi, Maharao of Kotah, Maharaja of Kishengarh, the Nawab of Tonk, and the Raj Rana of Jhalawar came to Ajmer to meet the Governor General.
	Lord Mayo visited Nasirabad on 25 October.
1871	Ajmer-Merwara was taken away from the N. W. P. Government and placed under the Foreign and Political Department of the Government of India.
	The Merwara Battalion was transferred from Beawar to Ajmer.
	An Assistant and a Sub-Assistant Conservator of Forests were appointed at Ajmer.
	The Tahsil of Ramsar was abolished.
1872	The present Jail building was constructed at Ajmer.
1873	A Jagir Committee with Captain Repton as President was appointed to enquire into the Jagir tenures.
1874	The Ajmer-Merwara Forest Regulation VI of 1874 was passed.
1875	The first regular Twenty Years Settlement of the province was made by Mr. La Touche.
	A Topographical survey of Ajmer was completed.
	Dec. 2. The Viceroy, Lord Northbrook paid a visit to Ajmer.
	August 1. The Railway first came to Ajmer from Agra.
	The foundation stone of the Mayo College building was laid at Ajmer.
1875-1876	Six stone inscriptions in Sanskrit were found during excavations in Adhai-Din-ka-Jhonpra. They are now in the Rajputana Museum, Ajmer.
	Feby. 14. Nasirabad was connected by Railway with Ajmer.
1876	H. H. Maharana Sajjan Singh of Udaipur visited Ajmer.
1877	The Ajmer Courts Regulation I of of 1877, the Ajmer Land and Revenue Regulation III of 1877 were enacted.
1877-1878	H. E. the Commander-in-Chief of India, and H. E. the Governor of Bombay came to Ajmer.
1879	Decr. Lord Lytton, Viceroy of India, visited Ajmer.
	Railway Loco and Carriage Workshops were built at Ajmer.
	H. H. the Maharana of Udaipur visited Ajmer.
1880	The Ajmer Railway Workshops were opened. H. E. the Governor of Bombay came.
1881	The Malwa Branch of the Rajputana State Railway from Ajmer to Khandwa was opened on 1st December.
	A census of population was taken on 17 February.
	Nov. 19. The Marquis of Ripon, Viceroy of India, came to Ajmer.
	The Ajmer Arya Samaj was established.
1882	The present Church of England was constructed on the Visla Lake.
	The American Methodists established a mission at Ajmer.

A. D.

1883 October 30. (The Diwali Day) Mahrishi Dayanand Saraswati died at Ajmer in the Bhinai House, and was cremated the next day.

December. the Paropkarini Sabha decided to establish an *Ashram* (Institute) at Ajmer in memory of Mahrishi Dayanand Saraswati.

1884 Railway General offices were built at Ajmer.

Lord Randolf Churchill, Ex-Chancellor of Exchequer, Great Britain and Ireland, visited Ajmer.

Kaisargunj, Ajmer city extension to the south, was begun.

Sir Lepel Griffin visited Ajmer.

1885 The Mayo College building was completed.

Nov. 5. the Marquis of Dufferin, Viceroy of India, and Marchioness of Dufferin came to Ajmer.

Lord Mayo's Statue removed from the Mayo College Central Hall to the lawn outside the western front.

1886 The Arya Samaj Bhawan, Kaisargunj at Ajmer was constructed.

The Ajmer-Merwara Municipalities Regulation of 1886 was enacted.

Mr. Whiteway's Twenty Years Settlement was made.

The Ajmer Rural Boards Regulation was enacted.

1886 Visit of H. R. H. the Duke and Duchess of Connaught to Ajmer.

1887 Feb. 11. Col. Sir E. Bradford, A. G. G., Rajputana held a Durbar in the Kaisarbagh, Ajmer near Mr. Saunders *Chhatree*.

H. H. Maharaja of Mysore visited Ajmer.

1888 The Victoria Jubilee Clock Tower was built.

The Court of Wards was established in July, 1888.

The Arya Pratinidhi Sabha, Rajasthan and Malwa was established at Ajmer.

The Ajmer Merwara District Board was established.

1889 H. E. Lord Roberts, Commander-in-Chief of India, visited Aimer.

H. R. H. Prince Albert Victor accompanied by Sir Edward Bradford visited Ajmer.

The D. A. A. V. High School was established at Ajmer.

Nawab Sir Asman Jah Bashiruddaula built the Mahfil-Khana in the Dargah Khwaja, Ajmer.

1890 October 28. Lord Lansdowne, Viceroy of India, visited Ajmer.

H. R. H. the Czarewitch (late Czar of Russia) visited Ajmer

H. R. H. the Prince of Greece visited Ajmer.

The *Vedic Yantralaya* (printing press) was removed from Allahabad to Ajmer.

The Roman Catholic Mission began work in Ajmer.

February 17. H. R. H. Prince Albert Victor and Duke of Clarence visited Ajmer.

There was a severe famine in Ajmer-Merwara.

A. D.	
1891	The first Spinning and Weaving Mill, called the Krishna Mill was started at Nayanagar (Beawar).
	A Census was taken at Ajmer on 26th February.
1891-1892	The Ajmer Municipal Committee constructed the Foysagar lake at Ajmer.
1895	The construction of the Victoria General Hospital building began on 4th March, 1895 and was finished in 1898. It is now occupied by the Municipal Office, Ajmer. Vaccination was made compulsory in Ajmer.
1896	Nov. 10. The Earl of Elgin, Viceroy of India, came to Ajmer.
	Degree Classes were opened in the Government College, Ajmer.
1899	November 2. Lord Curzon visited Ajmer.
1900	There was a severe famine in Ajmer-Merwara.
1901	The Trevor Town Hall at Ajmer was built by public subscription as an Indian Club. Later, at Col. Trevor's request, it was made a Town Hall and was given over to the Ajmer Municipal Committee.
	A Census was taken on 1st March.
1902	The Court of Wards as a separate department under a General Manager was established.
	November 18. Lord Curzon, Viceroy, came to Ajmer.
1903	April 1. A *Daikhana* to train nurses in Rajputana was established.
1904	The Co-operative Credit movement was started in Ajmer.
1905	Mr. Leslie, Sanitary Commissioner of India, visited Ajmer to consider the question of water supply.
1906	April 4, Lord Minto, Viceroy of India, came to Ajmer.
1907	The restoration of the marble Baradaries on the embankment of the Anasagar lake was completed. Mr. Silk was sent by the Government of India to Ajmer to find out fresh sources of water supply for Ajmer.
	Jan. 3. H. H. the Amir Habibullah Khan of Afghanistan visited Ajmer.
1908	The Madras system of vend of country liquor was introduced in Ajmer. An Excise Superintendent was appointed for Ajmer-Merwara.
	Oct. 19. the Rajputana Museum was established at Ajmer.
1909	A severe outbreak of plague occurred in Ajmer.
	The Railway Bisset Institute was built at Ajmer.
1910	Mr. Lupton's Thirty Years Settlement was made.
1911	Dec. 21. Her Majesty Queen Empress Mary visited Ajmer. She visited Pushkar on the 22nd. On the 23rd she left for Deoli.
	A census of Ajmer Merwara was taken.
1912	November 16. Lord Hardinge, Viceroy of India, came to Ajmer.
	The Edward Memorial was built at Ajmer.

A. D.	
1913	Nov. 17. Dr. J. H. Caumont was appointed the first Roman Catholic Bishop, Ajmer. A Registrar of Co-operative Societies was appointed for the first time.
1914	The Bhaonta waterworks for Ajmer were established.
1915	H. E. H. Nizam of Hyderabad built the Main Gate of Dargah Khwaja Sahib.
1916	Nov. 17. Lord Chelmsford, Viceroy of India, came to Ajmer.
	Church of Scotland Woman's Mission Hospital was opened.
	The Ajmer-Merwara War Board was established during the World War of 1914-18.
1918	A Maternity Home was started at Ajmer.
1918-1919	The Influenza epidemic which was India-wide, took a toll of 29830 persons from Ajmer.
1919-1922	The Government High School building at Ajmer designed by Mr. Lutynes, was put up.
1920	The Government of India appointed a Committee with Mr. Ashworth, a U. P. civilian, as Chairman to report on administrative changes necessary to give the benefit of the Reforms to the people of Ajmer-Merwara. It reported that Ajmer-Merwara should be amalgamated with the United Provinces.
1921	A separate Superintendent of Education for Ajmer, Delhi and Central India was appointed.
	A census of Ajmer-Merwara was taken.
	On 22nd June, the Merwara Battalion (raised in 1822), now named 44 Merwara Infantry was disbanded.
	Nov. 28. His Royal Highness the Prince of Wales came to Ajmer. Lord Cromer and Admiral Halesey were with him.
1922	September. A branch of the Imperial Bank of India opened at Ajmer.
1923	Jany. 26, the Marquis of Reading, Viceroy of India, came to Ajmer.
	The post of the Superintendent of Education, Ajmer-Merwara was abolished.
	The Kerot estate was made a Tazimi Istimrari estate.
1924	Mr. Har Bilas Sarda was elected Member of the Central Legislative Assembly, when for the first time, Ajmer-Merwara was given the right to elect a member to it.
1925	A new Ajmer-Merwara Municipalities Regulation was enacted.
1926	A Judicial Commissioner was appointed for Ajmer-Merwara, and the Chief Commissioner ceased to exercise judicial powers.
1927	The Government handed over Primary Education in the city of Ajmer to the Ajmer Municipal Committee.
	Government College, Ajmer was affiliated to the Agra University.
1928	The New Victoria Hospital in Kaisar Bagh was opened in October

A. D.	
1929	The Board of High School and Intermediate Education for Rajputana, Central India and Gwalior was established at Ajmer.
1930	King George's Royal Indian Military School, Ajmer was opened.
	March 7. Lord Irvin, Viceroy of India, came to Ajmer.
	Ajmer city was electrified.
1931	Adarshnagar extension began to be built at Ajmer.
	A census of Ajmer-Merwara was taken on 16 February.
1932	December 4. Lord Willingdon, Viceroy of India, came to Ajmer.
	The Ajmer P.W.D. was placed under the Superintending Engineer, First Circle, Central P.W.D., Delhi.
	Post of Incometax Officer for Ajmer-Merwara was created.
1933	The semi-centenary of Mahrishi Dayanand Saraswati's death was celebrated at Ajmer, when Aryasamajists from Africa, Burma and all over India assembled.
1934	Ajmer Municipal Committee was superseded by a nominated Committee.
1935	The Government Railway Police, and the Ajmer Merwara Police were amalgamated
	A bridge on the Banas river was built near Deoli.
1937	April 1. Part III of the Government of India Act, 1935 A.D., was brought into force, and Ajmer-Merwara was taken away from the Political Department and placed under the Home Department of the Government of India. The U. P. Government for the first time lent two civilians from its cadre, for 3 years, to be Commissioner and Assistant Commissioner of Ajmer. The management of the Mayo College, Ajmer, was handed over by the Government to the Mayo College Council, elected by the Princes of Rajputana.
1938	Certain portions of Merwara which had been temporarily handed over to the British Government between 1823 and 1830 A.D. were retroceded to the Mewar and the Marwar States. Thus 93 villages went to Mewar, and 22 to Marwar. The area of Ajmer-Merwara was reduced to 2367.6 square miles, and population to 506,964.
	Supersession of the Ajmer Municipal committee came to an end in August and a new committee was elected.
1939	A most severe famine broke out in Ajmer-Merwara.
1940	A new Maternity Home was built on the Jaipur Road at Ajmer.
	March 7. Lord Linlithgow, Viceroy, came to Ajmer.
	A new Revenue Settlement was started in November.
	Famine of 1939-40 came to an end when good rains fell in July and August.

PART III

ADMINISTRATION

CONTENTS.

Though Ajmer-Merwara is now under the Home Department of the Government of India, its two principal officers—the Commissioner and the Assistant Commissioner—are borrowed for fixed periods from the United Provinces. The Chief Commissioner of Ajmer-Merwara belongs to the Political Department of the Government of India,which is under the Crown Representative in India. The judicial department is under an officer, who is Judicial Commissioner both for Ajmer-Merwara and Kathiawar in the Bombay Presidency. The District Judge is an officer of the U. P. judicial service. The Police department always gets its senior officers for limited periods from the U P. Police service. The Forest Department gets its Divisional Forest Officer also from the U. P Forest service. The forest programme for the province is laid down by the Conservator of Forests, U. P. The P.W.D. is under the Central P.W D., Delhi, and its officers are on the cadre of that department. It is under the Superintending Engineer, First Circle, who lives in Delhi. The Income-tax Department is under the Bombay Income-tax Department. The Assistant Commissioner of Income-Tax lives in Karachi and the Commissioner of Income Tax at Bombay. Education is under a Superintendent, who is Superintendent of Education for Delhi, Ajmer and Central India, and has his headquarters at Delhi; while the Government College, Ajmer, is affiliated to the Agra University. The present Civil Surgeon belongs to the medical branch of the Political Department of the Crown Representative. The Excise Department gets it expert advice from the Excise Commissioner who lives at Indore. The Co-operative department is supervised by the Co-operative department of the Punjab Government. The revenue settlements are always made by officers of the U. P. Revenue Service. For technical advice in sanitary matters, questions of water supply and others, recourse is had to the U. P. and Delhi Governments.

I—JUDICIAL

The Judicial Department is under an officer who combines in his person two offices, those of the Judicial Commissioner, Kathiawar and the Judicial Commissioner of Ajmer-Merwara, and has his headquarters at Rajkot in Kathiawar. He is always a Bombay civilian, and is the High Court for Ajmer-Merwara. Under him, there are a District and Sessions Judge

CHAPTER XX

GENERAL ADMINISTRATION

THE Resident in Rajputana, who is an officer of the Political Department which is under the Crown Representative in India (Viceroy), and as such is not under the Government of India, is the ex-officio Chief Commissioner of Ajmer-Merwara. His head-quarters are at Mt. Abu. Under the Chief Commissioner, is the Commissioner of Ajmer, and under him, an Assistant Commissioner. The Commissioner and the Assistant Commissioner have their head-quarters at Ajmer. An Extra Assistant Commissioner is stationed at Beawar, and is in charge of Merwara. A sub-divisional officer is in charge of the Kekri sub-division of Ajmer.

The Commissioner holds several offices. He is Commissioner and Collector of Revenue. He is the Inspector General of Jails. He is Inspector General of Stamps and Registration and is Registrar General of Births, Marriages and Deaths. He is Registrar General of Assurances. He is the Court of Wards, and the head of the Co-operative Department. He is Excise Commissioner and District Magistrate of Ajmer-Merwara. He is the Conservator of Forests. He is Chairman of theDistrict Board of Ajmer-Merwara, and is the Officer who hears appeals in Municipal matters against certain orders of the Municipal Committees.

The Assistant Commissioner also holds several offices. He is Revenue Sub-divisional Officer (Assistant Collector) and Additional District Magistrate. He is Registrar of Assurances. He is Collector of Excise. He is Sub-Judge, first Class for rent suits relating to agricultural land. He is Registrar of Charitable Societies, and also Registrar, Joint Stock Companies. He is Registrar of Births, Deaths and Marriages, and Collector of Stamps.

Ajmer-Merwara is a small province of British India situated in the midst of Indian States of Rajputana. It gets its higher officers from the regular services of other provinces in India. Its administration, therefore, has affiliations in its various branches of administration with the provinces of Bombay, the Punjab, the United Provinces, and Sindh.

and an Additional District and Sessions Judge for the whole province. In each of the sub-divisions, Ajmer and Merwara, there is a sub-judge of the First Class, stationed at Ajmer and Beawar respectively. There is also an Additional Sub-Judge at Ajmer. There is a separate judge of the Court of Small Causes at Ajmer. In Merwara, the Sub-Judge at Beawar exercises powers of the judge of the Court of Small Causes. The Sub-Divisional Officer, Kekri is Revenue Officer for the Kekri Sub-Division and has no civil powers. The Sub-Judge of Ajmer is Sub-Judge 1st Class and Judge Small Cause Court for Kekri. For the Cantonment of Nasirabad, at present the Sub-Judge, Beawar is Sub-Judge first Class and Judge, Small Cause Court. The Tahsildars of Ajmer and Beawar and the two Naib-Tahsildars of Ajmer and the Naib-Tahsildar of Beawar exercise Munsiff's powers within their revenue jurisdictions. Altogether, there are six Sub-Judges and ten Munsiffs.

For criminal justice, in addition to the two Sessions Judges, there is a Magistrate of the First Class for the city of Ajmer. The Assistant Commissioner of Ajmer is a Joint District Magistrate and hears appeals from the Courts of the Magistrates of the Second Class in Ajmer. The Treasury Officer, Ajmer; the General Manager, Court of Wards; and the Superintendent of Excise also do Magisterial work of the First Class and the Registrar, of Co-operative Societies, of the Second Class in the Ajmer District, except Kekri where the Sub-Divisional Officer is a Magistrate of the First Class. The Assistant Commissioner of Ajmer goes one day every week to dispose of criminal work at Nasirabad and exercises First Class powers.

A Magistrate of the first Class, called the Railway Magistrate exercises criminal jurisdiction within the Railway limits in Ajmer-Merwara.[1] Some of the Istimrardars of Ajmer are invested with civil and criminal powers within their respective Istimrari estates. In addition to the City Magistrate of Ajmer, there are four Honorary Magistrates of the first class who are Chairman of the four Benches of Honorary Magistrates of the second class, each Bench consisting of four Magistrates to do criminal work for the city of Ajmer. In addition to these Magistrates and Benches, there are six Honorary Magistrates of the Second Class to try cases arising under the Police Act and the Ajmer-Merwara Municipalities Regulation, and one First Class Magistrate for Urban Area.

1. His jurisdiction extends to all B. B. & C. I. Railway lands in the whole of Rajputana.

Altogether, there are eighteen stipendiary and fortyeight Honorary Magistrates in Ajmer-Merwara. There were six Panchayat Courts in six villages in 1937-38. They disposed of civil suits and criminal complaints. Seven more such courts were opened in 1938-39.

II—POLICE

Prior to 1862 A. D., there was no regular police in this small province, and the Merwara Battalion was responsible for peace and order.

Dr. R. H. Irvine, M. D. in his book, *General and Medical Topography of Ajmer*, p. 111, published in 1841 A.D., says: "The police of the city of Ajmer is generally vigilant and sufficient for protection. The attention of the police is also directed to preserving the city in as cleanly a state, as the means at the disposal of the Kotwal will allow."

In 1861, the total strength of the Merwara Battalion was raised to 1000 all ranks, and from the savings resulting from the abolition of the Mer Regiment, an organized constabulary consisting of 548 men was raised and placed under the control of a Superintendent of Police from the 1st of January 1862. It was from that date that the provisions of the N.W.P. Police Act were extended to Ajmer-Merwara. In 1870, the Merwara Battalion was restored to its purely military character.

In 1871, the Police was transferred from the control of the Inspector General of Police, North Western Provinces, to that of the Commissioner of Ajmer-Merwara. Several changes took place in the strength of the force between 1862 and 1882. In 1891, the strength stood at 703 of all ranks as below:—

Superintendent of Police ...	1	
Inspectors	3	
Sub-Inspectors	13	
Head Constables	93	
Constables	556	593
Mounted Constables	37	
	703	

Between 1920 and 1923 the post of Assistant Superintendent of Police was substituted by that of Deputy Superintendent of Police. In March 1935, the amalgamation of the Government Railway Police with that of the Ajmer-Merwara Police brought on transfer from the Government Railway Police, a force of 13 head constables and 57 constables making a total of 99 head constables and 805 constables. In the same year, a Sergeant's post was transferred from Government Railway Police to Ajmer-Merwara Police. In 1937, a post of a Sergeant was created at Nasirabad, and three constables of one of the Railway private guards came into reduction.

The strength of the Ajmer-Merwara Police Force at present is:—

Superintendent of Police	...	1
Deputy Superintendents of Police	...	2
Inspectors ...	...	4
Sergeants ...	...	2
Sub-Inspectors	...	33
Head Constables	...	98
Constables ...	...	793
		933

The proportion of police to the population of Ajmer-Merwara is one constable to 618 men, and the proportion to area is one policeman to 2.53 square miles.

Ajmer-Merwara is divided into three Police Circles, Ajmer Beawar and Nasirabad; and there are sixteen Police Stations.

The Superintendent and the two Deputy Superintendents live in Ajmer. Of the four Inspectors, two are in charge of Beawar and Nasirabad Circles; one is the Prosecuting Inspector and one is in charge of the Police Lines at Ajmer. One Deputy Superintendent is in charge of the Ajmer Circle. Every Police Station is under a Sub-Inspector's charge. The remaining sixteen Sub-Inspectors are distributed amongst the various Police Stations and the prosecution department. The three Police Circles and the Police Stations[1] are as under:—

I. *Ajmer Circle.*

1. Kotwali. 2. Imperial.

II. *Nasirabad Circle.*

3. Bhinai. 7. Nasirabad.
4. Gegal. 8. Pushkar.
5. Goela. 9. Sawar.
6. Kekri. 10. Srinagar.

III. *Beawar Circle.*

11. Beawar. 14. Pisangan.
12. Mangliawas. 15. Todgarh.
13. Masuda. 16. Jawaja.

1. In 1878, there were nine first class, and 8 second class Police Stations in Ajmer Merwara—*Waqai Rajasthan*, p. 177. In the times of the Mahrattas (1791 to 1818 A.D.), there were only eight *thanas*, Ajmer, Pushkar, Ausari, Piplaj, Bhinai, Kekri, Masuda and Beawar.—Maharaj Kishen's *Tarikhe Ajmer*, p. 44.

III—AJMER CENTRAL JAIL

The Ajmer Jail is a large square building with watch towers at the four angles, and one in the centre. It is situated on a healthy site to the north of King George's Royal Military School, at a distance of about one and half miles from the city. It was constructed in the year 1872 A.D. It is a central prison and provides accommodation for all classes of prisoners. Its capacity is 588, and the average number of inmates, 341.65. Non-criminal lunatics are also sent to the jail for medical observation and kept under detention, when accommodation in the Mental Hospitals at Agra and Lahore is not available.

Originally, the Jail was located in a walled enclosure containing the tomb of Nawab Abdullah Khan with a big gateway near the Moinia Islamia School, Ajmer. Later in 1872, the present jail was built and the old building was used as a *Sarai* for travellers and was known as Abdullahpura-ki-Sarai. When the Railway line was constructed from Ajmer to Ahmedabad, the road from Ajmer to Beawar was diverted and the old jail building was dismantled.

Describing the Jail in 1841 A.D., Dr. R.H. Irvine in his *General and Medical Topography of Ajmer* (p. 111-112) says:-

"The Jail is situated in an old patched up Muhammadan building, a few hundred yards from the town walls. It is separated entirely from other buildings; and is in a very airy and dry situation. The accommodation for the prisoners is sufficient in space. The security of the place against escape may be doubted, supposing the prisoners unite in an effort to do so, the walls being low, and the *burkundaz* guard small. The average monthly number of prisoners is about one hundred and fifty. The prisoners are generally muscular and powerful men, of marauding tribes. Every prisoner who pleases, does now and always will continue to, exchange some of his provisions, with the banya or others for opium, or whatever his favourite stimulant may be. Thus, the prisoner manages to pass a happy dreamy existence during his captivity."

The Commissioner and District Magistrate, Ajmer-Merwara, who is *ex-officio* Inspector General of Jails, exercises general control and superintendence over the Ajmer Central Prison. The Civil Surgeon of Ajmer-Merwara is the ex-officio Superintendent and Medical Officer of the Ajmer Central Prison. The strength of the other establishment is as follows:-

1 Jailor.	45 Warders (Male).
1 Deputy Jailor.	1 Female Warder.
1 Assistant Jailor.	1 Dyeing Master.
3 Head Warders.	1 Sub-Assistant Surgeon.
1 Head Warder on Condemned Guard.	

The approximate maintenance charges of the prison amount to Rs. 44,000/-. The cost in 1937-38 was Rs. 47,476-13-11, the average cost per prisoner being Rs. 131—10.

The Ajmer Central Prison manufactory is wellknown for its carpets and *durries*, and has the distinction of supplying goods for the Viceregal Lodge at New Delhi; to His Excellency the Commander-in-Chief of India; and the Governors of several provinces and other high personages. Other minor industries are also carried on in the Jail according to demand. Profit on jail manufactures in 1937-38 was Rs. 1544-10. In 1936, it was Rs. 2463-7-3.

A part time school has been started for the youthful offenders from the 1st July, 1938 and educational facilities provided for grown-ups also, outside working hours in addition to a library for their use. Arrangements have also been made for their religious and moral instruction as well as the physical development of the young by paid instructors, while the Sub-Assistant Surgeon attached to the Jail Hospital, gives them discourses on sanitary and hygienic matters and first aid.

IV—COURT OF WARDS

Constitution.—The Court of Wards department was established for the due preservation of the property of minor landholders, of incapacitated persons who hold lands, the education of the minors, and the care of their persons. The Commissioner is the head of this department, and the management is carried on through the General Manager, Court of Wards, subject to the general control of the Chief Commissioner, Ajmer-Merwara.

History.—The provisions of the 33rd of Victoria, Cap. 3, Section 1, were declared applicable to the province of Ajmer-Merwara, by a resolution passed by the Secretary of State for India in Council, on the 16th March, 1871. The *Ajmer Government Wards Regulation, 1888*, was proposed by the Chief Commissioner, Ajmer-Merwara, which received the assent of the Governor General on the 15th May, 1888, and came into force on the 1st July, 1888. The management of the Court is now carried on under the provisions of this Regulation.

Till 1902 A.D., the Assistant Commissioner, Ajmer, held charge of the estates under management, as Manager, Court of Wards. The post of the General Manager, was created on the 1st April 1902, under the Hon'ble the Chief Commissioner's Notification No. 12, dated the 23rd January 1902, to relieve the Assistant Commissioner of this work. This new post is pensionable and in foreign service, or non-pensionable, according as it is filled in from qualifying service or by a nominee of the non-qualifying service. The General Manager, also exercises civil and criminal powers as Sub-Judge and Magistrate, First Class, in respect of the estates, under the management of the Court of Wards, Ajmer. The General Manager has his office and court at Ajmer, within the compound of the District Court House. The expenses of the Court, including a part of the pay of the General Manager and that of his staff, are met from the contributions levied from the estates under management, at 5 p.c. of their ordinary income.

The following estates are at present under the management of the Court of Wards and are locally managed by managers and *Kamdars*:

1. Barli.
2. Govindgarh.
3. Bhagwanpura and Lalikhera.
4. Gangwana.
5. Lasaria.
6. Mandah.
7. Manoharpura.
8. Nilaseuri.
9. Rajosi.
10. Tiswaria.
11. Lavera (T. Bal Singh's estate).

Of these, No. 1 and 2 are Tazimi Istimrardars. The minor owners of the estates are receiving education at the Mayo College, Ajmer, and the Government High School, Ajmer.

V—EXCISE

The Excise administration is governed by the (1) Opium Act I of 1878, (2) Excise Regulation I of 1915, (3) Dangerous Drugs Act II of 1930, and the Rules made there-under.

The present Excise department was established in 1880 A. D. Before that year, it was known as the Abkari. Uptil 1908, the Assistant Commissioner as Collector of Excise, was in direct charge of the department. In that year, the post of Superintendent of Excise was created. That gazetted Officer is now in direct charge under the Assistant Commissioner as Collector, and the Commissioner of Ajmer Merwara as Excise Commissioner of this British Province.

Under the Superintendent of Excise are:—

1. Inspector (Bonded-warehouse Officer).
6. Sub-Inspectors including the Distillery Officer.
4. Jamadars.

Upto 1908, when the Madras system of vend of country liquor was introduced in Ajmer-Marwara, a contractor used to manufacture liquor. The exciseable articles are:—

1. Country Liquor
2. Foreign Liquor.
3. Opium.
4. Drugs including Ganja, Charas and Bhang.

The number of shops, where exciseable articles are sold, is as follows:—

		1900	1920	1939-40
Liquor Shops	...	133	114	94
Opium [1]	...	21	40	41
Ganja, Charas and Bhang	...	17	16	18
		171	170	153

The reduction in liquor shops is due to restrocession of parts of the district of Merwara, to Mewar and Marwar.

Excise Revenue (1850 to 1940 A.D.)

In 1850 the revenue (abkari) was				Rs.	4,920	10	9
1872-73[2]	,,	,,	,,	,,	28,734	0	0
1873-74	,,	,,	,,	,,	30,769	0	0
1890-91	,,	,,	,,	,,	1,08,998	0	0
1901-02	,,	,,	,,	,,	1,14,670	0	0
1911-12	,,	,,	,,	,,	3,46,320	0	0
1924-25	,,	,,	,,	,,	7,09,414	0	0
1934-35	,,	,,	,,	,,	6,96,816	0	0
1935-36	,,	,,	,,	,,	7,05,137	0	0
1936-37	,,	,,	,,	,,	7,30,529	0	0
1937-38	,,	,,	,,	,,	7,42,155	0	0
1938-39	,,	,,	,,	,,	7,31,810	0	0
1939-40	,,	,,	,,	,,	6,69,956	0	0[3]

There has been a tremendous increase in excise revenue during the last thirty years. It will also be noticed that the excise revenue forms 46 p.c. of the total Income (fourteen and half lakhs) of the province of Ajmer-Merwara for 1939-40. Taking the 1937-38 figures, the proportion is 41 p.c.

1. Cultivation of poppy is prohibited in Ajmer-Merwara.
2. *La Touche's Gazetteer*, p. 46.
3. The decrease in this year is due to severe famine that prevailed throughout the year.

The total excise revenue of Rs. 6,69,956 is made up as below:—

Opium	Rs.	1,07,329
Duty on country liquor (including rental)	Rs.	4,84,232
Foreign liquor	Rs.	9,931
Drugs including ganja, bhang & charas	Rs.	66,688
Miscellaneous	Rs.	1,776
	Rs.	6,69,956

Duty charged on each of the exciseable articles is given below:—

Country Liquor for Urban area	Rs. 6/-	per	L. P. gallon
" " Rural "	Rs. 4/3/6	"	"
Opium	Rs. 12/-	"	seer.
Ganja	Rs. 10/	"	"
Charas	Rs. 60/-	"	"
Bhang	Rs. 6/-	"	maund.

Besides the duty the privilege of selling these articles is given to shop keepers (licensees) in the places fixed by the Collector of Excise Revenue, Ajmer-Merwara, on payment of rentals fixed every year in accordance with the past sales.

Excluding the amount received on account of cost price of opium and poppy heads, the total Excise revenue for the year works out to Rs. 6,22,497. The incidence of Excise revenue per head of population is Rs. 1-3-8.

The total expenditure of the department in 1939-40 amounted to Rs. 27,734. The quantity of country liquor consumed in 1900-01 was 37.422. and in 1939-40. 52.708 gallons.

VI—INCOME-TAX

Prior to the year 1926 A.D., the Sub-Divisional Officers of this province used to exercise the powers of the Income Tax Officer in their respective sub-divisions. In 1926, the Extra Assistant Commissioner incharge of the Excise Department was made ex-officio Income-Tax Officer for the district of Ajmer-Merwara. This arrangement continued till the year 1932, when it was considered advisable to separate the Income-Tax department from that of Excise in the interest of efficient working of both these departments. A separate Income-Tax Officer was, therefore, appointed for this district in that year.

The income of this department for the last six years is as under :—

1933-34	... Rs.	2,58,263.
1934-35	... „	2,95,499.
1935-36	... „	3,27,004.
1936-37	... „	2,63,259.
1937-38	... „	2,08,073.
1938-39	... „	2,47,635.
1939-40	... „	2,52,192.

VII—STAMPS AND REGISTRATION

Stamps:—The Assistant Commissioner and the Commissioner of Ajmer, are Collector and Commissioner respectively, of Stamps and Registration. In 1939-40, the income from Stamps was Rs. 2,21,288.

Judicial stamps	... 1,48,321.
Non-Judicial stamps	... 53,202.
Revenue stamps	... 19,765.

The expenditure of the Stamps department was Rs. 23,743.

Registration:—In 1939-40, the number of documents dealing with immovable property, the registration of which is compulsory, was 2,803, of the value of Rs. 32,59,979/14/3. Documents registered, the registration of which is optional, were 520 of the value of Rs. 42,966/2. Documents regarding movable property registered were 240 of the value of Rs. 75,137/8. Ninety seven wills and eleven authorities to adopt were also registered. The income from registration was Rs. 12,375/-/6 in 1939-40 and expenditure Rs. 2,494/11/-.

VIII—PUBLIC WORKS DEPARTMENT

Prior to 1933, the Ajmer P. W. D. formed part of the local administration and was known as Rajputana P. W. D. It was under the charge of a Superintending Engineer, who was Secretary to the Local Administration in the Public Works Branch, and was also in-charge of the Public Works Division of the Western India States. In 1933, the Rajputana P.W.D. was abolished and the P. W. D. Division at Ajmer was amalgamated with the Central P. W. D., and is now under the charge of the Superintending Engineer, First Circle, Central

P. W. D., New Delhi. This Division has two Subdivisions, and the headquarters of both are located at Ajmer. The Abu Subdivision was abolished on the amalgamation of the Division with the Central P.W.D. It is at present under the charge of a Section Officer who works under the direct supervision of the Executive Engineer, Ajmer.

The Executive Engineer is the professional adviser of the District Board and the three Municipalities of Ajmer-Merwara. The activities of the Division are that, (1) it looks after all the Government buildings, their maintenance and repairs in this province and those at Abu. (2) Construction of any new works in this area, and maintenance of about 222 miles of roads in Ajmer-Merwara, and 25 miles of roads in Abu section. In addition, irrigation tanks which number about 270 are also maintained and looked after by this Division. The average annual expenditure on works is about five lakhs, and about one lakh of rupees on establishment.

All protected monuments such as the marble *baradaries* on the Anasagar Bund, Dhai Din-ka-Jhonpra, Sola Khamba and other protected monuments in Ajmer-Merwara are also looked after by this department. The following important works were constructed recently in this Division:

A. R. C. Bridge across the Banas River near Deoli, at a cost of about Rs. four Lakhs in 1935-36, consisting of 18 spans of 86 feet each and 10 spans 33′-6″ each.

Lakhagodah tank beyond Todgarh in 1937-38, at a cost of Rs. 35,000.

An Outdoor Patients Ward in the Victoria Hospital, Ajmer at a cost of Rs. 40,000/- in 1937-38.

The existing water supply for the city of Ajmer is inadequate for its growing population. At present, seven lakhs gallons of water is supplied from Foysagar and Bhaonta which comes to an average of 5.4 gallons per head based on a population of 1,30,000. The proposed water supply is being designed to cater for the requirements of a population of 1,70,000 and will supply 25 gallons per head of water. It is proposed to sink wells in the Saraswati valley near Pushkar and to pump up the water with electrically driven pumps.

The Public Works Department is in charge of all works in connection with famines, which, owing to failure of rains, are frequent in Ajmer-Merwara. Rains continuously failed during the last three years with the result that very acute famine conditions prevailed in this area. Famine was declared in August 1939. About 2,10,000 labourers excluding dependants were given relief daily. The daily expenditure was about Rs. 25,000/- and monthly, about Rs. 8,00,000/-. The nearest parallel to this calamity which befell this area in 1939-40 was the famine of 1899-1900, which was not so severe as the present one. The number of labourers relieved in 1899-1900 famine was about one lakh at the maximum, whereas there were nearly three lakhs labourers including dependants in 1939-40 A.D.

IX—FOREST DEPARTMENT

In the Settlement of 1850, Colonel Dixon demarcated the boundaries of each village, and included waste lands and hills in the *Shamlat* or common land of the villages, with the stipulation that the villagers, would preserve these forests and not destroy them. This agreement was not observed. After Colonel Dixon's death in 1857 A.D., forests were neglected. By 1869, these waste lands were badly denuded of vegetation. In 1869, Sir T. Brandis, Inspector General of Forests, N. W. P., visited Ajmer and found the forests ruined owing to unrestricted felling of trees.

The new settlement of 1870-74 attempted to resume control over certain of these waste lands. The villagers would not agree to the proposals, and recourse was had to legislation. "The Ajmer Forest Regulation of 1874" was enacted. Under this regulation, only one-thirteenth of the area of the waste land, far away from the villages, was reserved as Government forests, and the rest was allowed to remain as Shamlat land. In 1892, the "Preservation of Private Forests Act" was passed. It has remained a dead letter.

The total area of Ajmer-Merwara in June 1939, was 15,62,106 acres, as below:—

(1) Wastelands : (*a*) Government reserves (about)	...	3 p.c.
(*b*) Shamlat private wastelands	...	64 p.c.
(2) Lands cultivated	...	18 p.c.
(3) Current fallow	...	15 p.c.

The waste lands at present, can be classified as follows:—

1. Government Reserved Forests.
2. Private *Birs.*
3. Village commons (Shamlat).

The condition of the vegetation on these Shamlat lands is unsatisfactory: (*a*) Some of the areas are completely denuded of all vegetation; even Thor (Euphorbia) and grass do not grow on account of erosion which has set in. (*b*) On some areas, however, thor and other bushes still grow and there is grass growth during the rainy season only. (*c*) Areas where a few trees along with other bushes grow. The condition of private *birs* (forests) is better than that of Shamlat lands.

GOVERNMENT FORESTS.

According to Mr. Lupton's Settlement Report of 1910, the area reserved for forests was 142 square miles, 114 in Merwara and 28 in Ajmer. The total forest area in 1937 A.D. before retrocession, was 91134 acres. Now it is only 46674 acres, or 17967 and 28707 acres in Ajmer and Merwara respectively; in other words, half of what it was before 1938 A.D. To manage this area, the following staff is kept.

1 Divisional Forest Officer, who is a lent officer of the U.P. Forest Service
2 Deputy Rangers.
21 Forest Guards.
4 Foresters.
3 Range Clerks.
3 Range Orderlies.

Management.—The Government forests are managed by the Divisional Forest Officer according to the prescription of a Working Plan prepared under the technical supervision of the United Provinces Forest Department.

The total receipts and expenditure of the Ajmer-Merwara forests for the year 1937-38 and 1938-39 are:

	Revenue.	Expenditure.	Surplus.
1936-37 (before retrocession) ...	85780	64756	21024
1938-39 (after retrocession) ...	54260	47870[1]	6390

The details of expenditure are as below.

	1936-37.	1938-39.
Maintenance, conservation etc. ...	30956	16269
Pay of Divisional Forest Officer ...	9288	13362
Pay of Establishment	18068	12847
Travelling allowances	4009	3176
Contingencies	2435	2216
Total ...	64756	47870

1. This includes Rs. 3786, leave salary of the late Forest Officer, 1191/-, gratuity to retrenched staff, and Rs. 237, travelling allowance for a visit of the Forest Officer to Abu.

X—CO-OPERATION

The Co-operative Credit movement in Ajmer-Merwara owes its inception to the passing of the first "Co-operative Credit Societies Act" in the year 1904 A.D. The movement had an humble start. Difficulties of finance and management made it impossible for experiments being made in the Khalsa villages. The Istimrari Estates, which were then under the Court of Wards management, were therefore selected in which to start the movement.

At first eight societies were organised in the said area; but for want of a central agency to cater for their requirements, progress continued to be slow till 1910. From 1910 to 1913, progress was fairly rapid. The number of societies rose from 8 to 282 (including three Central Banks) with a membership of 8611 and a working capital of over ten lakhs. Though expansion was very satisfactory, yet, it became clear that the edifice had not been built upon strong foundations; the task of organising and supervising the societies had had to be entrusted to an unpaid agency without experience to guide and control the course of the movement.

In 1913, Government sanctioned the creation of the post of a wholetime Registrar and one Inspector as a temporary measure. This naturally accelerated the pace, and before the close of the year 1918, the number of societies rose to 362, besides four central institutions. Their working capital also rose from ten lakhs to twentyseven lakhs.

After the appointment of a trained official as Registrar in 1918, there was satisfactory progress in all phases of Co-operative activity, and by the close of 1929, the number of all kinds of societies had risen to 606 with a membership of 18656 and a working capital of Rs. 45,47,001/-. Since then, the movement in Ajmer-Merwara, as in the rest of India, is passing through anxious times. The economic blizzard which set in sometime in 1929 A.D., severely hit the paltry resources of the peasants; and agriculture being the mainstay of the people, inflicted severe suffering on them. Consolidation, rather than expansion, became the sole aim of the department during the days of stress and strain, and there has been steady progress. The number of societies by the end of the last Co-operative year *i.e.* 30th June, 1940 were 746, with a membership of 23653, and a working capital of

Rs. 62,55,070. In April 1938, 126 societies with 2341 members and Rs. 1,95,818 working capital were retroceded to the Mewar and Marwar Darbars.

It is, however, a notable fact that in respect of working capital, Ajmer-Merwara stands second to none in the whole of British India; and, in respect of membership and number of societies, it holds the second position. While the main work of the department lies in rural areas, the urban areas have not been neglected. There were on the 30th June 1940, 163 societies (including nine Housing Societies) consisting of 7811 members and a working capital of Rs. 19,35,707.

Out of a grant of rupees one crore, sanctioned by the Government of India in 1936, fifteen lakhs were reserved for the training and education of the members of Co-operative Societies and their staff. Of this amount, Rs. 11,160/- were allotted to Ajmer-Merwara. This was used to hold a training class for a period of two months, and to do some propaganda. This grant was used up by the 28th February 1939. A grant of Rs. 3,000/- a year is given now. Out of the Rural Development grant, a grant of Rs. 1,000/- was given for propaganda work for "Better Living Societies" in the villages. With this grant, two Sub-Inspectors have been appointed for one year as an experimental measure. As a result, nineteen Better Living Societies have been registered. The experiment having proved successful, a further grant of Rs. 1,000/- was given during this year; but the two posts were brought into reduction from 31st August 1939, as the severe famine in the province made it impossible to start such societies.

XI—GOVERNMENT TREASURY

When the British took Ajmer in 1818, they housed the Government Treasury in a building on the Anasagar Bund, standing on what is now a *chabutra* to the right as we ascend the stairs from the small square water reservior of the Daulat Bagh. When the present District Court-House was constructed, the Treasury office was shifted to its northern block. Attached to the Treasury office and the Treasury Officer's court room, are the "Double Lock", and the vernacular office.

The Ajmer Treasury was till recently the second biggest treasury in India. Till 1922 A.D., there were three Sub-Treasuries under it.

1. Beawar sub-Treasury.
2. Todgarh sub-Treasury.
3. Nasirabad sub-Treasury.

The Nasirabad sub-Treasury was abolished about 1924, and the Todgarh sub-Treasury in 1938. There is now only the Beawar sub-Treasury, with the Tahsildar of Beawar as Sub Treasury Officer. The Ajmer Treasury is under the control of the Accountant General, Central Revenues, New Delhi.

Prior to the opening of the Ajmer branch of the Imperial Bank of India, the Ajmer Treasury had to deal with cash, and the daily balance was about four or five crores of rupees in whole rupees, small coin and currency notes in the Double-Lock. A branch of the Imperial Bank of India was opened in 1922 A.D. at Ajmer, and the work of dealing with cash was transferred to the Bank in 1924 A.D.

The monthly accounts of payments and receipts are submitted to the A. G. C. R., New Delhi. The monthly figures of receipts and payments of the Treasury upto 1938 were very near 43 lakhs and 14 lakhs respectively. But in 1938, the B. B. & C. I. Railway separated its accounts from the Treasury; and the monthly figures of receipts and payments have since fallen to near six lakhs and eleven lakhs respectively. After the transfer of the cash department, the Double-Lock is used for storing non-judicial, judicial, revenue and postage stamps only.

Till a couple of years ago, the Ajmer Treasury used to remit small coins, whole rupees and currency notes to other Treasuries, as and when required. But now this work has also been transferred to the Ajmer branch of the Imperial Bank.

CHAPTER XXI

LAND AND LAND REVENUE

THE total area of the district of Ajmer is 2,070 sq. miles. Of this, three fifths[1] or 1281 sq. miles is held by Istimrardars, and 235 sq. miles by Jagirdars. The remaining 554 sq. miles is *Khalsa*. Thus, 61.4 p.c. is Istimrari, 11.35 p.c. Jagir, and only 27.62 p c. is Khalsa.

Khalsa is land that pays revenue to Government. Jagir is assignment of revenue of land granted from the Khalsa as reward for good service or for a religious endowment. "Jagir may at present be said to mean *merely* alienated revenue, and for administrative purposes, *there is no practical difference between Jagir and Khalsa*".—DeLassoe's *Famine Report for 1890-92*, p. 7.

Khalsa.

The Khalsa and Jagir areas have no rivers or streams bringing water-supply from elsewhere, except the Khari river along the southern border of the district, which benefits the one jagir village of Kania only. The Saraswati and the Sagarmati streams of the Pushkar and Ajmer valleys are merely flood streams running only in rains. And except four, Pushkar, Budha Pushkar, and the small lakes of Sargaon and Korantia in Beawar Tahsil, none of which irrigates, there are no natural lakes or reservoirs. Moreover, the soil of the tract is mainly a comparatively shallow covering-over hard rock, and contains therefore (except along a few sandy *nullahs* in the Ajmer tahsil) no spongy substrata capable of storing up a supply of water, which wells can subsequently tap. The tract, therefore, depends entirely on the local rainfall, which is itself notoriously uncertain; and this, from the physical nature of the tract would speedily run off the face of the country, were it not caught and stored up in a number of artificial reservoirs or tanks. These tanks are now the one vital feature of Ajmer-Merwara. They are formed by throwing

1. Lupton's *Settlement Report*, p. 18. There are no Istimrardars in Merwara.

embankments across gorges in the hills or depressions in the plains; and by now, practically every gorge or depression at all suitable for a tank has been thus embanked. Luckily, the country lends itself to this tank-construction.

The province is on the border of what may fairly be called the "arid zone", and is the debatable land between the north-eastern and south-eastern monsoons, and beyond the full influence of either. The south-west monsoon, sweeps up the Narbada valley from Bombay, and crossing the table-land at Neemuch, gives copious supplies to Malwa, Jhalawar, and Kotah and the countries which lie in the course of the Chambal river. The clouds which strike Kathiawar and Cutch are deprived of a great deal of their moisture by the influence of the hills in those countries, and the greater part of the remainder is deposited on Abu and the higher slopes of the Aravalli, leaving but little for Merwara, where the hills are lower, and still less for Ajmer. It is only when this monsoon is in considerable force, that Merwara gets a plentiful supply from it. The north-eastern monsoon sweeps up the valley of the Ganges from the Bay of Bengal and waters the northern part of Rajputana, but hardly penetrates further west than the longitude of Ajmer. On the conflicting strength of these two monsoons, the rainfall of the district depends.

The prevailing wind during the rainy season is a south-westerly one, but there is but little rain which comes from this direction. The south-west monsoon is exhausted before it reaches even Merwara, and if this monsoon is in the ascendant, the weather will be cloudy, and there will be light and partial showers, but no heavy rain. When the wind veers round to the west, as it often does, there will be no rain. It is from the north-east that Ajmer, Beawar and Todgarh get their rain. The central portions of the province often receive heavy falls from the north-west, the north- east monsoon being apparently diverted from its course by the winds from the desert. The direction of the wind is most changeable, and the rainfall is exceedingly partial.

Not only, however, is the rainfall most precarious and partial, varying in total amount very much from year to year and place to place and falling with fury upon one side of a hill while the other side is perfectly dry, but it is most irregularly distributed over the rainy season, and most uncertain as to the intensity of the fall. "This last question is a most important one with reference to the filling up of the reservoirs. If the rain falls in light showers, even though it be on the whole an average fall, the soil will absorb it, the nullah will not run, and the tank will remain empty. If the fall is sudden and heavy and at the same time general within the catchment area of a tank, the chances are that the embankment will be damaged. The best rainy season is one which includes a fall of three or four inches in the twenty four hours in June, and a similar fall in September with intermediate showers, then the tanks fill and are replenished for the Rabi harvest, and Kharif crop is not drowned with excessive rain".

A province subject to such conditions can hardly be free from famine or scarcity for any length of time. The mean rainfall of the decade comes to 19.32 inches. To a population absolutely dependent on the seasonal rain for a good harvest, this precariousness must be a source of continual anxiety. *The agriculturalist in Ajmer-Merwara can never rely on two good harvests in succession.*

Irrigation.

Khalsa or land paying revenue to Government is divided into (*a*) *Chahi* land, irrigated from wells, (*b*) *Talabi*, irrigated from tanks, (*c*) *Abi*, submerged during the rains, (*d*) *Barani*, or unirrigared land, dependent on rainfall.

Appendix B gives the annual rainfall of Ajmer for 81 years, from 1860 to 1940 A.D. The average rainfall of 41 years ending 1900 was22·4 inches; and for the succeeding 40 years ending 1940, 19.9 inches.

The Hindu kings who ruled Ajmer, built artificial lakes like the Anasagar and Visalsar at Ajmer, and the Ramsar lake at Ramsar. Col. Hall built a number of *talaos* in Merwara, and Col. Dixon who followed him, built an enormous number of such talaos. Col. Dixon's *Sketch of Merwara*, published in 1850 A.D. (p. 121) says, that during "the last twelve years, one hundred and six new hamlets were located on waste jungle lands". and 3,915 new wells, 2,065 *nadees* (small tanks) were dug and constructed "resulting in an increase of 60,634 in the population of the tract (p. 132). The stove-like wells that have been built throughout the tract are too numerous to be detailed."

Colonel Dixon gives in his *Sketch of Merwara*, pp. 124-131, a list of 290 embankments or talaos built in Merwara during the preceding eleven years, 1835-36 to 1845-46, besides twentythree weirs on *nadees* in Beawar, at a total cost of Rs. 2,41,112-7-11¾, causing an increase in revenue in those eleven years beyond the *jamma* of 1835-36, of Rs. 6,41,234-5-6½, thus resulting in a profit during this short period after paying for the cost incurred, of Rs. 4,00,121-13-6¾. This, says Col. Dixon, "is our gain in a pecuniary point of view. As far as it affects the normal improvement of the people, the advantages are beyond calculation." (p. 137). These embankments irrigate land as below:—

120 in Mewar Merwara irrigate	... 10,865	bighas.
12 in Marwar Merwara "	... 847	"
158 in British Merwara "	... 28,968	"
290	40,680[1]	

It may be noted that the yearly revenue in Mewar Merwara villages increased by 45,858-0-6½ and in Marwar Merwara villages, by Rs. 1,804-10-6½ as under:—

	1835-36	1846-47	increase.
Mewar Merwara	Rs. 54,298-13-7½	1,00,156-14-2	45,858-0-6½.
Marwar Merwara	" 7,212-4-7½	9,016-15-2	1,804-10-6½.

How much have the States of Mewar and Marwar benefited by entrusting their undeveloped villages to the Administration of Ajmer-Merwara and geting them back in a far more prosperous condition! When we note that of the above 290 embankments, 280 were constructed in Col. Dixon's time, seven in Col. Hall's and three before him, we realize how great and rapid was the development of Merwara in Col. Dixon's time, and what prosperity his regime brought to the people.

In the district of Ajmer, similar improvements were made, but no records comparable to what the *Sketch of Merwara* describes are available. But that there were in 1848 A.D., a thousand talaos in Ajmer-Merwara, is proved by two facts, (1) Col. Dixon in his *Settlement Report* (p. 20) says that there are "about 1,000 talaos in Ajmer-Merwara"; (2) In his report on the famine of 1848-49, he says that of "about one thousand talaos in Merwara and Ajmer, only one Jugpura near Nasirabad had the benefit of a smart shower."[2] Many of these talaos have unfortunately fallen in disrepair and are more or less ruined.

In 1891, there were 435 tanks,[3] of which, 283 were controlled by Government. The others were village tanks which belonged to the villages and not Government. In 1910, there were 542 talaos in the Khalsa area, of which 283 were looked after by the P.W.D. Government now maintains 434 tanks in Ajmer-Merwara. Of these, 108 have since been handed over to the Mewar and Marwar Darbars.

1. Jalia and Balad tanks near Beawar, irrigate 649¾ and 526 acres respectively.
2. DeLassoe's *Famine Report*, 1892 A.D., p. 163.
3. The 1891 *Census Report*, p. 93.

As regards *wells*, Mr. Whiteway gives the number in Ajmer-Merwara to be 16,360, of which 11,735 only worked. (*Settlement Report, 1886 A.D.* p. 8) Captain DeLassoe, in his *Famine Report of 1892*, (p. 26) says that there are 29,000 wells and that they irrigate 10,90,000 acres of land.

Mr. Lupton, in his *Settlement Report*, 1910, p. 51 says that the working wells in 1907-8 were 14,468 and not working, 6,325. In 1934-35, the wells and the irrigated area were:

	Wells.	Irrigated area acres.	Wells abandoned or not used.
Ajmer and Kekri...	11,835	45,640	6,293.
Merwara-before retrocession ...	9,955	25,006½	2,420
	21,790	70,646½	8,713

According to Mr. Lupton's *Settlement Report*, p. 19, the cultivated area on the average of 18 years upto 1907, was:—

Ajmer	...	1,11,318 acres.
Beawar	...	48,336 ,, .
Todgarh	...	23,635 ,,

In other words, in Ajmer	31·7%	of the whole of the Khalsa and Jagir.
in Beawar	25·3%	,, ,, ,,
in Todgarh	15·3%	,, ,, ,,

is cultivated (forest excluded). Of this cultivated area, that which was irrigated from tanks and wells was:—

22.4 %	irrigated in	Ajmer.
26.63%	,,	Beawar.
44.6 %	,,	Todgarh.

This shows that, of the area under cultivation, one-fourth is irrigated and threefourths is *barani* or dependent upon rain. In Ajmer and Beawar taken together, three-fourths is unirrigable; and in Todgarh, one-seventh is cultivated, and of this one-seventh, less than half is irrigated.

REVENUE ADMINISTRATION

The Commissioner of Ajmer is the Commissioner and Collector of Revenue. The Assistant Commissioner is Subdivisional Officer for Revenue. For collection of land revenue, supervision of tanks, deciding questions of demarcation, and other revenue matters, six Tahsils were originally established, three in Ajmer—Ajmer, Ramsar and Rajgarh—and three in Merwara—Nayanagar, Todgarh and Saroth. Rajgarh was abolished after Col. Dixon's death in 1857, and

Ramsar, after the recognization of the district in A.D. 1871.[1] Similarly Saroth was amalgamated with the Beawar or Nayanagar Tahsil after Col. Dixon's death, and Todgarh after the rendition of Marwar and Mewar portions of Merwara in 1938 A.D.

LAND REVENUE SETTLEMENTS

There have been several settlements during the 120 years of British rule in Ajmer-Merwara. There were five settlements for the district of Ajmer, one for Merwara, and the remaining three for Ajmer-Merwara :—

Ajmer District

In 1820, the first settlement was by Mr. Wilder Superintendent, for eight years for	Rs. 140,034.
It broke down in the first year and was followed by one,	
In 1821, for five years for	Rs. 164,700.
This was continued for two years more.	
In 1827, Middleton's Five Years Settlement for ...	Rs. 144,072
In 1835, Edmonstone's Ten Years Settlement for ...	Rs. 129,872.
(During 1842-49, Col. Dixon collected revenue at ⅜ of the produce).	
In 1850, Col. Dixon's Twenty-one Years Settlement for ... (slightly varying from year to year).	Rs. 171,219.

Merwara

In 1850, Col. Dixon made a settlement for Merwara for ...	Rs. 181,751.

Ajmer-Merwara

In 1875, Mr. La Touche's Ten Years Settlement at ...	Rs. 304,593.
In 1886, Mr. Whiteway's Twenty Years Settlement was for	Rs. 298,927
In 1910, Mr. Lupton's Thirty Years Settlement was for ...	Rs. 271,341
rising eventually to	Rs. 284,778

According to the last (Lupton's) Settlement Report, the Settlement was confined to 196 villages, of which 138½ were in Khalsa, 51½ in Jagir, and 6 in minor Istimrardari area, (Karel, Rajosi, Kharedki, Nawsar, Ajaisar and Kotri).

Of the 141 villages,	the Jats hold	52,	the Gujars	35.
	the Mers „	41,	the Merats	4.
	the Rajputs „	4,	the Mussalmans	5.

The area settled was 1,348 sq. miles; 821 sq. miles in Ajmer and 527 sq. miles in Merwara. Of this, 1,081 sq. miles was Khalsa and 267 Jagir and minor Istimrar.

1. La Touche's *Settlement Report*, p. 10.

In 1940, a new Settlement was started by Mr. A. K. Sharma, Settlement Officer.

Rabi Crops in Ajmer-Merwara consists of Wheat, Gram, Barley, Gulchina, Poppy, *Methi*, Carrots, Lucerne, Laherwa, *Gulab*, *Motia*, *Zira*, *Sarson*, and *Sanwa*.

Extra Crop Rabi: Melons, *Jawar* and *Makki*.

Kharif: Maize, Cotton, *Jawar*, *Til*, *Bajra*, *Kulath*, Raddish, Carrot, Chillies, Lucerne, *Moong*, *Gwar*, *Moth*, *Urd*, *Singhara*, Tobacco, *Chowla*, *Mandwa*, Rice, Sugarcane, Jute, *Gulab-Motia*, *Kanghli*, Indigo.

The following villages are well-known for producing certain grains and vegetables:

Kanpura ...	for wheat. Kanpura wheat is supposed to be the best in India.
Ramsar ...	„ *Dana Methi*, (Methi seed).
Bhaonta ...	„ red Chillies and Melons.
Amba Masena ...	„ Melons.
Harmara ...	„ *Zira*.
Nand ...	„ *Aira*.
Karel ...	„ Maize and Melons.
Chavandia ...	„ *Gur* is manufactured here.

Pushkar, Ganahera, Galti, Hokran, Chavandia, Nedlia and Kanas grow sugarcane.

neither 'Istimrari Estates' nor are the holders 'Istimrardars' within the meaning of section 20 of the Ajmer Land and Revenue Regulation II of 1877. The non-Sanadi Istimrardars hold their estates on fixed tenures, and their estates are not liable to resumption. They are, therefore, full proprietors of their estates and possess rights over minerals found in them.

Of the nineteen principal Istimrari estates, the holders of sixteen, in order of precedence, are, Bhinai, Sawar, Masuda, Pisangan, Junia, Deolia, Kharwa, Bandanwara, Mehrun, Para, Deogaon-Baghera, Govindgarh, Tantoti, Barli, Bagsuri and Kerot. They enjoy the honour of *Tazim* and are called Tazimi Istimrardars. Of these, the first four and the Istimrardars of Kharwa, are the heads of their respective houses, from which the remainder are offshoots. Of the sixteen Tazimi Istimrari Estates, only Sawar is Sisodia: the remaining fifteen are Rathor, descended from King Jodha, who founded Jodhpur in 1459 A.D. Except Masuda and Bagsuri, founded by a scion of the family of Duda, the eldest son of Jodha, the remaining thirteen were founded by the descendants of King Maldeva's two sons—Chandrasen (1562-1583) and Udaisingh (1583 to 1595)—Bhinai, Deolia, Bandanwara, Tantoti, Barli, Deogaon-Baghera and Kerot by Chandrasen's descendants; and Kharwa, Junia, Mehrun, Pisangan, Govindgarh and Para by Udaisingh's. The oldest of these estates is Masuda, founded in 1558 A.D., and the youngest, Kerot.

Before the time of Rao Jodha, a few descendants of the royal family of Marwar came to the district of Ajmer and settled there, but they never attained higher positions than that of the Bhomias. The descendants of Jodha founded various Istimrari estates, of which the chief estates were Masuda and Bagsuri. Later, Rao Maldeva's son Chandra Sen's grandson, Karam Sen, came to Ajmer and founded the estate of Bhinai, from which Tantoti, Deolia, Barli, Deogaon-Baghera are the chief offshoots. Some of Mota Raja Udai Singh's descendants migrated to Ajmer and founded the estates of which Junia, Mehrun, Pisangan, Para, Govindgarh, and Kharwa are the principal Istimrari estates. The Rathor Istimrardars and Bhomias, who are in possession of more than two-third of the entire area of Ajmer, are descendants of the Marwar kings, Rao Ran Mal, Rao Chonda, Rao Jodha, Rao Chandra Sen and Motaraja Udai Singh.

Of the 83 Istimrardars, fifteen are large land-holders possessing from 3 to 60 villages and having an income, varying from 15,000/- to 1,25,000/-, the chief being Masuda, Bhinai and Sawar.

CHAPTER XXII

ISTIMRARDARS, JAGIRDARS AND BHUMIAS

MORE than half the area of Ajmer is in the possession of Istimrardars. Istimrardars are so called from the fact that they hold their estates in perpetuity, on condition of paying an annual revenue to Government, which is not liable to enhancement. This privilege is subject to certain conditions of the *sanad*.

None of the Istimrari estates ever paid revenue till the time of the Mahrattas in 1755 A.D., but were held on condition of military service. Mr. Wilder, the first Superintendent of Ajmer, after considering the claims of Istimrardars of the district, ruled that only Bhinai and Sawar were entitled to claim the status of Istimrardars and that the others were Talukdars and liable to be assessed to revenue from time to time. In 1830 A.D., even Bhinai and Sawar were held to be Istimrardars only during the life-time of the Thakurs then alive. In pursuance of this decision, on the death of the Thakur of Sawar, the estate was re-assessed to revenue, but no action was taken, when the Raja of Bhinai died. In 1839 and 1841, all the estates were again declared liable to re-assessment and the Government of India issued explicit orders to assess them; but the orders were not acted upon. Finally, when Major Davidson was Deputy Commissioner of Ajmer, the Government of India in 1873 A.D. waived its right to re-assess them, and Mr. (later Sir) Alfred C. Lyall, Chief Commissioner of Ajmer-Merwara granted all Istimrardars, Istimrari Sanads on the 30th March, 1875 in public durbar.

"There are sixty-six estates, containing two hundred and thirty villages, with an area of 8,19,523 acres." The Istimrari revenue is 1,14,734-3-11 and the estimated rent roll of the Istimrardars is Rs. 5,59,198"[1]. Sixty out of sixty-six estates are held by Rajputs.

There are three classes of Istimrari estates in Ajmer Merwara, *viz.*, (*i*) the Tazimi Sanadi, (*ii*) the Non-Tazimi Sanadi and (*iii*) the Non-Tazimi non-Sanadi. The last are

1. Watson's *Gazetteer of Ajmer-Merwara*, 1904, p. 91.

JODHA
King of Marwar (1453-1486 A. D.)

- Duda.
  - Viramdeva.
    - Jaimal.
    - Isarji.
    - Jagmal.
      - Hanwant Singh 1558 got Masuda.
      - Ladsingh. (Founder, Bagsuri 1658.)
      - Kallaji.
- Suja.
  - Bhagji.
    - Gangaji.
      - Maldeva.
        - Chandrasen (King of Marwar 1562-1583).
          - Ugrasen.
            - Karmasen captured Bhinai.
              - Shamsingh.
                - Udai Bhan (Bhinai.)
                  - Kesrisingh. Bhinai.
                  - Surajmal. Bandanwara.
                  - Narsinghdas. Tantoti.
                - Akbairaj got Deolia.
                  - Isardas Deolia.
                  - Devidas Barli.
                  - Naharsingh captured Deogarh.
                  - Gajsingh was given Kerot. (Kerot became Tazimi Istimrardar in June 1923.)
        - Udaisingh, King of Marwar (1583-1595).
          - Madho Singh.
            - Kishensingh.
              - Rajsingh (Junia).
            - Karma Singh. Mehrun 1670 A. D.
            - Jhunjhar Singh Pisangan (Shah-Jahan's time).
              - Fatehsingh.
              - Sham Singh.
          - Bhagwansingh.
            - Govinddas (founded Govindgarh.)
          - Saktsingh Kharwa.

The estate holders of the first class, *i. e.* Tazimi Sanadi estates, enjoy the following rights and privileges:—

(*a*) They have the right of being presented in a body to the Viceroy.
(*b*) They receive 'attar' and 'pan' at the Chief Commissioner's hands in Durbars, at which he himself presides.
(*c*) They are allowed to maintain private stills for the distillation of liquor from mahua or molasses, solely for their own use, but the stills are open to inspection by superior excise officers, and liquor distilled by them is subject to the limits fixed by the Collector.
(*d*) They occupy seats in first row in Viceregal and other Durbars.
(*e*) They are entitled to a return visit from the Chief Commissioner when he meets them in their own estates.
(*f*) They are exempted from personal appearance in the Civil Courts.
(*g*) They are exempted from the provisions of sections 13-15 of the Arms Act.
(*h*) They enjoy the privileges conferred by sections 27-29 of the Ajmer Land and Revenue Regulation II of 1877.

Both the non-Tazimi Sanadi and non-Tazimi non-Sanadi Istimrardars occupy seats in the Viceregal or other Durbars in the first, second or the last row according to precedence given in the Viceregal Durbar of 1877, and are exempted from the provisions of sections 13-15 of the Arms Act; but the difference between them is, that the non-Tazimi Sanadi Istimrardars receive invitations to attend durbars direct from Government officers, enjoy the privileges conferred by sections 27-29 of the Ajmer Land and Revenue Regulations II of 1877, pay their revenue and royalty direct to Government and are subordinate to their *Patwis* only in matters social; whereas, the non-Tazimi non-Sanadi Istimrardars receive invitations through their *Patwis*, pay their revenue and royalty to Government through their *Patwis*, and are subordinate to their *Patwis* in every respect.

OBLIGATIONS OF ISTIMRARDARS TO GOVERNMENT.

The various obligations of Istimrardars to Government are given in the conditions attached to the *sanads* granted to them, a draft of which is printed at pages 694-96 of the Ajmer Regulations, Fourth Edition, Vol. II, H. to L. In modification of condition 7 of the *sanads*, a supplementary *sanad* was issued in 1923 A.D. to all Istimrardars sanctioning the abolition of *nazrana* on successions to Istimrari estates.

In all the Istimrardar families, with the unimportant exception of Karel, where sub-division is still the rule, succession is by primogeniture, the provision for younger sons

consisting generally of a grant of a well and a few bighas of land, which is heritable property until the line of the original grantee becomes extinct. In early times, as in Karel at present, all sons shared alike except the eldest, whose portion was generally larger than that of the rest, but the disruption of estates which ensued was so inconvenient that it was dropped in favour of an assignment, known as *gras*, of single villages to younger sons, an arrangement which in its turn, has given place to that now prevailing.

According to Mr. La Touche,

> "The tenure of the feudal chief was originally identical with that of the chiefs in the Indian States of Rajputana. The estates were Jagirs held on condition of military service, and liable to various feudal incidents. Col. Tod in his *Annals and Antiquities of Rajasthan*, Vol. I, page 167, thus sums up the result of his inquiries into these tenures:—"A grant of an estate is for the life of the holder, with inheritance for his offspring in lineal descent or adoption with the sanction of the Prince and resumable for crime or incapacity; this reversion and power of resumption being marked by the usual ceremonies on each lapse of the grantee of sequestration (Zabti), of relief (Nazarana), of homage and investiture of the heir. From all that can be discovered, the original tenure of the mass of the Istimrari estates in Ajmer is exactly described by the above quotation. The estates were life grants, but, like all similar tenures they tended to become hereditary."

The Istimrardars are by law incompetent to make alienations lasting beyond their own lives. Like the other estates in Rajputana, those of Ajmer were originally held on service tenure, and were subject to certain feudal liabilities. In lieu of these burdens, the Mahrattas (1791-1818 A.D.) substituted fixed cash payments, and exacted certain cesses. The latter were abolished by the British, and in 1873, it was finally decided that the assessments then levied should be fixed in perpetuity.

The Istimrardars have benefited most by British Rule, owing to especial legislation passed for their protection. This is clear from what Dr. Irvine says, about their condition when they first came under British rule. He says:

"The Istimrar lands, granted in perpetuity to the various Thakurs are generally deeply in pawn to the seths and "bohras"; the Thakurs gain very little by their property; such is chiefly the result of their own carelessness.....Owing to the circumstances stated, it is certain that the *cultivator of Ajmer is not benefited by coming under British rule*, so much as he otherwise would have done."

History of the Tazimi Istimrari Estates

Of the sixteen Tazimi istimrari estates, the Bhinai family holds seven estates—

Bhinai.	Tantoti.
Bandanwara.	Barli.
Deolia.	Kerot.
Deogaon-Baghera.	

The Masuda family holds two estates—

Masuda and Bagsuri.

The Pisangan family holds five estates—

Pisangan.	Govindgarh.
Mehrun.	Para.
Junia.	

The Sawar	"	1	Sawar.
The Kharwa	"	1	Kharwa.

No Istimrari estate existed in Ajmer-Merwara before the time of Akbar. The areas of these estates were held by Gor and other Rajput families, or were parts of the Ajmer Khalsa. Of the five principal estates, Bhinai, Masuda, and Kharwa came into existence in the time of Akbar; Sawar in Jahangir's and Pisangan in Shah Jahan's time.

Bhinai

Rao Chandra Sen succeeded his father, Rao Maldeva, on the throne of Marwar, but refused to acknowledge Akbar's suzerainty and was ousted by Mota Raja Udai Singh, with Akbar's help. Chandra Sen's (1563 A.D.) grandson, Karma Sen, came to Ajmer from Jodhpur. He was given a feast by Madhia Bhil, who held eighty-four villages including Bhinai, called the *chaurasi*. Karma Sen killed the Bhil during the feast and took possession of his estate. Akbar confirmed the possession of Bhinai by Karma Sen.

There is a story current in Rajputana about this Karma Sen, son of Ugarsen, son of Chandrasen. During Jahangir's reign, once when the emperor was about to go in procession, it was suggested to him that to add dignity to the procession, a Rajput prince should sit in *Khawasi*, that is, behind the Emperor in the howdah on the elephant with a *Chhavar* in his hand. The custom in Rajputana is that the most important noble in a state sits in Khawasi and waves the *Chhavar* over the reigning king. As no Rajput king of Rajputana agreed to sit in *Khawasi*, Karmasen was persuaded to do so on promise of a big reward. When the news got abroad, there was a stir amongst the Rajput princes in Delhi, and efforts were made to dissuade Karmasen from accepting such humiliation, bringing the Rajput name into degradation. A *charan* came to know of it and offered to dissuade Karmasen from bringing disgrace on the royal family of Marwar. Just as the procession was about to start, he pushed his way through the crowd and recited, in a loud voice, the following couplet, warning Karmasen of the disgrace he would bring on his parents by sitting in *Khawasi*:

कम्मा उग्रसेनरो तो जननी बलिहार ।
छवर व झल्ले शाह पर तुं झल्ले तलवार ॥

Karmasen, who had taken his seat in the *howdah*, as soon as he heard the couplet, realized the enormity of his act, jumped down, and refused to sit in the Khawasi.

The Bhinai estate consisted of eighty-four villages which were subsequently divided in the proportion of 46 to 38, between Udai Bhan and Akhai Raj in the fourth generation from Chandrasen, the former making Bhinai and the latter, Deolia, his headquarters. Udai Bhan, being at that time childless, adopted Narsingh Das a son of Akhai Raj, but on the subsequent birth of a son Kesri Singh, three villages were assigned to Narsingh Das, from whom is descended the present Thakur of Tantoti. Kesri Singh obtained Bhinai and twenty-four villages and a younger brother, Suraj Mal, who became the ancestor of the house of Bandanwara, received ten villages. Karmasen's second son Hardar Singh's descendants got Sanparda and Dabrela. The twenty-five villages of Bhinai yield a revenue of over Rs. 1,00,000/- a year. Three villages have been assigned to the subordinate Thakurs of Sholian, Sarana and Santola for maintenance, and one, Kotri, to a *charan*. Santola is held in mortgage by the Maharaja of Kishengarh. The Bhinai estate pays a revenue of Rs 7,717 to Government. The title of Raja was bestowed on the head of the Bhinai house in 1783 A.D. by the then ruler of Jodhpur as a reward for military service.

In 1737 A.D., Maharaja the Abhai Singh of Jodhpur took possession of Bhinai. In 1740, the Raja of Bhinai went with his levies to Merta, to join Maharaja Bakht Singh, when the latter attacked Ajmer and drove out the governor. In 1752, Maharaja Ajit Singh's third son Kishor Singh, with the assistance of the Raja of Banera (Mewar), took possession of Bhinai. But Maharaja Bijai Singh sent the Thakur of Ras to recover

Bhinai. Kishor Singh was killed in the battle. When in 1756, peace was made between the Scindia and Maharaja Ram Singh on one side and Maharaja Bijai Singh of Marwar on the other, Bhinai, Deolia and Masuda came to Ram Singh's share.

In 1791, Sivaji Nana became the Mahratta subedar of Ajmer. In 1797, he took Ratakot from Bhinai and annexed it to Ajmer. He imprisoned Raja Udai Singh of Bhinai in Ajmer for non-payment of revenue. The Rajputs of Bhinai retaliated and imprisoned Ram Bhau, Tahsildar of Ajmer, and began to plunder the district. Then peace was made, both the prisoners were released and revenue was reduced and permanently fixed.

In 1803, Raja Udai Singh of Bhinai attended Raja Man Singh's coronation at Jodhpur as a *Sardar* of Marwar.

Bandanwara

Bandanwara is held by a Rathor Rajput of the Bhinai family. He holds an estate of twenty-one villages situated to the south of Nasirabad Cantonment. The estimated annual income of the estate, including the subordinate jagir of Amargarh, which pays revenue to the Thakur, is Rs. 70,000/- and the yearly revenue payable to the Government, Rs. 6,735/-.

Suraj Mal, the second son of Udai Bhan, was dissatisfied with the maintenance allowance given him by his elder brother Kesri Singh. He went to Delhi and got into Aurangzeb's service in 1659 A.D. He rendered valuable military service and was granted the grade of 3,500 *hazari* with an elephant. The Emperor got the Bhinai estate partitioned amongst Udai Bhan's three sons, the eldest Kesri Singh keeping Bhinai. Suraj Mal after getting his share, established himself in Bandanwara in 1667 A.D., and founded the Bandanwara estate. The Emperor gave Suraj Mal, Ramsar and Srinagar also, as jagir. These two pargannahs were, however, later taken away by Maharaja Ajit Singh of Jodhpur, as the Thakur of Bandanwara did not go in *Peshwai*. Ajit Singh demolished the Bandanwara fort and plundered the town.

Surajmal's eldest son, Amar Singh, retained Bandanwara, and the younger sons got Padlan, Jaola, Kalyanpura, Jotayan and Amargarh. The estate of Jaola has also been included in Bandanwara, Thakur Lachman Singh of Jaola, having died heirless.

Deolia

Deolia is held by a Rathor Rajput, descended from Akhairaj, the son of the founder of the Bhinai family. He holds an estate of seven villages yielding an annual income of about Rs. 38,000 and paying Rs. 5,398-2-4 as revenue to Government. The estates of Shokla and Raghunathgarh have been included in Deolia, Thakurs Bhur Singh and Raghunath Singh having died heirless.

Akhairaj, on separation from Udaibhan, got Deolia with thirty-eight villages. Akhairaj had five sons. The eldest Ishwar Das got Deolia, Dev Das got Barli, Nahar Singh got Nandsi and Gudah; Gaj Singh got Kerot, and Hari Singh got Jaitpura Jadana.

Ishwardas' second son, Sanwat Singh got Gudha Kalan. Ishwardas' eldest son's son, Bakht Singh, got Patodi; Barisal got Shokla; and Chhatrasal got Rughnathgarh.

"On the accession of the Maharaja of Jodhpur to power, not only was no revenue collected from this estate, but a jagir of Rupees 36,000 in Marwar and a daily allowance of Rupees thirty-five were bestowed on the Thakur, in consideration of which, he was to perform personal service with thirty-six horsemen. Till 1806 A.D., the family remained in possession of the Marwar jagir and the daily allowance."[1]

In 1817, A.D., Maharaja Bijai Singh of Jodhpur granted a *sanad* to the Thakur of Deolia on payment of Rs. 2,100 yearly.—M. Jwala Sahai's *Waqai Rajputana*, p. 16.

Deogaon Baghera

Deogaon-Baghera is held by a Rathor Rajput of the Deolia branch of the Bhinai family. The estate consists of three villages, which yield an annual income of Rs. 31,000 and pays Rs. 5,925/8/2 to Government.

Nahar Singh, as stated above, got Nandsi and Gudha from his father Akhairaj, Thakur of Deolia. He attacked and took Deogaon from the Gor Rajputs of Rajgarh, and Baghera from the Sisodia Rajputs in 1685 A.D. In the fight with the Gor Rajputs, the Thakur of Junia with his son, Kishen Singh came to the help of Nahar Singh. After the victory, as Kishen Singh had done brave deeds and was killed, Nahar Singh gave, out of the Deogaon estate, Keronj, Deolia Khurd and Kalera to the Thakur of Junia.

1. J. D. La Touche's *Report on the Settlement of the Ajmer and Merwara Districts*, p. 62.

Nahar Singh's eldest son, Deokaran, kept Deogaon-Baghera; the younger son, Bharat Singh got Nandsi; Inder Singh, Salori; Tej Singh, Richmalian; Hathi Singh, Bagrai, and Arjun Singh, Kebania.

Tantoti

Tantoti is also held by a Rathor Rajput of the Bhinai family. He holds an estate of three villages of a total income of Rs 25,000 and pays Rs. 2,897/13/9 annually to Government. The Thakur holds Bhum lands in three jagir villages, namely, Keria Kalan, Keria Khurd and Morajhari.

Suraj Mal, founder of Bandanwara estate, had four sons. Narsinghdas, the third son of Udaibhan obtained Tantoti at the partition. In 1761, when Maharaja Bijaisingh laid siege to Taragarh, Ajmer, the Thakur of Tantoti was in charge of one of the *morchas*. Again, in 1790, when General De Boigne besieged Taragarh, Thakur Gulab Singh of Tantoti was one of the defenders of the fort in behalf of Maharaja Bijai Singh along with Thakur Bhopal Singh of Masuda.

Barli

Barli is held by a Rathor Rajput of the Deolia branch of the Bhinai family. He holds an estate consisting of twelve villages, of which the revenue is estimated at Rs. 27,000/- He pays Rs. 3,398/6/5 annually to Government. The village of Piplia, which formerly belonged to Barli, now forms a part of the Bhinai estate.

Dev Das as stated above, on partition got Barli. He had four sons. The eldest Sanwaldas had Barli. Durjansal got Goela, Jet Singh got Kanai Khurd, and Harnath Singh got Piproli Khurd.

Kerot

Kerot is held by a Rathor Rajput of the Deolia branch of the Bhinai family. The estate consists of three villages, yielding an annual income of approximately Rs. 16,000 and paying Rs. 1,964 (including cess) as revenue to Government. The Thakur was granted the dignity of Tazim by the British Government in June, 1923 A.D.

Gaj Singh, fourth son of Akhairaj of Deolia, had on separation, got Kerot. His son, Ratan Singh succeeded to the Kerot estate, but gave out of the estate, Kurthal and Kanai Kalan to his brothers Bhim Singh and Padam Singh respectively.

Masuda

Masuda is held by a Rathor Rajput of the Mertia family. It is the largest and richest estate in the district, consisting of 26 villages, yielding a revenue of about a lakh of rupees and paying Rs. 8,555-6 as revenue to Government. Several Mer villages in Merwara, which were formerly held by the Thakur of Masuda, were declared Khalsa, the Masuda Thakur receiving Rs. 4,000/- a year as compensation.

Rao Jodha's great grandson, Jugmal, had three sons, Hanwant Singh and Lad Singh being the younger ones. Masuda was a Mughal *Thana* under Akbar in the Ajmer district. The Panwar Rajputs drove Akbar's thanedar and took possession of it. Jugmal and his sons, when they went to Akbar's court, were asked to recover Masuda. They prepared themselves to attack Masuda. The Maharana of Udaipur, who was the overlord of the Panwars, sent men to help the Panwars. A battle was fought at Harmara, in which Jugmal was victorious. Akbar gave Masuda in jagir to Hanwant Singh and Lad Singh, sons of Jugmal by a sanad in 1558 A.D.

Hanwant Singh's great grandson Ajab Singh had four sons, the eldest Mohan Singh got Masuda; and the younger sons Kesri Singh, Bakht Singh, Jas Karan and Girdhar Das got Sathana, Kesarpura, Sakhrani and Jamola respectively as maintenance. Shersingh, second son of Mohan Singh was given Shergarh, Kesri Singh had three sons. The eldest Nahar Singh kept Sathana, Bhagwan Singh got Lamba and Anok Singh, Nagar.

Bagsuri

Bagsuri is held by a Rathor Mertia Rajput. The Bagsuri estate consists of two villages and a hamlet, yielding an annual revenue of about Rs. 17,000 and pays Rs. 1,410/4/8 to Government as revenue.

As Hanwant Singh and his brothers who were given Masuda were proceeding to Masuda, they saw a tiger and a pig fight, and the pig putting the tiger to rout. The Sakuni (augur) declared that a fort built on that spot would be invincible. So, Lad Singh, younger brother of Hanwant Singh, built a village and a fort there and called it Bagsuri. This is said to be the origin of the Bagsuri estate. The present Istimrardar, Rao Bahadur Onkar Singh is General Manager, Court of Wards, Ajmer-Merwara.

Pisangan

Pisangan is held by a Rathor Rajput of the Jodhawat family. The estate consists of eleven villages and is situated to the west of Ajmer. Its annual income is about Rs. 23,000/- and the revenue payable to the Government, Rs. 4,563/14/2. The title of Raja, which is held by courtesy by the Istimrardar of Pisangan, was granted by a Sanad of Maharaja Man Singh of Marwar in 1806 to Nathu Singh, in recognition of the services rendered by the latter in the famous marriage dispute between Jodhpur and Udaipur.

Motaraja Udai Singh's fifth son, Madho Singh, held a *Patta* of Sojat, Jaitaran, Taswana, valued at three lakhs. "Kesri Singh, son of Madho Singh, the fifth son of Motaraja Udai Singh of Marwar, came to seek his fortune in Ajmer, and by the favour of the Emperor Shah Jahan, ejected the Panwar Rajputs from Pisangan and obtained a grant of the fief. His son, Sujan Singh, further extended the property by taking Junia from the Gor Rajputs and Mehrun from the Sisodias. In 1670, Sujan Singh, Thakur of Pisangan divided his estate amongst his three sons. The eldest, Kishen Singh got Junia, the second Karan Singh got Mehrun, and Jhujhar Singh the youngest, got Pisangan because, as is stated, he had avenged the death of his uncle Bhim Singh, by killing Gudar Khan of Shamgarh.[1] Jhujhar Singh's share included Pisangan, Khawas, Sarsari, Pranhera, Para, Meoda Khurd, Kodah, Sadara and Gulgaon. Jhujhar Singh had three sons, the eldest, Fateh Singh, got Pisangan, Khawas, Sarsari and Pranhera. Sham Singh got Para, Meoda Khurd and Kodah. Devi Singh got Sadara and Gulgaon. Fateh Singh's grandson Zalim Singh had two sons, the eldest Nathu Singh got Pisangan, and Kalyan Singh was given Khwas, Sarsari and Pranhera.

In 1740, the Thakur of Pisangan with his levies joined Bakht Singh at Merta, when the latter invaded Ajmer and took the city. In A. D. 1759 (S. 1816), Madhvarao Scindia, the Mahratta subedar of Ajmer began to oppress the people. The Istimrardars imprisoned Madhvarao in the fort of Gulab Singh, son of Kalyan Singh of Khwas and kept him there for three months. Reinforcements from Gwalior arrived and released Madhvarao and imposed a fine of Rs. 15,000/- on Gulab Singh. As this money was not paid, Gulab Singh was

1. J. D. La Touche's *Report on the Settlement of the Ajmer and Merwara Districts*, page 54.

imprisoned. His son, Sunder Singh paid Rs. 7,000 and Khwas was mortgaged with Bagh Singh who paid the balance. Gulab Singh was released.

In 1785 A. D., the Mahrattas called on Kalyan Singh to give Rs. 3,000/ as revenue. He could not do so and Pranhera and Sarsari had to be mortgaged with the subedar of Ajmer. In 1791, Kalyan Singh paid the money and got back the villages. Khawas and Sarsari now form a separate estate. Pisangan has only eleven villages now. The Thakur of Pisangan obtained the title of Raja from the Maharaja of Jodhpur by giving him a large Nazarana. The title was recognised by the British Government in 1875, when the Istimrari sanads were given to all the Istimrardars.

Mehrun

Mehrun is held by a Rathor Rajput of the Pisangan and Junia family, who holds an estate of thirteen villages, yielding an annual income of about Rs. 38,000 and paying a fixed revenue to Government of Rs. 5,359-8-1.

Karan Singh, younger brother of Kishen Singh, the founder of Junia, was the founder of the Mehrun estate. Karan Singh's son Nahar Singh had five sons. The eldest Abhai Singh kept Mehrun. In 1755, the other four sons were given Tiswara, Nimod, Sankaria and Kadhera respectively.

"In the year 1811 A.D., Thakur Lal Singh of Kadhera, who complained that his "gras" was too small, made a night attack on the fort of Mehrun. He treacherously murdered Jagat Singh, the Thakur of Mehrun, after having promised him safety, and caused his son, Bharat Singh, to be hurled from the battlements. He then made himself master of Mehrun, but was forced to give it up and to return to Kadhera by the Sisodia Raja of Shahpura, who marched against him. The widow of Bharat Singh was placed in possession of the estate, and she remained in possess on till 1842. She adopted Jawahir Singh; but on the death of the latter without heirs, his cousin, Kalu Singh, succeeded in 1867. The village of Kadolai was originally a portion of Mehrun, and was given on a service tenure to Gaj Singh, Thakur of Kerot, on condition that he should do service with two horses and two footmen, and should pay nazarana. The Thakur of Kerot, however, gradually ceased to do service till on the murder of Jagat Singh, the village was merged in the Kerot estate."[1]

Junia

Junia is held by a Rathor Rajput belonging to the same family as the Raja of Pisangan. The Junia estate consists of

1. J. D. La Touche's *Report on the Settlement of Ajmer and Merwara Districts*, p. 56.

sixteen villages, yielding an annual income of Rs. 50,000, and paying Rs. 5,723-15 as revenue to Government. The Istimrardar of Junia is a hereditary bhumia of Kekri, and as such is bound to supply *sawars* whenever required. He holds 1,500 acres of bhum land and keeps up an establishment of watchmen. He also holds one village in Jaipur and one in Kotah as jagir. The town of Junia is an old one. Its fort was built by Gor Rajputs.

When Kishen Singh, son of Sujan Singh, gave Junia to his eldest son Raj Singh, he gave Karonj to his second son Sanwat Singh, and Deolia Khurd to his third son Dhiraj Singh, and they all separated. Raj Singh's grandson Bakht Singh gave the villages Bogla and Kalesra to his younger brother Dalel Singh.

Govindgarh

Govindgarh is held by a Rathor Rajput, descended from Raja Udai Singh of Marwar. It is a small estate of two villages and three hamlets to the west of Ajmer. The annual income is about Rs. 10,000, and the revenue payable to Government is Rs. 2,418/4/-.

The Thakur of Govindgarh is a descendant of Govind Das, a grandson of Motaraja Udai Singh. He built the fort at Govindgarh. The estate consists only of one *asli* and three *dakhilee* villages. One Dakhilee village, Jaswantpura, has been given in "gras", and the Thakur of Govindgarh gives maintenance to fourteen persons. The family is a large one. The estate being small, the younger members of the family became bhumias. When Maharaja Abhai Singh of Jodhpur, who had been appointed viceroy of Ajmer and Gujrat by the Emperor of Delhi, fought with Sarbuland Khan in Gujrat, Himmat Singh, a great grandson of Govind Das joined the expedition with his three sons, one of whom, Dalel Singh, was killed in battle. Abhai Singh, on return, gave a *bhum* holding of 1,331 acres in Nand to Himmat Singh and his surviving sons; and on the death of Himmat Singh, the property was divided by ancestral shares. At present, there are eleven shares.

The village of Ramner Dhani was given in jagir to Bhim Singh, a grandson of Govind Das, by Shah Jahan. The revenue-free tenure was resumed by Aurangzeb, and the village given on a quit-rent of Rupees 1,500. This tenure the Mahrattas resumed, but left 2,000 bighas as Bhum.[1]

1. J. D. La Touche's *Report on the Settlement of Ajmer and Merwara Districts*, p. 57.

Para

Para is held by a Rathor Rajput, who is the head of a junior branch of the Pisangan family. The estate, which consists of six villages, pays Rs. 2,492-2-5 as revenue to Government. To the villages originally separated from Pisangan and assigned to the first Thakur, Jhujhar Singh, two were subsequently added by himself and one by his son. Thakur Sangram Singh died on 30th November, 1918, leaving no issue and was succeeded by Thakur Ranbir Singh, who has a son named Bijai Bahadur, born on the 4th November, 1919. Jhujhar Singh's second son, Sham Singh, got Para from his father on partition. He took Chhaparya and Aekalsingh from Gor Rajputs. His descendant, Saman Singh, took the village of Nolakha from the Thanawat Rajputs. In 1823, Barisal got Meoda Khurd; and in 1803, Bakht Singh got Kodah from Para. One Devi Singh got Sadara and Gulgaon from Pisangan.

Sawar

Sawar is held by a Sisodia Rajput of the Saktawat family, who holds an estate of thirty-three villages, yielding an annual income of about Rs. 60,000/- and paying Rs. 7,215-8 as revenue to Government.

Mr. LaTouche, in his *Settlement Report*, p. 65, says "The estate (Sawar) is a portion of a grant made by Jahangir to Gokaldas. The fact is that Jahangir had rebelled against his father Akbar, and a skirmish took place between the forces of the father and the son at Benares. Gokaldas, who was in Jahangir's service, fought for Jahangir and received 84 wounds." The prince when he came to the throne in 1605 A.D. as Jahangir, gave Sawar, Kekri and some other places as *jagir* to Gokaldas. Only Sawar now forms the estate. Gokaldas had two sons, Sunderdas and Ajab Singh. Ajab Singh was given Deokheri. Later, Sunderdas' second son Jai Singh was given Piplaj, and the third son Ram Singh, Bassoondni. The eldest son Pratap Singh had two sons, Raj Singh and Chhtrasal. The latter was given Chand Thali. Raj Singh's second son Bahadur Singh, was given Chonsla. The fifth from Raj Singh, was Ajit Singh, whose eldest son Jaswant

Singh kept Sawar, and the younger son, Zorawar Singh, was given Tankawas. Piplaj gives revenue direct to Government. In 1737 A.D., Maharaja Abhai Singh of Marwar took Ghatiali, Piplaj and Chonsla from Sawar.

Kharwa

Kharwa is held by a Rathor Rajput of the Sakta family descended from Rao Jodha. The estate consists of fifteen villages, yielding an estimated annual revenue of Rs. 72,000 and pays Rs. 2,318-10-0 to Government. Seventeen villages, which formerly belonged to Kharwa, were incorporated in Merwara on the constitution of that district. The Istimrardar receives Rs. 1,000/- a year from the British Government, in full satisfaction of his claims to these villages.

The founder of the estate was Sakht Singh son of Mota Raja Udai Singh of Jodhpur. He rendered valuable service to Akbar in the campaign against Bengal. He had also saved the life of Akbar by pulling him out of water, when during a boating excursion, Akbar fell overboard. Akbar granted a sanad to Sakht Singh.

For seven generations, the estate remained undivided; but in the eighth, Chatar Singh son of Suraj Mal was given Deogarh. Later, Gulab Singh, younger son of Devi Singh Thakur of Kharwa, got Nasun; and Devi Singh's eldest son Pratap Singh's younger son Sham Singh obtained Bhawani Khera from the parent estate.

Motaraja Udai Singh's descendant in a later generation, Ram Singh, founded the village Mevadia in 1651 A.D. and became its Thakur. The Thakur has eleven relations, who hold land and are held to be bhumias.

I—ISTIMRARDARS

Statement showing the area and income of the Istimrari Estates of Ajmer, and the revenue they pay to Government.

S. No.	Name of Estate.	Tribe.	Total area in acres.	Estimated income in 1874 A.D.	Estimated income in 1933 A.D.	Government revenue.			Remarks.
	Junia Family		Rs.	Rs.	Rs.	Rs.	a.	p.	
1	Manoharpur	Gor	3,750	4,000	9,362	1,050	6	6	
2	Junia	Rathor	34,475	33,056	50,171	5,723	15	0	
	Manda	"	1,729	640	1,500	249	0	0	
	Lasaria	Charan	2,103	3,000	5,500	285	0	0	
3	Bogla, Kalahera ...	Rathor	5,403	2,200	6,048	1,600	3	2	
4	Keronj	"	4,597	4,277	4,033	1,713	5	1	
5	Deolia Khurd	"	2,153	1,500	2,051	799	13	9	
	Mehrun Family								
6	Mehrun	"	22,585	15,708	22,585	5,359	8	1	
7	Tiswaria	"	2,774	2,100	2,700	1,023	4	10	
8	Nimod	"	1,669	1,400	1,942	612	6	7	
9	Sankaria	"	3,836	1,700	3,282	407	0	0	
10	Kadera	"	5,841	10,255	9,395	1,914	7	9	
	Pisangan Family								
11	Pisangan	"	32,095	22,000	23,000	4,563	14	2	
12	Khawas, Sarsari ...	"	10,036	6,000	11.000	1,937	13	9	
13	Pranhera...	"	10,139	5,000	10,333	1,695	8	7	
14	Para	"	10,958	9,000	18,126	2,492	2	5	
15	Meoda Khurd	"	2,305	1,800	2,900	788	5	0	
16	Kodah	"	3,242	1,700	3,230	536	7	6	
17	Sadara	"	3,316	4,000	7,767	851	0	0	
18	Gulgaon	"	2,990	2,200	2,715	801	5	6	
	Govindgarh Family								
19	Govindgarh	"	} 10,362 {	8,000	10,000	2,418	4	0	
	Jaswantpura	"		1,500	...	......			

Statement showing the area and income of the Istimrari Estates of Ajmer, and the revenue they pay to Government.

S. No.	Name of Estate.	Tribe.	Total area in acres.	Estimated income in 1874 A.D.	Estimated income in 1933 A.D.	Government revenue.			REMARKS.
						Rs.	a.	p.	
	Kharwa Family		Rs.	Rs.	Rs.				
20	Kharwa	Rathor	50,901	29,000	72,000	2,318	10	0	
	Nasun	"	3,682	2,500	3,000	......			
	Bhawani Khera ...	"		1,000	...	......			included in Kharwa.
	Leogarh	"	778	1,000	...	......			
	Bhinai Family								
21	Mewaria	"	3,885	2,000	3,000	445	15	3	
22	Bhinai	"	79,674	53,674	1,00,000	7,717	7	11	
	Sarana	"	6,502	3,500	8,779	680	0	0	
23	Sholian	"	2,744	1,000	1,828	455	8	0	
24	Bandanwara	"	34,845	25,525	65,359	5,306	5	0	
	Amargarh	"	1,858	800	2,683	......			
25	Jotayan	"	5,883	3,750	7,265	1,207	7	0	
26	Padlan	"	5,386	3,100	6,455	1,424	7	6	
27	Jaola	"	4,624	3,000	7,800	1,429	5	5	
28	Kalyanpura	"	2,571	1,700	1,995	483	4	9	
29	Tantoti	"	12,620	8,000	15,977	2,897	13	9	
30	Baori	"	2,455	2,000	2,500	420	8	5	
	Deolia Family								
31	Deolia	"	18,415	18,000	29,939	3,380	2	0	
32	Arwar	"	2,889	1,500	1,645	690	9	2	
33	Shokli	"	1,258	1,300	876	257	10	8	
34	Shokla	"	5,028	4,025	5,600	1,365	9	3	
35	Raghunathgarh	"	2,663	1,900	2,874	652	7	1	
36	Gudhakalan	"	3,394	1,440	3,254	595	0	0	
37	Barli	"	22,401	15,000	29,837	3,398	6	5	

	Kanai Khurd	,,	3,139	1,000	1,893	......			
38	Nagelao	,,	6,968	2,200	8,500	1,100	1	6	
39	Goela	,,	8,253	5,000	8,341	2,138	9	0	
40	Deogaon Baghera ...	,,	22,598	15,163	31,086	5,925	8	2	
41	Nandsi	,,	6,979	3,673	4,000	1,020	12	3	
42	Richmalian... ...	,,	3,420	1,800	4,000	646	7	7	
43	Salari	,,	2,869	1,000	1,782	130	0	0	
44	Kybania	,,	5,239	6,700	3,633	1,486	1	2	
45	Kerot	,,	8,660	7,000	15,194	1,854	15	0	
46	Kurthal	,,	3,967	2,200	4,300	855	0	5	
47	Kanai Kalan ...	,,	3,834	1,760	4,626	273	2	4	
48	Jetpura Jadana ...	,,	6,332	4,000	8,677	1,479	7	3	
49	Santola	,,	3,613	2,000	3,622	701	6	9	
	Masuda Family.								
50	Richmalian ...	,,	6,239	1,000	2,158	51	8	4	
51	Sethan	,,	2,647	1,400	1,500	600	1	3	
52	Masuda	,,	98,773	70,000	1,00,000	8,555	6	0	
	Jayasinghpura ...	,,		1,200		281	0	0	included in Masuda.
	Nandwara	,,	6,039	2,500		598	0	0	
	Shergarh	,,	5,614	6,700	7,000	640	0	0	
	Fatehgarh	,,	1,256	1,900		275	0	0	
	Kaila	,,	2,490	1,000		175	0	0	
	Kesarpura	,,		600	1,000	24	0	0	included in Masuda.
	Akrol	,,	1,545	800	1,000	284	0	0	
	Dalawas	,,	908	600	1,000	...			
	Jamola	,,	6,258	3,000	3,500	658	0	0	
	Sheopuri	Jogi.	2,560	2,000	2,500	159	0	0	
	Asan	,,		1,600	1,000	715	0	0	included in Masuda.
53	Sathana	Rathor.	11,242	7,000	8,000	1,597	3	0	
54	Lamba	,,	2,530	1,812	3,900	413	14	0	

Statement showing the area and income of the Istimrari Estates of Ajmer, and the revenue they pay to Government.

S. No.	Name of Estate.	Tribe.	Total area in acres.	Estimated income in 1874 A.D.	Estimated income in 1933 A.D.	Government revenue.	REMARKS.
			Rs.	Rs.	Rs.	Rs. a. p.	
55	Nagar	Rathor.	2,573	2,400	2,500	422 1 7	
56	Sakrani	,,	6,265	3,000	4,000	1,032 12 0	
	Bagsuri Family.						
57	Bagsuri	,,	10,508	19,000	17,000	1,410 4 8	
58	Bobawa	,,	4,619	3,500	6,000	663 0 0	
59	Karel	,,	7,848	8,000		2,132 15 2	
	Sawar Family.						
60	Sawar	Sisodia.	61,443	32,000	60,857	7,215 8 0	
	Deokheri	,,	1,080	400	1,455	service.	
	Basundni	,,	2,168	1,600	2,168	213 0 0	
	Chand Thali ...	,,	813	700	1,265	service	
	Chonsla	,,	2,075	1,100	3,500	176 0 0	
	Tankawas	,,	2,101	800	1,406	service.	
	Mehrun Khurd ...	Charan.	818	600	1,045	85 0 0	
	Bhandawas ...	Charan.	1,452	800	1,155	81 0 0	
61	Piplaj	Sisodia.	4,654	7,040	9,398	262 0 0	
	Chauhan Merats.						
62	Rajosi	Chauhan Merat.	10,645	2,600		1,386 2 0	
63	Nausar	,,	1,175	800		105 1 0	
64	Khrekri	,,	4,487	1,200		212 15 6	
65	Ajaysar	,,	2,213	500		202 15 0	
66	Kotri	Charan.	800	800	833	123 6 9	

The above information, except that under the head Estimated income in 1933 A.D., is taken from La Touche's *Settlement Report*, 1875 A.D.

II—JAGIRDARS

The revenue-free holdings of Ajmer are of three kinds (1) *Jagir*, (2) *Milk* and (3) *Bhum*. The difference between the first two is that the Jagir is the grant of revenue of an entire village or share in a village, while the *Milk* means the grant of a definite number of bighas. The subject of Jagir estates was investigated by a mixed Commission of Government officials and Jagirdars in 1874 A.D., and their report[1] contains a history of each estate. "Out of a total area of 150,838 acres, yielding in 1874 A.D., an average rental of Rs. 91,000, 65,472 acres (yielding an income of Rs. 42,740)[2] belong to the endowments of shrines and sacred institutions. The remaining (85,366 acres) are enjoyed by individuals and certain classes, designated in grants. No conditions of military or other service are attached to the tenure of any jagir.[3]

In all jagir estates, the revenue is collected by an estimate of the produce, and money assessments are unknown. As was the case in the khalsa, before Colonel Dixon's settlement, the ideas of rent and revenue are confounded under the ambiguous term *hasil*, and until the year 1872, the relative status of the jagirdars and cultivators as regards the ownership of the soil was quite undefined. In that year, it was declared that all those found in possession of land irrigated or irrigable from wells or tanks, which were not proved to have been constructed by the jagirdar, were owners of such land. The jagirdar was declared owner of irrigated land in which the means of irrigation had been provided by him, or unirrigated and waste land. Altogether there are fifty-five jagir estates in Ajmer, fifty-two being entire villages, three being villages which are half jagir and half khalsa. The revenue-free holdings fall into three classes:

(1) Grants to charitable and religious institutions.
(2) Grants to individuals.
(3) Grants to corporations.

Of the fifty-four jagir estates, two were given by the British, one by Maharaja Ajit Singh of Jodhpur, twelve by Maharaja Scindia, and the remaining thirty-nine by the Mughal Emperors. Of the fifty-four jagir estates, twenty-six belong to class I or religious endowments. four being attached to Hindu and twenty-two to Muslim religious institutions. The biggest endowment of eighteen villages is attached to the Dargah

1. *Ajmer Regulations*, H. to L., p 580. 2. Ibid. 3. C. C. Watson's *Gazetteer of Ajmer-Merwara*, p. 92, (1904). La Touche's *Settlement Report*, p. 133, gives the total area as 1,37,955 acres, and revenue as Rs. 68,407.

Khwaja Muinuddin Chishti, and three to Dargah Miran Husain. Out of the remaining twenty-nine villages, twenty four villages are grants to individuals or are villages held by individuals. Five, (three by the khadims of Dargah Khwaja Sahib and two by the Brahmins of Pushkar) are held by corporations.

Of the twenty-four jagir villages held by individuals, sixteen entire and two half villages are held by Jagirdars of the first class, who number nine. While the Jagirdars of the second class, hold four entire and two half villages. The chief difference between the two classes of Jagirdars is that in the first class Jagirs, the law of primogeniture prevails, while the second class Jagirs are divisible amongst the heirs.

The following table shows the number of villages in each class and the origin of the grant.

Name of granter.	Religious Institutions.	Individuals.	Corporations.	Total.
Akbar	16	...	...	16
Jahangir	1	½	4	5½
Shahjahan ...	...	3	...	3
Alamgir	...	½	...	½
Furrukhsayar ...	2	6½	...	8½
Muhammad Shah ...	...	4	...	4
Scindia	5	6	1	12
Maharaja Ajit Singh ...	...	1	...	1
British Government ...	1	1	...	2
Total ...	25	22½	5	52½

The following religious institutions enjoy jagirs:—

Religious Institutions.	No. of Villages.	Names of Villages.
1. Dargah Khwaja Muinuddin, Ajmer. ...	14 villages	... Amba Masina, Budhwara, Picholian, Tilora, Kayar, Khwajpura Bherwai, Kadampur, Parbatpura, Khwajpura Khurd, Kania, Bada Keria, Koradi, Chandsen and Nabab.
Diwan of Dargah ...	3 villages	... Hokran, Kishenpura in Ajmer District, and Gelota in Jaipur State.
Mutavalli of Dargah...	1 village	... Dantra.
2. Dargah Miran Sahib at Taragarh, Ajmer ...	3 villages	... Dorai, Somalpur and Kheria.
3. Chilla Bada Pir, Ajmer	1 village	... Makhupura.
4. Nathdwara Temple in Mewar ...	1 village	... Bhawanikhera.
5. Chhatri Surjee Rao in Pushkar ...	2 villages	... Lalikhera and Bhagwanpura.
6. Charitable Trust of Dudhadhari ...	1 village	... Nila Sevri.

The Jagir Enquiry Committee Report, 1874, assessed the approximate revenue of the jagirs at Rs. 91,000/- of which Rs. 42,740/- belonged to the religious endowments. This revenue has largely increased since 1874 A.D.

The first class Jagirdars are:—

			Villages.
1.	Raja of Rajgarh	...	Rajgarh, Kothaj.
2.	Raja of Gangwana	...	Gangwana, Oontra, Mugra.
3.	Nawab of Kumarbao	...	Boraj, Kazipura, Kesarpura, Setawarian, Sedaria, half Derathu.
4.	Jagirdar Dodiana	...	Dodiana, half Dilwari.
5.	„ Jharwasa	...	Jharwasa, Bhattiani.
6.	„ Arjunpura	...	Arjunpura.
7.	„ Mangliawas	...	Mangliawas.
8.	„ Chawandia	...	Chawandia.
9.	„ Dilwara	...	Dilwara (1).

Rajgarh is held by a Gor Rajput of the Bithaldasot family. The estate consists of two villages and yields an annual income of Rs. 5,000/-. The title of Raja is held by courtesy by the head of family, and was conferred on Debi Singh by the British Government, as a personal distinction, in 1877 A.D.

Gangwana is held by a Rathor Rajput, descended from Kishen Singh, the founder of the Kishengarh State. Maharaja Raj Singh of Kishengarh (1706-48) died, leaving four sons of whom the eldest, Fateh Singh, became the ancestor of the Fatehgarh family. The second, Sanwat Singh, succeeded to Kishengarh. The third, Bahadur Singh on the failure of heirs to Sardar Singh, son of Sanwat Singh, became the ancestor of the present ruler of Kishengarh. The fourth, Bir Singh, got a share in Karkeri and left two sons, Amar Singh, and Surat Singh. It was intended by Sardar Singh that Amar Singh should succeed him; but Bahadur Singh, with the help, first of the Maharaja of Jodhpur and subsequently of Holkar, expelled Bir Singh, and his family from all their possessions except Ralaota, and procured the adoption of his own son, Birad Singh. Bir Singh, having joined the Mahrattas, was killed at the battle of Panipat, and his two sons Amar Singh and Suraj Singh received a jagir of six villages—three, Sarana, Mugri and Ararka (subsequently confiscated by the Mahrattas) being assigned to Amir Singh; and the other three, Gangwana, Oontra and Mugra to Suraj Singh. Of Suraj Singh's sons, the eldest, Jaswant Singh, received Ralaota; and the younger brothers, Arjun Singh and Sher Singh, Gangwana, Oontra and Mugra. Arjun Singh's sons, Balwant Singh and Sher Singh, divided the Gangwana estate, of which moieties are held by their descendants. The whole income of the Jagir is about Rs. 7,000/-.

Dodiana is a jagir consisting of Dodiana and half Dilwari village. The annual income is about Rs. 3,800/-.

Jharwasa holds a two-thirds share in a jagir of which the whole value is about Rs. 6,000/-.

The Nawab of Kumar Bao holds a jagir, consisting of four whole villages, one three-fourth village, and one half village valued at about Rs. 11,000/- a year.

The second class jagirs are:—

(1)	½ Akhri.	(4)	Morajhari.
(2)	Baneori.	(5)	½ Nandla.
(3)	Ganahera.	(6)	Hathikhera.

In these jagirs no one is entitled to be called a Jagirdar.

The third class Jagirs are jagirs to corporations, and consist of five villages. The Khadims of Dargah Khwaja Sahib hold three villages, Bir, Gegal and Bainja: and the Brahmins of Pushkar two villages, the Badi Basti Brahmins hold Pushkar, and the Chhoti Basti Brahmins hold Nedla.

PUSHKAR JAGIR

The history of the Pushkar jagir is a chequered one. Of the seven or eight *firmans* of the Mughal Emperors of India extant, the earliest grant is Emperor Jahangir's *firman* dated 2nd Khurdad A. H. 1024 (A.D. 1617) which says that the grant is given to all the *Zunardaran* (Brahmins) of Pushkar. There are three *firmans* of Emperor Shah Jahan. One dated 15th Rabiulsani 1043 (A.D. 1636), explicitly says that the grant is to all the Brahmins of Pushkar. جمیع زناداران موضع مذکور Two others are of the regnal year 33 (A.D. 1658)—the one dated the 19th Jamadulsani says, that the grant is to both the parties. "*The grant is in equal shares to both the parties of Pushkar*, those of Barapura (Chhoti Basti) and to Rama and other Pujarees." Another firman, torn in places, but also of Emperor Shah Jahan, gives the grant to all the Brahmins of Pushkar, and directs the Mughal court nobles Khwaja Srirang, Rai Mahidas, Rai Ram Chander and Rai Mukandas to divide the revenue of Pushkar in *two equal shares between the two parties, of the Brahmins of Pushkar.*

No grant with respect to the Pushkar jagir of the time of the Mahrattas or Rathors, who were in possession of Pushkar in the eighteenth century, has come to light. But the evidence recorded by Mr. Cavendish, Superintendent of Ajmer, in the course of the inquiry into the rent-free tenures of Ajmer in

1829 A.D. shows that during the Rathor rule in Ajmer, the grant of this jagir was cancelled, and a cash payment of Rs. 300 was made in its stead, and that eventually in 1791 A.D., when Ajmer passed into Scindia's possession, Madhaji Scindia assigned the revenue of the agricultural land of Pushkar with some reservations to the Brahmins of Pushkar.

It was only after the seventies of the nineteenth century, that the Badi Basti Brahmins succeeded in getting themselves entered in the records as the holders of the Pushkar Jagir. In 1873 A.D., a committee was appointed to enquire into the Jagir tenures of Ajmer-Merwara with Captain Repton, Deputy Commissioner of Ajmer, as Chairman, Mr. J. D. LaTouche, Settlement Officer of Ajmer, as Secretary, and six members, of which three were Muslims and three Hindus, one of the latter being M. Maharaj Kishen Extra Assistant Commissioner, Settlement Department. This committee's report dated the 16th May, 1874 and published at pp. 559-581 of the *Ajmer Regulations*, *Vol. H. to L.*, gives only twelve lines and a half to the Pushkar Jagir and five lines to Nedla. It mentions the dispute between the Chhoti Basti and the Badi Basti, and Emperor Jahangir's *firman* and the decision of Maharaja Jaisingh of Jaipur that the Brahmins of the Chhoti Basti only are Brahmins. The report does not say that the *jagir* of Pushkar belongs to any particular Basti. In fact, it makes no mention as to the holder or holders of the *jagir*. The proposition statements (printed at pp. 626-27 of the Ajmer Regulations, Vol. H. to L.) for the *jagir* grants, forwarded by Mr. LaTouche to the Commissioner of Ajmer on 12 January 1875, *for the first time* mentions the Brahmins of Badi Basti as Jagirdars of the Pushkar *jagir*, and the Brahmins of Chhoti Basti as Jagirdars of Nedla.

III.—BHUM

In addition to the istimrari and jagir tenures, there is a third, called *Bhum*, which is peculiar to Rajputana. "The word Bhum means 'the soil', and the name *bhumia* properly signifies 'the allodial proprietor,' as distinguished from the feudal Chiefs and the tenant of crown lands. A Bhumia is a holder of land which has descended to him by inheritance, subject to no burden but that of military defence. According to Colonel Tod's *Rajasthan*, Vol. I, page 168, the bhumias in

Marwar are the descendants of the earlier princes who, on the predominance of new clans, ceased to come to court and to hold the higher grades of ranks."[1]

"There are in Ajmer 109 bhum holdings,[2] and except in those cases, where a Raja or Istimrardar is also a bhumia, the property passes to all the children equally. It is probable that none of these holdings are original allods, but belong to the class of assimilated allods. These bhumias are nearly all Rathors, descendants of younger branches of the Istimrari families, and cannot claim an origin higher than that of the estates from which they sprang. Whatever the origin of the holdings, however, the rights and duties of all bhumias came in course of time to be identical. At first, the land was revenue-free, subsequently a quit-rent was imposed but irregularly collected, and this quit-rent was abolished in 1841 along with the extra cesses from the Istimrardars."[3]

The bhumias are a feudal militia bound to attend when called upon to put down riots or to pursue dacoits or rebels. Each bhum holding is to furnish a horseman or a footman, and yearly pay a fixed *nazarana.* They have to furnish twenty-three horsemen and eighty-six footmen, and pay yearly *nazarana* of Rs. 4,200.[4]

The total Bhum area is 21,819[5] acres and the total *malguzari*, Rs. 51,720/-. Owing to subdivision, the average rental enjoyed by a Bhumia is now only Rs. 17 a year.

Once a year, on the king's birthday, a Durbar is held by the Commissioner at Ajmer, where the Bhumias assemble, pay their Nazarana, bring their arms and horses for inspection, and are entertained at a dinner in the evening.

1. C. C. Watson's *Gazetteer of Ajmer-Merwara*, p. 92.
2. For a complete list, see La Touche's *Settlement Report*, pp. 156-61.
3. C. C. Watson's *Gazetteer of Ajmer-Merwara*, p. 93. "The Maharaja, of Kishengarh, and the Thakurs of Junia, Bandanwara and Tantoti are among the *Bhumias* of Ajmer."
4. La Touche's *Settlement Report*, p. 161.
5. Ibid.

CHAPTER XXIII

FAMINES IN AJMER-MERWARA

As Mr. LaTouche (later Sir Diggs La Touche), who made the first regular Settlement of Ajmer-Merwara in 1874 A.D., has observed, "*Ajmer-Merwara can never rely on two good harvests in succession.*" A province subject to such unfavourable natural conditions, owing to the recurrent failure of monsoons, must remain subject to scarcities and famines and lead a precarious economic life, if its revenue administration is conducted on the principles laid down for provinces like the U. P. or the Punjab, as has been done since Col. Dixon's death in 1857 A.D. An Administration with the best will in the world, having to reckon with this serious drawback imposed by nature, which hangs on its head like a Damocles' sword, often sees its efforts for improving the economic conditions of the people frustrated.

The isolated position of Ajmer-Merwara, cut off as it is from the nearest British territory by more than 200 miles, with a backward and old-world atmosphere of the Indian States of Rajputana all round it, subjects it to an existence which is economically and politically unenviable.

Famines, which disfigure the history of this otherwise beautiful little province of Ajmer-Merwara, distinguish it from all other provinces of India; for, there is no province or district in the country where famines occur so frequently.

Rajputana is exposed to famine whenever there is a scarcity of rain; for there are no rivers in the province and few lakes except in Mewar. The couplet, current in Rajputana, says :—

पग पुगल धड़ कोटड़े वांह्य बायड़मेर ।
जोयेा लाधे जोधपुर ठावेा जेसलमर ॥

TRANSLATION:—The feet of famine are in Poogal (Bikaner); the trunk in Kotra (Marwar); the arms in Barmer (Mallani-Marwar). He will be found in Jodhpur (Marwar), if you search for him. In Jaisalmer, you will find him for a certainty.[1]

1. Another version of it quoted by Mr. E. H. Kealy, in his Census Report of Ajmer-Merwara, 1901 A.D. is:—"Pag Poogal Sir Merta, Udrej Bikaner; Bhulochuko Jodhpur, Thavo Jaisalmer." (His feet are in Poogal, his head is in Merta, his belly is in Bikaner: in forgetful moments he goes to Jodhpur, but he is always present in Jaisalmer).

A Marwari proverb says: "Expect one lean year in three, and one famine year in eight."

Ajmer-Merwara, though a little more favoured than Western Rajputana, is, on account of its proximity to Marwar, always affected whenever there is a famine in Rajputana.

The earliest recorded mention of a famine in Ajmer is contained in the well known Persian historical work, *Muasirul Umra*, vol. II, p. 402, wherein it is stated that in 1613 A.D., wheat sold at Ajmer at a rupee a seer.

The next severe famine in Rajputana, of which an account has been handed down to posterity in writing, occurred in 1661 A.D. (S. 1717). It is commemorated by the beautiful marble embankment erected at Kankaroli in Mewar by Maharana Raj Singh of Udaipur, the famous opponent of Aurangzeb. It cost a crore and a half of rupees. "A noble work with a nobler object and of more beautiful execution was never conceived by the human intellect."—Col. J. C. Brooke's *Famine Report*, 1870 A.D., page 7.

Another famine came in 1746 A.D., followed by yet another in 1791-92. According to tradition there was a severe famine in 1796 A.D. (S. 1853) called *trepanya*.[1] The famine of 1812-13 (S. 1869) affected the people for five years; three quarters of the cattle died, and in the same way as was recorded of the famine of 1661 A.D., "man ate man." Large tracts of country became utterly depopulated, and the saying, "The place became a desert in *Unhattra*" (S. 1869) reminds people of that calamity. A famine occurred in 1819 A.D., the year following the British occupation of Ajmer. There was a famine in 1823-24, and another in 1832 in Merwara. The famine of 1832 was marked by the fact that emigrants to Malwa brought back poppy seed with them, which they sowed in Merwara; this was the start of opium-cultivation in the district which continued, until it was stopped about 1896 A.D. There was a famine in 1834, and a scarcity in 1840 A.D.

A severe famine occurred in Ajmer Merwara, in 1848-49 A.D. Colonel Dixon, Superintendent of Ajmer-Merwara, in his report of this famine says, that the famine was "much more severe than that of 1832-33. With the exception of a few bullocks in each village, the districts are wholly denuded of cattle, which have been driven to countries possessing forage, where large numbers have already died......................Of about

1. The saying in Rajputana आगेत्रीपनयो पड़्यो फिरी फिरी नव बार । says that the S. 1853 famine came nine t'mes in rotation, *i.e.* every fifty-third year in nine centuries.

one thousand *talaos* in Merwara and Ajmer, only one Jugpura near Nasirabad had the benefit of a smart shower. The agricultural improvement during the last nine years, by the construction of *talaos* and the augmentation of wells, have tended to diminish the severity of droughts."

The following couplet describe the famine of 1848-49 A.D. (S. 1905-06).

पांचा पग पाडिया छकै दियों छेह। मऊ गई मालवे लारे आयेा मेह॥

(The year S. 1905 compelled people to emigrate; year 1906 showed that all was lost. The agriculturists went away to Malwa: good rain came when they had gone).

Col. Dixon says that the *mahajans* supplied food to cultivators; and in Ajmer, the higher classes subscribed very generously for the support of the old and the infirm: several thousand hands were employed by public-spirited citizens in building *ghats* at the Anasagar lake. The revenue demand was lowered by Rs. 35,000. No lives were lost, though three-fourths of the cattle perished. A drought occurred in 1854, and one again in 1860, and a most disastrous famine occurred in 1868-70 A.D. There was a partial famine in 1877-78; a severe one in 1890-92, and another severe one in 1898-1900. There was a famine in Ajmer-Merwara in 1901-02, and again in 1905-06; the years 1915-16, 1925-26 and 1926-27 were years of scarcity, as also 1936-37 and 1937-38. The years 1939 and 1940 were years of the severest famine that has occurred in this province.

Of the famines, of which we have records, the worst were those of 1868-70, 1890-92 and 1898-1900 A.D. and the present one of 1939-40 A.D. The famine of 1868-70, called the *Pachhisakal* (S. 1925 famine) inflicted the greatest suffering on Ajmer-Merwara. It was a complete famine, *trikal*—famine of all the three things: grain, grass and water. The famine of 1890-92, afflicted Ajmer more than Merwara; while in the famine of 1898-1900, Merwara suffered more than Ajmer. The chief feature which distinguishes the famine of 1868-70 from the next two, was that the former was a famine of grain. People died with money in their hands asking for grain, while, in the two later famines, owing to the advent of the Railway, there was grain, but no money to buy it with.

The Famine of 1868-70 A.D.

This was not only the most widespread famine in Rajputana, but the worst that has visited it during the last hundred and fifty years. Its duration was nineteen months.

RAINFALL—Taking Ajmer-Merwara as a whole, the rainfall was 7·4 inches in 1868. Both the Kharif and the Rabi harvests failed entirely. Cattle were for sale at nominal prices, and half the growing crops in 1869 were devoured by locusts. The climax was reached in September 1869, when grain was unobtainable. Such was the scarcity of fodder that cows were offered for sale at a rupee each, and good plough-cattle at rupees ten a pair. Half the cattle had been driven into Malwa owing to absence of fodder. The people were reduced to the necessity of supporting themselves on the bark of the *Khejra* tree and roots, which they mixed with grain and ground up to make bread. Mr. LaTouche says: "Grain was now literally unobtainable. The highest price it reached was three seers, but men with money in their hands could not get food in the city of Ajmer."

REVENUE COLLECTIONS—"In this year, three-fifths of the Government revenue was collected. The people had to borrow money to pay it. Rupees 42,000/- only were remitted, and 'the balance', by a procedure hitherto unknown in Ajmer Merwara, added to the demand of the succeeding year. In that year, when, as we have seen, locusts devoured more than half of a very indifferent Kharif harvest, and when Government was feeding the agricultural population on the Relief Works,- *a sum in excess of settlement demand was collected*."[1]

The havoc caused by this famine was so great that it has stamped itself on the memory of the people of Ajmer Merwara. Calamities never come singly; "famine was followed by cholera; of the 3,078 attacks, 1,598 proved fatal; then the locusts came and ate up 75% of the 50% sown. The result was that 25% of the population and 33% of cattle died, and 50 p. c. of the ploughs were lost"[2] Mr. LaTouche says that in the 1872 Census, population was less by 1,09,678 than that recorded at the 1865 Census.[3] "At Todgarh in Merwara, the mortality is almost as high as in Marwar, or 1 in 3½." (Brooke's *Report on the Famine of 1868-70*, p. 19).

RELIEF WORKS—In Merwara, 4,06,777 persons received relief upto October 1869; and altogether 9,71,711 were fed at an anna a head. The poor houses at Ajmer, Nayanagar, and other places in the district had been opened before the end of 1868 A.D., "and were thronged with the helpless and the starving, but the people attending them were unable to work on the public works, as they were only fit to be tended and

1. LaTouche's *Settlement Report*, page 88. 2. Tucker's *Famine Report*, page 5. LaTouche's *Settlement Report*, p 87. 3. LaTouche's *Settlement Report*, page 33.

nursed and not to labour. Many who went to find work fell down and died before they had commenced, and others expired with the first exertion, lifting a spade or mattock.[1] People wandered about the bazar with money in their hands, seeking for grain, which was not to be procured in return, while the relief-houses and public works were almost paralysed: for, though money could be given, it could not be exchanged for food."[2]

The following amounts were spent in relief of various sorts in Ajmer-Merwara:

Famine Relief Works	Rs.	7,74.000
Poor Houses	,,	1,03,000
Road Poor Houses	,,	11.074
District Relief Works	,,	75,000
Grain imported from Agra and sold, balance ...	,,	57,000
Nasirabad, chiefly buildings	,,	5,00,000
Total (Govt.) ...	,,	15,20,074
Ajmer Road Fund	,,	10,000
Pushkar Road subscriptions from Indian States ...	,,	25,000
United Presbyterian Mission Relief subscriptions ...	,,	69,000
Total ...	Rs.	16,24,074

Famine of 1890-92 A.D.

The next big famine was the famine of 1890-92 A.D. The *Famine Report for 1890-92*, pp. 34-35, says: "Only insignificant revenue remissions were made and the usual revenue was recovered." The kharif crop had been an eight anna crop, but it was the fourth in succession of bad crops. "It became certain that there would be no *barani* crop, and only a two anna talabi crop. Mortality amongst cattle was excessive and cattle were being sent away. Twenty-five deaths from starvation were reported to have taken place." The District Officer asked for the opening of relief works, and said that three lakhs were required for the next three months. The Officiating Commissioner was At Abu. "The grant was sanctioned on 31st August 1891 A.D., but the sanction was *not communicated to the District Officers.*" The Officiating Chief Commissioner could not judge immediately of the actual degree of distress, called for reports and *nothing* was done till the villagers took matters into their own hands, and the September grain riots commenced.

1. "The poor-houses were soon crowded with gaunt and emaciated beings, many of whom died at once after taking a meal, others lingered on a few days to end their miserable existence in the same way."—Col. Brooke's *Report*, page 34.
2. Col. Brooke's *Report*, p. 32.

ORGANISED ATTACKS ON VILLAGES TO LOOT GRAIN AND DESTROY ACCOUNT BOOKS.

The first five cases of grain-robbing occurred in the second week of September. For eight days, this lawlessness prevailed without check or hinderence. Grain stores were looted and the account-books of the *banias* were destroyed. In two places, temples were defiled, idols broken and taken away. "Complaints of victims about loss of ornaments and other property were dismissed." On 15th September 1891, hundreds of villagers assembled and looted grain in Akhri. On the 16th and 17th, looting took place at Bir. Looting took place at Rajgarh on the 18th, Morajhari and Srinagar on the 18th and 19th; in Oontra (Gegal) on 19th, Kumharia (Bhinai) on the 20th and in Sithuria and Jethana (Masuda and Mangliawas Police circles) and at Lohari, (Masuda) on the 22nd,—DeLaessoe's *Famine Report*, p. 230. These lootings took place sometimes in daylight and sometimes at night; and the attackers all arrived marching into the villages with flags flying and drums beating. On the night of 22nd September, an attack was actually made by some hundreds of men on the village of Beawar about four miles from Nayanagar (miscalled Beawar town) the head-quarters of the district, (p. 232). On the night of 23rd of September, some 1,500 men at least were abroad, many being armed.

WATER SUPPLY: All the tanks were dry, even the Anasagar at Ajmer—a thing which had not happened since 1812 A.D. Even drinking water became exceedingly scarce. For the first time, water from Budha Pushkar was brought into Ajmer. Ninety-six tanks were built or restored, and 1,984 wells were dug or deepened. The largest work was the Kayar tank, eight miles from Ajmer, where nine thousand labourers were employed.

The average number of labourers during the period, October 1891 to September 1892, was 12,108; the highest monthly average being 22,732 in June 1892, and lowest 423 in September. Gratuitous relief was given to 9 87,302 people at the total cost of Rs. 43,160-2-9. The Municipal Committee, Ajmer constructed the Foysagar lake at Ajmer as famine work.

MIGRATION: There were in Ajmer-Merwara, 7.06,792 cattle in June, 1890. Of these 1,29,269 died in the district, 41,426 died in foreign territory, and of 62,309, there is no trace. 4,73,788 are present in the district out of a total of 7,06,792.

REMISSIONS: In Kharif 1890, Rs. 2,733-13-0, and in Rabi 1891, Rs. 3,526-4-9 remission was given.

FAMINE MORTALITY: "From July 1891 to September 1892, deaths reported were 16,474. The normal number for the same period is 9,816. The balance 7,000 must be taken to be deaths owing to famine. Fever following the 1869-71 A.D. famine had decimated the population. The same thing happened after the close of 1890-92 famine"[1]

EXPENDITURE: The total Government expenditure including revenue remissions was Rs. 10,03,307-4-0. "The total loss to the people caused by famine on crops, cattle, dairy produce, etc. may be taken to be :

Loss on crops 90-91	...	... 26,75,000
" " 91-92	...	... 43,60,000
Value of cattle lost	...	... 24,08,000
Loss on dairy produce	...	... 26,20,000
Loss on manure	...	... 3,20,000
	Total Rs. ...	1,23,83,000 or

Rs. 38/- per head of the rural population"[2]

The Famine of 1898-1900

It began in Merwara in November 1898, and was confined to it till September 1899. From September 1899 to 18th August 1900, the whole of Ajmer-Merwara was famine stricken. But Merwara, being a poorer district, suffered far more than Ajmer. The cause of the famine, as usual, was the partial failure in 1898-99, and total failure of rain in 1899-1900, followed by locusts.

MIGRATION: About 4·01% of the population of the district of Ajmer emigrated.[3] Out of 5,53,3779 cattle in the district of Ajmer, 1,10,859 or 20% migrated;[4] and, of the 2,40,498 in Merwara, 52,020 or 21% were taken away. In Merwara, out of 240498 cattle, 122512, or 50·98 p.c. died.[5]

RELIEF WORKS: "The population of Merwara being 119,999, the proportion of those on relief, to the general population was at one time as high as 73 p. c., and for a considerable period, 70 p.c. or thereabouts." (Tucker's *Famine Report*, p. 12 (a).) "Merwara suffered from a period of drought

1. Captain DeLaessoe's *Famine Report*, p 10.
2. Captain DeLaessoe's *Famine Report*, p 115.
3. Mr. Tucker's *Famine Report*, 1898-1900, p. 117.
4. Ibid, p. 124. 5. Ibid, p. 128.

and famine of probably unequalled duration. *Wages were cut down as the famine progressed, and still the workers were there.* The villages were empty and the people absolutely without resource. Even the village *mahajans* supported themselves by working on the works as labourers."—Tucker's *Famine Report*, p. 12b. In Ajmer, in the third week of June, the works figures rose to 50,063, and gratuitous relief to 12,665; total, 68,728. "Thus, 16% of the population were receiving relief in Ajmer." Excluding charitable figures, the highest figures for any one week in both districts were 1,56,076.—Tucker's *Famine Report*, p. 12c.

COST: The cost of departmental relief in Ajmer, including Rs. 50,900/- on account of tools and plants and other miscellaneous items, was Rs. 8,76,204[1] and Rs. 8,98,927 including work at Deoli. The number of units relieved was 95,96,386,[2] and 97,04,363 including the works at Deoli. The cost per head was one anna and four pies a day. In Merwara, the total cost was Rs. 20,25,750,[3] and the units relieved were 1,99,08,965,[4] at one anna and five pies a day. For Ajmer-Merwara :

Cost was .... Rs. 29,24,677
Men relieved were 2,96,13,328

CIVIL KITCHENS, POOR HOUSES AND GRATUITOUS RELIEF :[5]

	Ajmer		Merwara	
	Persons relieved.	Expenditure.	Persons relieved.	Expenditure.
Civil Kitchens...	8,75,521	47,694 11 10	27,74,413	1,22,949 12 2
Poor houses ...	5,15,617	44,837 5 8	1,40,025	11,194 12 11
Grat. Relief ...	1,46,550	8,512 0 3	15,42,933	1,06,709 14 11
Home Relief ...	9,867	648 9 9	Nil.	Nil.
Total ...	15,47,555	1,01,711 14 6	56,15,773	2,40,854 7 2

Total number of men relieved .... 3,67,76,656.
Total expenditure .... Rs. 32,67,243-5-8

REVENUE REMISSIONS: As regards remissions of land revenue and cesses, out of the demand of Rs. 2,08,453 for Kharif and Rs. 2,12,079 for Rabi 1899, the total demand for two

1. Mr. Tucker's *Famine Report*, p. 96. 2. Ibid, p. 96. 3. Ibid, p. 97.
4. Ibid, p. 97. 5. Mr. Tucker's *Famine Report, Appendices.*

harvests of Rs. 4,20,532 from Ajmer-Merwara, *only Rs. 390* were remitted in Merwara, and *nothing in Ajmer*. There were, however, large suspensions, and part of these was later remitted. The great famine of 1898-1900 ended in the cold season of 1900.

In 1901 A.D., the rains began well in July and August but failed later, giving Merwara an average of 10·81, and Ajmer, 12·9 inches. The result was famine. The Commissioner, Mr A. L P. Tucker, fixed four annas as wages for man, and annas two for woman on relief works.

Famine of 1905-06

In seven years from 1899 to 1905-06 A.D., there were three famines covering four years 1899, 1900, 1901-02, 1905-06.

Thus, after the countrywide famine of 1898-1900 A.D., and the famine of 1901-02; in the following three years there was not one sixteen-anna crop. Taken together, the crops were in Beawar $9\frac{1}{3}$ as in Kharif, and $8\frac{1}{5}$ as in Rabi; and, in Todgarh, $13\frac{1}{5}$ as in Kharif and $8\frac{2}{3}$ annas in Rabi. No wonder that where people live in a chronic state of scarcity, with no reserves for bad seasons, the failure of a single harvest brings a famine. In Merwara, there had been partial failure of monsoons for five years. In 1904, rains ceased early and in 1905, the severe frost killed the crops and destroyed trees, and there was *trikal*, famine of grain, fodder and water.

In February 1906, the ratio of persons relieved to the population of Merwara was 22·50. The aggregate numbers relieved in Merwara were 66,47,471, and the relief cost, Rs. 4,31,952. In Ajmer 39,47,497 were relieved at a cost of Rs. 3,67,230 or 17·9 pies per head.

LAND REVENUE: In Merwara, no remission was given (*Famine Report*, p. 23). In Ajmer, remission of land and water revenue amounted to Rs. 48,773/12/5. There were suspensions of land revenue to the extent of Rs. 1,98,558.

EMIGRATION: From Ajmer-Merwara, 31,066 persons emigrated: 8,915 cattle died in Ajmer.

The next ten years after 1905-06, with the exception of 1909-10 and 1910-11, were lean years. (The year 1911-12 was bad, the crops in Merwara being $4\frac{1}{4}$, kharif, and $9\frac{5}{12}$ rabi in Beawar, and $2\frac{1}{2}$ as kharif and 5 as rabi in Todgarh. The year

1915-16 was the next year of scarcity, when crops in Merwara were :—

		Kharif.	Rabi.
Beawar	...	$2\frac{1}{4}$ Annas.	$5\frac{6}{12}$ Annas.
Todgarh	...	$5\frac{3}{4}$ „	$6\frac{6}{12}$ „

The maximum number on works on any one day was 5,506. The units relieved were:

Men	...	162,509.
Women	...	279,356.
Children	...	212,133.

The P.W.D. relief works expenditure came to Rs. 1,00,673. Taccavi distributed was Rs. 1,64,472.

Remissions of revenue were Rs. 1,06,608, only Rs. 94,013 were collected. Over six lakhs of rupees were paid to the B. B. & C. I. Railway on account of concession rates for fodder brought by rail. Owing to bad years, remissions of Government revenue in Merwara in the five years, 1911-12 to 1915-16, were Rs. 1,43,439-12-1.

SCARCITY OF 1925-26.

There was a scarcity in 1925-26. The maximum number on famine works was 4,443 on 30th April, 1926. Rain came in July 1926, and all works were closed in August 1926.

Relief was given to 4,81,044 men, women and children at a cost af Rs. 74,036 by P. W. D. Works. The civil works gave relief to 49,532 people at a cost of Rs. 3,974.

Famine of 1938-40 A.D.

This was one of the severest famines that have ever afflicted Ajmer-Merwara. It was widespread. Not only the whole of Rajputana, but Kathiawar and the south-eastern part of the Punjáb also suffered severely. The rainfall of fourteen inches in 1936 was badly distributed and there was scarcity. Bhim and Barakhan in Merwara were specially affected. Twelve works were opened but closed in March 1937. Distress continued, and three works connected with tanks were again opened, and metal was collected at an expenditure of Rs. 73,022. Distress continued in 1938. Ordinary works were started by the P. W. D. on the Bir and Srinagar and Jillaora tanks; and by the District Board of Ajmer-Merwara on Ajmer-Srinagar and Srinagar-Kanpura roads, and in the Beawar and Kekri paragannahs at a cost of Rs. 34,243 to the P.W.D., and 13,985/- to the District Board respectively. The monsoon came to an end early in August. In 1939, it failed altogether. The rainfall in 1938 was 8·74, and in 1939, only 6·96 inches. The result was severe distress. It became necessary to feed men, women and children and provide fodder for the cattle. At first, ordinary works were opened on a large scale to relieve this distress, for which the Government of India sanctioned a supplementary grant in the latter part of 1938 A.D. Twenty-nine Irrigation works were started but the wages offered were too low to draw labour. Twenty-six of these works were closed, and it was hoped that July would bring good rain. As the monsoon failed, distress increased. Three test works were again opened in the beginning of August, 1939. This time, within three weeks, labour crowded beyond all expectation. As had happened in the famine of 1890-1892 A.D., the people during this famine too, took to looting owing to delay in opening famine works. "There was an extensive outbreak of crimes against property; large bands of men had begin looting villages. Cattle had been exported and many had died in the severest fodder famine." Ajmer-Merwara was then declared a *famine district*. The distress was so widespread that thirty-nine charges were established. The expenditure incurred on these works upto 31 March, 1940, was Rs. 31,76,000.

As the official report on the famine has not yet been prepared, a full account of this calamity, one of the worst that is on record, can not be given. Exact figures of expenditure are not yet available. No information is available about the emigration of men and cattle, and their return; or about the mortality of cattle that remained behind; or, whether any gratuitous relief was given or kitchens for the poor opened. Revenue remissions, however, were Rs. 36,539 in 1938-39, and Rs. 1,16,547-4-4 in 1939-40 A.D. The courtesy of the Famine Executive Engineer and the Divisional Forest Officer of Ajmer has, however, made it possible to give some facts and figures to show the magnitude of the calamity and the work done during the famine.

With the progress of famine relief operations, the work increased so much that on 2 February, 1940, a separate famine division had to be created and an Executive Engineer placed in charge of it. The work was divided into four sub-divisions and was concentrated on the improvement of tanks and roads. The following works were started:—

(*a*) Strengthening and improving of tanks;
(*b*) Silt clearance and restoring capacity of tanks;
(*c*) Construction of new tanks;

(*d*) Construction of fair weather roads;
(*e*) Construction of new metalled roads and metal collection for roads already in existence;
(*f*) Remodelling of roads and widening of *patrees*.

The wages paid to the labourers were based on the ruling price of grain; and were calculated on the assumption that the staple food, barley, sold at 9½ seers a rupee.

Workers.		*Wages.*	
Special	....	10 pice a day	18 chhatanks.
Diggers	....	9 ,,	18 ,,
Carriers	....	7 ,,	14 ,,
Working children	....	5 ,,	10 ,,
Dependants.			
Men	....	5 ,,	12 ,,
Women	....	4 ,,	10 ,,
Children			
10 to 14 years	....	4 ,,	8 ,,
7 to 10 years	....	3 ,,	6 ,,
Under 7 years but not in arms	....	2 ,,	4 ,,
Infants in arms	....	1 ,,	3 ,,

Thirty fair-weather roads were made at a total cost of Rs. 8,09,228/3/3, as famine works.

1. Kharwa-Masuda Road.
2. Beawar-Pisangan Road *via* Nagelao.
3. Bhawani Khera-Bandanwara Road.
4. Bithur-Naharpura Road.
5. Sarana to Bhinai.
6. Pisangan to Pushkar.
7. Balad Road at Junction of Beawar-Todgarh Road.
8. Goela to Bandanwara.
9. Masuda-Bagsuri Road.
10. Foysagar to Ajaisar.
11. Kekri to Baghera.
12. Deogaon to Molkie.
13. Deolia to Champaneri.
14. Deolia to Kadera.
15. Deolia to Sawar.
16. Barol to Dabrela.
17. Kekri to Kadera.
18. Kadera to Mehrun.
19. Circular road round the Anasagar lake at Ajmer (unfinished).
20. Kotra-Beawar Road.
21. Beawar Road to Model Farm.
22. Pushkar-Kharekri.
23. Minto Road (from 31/3 mile of Ajmer-Beawar Road to Makrera Tank
24. Ramner to Ararka.
25. Gegal to Ramner Dhani.
26. Ajmer to Ararka.
27. Deolia to Bijainagar.
28. Gegal to Khodan.
29. Bir Nasirabad Road.
30. Gughra to Bhudole.

Thirteen roads have been remodelled and their *patrees* widened, at a cost of Rs. 5,14,514/15/0 The following seven new roads were constructed and metalled.

1. Ramgarh Masuda.
2. Ramgarh Bijainagar.
3. Ramgarh Ratanpur.
4. Ramsar Barol.
5. Kekri Bhinai.
6. Kekri Sawar.
7. Ramsar Kanpura.

Silt was cleared from 82 tanks, 32 in Ajmer and 50 in Beawar subdivision; the cost in connection with the two most important of these tanks was Rs 1,34,552-15-9.

1. Kalikankar tank .... Rs. 1,10,389- 3-3.
2. Phulsagar tank at Jalia .... Rs. 24,163-12-6.

The following four *new* tanks were constructed.

			Cost.
1.	Kishanpura tank.	Merwara.	Rs. 21,825- 3-0.
2.	Kalinjer tank.		„ 58,769-15-9.
3.	Mayapur tank.	Ajmer.	„ 43,439-14-6.
4.	Somalpur tank.		„ 39,018-15-3.
		Total	Rs. 1,63,054- 0-6.

Metal for twenty-eight roads was collected, the most important road being the Nasirabad-Deoli Road.

The three largest famine works were :—

Roads.	Men relieved.	Cost.
1. Pushkar-Pisangan Road	37,63,517	4,08,476-13-6
2. Barakhan-Todgarh Road	25,52,490	2,29,636-12-6
3. Kekri-Bhinai Road	22,16,851	2,13,055-11-9

The highest number of persons relieved on any one day was 2,09 316 on 29 February, 1940. On 31st January 1940, the number on the works was 2,06,151. On 31st May, 1940 the numbers fell to 1,71,779. On 15 October, 1940 all works were closed. The distress was more widespread and acute in the first half year of 1940. The total expenditure on works was *about sixtyfive lakhs*, and the total units relieved were in Ajmer, 3,33,87,042, and in Merwara, 2,25,63,313, total 5,59,50,355.

FODDER

As the monsoon came to an end early in August 1938, shortage of fodder began to be felt in January, 1939 and acutely after March, 1939. Measures taken to relieve the distress caused by the fodder famine, consisted of :

(1) Import of grass. Altogether 9,20,000 maunds of fodder (hay, *karbi*, *kutti*, and *bhoosa*) were imported through contractors under Railway freight concession certificates and sold to the public, under Government control.

(2) Taccavi to cultivators was given chiefly in kind, *i.e.* in hay, *karbi*, *kutti*, and *bhoosa* and not in cash. Fodder of the value of Rs. 2,65,000 was thus given as Taccavi.

(3) Grazing was allowed over reserved forests.

(4) Rightholders were allowed to cut grass over the whole of the *Hakuk* area.

(5) Famine Insurance hay collected in previous years was given back to the villagers. In this way, 3,708 maunds was given to the right-holders, who had deposited it in previous years.

Railway Concession Certificates were given to zamindars, cultivators, and charitable bodies, who wished to import fodder themselves. When the distress was very acute, demand for fodder rose to 6,000 maunds a day, requiring about seventy wagons to carry it. Seventy-five hay depots were opened in Ajmer-Merwara; 28 in Ajmer; 13 in Nayanagar (Beawar); 9 in Nasiradad, and the remaining 25 in other places. Of the 9,20,000 maunds of grass imported, 5,05,000 came to Ajmer; 2,25,000 to Beawar; and the rest to the six other stations where there were depots.

Hay was sold from -/14/- to 1/8/- a maund.

Karbi from -/14/- to 1/5/- a maund.

Jawar kutti from -/15/- to 1/7/- a maund, and

Bhoosa from -/13/6 to 1/2/- a maund.

The total cost to Government for providing grass for cattle was Rs. 3,62,036-1-3, of which Rs. 3,56,175-1-0 represented the Government share of the freight paid to the Railway. In addition to this, seventeen wells in or near the forest grazing grounds were deepened at a cost of Rs. 800. Owing to adequate arrangement for the supply of fodder, cattle that had not migrated were saved.

COLONEL SIR DONALD FIELD, K. C. I. E., C. I. E., I. A.,
CHIEF MINISTER OF JODHPUR.

The large expenditure of about sixty-nine[1] lakhs of rupees incurred by Government in relief works shows the magnitude of the calamity, and the liberal spirit in which the Government for the first time in the history of famines in Ajmer met it. The total expenditure incurred by Government in the three great famines of the last century—the 1868-70, the 1890-92, and the 1898-1900 famines—was Rs. 57,90,614-9-8; while the famine of 1938-40 alone cost Government about Rs. 68,75,408-15-6.[2] The units relieved in the 1898-1900 famine were 3,67,76,656; while those relieved in the 1938-40 famine were 5,59,50,355. Taking the rural population of Ajmer-Merwara in 1939 after the rendition of parts of Merwara to Mewar and Marwar, in accordance with the last census, to be 3,87,440, the figures of men relieved show that when the famine was at its peak, nearly 54 per cent of the rural population was on famine relief.

Marwar too was equally hard hit by the 1938-40 A.D. famine, and the relief operations under the direction of Colonel Sir Donald Field, the Chief Minister of Jodhpur, were also, for the first time, conducted in a liberal and systematic manner and were most helpful to people.

MEDICAL ARRANGEMENTS

A sub-assistant surgeon and compounders were appointed to look after each camp having over 6,500 workers; and a dispensary was opened in almost every charge. Indoor-patients wards were provided in a number of camps, and nurse midwives in certain camps. To prevent scurvy, sprouted gram was given to workers. In fifteen cases at Gegal, owing to *lack of firewood*, the workers mixed flour with *gur* and water, and ate it uncooked. This brought on *gastro enteritis*. They were treated and recovered. All wells and water were disinfected with potassium permanganate. Workers were vaccinated for small-pox. The total number of deaths in the rural areas of Ajmer-Merwara, from September 1938 to September 1940, was 20,459, including deaths, of children under five years, which were 10,364. There were altogether 454 cases of small-pox; none of cholera. There were 1,078 cases of diarrhoea from October 1939 to June 1940. There were several deaths from heat-stroke. In one charge, there were six in a week. The monthly deaths from fevers in the first six months, of

1. Actual figures are not yet available: adjustments are being made.

2. This amount is made up of about Rs sixty-five lakhs on famine works, (exact figures are not available), and Rs 362,036 expenditure on providing cheap fodder, and Rs. 13,372-15-6, expenditure on medical staff in famine camps. The latter does not include the pay of the Famine Medical Officer, cost of medicines, and other expenditure.

1939 were 691·5, and of 1940 were 1,193. A mobile dispensary was run for four weeks. People welcomed it. Gram was at first purchased from two Seths, who charged no profit. The Audit officer, however, insisted that it should be purchased only from a contractor, and so *higher price* had to be paid.

Captain C. J. H. Brink, I.M.S., Famine Medical Officer, who had full experience of famine work in Ajmer-Merwara says in his report that, "mothers with children under five years, should not be forced to come to work in the hot weather, but spinning or other suitable work should be provided, which will give the mother an income without the necessity of taking the children to work in the hot sun, especially in some areas where there is no shade from trees for miles around, namely Kekri. It was pathetic to hear the numerous reports from Sub-Assistant Surgeons, where it was observed that *a mother leaves the infant under a cloth in the shade of a shrub and returns after several hours of digging or moving of stones or earth to find the child lifeless; and it happened to better nourished infants too.*"

He adds "As many as six deaths from heatstroke in one week were recorded in one charge. The bigger children especially became listless and died in the early morning after headache, vomiting and with slight temperature. It is strongly held that huts should be erected near the works, where mothers can leave their children under the proper care of a specially appointed person to look after them. There were famines in 1891, 1898, and in 1900 A.D. and no time should be lost to amend famine codes and make the necessary preparations at once, *there being nothing yet in Ajmer-Merwara to prevent a succession of famine years occuring again*, at any time, as in the last decade of the last century."

"The balance of the number of increased deaths is made up of the aged. They would apparently not have died, if they had had sufficient suitable food to keep up their failing strength for a year or two more. It is not proposed to enter into a discussion of gratuitous relief in villages, but due to the daily exodus of able-bodied villagers, the old crippled do not receive the usual care and attention and are bound to suffer.

"This is a subject for which rules should be incorporated in every Famine Code. Trained nurses and *dais* should be included, as essential members of the medical staff and they should not only deal with the confinements of pregnant women but should give antenatal and postnatal advice to mothers on their health and on the feeding and care of children."

GENERAL OBSERVATIONS.

A number of broad facts emerge from the foregoing account of the famines that have occurred in Ajmer Merwara during the British rule. These facts fall under three heads:

(1) Prevention of famines, and

(2) Measures to be taken to deal with famines when they break out.

(3) Revision of the Land Revenue policy which has been pursued in Ajmer-Merwara during the last eighty years.

The cause of famine in Ajmer-Merwara is the failure of the monsoon. The plateau on which the town of Ajmer stands, marks the highest point in the plains of Hindustan. The rain falling on one side of the Madar hill near Ajmer drains to the Bay of Bengal and that on the other side, to the Gulf of Cambay, and this is continued along the edge of the highland down the whole length of the district. As the slope of the land is in every direction away from the district, there is no permanent undercurrent of percolation to feed the supply in the wells.[1] The rainfall is precarious, never abundant, often falling irregularly, too early or too late, and generally local.

Col. Dixon, who passed his whole active life from 1821 to 1857 A.D. in Ajmer-Merwara, studying the needs of these districts and understanding the character, the traditions and the habits of the people, and was thus best-fitted to administer the districts, was fully alive to the need of guarding against the frequent occurrence of famines. His view was that if a monsoon failed, but there was sufficient water available in tanks and wells for irrigation, there would be no famine. He, therefore, laid down two principles, by acting on which, the famines would be avoided or their rigour greatly reduced. Those principles were:

(1) *To collect and store as much of the rainfall in normal years, as possible, and*

(2) *So to adjust the revenue demands by making timely remissions, and modifying the settlement, wherever necessary, as not to impoverish the cultivators, but leave them some reserves to fall back upon in times of distress.*

Acting on the first principle, he covered both the districts with *talaos* (tanks), putting a bund to close every gorge, embanking every depression in the soil, and storing water running down the hill-sides with which the country abound, thus providing almost every village with a talao or a *nadi* and

1. DeLaessoe's *Famine Report for 1890-92*, p. 127.

make the subsoil water available to wells which were dug in every village, commensurate with its resources. These lakes and wells were helpful in normal years and served as insurance against abnormal years of scanty rainfall. "Tanks", says Mr. Lupton, the last Settlement Officer of Ajmer Merwara, "are an excellent form of insurance against famine." [1]

As regards the settlement demands, they were collected by Colonel Dixon in a liberal spirit, varying from year to year according to the capacity of the people to pay. The result was that, during his rule from 1842 to 1857 A.D., there was no famine of the intensity or extent of the famines of 1868-70, 1890-92 or 1898-1900 or 1938-40. Despite the fact, that no facilities for import of grain existed in those days, such as the Railway provided during the famines of 1890-92, and 1898-1900, and the 1938-40, there was only one severe famine in his time, that of 1848-49 A.D., which by his tactful and sympathetic treatment of the people, and the immense influence he had with all classes, he tided over *without any Government expenditure, and without the loss of a single life.*

The second principle, which is the most important one, has, as the history of revenue collections since Colonel Dixon's death shows, been consistently ignored with results disastrous to the province.

The constructive administration of Ajmer-Merwara, independent of the reactions or results of the general progressive administration of India came to an end with the death of Colonel Dixon in 1857 A.D. "*With the death of Colonel Dixon*", *says Mr.* (*later Sir Diggs*) *LaTouche*, "*closes what may be called the second period of the history, the era of material improvement; and the era of inflexible realization of the revenue commenced. The principle of Col. Dixon's settlement was forgotten, and the idea gradually gained ground that the assessment was an equal annual demand to be collected in full each year.*" Discussing the condition of the villages during the famine of 1868-70, Col. Brooke says: "In some villages the remissions required did not exceed one-third to one-fourth; but in others, *remissions of* half to two thirds, *if not the whole,* were considered necessary." But as a matter of fact, out of the three years' total demand of Rs. 5,50,907 for the three famine years 1868-69 to 1870-71, *only Rs. 42000 were remitted and the rest collected.*

Mr. LaTouche, who conducted the 1874 A.D. Settlement in Ajmer-Merwara, arrives at the conclusion that the average net

1. Lupton's *Settlement Report*, p. 117.

earnings of an agriculturist, *i.e.*, *the amount left for the maintenance of his family is Rs. 3-14 per mensem*. Capt. DeLaessoe says that, "If we leave out the dairy produce as an uncertain factor, the *cultivator has Rs. 2-10 per mensem left for the maintenance of his family*." (p. 22). He adds that "the average number of persons in a family is four." Thus the *cultivator has to exist on 10½ annas, a month*. What wonder that he is steeped in debt! How could he possibly avoid falling a victim to the famine when grain becomes much dearer that in normal years. *When in normal years, he has not enough to eat*, he must die, if no relief works employ him in a famine. *The agriculturists have thus been reduced to dire straits owing to the abandonment of Col. Dixon's revenue policy.*

To carry out Col. Dixon's second principle regarding the adjustment of revenue demands, remissions are necessary whenever the harvest is below the average. The policy of insisting on the collection of the last pie of the demand, even when there was a total failure of crops and the cultivator had to sell every thing he possessed and borrow money on the security of future earnings, to pay the revenue demand, was disastrous to the people of Ajmer-Merwara during half a century from 1857 A. D. to 1905 A. D. Happily, it has now been modified, though something more remains to be done to come back to Colonel Dixon's reasonable and fair policy of collecting in proportion to the produce; for, as Mr. LaTouche admits, "*the settlement demand is very heavy*".—La Touche's *Settlement Report*, p. 132.

It may be well to put on record here an observation, the result of experience of officers in-charge of the revenue administration of Ajmer-Merwara. It is this. "Thirty years records show that when the total fall in June and July is below half the average for those months, the total fall for the season will be largely deficient", and that when the "grass is not well-up by the end of July, the produce will be scanty."[1] As soon, therefore, as it is found in any year that the rainfall in June and July is less than half the average of those months, the matter, should be taken up at once, and plans should be immediately made ready, so that measures can be taken at the first appearance of distress. Similarly, if the rains cease too early, much before the middle of September, it will be known whether the tanks are full or not, and the total fall will indicate the nature of the well-supply. In either case, scarcity is probable if the preceeding harvest has been poor, and plans are needed in good time to cope with the situation. If the

1. DeLaessoe's *Famine Report*, 1892, p. 27.

precaution contained in this observation had been acted upon in time, the lootings and dacoities that occurred in the rural areas of Ajmer in 1891 A.D. and in 1940 A.D. would not have occurred.

A careful consideration of the records of the three great famines of the last century shows, that the District Officers of Ajmer-Merwara were from the beginning, alive to the requirements of the situation and did, all they could, to relieve distress when it occurred. They worked indefatigably to mitigate the sufferings of the people and helped them as much as they could. If the relief was inadequate, or was too late, or the wages were insufficient, the fault was not of the District Officer.

It is fortunate that, owing to the advent of the Railway and motor transport, and the development of the roads programme, there is no longer any likelihood of the occurring of a *pachisya* or 1868-70 A.D. famine, when people wandered in the bazars with money in their hands, asking for grain and died for want of food.

It is matter of satisfaction, that during the last thirty years, possibly because it saw that in the six years, 1899-1900 to 1905-06, there were three famines, the Government have abandoned the policy of rigorously collecting the whole of the revenue demand, and have been liberally giving remissions. We find that from 1908 to 1940 A. D., as much as Rs. 14,66,935 of revenue[1] have been remitted. Of this, such a large sum as Rs. 10,11,524, had formed part of "suspensions" in various years.

The policy of suspensions of revenue should be altogether given up; and *what is now suspended should not be suspended, but remitted.* If this is done, not only would the economic conditions of the agricultural population of this famine-exposed province be greatly improved, but it would be possible for the agriculturists to accumulate some reserve to fall back upon in bad years, and to acquire some power of resistance to famine, and Government will not have to open works during scarcities. Apart from this financial gain to Government, Excise, Stamps and Incometax would bring in more money; and better material would be available when military enlistment becomes necessary.

Another matter that should be seriously considered now, when a new settlement is about to be made, is the fixing of the future revenue demand from the province.

1. See Statement B, p. 337.

It may be noted, that Mr. J. D. La Touche, when he made the Settlement in 1874 after the disastrous famine of 1868-70 A. D., reduced the demand by 19 p. c.[1]. Considering the crop out-turn in Ajmer-Merwara, during the last thirty-eight years, the *demand should be greatly reduced* so as to bear a just and fair ratio to the actual produce of the land. *Statement A*, attached to this chapter, contains information taken from the Ajmer-Merwara Administration Reports about the actual out-turn of the crops in the two districts. The statement shows that during the last forty years, there have been only six sixteen-anna rabi crops, and not even one sixteen-anna kharif crop in the district of Ajmer; and that there were only six sixteen-anna rabi and three sixteen-anna kharif crops in the Beawar Tahsil.

The third broad fact that emerges from a study of the famines that have occurred in Ajmer-Merwara during the last eighty-one years—1860 A.D. to 1940 A. D.,—is that the Land Revenue policy of Government pursued in Ajmer-Merwara has not been a success. As Mr. (later Sir Diggs) La Touche has remarked, "with the death of Colonel Dixon closed the era of material improvement; and the era of inflexible realization of the revenue commenced." This policy which brings to mind the Shylock of the *Merchant of Venice*, has not only been detrimental to the people, but has not been financially a success for the administration of the province. A careful study of the famines and their causes during the last fifty years shows not only that the rigorous enforcement of the revenue demand and the full realization (when necessary by attachments) of the revenue due, which, as Sir Diggs La Touche clearly admits, is very heavy, has not only left the agriculturists of Ajmer-Merwara steeped in poverty and debt, and has rendered them incapable of tiding over a scarcity, however mild, but has compelled Government, in consequence of the agriculturists' utter impoverishment to spend a far larger sum to keep them alive than the whole of the revenue it realized during this period.

Though, owing the advent of the Railway to Ajmer, the question of lack of grain supply has been eliminated, the other two factors—want of water to irrigate the fields, and fodder to feed the cattle—still remain. The first famine after the coming of the Railway to Ajmer occurred in 1890-92 A. D. If, therefore, we take the period from 1890 A. D. to 1940 A. D., a period

1. La Touche's *Settlement Report*, p. 127.

of fifty-one years, we find that Government expenditure[1] on famine relief alone during this period, comes to the huge amount of Rs. 1,27,23,824-9-5 as shown below:—

Government Expenditure on Famines.

		Rs.	a.	p.
1890—1892	famine	10,03,307	4	0
1898—1900	„	32,67,243	5	8
1905—1906	„	7,99,182	0	0
1915—1916	„ works	1,00,673	0	0
„	„ paid to Railway for fodder	6,00,000	0	0
1925—1926	„	78,010	0	0
1938—1940	„	68,75,408	15	9
	Total	1,27,23,824	9	5

Now, the whole of the revenue demand for the twenty-one years from 1890 to 1910, at Rs. 2,98,927 a year, comes to Rs. 62,77,467; and for thirty years from 1911 to 1940 at Rs. 2,71,341 a year to Rs. 81,40,230, total Rs. 1,44,17,697. If we deduct from this amount, the amount of remissions, Rs. 14,66,935, stated in the Administration Reports to have been given from 1901 to 1940 A. D. (details given in Statement B); and an approximate sum of four lakhs[2] of remission given between 1890 and 1900 A. D., the total revenue collections, assuming that the revenue dues were collected in their entirety, come to Rs. 1,44,17,697 *minus* Rs. 18,66,935 remissions = Rs. 1,25,50,762. Thus, while Rs. 1,25,50,762 were realized from the agriculturists as land revenue, during the last fifty-one years, 1890 to 1940 A. D., Rs. 1,27,23,824-9-5 were expended by Government in keeping them alive during the same period. In addition to this direct expenditure, Government have, owing to recurrent famines during this period, had to incurr extra expenditure in the shape of Famine allowances to its servants, and otherwise owing to dearness of prices, and have lost large amounts of money in Incometax, Excise, Stamps and other sources of revenue.

Colonel Dixon, with his policy of adjusting revenue to produce, tided over the famine of 1848-49 A. D. without

1. When in the 1890-92 A.D. famine, Government expenditure was Rs. 10,03,307-4, Captain DeLaessoe (*Famine Report*, p. 115) estimated the total loss to the people, caused by the famine, on crops, cattle, dairy produce &c at Rs. 1,23,83,000. If an estimate on the same lines is made of the total losses suffered by the people during the famines between 1890 and 1940 A.D. the amount of loss would be found to be several crores

2. Exact figures of remissions given during the years 1890 to 1900 A. D. (including two big famines) could not be had.

any Government expenditure. It is true that, even with less heavy assessments, famines will occur; but the agriculturists would then be able to tide over ordinary scarcities without any demand on Government expenditure; and even famines, when they occur, would not entail such large expenditure. In view of the facts given above, the question of revising the Land Revenue policy deserves to be carefully considered.

To sum up, the requirments of Ajmer-Merwara are :

(1) All tanks should be kept in proper repair, and all village tanks should be taken up and maintained by Government. Mr. Lupton strongly urges that "*Government should take over all village-tanks and maintain them.*"[1]

(2) New tanks to be constructed, wherever possible. Four new tanks were constructed in 1940 A. D. (See p. 325 above).

(3) Digging of wells to be encouraged.

(4) *Settlement demand to be greatly lowered and brought to bear proper relation every year to the actual produce.*

(5) *Suspensions to be abolished, and whenever necessary, remissions to be given.*

(6) Rainfall to be carefully watched every year, and plans of relief to be prepared and kept ready whenever rainfall is deficient in June and July, or stops too early. And above all,

(7) To give the agriculturists in the *Istimrari* and *Jagir* areas in Ajmer, *which form nearly two thirds of the entire district of Ajmer*, the same rights in land, and place them in the same position *visa vis* the Istimrardars and Jagirdars, as in the Khalsa area.

(8) To amend the Famine Code (for Ajmer Merwara in view of the peculiar conditions prevailing in this province) in the light of suggestions made by Captain C. J. H. Brink, I. M. S., Famine Medical Officer, especially with regard to employment in famine labour, of women with infants in arms, and to provide for payment of adequate daily wages to men on works, as was done by Mr. A. L. P. Tucker, Commissioner of Ajmer, in the famine of 1901 A.D.

1. Mr. Lupton's *Settlement Report*, p. 117.

STATEMENT A.

Harvest Outturn.

	Ajmer.		Beawar.		Todgarh.	
	Rabi.	Kharif.	Rabi.	Kharif.	Rabi.	Kharif.
1900-1901 ...						
1901-1902 ...	good	poor	fair	poor	fair	poor
1902-1903 ...	poor	6				
1903-1904 ...	...	12				
1904-1905 ...	fair	10	good		good	
1905-1906 ...	damaged	failure	damaged	failure	damaged	failure
1906-1907 ...	10	13·5	poor	14·5	poor	14·5
1907 1908 ...	good	failure	satisfactory	poor	satisfactory	poor
1908-1909 ...	14	13	16	9	11	7½
1909-1910 ...	16	13	over 16	12	16	14
1910-1911 ...	16	13 to 14	16	13 to 14	16	13 to 14
1911-1912 ...	wet 15 dry 8		wet 12 dry 4		wet 13 dry 2½	
1912-1913 ...	14	12	12	10	15	16
1913-1914 ...	9¾	wet 14 dry 2	10	5	15½	5
1914-1915 ...	11 in wet & 3 in dry area	10	2	13	4	16
1915-1916 ...	16	8	14	2·3	16	6
1916-1917 ...	4 to 8 as 1½ in dry area	above normal	5	16	6·8	16
1917-1918 ...	9·5	4·1	above normal	8·10	above normal	9·5
1918-1919 ...	10	4·6	above normal	5·2	above normal	7·1
1919-1920 ...	10·10	12	11·2	16	4	11·2
1920-1921 ...	10·8	7·9	12·9	13·9	14	15·4
1921-1922 ...	13·11	10·2	16	14·6	11·6	16
1922-1923 ...	14·5	10·8	16	16	10·8	16
1923 1924 ...	10·9	6·10	16	8·9	8·4	13·3
1924-1925 ...	8·1	11·8	11·2	full	12·6	full
1925-1926 ...	above normal	7·5	above normal	8·4	1·10	8·7
1926-1927 ...	8·10	12·6	7·3	12·4	2·8	full
1927-1928 ...	15·5	9·3	full	9·4	full	11·7
1928-1929 ...	full	13·4	"	full	"	full
1929-1930 ...	12·5	7·5	full	15·5	"	15·1
1930-1931 ...	full	10·10	"	14·3	"	full
1931-1932 ...	14·8	12·1	"	"	13	13·2
1932-1933 ...	14·9	6	"	9·9	full	10·10
1933-1934 ...	11·4	12·8	full	full	14·1	14
1934-1935 ...	12·10	13·2	"	"	full	full
1935-1936 ...	full	13·5	"	"	"	"
1936-1937 ...	"	9·7	"	12·2	"	9·5
1937-1938 ...	12·10	12·2	"	full	8·11	full
1938-1939 ...	11·6	9·3	12	14		

STATEMENT B.

Revenue Remissions in Ajmer-Merwara, *vide*, Annual Administration Reports of Ajmer-Merwara.

	Current Year. Rs.	Previous Year. Rs.	Total. Rs.
1900-1901 ...	Nil.	Nil.	Nil.
1901-1902 ...	"	"	"
1902-1903 ...	"	2,42,892	2,42,892
1903-1904 ...	112	1,73,973	1,74,085
1904-1905 ...	12	542	554
1905-1906 ...	Nil.	16,991	16.991
1906-1907 ...	199	41,316	41,515
1907-1908 ...	Nil.	58,318	58,318
1908-1909 ...	334	1,15,748	1,16,082
1909-1910 ...	2.327	1,77,385	1,79,712
1910-1911 ...	Nil.	343	343
1911-1912 ...	Nil.	Nil.	Nil.
1912-1913 ...	27,836	39,001	66,837
1913-1914 ...	6,155	2,121	8.276
1914-1915 ...	42,221	25,069	67,290
1915-1916 ...	973	Nil.	973
1916-1917 ...	52,709	47,094	99,803
1917-1918 ...	101	...	101
1918-1919 ...	Nil.	Nil.	Nil.
1919-1920 ...	44,359	42,979	87,338
1920-1921 ...	3,627	3	3,630
1921-1922 ...	Nil.	Nil.	Nil.
1922-1923 ...	...	...	...
1923-1924 ...	...	...	...
1924-1925 ...	774	...	774
1925-1926 ...	...	5	5
1926-1927 ...	36 311	16,882	53,193
1928-1929 ...	Nil.	Nil.	Nil.
1929-1930 ...	25,752	...	25,752
1930-1931 ...	7,003	...	7,003
1931-1932 ...	...	...	...
1932-1933 ...	24,672	...	24,672
1933-1934 ...	20,749	...	20,749
1934-1935 ...	Nil.	Nil.	Nil.
1935-1936 ...	Nil.	Nil.	Nil.
1936-1937 ...	10,070	...	10,070
1937-1938 ...	6,891	...	6,891
1938-1939 ...	36.539	...	36,539
1939-1940 ...	1,05.685	10,862	1,16,547
Total Rs. ...	4,55,411	10,11,524	14,66,935

CHAPTER XXIV

LOCAL SELF-GOVERNMENT

1—The Municipal Committee, Ajmer

THE town of Ajmer has been a Municipality since 1869 A.D.; and till 1886, was governed by the provisions of the N. W. P. and Oudh Municipalities Act VI of 1868 A.D.[1] The principle of election was first introduced in 1884 A.D., previous to which, the Municipal Committee consisted of members nominated by the Chief Commissioner, with the District Magistrate as President. The report of the Municipal Committee for 1886 A.D. shows that there were then fourteen members; nine Indians and five Europeans.

A separate Regulation for this small province, the Ajmer Municipalities Regulation V of 1886, was enacted by the Government of India, and brought into force in 1888 A.D. Under this regulation, the committee consisted of twenty-three members, eighteen of which were elected and five nominated. For purposes of election, the Municipality was divided into four wards:

(1) City (sub-divided into 8 sub-wards) elected 9 members, 6 Hindus and 3 Muhammadans.

(2) Kaisargunj elected 2 members, one of whom was to be a Muhammadan.

(3) Suburban Ward elected 3 members, one of whom only might be an Indian.

(4) Railway Ward elected 4 members, only one of whom, might be an Indian.

The Committee was sub-divided into five sub-committees: (1) Finance, (2) Conservancy; (3) Public Works; (4) Garden and Nazul; (5) Lighting.

The Committee had an elected Chairman, a Secretary, an Overseer, a Sub-overseer, a Sanitary Inspector and two Sub-Inspectors and an Assistant Health Officer.

1. La Touche's *Gazetteer*, p. 50.

The Municipalities Regulation V of 1886 was revised in 1925 A.D., and a new Regulation called the Ajmer-Merwara Municipalities Regulation VI of 1925 was enacted by the Government of India on the lines of the United Provinces Municipalities Act. This Regulation came into force on 1 January, 1926. Under this Regulation, the city and the suburbs were divided into the same number of wards and elected the same number of members as laid down in the Regulation of 1886 A.D.

In 1933, the Local Government, having received several complaints of the maladministration of the Municipal Committee, appointed a Committee consisting of the Commissioner of Ajmer as Chairman, and three members to enquire into the complaints. On the receipt of the report of the Committee, the Chief Commissioner superseded the Committee for three years, under Section 243 of the Regulation with effect from the 1st August 1934, and nominated a committee of eleven members including the Commissioner of Ajmer as Chairman, which number was later increased to eighteen, including the Chairman. This committee introduced various reforms. It framed bye-laws for the work of the Committee, appointed a qualified Medical Officer of Health, widened the roads and macademised many of them. Part of the Nullah Bazar road was improved by providing cement. It took up town-planing and the laying out of several suburban areas. It disposed of several thousand building applications and cases which had been in arrears. It constructed several pucca drains in the city; had an aerial survey of the Municipality made, at an expense of Rs. 18,000; dug a well after trial boring in Dumada to supplement the water supply from Bhaonta, and unanimously passed a resolution in 1936 A.D., to introduce compulsory free primary education in Ajmer. No effect, however, has so far been given to the resolution, as Government have not yet framed a Primary Education Act for Ajmer-Merwara.

The Chief Commissioner's notification superseding the elected Committee having been withdrawn, a new elected Committee came into existence on 1 May, 1939. The Executive Staff of the committee consists of a Chairman, an Executive Officer, a Secretary, a Medical Officer of Health, a Chief and four, Sanitary Inspectors and a medical man in charge of vital statistics; a Municipal Engineer, a Supervisor and six overseers; a Taxes Superintendent and a Superintendent of Octroi.

The electorate having largely increased in recent years, the Committee has also been enlarged. It consists now of thirty-three members (including the Chairman), of which twentyfour are elected and eight nominated; the city being divided for purposes of election into twenty wards. Joint Elections with reservation of seats for Muslims, Europeans and Indian Christians has always been the system in vogue in this province. The committee is divided into the following sub-committees:

(1) Public Works (2) Finance (3) Conservancy (4) Education and Library (5) Water Works (6) Hackney carriage (7) Garden and Nazul (8) Purchase and Supply and (9) Lighting, sub-committees.

The finances of the Committee have improved with the growth of the population of Ajmer. The following table shows the financial progress of the committee.

Year	Income.			Expenditure.		
	Rs.	a.	p.	Rs.	a.	p.
1872	26,006[1]					
1890-1891	99,608	0	7	89,478	3	3.
1900-1901	178,157	12	8	185,997	14	7.
1910-1911	345,195	13	5	264,057	3	0.
1920-1921	416,835	0	5	435,095	3	9.
1930-1931	552,903	4	7	530,420	1	0.
1938-1939	557,666	3	11	614,467	15	8.
1939-1940	590,400	2	3	606,308	8	4.

Thus, the net income of the Committee which was Rs. 99,608-0-7 or below a lakh in 1890-91 has become Rs. 557,666-3-11 or almost 5·60 times as much as it was 49 years ago. The years 1938-39 and 1939-40 were years of severe famine in Ajmer-Merwara.

WATER SUPPLY.

The principal drawback and handicap, from which Ajmer suffers is insufficient Water Supply. With abundant supply of water, Ajmer, owing to its great stratagic importance, its picturesque surroundings and its excellent climate, would undoubtedly have been one of the most populous cities of India, and might possibly have displaced Delhi as the metropolis of India. The water supply is the chief problem with the Municipal administration of Ajmer. In old days, when Ajmer was a small town, the wells and the Anasagar lake furnished sufficient supply. As the town grew bigger, particularly with the transfer of the head-quarters of the Rajputana State Railway (later Rajputana Malwa Railway), water requirements of the

1. La Touche's *Gazetteer of Ajmer-Merwara*. p. 50. Of this income, octroi was Rs. 22,278/-.

city rose; and the Anasagar, the only source of supply being contaminated, it was proposed to store water somewhere before it came to the Anasagar. An embankment was, therefore, constructed near the village Ajaisar, and Foysagar was built in 1891-92 by the Ajmer Municipal Committee, to supply water to Ajmer, at a cost of Rs. 2,68,900. Of this amount, one lakh was spent on the embankment and the deepening of the bed. A twelve inch pipeline for a distance of three and a half miles was laid. It can supply four lakhs of gallons of water by gravity, and two lakhs by pump, daily. Even this water has, however, been declared unfit for potable purposes.

The daily requirements of water in Ajmer in winter months is nine to ten lakhs; and in summer, thirteen to fourteen lakhs of gallons. The B. B. & C. I. Railway requires two and a quarter lakhs of gallons in winter, and three to three and a half lakhs gallons in summer, in its workshops and other works. Foysagar supplies normally six lakhs gallons daily. As this quantity was insufficient for the requirements of Ajmer, the sacred lake of Budha Pushkar was laid under contribution, and the Railway was granted a license to take water from it in years of scarcity. The Railway erected its plant there at its own expense, and takes water from it. The terms of the renewed license which is for thirty years, and is dated the 5th August 1930, are as below :—

1. The Railway may sink masonry wells and tubes in the bed of Budha Pushkar lake, and lay down and erect and maintain pipes, pumps, boilers and similar works in the area outlined by the Committee.
2. That the Railway will take water from the Foysagar lake so long as the level of the said lake is 7 feet or more on the guage, and will pay therefor to the Municipality, at the rate of annas nine per thousand gallons.
3. That when the supply of water from the Foysagar lake or Bhaonta Water Works available for the city and suburbs shall fail to reach the quantity of 4,00,000 gallons per day, the Railway Company will, upon a request being made, supply the deficiency to the Municipal Committee from Budha Pushkar lake, provided that the water to be supplied from it to the Committee shall in no circumstances exceed two thirds of the quantity of water capable of being pumped in every twentyfour hours, and that the Municipal Committee shall pay to the Railway for water supplied from Budha Pushkar at the rate of nine annas per thousand gallons.

Budha Pushkar has the capacity to supply four and a half lakhs of gallons of water daily.

1905 A.D., the Sanitary Commissioner of India, Mr. Leslie came to Ajmer to look into the question of its water supply and submitted his report. The following year, Mr. Vrendenburg, of the Government of India, Geological department, came to investigate the geological side of the question and in 1907, the Government of India sent Mr. Silk, a Bengal Sanitary Engineer, to consider the sanitary surroundings of Ajmer with a view to find out fresh source of supply. Mr. Silk's view was that the two sources of supply were, the river beds of the Sagarmati at Bhaonta, ten miles south of Ajmer, and the Saraswati at Pushkar, seven miles west of Ajmer; and any one of the two would supply sufficient drinking water for Ajmer, the Foysagar water to be used only for garden and house-hold purposes. The Municipal Committee thereupon employed a P. W. D. Engineer, Mr. Heinneman, who in 1912 prepared a scheme to set up water works at Bhaonta. Some wells were dug in 1914 A.D. The scheme was completed in 1915, at a cost of Rs. 5,75,204, Government contributing a sum of only Rs. 1,20,000 towards it. Fifteen wells were sunk in the bed of the river, and a main connected it with the Foysagar pipe-line.

After the outbreak of the influenza epidemic in 1919, A.D. attention was centred on a system of drainage for Ajmer, without which no great improvement in sanitation is possible, and Mr. Hoey prepared a scheme which was estimated to cost 1,50,000/-.

In 1921, there was scarcity owing to the failure of the monsoon and the Bhaonta supply was found insufficient. In 1923, after three bad years, the supply fell to three and half lakhs of gallons. More wells were dug in 1923 at a cost of Rs. 35,973. The total outlay on Bhaonta thus comes to Rs. 6,11,177. The utmost capacity of the Bhaonta pumping plant is 7,00,000.

Owing, however, to the rapid growth of the city, the question of water supply again began to cause anxiety. The services of a water-engineer, Mr. Mallet, were obtained in 1923, and the B. B. & C. I. Railway, which is equally concerned in the matter, sent another water engineer, Major Pogson. The latter advised sinking wells at Dumada, eight miles south of Ajmer and also recommended a boring behind the Mayo College, "due south of Madar Hill and due west of Kiranipura." Messrs. Lane Brown and Hewlett, a sanitary engineering firm of Lucknow, were commissioned to prepare a drainage scheme; but their scheme of underground sewerage was rejected, owing to lack of necessary supply of water.

In 1936, Mr. J. A. R. Bromage, M.I.C.E., Superintending Engineer, Health Services, Delhi, was sent by Government to Ajmer, and he submitted his report on 4 April, 1936. He advocated the sinking of wells at Dumada and installing pumps at Jhalra, Diggi, and Katan Bao in Ajmer. As Ajmer experienced a scarcity in 1936-37, and again in 1938, a well was dug, as an experimental measure, at Dumada in 1938 at a cost of Rs. 4,140.

During the last few years, several colonies have sprung up round Ajmer; and it has been found that the supply from the Foysagar, Bhaonta and Dumada, in addition to that from the open lake and wells of Ajmer is not sufficient for the growing city of Ajmer. As the year 1938 was a year of great scarcity, and the year 1939 developed into a severe famine, and the rainfall in the Foysagar catchment area fell from 20·98 inches in 1837, to 7·01 inches in 1938-39, it became necessary to find out a new source of water-supply. The Railway gets[1] its supply normally from the Foysagar, but when it fails, or its level goes below seven feet, the Railway gets its water from Budha Pushkar. The city also gets a part of its supply then from Budha Pushkar. Ordinarily, the daily supply of water to Ajmer and the Railway is from :

Foysagar, 5 lakhs of gallons a day.
Bhaonta, 4 to 7 lakhs of gallons a day.

It is only in times of scarcity that recourse is had to Budha Pushkar.

The population of Ajmer was 1,19,524 in 1931 A.D. All estimates say that in 1941, the population will be found to be 1,35,000; and in a few years, it will go up to 1,50,000. At present, there are only 946 private connections (31st March 1939) and hundreds of applications for new connections are held in abeyance. Most of the suburban extensions, Adrashnagar, Gulabbari, Ramgunj, Bhagwangunj, Christiangunj, Pal Bisla, Bhairongunj, Nagla and others are without any water connection. The Committee has to arrange a water supply of twenty lakhs of gallons a day and has to find a source of fresh supply of about eight to ten lakhs gallons a day. Mr. J. A. R. Bromage, in his report, says that "any comprehensive scheme should provide for at least two million gallons domestic supply daily." If the population expands to 1,50,000, as is likely, a daily supply of two and a quarter million gallons would be necessary for domestic purposes.

1. In 1938-39, the Railway got 664,95,901 gallons at a cost of Rs. 37,405/2/-; and private consumers, 1,00,473,504 at a cost of Rs. 60,103/7/-. The total quantity consumed was 37,83,40,000 gallons or 10,36,551 gallons a day. The maximum quantity consumed on any one day, was 13,46,000 gallons.

Government has sanctioned a grant of eight lakhs and a loan of eight lakhs of rupees for the water supply and drainage of Ajmer. As an experimental measure, digging of wells in the Saraswati river, about four miles west of Pushkar, has been taken in hand. If the test works are successful, these wells will become an additional source of supply of water to Ajmer.

It will be seen that with the growth of the city, fresh sources of supply have from time to time been tapped. Foysagar, Budha Pushkar, Bhaonta and Dumada have, one after another, been laid under contribution; but none has so far removed anxiety for water supply. If the Saraswati river scheme turns out to be of a piece with the others, the problem will remain unsolved, and several lakhs of rupees shall have been spent only in finding palliatives. The true remedy lies, it seems, in the scheme put forward by Mr. Fraser, late Superintendent of the B. B. & C. I. Railway Workshops. His scheme was to bring water from the Chambal, the nearest river to Ajmer. It is a costly scheme, but one which would remove all future anxiety, and secure for Ajmer and the large Railway workshops there, a perennial supply of water. The rainfall all over Rajputana, including Ajmer-Merwara, shows a decrease, decade after decade, and all schemes based on utilizing soil and sub-soil water for consumption in a growing city like Ajmer will eventually prove to be temporary expedients. Geographical, political, educational and social reasons unmistakeably point to a progressive development of the city of Ajmer, and a great extension of the Railway workshops there. In order to secure for Ajmer, a constant and adequate water supply, apparently the only thing to do is to accept and carry out the Chambal river scheme.

The sanitation of the town, which depends primarily on water supply, drainage, and provision of open spaces, parks, gardens as lungs of the town, demands that an adequate supply of water should be secured.

DRAINAGE.

Upto the year 1934 A.D., all the sullage water was collected in cess-pools, of which there were thousands in Ajmer, and they were emptied by Municipal carts, which could never be done efficiently. The necessary result was dampness and obnoxious smell, due to the overflow of the cesspools. In 1938, an attempt was made to provide surface drains in all the streets, of which by now, five miles have been provided at the cost of the house owners. If Government gives a grant, as promised, the drainage scheme for the city will be undertaken almost simultaneously with that of water-supply.

II—Ajmer Merwara District Board.

The Ajmer Rural Boards Regulation was passed in 1886 A.D. to establish Local and District Boards in this province. A District Board for Ajmer-Merwara, and two Local Boards for Ajmer and Merwara respectively, were established. The Local Boards were, however, abolished from 1 July 1892. The functions of the District Board as laid down in the said Regulation, are:—

(*a*) The construction, repair and maintenance of public roads and other means of communications;

(*b*) The management and maintenance of schools, hospitals, dispensaries, markets, rest-houses, *sarais* and other public institutions and the construction and repair of all buildings connected with them;

(*c*) The construction and repair of public wells, tanks, and other waterworks, the supply of water from them and from other sources, and the preservation from pollution, of water;

(*d*) The planting and preservation of trees on the sides of roads and on other public ground;

(*e*) The establishment and maintenance of relief-works in time of famine or scarcity, if required by Government.

(*f*) The establishment and management of pounds;

(*g*) The regulation of camping-grounds;

(*h*) The holding and management of agricultural shows and industrial exhibitions;

The Ajmer-Merwara District Board consists, at present, of 51 members including the Commissioner of Ajmer as permanent Chairman. (Chief Commissioner's Notification No. $\frac{246\text{-c}}{516\ \text{A}/37}$ of 15 September 1938). Of the 50 members,

16 are Tazimi Istimrardars, and

14 members[1] are nominated by the Chief Commissioner, and 20 are elected members.

1. Under notification no. 379-586-11 of 20 April 1892, the Board consisted of 40 members of which 16 were elected and 9 nominated by the Chief Commissioner, in addition to the Tazimi Istimrardars.

The income of the Board consists chiefly of :—

(1) The local rate levied on land in Ajmer-Merwara including all Istimrari, Jagir and Khalsa estates, which at present is 4½ pies per rupee of the annual value of an estate;
(2) Tolls levied under the Indian Tolls Act 1857;
(3) Horse and Cattle Fair Capitation Tax:
(4) District Fund contribution towards medical aid by Istimrardars and others;
(5) Cattle Trespass Act receipts;
(6) Dak-Bungalow charges.

The total estimated income from these sources in 1939-40 amounted to Rs. 1,13,720. Including the opening balance, it was Rs. 1,23,873. The expenditure for the year was Rs. 1,17,110, leaving a balance of Rs. 6,763. The main headings of the 1939-40 budget, will give an idea of the work of the Board:

RECEIPTS.

Interest from investments	Rs.	1,690
District Fund Cess	"	26,000
Cattle Tresspass Act income	"	4,550
Medical contributions from Istimrardars and others.		4,770
Government grant (medical)	"	2,500
Scientific and other departments, including Government contribution	"	8,070
Horse and Cattle-Fair Capitation Tax ...	"	26,000
Tolls on Roads	"	12,000
Miscellaneous, including grants from Government for roads from Road Development Fund ...	"	28,140
Total ...	Rs.	1,13,720

EXPENDITURE.

Establishment, Pensions, etc.		Rs.	7,920
Cattle-pounds		"	760
Education: Primary Schools	12,100/-		
Grants to Schools	950/-	"	14,320
Inspection etc.	12,70/-		
Medical: (contributions to Govt. hospitals etc.,) ...		"	7,420
Agricultural Farms at Makrera and Tabiji ...		"	11,570
Cattle-Fair at Pushkar		"	7,600
Tolls		"	210
Veterinary Charges at Ajmer, Beawar and Kekri...		"	7,500
Repairs to dak-bungalows, school building, etc. ...		"	5,350
16 Roads: Ajmer to Srinagar, Mangaliawas to Pisagan and others, and establishment, tools etc.		"	39,280
Water Supply		"	1,000
Dak Bungalow Establishments		"	1,620
Contributions to Ajmer-Pushkar Road ...		"	4,990
Miscellaneous		"	7,570
Total ...		Rs.	1,17,110

CHAPTER XXV

EDUCATION

I—The Government College, Ajmer

"AJMER", as Colonel Tod, the Father of Rajput History, says, "is the heart of Rajputana," from which emanate all those vital impulses which help its development. It is natural, therefore, that the enlightenment that shapes the mind and the character of the people should arise in Ajmer and radiate over the province from this central point of vantage.

With the beginning of the nineteenth century, the unsettled conditions of the country that had during the preceding century, rendered life and property precarious, and had proved fatal to all intellectual and economic progress, gave place to order and security; and in their wake, followed peaceful development. Progressive and enlightening influences, born in Ajmër, began to spread and beneficially affect Rajputana. Ajmer-Merwara had passed into the hands of the British Government, and not many years elapsed before a public school was established in 1836 A.D. by the Court of Directors of the East India Company. This school developed into a High School in 1847 A.D., and was firmly established in 1851 A.D. It was affiliated in 1861, to the First Arts standard of the Calcutta University, the only University then in existence in North India.

The Government College, Ajmer, enjoys the rare distinction of being one of the oldest educational institutions in the country. Only three years back, in February 1937, the College celebrated its centenary. The East India Company founded at Ajmer a High School in 1847 A.D. at a time when the Punjab was governed by the Sikhs; Oudh was still in the hands of the Nawab Viziers, and a powerless Mughal was still on the throne at Delhi, as the puppet Emperor of India.

Upto 1875, thirty-seven pupils matriculated, and eight passed the First Arts Examination from the Ajmer Government College. In 1872, there were 235 students in it, 181 Hindus and 54 Muslims. The income of the College was Rs. 32,718 and expenditure, Rs. 32,063. Facilities for further education not being available at Ajmer, students began to go to the Agra and Allahabad Colleges to get University degrees.

The demand for a Degree College now grew apace and in 1892, the ex-students of the Government College, resident in Ajmer, formed an Ex-students Association, and started an agitation to raise the College to a Degree College. They gave most splendid proof of their love of their *alma mater* by raising among themselves the sum of Rs. 44,000. They handed this amount to Government, who opened the Degree Classes (Arts) in the year 1896. The B.Sc. Classes were opened in 1913 A.D. Since then, the College has been going from strength to strength. It was affiliated to the Allahabad University when the latter came into existence, and to the Agra University in 1927 A.D. It is now equipped with an excellent library, and with the facilities for the study of nearly all subjects of Arts and Science, including Biology.

COLLEGE COURSES: For Degree Examinations, the Courses are:

B.A. DEGREE: English with any three of the following:

(1) English Literature. (2) Philosophy. (3) Economics. (4) Mathematics. (5) Sanskrit. (6) Persian and (7) History.

B.Sc. DEGREE: Chemistry with group A—comprising (*a*) Physics and (*b*) Mathematics; or group B—comprising (*a*) Botany and (*b*) Zoology.

STAFF: Besides the Principal, the staff consists of ten professors of the Provincial Educational Service and six assistant professors.

STUDENTS: The number of students in the Intermediate classes and the B.A. and B.Sc. classes are:—

		Arts.	Science.
Intermediate	....	105	100.
Degree Classes	....	80	50.

A large number of students are refused admission every year owing to want of room, the expansion of education in Ajmer itself making it difficult to admit outsiders.

The College has a well-stocked Library, containing about ten thousand volumes on all subjects. It is the oldest library in the province. There is a Reading Room where about fifty periodicals and a dozen daily papers are kept on the table in addition to those received in exchange for the *Ajmer Government College Magazine*, which publishes three issues every session.

The students have formed a number of clubs and associations to promote literary activity and provide social amenities. There are: The College Union, the History Seminar, the Philosophy association, the Economic Association, the Natural Science, and the Mathematical Societies, the Amateur Dramatic Club, the Hindi Sahitya Sabha, the Bazme Adab, the Social Service League and the Olympian Club.

BUILDINGS: The College was originally housed in 1851 A.D., in an old building now called the Blue Castle, situated in the city camping ground. The growth of the institution soon demanded more liberal accommodation; and General Keating, the A. G. G. Rajputana, laid the foundation-stone of the present commodious building on 17 February, 1868 A.D. Additions to it have been made from time to time. The Biology block was added in 1929, and the Chemistry block in 1935 A.D. A Sports Pavilion on the main play-ground was built in 1938 with money subscribed for the purpose, by the old boys of the College and sympathisers when the Centenary of the College was celebrated in 1937 A.D. A marble fountain in the quadrangle, separating the old and the new blocks was presented by Mehta Fateh Lal, an old pupil of the College.

The Hostels for students contain accommodation for fifty boys.

PLAY GROUNDS AND GAMES: There are two big play-grounds in the College compound, seven Tennis Courts, and four Volleyball Courts, providing facilities for Cricket, Hockey, Football, Tennis, Volleyball and Athletic Sports. The College holds a record of distinctions in Rajputana.

The College has had eminent scholars as its Principals. The lexico-grapher Dr. Fallon, and Dr. Hall, were amongst its earlier Principals. Mr. F. L. Reid, a highly cultured and noble minded Englishmen, and Mr. E. F. Harris, who devoted his whole life to the progress of education in this province, and at one time saved the College from abolition, have adorned the Principal's chair. The present Principal, Mr. P.

Seshadri, is an educationist of International repute. In his time, great expansion has taken place in the College and the numbers have risen from 150 to nearly 350, and numbers of students who wish to join the College have to be refused admission every year, for want of room.

The College has supplied the province with a large part of its intelligentsia, and has, among the long succession of Old Boys, many distinguished scholars, politicians and administrators who have made their mark in the history of the country. The moral influence of this institutions on the life of Rajputana has been incalculable. It has been a beacon-light throwing its rays into the remotest quarters of this backward province. The College has done valuable work in spreading enlightenment in Rajputana. But its usefulness is at present limited; its natural growth arrested. It ought long ago to have been raised to the status of a University. Many Colleges in other provinces that came into being long after it the establishment of this institution, have developed into Universities; while others have pushed forward. The Ajmer Government College has lagged behind. This is due not to any weakness of the College itself, but to reasons which must be removed, and which being against the spirit of the times, cannot last. A separate University for Rajputana is a crying need, and the Government College offers the best possible ground for the erection of this new edifice. The establishment of a University is desirable not only because it offers facilities for higher education in all branches of learning, but because a University alone can create that atmosphere of culture and learning, and can become the fountain-head of that new spirit, which alone can give this historic province, the place and position in India due to it because of its glorious achievements. A seat of learning like a University alone provides that atmosphere which will enable its alumnii to preserve its noble traditions and all that is beautiful and great in this land of Romance and Chivalry. It may be remembered that Rajputana is bigger than Great Britain and Ireland combined or Italy.

II—Secondary Education

There are in all sixteen secondary schools in the city of Ajmer, out of which, ten are for boys and six for girls. Of the ten secondary Schools, six are High Schools for boys and are full to their accommodating capacity. Besides the four recognised Middle schools for boys there are two or three private ones which, though not recognised by the Education department, are attended by a large number of boys. This, along with the fact that there is a great rush of boys for admission to recognised schools in Ajmer every year, shows that the demand for secondary education in the city is increasing and there appears to be a real need for two more High Schools.

There are two Government High Schools in the city which are getting over-crowded in the matter of accommodation. Large number of applications for admission are refused. The Government High School, Ajmer has large and spacious buildings, including a hostel, designed by Mr. Lutynes and put up in 1919-1922 at a cost of Rs. 5,30,407/10,[1] and extensive grounds for outdoor games. The other Government High School is the Moinia Islamia High School. The four private schools are the D. A. A. V. High School, Husband Memorial High School, Oswal Jain High School, and the St. Anselm High School. These privately managed schools supply a great want, but they need proper buildings and extensive grounds for outdoor games. The D. A. A. V. High School, the largest of these, finds its present building inadequate owing to the increasing demand for admission. A more commodious building is being constructed for it on the Beawar Road.

Of the six High Schools for boys, the Government High School and the D. A. A. V. High School are the largest, each with over 600 pupils on its rolls. The St. Anselm High School, run by the Roman Catholic Church is the smallest with 278 boys inclusive of the primary section, and is meant for European and Anglo Indian boys.

The four Middle schools for boys all contain 550 boys in the Middle and 348 in the Primary sections, total, 898 boys.

The Hitaishini Sanskrit Pathshala, a private institution, is a school where Sanskrit and Hindi are taught. It has 143 pupils. They pay no fees. It was started in 1888 A.D. In 1921, the Municipal Committee, Ajmer granted it a site, and the present building was put up by public subscription. Its students sit for the *prathma* examination of the Benares University. There is also an Ayurvedic class in the school, and a dispensary is attached to it, where free treatment, including medicines, is given.

1. Main Building ... Rs. 1,78,627 — Drainage, Play-grounds Rs. 1,29,146-14-4
Hostel ... ,, 1,60,451-15-7 — Other buildings ,, 62,181-12-1
Total Rs. 5,30,407-10

III—Board of High School and Intermediate Education

The Board of High School and Intermediate Education for Rajputana (including Ajmer-Merwara), Central India and Gwalior was inaugurated in the year 1929 A.D., with headquarters at Ajmer. Prior to the year 1929, institutions in the areas now represented by this Board, had to look to the Allahabad University, and thereafter, to the Board of High School and Intermediate Education, U. P., Allahabad, for recognition of their High School and Intermediate Examinations. Since the establishment of this Board, all educational Institutions working under the control of the Board of High School and Intermediate Education, U. P. and situated in the areas covered by this Board, were transferred to it, and the first examinations of the Board were held in 1930 A.D.

Till the year 1932, the Board mainly supervised and regulated the High School and Intermediate Education in Rajputana (including Ajmer-Merwara), Central India and Gwalior. But in 1932, the training of teachers was also put under its care and a Teachers' Training Certificate Examination is now being conducted by the Board. A scheme to establish a first class Training College to prepare candidates for a University degree in Education, under the direct management and control of the Board, is under consideration and negotiations with the Government of India, through the Local Government to give shape to the scheme are in progress, and the College would possibly open in July 1941.

Constitutionally, the Board consists of the Principals of the Degree Colleges, the Principals of the Chiefs' Colleges, representatives of the Agra University, and of the States and British areas in Rajputana and Central India and Gwalior. The total strength of the Board is at present fortytwo. There are several committees appointed by it, which work for the proper execution of the business of the Board, prominent amongst them being the Examinations Committee, the Recognition Committee, the Finance Committee and the Curriculum Committee. The term of office of the members of the Board and its Committee is three years. The Hon'ble the Chief Commissioner, Ajmer-Merwara, is the Controlling Authority of the Board. The other two chief officers of the Board are the Chairman and the Secretary of the Board. The Chairman is an honorary officer. He is appointed by the

Controlling Authority from a panel of three persons nominated by the Board from among its members. He holds office for a term of three years. The Secretary too is appointed by the Controlling Authority and is the Chief Administrative Officer of the Board. He is a wholetime paid officer.

The Board prescribes courses for the High School, Intermediate, Intermediate in Commerce, and Teachers' Training Certificate Examinations on the recommendations of the Committee of Courses, appointed by it for the purpose. It publishes its own text-books in English both for the Intermediate and the High School, and in Sanskrit and Hindi for the High School Examinations.

The Examinations of the Board are said practically to be of the same standard as that of the other Boards and Universities in India, and are recognised by them as equivalent to their examinations.

Examination fees from the examinees constitute the main revenue of the Board. The Board has got a permanent reserve fund, which at present amounts to Rs. 40,000. Its offices are housed in a large building of its own, put up in 1935 A.D. at a cost of Rs. 88,592-2-0.

FINANCES:—The year 1939-40 commenced with an opening balance of Rs. 1,06,379-1-0. During the year, the total income of the Board was Rs. 1,52,196-0-5. The net receipts including the opening balance amounted to Rs. 2,58,575-1-5. Against this, there was a net expenditure of Rs. 1,19,898-4-3. The gross expenditure including advances made and deposits paid amounted to Rs. 1,26,225-4-7.

The Board has finished eleven years of its existence. There are one hundred and twenty-four High Schools (fifteen in Ajmer-Merwara; fifty three in the Indian States of Rajputana; forty one in Central India; and fifteen in Gwalior); twenty Colleges (three in Ajmer-Merwara, seven in Indian States of Rajputana, seven in Central India, and three in Gwalior); seven Intermediate Colleges in Commerce (one in Ajmer-Merwara, four in Rajputana and two in Central India).

Of these, there are fourteen girls' High Schools and one Girl's Intermediate College. The number of examinees has risen to an appreciable figure. In the last Examinations, conducted by the Board in March 1940, there were 6,414 candidates, as detailed below, as compared to 3,091 in 1930 when its first examinations were held.

1.	High School Examination	4,727
2.	Intermediate Examination	1,515
3.	Intermediate Examination in Commerce ...	170
4.	Teachers' Training Certificate Examination.	2
	Total ...	6,414

Girls' Education

Girls' Education in Ajmer-Merwara has been sadly neglected. In the city of Ajmer, there are only three High Schools, two of them, the Convent High School run in European style, and the Sophia High School are managed by the Roman Catholic Church, and are meant chiefly for European and Anglo-Indian girls. The third, the Savitri Girls High School is a private institution and is the only High school for Indian girls. There is no Government High School for girls. In addition to these, there are three middle schools for girls. All the schools are full to their utmost capacity. There are nineteen primary schools for girls, maintained by the Municipal Committee, Ajmer.

The state of girls' education is mirrored in the literacy of the women of Ajmer-Merwara. Of the total number of women 2,64,211, only 7,839 or 2·9% are literate. If we exclude the European and Indian Christian women, the percentage will become still lower, *i.e.*, 2·2%.

	Total.	Literate	p. c.
Women	2,64,211	7,839	2·96
Hindu and Muslim (women)!...	2,61,264	5,851	2·2
Christian (women) ...	2,947	1,988	67·5

The progress of education is reflected in the literacy of women. Out of 1,000 women, there were :—

	Census. 1921	Census. 1931		p. c.
Literate European and Parsi women	975	929	or	93·0
„ Indian Christian ...	414	695	or	69·5
„ Jains „ ...	60	82	or	8.2
„ Muslims „ ...	18	28	or	2·8
„ Hindus „ ...	15	23	or	2·3

The Ajmer-Merwara Administration Report for 1937-38 the latest published report, shows *that Hindus are much behind the Muslims in secondary and primary education.* The Report says that in recognised schools, there are 12,509 Hindus and 4,094 Muslim boys. Of the population of Ajmer-

Merwara (1931 Census) 5,60.292, there are 4,54,0C6 Hindus and 97,133 Muslims *i. e.* 81·03% are Hindus and 17·3% are Muslims. In education however, the Muslims have outstripped Hindus; for, only 2·7 of the Hindus population is receiving education in High and lower schools; while as much as 4·2 p. c. of the Muslim population is in the High, Middle and Primary Schools. The Report also says that in unrecognised schools, there are 1,624 Hindu, and 1,422 Muslim boys. This gives the percentage of Hindu and Muslim boys in unrecognised schools as ·35 and 1·4 p. c. respectively, that is to say, that proportionately speaking, for *every one per cent Hindu boys there are three per cent of Muslim boys at school in unrecognised schools.*

As for girls' education, according to that report, the number of Hindu girls at school in recognised institutions is 3,105 and Muslim girls 670, or ·686 and ·689% respectively; and in un- recognised schools, 222 and 197 or ·048 and ·20% respectively.

Thus, in school education, *Hindus of Ajmer-Merwara are the backward community and not the Muslims*, in regard both to boys and girls education.

The 1931 Census Report also shows that owing to special measures adopted to spread education among Muslims, there is greater literacy among the Muslims than amongst the Hindus in Ajmer-Merwara. The Census Report (Vol. XXVI) p. 66., Table 3, gives the literacy among Hindus and Muslims per *mille* as below :—

		Males.	Females.
Hindus	...	164	23
Muslims	...	196	28

Taking the percentage, we find that of the

Hindus,	8·37%	are literate and of the
Muslims,	9·1 %	are literate.

IV—Primary Education

There were many *Pathshalas* in Ajmer, and a *Poswal* (pathshala) in every important village in this province before the British came. The first public school was started in Ajmer by the British sometime before 1833 but the famine of 1834 A.D. disorganised it. Dr. R. H. Irvine, M.D. in his *General and Medical Topography of Ajmer*, published in 1841,[1] says:—

1. Pages 108-110.

"The Government has twice established an English school at Ajmer. The first attempt failed; and the school was judiciously abolished by Lord William Bentinck. An English school was again established in 1836, on a more extensive and expensive scale. The annual expenses of the Ajmer school is five thousand and fifty-two Company's Rupees. The number of scholars varies, but average one hundred and fifty per mensem. The cost per annum to Government, for each scholar (most of whom are little boys learning vernacular), thirty-three Company's rupees"

Mr. Thomason, Lt. Governor of the N. W. P. (now U.P., Agra and Oudh) visited Merwara in 1847, and sanctioned the established of one Urdu and eight Hindi schools in that district. In 1853 A.D., there were eleven schools in Merwara.

Col Dixon's *Sketch of Merwara* (p. 106) dated the 20th June 1848, says: "The town (Nayanagar) contains ten schools in which Hindi is taught, and two for instruction in Persian (Urdu)."

Mr. J. D. La Touche in his *Settlement Report*, 1875 A.D., p. 103, says:—

"There are eighteen Elementary Schools supported by Government in Ajmer, and eleven in Merwara. The former are attended by 671 pupils, the latter by 236, giving a total of 932, including 25 pupils attending the College with scholarships. Of this number, 910 are Hindus, and only 22 Muhammadans. Of the Hindus, 412 belong to the shopkeeper class, 131 are classed as agriculturalists, and 94 as artizans and labourers. The total cost of these schools during the year amounted to Rs. 13,244, of which Rs 12,778 was a Government grant. The average daily attendance was only 668.

"No arrangements were made at Colonel Dixon's settlement in 1850, for the levy of a school cess, but shortly after the announcement of assessment, 75 schools were established in Ajmer-Merwara; and Colonel Dixon possessed sufficient influence to induce the people to defray a large portion of their cost. The number was subsequently reduced to fifty-seven and the contributions were continued as long as Colonel Dixon lived. After his death, all schools except those supported by Government were closed."

Besides these Government schools, "the Rajputana United Presbyterian Mission," continues Mr. LaTouche, "has established four Anglo-Vernacular Schools, one at Ajmer, one at Beawar, one at Nasirabad, and one at Deoli, besides 52

Vernacular Boys' Schools and six Vernacular Girls' Schools; 2,142 boys and 290 girls are taught in these schools, total 2,432, and the average attendance in 1872 was 1,975. Most of the girls and a small proportion of the boys are the orphans who were left destitute in the famine of 1868-70 and who have since been fed, clothed, and educated by the Mission. The hamlet of Asapoora near Nasirabad; and another near Ajmer, have been founded on land purchased by the Mission, for the purpose of opening a career of agriculture to the young community. There are nine Missionaries including two medical practitioners in the district."[1]

In old days, the Principal of the Government College, Ajmer was *ex-officio* Inspector of Schools, and under him there were two Deputy Inspectors, one for Ajmer, and the other for Merwara. The Commissioner of Ajmer was the Director of Public Instruction. In 1921, a Superintendent of Education was appointed, relieving the Commissioner and the Principal of the Government College of their duties as Director of Public Instruction and Inspector of Schools respectively. As he was Superintendent of Education for Delhi, Ajmer and Central India, he was not able to devote all his time to Ajmer. In 1923, owing to financial stringency even this appointment was abolished, and the Educational Commissioner to the Government of India was made ex-officio Superintendent of Education. His visits to Ajmer were rare, and education suffered. The old arrangement was revived in 1931 A.D. but until a full-time Superintendent of Education is appointed for Ajmer-Merwara. education will not make satisfactory progress.

At present, under the Superintendent of Education, who has his Headquarters at Delhi, there is a District Inspector of Schools, and under him, there are three Assistant District Inspectors in charge of schools in Ajmer, Kekri and Merwara circles. There are 177 schools in the rural areas of Ajmer—72 in Ajmer, and 50 in Kekri, and 55 in Merwara. In the city of Ajmer, primary education was transferred to the Municipal Committee in March 1927, Government washing its hands off it. When transferring, Government made it a condition that Government will not let secondary education suffer, and that it will pay part of the expenses of the future expansion of primary education. When the Government was in charge of primary education, there were only two boys and

1. *Report on the Settlement of the Ajmer and Merwara Districts*, by La Touche, p. 104.

one girls' school. At present, there are thirteen boys and ten girls schools. During the twelve years that have since passed, Government have not contributed a single pie towards the Primary Education in the city of Ajmer. This ommission on the part of Government becomes still more significant when it is seen, that Ajmer is still a stranger to compulsory primary education. There is no city in the Punjab or the U. P. or Delhi of the size or importance of Ajmer, where compulsory primary education was not introduced long ago. The Municipal Committee, Ajmer unanimously passed a resolution on 26 September, 1936 sanctioning the introduction of Compulsory Primary education in Ajmer and asking the Honorable the Chief Commissioner either to frame a Primary Education Act for this province, or to apply the Punjab or the U. P. Primary Education Act to Ajmer. More than three years have passed and nothing has been done. The matter has not even gone up to the Government of India, being still under the consideration of the Commissioner and the Honorable the Chief Commissioner. If Ajmer had remained a part of the United Provinces, as it was before 1871, Ajmer would not have lagged so far behind other provinces in primary education.

The Ajmer Municipal Committee took over two boys and one girls' school from Government in 1927 A.D. During the last twelve years—1927 to 1939,—the progress under the Municipal Committee has been continuous, as will appear from the figures given below :—

Year.		Expenditure.	Number of Schools.
1927-28	...	Rs. 12,021	3
1928-29	...	Rs. 15,140	4
1929-30	...	Rs. 19,845	6
1930-31	...	Rs. 24,288	7
1931-32	...	Rs. 26,324	9
1932-33	...	Rs 28,254	11
1933-34	...	Rs. 31,133	11
1934-35	...	Rs. 32,425	11
1635-36	...	Rs. 32,060	12
1936-37	...	Rs. 33,034	14
1937-38	...	Rs. 40,474/4/8	21
1938-39	...	Rs. 43,002/14/7	23
1939-40	...	Rs. 46,728/15/4	23
1940-41	...	Rs. 48,000 (budgetted amount.)	23

Of these, two are Harijan Schools.

In addition to these schools maintained by the Municipal Committee, there are 35 private schools which receive grant-in-aid from the Municipal Commitee. This grant-in-aid which was Rs. 9,000 in 1938-39, has been reduced to 6,000 in 1939-40 A.D.

Physical education has been introduced in Municipal Schools, and a Physical Instructor has been engaged. In the largest primary girl school, a Music Class has been opened; and in one school, there is a troop of Girl Guides. There are 1,024 students in the thirteen boys schools, and 965 in the ten girls schools. Primary Education in the rural areas is mostly in the hands of Government, and altogether, there are 177 schools. The fact that of the 177 schools, 37 are private schools, shows that Government expansion of primary education is very slow. On 31 March 1940, there were in

		Government.	Private.	Total schools.
Ajmer Circle	...	52	20	72
Kekri Circle	...	45	5	50
Merwara	...	43	12	55
Total	...	140	37	177

Thus, leaving the city of Ajmer, there were 177 primary schools in Ajmer-Merwara, in a population of 3,87,440, or one primary school for 2,188 people. In Merwara, taken separately, with a population of 1,36,374, there were only 55 primary schools, or one school for 2,479·5 people.

Public Information

BOOKS, NEWSPAPERS AND PRINTING PRESSES

BOOKS: In 1939-40 A.D., 151 books were printed and published in Ajmer-Merwara :

10 English or other European languages.	9 Urdu
2 English-Hindi.	117 Hindi.
10 Sanskrit.	3 Prakrit.

It is remarkable that one hundred and seventeen books were published in Hindi and only nine in Urdu. Hindi and Marwari, are the languages spoken in the province, by all except the educated Muslims, who speak Urdu.

NEWS-PAPERS AND JOURNALS: Twelve newspapers and sixteen periodicals are published in Ajmer-Merwara. Of these, seven are in English, eighteen are in Hindi, and only three in Urdu.

PRINTING PRESSES: There were forty-two Printing Presses in Ajmer-Merwara in 1939 A.D., of which thirty-four were in the city of Ajmer.

CHAPTER XXVI

MEDICAL AND PUBLIC HEALTH

I.—General Hospital.

THE first public hospital in Ajmer was opened in connection with the jail here. Dr. Irvine, writing about it in 1840, says, "The Hospital is hardly worthy of the name, being an arched stone-shed in one of the angles: small, but, sufficient for the average number of sick; protection from the sun and rain is afforded, but the ventilation is insufficient."[1]

On 15 January 1851, at Col. Dixon's initiation, the first dispensary called the Sadar Charitable Dispensary was opened at Ajmer, and a building for it was built adjacent to the Balaji temple by the Agra Gate, inside the city-wall at a cost of Rs. 6,000 subscribed by the public. It had accommodation for twenty-five beds—twenty-one for men and four for women. The building was of the shape of a *haveli* and still stands intact. Later, a lunatics' ward was built behind this hospital.

As the demand for accommodation and operations increased, a new general hospital was built at a cost of Rs. 43,253, and opened on 4 March, 1895. It was called General Hospital. Government contributed nothing towards the building. The site was presented free by the Ajmer Shamlat, and the cost of the building was met as follows:

Sale proceeds of the old dispensary sold to Bhimraj Chhogalal of Nasirabad	Rs. 10,000
Ajmer Municipal Committee ...	Rs. 7,350
Dispensary Fund	Rs. 6,203
Walter Memorial Fund account ...	Rs. 8,200
Seth Sobhagmal Dadha	Rs. 5,000
Seth Nemi Chand Soni	Rs. 4,500
Seth Samir Mal Lodha	Rs. 2,000
	Rs. 43,253

1. Dr. Irvine's *General and Medical Topography of Ajmer*, p. 112.

In 1898, this General Hospital was re-named the Victoria Hospital on the occasion of Her Majesty's Diamond Jubilee. Seth Sobhag Mal Daddha presented a bronze bust of Her Majesty, which was placed in a small marble *chhatri* over the porch of the Hospital. Later, quarters for the assistant surgeon and sub-Assistant surgeons and menials were built, as also a Women's Out-patient Department.

As the increased population of the city demanded a much bigger hospital with accommodation for family wards, for X rays, maternity cases, and for higher-class Indian and Europeans, it was decided to build a new hospital in an open place, and a new site was selected for it in the Kaisar Bagh. The old hospital and the grounds were sold; the old hospital building is now occupied by the Municipal Committee, Ajmer, for its office. A small dispensary is kept in the building and is maintained by the Ajmer Municipal Committee at an annual cost of Rs. 10,720.

New Victoria Hospital.

The New Victoria Hospital was opened in 1927. It is a three storied building of cement and stone, and is situated in the north-western corner of Kaisar Bagh. The building and equipment cost Rs. 4,02,975. The main Hospital building, Staff quarters, Sanitary fittings, Electric Installation, Septic tanks &c. cost Rs. 3,83,793-12-2, and equipment &c. Rs. 1,09.271-3-10, total Rs. 4,02,975-0-0. This expenditure was met from :

1.	Hospital Fund (made up of public subscriptions and donations ...	... Rs. 2,44,163-14-0
2.	Sale proceeds of hospital land sold to S. Sobhagmal Lodha ...	... Rs. 1.07,493-12-0
3.	Government of India grant ...	... Rs. 1,00,000- 0-0
4.	Ajmer Municipal Committee grant	... Rs. 10,000- 0-0
5.	R. B. S. Biradhmal Lodha, for X Ray apparatus ...	... Rs. 8,000- 0-0
6.	Donation for building three Family Wards.	Rs. 9,000- 0-0
7.	Miscellaneous ...	... Rs. 2,025-13-0
	Total	... Rs. 4,80,683- 7-0

In the old General Hospital there was accommodation for 52 beds; in the new, when first built, there was room for 99 beds: this is now increased to 130. The buildings occupy an area of 20,000 square feet. The total compound area is 8·57 acres. The hospital is administered by a committee of local gentlemen with the Commissioner, Ajmer-Merwara as chairman, and the Civil Surgeon as Secretary.

The New Victoria Hospital is a Government aided institution and the only big Hospital in Ajmer-Merwara. It has separate departments for men and women. The Men's department is run by two Sub-Assistant Surgeons. The women department is run by a lady Assistant Surgeon. An Assistant Surgeon is in charge of the whole of the hospital. The New Victoria Hospital consists of two departments: (1) Outdoor Department, (2) Indoor Department.

The new Out-patient department is a separate block which was constructed in 1937 A.D., at a cost of Rs. 55,127, out of which, Government paid Rs. 50,700/-, the balance being met from the Victoria Hospital Fund. Government have also paid Rs. 2,500/- for the equipment of this department. Rooms have been provided in this building for holding special clinics in Tuberculosis, Eye, Dental and Venereal diseases. The T. B., Eye and Dental clinics have already been started, but special clinics in venereal diseases have not yet been opened.

The Out-patient department is open to the public for five hours in the morning, and two hours in the evening. In addition to this, one Sub-Assistant Surgeon, a compounder and a ward boy are always on duty, to attend to accidents and other emergencies. Only well-to-do patients are charged the price of medicines, while the majority of the patients who are poor, are supplied medicines free. The total number of out-patients treated in the Victoria Hospital during the year 1939, were 47,880, with a daily average of 512·52.

The Indoor department consists of the following wards:

1. Men's Medical Ward having twenty beds.
2. Watson Ward (Surgical Ward) having twenty beds.
3. Women's Medical Ward having twenty beds.
4. Lady Reading Ward having twenty beds.
5. Men's T. B. Ward, having 10 beds.
6. Women's T. B. Ward, having 10 beds.
7. Special Ward, having 6 beds.
8. Infectious Diseases Ward, having 20 beds. Total, 130 beds.

This accommodation is quite insufficient and the Wards are often overflowing. Patients are sometimes kept in the Verandahs. In order to make it an efficient institution, Government should take it over and maintain it as a Government Hospital.

The authorised scale of diet for the In-patients is about one anna six pies per patient. Since this is not sufficient in many cases, it is often supplemented by milk, fruits, eggs and liver. The patients in the family wards and the women patients in the Hospital Wards, are looked after, by the nursing staff which consists of one matron, two sisters and twelve Indian nurses. Those in the men's wards are looked after by the compounder and the ward boy, attached to that ward.

In the Indoor block, there are an X-ray room, the Laboratory and the Operating theatres, the offices of the Civil Surgeon, the Additional Civil Surgeon, the Assistant Surgeon, the matron, a small hospital office and linen godown and the various wards except the family wards, which are separate buildings situated to the west of the main block. The new X-ray plant was purchased in the year 1938-39 A.D. at a cost of Rs. 26,120. The Additional Civil Surgeon is in-charge of the X-ray department. All Out-patients and the Indoor patients in the paying wards have to pay for X-ray examination; those in the general wards are examined free of charge. There is a small clinical laboratory attached to this Hospital, where all important bedside laboratory tests are carried out. Out-patients have to pay for all laboratory tests. Those who are very poor are not charged.

The Anti-Rabic treatment is carried out in the Out-patients department of this Hospital.

T. B Wards: The two T. B. Wards (Tara Devi Wards) were built in the year 1935 A.D. and named after Taradevi, the deceased wife of R. B. Seth Bhag Chand Soni, M. L. A.

Isolation Block: This ward was opened in the year 1933 for the treatment of infectious diseases and is maintained at the cost of the Municipal Committee, Ajmer. There are no maternity wards; nor is any special facility for maternity cases provided. The whole hospital is provided with a water system and septic tanks.

The staff of the New Victoria Hospital, Ajmer is.

1 Additional Civil Surgeon
1 Assistant Surgeon
1 Lady Assistant Surgeon
5 Sub-Assistant Surgeons
1 Matron
2 Sisters
1 Clerk
1 Mistri
14 Compounders
11 Nurses
28 Ward attendants including one women attendant
2 Cooks
1 Mate
1 Bhisti
2 Dhobies
8 Sweepers
1 Peon

VACCINATION: Vaccination is compulsory in Ajmer since 1895 A.D. (as also in Kekri and Beawar since 1901 and

1902 A. D. respectively). It is perhaps not generally known that vaccination was known in India long before it was discovered in Europe by Jenner.[1]

Though, with the decline of the Hindu system of medicine, vaccination fell into disuse; inoculation by small-pox virus has always been, in use in India, and was to some extent practised in Rajputana before the introduction of vaccination. Vaccination was first introduced in England by Dr. Lord in 1853 A.D.

HOSPITALS IN THE PROVINCE.

The following hospitals and dispensaries exist in Ajmer Merwara, and are financed by the Government and by the Ajmer-Merwara Dispensary Fund. The expenditure incurred during 1938 A.D. was:—

	By-Government.	From Hospital Fund.
Kekri	Rs. 3,089	878
Pisangan	Rs. 1,704	247
Bhinai	Rs. 2,681	792
Masuda	Rs, 2,276	1,531
Beawar	Rs. 10,371	2,368
Srinagar	Rs. 2,576	1,189

Ramsar and Sawar opened in June, 1939 A.D.

Their annual probable receipts are as follows:—

Interest on investments	Rs. 1,700
Contributions from Istimrardars	Rs. 640
Jagir and Khalsa	Rs. 1,360
Municipal Committee, Beawar	Rs. 2,000
" " Kekri	Rs. 300
Dharmada " "	Rs. 100
Shamlat " Ramsar	Rs. 300
Government Grant	Rs. 900 } 1,600 }
District Board Grant	Rs. 900
Vaccination contributions from Istimrardars ...	Rs. 170

1. H. E. Lord Ampthill (sometime Viceroy of India) at the opening of the King Institute of Preventive Medicine in Madras, in February 1905 A.D., said: "The ancient Hindus used animal vaccination secured by transmission of the small-pox virus through the cow, and Colonel King bases this interesting theory on a quotation from a writing by Dhanvantri, the greatest of the ancient Hindu physicians, which is so striking and so appropriate to the present occasion that I must take the liberty of reading it to you. It is as follows:—

"Take the fluid of the pock on the udder of the cow, or on the arm between the shoulder and elbow of a human subject, on the point of a lancet, and lance with it the arms between the shoulder and elbows until the blood appears. Then mixing the fluid with the blood, the fever of the smallpox will be produced. This is vaccination pure and simple. It would seem from it that Jenner's great discovery was actually forestalled by the ancient Hindus."

The charitable Dispensary at Deoli is financed partly by the Government and partly by the Deoli Charitable Funds.

Women's Mission Hospital, Nasirabad.

The Rajputana Branch of the Scotish Presbyterian Mission started a Hospital at Nasirabad soon after it opened mission work there. After the departure of Dr. MacLaren in 1916 A.D., it was converted into a Women's Hospital. The Lady Doctor in charge of it, Dr. T. Martin, is an Assistant Surgeon. She joined the hospital in 1907 A.D., before its conversion into a purely Women's hospital, and has devoted her whole life to its service. The institution serves not only Nasirabad and its environs; but owing to her popularity, numerous cases go to her from Ajmer, Beawar, Jodhpur and Jaipur and other parts of Rajputana; she is in demand amongst the Istimrardars and the neighbouring Indian States.

The Hospital started with eight beds for women. The number is now forty, and very often there are forty-five In-patients. It is run wholly by an Indian staff. There are three qualified nurses and four qualified *dais* in addition to three trained nurses. There is an Assistant Lady Doctor. The Hospital building is Cantonment property, and the Cantonment Committee gives a monthly grant of Rs. 50 towards the upkeep of the hospital. Mrs. Martin herself performs all major and minor operations. Well-to-do people are charged fees, and the poor are served free. The annual expenditure is about Rs. 13,000. The Mission has borne the entire expenditure of the Hospital from the beginning. Only latterly, the expenditure is met partly by the mission and partly by fees. In 1940 A.D., there were 941 Indoor patients in the hospital. There were 337 mid-wifery cases; and 108 major, and 216 minor operations were performed. The dispensary department served 13,094 new, and 1,27,341 old patients. 487 Operations were performed in it.

Mrs. Martin, in addition to running this hospital, used to carry on Welfare work in Nasirabad, Kekri and Bhinai; but owing to pressure of hospital work, she has had to give up this work at Kekri and Bhinai. She also runs a Women's Club at Nasirabad.

Church of Scotland Women's Mission Hospital at Ajmer

Women's medical work under the Church of Scotland Mission was begun in the city of Ajmer towards the end of last century. The present hospital was opened in 1916. The hospital, built in a spacious compound out-side the Delhi Gate, lies at the foot of one offshoot of the Taragarh hill. The land was presented free by the Municipal Committee. It has 65 beds, in which are included private rooms, free wards, and a maternity ward, with a nursery for the babies attached. In addition to the in-patients, an out-patient's dispensary is open daily to which women from the city and from the district come. The hospital is financed by the Church of Scotland and by fees paid by patients. It has a training school for nurses who sit for the examination of the Punjab Nurses Board.

Maternity Home and Child Welfare Centre, Ajmer.

The work of training *dais* in Rajputana was started on 1st April 1903, by a Branch Committee of the Victoria Memorial Scholarship Fund, and a *dai khana* was opened in Kaisargunj. By 1918, no less than 128 *dais* had received training. In that year, the work was re-organised and a Maternity Home was started. In 1928, the Maternity Home was moved to the *Dai Khana* and Maternity Home, situated outside the Agra Gate, opposite the Scottish Free Church in a rented building. In September 1940 A.D., it moved into a building of its own, constructed on the Jaipur Road at a cost of Rs. 48,405-12-0. The Maternity Home has twelve beds. A Lady Doctor has been appointed as Superintendent, since February, 1941. There is already a European matron in charge, and eight nurses are employed.

The work of the Maternity Home is

1. To provide a Home where women can go for confinments.
2. To hold anti-natal clinics at which advice and assistance may be given to expectant mothers.
3. To hold child-welfare clinics
4. To provide a training centre for midwives,
5. To provide a centre from which midwives can be obtained for cases conducted in their own houses.

In 1940 A.D., 298 labour cases were attended to in the Maternity Home, and eighteen at the patients' homes. Rs. 2,275-2 were realized as fees.

The *Dai Khana* and Child Welfare Centre is not a Government or a Municipal institution. It is managed by an independent committee and supported by donations from the Victoria Memorial Scholarship Fund, Lady Chelmsford League Fund, and Red Cross Society. The total expenditure for 1940 A.D. was Rs. 10,211-7.

The Maternity Home conducts a *Dai* class, in which there were thirteen pupils in 1940 A.D. For a small Maternity Home, a European Lady Doctor and a European Matron, each one on Rs. 250/- a month, and an Assistant Matron on 125/- per month is an arrangement which will hardly commend itself to anybody.

Child Welfare Clinics

There is a Municipal Child Welfare clinic in Lakhan-Kotri, Ajmer. It was started in 1937 A.D. It is visited twice a week by the lady doctor of the Victoria Hospital. During the year 1940 A.D., 119 births were conducted in the centre. The expenditure for the year 1940 was Rs. 1,300. This clinic serves a population of about 4,400 persons. The number of births in this population was 313 in 1940. The centre visits were 3,155 and the home visits 4,536.

At Beawar, there is a *Srimati Sethani Ganga Bai Maternity Home*, started on 19th October, 1939. A qualified Indian lady doctor is in-charge of it. It is self supporting. It serves a population of about 30,000 people. 35 labour cases were conducted during the year in it. Its income and expenditure in 1940 were Rs. 3,958-13 and Rs. 2,701-12-6 respectively.

In Kekri, there is Mrs. Gidney Zenana Hospital and Maternity Home. It is managed by a Committee of thirteen members, with the Sub-divisional Officer, Kekri as Chairman. A qualified lady doctor is in-charge. It serves a population of 7,500 persons. Its total income and expenditure for 1940 were Rs. 1,952-14-0 and Rs. 1,960-8-3 respectively.

II.—Public Health.

There is no Public Health organisation in the rural areas of Ajmer-Merwara; and, in this respect, this centrally administered area is very much behind other provinces of India. As regards urban areas there are three Municipalities in Ajmer-Merwara, out of which, the Beawar and Kekri Municipalities have made no attempt at Public Health organisation for their towns. Ajmer, the chief town of the province, was provided with an Assistant Health Officer as long ago as 1897. The officer appointed was a retired sub-assistant surgeon from the local hospital. He was succeeded by similar officers, with no pretentions to knowledge of public health affairs. In 1923 at last, an officer with public health qualifications was appointed, but he was not placed in charge of the Public Health department. He was supposed to work as Assistant Health Officer under the supervision of the Civil Surgeon of Ajmer.

The statistics for the last sixteen years show, that it is only during the last five years, that the death-rate has become lower than the birth-rate. Upto 1935-36, the death rate was always higher. Though the death rate is now lower than the birth-rate, it is still high.

	Birth.	Death.
1935-36	45·07	32·54
1936-37	46·81	32·47
1937-38	45·90	42·75
1938-39	51·06	39·53
1939-40	52·14	40·79

The statistics also show that during the last fourteen years, 1926-27 to 1939-40, there has been little improvement in the death rate. From 1926-27 to 1930-31, the average for five years was 39·4, and during the same period from 1935-36 to 1939-40, the average was 38·21. Table X, on p. 51, of the Report of the Ajmer Municipal Committee for 1938-39, shows that the infant mortality, though lower than it was ten years ago, is still very high. The figures for the last four years are:-

1935-36	252·41	per 1,000 births.
1936-37	235·74	
1937-38	311·29	
1938-39	279·21	

Though epidemic and dangerous diseases like cholera and plague, seldom appear in this area, due probably to its extreme dryness and low humidity; diseases like enteric and dysentery are as common as in other towns of India. In recent years, an effort was made to protect the population against small-pox; and as many as 65,000 vaccinations were done in the year 1940, which is a record figure in the history of Ajmer. Tuberculosis, however, is spreading in Ajmer as it is doing in other urban areas of the country. The local Red Cross Society carried out a tuberculosis survey in 1939-40, and about twenty beds have been provided in the local new Victoria Hospital.

GENERAL OBSERVATIONS.

The matter of Public Health is the most important of all questions connected with Ajmer-Merwara. When Ajmer was a small town containing about 24,000 people during the early period of British Rule, the public health question was not acute. But now that the population has increased tremendously—it was 1,19,524 in 1931 and is likely to be 1,35,000 in 1941 A.D. and would probably have been much more but for the severe famine of 1939-40—the situation has become grave, and steps have to be taken to protect public health. The city of Ajmer is neither a commercial centre, nor an industrial city, and the resources of its Municipal Committee are limited. If taxation is increased beyond a certain limit, the law of diminishing returns will come into operation, and defeat its object. In all major provinces, the provincial resources enable provincial governments to look after the sanitation and health of the towns and the rural areas under their jurisdiction, with the aid of the Public Health Service, and the provisions in the provincial budgets. Ajmer-Merwara is too small a province to permit of that. It behoves the Government of India to do in Ajmer, what it is doing so liberally in Delhi, which also, like Ajmer, is under its direct administration. Because it is a small province, and unlike Delhi is out of its sight, Ajmer-Merwara ought not be out of its mind too.

It is a notable fact, that during all these years—from 1869, when a Municipal Committee was established in Ajmer, to 1940 A.D.—Government have not given a single pie to the Municipal Committee to improve the health conditions or the sanitary arrangements of Ajmer. In Delhi, the Government of India have financed the scheme of removal of refuse, costing thirteen lakhs, the Municipal Committee paying nothing towards it. In Delhi, in 1938, even in the anti-malarial campaign in the urban area, costing Rs. 14,000, Government contributed Rs. 5,000. In Ajmer, the Municipal Committee is spending six to seven thousand rupees every year on anti-malarial measures, but the Government does not contribute a pie towards it. The new drainage scheme of Delhi costing forty-six lakhs is being financed entirely by Government, the Municipal Committee paying nothing towards it. Everywhere, Capital Public Health works are established and financed by Government. Government also gives substantial grants towards maternity and child welfare and anti-tuberculosis schemes. The Bombay Government pays fifty per cent of the salary of sanitary Inspectors. In the United Provinces and in Madras, the cost of Public Health Officers is borne entirely by Government. In the Punjab, the lady Health visitors are paid by the local bodies in the first instance, but Government pays the entire expenditure at the end of the year. It is time that Government took this matter into its consideration.

Just as the Ajmer-Merwara P.W.D. has, in order to make its work efficient, been made a division under the Central P. W. D. Delhi, and is looked after by the Superintending Engineer, First Circle, Central P. W. D., Delhi; so also, the Public Health department of Ajmer-Merwara should be placed entirely under the Public Health Service of Delhi, or the United Provinces, under which it should form a Division. Without the constant technical supervision, control, and guidance, based on wide experience of the Delhi or the U. P. Health Department, little progress can be expected.

Government ought to instal a plant for the disposal of sullage and nightsoil for Ajmer, and should also instal filtration plants at Foysagar, Budha Pushkar, the Jhalra and all other tanks in Ajmer. No real and permanent improvement is possible, unless Government has a Public Health Service however small, to look after the Public Health of the province. The *Report of the Royal Commission on Labour* (p. 254) distinctly lays down that Public Health Officer should always belong to Government cadre, for the protection of the public health is eventually Government and not Municipal responsibility.

CHAPTER XXVII

MILITARY

ON the termination of the Pindari War in 1817-18 A. D., the Government of India decided to station three Corps complete with Artillery, one in Rajputana, another at Neemuch and a third at Mhow. At first, the Rajputana Force was proposed to be stationed at Tonk-Rampura; but when Ajmer was ceded to the British by the Scindia, its supreme strategical position was at once realised, and it was decided to place the troops near Ajmer. Soon after taking Ajmer on 26th July 1818, General Ochterlony marched to Neemuch with a small force, leaving a garrison at Ajmer. The rest of the division under the command of Brigadier Knox marched to the village Nandla, and fixed upon the plains between Nandla and Bir for a cantonment. A cantonment was established there on 20 November, 1818 and was named Nasirabad after the title of Nasiruddaula, conferred on General Ochterlony by Emperor Shah Alam in 1804 A.D.[1]

When Merwara was conquered in 1821 A.D., Sir David Ochterlony, Resident in Rajputana and Malwa, recommended on 6 November. 1821, the establishment of a local corps to keep order in that district and give employment to the Mers, who, from time immemorial, were a race of robbers and dacoits. The proposal was sanctioned on 28 June, 1822, and Captain Hall of the 16th Bengal Native Infantry under the Quarter Master General, Nasirabad, was appointed commandant of this force and Superintendent of Merwara. It was located at Beawar. In 1861, it became the Merwara Police Corps. After the regular Police was formed, it became "Merwara Battalion" and later was converted into 44th Merwara Infantry. It was transferred from Beawar to Ajmer in 1871 A D. It had 712 men and four British Officers. It was finally disbanded on 22nd June, 1921 A.D.

In 1857 A. D., a cantonment was established at Deoli, seventy miles from Ajmer and situated in the midst of Indian States territories with easy access to Bundi, Kotah, Tonk and

1. *Rajputana Gazetteer, Ajmer-Merwara*, Vol. I-A, p. 118 (1904).

Udaipur. A regiment called the Meena Battalion was raised that year. In August 1857, fearing that enlistment was a cloak for imprisonment, 205 Meenas deserted. The Meenas were not given rifles: only swords and muskets were allowed, and pay was given to them every day, not monthly. In 1858, the Deoli force, when sent to Kotah after the troops there had mutinied, did every good work. It was later called the 42nd Deoli Regiment. It had 812 men and seven British Officers, and was divided into a squadron of Cavalry and a battalion of Infantry. In 1860, it was named the Deoli Irregular Force. It was disbanded in 1921 A D. In addition to the Merwara Battalion and the Deoli Irregular Corps, there was the Erinpura Irregular Force at Erinpura of similar strength as the Deoli Irregular Corps.

Ajmer is now a centre only for recruiting operations for Ajmer and Central India; and a Recruiting Officer and an I. M. S. Officer reside here. The recruits are supplied principally to the 10/6th Rajputana Rifles, stationed till a few months ago at Nasirabad, and to other Infantry and cavalry regiments containing Rajputana classes (*e. g* Sam Brown's Cavalry, Hyderabad Regiment, etc.). Only Rajputs, Gujars, Jats, Mussalman Rajputs and Ahirs are recruited.

Ajmer is also the headquarters of the Auxiliary and Territorial forces. The Auxiliary Force is the second Battalion of the B. B. & C. I. Railway Regiment AF (1). This corps consists of a Head quarters Company and three other Companies, including a Company at Mount Abu. In 1903, its strength was 344: in 1939, 400.

The Territorial Force is the 11th Battalion, 4th Bombay Grenadiers (ITF) and consists of four companies, with a total strength of 700 men, and nineteen Junior grade and eight Senior grade Indian, and four British Officers.

THE NASIRABAD CANTONMENT.

Nasirabad is now the only cantonment in Ajmer-Merwara. When it was laid out, Nasirabad Cantonment "was the largest cantonment then in India".[1] This cantonment was marked out for a force consisting of one regiment of Irregular Cavalry, two companies of Artillery, two companies of Pioneers, five Regiments of the Line and two Local corps. As so large a space of ground, waste and unoccupied, was not available, it became necessary to include a portion of the lands

1. *The Story of Merwara or Our Rule in India*, p. 125, (Longmans Green and Coy., London. 1868 A.D.).

belonging to the villages of Deranthu, Dilwara, and Nandla, for which compensation was sanctioned, the payment to be continued annually so long as the ground should be actually required.

The present area of the Cantonment was settled in 1872. The Cantonment pillars enclose an area of 8·5 square miles. Nasirabad is situated in latitude 26·18 and 45″ North and longitude 74·47 East, and is about 14 miles, in a south-east direction from Ajmer, with which it is connected by a branch line of the Rajputana Malwa Railway, and also by a good mettled road. Its elevation above the sea is about 1,460 feet—forty feet above adjacent country, and from 30 to 40 feet above the nearest water.

The station itself is on a bleak, bare plain, which slopes eastwards from the range of the Aravalli Hills lying nearest to Ajmer and is dotted with cultivation, dwarfed trees and numerous tanks. Very little wood or jungle is to be found in the vicinity. The Aravalli Hills are about six miles to the north-west, and are about 1,200 feet high, and 2,800 feet above the sea.

To form a correct judgment of the importance of Nasirabad as a military centre, it is necessary to bear in mind its proximity to some of the more powerful Indian States in Rajputana and Central India, such as Jaipur, Jodhpur, Udaipur, Kotah, Bharatpur in Rajputana, and Gwalior and Indore in Central India. *The Rajputana Gazetteer* says: "As a military station, Nasirabad is important in being most centrally situated for operations in Rajputana. It is the nearest considerable military station to Jaipur and Jodhpur and well-placed for rapid despatch of troops in the direction of Udaipur, Bikaner and Indore."[1] "The actual presence of British troops at Nasirabad becomes all the more important, as it permits independent action in troublous periods, and strengthens, during peace time, the hands of the various Political Agents. The Cantonment at Nasirabad has also a wholesome effect on local forces, police, and Indian States generally and assures the safety of Ajmer, a commercial centre of yearly increasing importance". "From past experience it may be fairly concluded that to ensure the proper administration of the vast tract of country concerned, a Battery, six companies of British Infantry, a squadron of Native Cavalry, and a regiment of Native Infantry should form the minimum garrison of Nasirabad."

1. C. C. Watson's *Rajputana Gazetteer*, p. 118.

Taking into consideration the original object of the entry of a British force into Rajputana in 1818, it is clear that, situated as the Cantonment is in the midst of an extensive flat plain, undulations being trifling, the field operations would be the system of opposition to any invading force. The station itself possesses no fortified position. In disturbed times, the chief objects of the garrison would, therefore, be;—

(1) Keeping open communication with Ajmer,
(2) The retention of the Water-supply,
(3) Keeping open tne Railway line, if possible, without endangering (1) and (2).

"With the normal garrison, unhindered communications with Ajmer and the safety of the water-supply may be regarded as feasible; the holding of the line of Railway only probably so. Without the artillery or the Infantry, successful defence and securing water only could be reckoned upon."

When Victor Jacquemont, the French naturalist, visited it in 1832, there were three Regiments of Infantry, two of Cavalry, two of Artillery, and Sappers and Miners. There were 60 Europeans there at that time. In 1878, when Nasirabad was a large cantonment, the troops there consisted of:

130 Artillery men and six Cannons	794 European Infantry.
149 Indian Cavalry.	691 Indian Infantry.

Captain E. G. T. Welch's *Compendium of Information regarding the Nasirabad Contonment* says (page 6) that the normal strength of the Nasirabad garrison is as follows:—

1 Field Battery.	1 Regiment Indian Infantry.
6 Companies of British Infantry.	1 Squadron Indian Cavalry.

The garrison at Nasirabad in 1939 A. D. consisted of one British Infantry Battalion, the Lincolnshire Regiment, and the 10th Battalion of 6th Rajputana Rifles. The last was a purely training Battalion, where all recruits for the 6th Rajputana Rifles were trained. Attached to it were Indian Supply Depot, the Military Engineers' Services, the Indian Military Hospital and the Military Veterinary Hospital. Nasirabad was a Brigade Head-quarters till the year 1927-28; since when, it is only a Military Station under Mhow. There are Sanitary Camping grounds round Nasirabad as under:—

Nos. 1, 2 and 3 at Jharwasa, about five miles on the Neemuch road to east.

No. 4 beyond the race course, about two miles on the Neemuch road to east.

No. 5 beyond Artillery Hill, about one and half miles on the Neemuch road to west.

No. 6 to west of the Cavalry Hospital.

The camps at Jharwasa have never been acquired by Government, though used when needed. Nos. 4, 5, and 6 are in Cantonment limits.

The Native Cavalry lines are constructed to accommodate one squadron, and have also the required subsidiary buildings. They are of the old pattern, but in fair order.

HOSPITALS—There is one hospital for British troops, known as the 'Station Hospital.' It consists of two blocks, each double-storeyed, connected by a covered way, and standing in a small but neat garden. Outside the compound is a patchery on the north-west, which has been converted into wards. These buildings give accommodation for 106 men. There is also a womens' hospital attached, affording accommodation to eight women and children, total 114 beds.

There are two hospitals for Indian troops, one for Infantry and one for Cavalry, the former being at the south end, the latter at the north end of Camp, about two miles apart. The Infantry hospital consists of two large wards with accommodation for 48 beds. The Cavalry hospital has one large ward and gives accommodation for twelve beds. Both are supplied with the regulated subsidiary buildings.

BUNGALOWS: "The bungalows for military occupation in Nasirabad are fairly good, but most of them, though affording sufficient accommodation, are very old, thatched, and constructed of mudbricks. One or two only are of stone and have flat stone roofs. Rents are not excessive; indeed, are reasonable as compared with other stations, where the houses are worse. Excluding public buildings, there are fifty three bungalows for European residents."

Nasirabad is dependent on the arsenal at Mhow. The Field Battery has a regimental soldiers' garden attached to it, and the European Infantry has a garden and an Institute.

FIRE ENGINES: There are three fire-engines, the Royal Artillery, the British Infantry, and the Indian Infantry each having one.

RIFLE RANGES: The Rifle ranges of the British and Indian Infantry are side by side facing north, and are distant three-fourths of a mile from the British barracks, and one and a quarter mile from the Indian Infantry Lines. The Indian Cavalry carries on its practice on whichever range may be available.

ARTILLERY RANGE: The Royal Artillery use a piece of land near the village of Bulwanta as a range for the annual practice, the spurs of the Aravalli hills forming an excellent stop-butt and permitting change of site. Notice has to be given to the Civil authorities previous to the commencement of the practice.

COMMISSARIAT AND TRANSPORT: With a European garrison of only moderate strength, the Commissariat Department is on a small scale. The greater portion of the supplies are obtained by contract, but bread is made and issued under departmental arrangements, the flour being procured from the Government mill at Mhow. Fresh vegetables are also supplied departmentally from a garden of about sixteen acres, situated west of the barracks and leased from the Cantonment for Rs. 100 per annum. Should the interests of Government, through contract rates running very high, nècessitate the measure, the department undertakes all supply. The following is the strength of

The Army Transport	...	Pack mules ...	20.
		Draught mules ...	20.
		A. T. Carts ...	10.
The Ambulance Transport	...	Mate	1.
		Dooly-bearers ...	32.

The Executive Commissariat Office is located in a hired bungalow in the absence of a public-building. The Executive Commissariat Officer also resides there. The Commissariat stores are situated at the south-east end and very near the sudder Bazar. The accommodation is ample for all requirements. The cattle-pens and sheep-folds are conveniently placed a few hundred yards towards the south-east of the store rooms. The commissariat slaughter-yard is also a short distance in an easterly direction from the cattle-pens. The bakery is situated close to and east of the Artillery barracks.

STACK-YARDS: There are two stack-yards, one for the artillery on the plain facing the Artillery barracks and enclosed by a kutcha stone wall. Precautionary arrangements against fire are carried out. The other is near the Commissariat cattle-pens, and is enclosed by a mud bank and hedge. Here, hay is stacked for commissariat and transport cattle requirements, fire precautions being duly taken.

The Transport Lines are on the east of the sudder bazar, a few hundred yards due north of the Commissariat

Store-yard. A portion of the Cattle Lines is now in charge of the police.

WATER SUPPLY: The water-supply for the troops is derived from the Danta wells which are in charge of the Military Works Department. The Danta wells are situated in a nullah about four miles from Camp to the east of the Ajmer road.

PARADE GROUNDS: Within Camp limits, the ground available for the exercise of the troops is as in margin.

1. General Parade Ground.
2. The Regimental Parade Grounds.
3. Royal Artillery.
4. British Infantry.
5. Indian Artillery.

The General Parade ground affords ample space for all ordinary exercise parades, and no restrictions exist to manoeuvring troops of all arms beyond its limits, care only being required at certain seasons to avoid injuring such cultivation as is here and there found. Long distances can be traversed, the whole of the country for miles being of such open nature. As already stated, it, however, affords little opportunity for tactical display, and positions for attack and defence are not very suitable. When Field Firing is to be carried out, intimation has to be given to the Commissioner of Ajmer, the various grounds being beyond Cantonment limits. There is a pit near the cantonment plantation which permits of the troops being instructed in escalading.

The approximate cost of military buildings at Nasirabad including Royal Artillery Lines, European Infantry Lines, Station Hospital buildings etc., was estimated in 1892 A.D. at Rs. 22,12,869.

The earliest description of the Nasirabad Cantonment is to be found in Bishop Heber's *Narative of a Journey Undertaken in the Upper Provinces of India.* Writing in 1825 A.D., Bishop Heber says:[1]

"The Cantonments are very regular and convenient, the streets of noble width, and there are a sufficient number of stunted parkinsonia about the gardens to save the view from the utter nakedness which is usually seen in Rajputana. Many wells and two or three large tanks have been constructed since the English fixed here; but most of the water is brackish. Garden vegetables thrive well, though the soil is light, and the rock is very near the surface. In contradiction to all I had been previously told, I find that Nasirabad is, even now, perhaps the healthiest station in India; and the climate is pleasant at all times except during the hot winds."

1. Vol. II, p. 50, (1849 edition).

He adds; "I have not, in all India, met with a better informed, a more unaffected and hospitable society."[1]

The Civil Station attached to the Cantonment is a fairly large town, the population being 21,397.[2] The Cantonment Committee is in charge of all Municipal requirements, the executive work being disposed of by an Executive Officer. The judicial work—civil and criminal—of the Civil Station is disposed off by officers of the Ajmer-Merwara judicial department, the civil work by the Sub-judge, Beawar, and the criminal work by the Assistant Commissioner of Ajmer.

The Cantonment committee consists of three members, two military officers and a representative of the Bazaar. The Officer Commanding the Station is *ex-officio* President, and the Cantonment Executive Officer acts as Secretary of the Committee.

The Scottish Presbyterian Mission have a church, a High School for boys and an Orphanage. There is a good hospital for women, and a lady doctor is in charge. There is a Post Office and a Telegraph Office, a Freemason's Lodge, and an Ice Factory. An electric Power House having been established in 1937, the whole station is now electrified.

Owing to the scarcity of water, and the war with Germany, the Cantonment was temporarily abandoned early in 1940 A.D. The English troops returned to England, and the Rajputana Rifles left for Delhi in May. Thus, for the first time since 1818, Nasirabad was left without any troops. New troops, however, arrived in September.

1. "When ladies and gentlemen go out to dinner parties, they send their own chairs as well as their own plates, knives, and forks, a custom borrowed from the camp, and very sensible and convenient. At church also, every body was to bring their own chairs; but as the soldiers had very few of them anything like a seat, I begged that the ladies and gentlemen would send what supply they could spare for their use. A curious muster was accordingly made of all chairs in the cantonment, but there were still more people than seats,"——*Narrative*, Vol. II, p. 51. (1849 edition).

2. Including the Military.

CHAPTER XXVIII

B. B. & C. I. RAILWAY METRE GAUGE

THE advent of the Railway to Ajmer resulted in an enormous increase of its population and the physical development of the city. The population of Ajmer when the British took it in 1818, was 24,000. After fifty-four years of British rule, it was only 35,111 in 1872 A. D. Suddenly it rose to 48,735 in 1881 on the advent of the Rajputana State Railway; and on the transfer of the Railway Workshops and Offices from Agra to Ajmer in 1886-87, the population rose to 68,849 in 1891. Thus the population was doubled by the Railway. It has since 1891, during the last forty-eight years again risen by 80%, partly owing to the extension of Works connected with the Railway.

Till 1873, there was no railway in the whole of Rajputana. Agra and Ahmedabad were the two terminii of the two Broad-gauge lines, the E. I. R. and B. B. & C. I. Railway, near the borders of Rajputana. Government resolved to connect the two with a metre-gauge line called the Rajputana State Railway. Work began on the Agra side. From Agra to Bharatpur, the line was finished on 20 October, 1873. It came to Ajmer on August 1st, 1875 A.D. and was taken to Nasirabad on February 14th, 1876.[1] Nasirabad was thus connected with Agra in 1876. The Railway runs through Ajmer-Merwara north-east to south-east. On December 1st, 1881, the Malwa Branch permitting through communication between Ajmer and Khandwa was finally opened, sections of this line having been opened from 1874 onwards, and the whole system came to be called the Rajputana Malwa Railway.

An interesting fact connected with the advent of the Railway to Ajmer is that in the beginning, fare was not charged on the number of miles travelled but per station.[2] First Class fare from one station to the next station was eight annas; second class four annas and third class one and a half anna; and so on for every station. There were in the beginning twentyseven stations from Agra to Ajmer and the first class fare was Rs. 13-8-0 and the third class Rs. 2-8-6.

1. M. Jwala Sahai's *Waqai Rajasthan*, p. 137 (1878 A.D.). 2. Ibid, p. 127.

The Railway has greatly stimulated trade, and enriched one community immensely. The Khadims of Durgah Khwaja Sahib, who were a very poor community, have after the coming of the Railway, become a most prosperous and rich community;[1] and the Khadim *muhalla*, the part of the city where they live, once a sparsely populated muhalla of small houses and huts, has now become the most congested part of Ajmer with tall buildings. The chief means of livelihood of the Khadims is the offerings and presents made by Muslim pilgrims, who owing to the Railway, now come to the Dargah in large numbers all the year round, and flock to it during the annual *Urs Fair*.

Ajmer is the head-quarters of the B. B. & C. I. Railway, metre-gauge system. It was originally a State Railway and worked as such till 31 December 1884, when it was handed over to the B. B. & C. I. Railway Company on a contract which terminates on 31st December 1942 A.D., when the Government will again take up the management. The fact that it has sixteen independent administrative offices with officers and several thousand clerks, and workshops with seven thousand workmen, shows what major part the Railway plays in the life and activities of Ajmer. Apart from the large numbers, who live within the walled town, the extended suburbs of Ajmer, except the Mayo College, the Gunj outside the Agra Gate, the Civil lines and the Cavendishpura, are all populated by about thirty to forty thousand people who are either Railway servants and their dependants or caterers to them, or connected with them in one way or another.

The principal Railway buildings in Ajmer are:—

Railway Institute	built in	1878	A.D.
Railway General Offices	" "	1884	"
Railway Station (ground floor)	" "	1885	"
Railway Hospital	" "	1890	"
Bisset Institute	" "	1909	"
Railway Power House[2]	" "	1924	"

The following have their offices in Ajmer.

The Engineer in Chief.
The Traffic Superintendent.
The Deputy Chief Auditor.
The Treasurer, Metre-Gauge.
The Assistant Watch and Ward Superintendent.
The Compilation Officer.

1. Dyers have also greatly benefitted, as large quantities of cloth dyed in Ajmer is now exported to the U. P., Punjab, Central Provinces, Malwa and Bombay.
2 Cost, Rs. 13,00,000.

The Commercial Officer.
The Medical Officer.
The Superintendent of Stores.
The Divisional Electrical Engineer.
The Deputy Superintendent, Railway Police.
The Signal Engineer.
The Superintendent Railway Telegraphs.
The Executive Engineer.
The Loco and Carriage and Wagon Superintendent.

Trade has been stimulated by the Railway. Trade returns for 1936 A.D. for Ajmer show:—

Imports.	Wagons.	Maunds.	Freight Charged.
Salt, Petrol, Charcoal, Timber, Fuel etc.. ...	2,908	...	Rs. 2,79,425
Grain and Seeds, Sugar and Jagree	...	4,23,389	„ 2,98,738
Grain	...	2,65,658	
Seeds	...	69,102	
Sugar	...	62,097	
Jagree	...	26,532	
Exports.	**Wagons.**	**Maunds.**	**Freight charged.**
Live Stock	258	...	Rs. 15,555
All other goods	...	89,100	„ 83,822
			Rs. 99,377
Total Rail-borne Traffic ...	3,166	5,12,489	Rs. 6,77,540

The town of Beawar is a distributing centre for Mewar and Marwar. Its total imports (1938 A.D.) of all commodities was 7,91,236 maunds.[1] The imports and exports of cotton and wool were:

			Imports	Exports
Cotton	....	Maunds	1,00,946	Nil.
Wool	....	„	70,541	85,628

Taking an average of twelve months, October, 1936 to September 1937, the total amount of money received daily from the various metre-gauge Railway stations in the Railway cash Office was Rs. 1,14,128/-.

RAILWAY WORKSHOPS.

The Locomotive, and Carriage and Wagon Shops are the largest industrial works in Ajmer-Merwara. At one time, they

1. According to Mr. La Touche's *Gazetteer*, p. 49, the imports and exports by road were estimated at Rs. 23,19,170 and Rs. 19,27,090 respectively, as there was no Railway then.

employed nine thousand men. In July 1938, they employed 6,947 men and ten Officers: Loco. Shops. Carriage Shops.

	Loco. Shops.	Carriage Shops.
	3,632	3,315

OFFICERS: In addition to the Loco. and Carriage Superintendent and his Deputy, who arè common to both the shops, there are:

		Loco.	Carriage.
Other Officers	....	4	4
Foremen and Assistants	....	30	17
Chargemen	....	114	100

The total monthly wages for July 1938 paid to workmen was Rs. 2,54,706 and to Chargemen, Rs. 74,106.

The building of the Loco. and Carriage and Wagon shops began in 1877 A.D. and completed towards the end of 1879. They do all work of repairing and renewing locomotives, carriages and wagons of the B. B. & C. I. Railway (Metre Gauge Section). The housing of the Stores Department was separated in 1881 to a new site, and the Carriage and Wagon Department was separated and moved to their present site in 1884 A. D. Additions were made in 1885, and new buildings were put up for the Foundry, Smithy, Wheelshop, Boilershop and other shops.

LOCOMOTIVE SHOPS: The Loco. shops occupy an area of 32½ acres of which the covered area is fourteen acres. These shops employed 4,000 men in 1936 and are the only shops in India in which Locomotive building is carried on. This work began in 1896, and upto November 1937 A.D., 375 engines were constructed. Fifteen new engines per annum are built to meet the needs of replacements. The shops also manufacture parts for the Signal and Engineering departments of the Railway, and a certain amount of work is also done for other Railways. Owing to reorganization, there has been reduction in the number of daily paid men.

The work in the Loco. shops is divided into two branches: 1. Manufacturing and 2. Repairs.

1. The Manufacturing departments are:—

   (*a*) The Foundry. (*c*) The Machine Shop.
   (*b*) The Smithy and Forge. (*d*) The Tool Room.

2. The Repair Departments are:—

   (*a*) The Erecting Shop. (*c*) The Boiler Shop.
   (*b*) The Fitting and Repair Machine Shop. (*d*) The Coppersmith Shop.
   (*e*) The Millwright Shop.

The Boiler Shop turns out about twenty Boilers per annum.

The Locomotive Stores consists of several buildings, the main building being 162 by 80 feet, for the clerical staff and valuable metals It is under the Railway Stores Department and about sixteen thousand items are stocked in it.

The Home Board has recently sanctioned the building of Locomotives for Metre gauge lines in other parts of India, and nine locomotives are under construction for the A. B. Ry. That Locomotives can be built at Ajmer at a lower cost and of a quality, which is equal to the products of any of the first-class locomotive firms in Europe, speaks volumes in favour of the Locomotive shops at Ajmer.

CARRIAGE AND WAGON SHOPS: In the earlier years, the Workshops carried out repairs to all Rolling Stock, but constructed only bodies for coaches, the underframes and wagons being indented from abroad. Later on, with the introduction of more and better machinery, more and more parts of the complete vehicles were manufactured in the Work-shops, till now all the fittings of underframes and vehicles, with the exception of such fittings as axles, tyres, retaining rings, helical springs, commodes, wash-hand basins, and other patent stores, are manufactured from raw material, and complete carriages and wagons are built in the Workshops. Even Broad-Gauge coaching and goods stock have been built and made over to that system. The primitive types of carriages and wagons were four-wheelers, varying from 14′ to 18′, and bogies from 25′ to 40′ in length. Now, the length of four-wheeled stock is in some cases as much as 27′ for wagons, and 41′ in the case of bogie wagons, and 60′ in the case of bogie coaches.

Great improvements have been made and more facilities provided for the convenience of passengers. Latrines to suit Indian style with tiled floors and two water-taps have been provided in lower class carriges, while the upper class coaches have lavatories fitted with European type of commodes and wash-hand basins. Complete electrical equipment has replaced oil lamp lighting, and overhead water tanks to supply water to the latrines and lavatories have been fitted in the roofs ofc arriages.

The cost of a bogie third class carriage is about Rs. 23,000 that of a bogie first and second class is Rs. 36,000, that of a 43 ft. open wagon is Rs. 6,000, and that of a four wheeled covered wagon is Rs. 3,000.

The Carriage and Wagon Workshops comprise :—

1. Iron Underframes, bogies, wagon construction and repairs shop.
2. Wooden coaching and wagon bodies construction and repairs shop.
3. Tin and copper smith shop.
4. Painting and Trimming shop.
5. Blacksmith shop.
6. Millwright shop.
7. Steel Foundry. This is of the Tropenas process.
8. Machine shop.
9. Sawmill.

An electrically driven traverser facilitates transference of vehicles from one shop to another for immediate attention and enables more speedy outturn.

The maximum number of operatives employed in the Carriage and Wagon Workshop was 5,780 in the fiscal year 1926-27. Since then, due to Job Analysis and smaller capital programmes, the number has been reduced to 3,661. In 1887 at the opening of the Carriage and Wagon Workshop at Ajmer only some 500 men were employed. The average total amount paid on wages and salaries to the Workshop staff comes to Rs. 1,48,107/- per month in addition to the salary of the Administrative Officers and staff.

A feature of the Carriage and Wagon Workshop is the Chemical and Metallurgical Laboratory and Testing House. This was started in 1903 A.D., solely for the steel foundry work which had been started under Mr. Herbert, the steel chemist. Ajmer thus began producing steel for the first time in India (long before Messrs Tatas even thought of it). The Railway Company's attention was then turned to the problem of a suitability water supply for Loco. feed purposes. The Laboratory was therefore equipped with water analysis apparatus to test the suitability of water samples. Later, water softening plants were provided and at present eleven such plants are in operation on this Railway, producing about 500,006 gallons of softened water per day. This is the first Railway in India to instal a water-softening plant.

Besides the above work, the Laboratory carries out analysis and tests on a large variety of other material used in Railway work such as pigments, oils, coal, timber, greases, acids, disinfectants, butter, beverages, sewage cement, metals etc. Any material which can be subjected to a practical test is sent to this laboratory by the Controller of Stores for examination before placing final orders. The laboratory has recently been fitted with appliances for physical tests and a

RAILWAY GENERAL OFFICES, AJMER.

THE RAILWAY BISSET INSTITUTE, AJMER.

THE RAILWAY STATION, AJMER.

RAILWAY HOSPITAL, AJMER.

photomicrographic equipment has also been installed for examination of metal structure under very high magnification. The number of tests carried in 1936 was 16,000.

At a little distance from the Loco. shops, on the north side of the Martindale Bridge is situated, what used formerly to be the B. B. & C. I. Signal Manufacturing Workshops under the control of the Locomotive Superintendent, and employing about three hundred men. The work undertaken in these Shops included maintenance and the manufacture of signalling material and work in connection with points and crossings for the Metre Gauge section. From about the year 1935 A.D., manufacturing work has been stopped, and the Shop is used now for reconditioning signalling and interlocking apparatus and is known as the Signal Inspector, Ajmer Workshop.

THE RAILWAY STATION: The Railway Station, Ajmer is a commodious building with four well furnished retiring rooms for travellers on one side, on the first floor and the Station Master's quarters on the other. There are separate first class and second class waiting rooms for ladies and gentlemen and a refreshment room where European food is served.

RAILWAY HOSPITAL

The B. B. & C. I. Railway Hospital was built in Ajmer in the year 1890. At that time it was only a small Dispensary with one Assistant Surgeon, one Sub-Assistant Surgeon and two Dispensers. The Civil Surgeon, Ajmer was the Consulting Surgeon for this Hospital. With the exception of a small dressing room at the back of the Hospital, no addition was made to it till the year 1921. In the year 1910, it had its first Medical Officer, Dr. T. S. Jackson, who brought this Dispensary to the status of a Hospital. In the year 1914, it consisted of the old block only which has since been contructed into the present general and private wards, the matron's office, major operation room and the X-Ray room. In 1914, there were only two bungalows for the Assistant Surgeon and the Sub-Assistant Surgeon, and a block of twelve units for Dispensers and other low paid staff. There were only one Assistant Surgeon, one Sub-Assistant Surgeon, one Relieving Sub-Assistant Surgeon, one peon, one mali, two compounders, one Ward orderly, one shop cooly, one watchman and one sweeper. There was at that time only one General Offices Branch Dispensary attached to this Hospital. Later, another branch was opened for the benefit of the Railway employees residing in the city, which is called the Station Branch Dispensary and is situated near the Railway Luggage Office. An Ajmer Railway Hospital Samaritan Fund to give assistance to poor Railway employees, and extra comforts to very poor patients was also started. The following additions were made to the building in the year 1921 A.D. :—

(1) Out-patients block. (2) Indian surgical ward. (3) Bacteriological Laboratory. (4) X-Ray installation. (5) kitchen for European inpatients. (6) New quarters for Assistant Surgeon, Sub-Assistant Surgeons, compounders, ward orderlies and other staff.

The next improvement effected was the addition of an electrical lift in the year 1925. In the year 1927, two Indian private wards were generously presented by Khan Bahadur Ardeshir R. Dalal. In the year 1931, five units private wards were added. A dhobi ghat was added in 1937. Nine units of ward orderlies quarters and a compounder's quarter were added in 1936 and 1937 respectively. In the year 1937, two more Indian private wards was given by Khan Bahadur A. R. Dalal.

Since its foundation there have been the following Medical Officers in charge of this Hospital :—

Dr. T. S. Jackson.	Dr. E. Clarke,	Dr. R. A. Heatley.
„ A. Noble.	„ R. V. Clayton.	„ S. S. Banker.
„ S. A. Wilkinson.	„ C. D. Newman.	„ F. B. Khambatta.

At present this hospital is well equipped and compares very favourably with those of other Railways in India and gives the following amenities :—

Outdoor treatment. Indoor treatment. X-Ray examinations. Anti-rabic treatment. Bacteriological examination. Ultra-Violet rays treatment.

The statistics are as follows :—

Year.	*Inpatients.*	*Outpatients..*
1909	153	11,275.
1919	216	26,765.
1929	625	31,420.
1937	1,054	36,399.
1938	903	35,996.

At present the staff consists of the following :—

1. Medical Officer.	4. Clerks.	1. Naik,
2. Assistant Surgeons.	1. Matron.	2. Peons.
3. Sub-Assistant Surgeons.	2. Nursing Sisters.	21. Ward orderlies.
	5. Nurses.	1. Dispensary servant.
6. Dispensers.	1. Motor driver.	1. Indian Ayah.

and twelve servants, cooks, dhobees, sweepers &c.

The number of beds is as follows :—

Ward.	*No. of beds.*	*Ward.*	*No. of beds.*
European Male Ward	... 8.	Indian Medical Ward	... 8.
„ Female Ward	... 6.	„ Surgical „	... 12.
Private Wards	... 2.	„ Private „	... 4.
Isolation „	... 2.	Verandahs	... 8.
Total	... 18	Total	... 32.

The annual expenditure of this Hospital is approximately Rs. 1,19,000/-

The Railway has built two Institutes to provide amenities and recreation for its employees; the Railway Institute situated near the Loco. Shops for its European and Anglo-Indian employees, and the Bisset Institute for the Indians.

THE RAILWAY INSTITUTE

The Ajmer Railway Institute is an old established club which came into existence when the metre gauge Workshops were moved from Agra to Ajmer. On 1st December 1881, the Malwa section, then known as the Holkar-Scindia Neemuch State Railway, was extended to Ajmer, and formally opened by the Governor of Bombay. A ball on a very large scale was held in one of the newly built loco. sheds, specially arranged for the purpose, as the Institute building as it then existed, was much too small.

Since then various improvements in the building and grounds have been made from time to time. The grounds are extensive and include four Tennis Courts, a Bowling Green. A Recreation Ground (for Football, Hockey, etc.) with a large pavilion, a separate Hockey Ground and a Miniature Rifle Range. Inside the building a Cinema (Talkie) provides shows twice weekly; a circulating library, reference library and current periodicals are available in the large Reading Room and General Lounge; a Billiard Room with three tables caters for billiards, snooker, etc.; a Card Room is also available; the Bar is well equipped, having a large refrigerator and a well furnished Lounge as well as a 'High Stool Bar'. The main hall has an excellently sprung dance floor and a large stage; a smaller hall is available for indoor games, lectures, religious services etc.

Membership is some 275 persons and includes a few non-railway members, all of whom are elected at a Committee meeting. The affairs of the Institute are managed by a Committee consisting of :—

President (usually the Loco. and Carriage Superintendent).
Vice-President (usually a Railway Officer),
Bar Manager.
Honorary Treasurer.
Honorary Auditor.
and eight members.

The officebearers, and half the number of members are elected by the general body, the other members being nominated by the President. The Secretary is appointed by the Committee. Sub-committees carry on the following :—

Tennis, Library, Bar, Billiards, Entertainments.

The main committee meets monthly, and an annual general meeting is held to receive the report and accounts of the past year. The annual income is variable, but may be considered as about Rs. 20,000/- made up of subscriptions, hire of hall, profits from Bar, entertainments, etc. Expenditure is also a variable item and when no large special expenditures occur, is about Rs. 18 000/- per annum, covering pay of staff, cost of library, new books, papers, repairs to billiard tables etc.

The Bowling Green is a sub-club but with its own separate finances; similarly the Tennis and Indian games clubs. The Railway Institute and the Bowling Green are said to be amongst the finest of such institutions in India.

BISSET INSTITUTE

The Bisset Institute is situated on the Katchery Road where it joins the Mall Road and was built in the year 1909 A.D. The cost of the building etc. was Rs. 40 115/-. It is named after Col. W. S. S. Bisset, who was, at the time, Agent of this Railway. There are three Tennis courts as well as a Football and Cricket ground with a pavilion for spectators. There is also a Billiard room, a well-stocked Library and a reading room with a good supply of newspapers. There is a stage for theatrical shows in the main Hall. It is perhaps the biggest Indian club, in Ajmer and is meant for the Indian employees of the B. B. & C. I. Railway. It affords all the recreation and social amenities one can reasonably expect in an up-country station.

POWER HOUSE: The original power supply for electrical operation of Railway plant consisted of a small power house located in the Railway Carriage shops about 1906. The plant installed comprised Babcock and Wilcox water tube and Loco. type boilers and five reciprocating non-condensing steam sets, totalling 625 K. W. Subsequently when the advantages of electrical drives were appreciated, the adjacent Loco Workshops were installed with electric motors, and supply given from the Carriage Shops Power house. In 1620, the Railway staff quarters in Ajmer were equipped with electric lights and fans. In 1924, a new Railway Power House was built, on a new site off the Nasirabad Road, it being justified by a steadily increasing load over years and the more economical results obtainable from modern plant.

The new plant consisted of four Babcock and Wilcox water tube boilers operating at 200 lbs/0 pressure and two Fraser and Chalmers impulse type turbine sets, each driving 1,000 K W., G. E. C. 460 volt D. C. generators through reduction gearing. Condensers operating with a spray cooling pond were fitted, water supply being taken from the Ajmer Municipality. Results obtained by the new plant gave approximately 16 lbs. of steam per unit generated against 33 lbs. of steam per unit generated in the Carriage Shops Power house. The new plant generally has given satisfactory results, and the present day cost per unit generated is As. 0·5 per unit. In 1939 the maximum load was 1,200 K. W., and the monthly total units generated 1,73,685. In 1939, a bulk supply from the Ajmer Electric Supply Co. was arranged to deal direct with the distant Railway Cantonment load and also with the small Week-end and night Railway Workshops load. This enabled some reduction to be made in the operating costs of the Railway Power House as plant could be shut down at times of non-economical load.

All Railway workshop plant operates on 440 volts D. C., and a load during workshop hours of 600 K, W. in the Loco. Shops, and 400 K. W. in the Carriage Shops is daily carried on the present Railway Power House. Electrically operated pumps in wells and industrial motors in the smaller Railway Workshops are also installed.

WELFARE WORK.

The Ajmer Railway Welfare Centre was started in January 1927, and since then it has been, gradually enlarged, and there are now eight sub-centres. It is situated near the Loco. Workshop and has a staff of three trained midwives and one probationer nurse. It is governed by a committee consisting of the Medical Officer as President, an official's wife as Honorary Secretary, an Honorary Treasurer and one or two employees or wives of Railway employees from each Department in Ajmer. Its main functions are :—

Pre-natal work.
Midwifery.
Post-natal work.
Advise to mothers.
Care of children.
Distribution of milk.

During the last nine years :

Milk supplied free	...	...cost Rs.	12,773
Milk supplied at reduced rate	...	...cost „	6,450
Number of births	...	...	706
Children attended	...	...	835
Vaccinations	...	...	859
Anti-natal cases	...	...	673
Confinements at home	...	...	459
Confinements at the Clinic	...	...	55

There is also an arrangement, whereby difficult cases may be sent to the Church of Scotland Womens' Mission Hospital, Ajmer if a lady doctor is required.

PART IV

PUSHKAR AND MERWARA.

CHAPTER XXIX

PUSHKAR

SEVEN miles to the west of Ajmer, and separated from it by the Nag Pahar (Serpent Mountain), lies the sacred lake of Pushkar. An excellent road[1] constructed by Mr. Macnaughten, Superintendent of Ajmer, in 1840 A.D., connects it with Ajmer.

The town of Pushkar is picturesquely situated on the lake, with hills on three sides: on the fourth side, the sands, drifted from the plains of Marwar, have formed a complete bar to the waters of the lake, which has no outlet, though the filtration through the sand hills is considerable. "The town and lake of Pushkar form a romantic scene. The form of the lake is irregularly elliptical," says Dr. R. H. Irvine.[2] The lake is fed from the Nag Pahar. Bathing ghats have been constructed round the lake. Till recently, water lilies, yellow, pink and white, filled the lake.

SANCTITY: Pushkar is the most sacred place of the Hindus in India. It is the "king of sacred places", just as Benares is their "*guru* or preceptor." Col. Tod says: "Pushkar is the most sacred lake in India: that of Mansarovar in Tibet may alone compete with it in this respect."[3] No pilgrimage to Badri Narain (Himalayas), Jagan Nath (Orissa), Rameshwara (near Ceylon), Dwarka (Kathiawar), the four principal Hindu places of pilgrimage, is complete till the pilgrim bathes in the sacred waters of Pushkar. The ashes of well-to-do Hindu residents of Rajputana are either entrusted to the sacred waters of the Ganges or consigned to this holy lake.

The *Rajputana Gazetteer* says: "According to ancient charters, no living thing is allowed to be put to death within the limits of Pushkar",[4] on account of its great sanctity.

1. Dr. Irvine's *General and Medical Topography of Ajmer*, page 48. (A.D. 1841.) "The road passes through a defile on the far side of the range of mountains seen from the pavilions on the Ana Sagar."—Caine's *Picturesque India*, page 82.

2. *Medical Topography*, p. 49. In old days, the road to Pushkar lay by the village Kharekdi, round the southern end of Nag Pahar. The path made by Seth Daulat Mal exists across the hill. In 1840 A.D., a rock was cut asunder, and a cart road constructed. The road has since been greatly improved.

3. Tod's *Rajasthan: Personal Narrative*, chapter XXIX.

4. C. C. Watson's *Gazetteer of Rajputana*, Vol. II, p. 70.

Special sanctity attaches to an immersion in the waters of this lake, during the last five days of the month of Kartik, which falls in October or November, when people from distant places come in large numbers to Pushkar. A cattle fair is also held during this period, and a great trade is done in horses, camels and the famous Nagor bullocks. This is one of the principal cattle fairs in Upper India.[1]

Emperor Jahangir, in his *Tuzake Jahangiri*, says that "he had the lake measured round, and it was about one and half *Cos* (3 miles)."[2]

The Ajmer-Merwara District Board levies a road cess on all pilgrims and visitors to Pushkar, amounting yearly to from seven to eight thousand rupees.

Antiquity of Pushkar

Pushkar is one of the oldest places in India. Its antiquity has not yet been properly investigated, and it is difficult to say with any certainty when Pushkar first came into existence.

During the rains, people sometimes find here punch-marked Hindu coins, which are held to be the most ancient of Indian coins, as being of a date anterior to the fourth century B. C.; also Bactrian, Greek, Kshatrapa, and Gupta silver coins. These show that Pushkar was in existence in the fourth century B. C. Several kinds of silver and copper *Gadiya* coins; coins of Samantdeva, Ajaideva, and his queen Somaldeva, Someshwara, and Prithviraja's copper coins, as well as Pathan and Mughal coins are also found here.

1. At the last Fair in November 1940, owing to a severe famine in Rajputana, fewer cattle came to Pushkar. The sales were as below:

		For sale.	Sold.	Government sales-tax.
Horses	...	1,396	508	1,711-12-0
Cattle	...	9,273	5,920	11,714- 0-0
Camels	...	9,159	5,915	17,745- 0-0
Total	...	19,828	12,343	Rs. 31,170-12 0

Prices fetched were as below :—

		Highest Rs.	Lowest Rs.	Average Rs.
Horses	...	625	6	69
Cattle	...	300	3	50
Camels	...	300	10	77

Total sales amounted to Rs. 7,89,501-6-0.

2. *Tuzake Jahangiri*, Rogers, Vol. I, p. 255.

The Ramayana, the oldest epic poem in the world, mentions Pushkar, and says (*sarga* 62, *sloka* 28) that Viswamitra performed *tap* (devotion) here. It further says (*sarga* 63, *sloka* 15) that the *Apsara* Menaka came to Pushkar to bathe in its sacred waters.

The Mahabharata, whilst laying down a programme of Maharaja Yudhishtar's travels, says: "Maharaja, after entering the jungles of Sindh and crossing the small rivers in the way, you should bathe in Pushkar."

Inscriptions found in other parts of India show that this place was equally sacred to the Buddhists as to the Hindus. Four stone inscriptions of the second century B. C. in the Buddhist *Stupa* at Sanchi in Bhopal (Central India), mention the charitable donations made by Bhikshus Arhadina, Nagarakshita, Arya (venerable) Buddharakshita, Himgiri, Pusak and Isidata (a woman), all inhabitants of Pushkar. These inscriptions show that in the second century B. C., Pushkar was a populous town and a holy place.

A manuscript *Account of Ajmer and Jodhpur*, by one Gulam Qadir, written about 1830 A.D., says: "At Pohkur, near the Khut Mandir, is a stone with Sanskrit inscription of which the following is a translation. 'In the year S. 106 (A.D. 59) and twelfth day of the moon in *Asar*, the wife of Govind Brahmin, daughter of Vias Bikram burnt herself with her husband.' This inscription has disappeared and has not yet been traced.

An inscription of about 125 A.D. in the Pandu Lena Cave in the hills of Trirashmi, near Nasik (Bombay Presidency) says that Ushavdata, son of Dinik of the Shak dynasty, and son-in-law of the well-known King Nahpan of the Kshatrapa family, came to Rajputana, built a ghat on the Banas River, and in Pushkar gave in charity 3,000 cows and a village. This shows that the sanctity of Pushkar in the second century A.D. was as great as it is to-day.

The oldest inscription found in Pushkar itself is of the time of King Durgaraja, and is dated the year 925 A.D., which was presented to the Rajputana Museum, Ajmer, in 1909 A.D. A later inscription containing no date, but of the time of King Vakpati Rai, probably the Chauhan King of Ajmer (about 1000 A. D.) found in Pushkar, is in the Rajputana Museum.[1] In September 1910 A.D. during a further search for inscriptions, we discovered an

1. Both these inscriptions were found by the author of this book and Mahamahopadhyaya P. Gauri Shanker Ojha during a search for inscriptions at Pushkar.

inscription dated 1187 A.D. on a *Sati* pillar in the temple of *Ashtotar shat-ling Mahadeva.*

The famous Harsha Temple inscription of 973 A.D. in Shekhawati (Jaipur State), mentions the grant by the Chauhan King Sinharaja of four villages to the temple of Harshanath after a bath in the Pushkar.

The epic poem, *Prithviraja Vijaya*, written in the twelfth century A.D., dilates on the sacred character of the place, and mentions a celebrated temple of Ajagandha Mahadeva, which does not appear to be in existence now, unless it is the temple now known as the temple of Atmateshwara Mahadeva, the under-ground storey of which appears to be very old.

Origin of Pushkar

The origin of Pushkar is thus given in the *Padma Puran* of the Hindus: Brahma, the Creator of the world was in search of a suitable place to perform a *yagna* according to the Vedas. As he reflected, the lotus fell from his hand, and he resolved to perform the sacrifice where it fell. The lotus, rebounding, struck the earth in three places; water issued from all the three, and Brahma descending, called the name of the place Pushkar, after the lotus. The three places are situated within a circuit of about six miles, and are called the *Jyeshtha* (elder) Pushkar, the *Madhya* (central) Pushkar and the *Kanishtha* Pushkar (younger Pushkar).

The *Jyeshtha* Pushkar is the place where Brahma prepared to perform his *yagna*. All the gods attended. As, however, no important function, religious or social, can be performed amongst the Hindus by a man unless he is joined in it by his wife,—for according to Hinduism, a man and his wife both together form one entity, and the one without the other always remains only a part, and not a whole—Brahma had to wait for his wife *Savitri*, to begin the *yagna*. Savitri would not come without Lakshmi (wife of Vishnu), Parvati (wife of Siva), and Indrani (wife of Indra), whom the god *Pavan* (air) had been sent to summon. As the auspicious hour was getting very near, and Savitri would not come unless accompanied by the other godesses, Brahma was angry and asked Indra to get him a girl whom he could marry and begin the *yagna*. Indra brought a *gujar's* daughter named Gayatri. Brahma married her and the *yagna* commenced. A demon appeared and interrupted the sacrifice, at the instigation of Siva. Eventually, Siva removed the interruption on the condition that he should also have a temple to himself at Pushkar. Savitri appeared as the sacrifice was nearing its end. Seeing Gayatri in her place, she became enraged; Brahma tried to pacify her, but did not succeed. She went away in a rage to the hill called *Ratna Gir* (the hill of gems), to the south of Pushkar, on which stands a temple dedicated to her. The largest and the most fashionable of the fairs of Ajmer is held here every year on *Bhadva Sudi 8th* (August).

History of Pushkar

With the rise of Buddhism, which was nothing more than a protest against priestly dominance and the tyranny of the caste system in Hinduism, Pushkar, like other sacred places such as Benares, Muttra, and Gaya, took up the cause of Reformation and soon became a stronghold of Buddhism. With the decline of Buddhism, Pushkar also declined, and for a time was cast into the shade. After sometime, a Jain Raja, Padam Sen[1] founded a city called Padmavati Nagri, which according to tradition contained a lakh of houses. It extended to where now stand the villages Surajkund, Galti, Bansli and Kishenpura. The rivers Nanda, Parachi and Saraswati supplied water to the city and added to its beauty. Tradition says that whenever, a worthy but poor person came to settle in the city, each family gave a rupee, and with the lakh of rupees as capital, the new-comer commenced business. Jains called it *Kokan Tirath* in those days. It prospered for long, but eventually the river overtook it. The cause given is that once a *yogi* came to the place and lived for twelve years in devotion. One day, he saw his disciple with a wound on his head. The disciple at first refused to explain the cause, but when pressed, stated that the city was populated only by Jains, who did not give alms to anybody who was not a Jain, and he, therefore, had to eke out his living by selling head-loads of jungle thorns. The yogi's indignation was roused so much so that owing to his curse, a tornado of wind and dust descended on the city and destroyed it.

1. One of the descendants of Raja Padmasen is said to have founded a town at the foot of the Taragarh Hill, Ajmer, called Inderkot, which survives as a *muhalla* of the city of Ajmer.

It was restored in the beginning of the ninth century A.D. by the famous Parihar king, Narhar Rao of Mandor (Marwar) who ruled over the whole of Hindustan from the Sindh to the confines of Bengal. It is said that one day while out hunting, he felt thirsty, and finding some water in a pool, he took up a little in his hands to drink, when he found that the white spots on his hands disappeared with the touch of the water. Raja Narhar Rao was surprised at this, and thinking that the water possessed great healing qualities, began to investigate the history of the place. Finding that once it was a sacred lake, he had the place cleared and the lake restored, by making an embankment on the side the water flowed. The Swaroop Ghat (Ghat of the body restored to seemliness) commemorates the event. He re-built old places so far as he could find them, and had twelve Dharmshalas (free resting places) and ghats on the three sides of the Pushkar lake built. Portions of some of these, known as Pariharon-ki-shala, still exist. One in a good condition stands on the Rai Mukand Ghat and is in the possession of some Kayasthas of Ajmer.

Later, the place came into the possession of the *gujars*. In 1157 A.D., however, a body of Sannyasis fell upon them on the night of the *Dewali*, and killing them all, restored the place to the Brahmins, and left their own representatives in five of the principal temples. Their descendants still preside in those temples.[1]

Temples

Pushkar is full of temples, great and small. It is famous for its temple of Brahmaji, which is the only important temple dedicated to Brahma, the Creator of the world, in India; and because of this, it is sometimes called *Brahma Pushkar*. Besides the temple of Brahmaji, the other old temples are those of the Savitri Mata, Badri Nath, Varahji and the Atmateshwara Mahadeva. Even these temples have been rebuilt or repaired in recent times.

VARAHJI TEMPLE: The temple of Varahji was built by King Arnoraja (1123-50 A.D.), who built the Ana Sagar lake at Ajmer, and executed repairs to the Pushkar lake. The temple was repaired in the time of Akbar, by Sagar, a

1. In the temple of *Atmateshwara Mahadeva*, Prag Jati was left. In *Varahji* temple a *Bharati Sannyasi*. In Badri Nathji temple, Gyan Nath, and in the temples of Brahmaji and Savitri, *Puri* Sannyasis were left.

brother of the celebrated Rana Pratap of Chitor. Jahangir in his *Tuzak-e-Jahangiri*, says: "There are numerous temples in Pushkar. One of them was built by Rana Shankar (Sagar), who is one of my chief nobles, at a cost of many lakhs of rupees.[1] The temple was pulled down by Aurangzeb, and appears to have been rebuilt by Maharaja Jai Singh II of Jaipur. The inscription on the pedestal of the image shows that the present image was installed in 1727 A.D.[2] Aurangzeb also broke an old temple of Kesho Rai near the *Gau* (Cow) *Ghat* and built a mosque in its place.

TEMPLE OF BRAHMAJI: This temple was rebuilt in S. 1866 (1809 A.D.) by Gokal Chand Parekh,[3] a minister of the Scindia, at a cost of Rs. 1,30,000. A stone inscription (in Hindi) in the possession of the Mahant of the temple, says that during the time of Maharaja Sawai Jai Singh (1699-1743 A.D.) a Brahmin lady named Bai Phundi, daughter of Purohit Girdhardas, and mother of Shambhu Ram of Jaipur, repaired the temple of Brahmaji in Pohkar on *Maha Sudi 5th*, S. 1776 (1719 A.D.).

Colonel Broughton, who visited Pushkar on the 1st February, 1810, says: "Pushkar is a place highly venerated by the Hindus, as Ajmer is by the Mussalmans. The town is situated on the shores of a romantic Pohkar or lake, from which it takes its name. It is at Pushkar alone that the image of Brahma, at least of any celebrity, is to be seen; this temple is close to the margin of the lake—small, plain and evidently very ancient. The image which is about the size of a man, has four faces and is in a sitting posture, cross-legged." The temple of Varahji, as it now stands, presents only the small remains of the ancient temple which was overthrown by the bigoted zeal of Aurangzeb, and is said to have been 150 feet in height and covered with the finest specimens of Hindu sculpture. The old walls to the height of about 20 feet were left entire, and have been covered in to form the present temple by Maharaja Sawai Jai Singh of Jaipur."[4]

TEMPLE OF BADRI NATHJI, was repaired by the Thakur of Kharwa (Ajmer) about 1800 A.D. The present TEMPLE OF ATMATESHWARA MAHADEVA was built by Goomanji Rao,

1. Roger's *Tuzake Jahangiri*, Vol. I, p. 254.
2. The *Rajputana Gazetteer* (Vol. II, page 69) says that Raja Dhiraj Bakht Singh repaired it. A small Hindi inscription on the lintel of the low door of the *Katera* says that it (the Katera) was built on Thursday, Asar Sudi 15th, S. 1842 (1785 A.D.) by Pandit Naru Govind Kulkarni.
3. *Medical Topography of Ajmer*, p. 50.
4. *Letters from a Mahratta Camp*, p. 258.

the Mahratta subedar of Ajmer (1809-1816 A. D.). The present TEMPLE OF SAVITRI was built by the *purohit* of Maharaja Ajit Singh of Marwar (1687-1724 A.D.).

Of the modern temples, the largest are: (1) Behariji Temple (2) The Srirama Vaikuntha Temple and (3) The Rangji Temple.

BEHARIJI KA TEMPLE, popularly known as Baiji ka Mandir, was built in S. 1892 (A.D. 1835) at a cost of five lakhs of rupees by Sri Sirahkanwar Bai, daughter of H. H. Maharaja Man Singh of Jodhpur and married to Maharaja Jagat Singh of Jaipur. It is called Baiji ka Mandir by the Badi Basti Brahmins, who are purohits of the Jodhpur Durbar, but Raniji ka Mandir, by the Chhoti Basti people who are purohits of the Maharaja of Jaipur. She is said mostly to have lived in Jodhpur. A garden, now in ruins, stood on six bighas of land attached to the temple. A village named *Padu* in Marwar was given for the upkeep of the temple. Some say that the Maharaja of Jodhpur gave this village; others say that the Rani gave this village, as she had received it in dowry from her father.

SRI RAMA VAIKUNTHA TEMPLE: This is the largest and the most imposing of the modern temples, and is situated at the entrance to the town of Pushkar. It belongs to the Srivaishnava sect of the Hindus, which was founded by Sri Ramanujacharya, who flourished in the eleventh century of the Christian era. The Vaishnavas and the Saivas—the worshippers of Vishnu and Siva—are the two principal sects to which most of the Hindus belong. Vaishnavism is divided into four sub-sects or Sampradayas—the Sri Vaishnava, the Vallabh, the Madhava and the Naibarak. The Sri Vaishnava Sampradaya was founded by Sri Ramanujacharya, who was born in 1016 A.D in Bhutpuri, Madras Presidency and preached in Srirangam near Trichnopoly. Srirangam is the principal seat of this sect. The Vallabh Sampradaya was founded by Vallabhcharya, and its chief seat now is Nathadwara near Udaipur in Rajputana. Madhvacharya was the founder of the Madhava Sampradaya, and its centre now is Udipi in South India. All these three sects originated in South India. The fourth, the Naibarak branch of the Vaishnavas originated in Northern India, and its chief seat is now Salemabad in the Kishengarh State in Rajputana.

In Pushkar, the two temples of the Ramanuja or Sri Vaishnava creed are (*a*) the temple of Sri Rama Vaikuntha and (*b*) the Rangji-ka-Mandir. The Sri Vaishnava Sampradya is divided into three principal branches, according as they follow the Jayakhyam, the Satavata and the Paushkara Samhitas of the Panchratra, sacred literature of the Vaishnavas. The Srirama Vaikuntha temple belongs to the Jayakhyam; and the Rangji-ka-Mandir to the Paushkar sect. There are slight differences of ritual between the three branches of Ramanuja Vaishnavism, as well as in the outward marks on the foreheads of their followers, which distinguish them. But the real difference is that the Jayakhyam is the original and orthodox creed, and its ritual is wholly in Sanskrit, while the ritual of the others is both Sanskrit and Tamil, as they attempted to reach the masses, who are all Tamil speaking people, while the Sanskrit is the language of the Pundits of Northern India. The Srirama Vaikuntha follows the Jayakhyam Samhita, which according to its followers, was first preached by Bhagwan to Narad Muni, who in his turn recited it to five Rishis at Prabhaskshetra in the province of Gujrat.

The *Viman* or *Gopuram* over the inner temple of Srirama Vaikuntha was built in accordance with the rules of architecture given in the Jayakhyam Samhita, as also the size and the shape of idols. The idol in this temple is *Paramurti*, and in the Rangji temple, *Vibhava*. The Viman is built of stone and contains signs (चिन्ह) of 361 gods or Devtas. In front of the inner temple or *Nijmandir*, stands the golden Garud Dhwaja Khambha, representing the *garuda*, the *Vahan* of Vishnu. In the yearly *Mahotsava*, this Dhwajakhambha is worshipped for ten days. One of the earliest mentions of *Garud Dhwaja* is to be found in the Bhilsa inscriptions of the second century A.D., which says, that a *Garud Dhwaja* was erected by Helliodoros, a Greek convert to Vaishnavism.

The outer Gopuram, built over the principal entrance of the temple is of brick and mortar, which admits of elaborate carving. This was also built and decorated by South Indian masons imported for the purpose. At the four corners of the temple, on the walls are placed four images of Garuda, to show that it is a Vaishnava temple.

The Srirama Vaikuntha temple contains one principal temple called the Vaikuntha Vanktesh, and eight other temples, (1) the Lakshmiji temple dedicated to the first wife of Bhagwan (2) the Godambaji, the second wife of Bhagwan, (3) Rughnathji (4) Srirangnath Bhagwan (5) Sudarshan Bhagwan, illustrating the Sudarshana Chakra of Sri Krishna (6) Vishvatsen, the Commander-in-Chief of Bhagwan's forces (7) Ramanuja Mandir and (8) Vedantdeshik, dedicated to the man who resuscitated and strengthened the Ramanuja cult four hundred years after it was founded.

The principal temple contains two idols: that of Bhagwan which was made in the temple by Dravid architects; and that of Lakshmi Narsingh which was brought from the village Ahobal in the Deccan by men who walked on foot from Ahobal to Pushkar with the idol, which journey took them six months. According to the creed of Jayakhyam, the approach to Bhagwan (God) is through his wife Lakshmi; while in the other branch, the approach is direct, and there is no mediator.

In the principal or Vaikunthvanktesh temple, worship is performed six times a day: in the remaining eight temples, only five times. The priests are all Dravid Brahmins. *Bhog* or food for all the nine temples is cooked in one common kitchen, and after presentation to the idols, is distributed morning and evening to people. On *Utsavas* (festivals) food is distributed three or four times a day.

The festivals or *Utsavas* observed every month in this temple are ten; the four Fridays, when the goddess Lakshmi is taken in procession to the garden attached to the temple; the two Ekadashis or the eleventh days of the two fortnights in the month; the fifteenth and the last day of the month; every Sankranti in the month, and the Revti and Satri nakhshtras, when the god too is taken round in procession. Three special festivals observed are : (1) *Hindolas* in the month of *Sravan* which last for fifteen days, and attract large crowds from Ajmer; (2) *Brahmaseva* in Chaitra, (March April) lasting ten days, which is the most important of all Utsavas; the third is the Kartik fair which lasts for six days.

There is a temple of Lakshminarain, situated outside the temple proper, but inside the compound of the Sriram Vaikuntha Temple. The compound contains several residential quarters and a garden, and occupies an area of about twenty bighas. The temple was built by Seth Magniram Bangar of the Maheshwari caste of Didwana, Marwar, at a cost of eight lakhs of rupees. The foundation of the temple was laid in S. 1976 (A.D. 1920), and it was finished in S. 1981, (A D. 1925).

In the compound, there is a small *pathshala* (school), where Sanskrit upto the Sastri degree, and Hindi are taught. About twenty boys attend the school. The annual expenditure of the temple is about Rs. 26,000 a year, for which a special fund has been created and set aside by the firm of Seth Magniram Bangar. No presents or offerings by worshippers or visitors are accepted by the temple.

SRI RANGJI TEMPLE, is the third important modern temple. It is also dedicated to Ramanuja Vaishnava worship. The priests of this temple are also Dravid (Madrasi) Brahmins. The followers of this sect, no matter to what caste they may belong, will sit together and take their food in the temple without observing any *Chauka system.*[1]

The Rangji temple was built in 1844 A. D., (S. 1901) by Seth Puran Mal. He had, before this, built two temples at Hyderabad, Deccan, where he had a flourishing business. These temples were called Sita Ramji temple and Viradh Raj Bhagwan. His Highness the Nizam donated a Jagir of two villages with an income of about Rs. 50,000 a year for maintenance of the temples. Out of this Jagir, Rs. 8,000 a year were allotted for the maintenance of the Pushkar Rangji temple. Later, the widow of the Nawab of Elichpur, when she came to Pushkar, gave two villages, Akoli and Bordi in the Akola district, for the temple. The Rao Raja of Sikar gave the village Rampura, and the Raja of Khetri, gave some land and wells to the temple. Seth Ram Lal, a descendant of Seth Puran Mal made all these properties his personal estate, and now his descendants give Rs. 100 a month for the maintenance of the temple.

One of the finest of the modern temples is THE MAHADEVA TEMPLE, raised over the remains of the Mahratta General, Jai Appa, who was assassinated near Nagor in 1756 A D. Of this temple, Colonel Broughton says:—

"Of the modern temples, the one dedicated to Mahadeva, is by far the most remarkable, for the elegance of its structure and the nature of its ornaments, of all the temples that Pushkar boasts of. It was built by Anaji Scindia, the grandfather of the present Maharaja (Daulat Rao). The image and the altar on which it is placed, are of fine white marble, highly polished and executed in a style superior to anything of the kind I have seen in India, The idol is *Panj Mukhi* or five faced, each face crowned with *jatta* or matted hair of the *uteet*." [2]

Other wellknown temples are (*a*) BHURIYA NARSINGHJI temple, built by the Seth of Kuchaman to the north of Sri Rangji Temple. Attached to it is a garden. (*b*) NARSINGHJI Temple built over the Narsingh *Ghat*, by the

1 People taking their food in the kitchen without touching each other is called the *Chauka* system.

2. *Letters from a Mahratta Camp*, p. 259. Colonel Broughton further says: "Besides the temple which I have described, the banks of the lake are covered with a number of smaller ones, Pavilions, Choultrees, etc., built by the neighbouring Rajas at various periods. Many of these buildings are at present nearly, and some of them altogether, immersed in the water, the springs of the lake having risen within the last six weeks to height beyond any that is on record. Some of the streets of the town are inundated, and the domes of the buildings upon the shore, with the trees about them, appear above the surface of the water at some distance in the lake."

Mahajans of Ajmer and Pushkar. (*c*) TONK KA MANDIR built by a *Mahajan* of Tonk. (*d*) NANAJI KA MANDIR, and (*e*) Ral Bahadur Harkishandas BHATAD'S TEMPLE. The temples by the Thakurs of Ras, Nimaj, Raipur, Riyan, Balunda, Babra, in Marwar; and Pisangan, Masuda and Tantoti in Ajmer, have large residential quarters attached to the temples, and are all situated in the sandy plain near Brahmaji Temple. Colonel Broughton also says :—

"A large building erected by Madhaji Scindia next attracted our notice. It contains images of Bhawani, Mahadeva, and some others of the Hindu deities, all of white marble, but executed in a manner very inferior to the one I have just described. The interior apartment is surrounded by a range of piazzas, also of marble, designed for the accommodation of the numerous Beragees or mendicants, who make pilgrimages to Pushkar; and for whose support, the revenues of ten small villages in the district were allotted by the illustrious founder."[1]

Ghats

Of the numerous ghats surrounding the lake, the best known are the Gau Ghat, the Varah Ghat, and the Brahma Ghat. The Gwalior Ghat. the Chandra and the Indra Ghats, the Jodhpur and the Kotah Ghats are of modern date; and are amongst the finest on the lake.

1. THE SARASWATI GHAT, is the first ghat, beginning from the north-east. There is no masonry work in the ghat and no steps: cattle drink water here.

2. RAJGHAT is the next ghat. It belongs to the Jaipur State. Upto 1870 A.D., the Pushkar purohits of the State were in charge of it. A grant of four villages, Tangwada, Banowda, Dholka and Mahajanpura were attached to it. Now, a state servant looks after the Ghat. Attached to it is the *Man Mandir*, a square cloistered building of brick and mortar built by Maharaja Man Singh of Jaipur. This memorial of the greatest man in Emperor Akbar's court—"to whom," says Col. J. Tod, "Akbar was indebted for half his triumphs,"—had been sadly neglected but has recently been

1. *Letters from a Mahratta Camp*, p. 259. After visiting Pushkar and the Dargah at Ajmer, Col. Broughton says :—

"We returned to camp in the afternoon, very highly pleased with our trip, and sensibly struck by the decency and civility of the Hindu priests, as contrasted with the clamorous, and almost insolent, demands of the Muhammadans at the Dargah."

repaired by the Jaipur State, the brighest page of whose history is the record of the exploits of Raja Man Singh.

"Let the eye embrace these extremes of his conquests, Cabul and the Paropamisus of Alexander, and Aracan (a name now well-known) on the Indian Ocean, the former re-united, the latter snbjugated to the Empire by a Rajput prince and a Rajput army."—Tod's *Rajasthan*, Vol. I, page 336.

3. The next ghat is the Kishangarh Ghat known as *Panch Vir Ghat* (Five Heroes Ghat). This ghat was originally built by the Jaisalmer State and was known as Jaisalmer ghat when built (M. Jwala Sahai's *Waqai Rajasthan*, p. 203). It is said that the Jaisalmer State being far away could not look after it, and placed it under the supervision of the Kishangarh State, which is near Ajmer. The origin of the ghat and its name is as under:—

In 1679 A.D., Aurangzeb demolished the *Keshoraiji* temple near the Gau Ghat at Pushkar and built a mosque in its place. When the mosque was finished, Tyber Khan, the Mughal Governor of Ajmer, came to Pushkar with one hundred cows to sacrifice them in the mosque. The Brahmins of Pushkar appealed to the neighbouring Rajput chieftains to prevent the slaughter. The Thakurs of Riyan, Alniawas, Govindgarh and others came with their men, and passing between the Pushkar lake and the Nag Pahar, came to the eastern bank of Pushkar. An engagement took place here between the Thakurs and Tyber Khan, in which the Thakurs of Alniawas, of Bajoli near Chandaroon (Marwar), of Manji, and T. Kesri Singh of Riyan, most of them Mertia Rajputs, were killed. Five of them died where this *ghat* stands. The Alniawas Thakur attacked and wounded Tyber Khan in the Varahji Temple.

The following couplet celebrates this event.

राजड़ गोकल रूपसी, चत्र हटी जगतेश ।
सुजो अणदो केशरी, नव रण रहया नरेश ॥

Translation: Rajad (Raj Singh) Gokal Singh, Rup Singh, Chatra Singh, Hati Singh, Jagat Singh, Suja (Suraj Singh), Anand Singh and Kesri Singh, nine chieftains were killed in the fight. Raj Singh was Thakur of Alniawas; Gokal Singh, of Bajole; Rup Singh, of Majis; Kesri Singh, of Riyan in Marwar.

The case of Thakur Kesri Singh of Riyan, is characteristic of the Mertia Rajputs and proves their heroism. When the messengers from Pushkar reached the town of Riyan, the dowager Thakurani asked the young Thakur, her son, 16 years of age, who had just been married, as to who would go from

Riyan to take part in the fight to rescue the cows. Kesri Singh said, his uncle was going. The mother said, "No, my son, the occasion demands that you should go." And the son went and was killed.

There is a tomb on the Ghat. A faqir lives there during the day. At 5 p.m. the ghat is locked by the Kishangarh man and the faqir goes away. On the ghat, there is a house called the Goron ki haveli (house of Gor Rajputs) also in the possession of the Kishangarh State. The faqir gets a *petia* (daily provisions) from the Kishangarh State.

4. The next ghat is the BUNGALOW GHAT said to have been built by the Mahrattas in 1812 A.D. It is so called as a bungalow built by a *gosayin* stands on it. Gokalpuri, Jagirdar of Chavandia is in possession of the ghat, and a servant of his, looks after it.

5. Adjacent to it is the KOT TIRTH GHAT also called "Chhatree Ghat," as a Chhatree on the remains of Jai Appa Scindia stands on it. An idol of Koteshwar Mahadeva stands on the ghat. Daulat Rao Scindia repaired the ghat at an expense of a lakh of rupees in S. 1872 (1815) A.D.). The tradition is that when Brahma performed the yajna to inaugurate Pushkar, he brought water of numerous *Tiraths* (places of pilgrimage) and poured it here. A grant of four villages Chavandia, Rampura, Nand and Harmara was made to maintain it. By an agreement dated 12th December 1860, three of the villages became British Khalsa and Chavandia remained with the ancestors of Gokalpuri Gosain as a grant for the maintenance of the ghat. The Gwalior Darbar gives Rs. 400/- a year for the upkeep of the Chhatree now. The British Government has given *Maafi* land in Suraj Kund (20 bighas), in Bansli (2 bighas) and some in Harmara.

6. SHIV GHAT is the next ghat called after Shivji (Mahadeva), who had been appointed by Brahma to keep the peace at the time of the *yajna*. The Mahratta subedar of Ajmer, Govind Rao, repaired it and at an expense of twenty-five thousand rupees, built a temple of Govindji on it, and a house. Govind Rao's purohits are in-charge now. maafi land, twenty-five bighas in Bandi. 150 bighas in Narwar (Kishangarh State), 25 bighas in Rampura (Srinagar circle), and 25 bighas in Ladpura (Marwar State) is attached to the temple and the ghat.

7. INDRA GHAT, called after the god Indra, whose temple stands on it. It was built by Bakshi Sunder Lal, Kayasth of Jaipur at an expense of fourteen thousand rupees

about S. 1908 (A.D. 1850). The land of this ghat was in the possession of some Brahmins, who were made priests of the temple in lieu of the land, they gave for the ghat and the temple.

8. CHANDRA GHAT was built by Sham Lal Kayasth, Naib Bakshi of Jaipur in S. 1908 (1850 A.D.). He installed an idol of Chandrama (Moon) on it.

A *Qabuliat* dated Ashad Vadi 5th, S. 1908 (1851) executed by Sunder Lal and Sham Lal, builders of these two ghats and filed in Civil Suit No: 42 of 1914, Court of Sub-Judge Ajmer, stating that they had built ghats at Pushkar with the permission of the Brahmins of *Chhoti Basti* shows, that the ghat had been built before *ashad*; s. 1908 (July A.D. 1851).

9. EKSO-ATH (108) MAHADEVA GHAT Kunj Behari and Rasak Behari Brahmins are in possession. A temple of 108 Siva stands on the ghat.

10. BANSILAL GHAT lies next to it. An old ghat was renovated in S. 1926 (A.D. 1869) by L. Bansi Lal, E.A.C. Ajmer. It is called after him.

11. VARAH GHAT evidently called after the famous Varahji temple in *Chhoti Basti*. A temple of Rameshwara, built by Brahmin Dataram about 200 years ago, stands on it.

This ghat was built by Raja Narhar Rao Parihar. He built also twelve *Dharmshalas* and twelve temples in Pushkar. Five of these *shalas* still exist on the Varah Ghat.

A Dharmshala built and endowed by the famous Queen Ahalyabai of Indore, called *Annakeshetra*, stands on it. One hundred and eight Brahmins were fed every day at the place when it was started. A temple called *Pachdevri* consisting of five small temples built by four peasants whose names are not remembered, at a cost of Rs. 4,000 in the time of Govind Rao, Mahratta Governor of Ajmer, about S. 1812 (A.D. 1755) stands on it. There is a Ganesh temple on the Ghat, some Maheshwari gentlemen built a Raghunathji temple on it, about 145 years ago.

12. MODIGHAT is the next ghat built by Modi Mahram of Kishangarh in S. 1820 (A.D. 1763). A temple of Murli Manohar was built along with the ghat. Modi Mahram gave the temple to his purohits, to whom the land of the ghat had belonged, and who are now priests of the temple. Maafi land at the villages of Oontra and Ararka in Ajmer, and Parasar in Kishangarh, and a Kunj (residential quarter) are attached to the temple.

13. NARSINGH GHAT called after the Narsinghji temple built on it, by the Maheshwari and Agrawala Mahajans of Ajmer at a cost of Rs. 12,000, about 270 years ago and given to the Mahant of the Narsinghji temple at Ajmer. It is maintained by offerings and presents.

14. VISHRAMGHAT with a temple of Siva on it, built byHindu Rao Mahratta, about 120 years ago. A *chhatree* of Sarji Rao Mahratta stands on the ghat. It was given away to Parmanand Dudhadhari, Jagirdar of Lilasevri. Jagir in the villages of Bhagwanpura, Lalikhera and Sawaipura is attached to the temple. A *haveli* (house) attached to the Ghat also belongs to the owner. A Bhandari Mahajan of Jodhpur built a large house called Bhandari-ki-haveli about 200 years ago and entrusted it to a woman mendicant, after whose death, the heirs of Nana Sahib's temple became owners of it.

15. BHADAWAR RAJA'S GHAT, with a temple of Indreshwar Mahadeva built by Raja Gopal Singh of Bhadawar is S. 1766 (A.D. 1709) at a cost of Rs. 50,000. It is now known as the Thana (Police Station); for, the British Government took possession of the ghat after the Mutiny, and built a Thana (Police Station) there. It is now used as a Dak Bungalow and is in the possession of the Disrtict Board of Ajmer, a new police station having been built. The Raja of Bhadawar is said to have joined the mutineers in the Mutiny of 1857 A.D.

16. BADRI GHAT: It was originally attached to or named after the temple of Badri Narayanji, which is situated at a little distance, to the north, from the ghat. It was built about 270 years ago at a cost of Rs. 20,000.

17. RAGHUNATH GHAT: On it, stands the Raghunathji temple also called the *Asthal*. It is said to have been built in S. 1608 (A. D. 1551)) by a Deccani Brahman at a cost of Rs. 50 000. In old days, the Government used to give Rs. 15 a month for the upkeep of the *Asthal*. This allowance was stopped about 1866 A.D.

18. GANGOR GHAT is an old ghat with a Dharmshala on it. Kayasth Lalji Malji family of Ajmer are in possession now. Here come all the *jels*[1] of Pushkar during the *Jel fair*.

19. RAM GHAT built by Ram Saran, a Deccani Brahman, about 225 years ago. A *haveli* with three storeys

1. Just before the Gangor festival in Chaitra (spring), groups of women go to a lake or a well outside the town and bring water in brass vessels on their heads, piled one upon another, accompanied with music. These are called जेला, *Jelan*.

The Gau Ghat at Pushkar.

built by Hemraj, kamdar of Kuchaman, on the ghat is in the possession of his descendants. The ghat was presented to his purohits by the builder A monthly allowance of Rs. 4 for *Bhog* (food offering) is still paid to the priest. A *tibari* and two small rooms stand on the ghat. *Saligram Nazir* of Jodhpur built a temple, called Nazirji-ka-temple at a cost of Rs. 10,000 about 160 years ago. A maafi village, Tajuwas, is attached to it.

20. RAI MUKAND GHAT built by Rai Mukand, Kayasth of Narnaul, about 460 years ago, projects between the two Ramghats. A haveli on the ghat is in the possession of Mukand's descendants.

21. RAM GHAT built by Madho Rao Jyotishi of Deccan with a temple of Rameshwara Mahadeva, in S. 1893 (A.D. 1836)).

22. SHEKHAVATJI-KA-GHAT built by Rani Lakhmavat of the Raja of Kheri about 270 years ago.

23. HATHI SINGHJI-KA-GHAT built by Hathi Singh, a mahajan of Kishangarh about 170 years ago. The ghat and the residential quarters are in the possession of Hathi Singh's *purohits*.

24. BALA RAO-KA-GHAT built by Bala Rao. Musammat Rodi of Alwar built a temple on it, known as Rodiji ka temple, dedicated to god Shiva. Two wells with some land in the village Rajpura, Alwar State, are attached to the temple for its maintenance. Adjacent to the above ghat, is the temple of Gopalji, built about 140 years ago by the Thakur of Meora, Kishangarh State. A maafi well in village Buvaroo, Kishangarh State, is attached to the temple.

25. CHEER GHAT with a Seetla Mata temple, built about 280 years ago. A temple of Mahadevaji built by one Gangadhar of Nagor, and a temple of Ganeshji stand on the ghat.

26. GAU GHAT: This is the largest ghat in Pushkar. About 260 years ago, one Kalu Ram Kayasth of Jodhpur built a Zenana Ghat on it. This Zenana Ghat was demolished, and a new Zenana Ghat for women called Queen Mary's Zenana Ghat, to commemorate the visit of Queen Mary of England in December 1911 A.D., has been built in its place. The Queen presented Rs. 1,500 to Pushkar, of which Rs. five hundred were given to *Chhoti Basti*. With the remaining Rs. one thousand, and twentyfive thousand rupees out of a lakh of rupees presented by the Maharana of Udaipur to the Prince of Wales during his visit to that State, as also Rs. 7,000 given

by the Maharaja of Jodhpur and Rs. 1,000 by the Maharaja of Karauli, this Zenana ghat was built in 1913 A.D.

The Raja of Bhinai built a Shiva temple on the Gau Ghat about 200 years ago. A chhatree called Santuji Baola ki chhatree is said to have been built at a cost of Rs. 100,000. In 1866 A.D., a Shiva temple was built by a *jyotishi* of Jodhpur at a cost of Rs. 10,000, but no idol has been placed in it. A Tripolia gate and some shops belonging to the Jodhpur State stood here, but the gate was removed sometime ago.

Bharatpur-ki-kunj, and a temple of Radha Madhoji and Anna Poorna, built by the Raja of Bharatpur about 270 years ago, stand on the southern end of the ghat. An allowance of Rs. 180 is given by the Bharatpur State for their upkeep. Separate places for men and women pilgrims and visitors have been built here.

27. YAGYA GHAT with a temple of Shivji was built by Jagooji, *purohit*, of the Jodhpur Darbar. The tradition is that Brahmaji performed his *yajyna* here at the inauguration of Pushkar.

28. CHHEENK GHAT so called because a Chheenk Mata's temple built about 570 years ago, stands on it.

29. There is a ghat next to it, but no one is in possession of it. A Gaurji-ki-haveli, said to have been built by a Gaurji Brahman, about 600 years ago stands here.

30. GALIKA GHAT. Public women generally bathe here.

31. HADON-KA-GHAT with a temple of Anna Poorna on it, built by H.H. the Maharao of Bundi about 200 years ago. Worship is conducted in the temple by the priest of Brahmaji temple. A temple of Raghunathji built by the Maharao of Bundi about the same time as the ghat, also stands on the ghat. During the outbreak of plague, the idol was removed and has not been replaced. Now, a grant of Rs. 200 a year is made by the State for its maintenance.

32. BRAHMA GHAT: This is a very old ghat. It is said that the Thakur of Kaka, Jodhpur State, more than a thousand years ago, repaired it A temple of Murli Manoharji built by Gordhan Khichi of Soliyana near Nagor, stands on it. The State gives Rs. 100 a year. A well in the village Nanya near Parbatsar (Marwar) is attached to it. A Gujrati Dharmshala was recently built on it. A temple called the Pisangan temple without an idol in it stands here. There is a Zenana Ghat, and a Tibara (room) on it was built by P. Brahmanand, Revenue Officer of Jodhpur.

33. SAVITRI GHAT also built by the Thakur of Kaka at the same time as the Brahma Ghat.

34. PARAS RAM GHAT A *Dwara* (monastry) was built by Acharya Parasramdeva of the Naibarak sect with a temple of Radha Madhoji. The Mahant of Salemabad once repaired the ghat and the buildings. The ghat is a very old one and the mahant pays Rs. 100 a year for its maintenance.

35. Open Ghat where elephants and cows drink water.

36. KARNI GHAT: The Karni Mata temple on it is said to have been built by the *Charans* about 160 years ago. The Charans pay Rs. 100/- a year for the maintenance of the temple. The Bikaner State built a small temple here two years ago.

37. A delapidated Ghat with open land behind it, on which stands the Chhatree on the remains of Maharaja Abhai Singh, who died at Ajmer on Asad sudi 15th, S. 1806 (A.D. 1749) and cremated at Pushkar. It is a pity that a chabutra in ruins alone marks the last resting place of a king who, in his time, was the most powerful sovereign in Rajputana, and who had the courage to accept the request of the Mughal Emperor to reduce to submission Sarbaland Khan, Viceroy of Gujrat, when no noble in the Imperial Durbar dared do it. One hundred and twenty-five bighas of land and a well are said to have been given for its maintenance. A temple of Kalyanji stood here. The idol has recently been removed to Gau Ghat. The Jodhpur Darbar would surely put the land in proper order and repair the *Thada* or build a Chhatree over it, if the matter is brought to its notice.

38. CHAUDI PEDYA-KA-GHAT is another ghat in ruins with only some steps leading to the lake left, and is so called because the steps are more than ordinarily wide. By it, stands Hingor Mal's Mahal. Pillars and stones used in the palace remain to mark its place. It is said to have been built by a Bharmalot Thakur of Badnagar who later migrated to Khandwa.

39. SWAROOP GHAT with a temple of Mahadevaji on it, built at a cost of Rs. 12,000. It is a very old place and was repaired by H. H. Maharao of Kotah. Whenever the eighth day of *Sudi Paksha* is a Wednesday, the people bathe here.

40. KOTAH GHAT. Behind it is Maha Prabuji-ki-Baithak built by Gulab Rai, *Paswan* (mistress) of the Maharaja of Jodhpur, who also built the Gulab Sagar at Jodhpur.

41. SWAROOP GHAT also called Ballabh Ghat, because Swami Ballabhacharya came and read *Bhagwat* here. He is said to have read it in eighty-four places, one of which is this place.

42. Next is a ruined ghat, where *Bhopas* (pujaries of Bheroonji) bathe.

43. BUNDI GHAT built by K. Bheem Singh's widow (Ram Singh's son, and brother of Maharao Raghubir Singh).

44. JODHPUR GHAT built by Maharaja Man Singh of Jodhpur. The *gosayeens*, who were *gurus* of the Maharaja, later established foot-prints of Nathji here. The Jodhpur State gives Rs. 100 a year for its up-keep. There was an old ghat here, which was demolished and a new one built by the State.

45. SAPTARISHI GHAT named after the seven great Rishis of India. Only steps leading to the water remain now of the old ghat.

46. TIJAMAJI KA GHAT AND TEMPLE: Pratap Kunwar Bai, daughter of the Bhati Thakur of Jakhan who was the third queen of Maharaja Man Singh of Jodhpur and was called Tijamaji built it after the Jodhpur Ghat had been built.

OTHER BUILDINGS

The Chhatree in the Pushkar lake was rebuilt by the Thakur of Khimsar in S. 1848 (A.D. 1791).

Another building in Pushkar which has not received proper attention deserves notice here. It consists of two red stone pavilions built by Emperor Jahangir on the margin of the lake, near the cremation grounds, behind the Jodhpur Ghat. The pavilions are identical in construction, and were built in H. 1024 (1615 A.D.). The following inscription appears above the door in the western wall of the southern of the two pavilions :—

الله اکبر

شاه نور الدین جهانگیر ابن اکبر بادشاه تاجهان باشد به تخت بادشاهی شادباد

کرد فتح ملک رانا در دهم سال جلوس هو زمان فتحی ز غیبش بامبارک باد باد

شد بحکمش این همایون قصر در پهکر تمام قصر جاهش را فراز از آسمان بنیاد باد

سال تاریخش طلب کردم ندا آمد زغیب پهکراین قصر جهانگیری مدام آباد باد

باهتمام انیرای سنگهدلن ۱۰۲۴

TRANSLATION.—King Nur-ud-din Jahangir, son of King Akbar: May he remain happy on the throne while the world lasts. (He) conquered the territory of the Rana (of Chitor) in the tenth[1] year of his accession to the throne, May welcome victories come to him from the unknown at all times. By his order this auspicious palace in Pushkar was completed. May the foundation of the palace of his grandeur be as high as the sky. I asked for its chronogram, and a voice came from the unknown; "May this palace of Jahangir in Pushkar always remain inhabited."

Under the management of Anirai Singhdalan,[2] H. 1024 (1615 A.D.).

Pushkar, till very recently, was famous for its fruit gardens. Emperor Jahangir, in his *Autobiography* praises the fruit, Pushkar yielded in his time. Even so late as 1825 A.D., when Bishop Heber visited it, Pushkar grapes were famous. He says: "Pushkar is renowned for its gardens and vineyards. The *grapes are by far the best and largest in India and equal to those of Shiraz*" (*Persia*).[3]

BADI BASTI AND CHHOTI BASTI

The town of Pushkar is divided into two parts. That in which the temples of Varahji and Sri Rangji are situated, is called the *Chhoti Basti*; and the other, the *Badi Basti*. The *Chhoti Basti* was originally called Varahpura after the famous Varahji ka Temple there. The Brahmins of the two *bastis* have always been on unfriendly terms with each other; the reason being that the Brahmins of the Chhoti Basti allege that the Brahmins of the Badi Basti are not true Brahmins, but are Shakadwipi Brahmins, *i. e.*, Mag (Magii of Persia), and that they later began to call themselves Parasar Brahmins. The earliest mention of this disagreement between the two Bastis is found in Emperor Jahangir's *Firman* dated 2nd Khurdad, H. 1024 (A.D. 1615) which states that there were two parties, and as they quarrelled with each other, the grant was first withheld, and later granted.

The Brahmins of *Badi Basti* claim that they are the original Brahmins of Pushkar and that they are descended from Parashar Muni who was the father of Veda Vyas. The last descendant was Bhopat. Bhopat's descendants became divided into seven *thoks* or groups. These seven thoks are (1) Allavat from their progenitor, Alla (2) Devavat from their progenitor, Deva (3) Dharmavat from their progenitor, Dharma (4) Adhari from their progenitor, Lachman. (5)

1. The tenth year of Jahangir's accession to the throne began with the 10th March, 1615 A.D., *vide* Elliot's *History of India*, Vol. V, page 341.

2. Anirai Singhdalan was the title of Raja Anup Singh Badgujar—*Maasir-ul-Umra*, Vol. II, p. 220.

3. Heber's *Narrative*, Vol. II, page 50. The residents of Ajmer prize the radish grown in Pushkar, and the neighbouring village Thaonla.

Krishna Kalyan after their progenitors, Krishna and Kalyan. (6) Chokhavat after their progenitor Chokha, and (7) Chandavat. They say that about eighteen generations have passed since Bhopat. They also claim that when in old days, Brahmins were divided into ten classes; they, like the Brahmins of Muttra and Gaya, were excluded from this classification, and that when Maharaja Narhar Rao renovated this sacred place, he, after investigations, made them his Pushkar *gurus*.[1]

Pt. Maharaj Kishen, the author of *Tarikhe Ajmer* (History of Ajmer) published in 1876 A.D., rejects this claim of the *badi basti* Brahmins, and says that Bhopat was known to be a Mer. He also says that Parasar Brahmins are nowhere to be found in India except Pushkar and a few families in Nagor and Mundava (Marwar) to which places, they migarated from Pushkar. He relates that Maharaja Sawai Jai Singh (1699-1743 A.D.) during one of his visits to Pushkar, after a bath in the sacred lake, presented his rich garments to his *Purohit* (priest). The Purohit gave these clothes to his son-in-law, who was a *sevak* in Jaipur, at his marriage. Later, when the Maharaja was passing one day through a bazaar in Jaipur, he saw a funeral procession approaching and a sevak according to custom leading it, clad in the clothes which Jai Singh at once recognised as his. On enquiry, the Maharaja found that his Pushkar purohit had given the clothes to his son-in-law, who was a *sevak* by caste. The Maharaja then concluded that the Pushkar Brahmins were not Brahmins at all, and abandoned his Pushkar purohits, and made Chhoti Basti Brahmins, his *purohits* and gave them a *sanad* dated *Mahabadi* 9, S. 1789 (A.D. 1732), which says that he (Maharaja) had taken away his *Purohitai* from Hira and others who were Bhojaks, and given it to Durga Das, son of Jai Kishan Brahmin Sanadhya, Jiwaraj son of Saroman Gaur, and Ghanshyam son of Jogidas Sanadhya. Maharaja Sawai Jaisingh, in his order of Falgun sudi 5th, S. 1789 (A.D. 1732) declared the *Badi Basti* people as Bhojaks and not Brahmins. A fact which distinguishes the *Badi Basti* Brahmins from all other Brahmins is that they intermarry with *Sevaks*, the servants of the Jain Shravaks (Saravgi), who eat *rotees* (chapaties) given by the *Saravgis*.

1. The *Wajibul Arz* or the Record of Rights attached to the *Ten Years Settlement Record*, Ajmer-Merwara, (1875 A.D) says that Raja Narhar Rao brought, from the village Goela near Pushkar, ancestors of the Brahmins of Parasar *gotra*; and from Teharya in Marwar, Mers of the *gotra* of Pakharya and settled them at Pushkar to protect the town in S. 744 (A.D. 687).

Whatever the origin of the *Badi Basti* Brahmins, whether they are descendants of Sukhdeo Muni, or are Parasar Brahmins or were Bhojaks or Sevaks, they have for several centuries, *vide* the Mughal Emperor's *firmans*, been held to be Brahmins and must now been accepted as Brahmins. History records innumerable instances of people in India who became Brahmins from Kshtriyas and Vaishas; some even from the aboriginal tribes of India. Valmiki is a conspicuous instance.

ENVIRONS OF PUSHKAR.

The Prachi Saraswati river which passes by the village of Hokran, disappears in the sands, but reappears in five channels further on. Brahmins are enjoined to bathe in them:

Suprabha	falls in Jyestha Pushkar.
Sudha	falls in Madhya Pushkar.
Kanka	falls in Kanishtha Pushkar.
Nanda	flows passed the Nand village.
Prachi	passes by Hokran.

The town and the lake of Pushkar are surrounded by hills, on which stand sacred temples. The biggest of these is the Savitri temple. To the north of Pushkar on a hill, stands the temple of Pap-Mochini Mata, where also a fair is held every year. About a mile behind the temple of Brahmaji, on the way to the Nand village, is a picturesque place with the temple of Kapaleshwar Mahadeva, where a fair is held every year on *Sawan sudi* 14th. To the east of the Pushkar lake, stands the famous Nagpahar (Serpent Mountain), part of the Aravalli Mountains. Col. Tod says of this mountain :—

> "There are many beautiful spots about the Serpent Mount which, as it abounds in springs, has from earliest times been the resort of Hindu sages, whose caves and hermitages are yet pointed out, now embellished with gardens and fountains."—*Annals and Antiquities of Rajasthan*, Vol. I, p. 776.

The western slope of this Nag-Pahar is studded with picturesque spots. There is the *Agast Muni ki gal* or Savitri *gal* (glen) a wooded and secluded place, where a fair is held on Bhadrapad sudi 12th, every year. Next to it, is the Nahrol, which carries the water from the hill into the Pushkar lake. Then, there is the Bhartrihari cave, where also a fair is held every year. Near it, is the *Bamdevaji ki gupha* (Cave). At the foot of the hill near it, is the Daurani-Jethani ki Baori (well with steps leading to the water) built by a Pushkarna *purohit* of Jodhpur. Near it again, is the Yamdagni Kund, where a fair is held yearly on Kartik *sudi* second. Further to the north, is the Punch Kund so called as there are five reservoirs of water near each other. Pilgrims bathe in all the five kunds. A big fair is held here every year on *Nag-Panchmi*, Sravan Vadi 5th (August). The people of Ajmer and Pushkar go to the Serpent Mountain, and a fair is held there on *Haryali Amavasya i. e.*, Sravan Vadi 15th, which ushers in the rainy season. At the foot of the hill on which the Punch Kund are perched, is the Government nursery garden. Picnics are held every day during the rainy season at the Punch Kund and this garden, and often during the rest of the year. Further north, is another sacred place called *Gau Mukh* where the *malti* flower flourishes in abundance. It is a beautiful spot. Water flows down the hill during the rainy season and is collected in a big reservoir.

It is said that the hermitage where Sakuntala was born and grew up was situated on the western slope of this hill, and that the poet Kalidas had the scenery of this place in his mind when he painted the picture of the hermitage of Rishi Kanwa, in his world-renowned Sanskrit drama Sakuntala. Pushkar is thus related to one of the world's greatest master-pieces of literature

DISTRICT

MERWARA

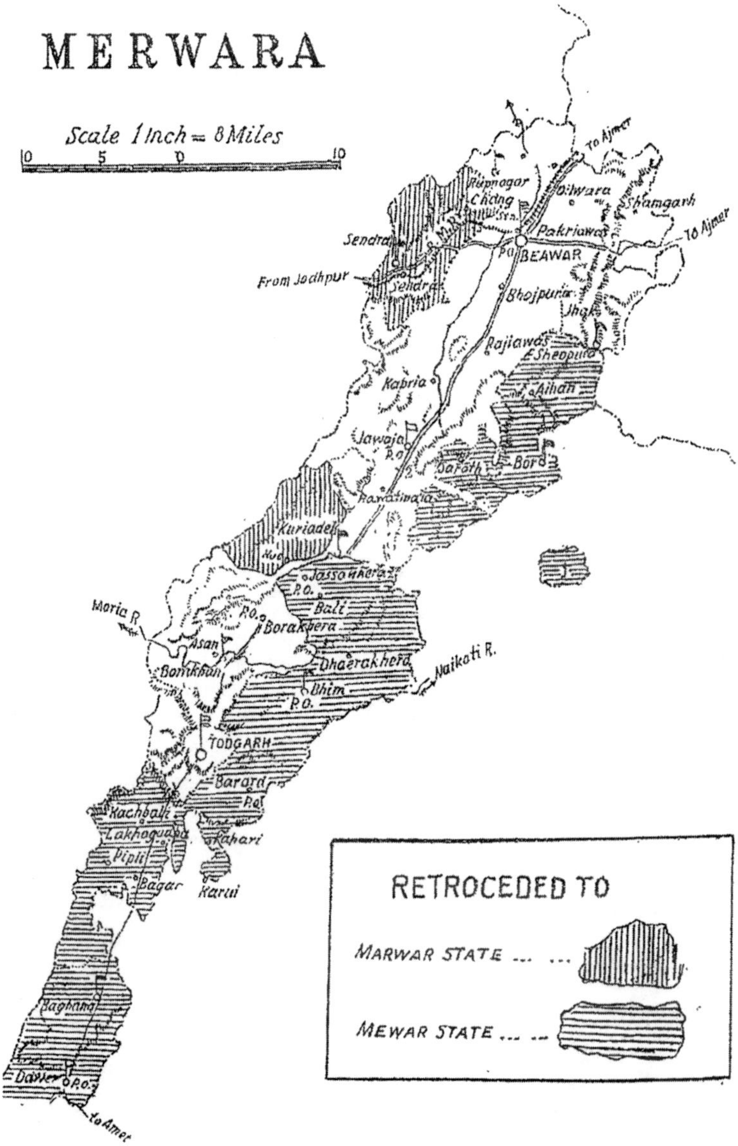

CHAPTER XXX

MERWARA

MERWARA—the land of the Mers—"is a mountainous tract consisting of a number of parallel ridges extending in a direction from the north-east to south-west," and extends from Komalmer in Mewar to Ajmer. It separates Mewar from Marwar.[1] The Aravalli, or, to give the hills the original Indian name, Araballa range of hills, which runs through Rajputana, assumes to the south of Ajmer, the form of a double range enclosing the greater part of Merwara. The area enclosed was at one time covered with dense impenetrable forests.

Merwara is bounded on the north, by Marwar (Jodhpur) and Ajmer; on the south, by Mewar (Udaipur); on the east by Ajmer and Mewar; and on the west by Marwar. It lies between north latitude 26°11′ and 25°23′ 30″, and east longitude 73°47′ 30″ and 74°30″. Its area was 641 miles, before the rendition of the Mewar and Marwar villages to these two States in 1937 A.D. It is now only 370 square miles with a population of 83.065. The longitudes and latitudes of British Merwara since 1937, are latitude 26°11′ 50″ and 25 39′ 45″; longitude 73°54′ 45″ and 74°29′ 10″. It was a narrow strip seventy miles long with a varying breadth of fifteen to one mile in 1937. It is now forty-eight miles long and fifteen miles broad. There are no mountains, the highest hills are about Todgarh, where the highest peak of Goramji[2] attains the height of 3,075 feet above sea-level. The average level of the valleys is 1,800 feet.

There were nine passes in the whole of Merwara. Only three are left in British Merwara—the Barr Pass and the Pakheria and Sheopura Passes. There is no river. The beds of drainage channels are rocky. The rainfall, if unarrested, rapidly flows off into Mewar and Marwar, and but little benefits the country, as the soil is shallow and does not retain moisture. The large tanks of Dilwara, Kalinjar, Jawaja, and Balad date from long before the British rule. They are wide earthen embankments; faced on both sides by

1. Thornton's *Gazetteer*, p. 583. 2. Now in Mewar.

flat stones laid horizontally, and closing gorges through which the hill streams had worked passages.

LAKES: There are two natural lakes, Sargaon and Karantia, both near Beawar. The former is used for irrigation; but the latter lies amongst hills and is of no use for irrigation. With the exception of a few tanks built before 1818 A.D., and those built by Col. Hall, the Superintendent of Merwara from 1822 to 1835 A.D., all tanks were built by Col. Dixon, who administered Merwara from 1835 to 1842 A.D., and both Ajmer and Merwara from 1842 to 1857 A.D. When the rendition of Mewar and Marwar portions of Merwara was made in 1937 A.D., as many as ninety-four embankments, including village *nadis*, were transferred to Mewar, and fourteen to Marwar.

From an agricultural point of view, the difference between Ajmer and Merwara is very marked. Mr. Lupton says:

> "While Ajmer may be described as mainly a series of plains intersected by hills, Merwara, on the other hand, is by far the greater part, a confused mass of hills with small intervening valleys, or deep hollows and pockets of soil in which the cultivation mainly lies; further, while, for the most part the cultivation in Ajmer and Beawar plain (where it occurs, as it is very dispersed by large stretches of barren rock or waste or scarcely culturable shallow stony soil) lies in broad open fields; in Merwara, on the other hand, it lies in small carefully terraced fields in these hollows or pockets, or in ledges along the *nullas* or on the slopes of the hill sides, these terraces being necessary both to catch the silt scoured down by the rain, and to retain the soil in *situ*, when the field is once formed and prevent its erosion, and to catch and retain all available moisture."[1]

FAUNA: An occasional tiger is met with in Merwara, while leopards and hyenas are to be found in the hills upto Dewair. A few Sambhar are also to be found.

CLIMATE: The climate is healthy. It is dry and hot in the summer, and cold and bracing in winter. The south-west monsoon exhausts itself before it reaches Merwara or Ajmer. The clouds which strike Kathiawar and Cutch are deprived of a great deal of their moisture by the influence of hills in those countries and the greater part of what remains is poured over Abu. It is only when this monsoon is very strong that Merwara gets a plentiful supply. The north-eastern monsoon sweeps up the valley of the Ganges from the Bay of Bengal and waters the northern part of the Rajputana, but hardly penetrates further west than the longitude of Ajmer. It is from the north east that Merwara obtains its heaviest rainfall, though Todgarh gets more benefit out of the Arabian Sea monsoon than Ajmer. The average rainfall is eighteen inches.

1. Lupton's *Settlement Report*, 1910.

The Origin of the Mers.

Mer is a generic term applied to the inhabitants of this hilly tract. The Mers or Rawats as they call themselves, declare that they are the descendants of Emperor Prithviraj[1] of Ajmer, whose son, Jodh Lakhun, married a girl of the Mina tribe, supposing her to be a Rajput. Later, when he discovered her origin, he sent her away with her two sons, Anhal and Anup. They wandered to Chang near the village of Beawar and settled there. Their descendants became *Chitas* and *Barar*. Anhal settled at Chang, and his descendants exterminated the Gujars who had given asylum to Anhal and his mother. They multiplied and founded the villages of Jhak, Shamgarh, Lulua, Athoon, Kot Kirna, Nai and others. This clan now holds one hundred and seventeen villages in the Beawar Tahsil, besides sixteen entire villages and portions of fifty-three in Todgarh. In Ajmer there are twentyone entire Khalsa and Jagir villages belonging to Chitas. Of the sub-divisions of the clan, the most important is the Merats, a term which is a patronymic derived from Mera, the common ancestor of Katatas and Gorats Harraj, grandson of Mera, a Chita, became a Muslim in Aurangzeb's time in Delhi. As a brave soldier is called *Kata* in Merwara, he was called *kata* by Aurangzeb, and his descendants are Katat Merats. They hold seventy-eight villages in Beawar Tahsil. Harraj's brother Gora, remained a Hindu and his descendants hold twenty-one villages in Beawar and thirteen in Todgarh, and one in Ajmer. Four villages in Ajmer, Nausar, Rajosi, Ajaysar and Kharekdi—are held by Katats on Istimrar tenure. The chief men of Katats and Gorats call themselves Thakurs, but the chief of Athoon, Chang and Jhak who are Katats are called Khans.

Anhal's brother, Anup, settled in what is now Todgarh Tahsil and founded the Barar clan. They hold eleven villages in Beawar of which the chief are Kalinjar, Sendhra, Bhailan and Khera Sagnotan. They hold the south of the Todgarh Tahsil and forty-eight villages in it. "They call themselves Rawats, and are more honest and straight forward. Their chiefmen are called Raos." Thus, of the descendants of Anup and Anhal, those of Anhal are all Hindus: of those of Anup, the Katats are Muslims and the Gorats, Hindus. Till recent time, they all intermarried, and *the Brahmins performed their marriage ceremony according to Hindu rites*. Now, they are discarding Hindu customs and dress, and intermarry amongst other Muslims.

1. History makes no mention of any son of Prithviraja called Jodh Lakhun.

Apart from the descendants of Anup and Anhal, who are Chauhan Mina Mers or Rawats there are other Mers who claim descent from Dharanath Parmar, who founded the town of Dharanagar in Marwar, long before the Rathors spread in Marwar, and the Gehlots became predominent in Mewar. Rao Bahar, a descendant of Dharanath, came and settled in Rudhana in Beawar Tahsil and his descendants founded the villages of Biliawas, Jawaja, Hahar, Bar Kochran, Rawatmal, Lusani in the Beawar, and some in the Todgarh tahsil. The tribe has six *gotras*. Of these, the Delats are more numerous and hold fourteen villages in Beawar and five in Todgarh. The other *gotras* hold eleven whole villages in Ajmer, and parts in eight more. Another tribe claims descent from Dharanath, that of Moti Rawats. They hold fourteen villages in Bhailan and two in Beawar.

Two brothers of the Rajputs Gehlot caste came to Borwa after the sack of Chitor by Allauddin Khilji, and intermarried with *minas*. Their descendants are divided into sixteen clans. They hold eleven villages in Beawar, one in Todgarh, and six in Ajmer—Amba Masina, Partabpura, Borak Ausari, Mayapura, Lachiapur. They call themselves *Suryabansi Rajputs* and are called Rawats. The *Balai* caste holds four villages in Beawar. Jats and Gujars[1] hold eleven, and Mahajans hold two, Narsinghpura and Dunger Khera. There are some other clans who also claim descent from other Rajput clans.

The above summary account shows that the present Mers are not the descendants of a foreign tribe pushed into the hills by the Rajputs, but are the offspring of Chauhan, Gehlot, Parmar and other Rajputs, who married *mina* and other wives and settled in this hilly tract, and that, except the Katats, all are Hindus. A point worth noting is that from the earliest times, all the Mers or Rawats and Merats intermarried and interdined, dressed alike and lived the same life, though some of them later became Mussalmans, and all observed the Hindus rites of marriage, and worshipped Hindu deities. With the introduction of the franchise and communal representation in British India in the wake of the Minto Morley Reforms, the Muslims began to separate from the Hindus. This trend is becoming more and more marked during the Montford Constitution. The movement is spreading in all strata of society and the Merats are leaving the Mers, adopting the customs and dress of the town Muslims and discarding social

1. There are no Bhil villages. In Mewar, according to the last Census, there were 625 Bhil villages.

relations with Mers. The Mers or Rawats too, are coming closer to the Hindus and are giving up some of their old habits and practices.

History of Merwara.

Little is known of the history of Merwara as a province before 1818 A.D. The land was covered with dense forests and inhabited by people in inaccesible fastnesses. Protected by difficult passes, behind impenetrable jungles, they continued to ply their trade of plundering the neighbouring villages of Marwar and Ajmer. It is after the British came to Ajmer, that Merwara has seen settled and peaceful life.

Mr. Victor Jacquemont, the French naturalist, after visiting Ajmer-Merwara in 1832, says:—

"I saw a country whose inhabitants since an immemorial time had never had any other means of existence but plunder in the adjacent plains of Marwar and Mewar, a people of marauders now changed into a quiet industrious and happy people of shepherds and cultivators. No Rajput Chief, no Mughal Emperor had ever been able to subdue them; fourteen years ago, everything was to be done with them, and since six or seven years, everything is done already."[1]

The Mers only once again took to the life of marauders and that was due to famine. Mr. Kaye says:—

"In 1832, there had been a drought, the country had been nearly depopulated. The industrial energies of the people were paralyzed by this calamity. They lost all faith in agriculture as a means of subsistance, and fell into their old marauding habits. This indeed in a greater or less degree was the result of every drought, and droughts were of frequent occurrence."[2]

Whatever the truth in the tradition of their origin so well preserved by the Rawats there is little doubt that Merwara was inhabited by a war-like people before Emperor Prithviraj's time. The Gujars of Chang according to tradition gave asylum to Anup, Anhal and their mother, and we must conclude that they were amongst the warlike people who peopled Merwara towards the end of the twelfth century A.D.; for, we find that soon after the death of Prithviraj in 1192 A.D., when Qutbuddin Aibak, in 1195 A.D., started from Ajmer to attack Anhalwara Patan, the Mers combined with the Rajputs of Gujrat and inflicted a defeat on Qutbuddin, who fled wounded to Ajmer, and shut himself up in the fortress of Taragarh. The Mers invested the fortress, and only retired to their hills after a six months' siege, when reinforcements arrived from Afghanistan.

1. *Letters from India*, by Victor Jacquemont, 1834 A. D.
2. Kaye's *History of the Administration of the East India Company*, p. 468.

We also find that Maharaja Hammira of Ranthambhor conquered Chang and Vardhanpura (Badnor) between 1285 and 1290 A.D. Vardhanpura, Chang, Athoon and Jhak were amongst the principal settlements of the Mers. With the rise of the Sisodia power in Mewar, the Mers were pressed back on the Mewar side, and by the time of Maharana Lakha (1382-1397 A.D.), Vardhanpura had passed out of their hands and incorporated in Mewar. The Maharana after razing Vardhanpura in 1383 A.D. built the present town of Badnor; and, in order to protect it from future Mer raids, he brought about an alliance between Badnor and Athoon. This is proved by the fact that on the death of the Khan of Athoon, the Thakur of Badnor always performs the ceremony of *sword binding* at the accession of the new Khan, and *vice versa*.

Athoon had acknowledged the suzerainty of the Maharana of Udaipur, and its Khan always presented a *Nazar* of rupees one hundred, whenever he went to the Maharana, who rewarded him with a horse. The fort of Athoon was one of the chief strongholds of the Mers. According to tradition, it was built about six hundred years ago. Before the building of this fort, the principality was known as Dhawalgarh and the Raja of Dhawalgarh was entitled to the seventeenth seat in the Maharana's *durbar*, the first sixteen were those of the principal nobles of Mewar.

Maharana Mokal (1420-1433) sent armies to subdue the Mers. Maharaja Sangram Singh II made attempts to conquer Merwara in 1723, when the Bhibeda Thakur Amar Singh and his eldest son, Akhshai Singh were killed.

The Mers plundered the camp of Emperor Jahangir, when in 1616 A.D. he moved out, after three years' stay in Ajmer, to go to Burhanpur. In 1632 A.D. (S. 1689) Maharaja Gaj Singh of Jodhpur sent his minister Muhnot Nainsi, the famous annalist of Marwar, on a punitive expedition against the Mers, as they had plundered some Marwar villages. Muhnot Nainsi, burnt fifteen villages of the Mers, and returned to Jodhpur. In 1645 A.D., Muhnot Nainsi, minister of Maharaja Jaswant Singh again attacked Merwara and burnt the villages of Kukda, Kot Kirana and others to punish Rawat Narain. Later, when Emperor Aurangzeb, failed in his attempt to conquer Mewar, departed for the Deccan to meet the advancing forces of the Mahrattas on 7 March, 1679 A.D., the Mers harassed his army and inflicted severe losses on it.

Mewar was exhausted by wars with the Imperial Mughal power; internecine quarrels reduced her strength still further after the decline of the Mughal power in the eighteenth century. Her western neighbours, the Mers of Merwara, began to plunder her people. Mewar, and later both Jaipur and Jodhpur, made several sporadic attempts to conquer the Mers. The history of Badnor says that in Kartik, S. 1762, (November 1705 A.D.) the Mers of Mugra Merwara and the Khans of Athoon, Chang and Jhak began to make depredations in Mewar and the Maharana sent an expedition against them under Dhabhai Nagji. But he failed to overpower them. The Maharana then sent Thakur Jaswant Singh of Badnor who attacked Haji Khan at Kalinjar and inflicted a defeat on him. The same year, Haji Khan of Athoon raided Hurda in Mewar and carried its Hakim, prisoner to Athoon. Thakur Jaswant Singh thereupon invaded Merwara, killed Haji Khan in a pitched battle and destroyed the fort of Chang and released the *hakim* of Hurda from captivity.

The Mers raised their heads again in 1713 A.D. and the Maharana sent Thakur Amar Singh of Nibhera against them; but Amar Singh and his son Akhshai Singh were killed in the first encounter, and the army retired. The Maharana then sent Thakur Jawahar Singh of Badnor, who attacked Athoon, and a battle was fought on Kartik Sudi 9th S. 1770; (1713 A.D.) but it was indecisive. In the meanwhile, Sahib Singh, brother of Thakur Amar Singh of Nibhera who had gone to Delhi with presents from the Maharana on King Farrukh-sayar's accession to the throne, returned and determined to avenge his brother's death. Assisted by the troops of Badnor, Deogarh and Shahpura, he inflicted a decisive defeat on the Khan of Athoon, who also had been reinforced by other Mer chieftains.

In 1725 A.D., Thakur Devi Singh of Parsoli in Jaipur incurred the displeasure of Maharaja Sawai Jaisingh[1] and fled to Jhak in Merwara. The Maharaja demanded his surrender. The Mers refused to surrender Devi Singh. The Maharaja thereupon invaded Merwara with a large army. He destroyed the strongholds of Jhak and Kalinjar, which had been vacated by the Mers. When the Maharaja advanced in the interior, the jungle was so thick, and the Mer guerrilla warfare so effective, that Maharaja Jai Singh failed to reach the Mer fastnesses, and after suffering losses, returned to Jaipur.

In 1730, the Maharana sent an expedition under Thakur Jai Singh of Badnor against the Khan of Athoon and other Rawat Thakurs. Thakur Jai Singh invited Thakur Sultan of Masuda to co-operate with him in the enterprise. In the

1. For a full account of this event, see Colonel Dixon's *Sketch of Merwara*, pp. 15-16.

war that followed, Sultan Singh was killed and Jai Singh was wounded, but the Mers were defeated.[1]

In 1778 A.D., Maharaja Bijai Singh of Jodhpur[2] sent a considerable force under a Bhandari Minister against Chang. This force was routed. The following year, the Maharaja sent Thakur Arjun Singh of Raipur with an army from Jodhpur against Kot Kirana. The Mers took the initiative, attacked the army on its march and defeated it with great slaughter. In 1790, the Thakur of Kuntalia[3] having assembled his men, and with reinforcements from Jodhpur attacked Bhailan. He was killed in the battle that followed. The Mers put his men to flight and plundered his camp.

Hari Khan, Khan of Athoon, again commenced his depredations in Mewar. Thakur Jai Singh now resolved to rid the country of the Khan, and took up his position in a pass with his two brothers, Sangram Singh and Nahar Singh. As Hari Khan returned with booty after one of his expeditions, he was attacked and killed by Jai Singh after a sanguinary fight. Later, in 1793 A.D. (Samvat 1850) Jai Singh, son of Gaj Singh, the great grandson of Jai Singh of Badnor attacked Athoon and took possession of it, and demolished the forts of Saroth and Ajitgarh, and excavated a lake at the latter place.

In 1800, Sivaji Nana, the Mahratta Subedar of Ajmer, on behalf of the Scindia, commenced hostilities against the Mer villages of Jhak and Shamgarh, but obtained no advantage over them.[4] He continued, however, for nearly three years, to make attempts at reprisals and revenge for the ravages committed by the Mers in the Ajmer district.

In 1807 A.D., Bala Rao, the Mahratta Governor of Ajmer,[5] brought a force of 60,000 men into Mugra Merwara, with the determination of crippling the Mers, at least for a season. This was a signal for a general rising of the whole of the inhabitants of the tract; and the Mers, Merats, and Rawats attacked and defeated Bala Rao who was obliged to retire.

About the year 1810, Muhammad Shah Khan[6] and Rajah Bahadur, dependants of Nawab Amir Khan of Tonk, either at the suggestion of Man Singh, Maharaja of Jodhpur, or of their own accord, came with a force to Jhak, ostensibly to seize the property of Dhonkul Singh, the posthumous son of Maharaja Bheem Singh and unsuccessful pretender to the throne of Jodhpur, who had fled and was supposed to have left his

1. Hindi *History of Badnor*, p. 231 (A.D. 1932).
2. Dixon's *Sketch of Merwara*, p. 11.
3. Ibid.
4. Col. Dixon's *Sketch of Merwara*, p. 17. 5. Ibid. 6. Ibid.

property in one of the Mer villages. These chiefs accomplished nothing and were eventually obliged to withdraw their troops from the neighbourhood of the hills.

Lastly in 1816 A.D., Maharana[1] Bheem Singh sent an army against Barar, but failed to take it, the chief of Bhagwanpura having lost his life during the operations. As a matter of fact, neither Mewar nor Marwar nor the Mahrattas, made any serious attempt to clear the thick forests of Merwara, and destroy the strongholds of the Mers or Rawats.

With confusion prevailing everywhere on the decline of the Mughal power in India, and the failure of the half-hearted attempts of the Rajputs and the Mahrattas to conquer the Mers, the latter became still more bold, and began to plunder all round. They destroyed several villages of Mewar, and plundered the adjoining tracts of Ajmer and Marwar freely.

Colonel Dixon, in his *Sketch of Merwara*, describes the extent of the territory, to which the predatory visits of the Mers were made. Six miles to the south of Shamgarh, located in the midst of the hills, are the towns of Jhak and Lulua. They maintained 250 horsemen and 600 armed men on foot. Their beat extended over the northern portion of Mewar including Shahpura. The Khan of Athoon with his brethren of Borwa and Saroth, commanded eighty sowars and six-hundred matchlockmen. Their beat extended to central Mewar including Banera, Bhilwara, Mandal, Chitor and Badnor. The Khan received a fourth of the plunder.

Southward along the hills, stood the Mer towns of Madlan, Barar, Barsawara and Chhapalian exercising their predatory calling over the southern portion of Mewar, and to Malwa. Mandsaur and other towns are said to have suffered from Mer inroads. On the western face of the hills, were Chang, Maunpura and Kuneja, Bagri and Kot Kirana; and the Mers of these villages used to prey on Marwar, from Nagor to Godwar, their forays extending to the gates of Jodhpur.

Shamgarh and its villages situated on the eastern face of the hills and within six miles of Masuda is said to have held five hundred *sowars* and a like number of foot armed with swords, and matchlocks. Their beat extended from Kharwa to Pisangan, thence by Narwar to Kishangarh, and round by Kekri and Bhinai to the banks of Khari river, thus embracing the district of Ajmer and Kishangarh. Marriage parties and people bound on a pilgrimage to Pushkar and Dargah Khwaja Sahib, Ajmer were the game mainly sought by these highway-

1. *Sketch of Merwara*, by Colonel Dixon, p. 17.

men. Footmen were engaged in cattle-lifting and robbing travellers.

Twelve thanas, garrisoned by 350 sowars, were established on the southern frontier of Ajmer to check these marauding excursions. The Rajput Chiefs kept sowars and matchlockmen in addition.

As each village required protection, Bhumias were appointed who had a free grant of land, and who maintained watch and ward, and protected the cattle and crops of the village. In all villages, 61,031 bighas of land were thus set apart. The Bhumias were the feudal police. Even the protective arrangements were not enough, and immunity from plunder was purchased by paying the Mers, blackmail. Some villages gave the produce of one or more wells, some paid course cotton cloth and a maund and half of grain from each well. The Chief of Kharwa is said to have given 1,000 maunds of grain from the village Liri. The Gor Rajputs of Rajgarh made over the produce of one village. Others paid a fixed sum of money. Colonel Dixon says: "At the time, Ajmer reverted to us (1818 A.D.), it was unsafe for unarmed people to appear outside the walls of the town after sunset, at which time the gates were closed."

The present British province of Ajmer-Merwara never formed one single province. The Mughals, the Rajputs and the Mahrattas, who possessed Ajmer, were in possession of the town of Ajmer and a portion of what is now called the district of Ajmer. But Merwara always remained independent, and the jurisdiction of the governor of Ajmer never extended to it.

Mr. Wilder, the first English Superintendent of Ajmer, soon found that there could be no peace in the district till the Mers ceased to plunder the villages near the border of Merwara. He entered into an agreement with the Mers of Jhak, Lulwa, Shamgarh, Kana Khera and Kheta binding them to abstain from plunder. The pledge was not respected, as the predatory instinct of the Mers, the life of robbers they had lived for centuries, and the failure of the Mughals, the Rajputs and the Mahrattas to subdue them, emboldened them to defy the British.

Mr. Wilder represented to Marquis of Hastings, the Governor General of India, that the aggression of the Mers would not cease till Merwara was subdued and the marauders compelled to settle down on land. The Governor General directed Colonel Hall, Quarter Master General at Nasirabad, to start operations against the Mers.

With a view to gaining knowledge of the features of the country so necessary for the successful conduct of military operations, a party of four officers, accompanied by a strong escort of a company of infantry, a troop of cavalry, and a number of *harkaras* (runners), proceeded from Nasirabad, *via* Lulwa to Shamgarh in Merwara. Of this party, was Colonel (then Captain) Hall, of the Quarter-Master General's department, who afterwards was entrusted with the charge of the district. There was in the party, also an officer of Engineers. The party was accompanied by Devi Singh, the Thakur of Masuda. Having proceeded thus far without molestation, they attempted to penetrate by the Jhak *ghata* to Dilwara; but the Mers collected in force and occupied the pass *via* Surajpura to Kharwa, where they halted for the night. Some considerable robberies were committed during the night, and a sentry and chaprassi were wounded; but no serious attack was made upon them. The necessary local information having been gained, the party returned to Nasirabad.[1]

The Mers were also rather anxious to ascertain the character of their new neighbours. It is said that about this time, a man was sent from Jhak to Nasirabad, as a spy to inspect and report upon the boasted power of the British. "The first thing he saw, was a number of Sepoys undressed, bathing and eating; and observing so many of them with the *Janau*, or Brahminical thread, across their bodies, he conceived the idea that the regiments were composed chiefly of Brahmins, seeing that in Rajputana this distinction is almost entirely confined to that caste, and held in light esteem accordingly. He next saw them in the evening, dressed in their red coats, and drilling on their respective parades: the exhibition seems to have fairly puzzled him, and on returning to his friends, he reported that the British regiments were composed of Brahmins and women.[2]

In old days, the Maharana had constantly to fight with the Mers, who acknowledged him as their overlord, but gave him only nominal allegiance. He too was anxious to settle matters with this wild people. Colonel (then Captain) James Tod, the great historian of Rajputana, and the best friend the Rajputs have ever had, outside their own people, happened at the time to be the Political Agent at the court of the Maharana. Under his advice, the Maharana co-operated with the British authorities to reduce the Mers to submission.

1. *Sketch of Merwara*, by Col. Dixon, p. 19.
2. Ibid, pp. 19 20.

In March 1819. a detachment of three regiments of infantry, a squadron of cavalry, and some light guns mounted on elephants marched from Nasirabad under Major Lawry, of the Second battalion, 7th regiment Native Infantry. Mr. Wilder accompanied the expedition. Three columns of attack were formed, one to attack Lulua, and the other two to attack Jhak, all to meet finally at Jhak at the same time. They met with little resistance, the Mers having retired to the hills. Some attempts were made to beat up the hills and jungles but to no purpose. After destroying some Mer villages and making terms with the Mers, binding them to abstain from plunder, and establishing three Police Thanas at Jhak, Lulua and Shamgarh, the troops returned to Nasirabad.

While the British troops had attacked Merwara from the north, the Maharana's army numbering about 1,000 men under Thakur Salim Singh of Rupaheli invaded Merwara from the east on Baisakh Sudi 10, S. 1876 (1819). It attacked and took Entally and established *thanas* in various places and pushed the Mers back all along the hilly tract extending from Masuda to Badnor and Amet. The Mewar troops advanced and fixed their headquarters at Rampura and attacked and took Borwa. The Mers were thus confined to their hill fastnesses. As, however, the Jodhpur Durbar did not so far co-operate in this venture, the Mers were able to retire further west. Captain James Tod, the Political Agent, Udaipur himself went to Jodhpur in November 1819 A.D. and persuaded the Maharaja to co-operate with Mewar and the British. The Jodhpur Durbar strengthened their outposts and began to push the Mers from the west, as the Mewar troops were doing from the south and the east. Several skirmishes took place and in a few months, half the tract was brought under control, and Police thanas established in many places. With the advent of the rainy season, Thakur Salim Singh and several other Thakurs returned to their estates, as the British troops had also returned to Nasirabad.

The Mers, finding the field clear, issued from their fastnesses, killed at Borwa, a Kayastha officer sent by Colonel Tod to Rampura, a town of Mewar, attacked and destroyed the thanas and started plundering all round. They cut off the British thanas at Lulua and Jhak, murdered the Thanedar of Jhak, attacked Anaqur and laid siege to Bheemgarh, which had been built and garrisoned by the Mewar troops in 1820 A D. When the news of this insurrection reached the Maharana, he ordered Thakur Salim Singh to go back to Merwara and reduce the Mers to submission. Thakur Salim Singh started on 19 September, 1820 and took Rampura and Sapola, and re-established the old *thanas* and advanced to attack the Merat strongholds of Borwa, Jhak, Athoon and Lulua. Re-inforcements arrived under Thakur Jai Singh of Badnor. The Rao of Bhagwanpura was killed fighting the Mers in November 1820.[1] The Thakur of Masuda was asked to join, and Thakur Devi Singh came with his men. After a battle lasting three days, Borwa was taken. After a few days, Athoon was also taken, but the Merats of Jhak resisted for another year. As Salim Singh returned to his estate Rupaheli for a few days, the Mers and Merats attacked and took back Borwa. Hearing this, Thakur Salim Singh returned post-haste to Athoon and advanced to Borwa, and after two days' severe fighting, took it and made it the headquarters of the Mewar forces. During the winter months, Kookda, Chang, Saroth, Jawas, Shamshergarh, Surajpura, and some other villages belonging to Jhak and Lulua, were also taken.

As the thanas established by the British were destroyed and the Mers began to plunder Ajmer villages again, Lt. Col. W. G. Maxwell of the 1st battalion, 13th regiment Native Infantry, at Mr. Wilder's request, advanced from Nasirabad with a detachment, took Shamgarh, Lulua and Jhak, and advanced to Borwa. The fort of Athoon was the *point d'appui* during the operations. This force divided itself into three parts and invaded Merwara from three sides, Todgarh, Kharwa and Masuda respectively. The chief objective was, "the strongholds of Athoon and Barar in which the Mers had been accustomed to defy whatever troops the Indian States might send against them."[2]

Borwa was taken without much difficulty, but Athoon offered stout resistance. Bhopat Khan, the Khan of Athoon, shut himself up in the "strong fort built of pucca masonry, capable of resisting any force not provided with breaching artillery." As there were no metalled roads, it was not easy to bring heavy artillery from Ajmer. This was a strong position, from having several stone enclosures in front of it, placed with considerable judgement, and capable of resisting infantry. The artillery, which had been previously augmented by the addition of a few pieces of heavy metal, was allowed to play for some time, and eventually both the centre and the flanks were attacked simultaneously, when the Mers immediately gave way. In this engagement, the Mers attacked the six pounders sword in hand, as the guns just taken from the elephants were being mounted on their carriages. The attacking party was, however, repulsed and a few rounds of grape induced the enemy to retire behind his walls. A second similar attack was made on two five-inch howitzers which had taken up another position. There, the European artillery men seizing the muskets from the sepoys, drove the enemy back until the howitzer

1. Col Brooke's *History of Mewar*, p. 24.
2. Col. Brooke's *History of Mewar*, p. 125.

could be loaded with grape and Mers driven within cover of their defences. An attempt to blow up the gateway with a six pounder failed. Order was then given to abandon the gun and retire, so hot a fire was kept up from the walls. This was not done before a great number of men had been killed and wounded on our side.''

During the night, however, Bhopat Khan evacuated the fort and retired to Ramgarh Sarotan. After taking Athoon, the force advanced to Barar and then to Barsawara, where the Mewar army built a fort and called it Todgarh, after Col. Tod, Political Agent of Mewar. News came here that Bhopat Khan and other chiefmen had retired to Ramgarh, "a place situated in the midst of fastnesses." A detachment of eight companies, a party of cavalry and a few guns were sent at once against Bhopat Khan. After a difficult all-night march, this force reached Ramgarh early in the morning and surrounded the place. In the fight that ensued, Bhopat Khan was killed with 150 men, and his son Lakha Khan was captured with 200 followers.[1] The Mewar contingent joined the British troops now, and both advanced to take Barar. After some fighting Barar was taken, and the following day, Barsawara (Todgarh) and Mandlan were also taken. A halt was made in order to support the Udaipur measures for retaining possession of the country. On these being considerably advanced, and the building of three forts nearly completed, five companies and two guns were ordered to remain till their completion, while the rest of the combined Mewar and British forces, except the artillery, moved forward on Kot Kirana and Bagri which were taken and made over to Jodhpur. A detachment of cavalry and infantry being left at Jhak, the main body of the force was withdrawn at the close of January 1821.

The Mewar forces having handed over Borwa to the British authorities, and on Masuda laying claim to it, retired on 29 March 1821 to Shamshergarh.

On Thakur Salim Singh's return to Rupaheli, and the British forces to Nasirabad, owing to the rainy season setting in, the Mers revolted again. The Maharana, therefore, sent Thakur Salim Singh for the third time in December, 1821 A.D. He came upon the Mers at Surajpura and defeated them, and established a cantonment there. Salim Singh returned to Udaipur to join the marriage festivities of Jawan Singh, the heir-apparent of Mewar. But hearing of Mer disturbances, he returned to Merwara.

1. *The Story of Merwara*, p. 27. (London, 1868 A.D.).

Organised resistance having been overcome, the work of establishment of permanent peace was taken in hand measures began to be taken to settle the Mers and Merats on land. Hundreds of prisoners taken during the campaign were settled on land in the parganas of Bheemgarh and Shamgarh. The Thakurs and Khans of Borwa, Jhak and Athoon having submitted, some more land was given to them and they settled in their estates.

Udaipur claimed thirtyone villages of the parganah of Beawar, and Thakur Salim Singh requested the Agent Governor General at Ajmer in March 1822 A.D., to restore them. But as the Jodhpur Durbar also claimed these villages, on the plea that these villages had been in the latter's possession for sometime before the Mahrattas took possession of the the district of Ajmer and Beawar in 1806 A.D., the British Government rejected the claims of both Mewar and Marwar, and incorporated them with Beawar, where a new town called Nayanagar was later founded. The history of Badnor says that the British Government did "the monkey and cat justice" in the matter. Government instituted an enquiry into the claims of Mewar and Marwar Darbars in 1822. In 1823, certain decisions were arrived at by which Jhak, Shamgarh, Bahar, Barkakra, Beawar and Bhailan Parganas were kept for Ajmer (British). Kot Kirana and Chang were given to Jodhpur; and Todgarh, Dewair and Saroth to Udaipur. Some villages were reserved in trust by the British Government to be eventually handed over to Mewar. Sixteen villages were given to the Rao of Deogarh (Mewar) and three to the Rao of Amet (Mewar).

In the discussions which took place during the investigation of claims to portions of the tract, after it had been conquered, the Chiefs of Masuda and Kharwa in Ajmer, asserted their rights to the villages nearest their estates; Masuda laying claim to Jhak, Lulua, Shamgarh, Kheta Khera and Ragpura; while Kharwa set forth her right to Kana Khera and Kesarpura. The claims of these Chiefs were admitted; that of Masuda, based on good service during the reduction of the country. The Governor General-in-Council eventually accorded half the net revenue of these villages, after debiting them with a fair charge for the district expenses, *vide*, Mr. Secretary Swinton's letter under date 8th July, 1825.

On the 29th June, 1823 A.D., Sir David Ochterlony[1] gave one quarter of the revenue of Fatehpur to Kharwa. Borlass's Horse was disbanded at Nasirabad in 1922 A.D.,

1. Dixon's *Settlement Report*, page 119.

Some of the disbanded Pathans offered service to Mr. Wilder, Superintendent of Ajmer. As Mr. Wilder, was afraid of the Mers' depredations, he accepted the Pathans' offer and assigned to three of the discharged Risaldars who settled there, one-twelfth of the produce of the villages of Myrean, Bulad and Beecharli.[1] In January 1835, Col. Hall[2] gave a quarter of the rent of Tikrana to Kharwa.

On behalf of the Maharana, Captain Tod, appointed a governor of Mewar-Merwara and raised six hundred matchlocks to keep the peace. The villages given to Marwar were made over to the adjoining Thakurs. The Thakurs of Masuda and Kharwa were held responsible for keeping order under Mr. Wilder's superintendence.

This triple government was, however, no government. The criminals of one portion found security in another: Merwara was infested with a gang of plunderers. It was, therefore, determined that the three portions should be brought under the management of one officer vested with civil and criminal powers, and a battalion of eight companies of seventy Mers each, and 240 of Amir Khan's drafts should be enrolled.

In May 1823, the Maharana of Udaipur, at the request of Sir David Ochterlony, Agent Governor General for Malwa and Rajputana, agreed to hand over administration of the most refractory part of Mewar-Merwara, consisting of seventy-six villages to British Government for ten years and to pay Rs. 15,000 (Chitor coin) for civil and military expenses. In March 1824, similar arrangements were made by Mr. Wilder with the Jodhpur Darbar, who handed over twentyone villages in the parganahs of Chang and Kot Kirana for eight years. The Maharana of Udaipur and the Maharaja of Jodhpur were to receive the revenues of their respective portions. On 7 March 1833,[3] the agreement with the Udaipur Darbar was renewed at Beawar by Colonel Locket, Agent Governor General for Rajputana for eight years more from 31st May 1833 to 31st May 1841, the Maharana agreeing to continue to pay the amount originally fixed Rs. 15,000 (Chitor coin) and in addition, pay Rs. 5,000 for the cantonment of Beawar. The agreement with Udaipur expired in 1841. It was renewed, and Maharana Sardar Singh (1838 to 1842 A.D.) agreed to let the tract remain under the British as long as it might suit their convenience. (*Aitchison's Treaties*, Vol. III, p. 19).

1. Dixon's *Settlement Report*, page 120. 2. Ibid, page 121.
3. Col. Brooke's *History of Mewar*, p. 36.

The agreement with Jodhpur was renewed for nine years on 23rd October 1835, when seven more villages were handed over. But these were returned to Jodhpur in 1843 A.D., and the Maharaja also agreed to leave the twenty-one villages with the British Government for such time as might suit their convenience.

Colonel Hall was appointed the first Superintendent of Merwara, and he ruled it for thirteen years, from 1823 to 1836. Colonel Dixon who succeeded him, was Superintendent upto 1853 A.D. On June 28, 1837, half the revenue of nine villages was assigned to the Maharana of Udaipur, and the villages incorporated in the Beawar Tahsil. (Dixon's *Settlement Report*, p. 119).

The Mewar and Marwar Darbars have been periodically asking for the return of their villages. The first request was made in 1832, when the treaties were renewed. The second request was made in 1843, but Colonel Dixon, Superintendent of Merwara protested against it and the matter was dropped, Colonel Sutherland also opposed the transfer. Emboldened by the success of the Mysore Party which had resulted in the rendition of Mysore, Mewar and Marwar claimed their portions of Merwara in 1866-67 A.D. The Maharaja of Jodhpur sent Colonel Taylor, formerly an employee of the East India Company, but at the time in Jodhpur service, to London to press his employer's claim. Colonel Hall and other British officers who were in Britain, helped the storm of protest raised against the return of the villages, and the matter was dropped. "*The Story of Merwara*," published by Longmans Green and Co., London, in 1868 A.D., gives a full account of this agitation.

In 1872 and 1874 A.D., the Maharana reopened the question, and asked that in place of the Mewar portion of Merwara, held by the British, the districts of Jawad, Jiran and Neemuch, which originally belonged to Mewar, but at the time were held by the British Government from Scindia in payment of the Gwalior Contingent, and the restoration of which the Maharana claimed under article 7 of the Treaty of 1818 A.D., may be returned to Mewar. The British Government did not accede to this request, but proposed to accept the revenues of the Mewar portion of Merwara in full discharge of Mewar Darbar's contribution towards the upkeep of the Mewar Bhil Corps (first raised in 1841) and the Merwara Battalion, and the arrears already due. And by Lord Ripon's *Kharita* of 16th October 1833, the Maharana was definitely assured that his rights of sovereignty over Mewar-Merwara will always remain intact.

It was further stipulated that, should the receipts from the district at any time exceed Rs. 66,000, the sum representing the contributions payable by Mewar for the administration of Mewar Merwara and the expenses of the two local corps, the surplus money would be paid in full to the Mewar Darbar, and that the Resident in Mewar should annually, intimate to the Maharana in a *kharita*, the aggregate revenue derived from the district during the preceding twelve months. The Maharana signified his assent to these arrangements in a kharita addressed to the Governor General under date the 13th November, 1883 A.D.

In the case of Marwar-Merwara it was agreed in 1885 A.D. that Jodhpur should retain its sovereign rights in these villages, and receive Rs. 3,000 a year from them; and that, if there is a profit, it should also receive forty per cent of it.

The question was again recently re-opened by the two Darbars, and the British Government have duly considered the representations made to it regarding the changed circumstances of the country. The Governments of Mewar and Marwar, it has been represented, are now conducted more or less on the lines on which British India is governed; there is reign of law in these States as in British India. There is complete peace in the country and the object with which the Mers of Merwara, Marwar and Ajmer were placed under one officer, which was to turn the predatory Mers, whose sole profession had been to plunder, into a peaceful agriculturist community, has been fully achieved. This having been accomplished, the necessity for keeping the Mewar and Marwar portions under British administration has disappeared. The agreement between the British Government and the two Indian States in its final form stipulated that "They (these portions) should be held by us (British) as long as may suit our convenience." It is thus clear that the Government of India always contemplated the return of the territories placed by the Mewar and Marwar Darbars for a purpose under the British Government only reserving the right to return them at a time when it suited its convenience to do so. The British Government therefore decided that the time had come to return the villages to the two States.

There is another important reason why the British Government has agreed to reopen the question and return the villages to Mewar. The arrangement arrived at between the Mewar Darbar and the British Government in 1883 A.D. was to the effect that the revenues of the Mewar portion of Merwara upto Rs. 66,000 a year will be considered as the Mewar contribution towards the upkeep of the two military corps established to keep order in the hilly tracts of Mewar—the Mewar Bhil Corps and the Merwara Battalion—and that the revenue exceeding that sum would be yearly returned to the Mewar Darbar. Now that perfect peace has been established in Merwara, and both the Mewar Bhil Corps and the Merwara Battalion *disbanded* as no longer required, the British Government had to pay to the Maharana this Rs. 66,000 a year, which had so long been appropriated towards the expenses of the two corps. It suits the convenience of the British Government to return the villages and not incur this additional yearly payment of Rs. 66,000 to Mewar.

In order to allay the fears of the people of these villages, who, having lived for over a hundred years under the British Government, are now transferred to the rule of an Indian State, Government have arranged that the transferred portions shall for sometime be administered as hitherto by a British Officer (under State employment) and shall be governed by the same laws and regulations, and enjoy the same educational, medical, forest and revenue facilities as they did before such transfer. For this purpose, the services of the revenue, educational, forest, cooperative, medical and other establishments hitherto administering the portions of Merwara have been transferred to Mewar and Marwar.

Thus, Merwara, which has had a chequered career in history during the last century, has in 1938 taken the same shape as it had assumed in 1822, after its conquest by the combined British and Mewar forces. It should not, however, be forgotten that very large numbers of Mers have lived for centuries in Mewar under the Maharanas of Mewar.

In 1822 A.D., the Mers lived under three governments. the British, the Mewar and the Marwar Darbars. They were, however, all brought under one Government—the British—in 1825 and lived under it for a hundred and twelve years enjoying the advantages of the British rule. In 1938, they have again been divided into three parts, one part continuing to live under the British, the other two being handed over to Mewar and Marwar.

The Census Report for 1931, Vol. XXVI, Table I, gives the area and population of the transferred portions as under:—

		Area Miles	No. of Villages.	Population.
Mewar-Merwara	....	221	93	44,463
Marwar-Merwara	....	50	22	8,846
Total	....	271	115	53,109

Table II gives the total population of Merwara as 1,36,374. The population of British Merwara is, therefore reducedf rom 1,36,374 to 83,065.[1] It is interesting to note that the population of Merwara had increased from 91,434 in 1881 A.D. to 1,36,374 in 1931 A.D. The population of the transferred portions now is 53,309. It is difficult to say what it was when they were taken by the British Government. While the two States have gained by this transaction, by handing over to the British Government sparsely-populated territory and receiving it back thickly papulated, the province of Ajmer-Merwara has suffered a loss. Its area has been reduced from 2,711 to 2,440 miles, and its population from 5,60,292 to 5,06,983; and the energy, time, and money spent on improving the transferred territory have been lost to it.

The average rainfall in Merwara during the twenty years upto 1904, was 20 inches. There were no roads in Merwara before the famine of 1869 A.D. There is a good road now upto Dewair; and fair weather roads to all important places in it. Up to 1937 A.D. when the Mewar and Marwar portions of Merwara were handed over to those States, there were two Tahsils, Beawar and Todgarh[2]; now there is only one, Beawar. In Colonel Dixon's time, the Beawar Tahsil contained two towns, 127 villages and 84 hamlets. There were three parganahs Beawar, Jhak-Shamgarh and Bhailan.[3]

A Subdivisional officer called the Extra Assistant Commissioner, Merwara is in direct charge of the administration under the Commissioner of Ajmer-Merwara, and under him is a Tahsildar and a Naib Tahsildar. A Sub judge, first class, decides civil suits. Appeals lie to the District judge, Ajmer-Merwara. A Senior Inspector of Police called the Circle Inspector, resides in Beawar and is in direct charge of the Merwara Police under the Superintendent of Police, Ajmer-

1. Thornton's *Gazetteer* (1850 A.D.), p. 589, says: "British Merwara contains an area of 282 sq miles with a population of 37,715. The portion allotted to Udaipur, was an area of 305 sq. miles and that to Jodhpur, 67 square miles.

2. For sometime, there was a third Tahsil, Saroth, *Vide*, La Touche's *Gazetteer of Ajmer-Merwara*.

3. Dixon's *Settlement Report*, p. 129.

Merwara. Forest, Excise, Co-operative, Income Tax departments are under the Officers who hold charge of these departments in Ajmer.

The chief town of Merwara is Nayanagar. After the subjugation of the Mers in 1819-21, it took a little time for things to settle down. Colonel Dixon founded a new walled town in 1835 A.D. to be the head-quarters of the administration of Merwara, and at the request of the people of the place,[1] gave it the name, Nayanagar.

"The site chosen was a place near the cantonment, where the Merwara Battalion was housed. There existed thirty or forty huts at the time when Captain Dixon issued a proclamation regarding the building of a town. Candidates for forty shops appeared, and work commenced. Streets at right angles were marked off, the main street being 72 feet wide with trees planted on both sides. Muhallas were allotted to the various castes."[2] The proclamation said that no octroi would be levied for two years and that concession would be given for four years. A city with a spacious bazar sprung up at his bidding. It rose with the rapidity of magic.

The trading classes asked that a wall should be built around the town for their protection. And so a city-wall with four gates and thirty two bashions, was built by Government at a cost of Rs. 23.840.[3] Colonel Dixon himself laid the foundation of the Ajmer Gate in February, 1836 A.D. The Police thana and the Octroi office were built opposite to each other in the bazar. The temple of Rughunathji and the Mahadevaji Chhatree were built in the bazar. Three wells, each twenty seven feet in diameter, were dug.

The Mahajans brought in their goods, and on 1, May, 1836, the bazar opened for traffic In a short time, it was reported that nearly two thousand families engaged in various manufacturing and commercial operations, were located within the wall, Col. Dixon built a hospital in Nayanagar in 1850 A.D. In his *Sketch of Merwara*, written in June, 1848, and published in 1850, page 105, Col. Dixon says:—

> "The Jail built in 1823 is within forty paces of the city wall. There are five hundred shops of pucca masonry within the walls of the town, three hundred of which are opened for trade, while two hundred are reserved as store-houses for merchandise............Sixty shops are occupied by native bankers and shroffs...............Ten shops are occupied by Fatehpuria Mahajans who are extensive traders."

1. *Sketch of Merwara*, p. 111. 2. La Touche's *Gazetteer*, p. 55.
3. *Sketch of Merwara*, by Colonel Dixon, p. 105. The total length of the wall is two miles. The bastions are twenty one feet high.

Nayanagar is now being wrongly called Beawar. It is a pity that the name given to it by its founder Colonel Dixon, is being changed. Throughout the *Sketch of Merwara*, published in 1850, Col. Dixon calls the place *Nayanagar*. In the *Story of Merwara*, published in 1868 in London, the place is called, Nayanagar. Beawar is nowhere used. Beawar, as a matter of fact, is a good-sized village, four miles away from Nayanagar, and is an old place. People of Ajmer-Merwara, except those connected with the administration, still call it Nayanagar. The reason why Nayanagar has come to be called Beawar appears to be as follows :—

Merwara was finally subjugated in 1821 A.D. In 1822 Captain Henry Hall (later General Hall) was appointed its Superintendent, and a local corps of Mers was raised and located four miles from the chief village in the plain. Beawar at the mouth of the hilly tract of Merwara, and was called Beawar Cantonment. As the Superintendent of Merwara was also the Commandant of this force, he lived in a house in the Beawar Cantonment and thus Beawar Cantonment became the head-quarters of the Merwara administration. The severe famine of 1834 disorganised life in Merwara and in 1835 Captain (later Col.) Dixon succeeded Captain Hall as Superintendent. In 1836, he founded a new town by the Beawar Cantonment, on the site of a hamlet called Bicherli, and named it Nayanagar (new city). As however, the Superintendent lived in the Beawar Cantonment, Beawar continued to be used as the name of the head-quarters of the administration. Till the year 1870 A.D. the town founded by Col. Dixon was called and known exclusively as Nayanagar in official and private records. In 1871, the Cantonment was abolished. and the Merwara Battalion was transferred to Ajmer, but as the Assistant Commissioner of Merwara who had taken the place .of Superintendent, continued to live in the same place as the Superintendent, the head-quarters of the administration continued to be called Beawar, though as a matter of fact, Nayanagar had now become such headquarters. In official correspondence, the seat of the Assistant Commissioner; which, after 1871 A.D., had become Nayanagar, after the transfer of the Merwara Battalion to Ajmer, continued to be called Beawar.

Nayanagar has a population of 28,342[1] (1931 census), and after Ajmer. is the most populous place in Ajmer-

1. The population of Nayanagar has risen as below :—

1847 A.D.	... 9,000		1911 A.D.	... 22,800
1887 ,,	... 15,829		1921 ,,	... 22,362
1891 ,,	... 20,978		1931 ,,	... 28,342
1901 ,,	... 21,928			

Merwara. Nayanagar (Beawar) is a Municipality. The Municipal Committee is composed of fifteen elected,—nine Hindus, four Muslims, two Christians—and six nominated members, including an official Chairman, who is the Extra Assistant Commissioner of Merwara. Thetotal income of the Committee in 1939-40 (famine year) was Rs. 1,69,943-13-0, and expenditure, Rs. 2,00,884-9-10.

EDUCATION:—In addition to a private Intermediate College called the Sanatan Dharm College there is a High School, a Municipal Middle School, and a Commercial School at Nayanagar.

Nayanagar or Beawar is a trade centre and is the most industrialized town in Ajmer-Merwara. It imports cotton, wool, foodstuffs and cloth, and distributes them to the adjoining parts of Mewar and Marwar. Wool, cotton, ghee, gur, sugar, *methi*, *zira*, cottonseed, *til* (Oil-seed) and several other commodities are stored in far larger quantities in Beawar than in Ajmer. After Fazilka in the Punjab, Beawar is the most important centre of wool trade in India.

It has three flourishing spinning and weaving mills, seven cotton presses, a hosiery factory and a ginning factory. The first mill, Krishna Mills, was started as early as 1889 and the last, Mahalakshmi in 1925. A.D., The mills are:—

Date of starting.	Name.	Capital. Rs.	Spindles.	Looms.	Managing Agents.
17 June 1889.	The Krishna Mills...	7,00,000	20,320	636	Messrs. Thakur Das Khimraj & Co.,
1 August 1908.	The Edward Mills...	6,40,000	18,312	376	Rai Bahadur Seth Gadhmal Lodha and R.S. Motilal Raniwala.
29 January 1925.	The Mahalakshmi Mills.	Issued—13,00,000 Paid up—12,99,600	13.726	416	Seth Lalchand Kothari and Rai Sahib Seth Vithal Das Rathi.

The following Cotton Presses and Factories exist in Nayanagar.—

1. The West Patent Press Co., Ltd.
2. The New Cotton Press.
3. The Hydraulic Cotton Press.
4. Khimraj Rathi's Ginning and Pressing Factory.
5. The New Barar Company, Limited.
6. The Mahalakshmi Cotton Press.
7. The Rajputana Cotton Press.
8. Sacheti Hosiery Factory.
9. Sacheti Ginning Factory.

Appendix A.

I

NOTABLE BUILDINGS IN THE CITY OF AJMER, WITH DATES OF CONSTRUCTION.

Buildings inside the city wall.	Date of construction, A.D.
Dargah Khwaja Muinuddin Chishti.	
a. Buland Darwaja in it	1469-1500
b. Akbari Mosque	1570
c. Khwaja's mausoleum	1636
d. Juma Masjid	1636
e. Mausoleum of Sheikh Hasan (Sola Khamba) ...	1638
f. *Mahfil Khana*	1889-91
g. Nizam's Nakkarkhana (Main Gate)	1915
Principal *Havelies* (big residential houses).	
a. Gajmalji ki haveli (Nahar Muhalla)	1791-1800
b. Patwan ki haveli (Karakka Chowk)	1830-40
c. Narsinghdasji ki haveli (Karakka Chowk) ...	1840-50
d. Ram Pershadji ki haveli (Nahar Muhalla) ...	1840-50
e. Lodhon ki haveli (Naya Bazar)	1850
f. Haji Muhammad Khan[1] ki haveli (Dhan Mandi) ...	1860-67
Ganpatpura Gate (*Sarai* in Mughal times)	1560-1570
Magazine (Akbar's palace)	1571
Audience Chamber in it, converted into a Museum in ...	1908
City wall and Delhi and Tripolia Gates	1571
Agra andUsri Gates	1820
Jhalra. (tank)	
a. Built about	1571
b. Emperor Shahjahan deepened it in	1643
c. Col. Dixon, Commissioner of Ajmer, repaired and enlarged it for the use of the city	1852
City Branch School, (now Girls' School) about	1880
Ajmer Municipal Office (formerly Victoria Hospital) ...	1895
Buildings outside the city wall.	
Taragarh (Garh Beetli) about	600 A. D.
a. Kutchery known as Prithviraja's Kutchery ...	1180-92
b. Dargah Miran Sahib: Buland Darwaja ...	1569
Mausoleum	1615
The Jain Chhatrees (north of Anasagar) containing inscriptions of	760 to 871 A.D. & later.
Anasagar Lake	1123-50
Visaldeva Vigrahraj IV's *Vidyalaya* (College)	
a. Built	1152-63
b. converted into Adhai-din-ka-Jhonpra.	1198-1210
Visalsar (Visla tank)	1153-63
Marble Baradaries on Anasagar Lake	1637
Abdullah Khan's Tomb (near Railway goodshed) ...	1710

1. Haji Muhammad Khan was assassinated at Pushkar on 10, November, 1867 A.D.

NOTABLE BUILDINGS IN AJMER WITH DATES.

	A. D.
Blue Castle (city encamping ground)	1710-25
Chishti Chaman Sarai, originally a garden (opposite the Victoria Jubilee Clock Tower)	1769
Idgah in Kaisargunj	1773
Bapugarh Hill Temple and Bajranggarh Hill Temple	1816-18
Ghats on the Anasagar Lake *1834-48* :—	
Khazanchion ka Ghat	1839
Ram Pershadji ka Ghat	1841
Gulkhandyon ka Ghat	1844
Navagarh Ghat	1846
Lodhon ka Ghat	1848
Paropkarini Sabha ka Ghat (originally Shahpura Ghat)	1847-48
Suraj Kund outside Madar Gate	1854
Nasiyan or Red Temple	
a. Temple (Sidhkut Chaitalaya)	1865
b. Svarnanagri Hall	1896
Government College, Ajmer	1869
New Wings of the College containing laboratories added in (Cost Rs. 2,58,300)	1929-35
Free Church of Scotland (Ry. Station-Kaisarbagh Road)	1862
Central Jail (Jaipur Road)	1872
Residency (on the Anasagar Lake)	1875-80
Railway Buildings at Ajmer :	
a. Railway Institute	1878
b. Railway Loco and Carriage Shops	1877-79
c. Railway General Offices	1884
d. Railway Station	1885
e. Railway Hospital	1890
f. Bisset Institute	1909
g. Railway Electric Power House	1924
Mayo College	1877 82
Arya Samaj Bhawan (Kaisargunj) (second storey built later)	1886
District Court House	1887
Queen Victoria Jubilee Clock Tower (opposite Railway Station)	1889-90
Dayanand Ashram (Kaisargunj)	1889-90
Roman Catholic Cathedral (Kaisargunj)	1898 Dec.
St. Anslem's School Concert Hall	1935 Jan.
Trevor Town Hall	1899-1901
Tikam Nivas (overlooking the Daulat Bagh)	1910
King Edward Memorial	1912-13
Moinia Islamia High School	1917
Government High School and Hostel (Cost Rs. 5,30,407).	1919-23
Court of Small Causes (Cost Rs. 55,140)	1921
Government Normal School (in Mir Shah Ali garden, Jaipur Road) (Cost Rs. 39,000)	1927
Moinia Islamia High School (Cost Rs. 1,33,240)	1928
Ajmer Electric Power House	1929
Police Lines and Buildings (Jaipur Road) (Cost Rs. 3,80,003)	1930
High School and Intermediate Education Board Office (Government Encamping ground) (Cost Rs. 88,592)	1935

II

PUBLIC DURBARS HELD AT AJMER.

Date A.D.			Convener.
3 January	1823	...	General Sir David Ochterlony, Agent Governor General, Rajputana and Malwa.
16 November	1826	...	Sir C.J. Metcalfe, Agent to the Governor-General in Rajputana.
2 December	1846	...	Mr. Thomason, Lieutenant Governor, North-West Provinces (now U. P.)
22 October	1870	...	Lord Mayo, Viceroy and Governor General.
5 November	1872	...	Colonel J. Brooke, Agent Governor General Rajputana and Chief Commissioner, Ajmer-Merwara.
28 June	1873	...	Colonel Pelly " " "
30 March	1875	...	Mr. Alfred Lyall " " "
11 February	1886	...	Sir Edward Bradford " " "
7 April	1911	...	Hon'ble Mr. E. G Colvin " " "
2 April	1913	...	Sir Elliot Colvin " " "
8 March	1919	...	Colonel Manners Smith " " "
22 August	1919	...	The Hon'ble Mr. A. T. Holme. " " "

Lord William Bentinck, Governor General of India, met the Princes of Rajputana on 17 January, 1832 A. D. at Ajmer but held no Durbar.

III

VISITS OF GOVERNORS GENERAL AND VICEROYS OF INDIA TO AJMER.

1. Lord William Bentinck, Governor General.	17-18	January	1832	A.D.
2. Earl of Mayo G. G. and Viceroy ...	20	October	1870	"
3. Lord Northbrook...	2	December	1875	"
4. Earl of Lytton	1	December	1879	"
5. Marquis of Ripon	19	November	1881	"
6. Marquis of Dufferin	5	November	1885	"
7. Lord Lansdowne...	28	October	1890	"
8. Earl of Elgin	10	November	1896	"
9. Lord Curzon	2	November	1899	"
" "	18	November	1902	"
10. Lord Minto	4	April	1906	"
11. Lord Hardinge	16	November	1912	"
12. Lord Chelmsford...	17	November	1916	"
13. Marquis of Reading	26	January	1923	"
14. Lord Irvin	7	March	1930	"
15. Lord Willingdon	4	December	1932	"
16. Lord Linlithgow	7	March	1940	"

Appendix B.

I

RAINFALL IN AJMER FROM 1860 to 1940. A.D. (81 years)

Year A.D.	Inches.	Year A.D.	Inches.	Year A.D.	Inches.
1860	10.77	1887	23.7	1914-15	23.24
1861	25.50	1888	22.3	1915-16	11.10
1862	43.40	1889	23	1916-17	28.42
1863	27.34	1890	16.34	1917-18	48.68
1864	17.64	1891	8.18	1918-19	5.81
1865	16.47	1892	22.18	1919-20	17.24
1866	26.16	1893	31.22	1920-21	20.44
1867	27.27	1894	26.61	1921-22	11.69
1868	9.28	1895	23.53	1922-23	13.61
1869	23.92	1896	22.26	1923-24	13.54
1870	16.97	1897	22.61	1924-25	34.09
1871	21.70	1898	12.35	1925-26	13.66
1872	32	1899	6.64	1926-27	24.24
1873	21.27	1900-01	26.27	1927-28	25.35
1874	17.75	1901-02	10.03	1928-29	24.61
1875	36.37½	1902-03	17.73	1929-30	28.77
1876	24.09	1903-04	18.19	1930-31	20.93
1877	11.76	1904-05	15.58	1931-32	20.51
1878	31.05	1905-06	7.44	1932-33	14.26
1879	27.50	1906-07	18.79	1933-34	34.39
1880	19.2	1907-08	13.14	1934-35	27.18
1881	22.1	1908-09	37.02	1935-36	28.97
1882	26.5	1909-10	29.96	1936-37	18.30
1883	17.3	1910-11	17.04	1937-38	24.64
1884	26.9	1911-12	8.04	1938-39	8.74
1885	24.6	1912-13	13.38	1939-40	6.96
1886	15.2	1913-14	15.13	1940-41	27.97

The above figures are taken from the following:

For 1860 to 1873 A.D. ... Mr. La Touche's *Settlement Report of Ajmer-Merwara*, p. 11.

For 1874 to 1879 ,, ... Ajmer Observatory, DeLaessoe's *Famine Report*, p. 130.

For 1880 to 1899 ,, ... Ajmer Observatory, *Rajputana Gazetteer*, Vol. 1. I—B p. 3.

For 1900 to 1940 ,, ... Supplied by the Executive Engineer, P. W. D., Ajmer.

II

TEMPERATURE CHART.

Year.	Month.	Date.	Highest Maximum.	Departure from normal of the month.	Month.	Date.	Lowest Minimum.	Departure from normal of the month.
1901	June.	11	114	+13	Jan.	5	38	− 8
1902	May	7	108	+ 5	Feb.	8	35	−12
1903	June	14	112	+11	Dec.	28	38	− 7
1904	May	21	109	+ 5	Jan.	9	39	− 7
1904	,,	21	109	+ 5	,,	20	39	− 7
1905	,,	11	113	+10	Feb.	1	30	−17
1906	,,	12	112	+ 9	Jan.	6	39	− 7
1906	,,	13	112	+ 9		9	39	− 7
1907	,,	17	109	+ 6	Dec.	28	42	− 3
1908	June	16	109	+ 9	,,	28	39	− 6
1909	,,	7	110	+ 7	Feb.	6	40	− 7
1910	May	24	107	+ 3	Dec.	22	40	− 6
1911	,,	17	109	+ 6	Jan.	5	41	− 5
1911	,,	18	109	+ 6	Feb.	4	41	− 6
1912	,,	15	114	+11	Dec.	10	42	− 5
1912	,,	16	114	+11	,,	10	42	− 5
1913	,,	31	109	+ 5	Jan.	24	41	− 6
1914	,,	26	112	+ 8	Dec.	12	38	− 9
1915	,,	4	111	+ 9	Jan.	10	37	− 9
1916	,,	26	109	+ 5	Feb.	7	34	−13
1917	,,	8	107	+ 4	Dec.	22	40	− 6
1917	,,	8	107	+ 4	,,	23	40	− 6
1918	,,	16	108	+ 5	Jan.	29	34	−13
1919	,,	2	110	+ 8	,,	15	37	−10
1920	June	9	110	+ 7	Feb.	6	32	−15
1921	May	3	110	+ 8	Jan.	22	38	− 9
1922	,,	19	110	+ 7	,,	3	35	−11
1923	June	3	109	+ 5	,,	1	39	− 7
1923	,,	6	109	+ 6	,,	1	39	− 7
1924	,,	16	107	+ 7	,,	22	36	−11
1925	April	24	109	+ 9	,,	22	34	−13
1926	June	6	108	+ 5	Dec.	28	35	−10
1927	,,	3	109	+ 5	Jan.	10	32	−14
1928	May	7	109	+ 6	Dec.	29	34	−11
1929	,,	4	109	+ 7	Jan.	31	27	−20
1930	,,	7	107	+ 4	Dec.	25	36	−10
1930	,,	8	107	+ 4	,,	25	36	−10
1930	,,	9	107	+ 4	,,	25	36	−10
1930	,,	10	107	+ 4	,,	25	36	−10
1930	,,	12	107	+ 4	,,	25	36	−10
1931	June	5	110	+ 6	Feb.	4	37	−10

TEMPERATURE CHART—*Contd.*

Year.	Month.	Date.	Highest Maximum.	Departure from normal of the month.	Month.	Date.	Lowest Minimum.	Departure from from normal of the month.
1932	May	24	113	+ 9	Dec.	30	37	− 8
1932	,,	25	113	+ 9	,,	30	37	− 8
1933	,,	30	107	+ 3	Jan.	15	33	−14
1933	,,	31	107	+ 3	,,	15	33	−14
1934	June	15	110	+ 9	,,	22	29	−18
1935	May	28	109	+ 5	,,	15	27	−20
1935	,,	28	109	+ 5	,,	16	27	−19
1936	,,	12	110	+ 7	Dec.	28	33	−12
1936	,,	13	110	+ 7	,,	28	33	−12
1936	,,	14	110	+ 7	,,	28	33	−12
1936	,,	15	110	+ 7	,,	28	33	−12
1937	,,	18	109	+ 6	Jan.	6	31	−15
1937	June	15	109	+ 8	,,	6	31	−15
1938	May	9	109	+ 8	Dec.	1	37·6	− 6
1939	July	9	106	+ 8	,,	1	44	− 6
1940	May	20	109	+ 5	Jan.	1	36	− 6

III

P. W. D. INSPECTION BUNGALOWS (17)

Ajmer.
Kishangarh
Mangliawas
Nasirabad
Goela
Deoli
Bir
Barol
Beawar
Sendra
Bandanwara
Barl
Jawaja
Jassakhera
Bhim
Todgarh
Chhaplian.

IV

POST AND TELEGRAPH OFFICES INCLUDING BRANCH OFFICES IN AJMER-MERWARA.

Head Offices	Sub Offices.	Branch Offices
1. Ajmer General Post Office.	Ajmer City.	1. Baghera
	1. Dargah Bazar T.	2. Bagsuri
	2. Diggi Bazar	3. Beer
	3. Jonesganj	4. Bhinai
	4. Kaisarganj T.	5. Bandanwara
	5. Kutchery-Ajmer T.	6. Champaneri
	6. Mayo Ajmer T.	7. Dewalia
	7. Naya Bazar	8. Gegal Akhri
	8. Regimental Bazar	9. Gobindgarh
	9. Bijainagar T.	10. Goela
		11. Harmara
	District	12. Jalia
		13. Kadera
	10. Deoli T.	14. Karel
	11. Kekri T.	15. Kharwa
	12. Nasirabad T.	16. Junia
	13. Pushkar T.	17. Ladpura
	14. Beawar town T.	18. Mangaliawas
	15. Todgarh T.	19. Masuda
	16. Beawar R. S.	20. Mehrun Kalan
		21. Pisangan
		22. Pranhera
		23. Ramsar
		24. Saradhna
		25. Sathana
		26. Sawar
		27. Singawal R. S.
		28. Srinagar
		29. Tantoti
		30. Thaonla
		31. Tilaunia R. S.
		32. Adarshnagar
		33. Ka'era Bogla
		34. Barakhan
		35. Barakhera
		36. Jawaja

TELEGRAPH OFFICES.

1. Ajmer General Telegraph Office.
2. Dargah Bazar (Ajmer City)
3. Kaisargunj (Ajmer City)
4. Mayo-Ajmer (Ajmer City)
5. Kutchery (Ajmer City)
6. Deoli
7. Kekri
8. Nasirabad Cantonment
9. Pushkar
10. Beawar
11. Todgarh
12. Bijainagar

Appendix C.

PRINCIPAL TEMPLES, MOSQUES AND CHURCHES.

I

HINDU TEMPLES.

1. Narsinghji temple, in *muhalla* Holidara. Nimbarak Acharya Tatwavetta possessed an idol, which was installed in this temple. It is dedicated to the Narsingh incarnation of God. Maheshwari Mahajans built the temple. Government gives an yearly grant of Rs. 75 to Narsinghji temple.
2. Lakshmi Narainji temple, in *Muhalla* Pattikatla. The Mahratta Governor Sivaji Nana (1791-1797 A. D.) put up a temple in the *Magazine*. In 1822 A. D., the idol was removed to the present temple. Some say it was removed in 1857 A. D. Government gives a grant of Rs. 56 a year to the temple since its removal from the *Magazine*.
3. Charbhujaji temple in the Kayasth *Muhalla*, built during Mahratta Rule.
4. Mohanji temple in Chaudhar *Muhalla*, built by Malu Maheshwaris 100 years ago, during Rathor Rajput period (eighteenth century).
5. Charbhuja temple near Ghee Mandi (Solthambha). Agarwals of Merta built it in 1859 A. D., (S. 1916.)
6. Raghunathji temple in Ghaseti, built about the same time as the Mohanji temple, during Rathor Raj in Ajmer.
7. Lakshminarainji temple in Ganj outside Agra Gate, built during Mahratta times.
8. Raghunathji temple in Naya Bazar (Ramanandi sect), built 100 years ago, by one Kani Ram, a military man.
9. Chhota Narsinghji temple in Naya Bazar, built by S. Ram Prasad about 1840 A. D.
10. Murli Manohar temple in Kaisarganj, built fifty years ago.
11. Khobranath on Anasagar Lake (Bheroonji temple). It is very old and is mentioned by Princess Jahan Ara, the eldest daughter of Emperor Shah Jahan in her book, *Munisul Arvah*.
12. Satyanarain temple of the Tambolees (betel sellers) in Lakhankotri.
13. Raghunathji temple in Lakhankotri, built by the tailors of Ajmer.
14. Raghunathji temple near Usri Gate built during Mahratta times.
15. Balaji temple near Agra Gate, built when Agra Gate was built.
16. Balaji temple, opposite Railway Station (very old, built before Mahratta times).
17. Lakshmi Narainji temple in Ghaseti *Baghichi* outside Usri Gate, built by the *chhipas*, more than 150 years ago.
18. Deoji temple in Gughra Ghati, near Mirshahali said to date from Chauhan times (sixth to twelfth century A. D).
19. Satyanarain temple in Holidara, built in 1910-11 A.D. by Solthamba Agarwals.

20-21 Babugarh and Bajranggarh temples, (see p. 126).

22. Anted Mata temple very old.
23. Chavanda Mata temple (see p. 125).

24. Vishnu temple in Bhata Bai, (Brahmania *sunars* (goldsmiths) built it and worship in it).
25. Vishnu temple in *Tulsi ki Baghichi*, built in Mahratta times, (Ramanandi sect.).
26. Two Shiva temples, one in *Sarafapol*, and the other in *Modania Gali* called Bhuteshwara Mahadeva Temple.
27. Shiva temple in city wall, near old Diggi gate, built by S. Ram Prashad about 1840 A.D.
28. Shiva temple in Shiva Bagh, Nayabazar, called Ardha Chandreshwar, built by the Mahratta Rulers of Ajmer.
29. Shanteshwara, temple, outside Madar Gate, built by the Mahratta governors of Ajmer.
30. Agreshwar Mahadeva temple outside Agra Gate, built by labourers who melted lead here in Mahratta times.
31. Jharneshwar Mahadeva, rebuilt in Mahratta times. (see p. 125.)
32. Shiva temple on the Koteshwar Hill near Foy Sagar (see p. 125).
33. Ajgandeshwara Mahadeva temple in Ajaipal valley, (see p. 122).
34. Ardhchandreshwara Mahadeva near the original brick tomb of Khwaja Muinuddin Chishti in the closed cellar under the present mausoleum of the Khwaja.
35. Baijnath Mahadeva temple in the Hokran hill.
36. Dudiya, contains Shiva, Hanuman and Vishnu temples built by Mahrattas.
37. Shiva and Hanumanji temple in *Keval ki Kui*, built by the Mahratta Governors of Ajmer.
38. Shivakund temple contains idols of Hanumanji and Ganeshji, of Colonel Dixon's time.

JAIN TEMPLES.

39. Paraswanath temple in *Goda Gali* Nullah Bazar. Tradition says that the Adhai-din-ka-Jhonpra was originally a Jain Temple, that when Shahbuddin Ghori converted it into a mosque, the idol was removed, and this temple was built. This is the earliest of the present Jain temples. The Bhattarak *gadi* was established in Ajmer in 1207 A.D. A Pandit, as disciple of the Bhattarak, conducts the worship. Connected with this, are the following temples:—
40. Bada Mandir, with the idol of Paraswanathji. This was built by the *panchayat* three or four hundred years after the *Goda Gali* temple.
41. Dharmdas Gangwal's temple adjacent to the Bada Mandir, built in s. 1852 (A.D. 1795) in the same compound.
42. Padmavati Mata's temple across the road.
43. Nasiyan containing an idol of Padam Prabhuji near Daulat Bagh.
44. Nagori Mandir opposite the Khatolan Pol *muhalla*, and a *Nasiyan* connected with it, containing an idol of Adi Nathji.
45. Godan ka Mandir, near Dharmdas Gangwal's temple and a *Nasiyan*, adjacent to Badamandir Nasiyan near Daulat Bagh.
46. Nayadhara Mandir also in Saraogi Muhalla.
47. Mul Chand Soni's temple. This is the largest and the most recent Jain temple, situated at the corner of Saraogi Muhalla. The Nasiyan connected with it, has been fully described on p. 114. This temple belongs to the *Terahpanthi* sect of the Digambar Jains.
48. Daryaoji temple of the *Khatrees* inside Madar Gate,

SIKH.

49. Sri Gurudwara, Ry. Station Daulat Bagh Road, 1890 A. D.

II

CHRISTIAN.

1. St. Mary's Church, Church of England, on the Visla Lake.
2. St. John the Evangelist, S. P. G. Mission, near Usri Gate. 1895 A.D.
3. Church of Scotland Mission, Jaipur Road, ... 1862 A.D.
4. Methodist Church, Jaipur Road, ... 1900 A.D.

III

PARSI.

Agiari (Fire Temple) on Nasirabad Road ... ... 1898 A.D.
The *Aram Gha* or *Dukhina* (Tower of Silence) near the Government Distillery ... ... 1887 A.D.

IV

MUSLIM.

1. The Adhai Din ka Jhonpra, originally a College built by Emperor Visaldeva, converted into a mosque (see page 68-82) 1195-1213
2. The Akbari mosque in the Dargah Khwaja Sahib, built by Emperor Akbar (see p. 87) 1571
3. The Juma Masjid in Dargah Khwaja Sahib, built by Emperor Shah Jahan (see p. 95) 1638
4. Mosque in Dargah Bazar, built by Tiloki, daughter of the famous musician, Tansen 1652
5. Mosque in Dargah Bazar opposite Moti Katla, built by one Miya Bai 1643
6. Mosque in Dargah Bazar built in Mughal times ... 1692
7. Mosque in Dargah Bazar 1780
8. Mosque in Imli Muhalla, Mahratta times 1761-1818
9. Mosque, Tekawalan, in Khazanchi gali ... ...
10. Mosque in *Ajmeri Dara* ... ...
11. Mosque, Deshwalian, in Purani Mandi 1860
12. Mosque in the City Encamping ground 1841
13. Mosque in Abdullahpura ... ... about ... 1720
14. Mosque, opposite the Railway Station 1850
15. Mosque, Bocha's mosque in Purani Mandi... ... Seventeenth century.
16. Mosque of Bohras in Cavendishpura built 20 years ago..

BIBLIOGRAPHY

I.—INSCRIPTIONS.

CHAUHAN PERIOD.

1. Inscription dated A. D. 760 in a Jain *chhatri* at Ajmer on Pandit Hemraj's remains.

2. Inscriptions dated A. D. 845, 854, and 871 A. D. in the Jain *chhatrees* and *Chabutras* at Ajmer built on the remains of Jain Bhattaraks, see *supra* p. 123.

3. Stone Inscription dated 18th June 973 A.D. (S. 1030 Asadh sudi 15th) of King Vigrahraj II in Harshnath Temple (Jaipur State), containing the genealogy of the Chauhan Kings of Ajmer from King Guvak to Vigrahraj II (Visaldev) and some account of their reigns—*In. Ant.* Vol. II, p. 119.

4. Kinsarya (Jodhpur State) stone Inscription of Baisakh sudi 3, S. 1056 (21 April 999 A. D.) of King Durlabhraj of Ajmer, containing an account of Dahyas, *samants* of the Chauhans—*In. Ant.* vol. XII, p. 59.

5. Stone inscription in the temple of Sankrai Mata in Shekhawati (Jaipur territory) of A. D. 1099 (Srawan vadi 1, V. S. 1156), mentioning that the temple was built by Shivahari's son Siddhraj during the reign of king Durlabhraj II. *Vide*, Report of the Rajputana Museum Ajmer for 1934, p. 3.

6. Pillar inscription in the temple of Jin Mata in Shekhawati (Jaipur State) of A. D. 1105 (S. 1162) of the time of king Prithviraj I of Ajmer mentioning the renovation of the temple through Hathhada son of Bohil—*The Rajputana Museum Report* for 1934, describes this inscription.

7. Pillar inscription of 1139 A. D. (1196 V. S.) in Jin Mata temple in Shekhawati (Jaipur State) mentions the name of king Arnoraj. The lower part of the inscription is not readable. Also described in the Rajputana Museum Report for 1934.

8. Pillar inscription in Jin Mata temple in Shekhawati (Jaipur Stase) of Baisakh vadi 11, S. 1196 (A. D. 1139) says that during the time of king Arnoraj of Ajmer, Alhan son of *Bavadatta* renovated the temple. *Vide*, Report of Rajputana Museum for 1934.

9. Revasa (in Shekhawati, Jaipur State) Stone inscription of V.S. 1196 (A.D. 1139) (unpublished) giving the name of king Arnoraja and his era.

10. Mokalji temple inscription (Chitor) of king Kumarpal of Anhalwara of A.D. 1149-50 (S. 1207) about the invasion of Ajmer.—*In. Ant.* vol. II, p. 422.

11. Stone inscriptions dated 27th November, 1153 A. D. Margshirsh sudi 5, S. 1210) of Emperor Vigrahraj IV (Visaldeva) in the Adhai din-ka-Jhonpra, Ajmer containing the *Harakeli* drama, (Part published in *Ep. In.* Vol. XX, p. 210). and *Lalita Vigrahraj Natak* by Emperor Vigrahraj IV now, preserved in the Rajputana Museum, Ajmer.

12. Lohari (Udaipur State) Stone, inscription of V. S. 1211 (A. D. 1154) of the time of Emperor Vigrahraj IV (Visaldeva) of Ajmer about the construction of Bhuteshwara Mahadeva temple. An account of it is published on p. 2 of the *Rajputana Museum Report* for 1922-23 A. D.

13. Siwalik Pillar inscription (Firozshah's Pillar) in Delhi, of 20 April 1163 (Baisakh sudi 15, S. 1220) of Emperor Vigrahraj IV (Visaldeva) It says that the Emperor had conquered the whole of Upper India. Edited by Dr. Keilhorn in *Ep. In.* vol. XIX, p. 218.

14. Two inscriptions of Emperor Vigrahraj IV (Visaldev) on the lintels of the small stairs in the backwall of the cloistered hall of the Adhai-din-ka-Jhopra at Ajmer saying that the building was put up by that Emperor.

15. Hansi (Punjab) Stone inscription of Magh sudi 7, S. 1224 (19 January 1168 A. D.) stating that King Prithviraj II, also called *Prithvibhatt*, son of Jagdeva, son of Arnoraj, built the gateway of the Hansi fort—*In. Antiquary*, vol. XII, p. 19, edited by Dr. Bhandarkar.

16. Menal (Mewar) Stone inscription of Jyeshtha vadi 13, S. 1225 (7 May, 1168 A. D.) of Prithviraj II containing an account of the construction of a temple and a well. A summary is given in the *Rajputana Museum Report* for 1922-23 p. 2.

17. Menal (Mewar) Stone inscription of V. S. 1225 (A. D. 1168) in the temple built by Queen Suhad Devi of Prithviraj II or Prithvibhatta.

18. Menal Pillar inscription of king Prithviraj II of V. S. 1226 (A. D. 1169) about erecting a monastry, published by Kaviraj Shyamaldas in the *Journal of the R. A. S.* Bengal, vol. IV, Part I p. 46.

19. Bijolian Rock inscription (Udaipur State) of Falgun Vadi 3 Thursday, V. S. 1226 (5 February 1170 A. D.) of king Someshwara's time, gives the Chauhan genealogy from king Samant Raj to Someshwara, and throws light on the reigns of Arnoraj, Vigrahraj IV and Prithviraj II. Published by Kaviraj Shyamaldas in the *Journal of the A. S. of Bengal*, vol. IV, Part I, p. 40.

20. Menal Stone inscription of Jyeshth sudi 10. S. 1228 (A.D. 1171 February 16) of Maharaja Someshwara's time. Mentioned in the *Rajputana Museum Report for 1922-23*, p. 2.

21. Inscription of V. S. 1228 (1171 A. D.) in the Chhatree of Rajkirtiji, Jain Acharya, at Ajmer.

22. Pillar inscription in Ruthi Rani temple at Menal (Mewar) of Sravan sudi 13, S. 1229 (3 August 1172 A. D.) of Chauhan king Someshwar's time containing an account of the construction of the temple of Nityapramodit, and an *ashram* for Bhattarak Prabhasrashi. An account of it is published in the *Annual Report of Rajputana Museum for 1922-23* p. 2.

23. Pillar inscription in the *Mandap* of Jin Mata temple, in Shekhawati (Jaipur State) of Asadh sudi 9, S. 1230 (A. D. 1173) of the time of king Someshwar, father of Emperor Prithviraj, mentions the renovation of the *mandap* of the temple, *Vide, Rajputana Museum Report for 1934 A.D.* p. 3.

24. Stone inscription of Amalda (Udaipur) of king Someshwar's time of Bhadrapad sudi 4, S. 1234 (29 August 1177 A. D.) mentioning the death of Dodiya Singharao, and his wife becoming *Sati*, and the erection of a memorial, *Vide. In. Ant.* vol. 56, p. 49.

25. Stone inscription in Lohari (Udaipur State) of Emperor Prithviraj's time of Asadh sudi 10, S. 1236 (16 June 1179) about erecting a pillar to commemorate the death of Jaisal Bagdi, and his wife becoming Sati—*In. Anti.* vol. 56, p. 49.

26. Stone inscription of Asadh sudi 10, S. 1236-37 (4 June 1180 A. D.) of Emperor Prithviraj's time in Phalodi Pokaran stating the gift of Parmar Rana Katia. Published by Mr. Tessitori in the *Journal of Bengal A. S.* Vol. XII, p. 3.

27. Stone inscription in Madanpur (Bundelkhand, C. I.) of V. S. 1239 (A. D. 1182) regarding the conquest of Mahoba by Emperor Prithviraj, after defeating Parmardideva the Chandail King of Mahoba. Published in *Archaeological Survey Report* vol. X p. 98 by General Cunningham.

28. Rewasa (Jaipur State) inscription of Margshirsh sudi 11, S. 1243 (A. D. 1186) of Emperor Prithviraj's time. It mentions the death of Chandail Nanava, son of Sinharaj, and a memorial to him. *Vide, Report of Rajputana Museum for 1935 A. D.* p. 8.

29. Stone inscription of 1187 A. D. (Sravan S. 1244) of Emperor Prithviraj's time mentions the erection of the *Mandap* of Gokarneshwar Mahadeva at Vigrahpur—*Arch. Survey of India Report*, Vol. VI. p. 136.

30. Inscription on the image of god Ganesh, discovered in Bajta near Sawar (Ajmer District) of V. S. 1245 (A. D. 1188) of Emperor Prithviraj's time. See *Report of Rajputana Museum for 1911-12 A. D.* page 2.

31. Stone inscription in Amalda (Mewar) of Falgun sud 12, S. 1245 (A-D. 1189) of Emperor Prithviraj's time, about erecting a memorial to Dood Rajehed ?

32. Inscription engraved in the Baradari in Madanpur (Bundelkhand C. I.) of the time of Emperor Prithviraj mentioning the conquest of Mahoba.

33. Inscription on an image found in Tantoti (Ajmer District) of V. S. 1251 (A. D. 1194) of the time of king Hariraj, brother of Emperor Prithviraj. It mentions queen Pratapdevi of king Hariraj, and the fact that the village was in her *Jagir*, vide, Report of Rajputana Museum, Ajmer for 1911-12 A. D., p. 2.

PATHAN PERIOD.

34. Inscription of H. 595 (1199 A. D.) on the Imamgah in the Adhai-din-ka-jhonpra, Ajmer.

35. Inscription of Zilhijj H. 596 (September, 1200 A. D.) about conversion of the Adhai-din ka-jhonpra into a mosque.

36. Inscription on the central arch in the *Facade* of the Jhonpra at Ajmer about the building of the *facade* in Sultan Shamsuddin Altmash's reign. (1210-36 A D.)

37. Inscription consisting of date S. 1535, Asadh sudi 6 (1478 A. D.) on the image of Paraswanath in the Dadabari, Ajmer.

38. Inscription of H. 939 (1532-33) on the northern wall of the Khwaja's mausoleum at Ajmer giving the date of the decoration of the dome.

MUGHAL PERIOD.

39. Inscription of Akbar's time on Buland Darwaza in Dargah Miran Sahib in the Taragarh fort of H. 976 (1569 A. D.)

40. Inscription of Jahangir's time, consisting of a couplet dated A. D. 1613 on the Hathibhata at Ajmer.

41. Inscription of 16 Rajab H. 1022 (1613 A. D.) giving date of a tomb in Charyar, Dargah Khwaja at Ajmer.

42. Inscription of H. 1024 (1615 A. D.) on the summit of the arch of the *Dalan* in Chashma at Ajmer, giving the date of its building by the order of Emperor Jahangir.

43. Inscription on Emperor Jahangir's pavilion at Pushkar, of A. D. 1615, mentioning construction of the pavilion under the supervision of Raja Anirai Singhdalan.

44. Inscription consisting of 33 verses under the eaves of the Juma Masjid in the Dargah at Ajmer giving date of the building H. 1047 (A. D. 1638)

45. Inscription of H. 1047 (1638 A. D.) on the entrance door of Allauddin's tomb in Dargah Khwaja Sahib at Ajmer.

46. Inscription, consisting of ten verses, of H. 1207 (1793 A. D.) giving date of the building of the *Dalan* by Nawab Walajah in the Dargah at Ajmer.

MAHRATTA PERIOD.

47. Inscription in the south *Tibari* of the mausoleum of Miran Sahib at Taragarh (1807-8 A. D.) built by the Mahratta governor Balarao Inglia.

48. Inscription of H. 1225 (1810 A. D.) on the southern door of the *Katera* of Miran Sahib in the Taragarh Fort.

49. Inscription H. 1227-29 (1812-14 A. D.) in the west *Tibari* of Miran Sahib's mausoleum built by Gumanji Rao Scindia.

II.—BOOKS.

ENGLISH.

Account of Ajmer and Jodhpur, A manuscript, by one Gulam Qadir.

A Chapter of the Indian Mutiny, by Col. G. H. Trevor, A. G. G., Rajputana.

Adam's *Western Rajputana States.*

Administration Reports of Ajmer Merwara.

Aitchison's Treaties, Vol. III.

Ajmer Regulations, Vols H. to L. and M. to P.

Akbar, the Great Moghul, by Dr. Vincent Smith.

Annals and Antiquities of Rajasthan, by Col. James Tod.

Annual Progress Report of the Archaeological Survey, Northern Circle for 1905 A.D.

Annual Reports of the Rajputana Museum, Ajmer.

Archaeological Survey Report for 1883-4, Vol. XXIII, by H. R. H. Garrick.

Archaeological Survey Report (1893) by Dr. Fuhrer.

Archaeological Survey Report for 1902-3.

Archaeological Survey Report, Western Presidency, by Dr. Cousens.

Asiatic Researches, Vol. VIII.

Bacon's *Essay on Plantations.*

Baillie Fraser's *Military Memoirs of Lt. Col. James Skinner.*

Bayley's Sir E. C., *History of Gujrat.*

Bernier's *Travels.*

Brooke's *Account of the Famine in Rajputana including Ajmer-Merwara.*

Caine's *Picturesque India.*

Calcutta Chronicle.

Cavendish's *Enquiry into the Rent-free Tenures in Ajmer-Merwara.*

Census Reports of 1881, 1891, 1901, 1911, 1921, and 1931 A.D.

Chambers' *Encyclopaedia.*

Chronicles of the Pathan kings of Delhi, by Edward Thomas.

Chronology of India, by Miss Duff.

Compton's *European Military Adventurers of Hindustan.*

Compendium of Information regarding the Nasirabad Cantonment, by Captain E. G. I. Welch.

Count Noer's *Akbar.*

Crofton's *Inscription on Tombs and Monuments in Rajputana and Central India.*

Dixon's *Settlement Report.*

Dixon's *Sketch of Merwara.*

Elliot's *History of India as told by its own* (Muhammadan) *Historians.*

Elphinstone's *History of India.*

Epigraphia Indica.

Embassy of Sir Thomas Roe.

Ferishta's *History of India, translated* by Briggs.

Foster's *Early Travels in India.*

Famine Report for 1890-92 by Captain Delaessoe.

Famine Report for 1898-1900 by Mr. A. L. P. Tucker.

Famine Report for 1905-6.

Gazetteer of the Bombay Presidency Vol. I. Part I (1896).

Gazetteer of Rajputana by C. C. Watson.

Gazetteer of Ajmer-Merwara by C. C. Watson.

Gazetteer of Ajmer-Merwara by J. La Touche.

Gazetteer of India by Thornton, 1850 A.D.

History of Eastern and Indian Architecture, by Fergusson.

History of Jahangir by Dr. Beni Prasad.

Hindustan under Free Lances by H. G. Keene.

History of Mewar by Col. Brooke.

History of the Mayo College Vol. I and II by H. Sherring.

India and its Native Princes, by Rousselet.

Indian Antiquary (Bombay)

Journal of Sir Thomas Roe (Hakluyt Society).

Journal of the Bengal Asiatic Society, Vol. LV.

Kaye's History of the Administration of the East India Company.

Kaye's Sepoy War.

Later Mughals by Irvine.

La Touche's *Settlement Report of Ajmer-Merwara,* 1874, A.D.

Letters from India by Victor Jacquemont.

Letters Written from a Mahratta Camp. by Col. Broughton.

Life of Madhava Rao Scindia by H. G. Keene.

Lupton's *Settlement Report of Ajmer-Merwara* (1910 A.D.).

Maharana Kumbha by Har Bilas Sarda.

Narrative of a Journey Undertaken in the Northern Provinces of India by Bishop Heber.

Orme's *Historical Fragments of the Mughal Empire.*

Purchas, Travels, (Translation) Vol. I.

Presërvation of Ancient Monuments in Rajputana (1881) by Captain H. H. Cole.

Pritchard's *Mutinies in Rajputana.*

Qanungo's *Sher Shah.*

Ras Mala by A. K. Forbes, I.C.S.

Repton, Major, *Report on Ajmer-Merwara.*

Ruling Princes, Chiefs and Leading Personages of Rajputana and Ajmer. (1939 A.D.).

Sir J. N. Sarkar's *History of Aurangzeb.*

Sir J. N. Sarkar's *Fall of the Mughal Empire.*

Sir J. N. Sarkar's *India of Aurangzeb.*

Some Account of the General and Medical Topography of Ajmer by Dr. R. H. Irvine M.D., (1841 A.D.) Calcutta.

Speeches and Writtings of Har Bilas Sarda.

Story of Merwara or our Rule in India. (London) 1868 A.D.

Storia Do Mogor by N. Manuchi, CC.

Tabqat-i-Nasiri, translated by Major Raverty.

Tavernier's *Travels.*

Thomas Coryat, Traveller, for the English wits, Greeting from the Court of the Great Mughal at Ajmer.

Travels in Western India by Col. James Tod.

Transactions of the Royal Asiatic Society of Great Britain and Ireland.

Tuzak-i-Jahangiri, by Rogers,

Wheeler's *History of India.*

Whiteway's *Settlement Report*, 1886.

SANSKRIT AND HINDI.

Ajitodaya (Sanskrit).

Gaudavaho (Bombay Sanskrit Series).

Hammir Mahakavya (Sanskrit) edited by Kirtane.

History of Badnor (Hindi) by Gopal Singh.

Jodhpur Khyat (Hindi).

Kiratarjuniya, (Sanskrit) by Bharavi.

Kirti Kaumudi (Sanskrit).

Khartargachha Gurvavali (Sanskrit) by Jinpalodaya.
Mahabharata (Sanskrit).
Muhnot Nainsi's *Khyat.*
Padma Purana (Sanskrit).
Prabandha Chintamani (Sanskrit).
Prabandh Kosh (Sanskrit).
Prithviraja Rasa (Hindi) by Chand Bardai.
Prithviraja Vijaya (Sanskrit) by Jayanak.
Ramayana (Sanskrit) by Valmiki.
Reu's *History of Marwar* (Hindi).
Vir Vinod, by Kaviraj Shyamaldas (Hindi).
Yuga Pradhan Jinchandra Suri by Agarchand Nahata (Hindi).

PERSIAN AND URDU.

Ain-i Akbari by Abul Fazal.
Akbar Nama by Abul Fazal.
Akhbarul Akhyar.
Alamgirnama.
Badshahnama.
Chahar Gulzar by Harcharandas.
Char Chamanchitraman.
Khulasat-ul-Tawarikh.
Tarikhe Ajmer, by P. Maharaja Kishen (Urdu).
Mirat-i-Alam.
Miratul Israr by Abdul Rahman.
Maasir-i-Alamgiri.
Maasir-ul-Umra.
Munisul Arvah by Princess Jahan Ara Begum.
Muntakhabul Tawarikh, by Abdul Kadar Badayuni.
Sairul Mutakharin.
Shahjahannama.
Tajul Maasir.
Tabqate Akbari by M. Nizamuddin.
Tarikhe Daudi.
Tarikhe Ferishta
Tarikhe Muzaffari.
Waqai Rajasthan, by Jwala Sahai (Urdu).

ADDENDA AND CORRIGENDA

Page	24	Line	34	for	677 miles	read	609 miles.
,,	25	,,	28	,,	60 years	,,	40 years.
,,	32	,,	10	,,	Swatambari	,,	Swetambari
,,	41	,,	13	,,	نیک زیا	,,	نیک زیبا
,,	47	,,	7	,,	1898	,,	1895
,,	57	,,	4	,,	built by the Jabbar Khan	,,	built by Jabbar Khan
,,	62	,,	16	,,	Century"	,,	Century"4
,,	62 Note	,,	2	,,	Topagraphy of India	,,	Topography of Ajmer
,,	65 Note	,,	1	,,	Tuzaci Jahangiri	,,	Tuzake Jahangiri
,,	67 Note 3	,,		,,	Minor sites	,,	Minor sights
,,	72	,,	35	,,	Anhalwarra	,,	Anhalwara
,,	76	,,	33	,,	Chahumana	,,	Chahamana
,,	85	,,	7	,,	Khown	,,	Known
,,	87	,,	33	,,	Nakarkhana	,,	Naqqarkhana
,,	89	,,	5	,,	Customs.	,,	Customs,
,,	92	,,	37	,,	Mutwalis	,,	Mutvallis
,,	94	,,	31	,,	Chhabutra	,,	Chabutra
,,	95	,,	5	,,	Omit comma after Mulk		
,,	95	,,	21	,,	Mutavalli	,,	Mutvalli
,,	98	,,	24	,,	Mutavalli	,,	Mutvalli
,,	99	,,	16	,,	Shrinesa	,,	Shrines
,,	99	,,	18	,,	Behar	,,	Bihar
,,	101 Note 3	,,	2	,,	Gushalkhana	,,	Ghusalkhana
,,	111	,,	3 & 4	,,	Omit "And an Assistant Games Superintendent."		
,,	114	,,	3	,,	Sidhkut Chatalaya	,,	Siddhakut Chaityalaya
,,	114	,,	16	,,	Ajodhia	,,	Ajodhya
,,	114	,,	22	,,	Khshir Samudra	,,	Kshir Samudra
,,	115	,,	24	,,	Chaitalayas	,,	Chaityalayas
,,	,,	,,	32	,,	Ajodhia	,,	Ajodhya
,,	,,	,,	39	,,	Aphsara	,,	Apsara
,,	,,	Last line		,,	Sidhkut Chaitalaya	,,	Siddhakut Chaityalaya
,,	118	Line	18	,,	Sura, Mardini	,,	Sura-Mardini
,,	120	,,	33	,,	Mahamahopadhya	,,	Mahamahopadhyaya
,,	123	,,	18	,,	Shiveramji	,,	Shivaramji
,,	125	,,	5	,,	Chhattrees	,,	Chhatrees
,,	137	,,	21	for	Ahichetrapur	read	Ahichhatrapur
,,	139	,,	(27)	,,	Aparagangeya (A.D. 1177)	,,	Apargangeya (A D. 1167)
,,	139 Note	,,	3	,,	*Gaudavahi*	,,	*Gaudavaho*
,,	141 Note 4	,,	5	,,	Histoy of India	,,	History of India
,,	142		11	,,	Chaluca	,,	Chalukya
,,	,,		26	,,	Chalucas	,	Chalukyas
,,	,,	,,	31	,,	Chaluka	,,	Chalukya
,,	144	,,	34	,,	Vindhia	,,	Vindhya
,,	145	,,	21	,,	Amargangeya	,,	Aparagongeya
,,	146	,,	6	,,	Kalpbrikshes	,,	Kalpvrikshas
,,	146	,,	11	,,	Cheddi	,,	Chedi
,,	147	,,	15	,,	Swayamber	,,	Swayambar
,,	154	,,	12	,,	Subha	,,	Subah
,,	155	,,	1	,,	Chisti	,,	Chishti
,,	155 Note 2		Omit 1				
,,	157	,,	1	,,	Governer	,,	Governor
,,	159	,,	4	,,	Ordinance	,,	Ordnance
,,	169	,,	2	,,	Siddhi	,,	Siddi
,,	171	,,	13	,,	Mauzum	,,	Muazum
,,	172	,,	28	,,	Gave-up	,,	Gave up
,,	174	,,	33	,,	Badshai	,,	Badshahi
,,	177	,,	36	,,	Artilerry	,,	Artillery
,,	179	,,	22	,,	Jaisht	,,	Jyeshth
,,	182	,,	7	,,	Unexperienced	,,	Inexperienced
,,	185	,,	2	,,	Reciprocalties	,,	Reciprocalities
,,	185	,,	34	,,	Influene	,,	Influence

Page		Line		for		read		
Page	187	Line	29	for	Jesht	read	Jyeshth	
,,	190	,,	1	,,	Chursiawas	,,	Chaursiawas	
,,	192	,,	1	,,	Rieu's	,,	Reu's	
,,	193	,,	8	,,	Seige	,,	Siege	
,,	210 Note	,,	3	,,	Rajputaua	,,	Rajputana	
,,	211	,,	31	,,	Thompson	,,	Thomason	
,,	211 Note	,,	1	,,	Gazetter	,,	Gazetteer	
,,	211 Note 1	,,	10	,,	Ordinance	,,	Ordnance	
,,	,,	,,	16	,,	Cemetry	,,	Cemetery	
,,	213	,,	32	,,	Arbillery	,,	Artillery	
,,	217	,,	42	,	Martialed	,,	Martialled	
,,	232	,,	36	,,	Lord Irvin	,,	Lord Irwin	
,,	239	,,	9 & 11	,,	Delassoe	,,	Delaessoe	
,,	241	,,	28	,,	Chhattrees	,,	Chhatrees	
,,	242	,,	3	,,	Geneology	,,	Genealogy	
,,	242	,,	14	,,	Sakambari	,,	Sakambhari	
,,	243	,,	32	,,	Shahabuddin	,,	Shahbuddin	
,,	243	,,	14	,,	Amargangeya	,,	Apargangeya	
,,	246	,,	8	,,	Rajah	,,	Rajab	
,,	247	,,	1	,,	Rajput	,,	Rajputs	
,,	250	,,	29	,,	Vichetra Kumari	,,	Vichitra Kumari	
,,	258	1905	H. R. H. Prince Leopold of Saxe Coburg Gotha					visited Ajmer.
		1911	Mr. C. E. H. Hobhouse, under Secretary of State.					,, ,,
		1912	J. R. H. Crown Prince and Princess of Sweden					,, ,,
,,	259	1913	Mr. Ramsay Macdonald (later Prime Minister of Britain)					,, ,,
		1913	Mr. E. S. Montague (afterwards Secretary of State, India)					,, ,,
		1925	Her Majesty the Queen Mother of Nepal					,, ,,
,,	260	1929	Lord Peel, Ex Secretary of State, India					,, ,,
		1929	The Royal Commission on Labour					,, ,,
,,	260	Line	4	for	Irvin	read	Irwin	
,,	265	,,	35	,,	Chairman	,,	Chairmen	
,,	,,	,,	41	,,	Urban	,,	Urban	
,,	283	,,	18	,,	Marwar benefited	,,	Marwar been benefited	
,,	,,	,,	20	,,	Geting	,,	Getting	
,,	287	,,	14	,,	1930	,,	1830	
,,	288	,,	13	,,	Istimrardars	,,	Istimrardar	
,,	,,	,,	29	,,	Bhomias	,,	Bhumias	
,,	292	,,	36, 38	,,	Chhavar	,,	Chhanvar	
,,	298	,,	30 & 37	,,	Khwas	,,	Khawas	
,,	,,	,,	34,36 & 39		Madhvarao	,,	Madhavarao	
,,	299	,,	1	,,	Khwas	,,	Khawas	
,,	301	,,	14	,,	Barisal	,,	Bairisal	
,,	313	,,	27	,,	वांह्यं	,,	वांहां	
,,	,,	,,	28	,,	जेसलमर	,,	जेसलमेर	
,,	315	,,	29	,,	Pachhisalkal	,,	Pachchisakal	
,,	318	,,	5	,,	Hinderence	,,	Hindrance	
,,	323	,,	18	,,	Begin	,,	Begun	
,,	334	,,	30	,,	Incurr	,,	Incur	
,,	339	,,	23	,,	Macademised	,,	Macadamized	
,,	340	,,	33	,,	Stratagic	,,	Strategic	
,,	346	,,	43	,,	Pisagan	,,	Pisangan	
,,	357	,,	38	,,	University	,,	Govt. Sanskrit College	
,,	365	,,	4	,,	Scotish	,,	Scottish	
,,	374	,,	26	,,	Contonment	,,	Cantonment	
,,	377	,,	30	,,	Narative	,,	Narrative	
,,	380 Note	,,	1	,,	Benefitted	,,	Benefited	
,,	390	,,	22	,,	Womens'	,,	Women's	
,,	392	,,	25	,,	Somaldeva	,,	Somaldevi	
,,	398	,,	35	,,	Vallabhcharya	,,	Vallabhacharya	
,,	,,	,,	44	,,	Sampradya	,,	Sampradaya	
,,	436	,,	14	,,	Local	,,	Local	